BARNES WALLIS'
BOMBS

STEPHEN FLOWER

D1376861

AMBERLEY

In memory of Flt Lt Len Sumpter DFC DFM and Gefreiter Karl Schutte
These men met as enemies at the Möhne dam on the night of 16/17 May 1943
They met again as friends at the same dam on 21 May 1989

First published 2002

Amberley Publishing Plc
Cirencester Road, Chalford,
Stroud, Gloucestershire, GL6 8PE

www.amberley-books.com

British Library Cataloguing in Publication Data.
A catalogue record for this book is available from the British Library.

ISBN 978 1 84868 959 6

Typeset in 10pt on 12pt Sabon.
Typesetting and Origination by Fonthill.
Printed in the UK.

Contents

Acknowledgements

This book came about as a result of the research carried out by me since 1986 into Brooklands airfield and its wartime products. It could not have been written without the help of many people, who often unwittingly contributed towards it.

At the head of this list must come the staff of the National Archives at Kew, followed by their colleagues at the RAF Museum at Hendon and at the Department of Photographs at the Imperial War Museum at Lambeth. Their information and illustrations formed the backbone of the story and helped to correct some misleading impressions formed from previously published accounts of the Wallis bombs. Since the story's principal characters are no longer alive, the NA files were particularly important, giving useful insight into people's minds and attitudes at various times during the development and use of these weapons.

I must also thank Capt. Paul Snook and his ever-patient wife Barbara, of Holt's Tours, who put together the inaugural Dambusters Tour in 1989, enabling me to meet Len Sumpter and gain a first-hand account of Operation *Chastise* from the sharp end. Much useful knowledge also came to light from a second visit to the dams in 1993. A further Bomber Command Tour in 1997, again organised by Paul and Barbara, enabled me to renew an acquaintance with Maj. Alan Thompson, a pilot and 617 Sqdn historian, as well as stay at the famous Petwood Hotel. As a final contribution from Holt's Tours, it was through Lt-Col David Storrie and his wife Linda that I met Brad King, Public Services Officer of the Imperial War Museum's Film and Video Archive, who with his colleagues supplied several illustrations relating to Highball and Upkeep. Jim Shortland's contribution has been mentioned in Chapter 13.

Rob Owen, the 617 Sqdn Association's official historian, welcomed me into his home, to spend several hours patiently comparing notes and authenticating stories, so enabling me to avoid some errors while following up a number of new leads. It was through him that I was able to contact Tom Bennett, who gave permission for an article of his in *Flypast* magazine to be quoted.

Jim Brookbank, a bomb aimer turned author and poet, not only gave me permission to quote from his book *Before The Dawn*, but also passed on a message from me to several of his fellow 9 Sqdn veterans, enabling me to add much new material from a unit that all too frequently has been overshadowed by 617. My thanks to everyone who responded. It will be noted that some of 9 Sqdn's aiming point photographs are uncredited. These were supplied by a former squadron officer whose wish for anonymity has been respected.

Two witnesses of Operation *Catechism* are quoted by kind permission of Sir Ludovic Kennedy, from his book on the battleship *Tirpitz*. Mr Dewi Davies' account of the Maenclochog Highball trials appears by kind permission of Les Mullins, editor of the *Western Telegraph*.

Next, my gratitude to the patience shown by Andrew Spinetti, Christopher Cross and Ivan Lamanow, who on various occasions guided my fingers and none-too-willing brain through that modern mystery, the word processor. There have been occasions when a suddenly blank screen gave me something akin to heart failure, although I have to say that how anyone writes anything without one these days is beyond me.

Some wartime drawings referring to either the *Tirpitz* or Highball came from the National Archives. The series of illustrations on the Highball aiming problems are my own, while the remainder of the artwork was ably and patiently executed by Julie Anne Hudson, a former colleague of mine at Hampton Court Palace.

Simon Parry, a fellow aviation enthusiast, cheerfully put up with a series of questions and demands while also supplying a number of useful photographs from his own collection.

Last, but by no means least, my thanks to the wartime witnesses interviewed by myself and others. It has never ceased to amaze me how much these people could still recall, even though in some instances they were describing events of more than half a century before. In his letter to me Graham Rees, formerly of 9 Sqdn, ended with these words:

> I hope that this information will be of use to you in the writing of your book. I am sure that it will make interesting reading for us 'old sweats' and that it will serve to educate the many critics of our efforts in Bomber Command.

I hope it does. This is their story and my only regret is that some of them did not live long enough to see their words in print.

Stephen Flower
July 2010

Author's Note

The question when writing a book of this kind is to decide whether to do so with the aviation enthusiast or the general reader in mind, especially regarding the use of wartime jargon and abbreviations. Such terms are unavoidable and I have decided to aim the story at the enthusiast, but with a glossary at the back to make things clearer for anyone unfamiliar with air force terminology of 1939-1945.

Ranks and titles used in the story are those that were current at the time of the events described, some of those involved later being promoted or knighted. Where extracts from post-war interviews are quoted, the subjects are given their later titles, as in the case of Sir George Edwards. Foreign names and titles have been used where appropriate, mostly with their original spellings.

Prior to a description of each raid, the serial numbers and individual letters of the RAF aircraft involved, where known, are included, along with either the pilot's name or brief crew details. These have been taken from the squadron Operations Record Books held at the National Archives – not infallible guides, as researchers will know, but by cross-referencing, some obvious errors have been corrected. In the case of aircrew killed, taken prisoner or missing on operations, details have been based on the Bomber Command Losses books compiled by W. R. Chorley.

Some RAF squadrons, for reasons known only to themselves, chose to use Roman numerals. For the sake of consistency I have used Arabic ones throughout.

Foreword

As with my previous book, *Raiders Overhead*, this one came about as a by-product of my research into the wartime history of Brooklands airfield. It would have been impossible to do that without relating the story of how Barnes Wallis came to be employed by Vickers and why he turned his hand from aircraft to bomb design. One of the first questions that came to mind was 'How many Tallboys and Grand Slams were used in action?' The only way to find out was to consult the relevant documents held at the National Archives at Kew and elsewhere. One thing led to another, with this book being the result.

While the story of Barnes Wallis, 617 Sqdn and the raid on the Ruhr dams has been well covered by books, a popular film and documentaries, it became apparent that this same coverage did not extend either to the Highball bomb, which was also designed by him, or to the six-ton and ten-ton earthquake bombs, which proved to be far more useful weapons. Paul Brickhill's book *The Dam Busters* has set the tone for much of what has been said since, but, as he acknowledged, it was written at a time when these weapons were still surrounded by a wall of secrecy. Much more information has emerged since then, including the release of RAF documents at the National Archives, to which Brickhill did not have access.

This book is not a squadron history, but is intended to give a full account of how the bombs were designed, tested and, except for Highball, used in action. The legendary rivalry between 9 and 617 Sqdns has been noted, but I have tried to give an objective assessment of each unit's contribution. Surviving veterans may disagree with some of my conclusions regarding the effects of certain raids, but I have based these on what was said at the time, compared with what was later discovered on the ground.

Each raid, including those that were cancelled, is listed in chronological order, giving the bomber force employed, the number of Wallis bombs used, any other units involved, the results obtained and other background information. Where possible, the story has been told in the words of those who were there.

Some people may feel that too much detail has been included, but I feel it is not sufficient to say that on a certain date x aircraft dropped y bombs on z targets. Those involved deserve better than such superficial treatment.

It cannot be claimed that the Wallis bombs or the squadrons that took them into action won the European war on their own, but they certainly made a massive contribution to the cause of air power and its role in the Allied victory in 1945. At the time the courage and dedication of 9 and 617 Sqdns, with those units who supported them, set an example that could hardly be surpassed. It is one that deserves to be remembered.

1

Preparation

The Navy can lose us the war, but only the Air Force can win it. Therefore our supreme effort must be to gain overwhelming mastery in the air. The fighters are our salvation, but the bombers alone provide the means of victory. We must therefore develop the power to carry an ever-increasing volume of explosives to Germany, so as to pulverise the entire industry and scientific structure on which the war effort and economic life of the enemy depend, while holding him at arm's length from our island. In no other way at present visible can we hope to overcome the immense military power of Germany.

Winston Churchill, 3 September 1940

Sunday 16 May 1943

It was just after 2100 when a red Very light arced through the Lincolnshire sky. It had been fired by Flt Lt R. E. G. Hutchison, 617 Sqdn's Signals Leader, as the signal for the Lancasters of the first and second waves to start up. Merlins whined and clattered into life, magnetos were tested, pressures and temperatures checked. One by one the black bombers moved out from their dispersals onto the airfield's perimeter track.

Anyone hearing that roar across the flat countryside would, in the parlance of the time, have said to themselves that ops were on again tonight. They would have been right too, but few of them could have known the significance of this one, or the meaning of the strange huge cylindrical object that hung beneath the deformed, gutted fuselage of each bomber.

First away was Flt Lt R. N. G. Barlow, one of many Royal Australian Air Force aircrew serving with Bomber Command. At 2128 the green Aldis light, for which he had been watching, flashed from the controller's caravan by Scampton's grass runway. Barlow's hand reached down to push forward the throttles, then moved aside for that of his flight engineer, P/O S. L. Willis, to hold them forward fully against the stops. With such a cumbersome and heavy weight beneath the aircraft, even a momentary loss of power on take-off would be catastrophic.

The idling rumble of the four Merlins changed to a full-throated bellow, the worn grass streaked by below as Lancaster AJ-E rolled forward, the huge main wheels lifted and, as the bomber rose, the dark boundary hedge flashed by below. Confined in his turret, the rear gunner, Sgt J. R. G. Liddell, peered through the open panel between his four guns to watch the airfield disappear behind, relieved to have 'unstuck' safely and wondering if he would see it again. Liddell had falsified his age to join the RAF almost exactly two years before. He was now eighteen.

Someone else with much to ponder was Barnes Neville Wallis, Assistant Chief Designer (Structures) of the Aviation Section of Vickers-Armstrongs Ltd. Wallis had been at Scampton to brief the crews and now had to face what would seem like the longest night of his life in Bomber Command's 5 Group headquarters at nearby Grantham. There would be a long, tension-filled silence, endured under the harsh scrutiny of Air Chief Marshal Sir Arthur Harris, Bomber Command's AOC, who had vehemently opposed this project when it had first been put to him and who was still not convinced that it would succeed. Wg Cdr Gibson's force would maintain radio silence until they were over their respective targets, when a series of Morse messages would indicate that the prescribed attacks had been made. If all went as Wallis had predicted, then Gibson's late dog would achieve a measure of immortality when his name came crackling into the head-phones of 5 Group's Chief Signals Officer.

Scampton quietened down as the last of the bombers droned away into the distance. For the ground crews, burdened with work until almost the last minute, there would be time to relax and perhaps light a cigarette. The offices, crew rooms and living quarters were silent.

Flt Sgt G. E. 'Chiefy' Powell steeled himself to the sad task of burying the dog outside his master's office. He would never have described his CO as a sentimental man and had been surprised when Gibson had quietly asked him to carry out the interment at midnight. Gibson would be over Germany by then, and had had a feeling that both he and his late companion would be going into the ground together. For better or worse, Operation *Chastise* had begun.

The sequence of events described above will be familiar to most people, including those who consider themselves to be cinema buffs rather than aviation enthusiasts. It was initially recorded in Guy Gibson's book, dramatically entitled *Enemy Coast Ahead*, backed up by Paul Brickhill's post-war best-seller *The Dam Busters* and finally brought to a wider audience by the film of that name, shot during 1954 and released the following year.

However, Gibson's book had to take account of wartime censorship. Brickhill's writing was also restricted by the fact that all the Wallis bombs were then still on the Secret List, where they would remain until 1962. The film makers, inevitably, had to simplify and telescope the events which had led up to this raid, with no mention of the other special weapon attacks which would follow it during the final two years of the European war.

What follows in this chapter is the story of how Wallis came to be involved in bomb design and why it had been deemed so important to breach a series of Ruhr dams that few in Britain had heard of till now.

Operation *Chastise* and the series of 'special' raids that would follow it all had their roots in the theory of strategic bombing, which had come into being as a result of the rapid advances made in aerial bombardment during the First World War. Espoused by, among others, MRAF Sir Hugh Trenchard, the first Chief of the Air Staff, this theory had held that the bombing of the enemy's cities and his factories would cause a collapse of both his will and ability to make war. Trenchard and his senior officers considered that such attacks would in the end be far more profitable than costly frontal assaults.

It was inevitable that senior officers in the other two Services would oppose such thinking, especially as they had been forced to give up their air arms to the RAF in 1918, but, the newly created air marshals had argued, what alternatives had the Army and Navy been able to offer? During the 1914-1918 conflict the Royal Navy had still claimed to rule the waves, but the outbreak of unrestricted submarine warfare in 1915 had led to Britain coming close to starvation. On land, the situation had been no better. The armies of both sides had bogged down in the muddy stalemate of the Western Front. Artillery and machine guns, backed by magazine rifles, had dominated the front line to such an extent that for nearly four years neither side could make much progress against the other.

With infantry casualty lists stretching to horrendous lengths, and the British public angered by German bombs, it was not surprising that these new ideas became accepted. Trenchard's Independent Air Force – a heavy bomber force by the standards of the day – began to carry the fight back into Germany. Plans had been made for an attack on Berlin and the first of the new Brooklands-built Vickers Vimy twin-engined bombers was standing by to do so when the Armistice came. This gave the admirals and generals their opportunity to declare that such a strategy would never have worked, and for the RAF to reply that it had not been tried for long enough to have been proven.

In 1937 the RAF's Air Staff, as part of their preparations for another looming European conflict, turned once again to strategic bombing and focused upon German industry. In October a list of thirteen Western Air plans was drawn up, one of which highlighted forty-five industrial plants in the Ruhr, Rhineland and Saar as vital to the German war machine. In inevitable British fashion, committees were formed for further study, one being the Air Targets Sub-Committee. Its members pointed out that the destruction of these targets could prove difficult and put forward an alternative – the Möhne and Sorpe dams.

The Möhne dam, south-east of the city of Dortmund, had been built to collect rainwater during the winter months in order to prevent flooding, so providing hydroelectric power as well as sustaining industrial and domestic water supplies. Made of limestone and sandstone, it was 130ft high, 112ft across at its base and 2,100ft long. Behind the towers on its parapet were two other circular ones, to control the sluices. Its maximum capacity was 134 million cubic metres.

The Sorpe, six miles to the south-west of the Möhne, had a similar role, being fed by the river from which it took its name. Its concrete wall was 190ft high and its capacity, at 72 million cubic metres, was much less than that of the Möhne, but nevertheless it was an important target. Were these to be breached, widespread flooding and dislocation of industry would follow, as well as a subsequent lack of water for hydroelectric power and other needs. Aqueducts, canals and their locks were also vulnerable to air attack. Three different types of dam were studied and possible means of attack considered.

It quickly became clear that the gravity dams – which included the Möhne – were too solidly built to be effectively attacked by any bombs that were currently in the RAF's inventory. Many of these consisted of stocks left over from the First World War, for the powerful thin-cased 'blockbusters' that would become familiar later on were not yet available.

It was not only the bomb's size that mattered, but also the amount of explosive it carried. The most common high-explosive weapons were the 250lb and 500lb GP types. Impressive though these weights might have sounded, more than half of each one was taken up by the bomb's casing. This low charge-to-weight ratio meant that they were not particularly effective, as later experience against softer targets than the dams would show. Their fusing arrangements were none too reliable either, and they turn up on German city building sites to this day.

Then there was the bomb's filling to consider. Most people have heard of Alfred Nobel and dynamite, but explosive of this kind was suitable only for industrial purposes. For this reason, Amatol, a more powerful chemical combination, had been developed during 1914-1918 and until 1941 would be the only readily available filling. The situation would improve when a young scientist called S. J. Pooley came up with Torpex. Thirty per cent more powerful than Amatol, it was originally intended for torpedoes but would also be used in depth charges and bombs.

Treasury parsimony in the inter-war years, coupled with the Government's infamous Ten Year Rule, under which it had been confidently assumed that there would be no war for a decade, had compelled the RAF to spend most of its limited budget on the maintenance of existing aircraft rather than the development of new weapons. The average airman of 1915, assuming he survived, would have been quite at home with the silver biplanes of twenty years later. He would certainly have recognised the small yellow objects slung beneath their wings.

Although the RAF had retained a heavy bomber force of sorts, its matronly Vickers Virginias and Handley Page Heyfords were patently unsuited to the demands of the war to come and their crews lacked any recent active service experience. In this respect the best-qualified airmen were those who had dropped small GP bombs from Hawker Harts onto feuding tribesmen on the North-West Frontier of India, but this would not

The light bomber of 1935 – a Hawker Hart of 12 Squadron on active overseas service. This could carry up to 520lb of bombs, but experience after 1939 would show that their explosive content was too small. (S. Parry)

amount to much against a European enemy able to shoot back. Thanks to the RAF's expansion plans, a new generation of faster monoplane bombers was on the point of entering service, but their effectiveness would still be limited by the outdated ordnance they would have to drop.

During 1938 the idea of stick bombing from altitude was considered, but the chances of hitting a dam in such a manner were assessed as small. Torpedoes were another possibility, but would be useless if the Germans placed nets in a dam's lake. In July Air Vice-Marshal W. Sholto Douglas, Assistant Chief of the Air Staff, chaired a meeting of the Air Ministry's Bombing Committee, which included representatives from all three Services, the RAE at Farnborough and the Research Department at Woolwich. It was held that the dams, especially the Möhne, represented a potential enemy Achilles Heel, as industrial power was thought to be almost entirely derived from them. None of those present then knew that the Ruhr did not rely solely on water for electricity generation, or that an efficient grid system would be able to compensate for the loss of power caused by a breached dam. However, it was also claimed that the Ruhr consumed 25 per cent of Germany's water, the bulk of this coming from the Möhne, which from now on would begin to assume the status of an important target.

The previous March, a paper written by the Director of Armament Development had recommended an attack on the lower face of a dam, so that water pressure would make it collapse. A low-level attack would be necessary for this kind of accuracy and, as already noted, no existing bomb was suitable – the current armour-piercing types would penetrate no more than five feet. Stick bombing was rejected as being uneconomical and, although a preference was expressed for torpedoes by some of those present at the meeting, the idea of a propelled weapon was also mentioned. The question of earth dams, such as the Sorpe, was also raised, with the suggestion that a number of GP bombs could be dropped on the top of one. This was interesting in view of later attempts to breach the Sorpe in 1943 and 1944.

Not the least of the problems were those posed by the gravity and earth dams. Gravity dams were large concrete or masonry structures, roughly triangular in cross-section and held in position by their own weight. They were either straight or, like the Möhne, curved inwards towards the reservoir. Emergency sluices were installed on the dam face to allow rapid draining if necessary. To prevent sludge being taken up, water was usually drawn out through sluice towers. It would then be used for the driving of turbines to produce electricity. Merely breaching the wall would not be decisive, as water could still be used from below the level of it, while the time taken to repair the breach would not necessarily be long. Any worthwhile attack would therefore have to damage the sluices and water pipes as well.

Earth dams had a vertical concrete or clay core, which was stabilised by a massive earth bank at each side. Again, a sluice was used to remove any excess water, which would otherwise have spilled over the top and caused erosion on the air side. In such instances water was usually extracted from the reservoir upstream via an intake tower, which meant that there was no machinery at the dam itself. Although also triangular in cross-section, the earth dam had a much broader base than the gravity type and was therefore less vulnerable to shock waves. GP bombs dropped onto its crown would hardly affect it. Events at the Sorpe would later show that even the shallow depression caused by a bigger weapon would not mean collapse.

Two days after this meeting, a letter to the Secretary of State for Air from Air Chief Marshal Sir Edgar Ludlow-Hewitt, then Bomber Command's AOC, listed a number of power stations in Germany, including two that were served by the Eder dam. Thus this structure too came under the scrutiny of the Air Ministry.

The Eder was situated south of the town of Kassel and south-east of the Möhne. At 139ft high, 115ft wide at the bottom and 1,309ft long, it was the largest dam in Germany, holding back an 11-mile lake with a capacity of 44,400 million gallons. Like the Möhne, it was there to provide control over winter flooding of the Eder and Fulda rivers – the former having been notoriously unpredictable in the past. The lake acted as a reservoir for the Mittelland Canal, which ran from the Ruhr to Berlin. It also had the tasks of providing uncontaminated water for drinking, industrial and agricultural purposes, as well as hydroelectric power.

Other exotic schemes were considered. These included sabotage, crashing a pilotless drone aircraft at the foot of the Möhne, or the more practical idea of devising a skimming torpedo that on impact would sink to a pre-determined depth and then be exploded by a hydrostatic fuse. All were rejected due to the large amount of explosive that would have been required, irrespective of the delivery system used.

Not only RAF senior officers appreciated the catastrophe that would occur if any of the dams were breached. It had not escaped some German minds either. Someone who was only too well aware of the risks involved was Justus Dillgardt, chairman of the *Ruhrtalsperrenverein*, the organisation responsible for the dams. In August 1939, showing remarkable foresight, he argued that the problem was not so much one of direct hits on the dam walls, but of bombs exploding below the waterline some twenty to thirty metres away. 'The compressed effect of the water caused by the explosion might cause the dam wall to collapse.'

Dillgardt's superiors would later have good cause to remember his predictions. From early in the war the Germans sent police and flak units to guard some of their dams. The Luftwaffe considered attacking the Derwent and Howden ones near Sheffield, but made no move to do so as it too lacked the means.

To add to Bomber Command's problems, events during the first year of the war showed quite clearly that, contrary to what had been said before it, the bomber would not always get through. Attacks in daylight quickly proved too costly and those by night became notorious for their lack of accuracy. The crunch really came with the Butt Report in August 1941, which showed clearly that only one in ten of the RAF's bombers was getting to within five miles of its target. There were those, within the RAF as well as outside it, who began to wonder whether it would not be better for Britain's war effort if Bomber Command were disbanded and its resources reallocated elsewhere.

All this meant that for the moment the dams remained unassailable. It would take a highly original mind, from outside the Service, to devise a method that would breach two of them.

At the outbreak of war Barnes Wallis was close to his fifty-second birthday and could look back on an aeronautical career of some renown.

He had initially made his name designing airships during the First World War, gaining a reputation for being technically competent and imaginative, but arrogant, unwilling to delegate and difficult to get on with. As the Assistant Chief Designer (Structures) under the Chief Designer, Rex Pierson, Wallis had worked for Vickers at their Weybridge factory, next to the famous Brooklands race track, since 1930. He had previously been the Chief Designer for a Vickers subsidiary, the Airship Guarantee Company, at Howden in Yorkshire's East Riding.

Wallis had shown foresight – not for the last time – by coming to realise that airships were likely to prove an aeronautical cul-de-sac and that the future now lay with aircraft. His task at Howden, assisted by Nevil Shute Norway, who would later become a well-known novelist, had been to design an intricate network of wires to hold the hydrogen gas bags in place within the alloy girder frame of the R100 airship. Bringing this experience to Weybridge had resulted in the geodetic structure for aircraft, which he had put to good use on the Wellesley long-range monoplane. This was followed by the twin-engined Wellington, which would prove to be the best of the RAF's bomber designs during the first two years of the war.

It was due to this that structures had become his main responsibility. With two new and larger geodetic types, the Warwick and the Windsor, under development at this time, it might have been thought that his plate was full enough. However, Wallis had the kind of mind that always thought several moves ahead and he began to focus it on other matters apart from bomber design.

During 1940 Wallis and the Vickers Drawing Office staff were evacuated from the main factory to Burhill Golf Club, which was two miles to the east. This early dispersal, which took place some months before the factory's other departments, turned out to be prudent, for both the Hawker and Vickers works on the airfield were subjected to a string of Luftwaffe attacks as summer turned to autumn.

The move also gave Wallis even more freedom than he already had. Although officially responsible to the Chief Designer and to the director-in-charge of Vickers-Armstrongs' aviation, who from June 1941 was Major Hew Kilner, Wallis was an independent character, with a free hand to make use of whatever facilities Weybridge had to offer. It was at Burhill, when his other duties permitted, that Wallis began to look at means of destroying natural sources of energy, with coal mines, dams and oil all considered.

Some indication of his character is necessary at this point. Assertive, to the point of being cantankerous at times, Wallis was a good deal tougher than the rather mild-mannered professorial type depicted by Michael Redgrave in the film *The Dam Busters*. Never one to put up with fools, he was capable of fighting his corner with some vehemence. He had looked on geodetics as very much his creation and woe betide anyone in the Drawing Office who strayed from the path that he had picked out. When dissatisfied with something that was being drawn, he was known to rip it from its owner's drawing board, scrawl on it the damning words 'Not this! Barnes Wallis', throw it on the floor and walk away. In this he was not unique; Sydney Camm, Chief Designer of Hawkers and best known for the Hurricane, was apt to behave in a similarly belligerent manner.

Not surprisingly, there were few people at Vickers who would care to argue with Wallis, though one who occasionally did was George Edwards, a Drawing Office section leader, who became the wartime Experimental Department Manager. He would later comment that working with Wallis was not all sweetness and light. Nevertheless, there was the respect of one engineer for another, despite his boss's reputed motto of 'quality at all costs'. This stubbornness did not make Wallis too many friends, but it was to stand him in good stead in the three years to come.

Wallis devoted much of the first year of the war to learning about bombs, the chemistry of their contents and the types of targets that they might be used against. He too sought information on the construction of the Möhne dam, finding it in a variety of German and Swiss articles dating back to the Edwardian era, when it and the Eder dam had been constructed. Though not yet concentrating exclusively on dams, his calculations led him to believe that the RAF's 1,000lb GP bombs were inefficient. He therefore sketched a 22,400lb bomb, over 19ft long and nearly 4ft in diameter, whose shape was not unlike the late and ill-fated R100. For now there was no question of this monster weapon taking to the air since no aircraft in the RAF's present or anticipated future inventory would be capable of carrying it, but it would form the basis of Grand Slam some five years later.

During October 1940 a series of tests connected with the Möhne dam's destruction began at the Road Research Laboratory at Harmondsworth in Middlesex. In a meeting with senior members of the laboratory's staff, Wallis mentioned the Möhne, the Eder and an Italian dam as targets for a ten-ton bomb attack, the idea being to get at least one bomb in the lake within 150 feet of the dam wall. It was decided to use 1/50th scale models of the Möhne in the tests, with the charges scaled down to two ounces each.

A series of reports compiled by A. R. Collins, a scientific officer who headed the four-man team involved, were initially encouraging, but also warned that the first models had been roughly constructed. Another report in February 1941 said that severe damage was unlikely to occur unless a 15,600lb charge was exploded fifty feet from the wall. Other tests, using a more carefully prepared model, took place at the Building Research Station at Garston, near Watford. This model, also to 1/50th scale and complete with towers, was constructed in a wood whose stream could be dammed to simulate the Möhne reservoir. The two-ounce charges did no more than crack it, and further experiments were carried out at Harmondsworth.

Wallis was a frequent visitor, but acknowledged that at this stage it was Harmondsworth's staff who were the experts, not him. It was also clear that no matter how good the models, there was no substitute for the real thing, so negotiations began with Birmingham City Corporation for authority to destroy a redundant dam at Nant-y-Gro, near Rhayader in Wales.

So far results had not been encouraging, but Wallis remained convinced that the explosion of his ten-tonner, if dropped from 40,000ft, would undermine a target by creating a shock wave in the ground alongside it. If no current RAF bomber could carry this load to such a height, then the only answer was to design one that would. In 1938 the Air Staff had searched for 'an ideal bomber' and Wallis had contributed a document entitled *Bomber Aircraft Determination Of The Most Economical Size*. This had had a wide circulation, including Group Captain the Honourable Ralph Cochrane, who had first met Wallis during his airship days in 1914-1918. Later on, Cochrane was to play a significant part, not only in Operation *Chastise*, but also in the use of two other bombs that Wallis would create.

Wallis was not the only designer to advocate larger aircraft, for Rex Pierson also proposed a six-engined bomber with a twenty-ton bomb load. All this was too much for the Air Staff, whose rejection of it was hardly surprising as the new four-engined Stirlings and Halifaxes were not yet in service. To some of the more conservative minds in Whitehall, a six-engined design must have seemed on a par with the futuristic multi-engined models used in the 1936 film *Things To Come*. All right for the Alexander Kordas of this world, but not for the RAF. Not yet, anyway.

Lord Beaverbrook, who became the Minister of Aircraft Production in 1940, was more open to new ideas. Impressed by what Wallis had said, he encouraged him to put forward the so-called Victory Bomber, to carry a 20,000lb bombload at 40,000ft for 4,000 miles. This too would have six engines. Although Beaverbrook was unable to commit his own ministry, he instructed Air Vice-Marshal Arthur Tedder, in charge of research and development, to give Wallis full co-operation. Sir Charles Craven, the Chairman of Vickers, arranged for Wallis to visit the English Steel Corporation at Sheffield to consult experts on the feasibility of casting the ten-tonner's casing. Official approval of the ideas put forward by Wallis and Pierson was not by any means universal, but the wheels were beginning to turn.

Someone else who began to look favourably on the ten-ton bomb idea was Air Commodore Pat Huskinson, Director of Armament Development for Beaverbrook's Ministry. A burly and blunt individual, Huskinson's character was not unlike that of Beaverbrook. He too had had his doubts about the effectiveness of the GP bombs; doubts that proved justified when he set up a trials target at an abandoned ammunition factory near Gretna Green and noted that many of the existing bombs failed to function when tried on it. Lessons that should have been remembered from 1914-1918 would have to be learned once again, although not by the Germans, for the bombs they dropped during the Blitz proved twice as effective as British ones, due to the use of aluminium powder in the filling.

A hasty process of improvement began and Huskinson became noted for his aggressiveness in pushing forward the updated weapons that he knew Bomber Command would need. However, as far as the ten-tonner was concerned, Huskinson could spare little time from his other problems, which were added to when a German bomb fell on his flat and blinded him.

At the beginning of 1941 Wallis summarised his recent work by writing *A Note On A Method Of Attacking The Axis Powers* – rather a long one at 117 pages. He began it with the following axioms:

1. Modern warfare is entirely dependent upon industry.
2. Industry is dependent upon adequate supplies of power.
3. Power is dependent upon the availability of natural sources of energy such as coal, oil and water (white coal).

Wallis stated that at present all the air forces used small bombs that were intended to attack surface targets. Attacks upon industry could be countered by dispersing it, but this could not be applied to the sources of energy listed above. 'If their destruction or paralysis can be accomplished they offer a means of rendering the enemy utterly incapable of continuing to prosecute the war.'

He was critical of current bombing efforts by both sides, saying that only through stick bombing could any direct hits be obtained and that even then Luftwaffe attacks on British cities had shown that hits created only temporary inconvenience. Parachute mines had a greater blast effect, but were inaccurate.

His technique would mean that the most destruction would be caused, not by the bomb's charge detonating, but by the air, earth or water that surrounded it. In the case of concrete, if the applied energy was highly concentrated, the structure would break before it could absorb the strain. 'Concrete structures which are quite unharmed by a charge bursting in air are destroyed by an equal charge bursting at the same distance, when the explosion occurs in deep water or in earth.' All enemy targets were in contact with water or earth, so 'to attack these targets successfully it is necessary to inject the largest possible charge to the greatest possible depth in the medium (earth or water) that surrounds or is in contact with the target.'

Wallis moved on to consider high-altitude attack, citing recent experiments with the high-altitude version of the Wellington. He considered that such aircraft could be used to attack the German coal-mining industry. Oil fields would be difficult, but hydroelectric dams were more promising.

Completed during March 1941, this Note was undeniably impressive, saying much for Wallis' ability as an engineer and his determination to impress his point of view on others. However, his criticism of current bombing was guaranteed to raise hackles in both Service and Government circles. His method of dam attack looked good enough on paper, but what of the difficulties of carrying it out?

A wide circulation of the Note to over 100 military, political and scientific individuals guaranteed a certain amount of interest, but also a great deal of scepticism. The Air Ministry, like its sister Services, was the unwilling recipient of any amount of new and often wildly impractical 'war-winning' ideas, not a few of them from Beaverbrook or Churchill. One scientific objection was that the state of current explosive development was such that it would be difficult to simultaneously detonate the entire length of such a bomb in order to produce the required shock wave, and anyway to some senior officers Wallis' ideas must have bordered on science fiction.

Unknown to Wallis, his name had attracted attention of a different kind. Professor E. A. Lindemann, Churchill's scientific adviser, had in the early war years been given a list of some forty inventors considered by an inter-Service security body of being German agents. One of those named was Wallis. The reasoning behind it was that since the Germans would be trying to find out what new weapons the Allies were developing, one way to do this would be to provide the agents with bogus ideas that sounded plausible but which were unlikely to work. The agents would then submit them to various scientific branches of the Service ministries and from their reactions gain clues as to what was really being developed. It was therefore possible to submit an idea and, regardless of its origin, be unknowingly blacklisted. Lindemann showed this list to one of his former Oxford students, Dr R. V. Jones. Jones thought the whole thing preposterous, especially as one of the names on it had been his mechanic while he was at college! The list may have been one reason why the ideas Wallis put forward were not immediately accepted.

One sympathetic recipient of the Note was Wg Cdr E. W. Winterbotham, head of the Air Section of the intelligence service MI6, who unofficially contacted the Prime Minister's office. The view expressed was that this project could not come to fruition until 1942 at least. Wallis showed characteristic impatience with those who did not immediately accept his ideas, but Winterbotham encouraged him to send a copy of the Note to Churchill. This move was however stymied by Lindemann, who declared that neither this bomb nor its aircraft could be completed before the war's end.

The anger and dejection that Wallis had begun to feel was added to on 21 May when Sir Henry Tizard, scientific adviser to the MAP, wrote to him, saying that the Air Staff had no interest in a large specialised bomber. Nor would they accept his view that this aircraft and its one big bomb offered a high probability of winning the war. They did, however, want two of his geodetic-structured aircraft in production as soon as possible. These were the high-altitude Wellington V, followed by the Warwick. They were to take priority over the Victory Bomber – which meant that he could continue work on it if nothing else was required.

Tizard was not unsympathetic to Wallis and supported the idea of the ten-ton penetrating bomb, but under present circumstances he had to agree with the Air Staff's decision. It was sound enough, for at present Bomber Command was just beginning to accept four-engined aircraft, and so far introduction of new designs had taken up to six years.

In September Vickers put the final nail into the Victory Bomber's coffin, consigning it to a long list of British aeronautical might-have-beens. It was now beginning to look as if the sceptics had been right after all, and that without the means to carry it the Wallis bomb would never leave the drawing board either.

Towards the end of 1941 Wallis shelved his idea of high-level ten-ton bombing and began to seek other methods of destruction. Early in the following year he conceived the idea of a weapon that would be dropped on the water upstream of the dam, to reach it by bouncing across the surface. On striking the dam wall it would sink and explode in close contact with it.

He was unable to recall how this idea occurred to him. The process has been likened to the children's game of ducks and drakes, but this is not so, as the stones involved spin round a vertical axis, while his weapon would use a horizontal one.

The advantages of this unusual method of delivery are best explained by quoting from a later report on the Highball bomb, further details of which will appear in

Chapter 4. This report was compiled in 1944, with hindsight, by the Vice-President of the Air Ordnance Board:

> If a spherical missile is set spinning about a horizontal axis, and is projected horizontally in the same direction as the underside is moving as the result of the spin, it will be found in a greater or lesser degree 'to fly by itself', depending upon the amount of energy imparted to it in spin and in horizontal travel. Thus the spinning sphere is well adapted to extend the range of a bomb after leaving an aircraft.
>
> The spinning sphere has a further characteristic in its ability to ricochet on water … This ability is greatly increased by imparting a spin in the same direction as is required to develop the lifting force.

Spinning would extend the bomb's initial flight before its first impact on the water, as well as improving its accuracy. Also, the number of ricochets and the length of travel on the water after the first impact would both be increased by comparison with a non-spinning sphere projected with the same horizontal velocity.

There was therefore a clear need to spin the weapon in order for it to bounce ahead of the aircraft, across the surface of a dam's lake. However, while spinning it forwards might have seemed the obvious course of action, this was not as desirable as it appeared. Once the bomb struck the water, drag would tend to spin it forwards. Drag is resistance to forward movement – caused by water as well as by air – and backspin would counter this. Spinning it forwards would also create what was referred to as negative lift, tending to roll the bomb beneath the water before it reached its target. Therefore, although the bomb would fall forwards and down on release, to achieve the desired result it would have to be spun backwards before it left the bomb bay. Backspin would also cause it to adhere to the dam wall and run down it before exploding. Provided the bomb was in contact with the wall when this took place, the water would tamp the resulting shock wave and breach the dam.

All of this may seem obvious now, but in 1941 it had yet to be fully appreciated. Although this method took Wallis some time to establish, it was not as novel as it appeared. He knew that, in order to avoid flying too close to a well-defended vessel, Allied airmen had used skip-bombing during anti-shipping strikes. This had involved dropping conventional weapons from low level, but climbing at the moment of release so that the bombs struck the sea at an angle, to skip forward across the waves. Indeed, these ideas predated aircraft, for he later discovered that naval gunners in the 'wooden wall' era, by pointing their cannon slightly downwards, had made the balls ricochet across the sea to increase their range.

Navies had not been the only forces to try such techniques. Napoleon Bonaparte, who had been an artillery officer before going on to higher things, had tried using his cannon – known as 'The Emperor's Favourite Daughters' – to bounce 12lb round shot off the ground and through the opposing infantry's ranks. However, Wallis later said that such knowledge had served only to reinforce his idea, and not as the inspiration for it.

Attacking dams in this war would be nothing new. As if to highlight these targets, the British film industry had released a film entitled *Ships Have Wings* – a poorly titled, badly scripted and ineptly acted piece of propaganda that had been intended as a tribute to the Fleet Air Arm. The customary stereotypes were all on display, the Italians being portrayed as idiots and the Germans as ruthless. The British aircrew gallantly faced heavy opposition en route to their dam target, which at the last heart-stopping minute was successfully breached, washing away a load of miniature enemy vehicles perched on the top of it. A model attack, in every sense.

The real thing was a different story. On 2 February 1941 Vice-Admiral Sir James Somerville, commanding the Royal Navy's Force H in the Mediterranean, had sent torpedo bombers from the carrier HMS *Ark Royal* to attack the hydroelectric dam at Tirso in Sardinia. Due to strong anti-aircraft defences this attack had been unsuccessful, although the Italians had been sufficiently alarmed by it to equip all their dams with net defences. All this was a portent of things to come.

It was in April 1942 that a scene familiar to everyone who has seen *The Dam Busters* film took place – that of Wallis borrowing his daughter Elizabeth's marbles and using a catapult to bounce them across water in a tin bath in his garden. Replacing the marbles with half-inch wooden spheres, Wallis patiently noted the results. He explained to Winterbotham, by now a group captain, that if a spherical bomb was used and detonated from the centre, the force of the explosion would reach all points of the surface at the same moment – which took care of the previous objection to the ten-ton deep-penetration weapon. Fine, but how would such a weapon react when it struck the water? Winterbotham phoned an Air Ministry contact, who assured him that it would bounce like a football. To Winterbotham's surprise, Wallis exclaimed, 'But my dear boy, splendid! Splendid!'

Once again it was time to commit his ideas to paper, which he did in *Spherical Bomb – Surface Torpedo*. Considering this weapon as primarily one for the Fleet Air Arm, he approached Professor P. M. S. Blackett, scientific adviser to the Admiralty. Blackett was impressed, seeing it as a method of attacking German capital ships, but also saw it as an RAF weapon and contacted Tizard, who met Wallis at Burhill the following day. The two men got on well, which was particularly important as Tizard's influence was wide-ranging, taking in the MAP and the Chiefs of Staff. Within two days permission had been obtained to use the facilities of the William Froude Laboratory at Teddington in Middlesex.

In the meantime, in a scene that would have been delightful to witness, Wallis and his secretary, Amy Gentry, went out in a rowing boat on Silvermere Lake, which was south-east of Brooklands airfield. Amy Gentry was, conveniently, not only an oarswoman of some note, having reputedly trained to Olympic standards, but also a formidable person – no shrinking violet would have lasted long in her position – and she was prepared to argue with her boss if she thought the occasion warranted it. When Wallis stood up to launch projectiles of various shapes across the surface, she bellowed, 'Sit down, Wallis! You'll have us both in the water, and I'm in charge of this boat!' Her common sense could not be denied, but, perhaps while working from a crouching position, Wallis carried out his tests and as a result decided the sphere was the best.

Work at Teddington began in June, taking place intermittently until the last week in September, the task being to refine the method of delivery to the target. Something that had to be resolved was whether to spin the weapon and if so, in what direction. To drop it without spinning would cause it to sink like a stone and if it was spun forward there was the danger of it leaping over the dam wall, then exploding harmlessly on the air side of it.

When Wallis decided on backspin is not known, although George Edwards, the Experimental Department manager at Vickers and a keen cricketer, was reputed to have discussed spin bowling with him at the time of the Silvermere Lake experiments. As will be seen, this would prove crucial on the night of the raid.

Something else that may have influenced his thinking was the discovery, made by nineteenth-century golfers, that the smooth-bodied gutta-percha balls of the day travelled further once they had collected nicks and scratches. This led to the dimpled surface of the golf balls of today. Also, when hit by a golf club the ball had backspin, which gave it height. It was lifted by a force nearly twice its own weight, which was why it soared high into the air in a parabola.

Various dimpled and smooth two-inch spheres, made from lead, balsa and other materials, were tried; the bounces were timed and the sphere's underwater trajectory filmed at Teddington after it struck the target. The tests attracted many visitors, including Tizard, who saw them as very promising and recommended a full-scale test using a Wellington. Another important visitor was Vice-Admiral Edward de Faye Renouf, who was engaged in experimental work and immediately saw the weapon's potential. He returned the next day with other senior officers, for whose benefit Wallis used a wax battleship model as the target. They were duly impressed when the sphere passed underneath it and went away convinced that a version of this weapon could be fitted into the bomb bay of a Mosquito. This would lead to the Highball bomb later on.

Now the RAF had to be convinced. On 21 June Air Vice-Marshal E. J. Linnell, Controller of Research and Development, visited Teddington and four days later gave permission for a Wellington to be fitted with an experimental weapon of 4ft 6ins in diameter. The film scene, in which Michael Redgrave as Wallis requests a Wellington on the grounds that he designed it, is an oversimplification; the design of this aircraft, and the modifications to it that would now take place, were very much a team effort, as Wallis himself would have been the first to acknowledge.

This was progress, but an order to convert one bomber did not mean that the Air Staff had been convinced of the weapon's effectiveness against dams. Wallis had spared no effort to convert all concerned, but impatiently wrote, 'There is no doubt that the Air Staff have been singularly stupid over this point.' He must have been cheered up by the news that the Admiralty wanted twelve of these spheres dropped from a Wellington and that MAP had authorised the Oxley Engineering Company, based in London and Leeds, to manufacture them.

The point that the charge needed to be in contact with the dam to breach it has already been mentioned, but this was not fully appreciated until early 1942, when A. R. Collins, still carrying out the Harmondsworth tests, decided to see if a contact explosion would breach one of the damaged models. To his surprise, it worked – pieces were flung up to thirty feet away.

The next step, with the permission of Birmingham Corporation, was to breach the old and redundant Nant-y-Gro dam at Rhayader in Wales. However, the dam held after an explosion in its lake on 1 May. Collins therefore felt that nothing less than a charge of 30,000lb would destroy a gravity dam the size of the Möhne, if it went off at a distance from it. Such a weapon was clearly impractical; it would have been bigger than the ten-tonner that Wallis had originally put forward.

Although it had been unofficial, the Harmondsworth contact test had been reported to Wallis and would now have an important effect on his thinking. If an explosion in the Nant-y-Gro lake failed to work, then would a charge in contact with the wall do the trick?

On 24 July a 500lb submarine mine, containing 279lb of explosive, was used as a contact charge at the Nant-y-Gro dam. This was spectacularly successful, pushing out its centre. Scaling up the weapon from this test meant that a 7,500lb charge exploded thirty feet below the water level of the German gravity dams would cause a fifty-foot breach. The weapon's casing would mean additional weight, but even so it was within the carrying capacity of the Avro Lancaster; a new four-engined design which had been in service with Bomber Command since the previous April.

In spite of all this some of the great and the good were still far from convinced. Professor Lindemann, now ennobled as Lord Cherwell, was one of them, and since Wallis did not meet Churchill Cherwell's attitude could not be ignored, especially when this new Peer of the Realm loftily declared that he doubted if the dams were of any consequence. Perhaps he was still influenced in some way by the blacklist of inventors. However, at a meeting at Vickers House in London on 25 August it was decided that 'the Spherical Bomb' should be tried off Chesil Beach in Dorset.

Before being loaded into any of the trials aircraft, the balance of the bombs would be tested on a specially built rig at the Experimental Department's dispersed site at Foxwarren. Situated in Redhill Road, halfway between Brooklands and what would become a new airfield at Wisley, this consisted of a few basic but adequate buildings, which would be used for the construction and testing of a variety of projects, from the F7/41 high-altitude fighter to the post-war Vickers Valiant – the first of the V-bombers.

The Lancaster's capacious bomb bay is shown by this shot of NX611, the aircraft preserved at the Lincolnshire Aviation Heritage Centre, in October 1997. The bulge behind it housed the H2S scanner. (S. Flower)

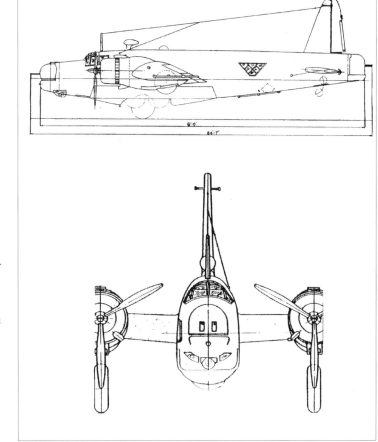

A pair of drawings, based on the original 1942 ones, showing the early experimental spheres as fitted beneath the trials Wellington. It can be seen that two were carried in the modified bomb bay. The other complete circles show the position of the undercarriage when extended. Also shown is a blister fitted to the bomb-aimer's window in the nose, enabling him to look forward as well as down. (S. Flower)

The trials Wellington in action at Chesil Beach. It is not known exactly when this was taken. (Imperial War Museum)

Summers dives the Wellington before releasing the first of the two bombs. (Imperial War Museum)

Moments later, the bomb bounces, but part of its casing flies off. This is visible just in front of the column of water. (Imperial War Museum)

Moving the Experimental Department to Foxwarren had been the idea of George Edwards, who had become its manager before the bombing of the Vickers works in 1940. Concealed among the abundant Surrey woodland, it was well away from Brooklands and, like Burhill, was less likely to be hit by any future Luftwaffe attacks.

By now Hawkers had left Brooklands to concentrate their workforce at a larger factory at Langley in Buckinghamshire, leaving their buildings at the Brooklands Flying Village to be taken over by Vickers. It was here, at a discreet distance from curious eyes at the Vickers factory across the grass airfield, that a Chester-built Wellington BIII, BJ895/G, was modified to take four of the Oxley Company's spheres.

Initial trials took the form of spinning a sphere on the ground, then in a rig fitted in a Wellington's fuselage to check the aircraft's stability. The next step was to load four of them into BJ895/G.

On 2 December Joseph 'Mutt' Summers, Vickers' Chief Test Pilot, flew this aircraft over the Queen Mary reservoir, north of Weybridge. Wallis, who was on board, spun all four spheres simultaneously at maximum revolutions, using the hydraulic system that had originally been installed to operate the bomb doors, which by now had been removed. As Summers was unaware that the spheres were spinning, it seemed that any fear of the aircraft being broken up by a gyroscopic effect was unfounded. However, not all of 617 Sqdn's crews would agree with this on the night of the raid.

Two days later, by now modified to spin two spheres, the Wellington flew to Chesil Beach with Summers as pilot, test pilot Bob Handasyde as flight test observer and Wallis as bomb aimer. The bombs were dropped into a stretch of water shielded from the open sea by a massive shingle bank. Although Wallis considered the experience exciting, it was also a disappointing one, for the welded spheres broke up on hitting the water. Nothing daunted, he ordered that the outer casings were to be reinforced with a mixture of granulated cork and cement.

The next attempt was made on 15 December, when Summers dived the Wellington at top speed and released two spheres, one smooth and the other dimpled, at sixty feet. Both appeared to shatter on impact, but Wallis eventually recovered one, to find that it was badly damaged, not broken. A meeting chaired by Vice-Admiral Renouf two days later noted the failure of the spheres and agreed to further strengthening of them, with Vickers providing another two standby wooden ones.

The third trial took place on 19 January 1943, one steel sphere breaking up on impact and the second one accidentally falling on land. Next day one repaired steel sphere was dropped from 100ft; according to Wallis it bounced as high as fifty-five feet before breaking up.

Far better results were obtained on 23 January, when a wooden sphere, dropped at 42ft, at 283mph and spinning at 485rpm, bounced thirteen times. The next morning another bounced at least twenty times and at dusk Summers bounced another over a special boom on the test range. On 5 February some wooden spheres of 3ft 10ins in diameter were dropped from various heights, achieving a range of 1,315 yards, which was twice that predicted by the model experiments.

By now two versions of the bomb were under consideration. These were code-named Highball, to be used by a Mosquito against surface vessels, and Upkeep, to be used by a Lancaster against the Ruhr dams. A third variation, code-named Baseball, involved mounting a mortar in the bows of an MTB or MGB of the Royal Navy's Coastal Forces to fire bombs at enemy shipping. This never saw the light of day, but would remain a possibility for the next two years.

With a certain satisfaction Wallis showed films of the trials on 28 January to mixed audiences of Vickers and Service staffs, including Winterbotham, Summers, Handasyde and Sir Charles Craven. Next day Vickers undertook to manufacture 250 Highballs at their Crayford works.

At last things looked to be going his way, but just to be certain Wallis drew up a third paper on the bombing of enemy industrial targets. Entitled *Air Attack On Dams*, but also including material on shipping attacks, it was sent to Vice-Admiral Renouf, then to other responsible Service officers and civilians.

On 30 January Wallis passed a copy to Lord Cherwell, with a covering letter stating that the Nant-y-Gro experiment had shown that it was possible to destroy the German dams if the attack coincided with them being at their maximum capacity, which would be May or June. Preparations for use of Highball were moving ahead and the potential deployment of this weapon against naval targets was threatening to overshadow the use of its larger brother against the dams. 'It is felt that unless the operations against the dams are carried out almost simultaneously with naval operations, preventative measures will make the dam project unworkable and that therefore the development of the large sphere of five tons' weight should be given priorities equal to those for the smaller weapon.'

Rather rashly, Wallis then went on to promise that if equal priority were given to both weapons, development of the larger one could enable it to be dropped from a Lancaster within two months. Modifications to the Lancasters would be small and the aircraft could be returned to their original use within a few days. This last assertion would turn out to be incorrect.

In his latest paper Wallis explained that the Nant-y-Gro dam had been a fifth of the size of the German ones, so a charge five times larger than that used in the second test there would be sufficient to breach them. Regarding the Sorpe, a more modern concrete-cored dam that had been built in the 1930s, he was of the opinion that such a dam would become self-destroying if a substantial leak could be established within the watertight core. In this he gave as an example the Dale Dike dam near Sheffield, whose collapse in 1864 had begun with a small crack on the crest. Wallis felt that if the Sorpe's concrete core could be cracked seepage would erode the earth bank on the downstream side, leading the core to collapse due to lack of support. However, he was wrong here; the Dale Dike dam had had a clay core and was therefore not comparable with the Sorpe.

Wallis concluded that in the Ruhr district the destruction of the Möhne would lead to a serious shortage of water, both for drinking and for industrial purposes. In the Weser district the breaching of the Eder and Diemel dams would seriously hamper transport on the Mittelland Canal and the river Weser.

Cherwell saw the Teddington film three days later, this time with less antagonism than before. Air Vice-Marshal Linnell approved preliminary design work on what was then referred to as Big Highball but was not prepared to sanction any further moves in case development of the Vickers Windsor bomber was adversely affected. This four-engined long-range geodetic design, not unlike a smaller version of the Victory Bomber, was yet another project that Wallis somehow had to find time for.

For Wallis and his team, February was a busy time, with conferences, working lunches and long working days that at times stretched almost to midnight. On 10 February came the news that Linnell had ruled that nothing more was to be done about the Lancaster project, although Highball work would continue. Linnell acknowledged that Upkeep was technically feasible, but Vickers were already some weeks behind on the Windsor project due to the Mosquito modifications for Highball. If Upkeep went ahead, this delay would stretch to months, also affecting Lancaster production at Avros at a time when Bomber Command were in need of as many of these aircraft as they could get. Linnell cautiously advised that Upkeep should wait until Highball tests had been satisfactorily concluded.

It was now time for those at the sharp end to be advised of what had been happening. Bomber Command's SASO, Air Vice-Marshal Robert Saundby, passed a copy of Wallis' latest paper to Bomber Command's AOC, Air Chief Marshal Sir Arthur Harris, with a minute stating that a particular squadron would have to be nominated, which would deprive the Command of that unit's strength for about three weeks. Saundby considered the operation feasible and concluded – wrongly – that the tactics would not be difficult.

Harris had become Bomber Command's AOC in February 1942, at a time of inadequate aircraft – with the exception of the Wellington – low bomb loads, few navigation aids and questionable morale among his crews. An ardent believer in strategic bombing, he seemed to regard his Command as the only force capable of winning the war for the Allies and was convinced that it should have priority over everyone else, including the rest of the RAF.

As far as Harris was concerned, what mattered was the breaking of German morale by the area bombing of cities. Anything that deviated from this was looked on by him as a 'panacea' – something seen by others as a universal cure-all but which in his opinion would turn out to be a waste of time and effort. His views had been reinforced by an unusual raid on the battleship *Tirpitz* at Asenfjord near Trondheim in Norway on the night of 27/28 April 1942. A force of Halifaxes and Lancasters under Wg Cdr Donald Bennett had gone in with the object of dropping 1,000lb spherical mines as well as bombs. The mines did not have contact horns but had carried hydrostatic fuses set to explode below the water's surface. The idea was that they would be dropped at low altitude, to roll down the side of the fjord and explode beneath the ship.

It had all seemed sound enough, but the raid turned out to be a failure and five bombers were shot down, including Bennett's Halifax, although he escaped to Sweden and was soon repatriated. His name will reappear in this story later on. A check by a PRU Mosquito showed that the *Tirpitz* had suffered no apparent damage. Indeed, her crew later confirmed that the mines had achieved nothing apart from scrape off some paint and kill a large number of fish! It may have been one reason why there was opposition to the Highball bomb later on.

With this fiasco in mind, it was hardly surprising that the AOC's reaction was a robust one. A blunt individual who, like Wallis, never tolerated fools, he was not impressed by what he read. His reply said exactly what he felt: 'This is tripe of the

Air Chief Marshal Sir Arthur Harris, AOC Bomber Command 1942-45. The look says it all. (Imperial War Museum, neg. no. CH13020)

wildest description. There are so many ifs and ands that there is not the smallest chance of it working.' He contended that if the bomb were not perfectly balanced it would either be torn loose by the vibration at 500rpm, or the aircraft would be wrecked. 'I don't believe a word of its supposed ballistics on the surface ... At all costs stop them putting aside Lancasters and reducing our bombing effort on this wild goose chase ... The war will be over before it works – and it never will.'

Nevertheless, an Air Ministry meeting on 15 February, which included Wallis and Summers, resulted in the go-ahead being given for one Lancaster to be modified for Upkeep. When this news reached Harris three days later, he promptly wrote to the Chief of the Air Staff, Air Chief Marshal Sir Peter Portal. Although he confused Highball with Upkeep, his feelings were plain enough:

> All sorts of enthusiasts and panacea mongers [are] now careering round MAP suggesting the taking of about thirty Lancasters off the line to rig them up for this weapon, when the weapon itself exists only within the imagination of those who conceived it ... I am now prepared to bet that the Highball is just about the maddest proposition as a weapon that we have come across – and that is saying something ... I am prepared to bet my shirt (a) that the Weapon itself cannot be passed as a prototype for trial inside six months; (b) that its ballistics will in no way resemble those claimed for it; (c) that it will be impossible to keep such a weapon in adequate balance either when rotating it prior to release or at all in storage; and (d) that it will not work when we have got it ... Finally, we have made attempt after attempt to pull successful low attacks with heavy bombers. They have been, almost without exception, costly failures ... While nobody would object to the Highball enthusiasts being given one aeroplane and told to go away and play while we get on with the war, I hope you will do your utmost to keep these mistaken enthusiasts within the bounds of reason and certainly to prevent them setting aside any number of our precious Lancasters for immediate modification.

Harris did not take kindly to advice from outsiders, including the Air Staff. Not only did he oppose this weapon, but also the idea of creating a special squadron to drop it. Special units of any size were anathema to him; on taking command in 1942 he had resisted the idea of a Path Finder Force, arguing that it would be a *corps d'elite* with a consequent adverse effect on morale within other units, who would be loath to send their best crews to it, and that it would be better if each bomber group developed its own marking techniques. His attitude would later have a certain significance for the Lincolnshire-based 5 Group and its AOC, Air Vice-Marshal the Honourable Sir Ralph Cochrane.

Air Commodore S. O. Bufton, head of the Air Ministry's Directorate of Bombing Research, had argued for the PFF force as far back as 1941. After consultation with the Air Staff his view had been backed by Portal, leading to the establishment of the PFF in August 1942 under Donald Bennett, who had rapidly risen to the rank of air vice-marshal while still under forty. It had become 8 Group the following January. All this had been much to the annoyance of Harris, who had regarded this as 'dictation' by a junior staff officer and had no doubt marked Bufton down as a panacea monger.

It was as well that Wallis had his supporters elsewhere. The First Sea Lord, Admiral Sir Dudley Pound, had described Highball as 'the most promising secret weapon yet produced by any belligerent'. Not that Pound's opinion would have cut any ice with Harris, whose contempt for naval officers was well known, but Wallis was making other converts to his cause by use of the trials films.

On 21 February he showed extracts from the Teddington and Chesil Beach films at Vickers House to an audience which included Pound, Craven and – significantly for Harris – Portal, although neither he nor Pound were fully prepared to commit themselves as yet. However, Portal did write to Harris, stating that Wallis' idea could not be dismissed out of hand, but promising that no more than three Lancasters would be diverted for Upkeep trials until the bomb had been thoroughly tested. He felt that a limited gamble was worthwhile.

Two days later, with Mutt Summers, Wallis finally entered the lion's den – Bomber Command HQ at High Wycombe in Buckinghamshire. The fact that he was now about to meet Harris owed much to the old boy network. Cochrane, as already noted, had known Wallis during 1914-1918 and had served under Harris in the inter-war years. As ever, it was not what you knew but who, and it had been Cochrane who had convinced his AOC to give them an interview.

The reception was warm but not welcoming. 'What the hell do you damned inventors want?' roared Harris. 'My boys' lives are too precious to be thrown away by you!'

He became a little less abrasive as Wallis outlined his scheme and agreed to see the Chesil Beach film. Despite his misgivings, Harris was aware of the need for security and curtly dismissed the projectionist, leaving Saundby to perform that task. Although he now had a clearer idea of what had been accomplished, Harris, like Portal, could not commit himself to setting aside a Lancaster squadron for one special operation, but he did reveal Portal's authorisation of the three trials Lancasters.

At last the CAS was coming round to favour the Upkeep attack, and on 22 February another hurdle was cleared when MAP finally gave its formal approval for two Mosquitoes to be modified at Brooklands for Highball trials.

Breaks, good or bad, come when they are least expected. On 23 February Wallis and Hew Kilner were summoned to Vickers House to see the company's chairman, Sir Charles Craven. They listened in shock and surprise as Craven told them that further work on Upkeep was to be stopped. Craven said that Wallis had made a nuisance of himself at MAP, was damaging his employers' interests and had offended the Air Staff. This had come about through Linnell urging Craven to stop this 'silly nonsense about destruction of the dams'. Linnell was evidently not aware of Portal's decision concerning the trial Lancasters, but, like Harris, was concerned about diverting them to this project. He also considered that the Windsor's development would suffer.

Seeking to make a dignified exit, Wallis quietly replied that if Craven really felt his conduct was damaging to Vickers, his resignation was at Craven's disposal. Now it was Craven's turn to display shock, which he did by slamming his fist on a desk top and shouting, 'Mutiny!'

Wallis left Craven's office, saying to Kilner that he really wanted to go, but his mood did not last long. He had come too far to give up now, and anyway three days later the situation changed again. At an MAP conference chaired by Linnell, to which Roy Chadwick, Avro's Chief Designer, had also been invited, Wallis was told that the CAS wanted every effort made to prepare aircraft and weapons for use during the spring of 1943. Upkeep had now been given priority over the Windsor and any other Lancaster projects at Avro.

The three trials aircraft would be followed by a further twenty-seven, to be delivered by 1 May. Due to the falling level of water in the dams, 26 May would be the last date by which they could be attacked that year. Vickers would handle the attachment arms for the bomb and the weapon itself, while Avro would deal with modifications to the bomb bay.

Torpex explosive would be made available to fill 100 Upkeeps, for which a self-destruct fuse would be necessary for security purposes in the event of an aircraft crashing in occupied territory. Work was also to continue on Highball, with the first modified Mosquito to be ready by 8 April.

Wallis left the meeting with the sudden and sick realisation that, far from being out of work, he was now to be pushed as never before. Everything that he had argued for over the last three years was about to be granted, but he had only three months in which to prove the feasibility of the weapon on which he had expended so much effort. Despite the trials, at this moment that weapon existed only on the drawing board. Past stresses and strains would seem as nothing compared to what now lay ahead.

2

Prelude

> There is no greater joy in life than finding something is impossible and then showing how it can be done.
>
> Sir Barnes Wallis, in a post-war television interview

With such a tight schedule there could be no question of taking weekends off. Even if there had been Wallis was by now so involved with this project that he would have found that impossible to do. On Saturday 27 February, he and his staff began work on the first full-size Upkeep drawings at Burhill. This task was done in a rather unusual area of the golf clubhouse, as Norman 'Spud' Boorer, a draughtsman who worked under him, later explained:

> In this squash court we had a big upright drawing board at the back, on the gallery of the squash court, which was, I think, 21 ft long and 7ft high. It had a rail along the top and a T-square hanging down, with the arms on, which you wheel about and do all your drawings ... Barnes Wallis, having been given the challenge to produce this weapon working by a certain date, got stuck in. Ernie Marshall and I drew the bomb up on this big drawing board in the squash court. We were then working for a section leader called Eric Allwright.

At the top of the golf clubhouse was the Centre of Gravity and Weights Office, one of whose draughtsmen was Jack Froude.

> I remember visiting a room in the house where I believe Spud Boorer, another senior designer, Marshall, and later a contemporary of mine, Ron Smithers, worked up the design. (I remember being somewhat envious of Ron at the time.) Of course secrecy was the order of the day during the war. I recall everyone in the building being called out onto the grass in front of the clubhouse to hear a speech by 'a Lord of the Admiralty' on the necessity of keeping quiet about what was going on. Perhaps it worked – the Luftwaffe left us in peace throughout the war.

In view of his own involvement in experimental work and his encouragement of Wallis after witnessing some of the Teddington trials, it seems likely that the officer concerned was Vice-Admiral Renouf.

Eric Allwright had previously worked in the Stress Office, then in the Drawing Office under Basil Stephenson, who had been Assistant Chief Designer at that time. Like the rest of the Vickers Drawing Office staff, Allwright had been moved to Burhill in 1940. By now he had a good deal of aircraft design experience, but like Wallis and the rest of the team, he had never designed a bomb until Wallis had come up with the ten-tonner and the Victory Bomber.

> When this bouncing bomb came along, we all knew what was going on, because he had one or two members of his own team working on it. We weren't involved in the project side of it at all, but we knew what was going on. He was getting little balls,

about the size of a golf ball, made up in Foxwarren at the Experimental Department, trying to get this thing to fly properly. So we knew all about this, and a lot of people rather derided it as 'the ball-game'. Then suddenly it started taking off.

Although Upkeep's outer casing would initially be spherical, its explosive would be contained within a steel cylinder. This was to be $^3/_8$in in thickness. It would be just under 5ft long and 4ft in diameter, with detonation to be provided by hydrostatic pistols of standard Admiralty design, as used in depth charges, set to explode at thirty feet below the level of the water. Three of these were fitted, the idea being that if one was put out of action when the bomb struck the dam wall, the other two would still be left to function as the bomb sank. The self-destruct fuse, a fourth item, was intended to be armed only after the bomb had left the aircraft.

The Vickers works at Crayford would deal with Highball, while Upkeep's steel cylinder and its wooden outer casing would be produced at other Vickers plants at Barrow, Elswick and Newcastle upon Tyne. Upkeeps for operational use would go to the Royal Ordnance Factory at Chorley in Lancashire for filling with Torpex, while those intended for trials would have an inert filling supplied by the ROF at Woolwich. It was intended that inert Upkeeps would be light grey in colour, while live ones, like other RAF HE bombs, would be dark green. Vickers staff would fit the wooden casings at a designated operational station.

Until he met Roy Chadwick, Wallis may not have realised that he too had been thinking along the lines of a big bomb. Sandy Jack, Chief Inspector of Avros' Lancaster Group, later recalled how far-sighted Chadwick had been:

The success of the Lancaster owed a good deal to Roy Chadwick's foresight in designing from the earliest Manchester project a bomb bay strong enough and roomy enough to carry the total maximum payload in one piece. This idea was not popular in 1936, when the largest bomb in production was the 2,000lb AP!

The Lanc was probably unique in being the only bomber aircraft in the world capable of carrying its maximum disposable load, if required, all in one piece. This ability was no accident, for Chadwick was a confirmed advocate of the big bomb. When the Manchester was still an early project I recall an argument with some Ministry and RAF officials. They were very concerned that the bomb gear should release an accurately aimed and evenly spaced row of bombs. Chadwick said, 'Gentlemen, if you dropped a stick of bombs spaced within three inches of the pattern you want, and they landed in a field fifty yards from my office, they would probably break the windows. If you dropped one 10,000lb bomb and missed by 500 yards, you would at least blow the complete roof off the building.'

All this had been said well before the Lancaster, which grew out of the unsuccessful Manchester, had first seen the light of day in 1941. Like Wallis, Chadwick had always been personally involved in all aspects of aircraft design; unlike Wallis he was more polite, quietly spoken, and preferred simple solutions to detailed ones. Chadwick's care, competence and good manners won him the respect of those he worked with, from shop-floor workers to flight test crews. It might therefore have seemed unlikely that he would have got on well with Wallis, but then Chadwick was no stranger to the abrasive characters that the aircraft industry seemed to breed in those days; Roy Dobson, the Managing Director of Avros, was a blunt Yorkshireman who tolerated neither fools nor delays.

Dobby, as he was nicknamed, possessed a fund of energy that was well known throughout his company. He was the kind of leader who was prone to visiting his factories at all hours, whose personality inspired his work force, who was accessible to just about everyone and was prepared to give them a fair hearing. If it became clear to him that modifications were necessary to improve the Lancaster's efficiency, he would go ahead with them at once, regardless of any bureaucratic objections. Once he had authorised such changes, Dobson would back his staff – to Cabinet level, if necessary.

These two were the kind of men who had turned the disastrous Manchester into a four-engined triumph. Their attitudes, their experience and the resources they commanded were exactly what Wallis needed to make his dream become a reality and meet the deadline that had been set.

Roy Chadwick now came up with what was called the Type 464 Provisioning Lancaster. These would be Lancaster BIIIs, fitted with Packard-built Merlin 28 engines. Apart from their bomb bay modifications, Chadwick suggested the mid-upper gun turret be removed to reduce drag. This was referred to the Air Staff, who subsequently approved it. A belt drive would be fitted on the starboard side of the doorless bomb bay, connected to a motor in the fuselage, and this would spin the weapon up to the required speed before dropping. Other modifications would be found necessary as the weeks passed and the Lancasters that would take part in Operation *Chastise* would be very different beasts from those used by Bomber Command's Main Force.

It was time to bring the modified Wellington back for another appearance, dropping two 3ft 10ins spheres at Chesil Beach. These had been filled with a cork and cement mixture to give 'the anticipated density of Upkeep', although they were not to the same size. More useful data was obtained before Wallis and his team moved to Reculver Bay on the north Kent coast.

During March the first three inert Upkeeps reached Brooklands and were rated 'a magnificent job' by Wallis. However, the total number of modified Lancasters was cut back to twenty-three, which meant that only twenty would be available for operational use. The three trials aircraft would be modified at RAE Farnborough by Vickers, while the remainder would be tackled by Avro. A small four-cylinder motor produced by Vickers for submarines would be used to spin the bomb. Spinning and balancing tests at Foxwarren settled a fear Wallis had had that Upkeep would leap clear of its retaining arms if spun at 400rpm or more. This all became part of Spud Boorer's job.

> When we got this thing going we had to test it first and balance it ... We built up an M-frame and suspended these things, drove them up to 400-500 revs. With that lot whizzing round no one in their right mind stood in front of it, because had it come off it would have gone all the way down and cut a swathe through the forest that was there. But they were all tested and balanced – they had to be balanced, otherwise they'd shake the aeroplane to bits – and delivered to Scampton. A chap by the name of Hill was the chargehand who went up to Scampton to see all this lot on its way, and of course Wallis went up to see the flight off.

By now sixty of each of the inert and live bombs were on order, with twenty of the inert ones to go to RAF Manston in Kent, in connection with the forthcoming Reculver Bay trials. The remaining forty inert Upkeeps, with all the live ones, would be sent to RAF Scampton in Lincolnshire.

The first Type 464 Provisioning Lancaster, ED765/G, arrived at Farnborough on 8 April, followed by two others, which would be based elsewhere as soon as Vickers had finished work on them. These were ED817/G, which went to Manston, and ED825/G, which was allocated to the AAEE at Boscombe Down in Wiltshire. The Manston aircraft bore the code letters AJ-C, but it should be explained that it was not the aircraft (ED910/G) that would be used by P/O W. Ottley on the raid – there were two Lancasters at the same time with the same code letters. The serial number G suffix was allocated to all the modified aircraft, denoting that because of the equipment they carried they had to be guarded while on the ground. At least one Highball trials Mosquito, DK290/G, is also known to have carried it, along with a number of the aircraft that would be issued to 618 Sqdn.

Spud Boorer ran into trouble while the three trials Lancasters were being modified at Farnborough.

Another one of my jobs on this was to lift this sphere, as it was early on, into the Lancaster. I got hold of Rex Pierson's globe, with the right scale, mocked up a Lancaster's bomb bay with cardboard and got ropes round it to see how you could lift it up into the bomb bay, because it was a pretty tight fit. Any rate, I did this and designed the necessary lifting gear for it – wire ropes about three-quarters of an inch diameter, which for the purpose I wanted needed to be wire-spliced at the end. We had an old boy in the shops by the name of Harry Couch, who'd been on the Vimy's first flight and who was a sailor in the early days and a wire-splicer.

As noted earlier, the Vickers Vimy twin-engined biplane had been intended to bomb Berlin in 1918, but instead had achieved more fame in post-war pioneering flights. Couch had been a rigger for the transatlantic pilots Alcock and Brown in 1919, so he would have been glad of the opportunity to revive his old skills.

I had a chat with him and we designed these ropes that way. Unfortunately I got called over by Wallis to Farnborough one day for a striping. I showed him this Lancaster with this bomb on the trolley and these wires to pull this thing up into the bomb bay, and he said, 'You're a clown, Boorer. This thing won't go in. Look! It jams.' I said, 'Let's have a look at that. It shouldn't do.'

What had happened – the Ordering Office at Weybridge – probably good-natured – had thought, 'Oh, wire-splicing's going to take a long time. We'll swage on some stainless steel Brunton ends.' These were solid stainless steel, so for the first foot or eighteen inches of the rope, instead of being flexible it was absolutely stiff. I explained this to Wallis and he calmed down a bit. 'Well, we've got to get it in somehow. We've got to drop this thing today. Time's getting short. What are you going to do about it?'

It is said that 'a call for engineering' is a polite phrase meaning 'give us a bigger hammer'. This time it turned out to be true.

I picked up this sledgehammer and belted this fitting round. I said, 'I hope there are no stress-men around, because they wouldn't let me do this.' 'No,' he said, 'I know they wouldn't. Nor would I really, but that's all you can do, isn't it?' We got it in and they made the proper ropes up afterwards and all went well.

All of this sums up the 'fit and make fit' situation that Wallis and his staff now found themselves in. Problems like this had to be speedily dealt with and there would be no time for elegant solutions. It all meant more red tape for Dobson and Chadwick to cut through, as Sandy Jack later recalled:

The modification work on the production line was extensive enough to cause comment in official circles. Some of the Ministry officials wanted the job to be done in a separate screened compound with attendant tight security. The Avro management and myself were completely opposed to this. We wanted to work as usual on one production line and leak information that this was a secret anti-submarine weapon. This was credible as the first trials were carried out at sea over the south coast. The Avro view prevailed; probably Dobby would not have done otherwise, even if asked.

The first modified operational Lancaster was ED864/G, which arrived at Scampton on 8 April. To further indicate how rushed things became, the twentieth and supposedly final one arrived there just three days before the attack took place. Even that was not the end of the story, for there would be one more last-minute addition, as will be seen.

Reculver Bay was secluded, with no houses overlooking it, which was why it had been selected for the task. Its only prominent feature was a ruined old Norman church, whose twin towers were clearly visible on a promontory. The church had been demolished by a vicar in the eighteenth century, but he had been obliged to leave the towers standing as a navigation marker for shipping. He could never have imagined the use that they would now be put to.

Handasyde used the modified Wellington to survey the trials area, while further balancing and spinning tests were carried out in Lancaster ED765/G at Manston. The weather and tide were deemed suitable on 13 April and among those gathered on the beach to witness the trials were two young officers from Bomber Command – Wg Cdr Guy Gibson and his Bombing Leader, Flt Lt Bob Hay.

Cameras on the shore would record the range and line of the drops, while inside the aircraft a bulb flashed when Upkeep was released. A. D. Grant of the Burhill staff was aboard, carrying four stop watches to time the first three bounces, to assist in determining their height and to record the duration of each run. In addition, on some of the drops a device worthy of Heath Robinson was mounted inside the aircraft to record the number of bounces. This consisted of a tripod with a peephole that rotated on a vertical axis, surrounded by a cylindrical perspex sheet. The operator looked through the peephole as the Upkeep was released, turned through 180 degrees to follow it down, then drew its track and the number of bounces onto the perspex. This was then transferred to tracing paper, leaving the perspex to be wiped clean for the next trial.

At 0920 on 13 April Handasyde arrived in the Wellington, flying along the beach at 289mph IAS towards two white buoys which were acting as markers. At a height of eighty feet an inert Upkeep, spinning at 520rpm, was released. On impact the wooden casing shattered, sending pieces in all directions, but the steel cylinder that had been inside it ran on. 'Excellent,' said Wallis.

Another pilot who would now be involved in the project was Sqdn Ldr M. V. Longbottom, whose stature of 5ft 6ins had led to the nickname of 'Shorty'. He was an RAF officer who had been seconded to Vickers for test flying. Later that morning and in the early evening he dropped two Upkeeps from the Lancaster. The first, dropped from 250 feet, shattered, leaving Wallis to wade out at low tide to recover the fragments. The second drop was to be at fifty feet, but this proved almost fatal, for the casing broke again and one piece of debris flew up to damage the Lancaster, which had some difficulty in landing at Manston. Once again it was noted that the cylinder ran on, without being affected by the abrupt loss of the casing.

For now Wallis had no intention of abandoning the original spherical design of Upkeep, believing that further tightening of the metal bands around the woodwork would keep it in place. However, on 18 April the Lancaster, this time piloted by Summers, dropped three bombs. Two sank altogether and yet again the third one broke free of its casing to bounce for some 700 yards.

The fact that this had now happened three times could no longer be discounted and overnight the wooden casings were removed from the remaining bombs at Manston. The bomb that 617 Sqdn would use in action would be cylindrical.

Eric Allwright remembered only too well the problems involved in Upkeep's design and building: 'A lot of work went on around it. Wallis was trying to do his ordinary job as well as all this – he was out at the Ministry and down to Fort Halstead and everywhere.'

Fort Halstead, near Sevenoaks in Kent, housed an Armament Design section, which would later provide the pistols for the earthquake bombs, and may have provided those for Upkeep as well. They had also queried whether such a large quantity of explosive would not burn, at least in part, rather than all explode simultaneously.

Eventually we drew this thing up, stressed it as far as we could, because it was cylindrical. It had these running tracks on it and the fuses inside. But it did have a wooden casing on it, to make it part of a sphere. Now, we didn't have time to develop that properly. The woodwork was all round, fitted up, and retained by very large continuous solid steel bands round it, about an inch in width, holding this lot

Upkeep in its original form, probably photographed at RAF Manston, with the wooden outer casing that was discarded shortly before the dams raid. A Mosquito can be seen in the right background. (A. Lane)

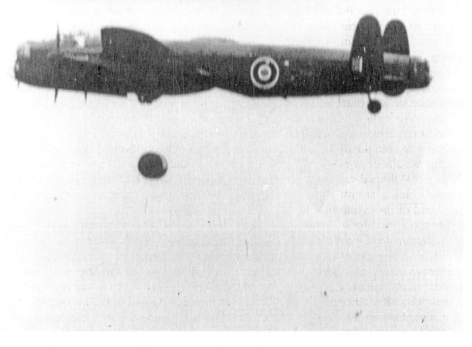

The final cylindrical version of Upkeep being dropped from a Lancaster at Reculver during 1943. (Imperial War Museum, neg. no. MH7294)

together. But even that wasn't satisfactory – it broke up when it hit the water. So things were getting desperate and Wallis said, 'Well, we'll try it without.' That saved the day … We hadn't got enough reinforcement on the woodwork and it was coming up to a date which was the only one available. It wasn't very easy doing this class of work. You couldn't spend weeks thinking about it – you had to get on with it.

However, even the course of the modified bomb did not run true at first, and an incident that occurred at this time showed another danger. A break-up on impact was likely to bring down the aircraft that had dropped it, as was seen when Capt. H. A. 'Sam' Brown, Avro's Chief Test Pilot, dropped two cylindrical Upkeeps, both of which came apart. This caused the first of a series of accidental damage problems for Sandy Jack:

Sam Brown flew the first modified Lanc to Boscombe Down, where it was promptly bombed-up with a missile of the then 'latest design.' Sam dropped it near Chesil Beach in relatively shallow water, whereupon it broke up on impact and sent up a cloud of spray that enveloped the tail of the Lanc. From then on Sam had problems with longitudinal control and on return to Boscombe Down we found that water containing many pebbles about the size of one's fist had done great damage to the elevators and tailplane. Many too were trapped in the structure and I still have one to this day.

The right time for the raid was now less than a month away and the pressure on Wallis was relentless, though he was to deny afterwards that he ever lost any sleep over it. Certainly he looked tired when he met Gibson and Longbottom at Burhill on 24 April. Well aware of the increased danger to Gibson's crews, Wallis stated that the operation would fail unless the bomb was dropped at precisely 60ft and 232mph groundspeed.

Gibson thought of the dangers he had faced in the past and would have to face again. He said, 'We'll have a go if it will work.' Wallis felt both gratitude and apprehension in equal measure, although when they were told the glad tidings Gibson's crews knew only apprehension.

On 29 April Longbottom dropped an Upkeep spinning at 500rpm at 50ft at 253mph. This one bounced six times in 670 yards, before deviating slightly left of its course towards the end of the run. Two similar performances were achieved over the next few days, and Wallis was now satisfied that the operation could go ahead as planned.

During the first week in May, two screens were erected east of the Norman church to simulate the dam towers. The Lancaster then 'attacked' towards the shore. The consequence was that several bombs landed on the shingle beach and film shows that at least one leapt over it to finish up in a field behind. Also visible, though with his back to the camera, was Wallis, waving his arms in exultation.

The size, weight and make-up of Upkeep had finally been determined. Its total weight would be 9,250lb, of which 6,600lb would be the Torpex explosive filling. The two V-shaped caliper arms which protruded from the bomb bay held the bomb across it and a twenty-inch disc mounted on their inside engaged a circular track at each end of the cylinder.

On the Lancaster's starboard side a belt was linked at a forty-five-degree angle to a Vickers Jassey Speed Variable Gear hydraulic motor in the bomb bay, causing the bomb to rotate backwards at 500rpm. Problems had been caused by trying to mount the motor above the bomb, so it was fitted inside the front of the bomb bay. The three bomb pistols remained set for thirty feet and the self-destruct fuse was timed to go off ninety seconds after release. Pressing the bomb release would operate powerful springs that would swing the caliper arms outwards, so dropping the weapon.

It all sounded fine, but would a live Upkeep work as Wallis had intended? Longbottom answered that question on 13 May by dropping one five miles off the resort of Broadstairs. This was recorded by a camera on the North Foreland and by another in a second Lancaster flown by Handasyde, with Gibson as an observer. The Upkeep spun at 500rpm, bounced seven times over some 800 yards, sank and detonated, with an enormous white spout of water that rose some 500 feet above Handasyde's Lancaster.

After all this, Wallis and Chadwick would certainly have agreed with a comment made by Alliott Verdon-Roe, after whom Chadwick's firm had been named: 'Achievement after incessant difficulties and obstacles is invariably sweeter than easily attained success for those who accomplish it.'

While the Upkeep trials had been going ahead, Harris had decided to allocate this task to 5 Group and the new squadron that was to drop it in action had been coming together at RAF Scampton in Lincolnshire.

Despite his long-winded 'Honourable' title, Cochrane was very much an airman's airman, with a keen interest in those below him and the problems that they faced. A reserved, austere man, he constantly sought to improve both the tactics and bombing accuracy of his command. Under his leadership 5 Group had become something of a law unto itself, earning the nickname 'Cocky's Private Air Force' – a reputation that at times led to strained relations between him and other bomber Group commanders, particularly Air Vice-Marshal Donald Bennett, the Pathfinder pioneer of 8 Group.

Although Harris could seldom be accused of sentimentality, he had himself commanded 5 Group earlier in the war and there were those who felt that he still favoured it at the expense of the other Groups, giving as an instance the fact that it had been the first Group to receive the Lancaster. However, this meant that if all the men for the new unit were selected from within 5 Group no conversion training would be necessary. Also, if anyone had cared to check back through the various Air Force Lists compiled in the 1920s they would have noted that Flight Lieutenants Cochrane and Saundby, now the AOC's deputy at High Wycombe, had served under the then Sqdn Ldr Harris as his flight commanders.

On 15 March Harris ordered Cochrane to form this new squadron without depleting the Main Force effort. The breaching of the dams would be its first task, but not its only

Air Vice-Marshal the Honourable Sir Ralph Cochrane, AOC 5 Group. (Imperial War Museum, neg. no. CH14564)

one. To command it Harris nominated Wg Cdr Guy Gibson, who had previously served under him in 5 Group. Harris, who did not give praise lightly, assessed Gibson as 'the most full-out fighting pilot in the whole of 5 Group in the days when I had it'. Inevitably all this would have led to moans about 'jobs for the boys', but if anyone had had the temerity to mention this in the presence of Harris he would no doubt have replied that it did not matter provided the right boys were slotted into the right jobs.

If any 5 Group boy was right for this job, it had to be Gibson. One of the RAF's few surviving pre-war regular officers who was still on operations, his experience had included Hampdens, Manchesters and Lancasters, with – unusually for a bomber pilot – a spell on Beaufighters with a night fighter squadron during the later stages of the 1940/1941 Blitz, instead of the OTU rest period that he would otherwise have taken. Wallis was to say of him: 'Men of a certain type will only become miserable if they are condemned to inaction, and their fate really lies in their own hands.'

During March 1943 Gibson, then CO of 106 Sqdn, recorded his last operation with them as being his seventy-first on bombers. At a time when few bomber crewmen, whatever aircraft they flew, could count on getting more than halfway through a tour of thirty operations, so far he had been fortunate indeed.

Expecting leave, Gibson's posting to administrative duties at 5 Group's Grantham HQ came as a shock. After more than three years at the sharp end, sitting behind a desk held no appeal for him and he readily agreed when Cochrane asked him to form a special squadron for one more operation. At this stage he was given no further details, but was told to practise low-level flying at night.

Squadron X, as it was initially known, came into being on 17 March and would be based at Scampton. This was a two-squadron station, but one unit had been moved out as part of the preparations for the laying down of hard runways. Squadron X would therefore be housed alongside 57, a Main Force unit.

The film has since given the impression that Gibson had a free hand to choose his crews from the whole of Bomber Command, with many well-decorated and 'tour-expired' crews volunteering, bringing with them a wealth of experience. The reality was different. His choice was restricted to 5 Group and men were posted in regardless of whether they had volunteered or not. He did not know all the pilots, not all crew members were decorated and some had not even finished one tour, let alone two. Some of them were 'posted across the station' from 57 Sqdn, including its entire C Flight, despite protests.

The reasons for joining were as varied as the men themselves. Some had had an offer made to them and took it up because it sounded interesting, or saw it as a means of remaining with crewmates they already knew and trusted. The hard-bitten types, who, like their new CO, preferred to remain in the front line, looked on it as a means of avoiding the instructing duties that they would normally have been given after finishing a tour. Others arrived with a certain sense of grievance, such as Sgt Stefan Oancia, the bomb aimer in Flt Sgt Ken Brown's Anglo-Canadian crew, who later commented that he did not recall volunteering for this transfer.

One pilot who was certainly determined to remain on operations for as long as he could was Flt Lt David Shannon RAAF, who had considerable respect for Gibson after previously serving with him in 106. He was later to say of him, 'He was my mentor. There was nobody quite like him ever again.'

Someone else with similar feelings was P/O Warner Ottley DFC, who arranged his crew's posting from 207 Sqdn to the new unit. A future star of the squadron was Flt Lt Harold 'Mick' Martin, an Australian who had earned a reputation for brilliant flying, especially at low level. Gibson had met Martin at a Buckingham Palace investiture and remembered that he had talked about the virtues of low flying. Now he asked for Martin and got him. Gibson's own crew were experienced men, although only Hutchison, his wireless-operator, had previously flown with him in 106 Sqdn.

As soon as Gibson arrived there was no doubt as to who was in charge. Some men saw him as straightforward but strict, while others nicknamed him 'The Boy Emperor' and saw him as a tyrannical glory-hunter. Corporal Beck Parsons, an electrical NCO and known as 'Joe' to his mates, described him, with evident restraint, as 'a typical regular CO'. Beck would now have the job of assisting in the fitting of this strange new bomb and its release mechanism to the squadron's Lancasters; a demanding task which Gibson's presence would not make any easier.

Gibson's feelings had hardened since 1939 and he was well aware that he had a lot to do in a short time. As the weeks went by he would come under increasing strain, which would sometimes manifest itself in publicly criticising men for trivial errors. Another method of relieving it was to take his black Labrador dog, Nigger, with him on walks around Scampton's perimeter. He needed to think, while Nigger loved to chase rabbits.

His concern was primarily with the operational side of his new command; he had little time for paperwork and was happy to delegate most of it to the Adjutant, Flt Lt Humphries, assisted by Flt Sgt Powell and Sgt Heveron, all of whom had previously been known to him and were good at their jobs.

One clue to the kind of pressure that Gibson was under, and his attitude to some of those below him, was illustrated by an incident that had occurred in his previous command. John Searby, an officer who had been posted to 106 Sqdn, met Gibson in his office and was asked what previous experience he had. When Searby replied that his service had been with Atlantic Ferry Command, Gibson's response had been curt. 'Ferry Command! This is the real thing – and anyone that doesn't like it can get out.'

Searby, who knew his next crew would value his experience even if Gibson chose not to, curbed his dislike when he noticed a pile of letters to next-of-kin on the desk. This was one administrative duty that Gibson did not delegate, so it was no surprise that he was in a bitter mood. Despite this unfortunate introduction, the two men became friends, Searby taking over 106's command when 617 was formed. Gibson was the kind of man to be either liked or loathed, but always respected.

With regard to the equally important non-flying side, every effort was made to sort this out by Flt Sgt Powell, who had previously been in charge of 57 Sqdn's administration. Having sorted out and swiftly reposted several unsuitable erks who had been dumped on him by other 5 Group units, he then submitted a list of requirements to the Station Stores Officer. When the latter, showing that helpful attitude so often assumed by storemen the world over, made a negative reply, Gibson soon intervened, backed up by an Air Ministry order that top priority was to be given to the new unit. Powell was fortunate in that 5 Group's pool of ground handling equipment was held at Scampton, so it was not long before the necessary paraphernalia required to service a bomber squadron began to appear. However, for the moment aircraft were a different matter and Gibson's crews had to make do with ten borrowed Lancasters until the modified ones arrived.

On 26 March X Sqdn was renumbered 617 and Gibson was informed that it would be required 'to attack a number of lightly defended special targets'. These attacks would necessitate low-level attacks by moonlight. The target details were not disclosed yet, but it was significant that it was deemed necessary to practise attacks over water. Gibson was inclined to think that their target would be the battleship *Tirpitz*, still lurking in a Norwegian fjord. If that were so, her defences would certainly not be light.

He learned a little more when he was summoned to Burhill to meet Wallis for the first time. After a journey by road and rail Gibson arrived at Weybridge station, to be met, to his surprise, by Mutt Summers, whom he had once met while seeking a test pilot's job at Brooklands before the war. The two of them then drove in a small Fiat car to Burhill, where their passes were rigorously checked – Gibson's buff-coloured one had been issued to him only that morning.

In his book *Enemy Coast Ahead*, Gibson, bound by wartime censorship, could say only that he met two characters named Mutt and Jeff – a rather thin disguise for Summers and Wallis. There was further surprise and not a little embarrassment when Wallis found out that Gibson had not yet received clearance to be told what the targets were! 'That makes it awkward, very awkward,' said Wallis, who contrived to get round it by giving Gibson a general summary of what had been achieved so far, illustrated by the trials films, and stressing that the bomb had to be dropped from 150ft at 240mph after coming out of a dive from 2,000ft.

Gibson had a good deal to think about as he took the train back up to London, but at least the target now seemed unlikely to be the *Tirpitz*. This was confirmed on 29 March, when Cochrane showed him two models of the Möhne and the Sorpe before sending him to see Wallis and Summers again, this time for a fuller briefing.

During April the squadron saw a great deal of sky. Gibson set a high standard and expected everyone around him to live up to it; those who did not could expect a swift posting back to the Main Force. The bomb aimer's additional duty of map reading from one navigational checkpoint to another while flying at night at low level had been mastered, as had flying at 150ft over water, although as a result of the Reculver trials this would be lowered to sixty feet, increasing the hazard to the crews.

For a successful run the Upkeep would have to be dropped absolutely level, for if one side struck the water before the other this could cause the bomb to turn away from the target. Indeed, this would happen to one aircraft at the Möhne on the night. The Lancaster would have to climb away after attacking the dams, but with a wingspan of 102ft and a fuselage length of 69ft 6in, this new height left little margin for error and even less chance of avoiding any flak. At such a height any violent evasive action was out of the question.

617 Sqdn's crews used ground targets at Wainfleet bombing range on the Wash, but two large white boards were also erected 700ft apart to simulate the Möhne dam's towers. Later the Eyebrook reservoir, near Uppingham in the Midlands, was used, with the same two boards re-erected on it. Their activity did not attract undue attention as aircraft often practised in that area. On 4 May an RAF working party under the appropriately named Flt Lt Lake replaced the boards with four canvas targets on the parapet wall, grouped in pairs to simulate the Möhne's two towers.

For local residents the rapid approach of four Merlins was deafening, but it was something that had to be accepted and many witnessed the nightly spectacle of huge black bombers pulling up sharply over the dam wall, firing flares as they went. The Abberton reservoir, near Colchester in Essex, proved a suitable practice target for the Eder dam and was used in the same way.

There were many civilian complaints, especially as advance warnings could not be given for security reasons. Sqdn Ldr Henry Maudslay, one of Gibson's flight commanders, once returned with foliage adorning his Lancaster after too low a flight, and airsickness was an unpleasant side-effect for several crew members.

An additional problem was the after-effect of the use of Synthetic Night Flying Equipment. Designed to simulate night visibility, but allowing training to be carried out by day, it comprised blue celluloid fitted to the two remaining turrets and the cockpit perspex. Crew members then wore amber-tinted goggles. This was fitted to two of the squadron's Lancasters, was used extensively and favourably commented on by Gibson, but the drawback was that when the goggles were taken off afterwards everything appeared red, which meant that crews had to don dark glasses until their eyes had readjusted.

Something that was more serious was the difficulty of maintaining accurate height at night over water. It was Benjamin Lockspeiser, MAP's Director of Scientific Research, who solved the problem, not – as the film later implied – Gibson watching spotlights on chorus girls in a theatre! Lockspeiser suggested spotlights shining down from the aircraft to determine their height, to which Harris commented, 'I tried that once with flying boats and it didn't work because the spotlight went through the water.' Indeed it had, but that had been on the open sea, in choppy water, not the calmer conditions of a dam lake.

After tests at Farnborough it was decided to fit two spotlights under each Lancaster's fuselage. Twenty feet apart, one would be under the port side of the nose and the other placed centrally in the rear of the bomb bay – it would not be obstructed due to the lack of doors.

Both lights were angled down to starboard and the only person able to see them would be the navigator, who would be looking out through the starboard blister window in the canopy, behind the pilot. On the navigator's command, the aircraft would descend until the two beams touched to form a figure of eight. The aircraft would then be flying at the correct height.

That was the theory, demonstrated by Maudslay before a sceptical audience at Scampton. More recent research has indicated that the beams were not perfect and that in some instances they converged below the surface, but despite this danger there were no accidents. After the crews had practised with them, they became convinced of their worth.

When the navigator was not required to give a commentary on the spotlights, he still had his usual trade to practise, now assisted by the Air Position Indicator, a device that had come into use the previous February. Designed to automatically and continuously maintain an accurate air plot, it showed the bomber's air position in terms of longitude and latitude, so that a ground position could be quickly plotted if the wind was known, or the wind speed and direction could be readily determined from fixes. There were no problems in installing the API and it was later reported to have worked well on the night of the raid.

Assuming accurate navigation to the target, another problem – there seemed no lack of them – was how to aim the bomb at low level. Conventional bombsights were intended for high-level area bombing and the only answer seemed another Heath Robinson-like contraption, devised by Wg Cdr C. L. Dann, one of three senior trials officers at AAEE, with responsibility for bombs. This sight was the ultimate in simplicity – a piece of wood with two nails banged through it, to coincide with the dam towers.

However, at low level the thicker air caused buffeting and the bomb aimer, prone on his cushion in the Lancaster's nose, could not use both hands to steady the Dann sight as he needed one for the bomb-release mechanism. Consequently three crews dispensed with this sight and made up one of their own. These were the crews captained by Flt Lt Les Munro, P/O Les Knight and Flt Lt David Shannon. This sight, even more basic in construction than the Dann one, was described by Flt Lt (then Flt Sgt) Len Sumpter, Shannon's bomb aimer, on his return to the Möhne in 1989:

> Three of us used the string and the chinagraph, and all the rest had the wooden bombsights. But Clay with Munro, they had to turn back, so there were only two of us left with string. And, coincidentally, all of the blokes that took part in the breach of this dam used the wooden sights and it only took two of us to breach the Eder with the string!

So, how did it work?

> On the front of a Lanc you've got the clear-vision panel – that round piece that you look through. Well, on that we put two thick chinagraph marks all the way down the panel, which corresponded with the nails on the piece of wood. Around the clear-vision panel were little nuts, so we loosened the inside of the nut on this side, tied the string on tight on that nut on that side, got a good run, put it round the other nut loosely, and then to scale again from the panel back to your nose – say you've got to get it seventeen inches – you pulled it back and measured it until it was seventeen inches, taut, you tightened that nut up, put a knot right in the middle and there's your bombsight! All you did was get the knot in your doings, hold it on your nose, look through your chinagraph marks and line up and that was it. That was the same as looking through the hole in the two nails on the sight and it was a lot easier, because you could put your arms on the armrests, you could have your bomb release in this, rest your hands together like that and there was no wobbling at all, whereas with the wooden one you were holding that end.

Using the string, the bomb aimer could hold himself rigid with his elbows. This would prove vital to the success of Shannon's and Knight's crews at the Eder.

Another change in procedure arose from the deletion of the mid-upper turret. On Main Force aircraft front turrets were seldom manned due to the rarity of head-on night fighter attacks. However, in this instance not only was there a displaced gunner, but also a need to provide some means, however slight, of firing back at any flak while making the bomb run. This meant moving one of the aircraft's two gunners into the front turret.

Most gunners were short in order to fit into the turrets, but, regardless of their size, most crews put the more experienced gunner at the rear. This time the other would go into the front one, with stirrups fitted to keep his feet out of the bomb aimer's line of sight.

Yet another modification, with which a lot of Main Force crews were already familiar, was the removal of the perspex between the guns in the rear turret. This lowered the temperature in the turret by only one degree – which indicates how cold it was in there – but improved the gunner's vision and therefore the crew's chances of survival. It also put a stop to incidents such as gunners firing at an engine oil dribble on the perspex, after mistaking it for the silhouette of a night fighter creeping up behind! All of 617's Lancasters would fly on the operation with their rear turrets so modified.

Ammunition was supplied in metal disintegrating-link belts, which in the case of the rear turret consisted of 2,500 rounds per gun and fitted into U-section channels that ran down the fuselage. On firing, empty cases and belt links were ejected via chutes below the gun barrels, at the extreme rear of the bomber. The usual mix was ball and armour-piercing, with every fourth or fifth round tracer to give the gunner an indication of where his fire was going and in the hope of frightening off any attacker. However, standard tracer, which glowed red or pink, did not ignite until it was some distance from the gun barrel. A special night tracer, known as G VI, which would burn continuously from the aircraft to the target, was devised by the Royal Army Ordnance Corps. It also used a white light, in the hope of fooling the Germans into thinking that cannon shells were being fired at them.

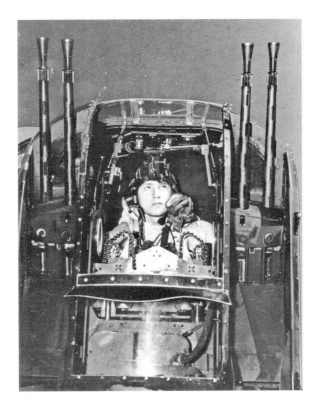

A Lancaster's rear gunner in his turret. The centre Perspex panel has been removed and ammunition can be seen feeding the guns from the centre (Imperial War Museum, CH12776)

Two 0.303in Brownings were carried in the front turret and four at the rear. A ventral position had been considered and indeed fitted to one of the trials aircraft, but was dispensed with before the raid. In the film, belted 0.5in ammunition is seen being loaded into one of the aircraft, which has the later Rose rear turret, but this is incorrect as only Frazer-Nash turrets were used by 5 Group at the time of this operation. All of this was the responsibility of Flt Lt R. D. Trevor-Roper DFM, who was Gibson's rear gunner and the squadron's Gunnery Leader.

There was also the question of communication. The TR1154 W/T radio sets normally carried by Bomber Command aircraft used Morse; something that was acceptable for Main Force raids, but which would take too long to pass on Gibson's commands over the targets. What was needed was a VHF R/T set of the type used by Fighter Command. The TR1196 set was considered, but rejected as the frequency band that it used suffered from severe interference at night. An alternative, the TR1143, was therefore fitted, proving excellent.

By the beginning of May Gibson was able to report that all his crews were ready for the operation. Eighteen modified Lancasters had also been received, with more following up until the day of the raid. On the night of 6/7 May an elaborate night exercise was staged, with nine aircraft in three flights of three flying to the Eyebrook and Abberton reservoirs in turn, to attack singly at precisely 60ft and 232mph, while being directed by Gibson. This was to simulate the attacks on the Möhne and Eder, while another six crews went to the Derwent dam to simulate the kind of attack envisaged for the Sorpe. The remainder – considered the reserve – were to practise bombing with spotlights over the Wash.

Following on from this, between 11 and 14 May, 617's aircraft dropped inert Upkeeps at Reculver, using the simulated towers on the promenade as aiming points. Wallis was impressed with their ability to put their bombs onto the beach. Someone who was not so happy was 617's Engineer Officer, who, now that the raid was almost on them, had the aircraft of Munro and Maudslay to repair. Munro's Lancaster had been damaged by dropping his Upkeep from lower than sixty feet, but was made ready in time for his part in the Sorpe attack. Maudslay's aircraft was in worse shape and his crew would go into action in another. With a decision to add one of the trials Lancasters to 617's strength, this made nineteen Lancasters for twenty-one crews, although sickness would solve this problem.

The squadron was at its peak now, but there would be no let-up until the last minute. Modifications to the Lancasters were still being carried out and the driver who brought an MAP Queen Mary trailer into Scampton with Upkeep rotation gear on board had been cautioned not to stop en route. Just in case he did, there had been a heavy escort to deter him from doing so. Parts were produced at Avros under the same tight security as anywhere else. Even the staff in the Design Office did not know what they were drawing, but Chadwick did. On the evening of 14 May, there was one more night exercise, again to the Eyebrook and Colchester reservoirs. Gibson noted it in his logbook as 'completely successful'.

While these final exercises had been taking place, on 13 May an Upkeep and Highball progress meeting, attended by Gibson, learned that while Upkeep had proved satisfactory, Highball, whose trials had been taking place in Scotland, had not. These bombs had broken up on impact.

At this time the Chiefs of Staff were in Washington and so the Vice-Chiefs met to confer over this latest turn of events. Air Chief Marshal Sir Douglas Evill argued that even if an Upkeep and its aircraft were captured, this would not mean that Highball would be compromised. His naval opposite number, who had received specific instructions from Admiral Pound before his departure, could not agree, so a signal was sent to Portal in Washington. The RAF argument won the day, for on 14 May the Chiefs of Staff replied that Upkeep should be used immediately without waiting for Highball. Thus Operation *Chastise*, which had come close to being cancelled at the last minute, finally went ahead.

It was now that a Most Secret Message was received at High Wycombe:

Op. *Chastise*. Immediate attack of targets 'X' 'Y' 'Z' approved. Execute at first suitable opportunity.

Behind these code letters lay the Möhne, Eder and Sorpe.

Activity at Scampton, already hurried, became frantic in the final two days before the raid. Mail services were temporarily suspended, phones were tapped and Gibson reminded everyone of the need to maintain tight security. Cochrane arrived to inform him of the decision, and as he left, taking Gibson with him to go over a draft operation order at Grantham, Wallis and Kilner landed from Brooklands in, of all aircraft, a white Red Cross Wellington flown by Summers.

Someone who was affected by it, even though he was not there, was Eric Allwright:

I remember on the day before the dams were knocked down there was some problem up at Scampton in Lincolnshire, where these things were, and of course we had two representatives up there. They wanted to talk to me about some of them. So it was all rushed. We were only allowed six minutes a call, because the lines were needed

The Möhne dam, photographed shortly before Operation *Chastise*. Torpedo nets can be seen in the dam lake and the power station that would be destroyed by Hopgood's bomb is visible between the base of the dam and the compensating basin. There were at least six gun positions, three on the dam wall and three by the crossroads at the lower left. (Author's collection)

for other things as well. So they rang up and it was chopped off, and we had to put a call back to them, and this went on all the morning until we'd resolved the problem … The other thing, which was rather nice, was that I was completely in Wallis' confidence. The day before we knocked the dams down I was called up to look at the aerial photographs taken the night before. I saw these things – I was very lucky in that way. He treated me very well.

On his return Gibson briefed his two flight commanders, his Bombing Leader, Bob Hay, and his Deputy Leader, Flt Lt J. V. Hopgood. This was as well, since Hopgood pointed out that the proposed route would take them close to a well-defended synthetic rubber factory at the town of Hüls. The route was amended accordingly.

Late in the evening Gp Capt. J. N. H. Whitworth, Scampton's station commander, regretfully informed Gibson that his dog Nigger had been run over outside the camp gates by a car. Contrary to what has been said elsewhere, the driver, a local doctor making his rounds, did stop, but there had been nothing he could do. It seemed like an omen and Flt Sgt Powell was surprised when Gibson quietly asked him to bury the dog outside his office window at a time when the squadron would be over Germany.

On Sunday morning the ground crews swarmed over each aircraft in the warm sunshine, but security had been such that it was still not apparent to most other people on the airfield that the operation was imminent. Many of those who were to watch 617 take off that evening were under the impression that they were witnessing the beginning of another exercise.

Compasses were swung with and without Upkeep in place, since it was found to have a strong effect on them. Any deviations were then noted on a card in the aircraft, although some instrument fitter slipped up in one instance, as will be seen. Gleaming belts of the special tracer ammunition, delivered at the last minute, went into the fuselage channels, fuel bowsers drove up to pump their loads into the wings and, with the aid of modified trollies, the Lancasters were bombed up. Even with conventional bombs, this was not only hard work, but also dangerous. The armourers were only too well aware of an incident at Scampton the previous March, when a 4,000lb 'cookie' had fallen out of a Lancaster and exploded. As well as the single Upkeep, each aircraft would carry six 4lb 'stick' incendiary bombs and other pyrotechnics, should target illumination be necessary.

It was to be expected that things would not go smoothly. At Flt Lt Mick Martin's aircraft, AJ-P, the crew were inside checking things over when the Upkeep fell from its arms onto the tarmac of the dispersal pan. Hay yelled that it might have fused itself and would go off in less than a minute. The crew and the armourers hurriedly exited from the Lancaster, anxiously seeking the nearest available cover. Martin dashed off in the flight van to fetch the Armament Officer, P/O H. 'Doc' Watson, who with some disdain declared, 'Flap's over. It's not fused.' Various airmen crept sheepishly back to the scene, to hoist the errant weapon back into position. It was then painted black by the crew.

Meanwhile the draft order for the attack was being updated and retyped. An appreciation of the defences stated that Target X (the Möhne) had three light gun positions on the crest of the dam. Two of these had been incorporated into the tops of the sluice tower roofs. A further three-gun flak position was situated near the village of Gunne and there was a double line boom with timber spreaders in the dam lake. That meant netting, which showed that the Germans had anticipated a torpedo attack.

The Möhne's flak defences had been put in place at the beginning of the war. They had then been removed for use in the western offensive during May 1940 and had not been replaced until two years later. There had also been some balloons, but these too had been removed and not replaced. It was thought unlikely – and correctly – that any dam other than the Möhne would be defended. This target was to have priority, followed by the Eder, which would be attacked once the Möhne had been breached.

The Sorpe would be attacked separately, in the hope of diverting the defences, but that did not mean that this dam was considered of lesser importance. However, three

The modified version of the Upkeep bomb, as mounted on Gibson's Lancaster, ED932/G. The belt drive to spin the weapon backwards before release can be clearly seen. (RAF Museum, neg. no. P11916CC)

other smaller dams that certainly fell into this category were the Diemel, Ennerpe and Lister, all of which would be marked down as secondary targets for the reserve wave.

Consequently the plan was that Gibson's wave of nine aircraft would fly a route across the Scheldt estuary to the Möhne, which he was to attack first. Depending on the result of his attack – and assuming he survived – he would then direct the others by VHF R/T to the Möhne, until it was breached, then the Eder. A second wave of five crews, with the Sorpe as their target, would follow a more northerly route across the North Sea to the island of Vlieland, then over the Zuider Zee to join the route taken by the first wave at the German border. The five aircraft in the reserve wave would act on coded signals to attack whatever was left standing, with the Möhne still taking priority.

Signals procedure was complicated. W/T silence was to be maintained as far as possible and throughout the raid all aircraft were to listen out on 4090 Kilocycles as no other aircraft would be using it that night. This would apply except when using the 'operation completed' signal on 3680 Kilocycles. To deny German direction-finding stations a 'fix' R/T silence would be maintained until ten minutes before they were due to arrive at the target, when the VHF sets would be turned on. The long list of codewords was as follows:

Cooler	Aircraft call sign
Pranger	Attack Möhne
Nigger	Möhne breached, divert to Eder
Dinghy	Eder breached, divert to Sorpe
Danger	Attack Lister
Edward	Attack Ennerpe
Fraser	Attack Diemel
Mason	All aircraft return to base
Apple	First wave listen out on button A (use VHF)
Codfish	Jamming on Button A – change to Button C (reserve VHF frequency)
Mermaid	Jamming on all R/T, control by W/T
Tulip	No.2 take over at Möhne (Flt Lt Hopgood)
Cracking	No.4 take over at Eder (Sqdn Ldr Young)
Gilbert	Attack last-resort targets as detailed

After dropping their bomb, whatever the result, aircraft were to change to 3680 Kilocycles to send the following:

Goner 1   Failed to explode
Goner 2   Overshot dam
Goner 3   Exploded more than 100 yards from dam
Goner 4   Exploded 100 yards from dam
Goner 5   Exploded 50 yards from dam
Goner 6   Exploded 5 yards from dam
Goner 7   Exploded in contact with dam
Goner 8   No apparent breach
Goner 9   Small breach in dam
Goner 10 Large breach in dam

While crossing the North Sea the aircraft were to descend to 60ft and set their altimeters, using the spotlights for calibration. They were to remain at low level to and from the target, especially when crossing the enemy coast. On reaching the target the leader of each section would climb to 1,000ft. The others would listen out on VHF and report in as they arrived. Spinning of Upkeep was to begin ten minutes before the attack. Attacks on the Möhne and Eder would be made at right angles at 60ft, but now at a slightly reduced ground speed of 220mph.

The Sorpe wave, led by Flt Lt Joe McCarthy, an American serving in the RCAF, would be controlled by him on the alternative VHF channel. Here, the bombs would not be spun and the attack would be along the length of the dam. Each Upkeep would be dropped just short of the centre and some twenty feet from the edge of the water. Aircraft were to attack 'from the lowest practicable height' at an indicated airspeed of 180mph. Harris had not thought much of this method of attack and subsequent events were to prove him right, but he had been overruled by the Air Staff.

The third wave would take the same route as the first and also at low level. They would be under the direct control of 5 Group's HQ, to attack the primary or last-resort targets as required.

Although low-flying bombers were harder to bring down than high-altitude ones, which meant that the heavy 88 and 105mm anti-aircraft guns would not pose much of a threat, the same could not be said for the light 20mm weapons. Six of these single-barrelled guns, capable of firing 120 rounds a minute, were emplaced at or close to the Möhne, each with a Luftwaffe detachment of six men.

Final PRU coverage of the Möhne before the attack had also revealed some other strange objects on the dam wall, which puzzled the interpreters at RAF Medmenham. They were not identified until after the war. In an attempt at camouflage, the Germans had begun to place clumps of artificial pine trees, garnished with camouflage scrim, on the dam parapet. Still, whatever they were, at least they were not barrage balloons, whose cables would have precluded a low-level attack. If these had been deployed at the Möhne, even at the last moment, *Chastise* would have been postponed and possibly cancelled altogether.

(A report written by a British disarmament team after the war stated that at the time of the attack there had been twenty small balloons, some on boats, in a ring around the Möhne. This was not correct, since a German report written after the attack clearly stated that there had been no balloons and only six guns to defend the dam at the time of the raid. Something else that could have led to *Chastise*'s cancellation would have been a searchlight, but there were none of these at the dam either.)

The German defences also comprised a comprehensive network of ground radar stations and a number of experienced night fighter units whose aircraft, although directed by ground control, carried radar of their own, plus a formidable cannon armament. There were five night fighter airfields along the route to the dams, and the airfield at Werl, also a night fighter base, was not far from the Möhne.

While a low-level attack favoured the bombers, for this was a complete departure from the tactics normally used at night and the night fighters' radar would find it difficult to track downwards, there were natural obstacles that were just as deadly. Each dam was surrounded by hills and even while flying across the flat countryside between there and the coast, one set of power lines suddenly looming up would spell disaster. As usual the crews would carry parachutes, but at so low a height, even if an aircraft survived such a collision, no one would have time to jump. Before the ejection seat, bailing out meant clipping on a parachute pack, scrambling along a cramped dark fuselage, opening a hatch and exiting smartly through it in the teeth of a 200mph-plus slipstream. If the aircraft had been carrying a normal load a crash-landing would have been a better option, but that was out of the question with the Upkeep hanging down beneath it.

By now it will be apparent just how complex and demanding an operation like *Chastise* was. It was not surprising that Martin's rear gunner, Flt Sgt 'Tammy' Simpson RAAF, later recalled the briefing as the longest he had ever known.

Shortly after noon Gibson and Wallis briefed all the pilots and navigators. 5 Group's Chief Signals Officer, Wg Cdr W. Dunn, gave the wireless-operators a separate briefing, which they certainly needed. After two hours those who were now in the know took a break, but were careful to say nothing about the targets, which for the moment puzzled the rest of their crews. Sgt Freddie Tees, the rear gunner in P/O Warner Ottley's Lancaster, thought that whatever it was it could hardly be worse than any other target. He did not yet know that what was to happen to him that night would change his life completely.

Realisation for the rest of the crews came during the afternoon as they all gathered to study models of the Möhne and the Sorpe. A model of the Eder had been ordered, but did not arrive until 18 September! Consequently, Shannon's bomb aimer, Len Sumpter, remembered things differently:

> Never saw any pictures of it, or anything. The only models there were the Möhne and the Sorpe. That one in the film – they made that for the film, that model of the Eder. The first time I saw the Eder was when I got there.

In addition to surprise, diversionary attacks would be important, especially as most of the Main Force had been stood down on this night, so a request was made to Fighter Command for night intruder operations over a defined area. As part of this diversionary effort, Bomber Command would provide nine Mosquitoes, six from 105 Sqdn and three from 139 Sqdn, each armed with four 500lb bombs. 105 were to attack Dusseldorf, Cologne and Munster, while 139's target was Berlin, although due to fuel problems one of their aircraft would bomb Kiel instead. These attacks would be made shortly after midnight and hopefully would draw away any night fighters from 617's area. Further activity included twenty-one Wellingtons, thirteen Stirlings and two Lancasters 'gardening' off the Friesian Islands, with another eighteen Wellingtons on the same task off the ports of Brest, Lorient and St Nazaire. Four more Wellingtons, probably from a training unit, would drop leaflets onto Orleans.

At Scampton nineteen Lancasters were available for nineteen crews, which meant there was no reserve aircraft to cater for any last-minute emergency. Commander H. C. Bergel of No.9 Ferry Pilots Pool – part of the Air Transport Auxiliary organisation which ferried aircraft from factories to the Services – was called on to fly the third trials Lancaster, ED825/G, from Boscombe Down to Scampton. Due to its gutted bomb bay this aircraft handled differently from the standard version, while the extra equipment in its cockpit was beyond him.

On arrival at Scampton Bergel's surprise was added to by the sight of other Lancasters in the same condition, each carrying an odd thing that looked like the front wheel of a steamroller. One of these objects was slowly rotating, but he was warned away before he could take a closer look. Glad to be out of this strange situation,

Modified Lancaster B III ED825/G prior to its last-minute delivery to RAF Scampton. Coded AJ-T, it would be flown by Flt Lt Joe McCarthy and his crew to the Sorpe dam and back. (Imperial War Museum, neg. no. ATP11384B)

Bergel boarded a waiting Anson and flew home. The aircraft he had just delivered would go to the Sorpe that night.

This now made twenty aircraft for nineteen crews, as follows:

ED932	'G'	Wg Cdr G. P. Gibson	ED929 'L' Flt Lt D. J. Shannon
ED937	'Z'	Sqdn Ldr H. E. Maudslay	ED934 'K' P/O V. W. Byers
ED877	'A'	Sqdn Ldr H. M. Young	ED865 'S' P/O L. J. Burpee
ED864	'B'	Flt Lt W. Astell	ED912 'N' P/O L. G. Knight
ED927	'E'	Flt Lt R. N. G. Barlow	ED910 'C' P/O W. H. T. Ottley
ED925	'M'	Flt Lt J. V. Hopgood	ED936 'H' P/O G. Rice
ED906	'J'	Flt Lt D. J. H. Maltby	ED924 'Y' Flt Sgt C. T. Anderson
ED909	'P'	Flt Lt H. B. Martin	ED918 'F' Flt Sgt K. W. Brown
ED923	'Q'	Flt Lt J. C. McCarthy	ED886 'O' Flt Sgt W. C. Townsend
ED921	'W'	Flt Lt J. L. Munro	ED825 'T' Reserve aircraft

As previously noted, G serial number suffixes had been allocated to all the *Chastise* Lancasters, but they appear not to have been carried on this raid. This is shown by a well-known photograph of Gibson and his crew at the door of their aircraft before take-off.

The final briefing began at 1800, with all aircrew assembled in a large briefing room whose door was guarded by Service Police. Wallis sat with Gibson and other senior officers on a dais opposite the door. It was Gibson who opened the proceedings to introduce Wallis, who explained why the weapon had been designed, some of the problems that there had been in its development and why the dams were to be attacked. Using his argument that such a raid would seriously affect German industrial capacity, he stated that the German method for making one ton of steel required eight tons of water. Many of the airmen present had previously flown in Wellingtons and some had heard of Wallis through them. Those who survived would later relate how strange it had seemed that this determined but kindly white-haired man should have taken up bomb design.

Afterwards, in a reference to the trials at Chesil Beach and Reculver, Wallis was quoted as saying, 'You gentlemen are really carrying out the third of three experiments. We have tried it out on model dams, also on one dam one-fifth the size of the Möhne dam. I cannot guarantee it will come off, but I hope it will.' As he sat down and looked at all those young faces, he is alleged to have quietly said to the officers beside him, 'They must have thought it was Father Christmas speaking to them.'

Cochrane now spoke, saying that he believed the crews would do a tremendous amount of damage and that this raid would be a historic one. He stressed the need for security afterwards and ended with the simple sentence: 'I know this attack will succeed.' It was this kind of quiet but strong leadership that drew respect from those under him.

Gibson went over the operational details again, ruling that no aircraft was to bring an Upkeep back – an order that would have unfortunate consequences for one crew the next morning. Dunn went over signals procedures once more and the crews, grouped in their three waves, conferred over their different responsibilities, the routes and the defences. The weather was assessed as fine, with light variable winds and good visibility over both Britain and Holland. Despite the obvious dangers, everyone was ready to go.

After a meal, that for many included a precious rationed egg, the crews returned to their quarters, some to write or rewrite and leave out letters to their next-of-kin if they did not return. Although this ritual was nothing new and provided some comfort when faced with the unknown, it was now that the confidence felt at the briefing began to ebb. Some men felt gloomy or sick and Hopgood, who had previously served with Shannon on 106 Sqdn when Gibson had commanded it, told him that this operation would be a tough one. Hopgood also felt he would not return. His navigator, Flg-Off K. Earnshaw RCAF, also correctly prophesied that eight aircraft – which meant fifty-six men – would not be coming back.

Earnshaw was not the only Canadian with a sense of foreboding, for P/O Louis Burpee, one of the reserve wave pilots, sought out a fellow countryman, Flt Sgt Ken Brown, shook his hand and said goodbye. By a coincidence, on this date Burpee's old squadron, 106, noted that he had just been awarded the DFM for his previous service as a flight sergeant. With 617 temporarily cut off from most of the outside world, it is doubtful if Burpee heard of it. He would certainly not have felt like celebrating.

Another member of Ken Brown's crew who was less than happy was his navigator, Sgt Dudley Heal, who said that, on being told the target, 'We all went to the bar and had a drink. Sixty feet. I ask you!' Sgt Basil Feneron, Brown's flight engineer, for some reason known only to himself, went out to the dispersal and tried to lift the Upkeep slung under his skipper's Lancaster. W/O Abraham Garshowitz, another Canadian and the wireless-operator on Flt Lt Bill Astell's aircraft, went out to it and chalked on the Upkeep the defiant phrase: 'Never has so much been expected of so few.'

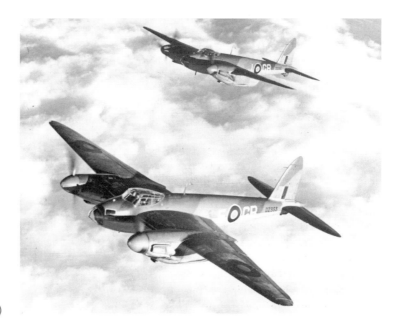

Diversions created by Mosquitoes of 105 Squadron (pictured here) and 139 Squadron would assist in drawing much of the Luftwaffe's attention from the *Chastise* attack. (RAF Museum, neg. no. P9547CC)

Flight Lieutenant R. E. G. Hutchison, Gibson's Signals Leader, helps his CO on with his parachute harness before taking off for Operation *Chastise*. (Imperial War Museum, neg. no. CH9682)

From 2000 the aircrew converged on their crew rooms to collect parachutes and other equipment. As this was a low-level raid in summer, there was no need for the fur-lined Irvin jackets, flying suits and other heavy impedimenta that were normally necessary. Most men wore life jackets and parachute harnesses over blue-grey Aircrew Suits – the RAF's equivalent of the Army's battledress uniform. Gibson elected to fly in shirt sleeves with a captured Luftwaffe fighter pilot's life jacket over the top. This was less bulky than the 1941 pattern 'Mae West' worn by his men and was envied by them.

Now there were ninety minutes to go and the warm evening was full of tension. Gibson packed his entire crew into his car and arrived at the crew rooms looking outwardly confident, although he later admitted that he had concealed his true feelings.

Something else to be concealed was the pain from gout in his feet – probably an illness brought on by the stress of the last few weeks. Over 100 operations and now this. It was three years, almost to the day, since his Hampden had struck a barrage balloon cable on a raid to Hamburg – something he had recently been reminded of when Longbottom had flown him into Brooklands in a Mosquito, touching down after a hair-raising flight through the cables there. The balloon held up the cable – and the cable would slice a wing off.

Being a former Boy Scout, Gibson had always worn their badge on his right wrist as a lucky charm. Perhaps he would need it, for, by a curious coincidence, his Lancaster had been given the letters AJ-G. These matched his father's initials – whose birthday it was today.

So, would Gibson's luck finally run out tonight, just as Nigger's had done? His sense of impending doom may not have been as strong as that felt by some of his men, but a feeling that he and Nigger would be going into the ground at the same time remained at the back of his mind.

Outside the hangar men tried to relax, either on the grass or in deckchairs. An hour or more to wait, while the Lancasters sat like giant pterodactyls, black, hunched and expectant in the distance. More than ready to be off, Gibson looked at his watch. At last it was time to board the three-tonners or crew buses for the drive to the dispersals.

After three years of debate and three months of intensive effort, Operation *Chastise* was on.

3

Operation *Chastise*

Destruction of the dam may take some time to become apparent, and careful reconnaissance may be necessary to distinguish between breaching of the dam and the spilling over the top which will follow each explosion.

Extract from *Chastise* operation order

Gibson hauled AJ-G over Scampton's perimeter fence and climbed away. Hopgood and Martin followed close behind, forming a fighter-like vic formation. This part of the route was well known to all the crews, passing as it did over the Wash and Wainfleet bombing range towards Southwold on the East Anglian coast. The sky was clear, with a full moon and the Northern Lights flickering behind them – a bizarre and unwelcome sight as they would be clearly silhouetted if night fighters should turn up.

Mick Martin later listed the defences:

From 7,000 feet upwards there was so-called heavy flak, and down to 3,000 feet there were night fighters. From 200 feet up to 4,000 feet there was light flak. Below 200 feet it's hard to hear low-flying aircraft approaching and it's damned difficult for ground gunners – if they did hear – to swing on and lay off the necessary deflection.

The first flight crossed the coast on track and on time, but over the North Sea the winds were stronger than anticipated, blowing them to starboard and over the heavily defended island of Walcheren. Perhaps the gunners below were surprised by the sudden appearance of this low-flying trio, for they did not react.

Being now over enemy territory, the bomb aimers carried out the initial arming of each Upkeep's self-destruct fuse, which would be fully armed on release. Turning to the east on an amended course, they picked up the Wilhelmina Canal, which ran between the night fighter bases at Eindhoven and Gilze-Rijen. Near the town of Helmond the canal met another at right angles and the Lancasters turned towards the Rhine.

Low flying gave a tremendous impression of speed as well as reinforcing the sense of vulnerability felt by each crew. Still, if the bombers were clearly visible in the moonlight, then so too were features on the ground below. Houses, haystacks, rivers, roads and even some people were glimpsed as they roared along. Crossing the German border, they were now less than forty-five minutes' flying time away from the Möhne, but they saw nothing in the moonlit sky except each other. Realising he was too far south, Gibson banked to port, following the Rhine to a bend in it near the town of Rees.

It was now that barges and gun positions on the river's banks reacted, as did the gunners in the three aircraft. No damage was incurred – yet – and Gibson, having reached the bend, turned east toward some lakes near Dülmen. Even with assistance from the bomb aimer, who was using maps on a special roller, accurate navigation at so low a height proved impossible. Concentrations of searchlights, backed up by light flak, caught them by surprise more than once, causing Gibson to break W/T silence to send back an amended flak warning, which 5 Group quickly passed on to all of 617's aircraft.

Near Dülmen Hopgood's aircraft sustained damage to its port wing. Its pilot may also have been hit, for one account quotes the flight engineer, Sgt C. Brennan, saying, 'Look at the blood,' to which Hopgood responded with, 'I'm okay.' Whatever the state of this Lancaster, there was no question of turning back now, not after all they had gone through to get this far. In any case, the Germans had clearly woken up and a lone damaged Lancaster limping home would be an easy target.

Hopgood's rear gunner, P/O Tony Burcher DFM RAAF, saw high-tension cables streak past above his turret and realised to his horror that his pilot had gone beneath them. Gibson skirted Hamm, whose marshalling yards had for years been a notoriously well-defended target, then turned again at a railway junction at Ahlen. Now heading almost due south between the towns of Werl and Soest, the latter distinctive because of its church spires, they rose up over some tree-covered hills and at last looked down on the Möhne lake.

The second flight, led by Young with Shannon's crew and that of Maltby, arrived soon after Gibson, having followed much the same route. Len Sumpter, in Shannon's aircraft, had not used a roller, but had carefully folded his maps, marking the high-tension cables in red. Well aware of the futility of baling out at this height, he did not wear a parachute – even if he had it would have been mounted on his chest and got in the way. Despite his best efforts, his navigation was not perfect either and Shannon arrived late at the Möhne, to be shot at by the gunners, who punched one small hole through AJ-L's fuselage.

The third flight, led by Maudslay, had also suffered from flak and in the light of later events at the Eder it was quite possible that his aircraft had been damaged. Astell and Knight followed him, but Astell's Lancaster met flak at Dorsten and was probably hit by it after delaying when the others turned at a pinpoint. Two lines of tracer came up, to which Astell's gunners replied, but the bomber hit high-tension cables and crashed in flames. A civilian witness then saw something roll away, with an explosion on the ground.

At the Möhne, Gibson assessed the defences. As reported, there were no balloons or searchlights, but the three positions near Günne were active, as were the two in the dam towers and one on the wall to the right of the right-hand tower as he looked at the dam from over the lake. Others would say that there were additional flak positions in the woods to the right of the attacking run, but subsequent German reports mentioned only the six guns. As Gibson made a dummy run over the dam to test the defences, through whose fire AJ-G passed unharmed, the second flight arrived, with Len Sumpter noting the steepness of the surrounding hills.

Each aircraft was to attack individually on Gibson's command. After flying over a bridge at Körbecke, they would use a spit of land as a convenient marker, then line up to attack the dam from a distance of 1,500m. The hills and trees would screen them until this final stretch, when they would be out in the open over the lake, trying to adjust their height and speed while under heavy fire.

Len Sumpter was waiting his turn while circling in David Shannon's Lancaster. Their Upkeep was already armed and rotating, as were those of the others.

On the run itself there were four people involved. There's the pilot taking note of the height and everything else, there's the engineer looking after the speed, there's the navigator looking out of the blister, getting the lights in line and telling the pilot up or down and there's the bomb aimer in front with his sight, waiting for the towers to come along and listening for everybody else to say that their part of the set-up is right and then he can drop the bomb, but if their part of the set-up wasn't right then he said, 'Abort,' and you had to go round. You had to get all these things absolutely correct before you could bomb.

Gibson dived across the spit, now with his spotlights on. Wondering why the crazy English were using what seemed to be landing lights, the gunners on the dam wall swung their weapons towards him. The Lancaster roared over the gleaming water, its front guns spitting white tracer back at the defenders and Gibson feeling suddenly vulnerable. The Upkeep fell away and the rear gunner, Trevor-Roper, saw it bounce three times, then explode ten seconds later. Hutchison fired a red flare, signifying that the bomb had been dropped and a tremendous sheet of water leapt skywards, but the dam held. It has since been said that Gibson's bomb struck the nets in the lake and tore a hole through them. If so, it may have created a path for those that followed.

Hopgood, bearing whatever wounds to man and aircraft he had already sustained, attacked next, with his bomb aimer, Flt Sgt J. W. Fraser RCAF, squinting through his Dann sight. As he crossed the lake tracer leapt out over it towards him, hitting both his port engines, the loss of the inner one cutting off power to Burcher's rear turret. More shells hit his starboard wing and as the aircraft rocked with the impact of these hits Fraser released the Upkeep, but too late. A red flare shot skywards from AJ-M – its wireless-operator, Sgt J. W. Minchin, having carried out his final task despite being wounded – and the aircraft turned away, trailing orange flame, trying to gain height and heading towards the village of Ostönnen. Attempts to quell the starboard wing fire failed and Hopgood ordered his crew to bail out.

Loss of hydraulic power meant Burcher had to crank his turret round by hand in order to scramble out backwards and reach his parachute, which was stowed in the fuselage. The recommended exit for him was to get back into the turret, turn it round and go out headfirst backwards, but there was no time now. Nor could he get out through the nose hatch or the crash exit further forward in the fuselage roof, not with Hopgood still trying to gain height. The only option was the starboard side entry door.

As Burcher clipped on his parachute he saw Minchin, who had donned his own, struggling over the Lancaster's infamous main spar. Burcher shoved Minchin out through the door, pulling his colleague's ripcord as he went out. He then pulled his own, held the billowing white silk in his arms and was blown clear as the Lancaster exploded. The next thing he was aware of was lying in a field on his back, which had been damaged when he hit the starboard tailplane.

At the front Fraser, being close to the nose hatch, was in a better position, but as he tugged it open the trees below looked frighteningly close. Like Burcher, he decided to pull the ripcord before leaving the aircraft, doing so as he knelt facing forward. The opening parachute pulled him out of the hatch headfirst, he somersaulted, the tailwheel narrowly missed his head, he swung to a vertical position and hit the ground a moment later. Fraser walked away without a scratch.

Hopgood's bomb had gone over the top of the dam wall and exploded by a powerhouse that was situated between it and the compensating basin. The wreckage of his Lancaster was now burning furiously in a field near Ostönnen.

Speed had become imperative, for surely the defenders would have called for support and this fire would draw night fighters the way blood attracted sharks. Now Martin came in, with Gibson, who had switched on his spotlights again, flying on his starboard side and slightly ahead in the hope of splitting the gunners' fire. Gibson roared over the dam's right-hand gun position, turning to port to allow Trevor-Roper's four guns to fire on the Günne flak positions.

To Martin, the right-hand tower was clearly visible but the other was obscured by smoke from Hopgood's Upkeep. A 20mm burst hit AJ-P in its starboard outer fuel tank and aileron, but Hay dropped their bomb and Martin pulled up safely, turning to port to avoid the Günne flak. There was a huge explosion, but the Upkeep, which may have struck the water at an angle when the aircraft was hit, was thought to have veered to the left and exploded some twenty yards short of the dam wall. Len Sumpter, still awaiting his cue, had a grandstand view of it all.

We were over there by Körbecke and we could see everything happening as the planes were all coming in. All the guns were firing and the flak that was coming up looked like lighted oranges that they were throwing at you. It was all tracer ammunition – orange. The flak reached us where we were circling round there, We were hoping for the best and watching it all going on and we weren't very happy because we were round there for about half an hour, circling round.

Young was next. Gibson flew on the air side of the dam this time, again to split the fire of the defenders, with Martin flying in on Young's left. This Upkeep bounced three times, struck the wall and exploded in contact with it. Still the dam appeared to hold.

Maltby attacked now, again with diversions from Gibson and Martin. Suddenly Maltby realised the crown of the dam was at last starting to crumble. His own Upkeep bounced four times, struck and exploded, its spout of water clearly silhouetted against the moon.

Next in line was Shannon, but it was a run he and Len Sumpter would never finish.

Just as Maltby was making his run Gibson was looking at the dam and he said, 'Right, Number 6.' That was us. We came over the spit there, to make a run round this way, just beginning to line up and Gibson said, 'The dam's gone. Call it off, Dave, and we'll go down to the Eder.'

The Möhnesee erupted as the centre of the wall finally split and fell away, unleashing the force of millions of gallons of water, which surged down the valley, sweeping away the burning remains of the powerhouse that Fraser had inadvertently hit. To Gibson, it looked like 'stirred porridge in the moonlight'. Hutchison signalled 'Nigger' back to 5 Group, who received his signal loud and clear despite the aircraft being 375 miles away and flying at less than a thousand feet. Shannon's Lancaster, its Upkeep still spinning, joined the others overhead to marvel at the sight. A single flak position on the wall still had some fight, but the gunners quickly silenced it.

Down below, Burcher's back injury meant that he had been unable to move from the field he had landed in, but although he was unable to see what had happened, that loud roar meant only one thing. After all this, was he going to drown? Fortunately for him he had landed on high ground to one side of the valley in which the dam lay and, like Fraser, he would survive. Minchin, whom Burcher had pushed out before making his own escape, had died from his injuries.

The greatest prize had been won, but the raid was not yet over. Gibson curbed his crews' excited R/T chatter, ordered those who had bombed to head for home and led the rest on to the Eder. The seventy-three miles between the two dams would be covered in twenty-six minutes.

Back at Scampton, Wallis and Cochrane had watched the first two waves take off before driving to Grantham to join Harris in 5 Group's underground operations room. To its staff the presence of so much 'brass' suggested something unusual was going on, and the quiet talk of the senior officers could not disguise the excitement in the air.

To Wallis, as he paced up and down, it was the longest night of his life. His request to fly on the raid had, not surprisingly, been turned down and now he faced an agonizing wait.

Wg Cdr Dunn was there to receive each W/T message, decode it and pass it on. At the first 'Goner' Wallis muttered, 'No, it's no good.' Despair was close now and a succession of 'Goners' made him bury his head in his hands. Had it all been for nothing?

Then the Morse spluttered again.

'Nigger!' shouted Dunn. 'It's Nigger! They've got it!'

Wallis leapt to his feet in triumph, waving his arms upwards in the warm glow of success. Those who knew him said afterwards it was the first time they had ever seen him show such emotion. Three years in the making, three months in the perfecting and now it was here. It seemed that everyone wanted to shake his hand. Harris declared, 'Wallis, I didn't believe a word you said when you came to see me, but now you could sell me a pink elephant.'

After this, anything seemed possible.

The second wave of five Lancasters, which had been given the Sorpe as their target, had been scheduled to take off some ten minutes before their CO, for they were to fly the more northerly route over the island of Vlieland before turning south-east over the Zuider Zee to join the first wave's track near Rees. These aircraft flew singly, not in formation, being timed to cross the Dutch coast at the same time as Gibson's formation, the idea being to appear as minor intruder raids.

One aircraft, AJ-Q, which should have been the first away, would not be going anywhere that night. Joe McCarthy, a New Yorker who had got round his country's neutrality by enlisting in the RCAF, found during the final run-up that his aircraft was useless due to a coolant leak in its starboard outer engine. His crew then dashed to the reserve Lancaster, newly christened AJ-T, which had arrived that afternoon. This aircraft lacked VHF radio and the spotlights, although neither of these would be needed due to the method of attack to be used at the Sorpe.

Concerned that another troubled crew would commandeer the reserve Lancaster and so leave them behind, McCarthy's crew frantically tossed out any unnecessary kit from AJ-T onto the tarmac and kicked out the centre perspex panel from the rear turret, only to find that the aircraft lacked a compass deviation card. There was no hope of accurate flying without it. For McCarthy, the last straw nearly came when his parachute accidentally opened and white silk billowed across the tarmac. Cursing, he freed himself from it, leapt into the truck and shot back to the crew room, on arrival announcing his frustration in a loud Brooklyn voice.

Flt Sgt Powell, one man who could be relied on to bring order out of chaos, dashed into the instrument section, found the missing card and handed it over to McCarthy. What about the parachute? McCarthy bellowed, 'Godammit, I'll go without one,' but Powell quickly found another and passed it to him as the vehicle was about to return to AJ-T's dispersal. Of such dramas were ground crews' lives sometimes made. McCarthy's crew finally left the ground over half an hour late, but as things turned out it was probably as well for them.

The other four members of the Sorpe wave met trouble as soon as they reached the Dutch coast. The first to go down was AJ-K, flown by Byers. He had strayed off track, flown over the heavily defended island of Texel, climbed to identify landmarks and was then hit by light flak, crashing into the Waddenzee. There were no survivors.

AJ-E, flown by Barlow, struck high-tension cables at Haldern, near Rees, at 2350, crashing with no survivors. His Upkeep failed to explode and would later be recovered by the Germans. It had not detached itself from the aircraft and consequently the self-destruct fuse was not fully armed.

Les Munro had taken off one minute after Barlow and the first stages of his crew's flight were uneventful. On reaching Vlieland his aircraft was hit by light flak, which tore a hole in the fuselage, damaging the rear turret's hydraulic pipes, the VHF radio, the crew's intercom and the master unit for the compass. For a while Munro flew on over the Zuider Zee, but after assessing the damage decided that there was nothing for it but to turn back. The crew could not even communicate with each other, let alone the rest of the force. Munro later commented, 'I was bitterly disappointed but I suppose that is why I am alive today.'

The last aircraft of this wave was AJ-H, flown by Geoff Rice. They too crossed the North Sea without trouble, fusing the bomb when two minutes short of Vlieland. Rice flew too low, pulled up to avoid a sand dune and having crossed the island he climbed to confirm his position, lost altitude again and turned south-east as briefed. As he was flying into the moon, height was not easy to judge and just as the altimeter registered zero a tremendous shudder shook the aircraft.

Realising his propellers were clipping the water, Rice instinctively pulled back on the stick, lost some forward speed in doing so and a second jolt was felt. Water poured in through the open bomb bay and ran back down the fuselage. There was a shout of 'Christ! It's wet at the back!' from Sgt Stephen Burns, the rear gunner, who was suddenly up to his waist in water and disinfectant from the Elsan toilet behind him. The only way it could drain out was via the turret's spent ammunition and link chutes. AJ-H staggered back into the sky, minus its Upkeep, which had been torn off in the first impact. The second one had been when the bomb struck the tailwheel and drove it up through the main spar of the tailplane.

Furious with himself, Rice made his exit between Texel and Vlieland, avoiding some flak and searchlights by flying under them. His bomb was thought to have exploded on its own a month later; certainly a massive explosion south of Texel was heard by people living on the island.

All this left only McCarthy, who on reaching Vlieland had made up some ten minutes of the time he had lost earlier. By now the island's defenders were thoroughly alerted, although McCarthy eluded them by flying between two large sand dunes – no mean feat in a four-engined aircraft.

His low flying enabled him to avoid further flak sites and also night fighters, which he frequently saw flying some 1,000 feet above them. None of the German pilots had expected heavy bombers to be at such a height and were unable to locate them. The gunners left these alone, concentrating on dousing searchlights and engaging flak. One even tried his hand at trainbusting, only to discover his intended victim was heavily armed and returned his fire with interest. McCarthy's aircraft took just one hit, which burst the starboard tyre. Navigation over Germany turned out to be harder than over Holland and when McCarthy reached the Sorpe at 0015 it was surrounded by thick mist, though the dam itself was clearly visible.

The Sorpe wave had been briefed to attack from the west over the village of Langscheid, lining up the nacelle of the port outer engine with the top of the dam to give the correct lateral position for the bomb's release. There were no defences other than natural ones, but these were enough to give anyone pause. Noting the tall church spire in the village, McCarthy realised that provided he avoided it he could use it to line up his bomb run along the dam's crest, but it took ten attempts before Sgt G. L. Johnson, his bomb aimer, was satisfied and the Upkeep's explosion crumbled some twenty feet from the crest. However, the Sorpe still held and after a final look in the hope of seeing a belated collapse, McCarthy turned for home.

Although Len Sumpter did not witness this attack, no one would have disagreed with his opinion:

> The Sorpe was a waste of time with this bomb. I mean, fancy trying to come across in this direction over a dam which has got a concrete core and earth each side and dropping that thing on the top of it, which is stupid. You just wasted the biggest part of it. Over on the side there you could see where the soil had fallen away. But there was no way you could breach the concrete core.

McCarthy's crew were to experience a hairy ride home. Due to compass trouble, he strayed over Hamm and was lucky not to be shot down. Unable to locate the briefed return route, he returned via the outward one, to land safely at Scampton despite the burst tyre.

So far it had been quite a night, but it was not over yet. Gibson's five aircraft met no opposition while in transit between the Möhne and the Eder, but locating the dam did not prove easy, as Len Sumpter found out.

> When we got down to the Eder – I don't know if the navigator made a mistake but – about ten or fifteen miles east of the Eder there's another tiny little reservoir and dam about half as wide as this, and we went to this one, you see! And we looked down at it, we thought, 'Well, that can't be it!' And then we called Gibson up. Gibson had found the Eder and fired a red Very up in the air and we went back and found him. But that was quite a laugh. Not enough water for a start!

The dam they had seen had been a small one at Rehbach, some two miles west of their target, but despite the confusion it was not long before all five aircraft were circling over the correct one.

The Eder's flak had been withdrawn two weeks earlier and as Gibson flew overhead he could see why. This long and winding lake had tree-lined banks steeper than at the Möhne. The dam itself, although higher from base to crown, was not as wide. Just to make things more difficult, early morning mist was beginning to gather on the water.

If this dam had been deliberately designed to be difficult to hit, the Germans could hardly have chosen a better site. The lake's irregular shape precluded a straight low-level approach, so the only option was to dive steeply down a gully to the right of Waldeck Castle, turn to port to fly over a spit of land that stuck out like a finger into the lake, level off and attack the dam, then all but stand the aircraft on its tail to avoid the hills at the side of the valley beyond. It would have been a difficult enough task in a light bomber such as the Mosquito; in an aircraft the size of the Lancaster it was going to be hair-raising.

According to Len Sumpter, Shannon's aircraft had covered the distance between the two dams with its Upkeep still rotating. Gibson ordered them in first, but after four attempts Shannon took a break because it had proved impossible to get the correct height after the steep dive and sharp turn. Next came Maudslay, who tried twice but suffered the same problems. Then Shannon tried again after two more dummy runs. Len Sumpter was still prone in the aircraft's nose, with a disconcerting view of the hills looming up ahead.

> We flew around and came over Waldeck Castle again and we were all keeping our fingers crossed that we were going to do it this time, because it was getting a little bit hairy and foggy and the time was getting on and we wanted to get the action going … This time Dave had cut the corner a little bit and went by the end of the spit of land, because, as I said, it's a team effort lining up … So I was thinking to myself, 'Well, I hope we're going to do it this time, because I'm getting a bit cheesed off with flying round here.'
>
> So anyway we came down over Waldeck Castle, across and just missed the spit of land and ran to the dam. This time the height was right and the speed was right and everything else was right, so I lined up my piece of string on the chinagraph marks and when the towers came in line with the chinagraph marks I pressed the button and away went the bomb. And I think you'll notice that the line from the spit to the dam is at right-angles … the breach was to the south of the dam, not in the centre. And the reason for that was because we attacked it at an oblique angle, I think.

AJ-L's Upkeep bounced twice before exploding on the shoreline, to the right of the dam. German witnesses later confirmed this. The resulting white plume of water was estimated to be 1,000ft high.

> We flew on and, as you'll see, when you come over the dam there's a hill there, about a thousand feet high, which you have to manoeuvre round and it gave us a bit of a heart attack going into it, because we wondered whether we were going to get over it or not. You see these films of planes just missing a hill – well, we didn't think we were going to miss this one!

Thankfully, they did and, having bombed, would not have to face that ordeal again. However, Gibson could not identify any specific damage from this attack and so Maudslay made his third run in.

The reason for checking the aircraft's speed was that Wallis had predicted the bomb would explode instantly if it struck the dam wall at too high a speed. As noted earlier, Maudslay's aircraft may have suffered flak damage en route. Gibson thought he saw something other than the bomb hanging down below AJ-Z, which might have indicated this. The aircraft flew too fast, the Upkeep fell too late and exploded on the parapet just behind the Lancaster with a vivid yellow flash which lit up the whole valley for several seconds.

Gibson called over the R/T, 'Henry, Henry – hello, Z Zebra, are you all right?'

Maudslay's response was a weak one: 'I think so, stand by.' Nothing more was heard, probably due to damage to Maudslay's VHF set or to reception being affected by the surrounding hills.

The film scene, in which this situation is dramatically resolved by having Maudslay's aircraft crash into a nearby hill, is not correct. The Germans were aware of what happened next but it was some years after the war before it became more widely known.

Being left with a damaged aircraft which was now limping along at low speed, with dawn due shortly and the threat of fighter attack, Maudslay turned for home, passing his W/T attack message to 5 Group as he did so. He then approached the town of Emmerich, whose oil refinery had been well defended for three years, to be shot down east of it, at Netterden. Again there were no survivors.*

This left only Les Knight and his crew in AJ-N to finish the job. Len Sumpter watched what happened.

> Les Knight came in after us – he went round a couple of times. Dave was talking to him, telling him how to do it, and Les Knight told him to get off the air … As I say, it was down towards the south end of the dam and we didn't go into it square. I don't think Les Knight went into it square either – he watched us go in and followed what Dave did.

Knight attacked in what he later described as 'perfect visibility', with a bright moon to starboard. The Upkeep bounced three times, hit the wall slightly right of centre and then exploded, causing an earthquake effect, which was clearly seen by Gibson, at the foot of the dam. A breach of some thirty feet opened up and a tremendous roaring torrent of water poured out, higher this time because of the steep sides of the valley.

Len Sumpter watched as this second flood claimed its first victims.

> The water came through just like a big wall … and it didn't have time to spread, like it did at the Möhne … Down there somewhere we could see cars going along and the water went over the car headlights and just drowned them … I think the wave was about forty or fifty feet high.

From Gibson's Lancaster came the splutter of Morse as Hutchison tapped out 'Dinghy', to the further delight of all at Grantham. It was time for what remained of Gibson's force to head for home.

One never made it. Young, who had bombed at the Möhne, flew too close to the port of Ijmuiden, was fired on and came down in the sea. This pilot had previously

---

* Maudslay was an Old Etonian and his name may be seen on a memorial wall at his former school. Curiously, other Etonians who survived the war, among them the writer and comedian Michael Bentine and the jazz trumpeter Humphrey Lyttleton, are also included.

acquired the nickname 'Dinghy' through twice having used one, but neither he nor his crew would survive to do so this time. The others returned safely, although Gibson was chased for a while by an unidentified aircraft. Whatever it was, it was the nearest the Luftwaffe's pilots came to exacting revenge, but it did not get within firing range and was left behind. The only damage sustained by AJ-G had been three small holes in its tail, probably during the repeated runs at the Möhne.

Two out of the three main dams had been successfully breached. It now remained to be seen how the reserve wave had fared against the others.

For those in the first two waves some of the tension that had built up on that Sunday evening had ebbed away once they had taken off. For the five reserve wave crews it was to continue for a further two hours. Possibly they would not be needed if Upkeep did everything that Wallis had claimed for it. Not so, for finally they too were ordered off, being directed to the various secondary dams.

The first away was Ottley, in AJ-C. En route he was told that the Möhne had been breached, was diverted to the Lister, which he acknowledged, and then to the Sorpe, but no acknowledgement of this change was received at Grantham. Nothing else was heard and it was not until after the war that the story of what happened next was pieced together.

At first little had happened to Ottley's crew until they reached the Scheldt estuary, where Sgt Freddie Tees in the rear turret exchanged fire with some searchlights and flak positions. At one point he saw a church steeple pass by above them. Perhaps Ottley saw it too and decided to climb.

By now on their return, several of 617's pilots, including Gibson, saw an aircraft fly too close to Hamm. Unlike McCarthy, Ottley would not get away with it. He was not only off track but was now too high and several searchlights coned his aircraft. Flak followed and the burning Lancaster crashed onto a 20mm ammunition dump at the edge of a wood, the Boserlagerschen Wald near Heesen, north-east of Hamm. The bomber's fuel tanks blew up in the air and the Upkeep exploded ninety seconds after it hit the ground. It was almost certainly due to this second explosion that there was one survivor – Freddie Tees, blown clear in his turret. He came to on the ground with severe burns, and spent the next two years first in hospital, then in a POW camp.

Louis Burpee and his crew, in AJ-S, who took off two minutes after Ottley, were to suffer a similar fate. His fellow Canadian, Ken Brown, to whom he had said goodbye before take-off, was a minute behind him in AJ-F when Burpee strayed off track and, like Ottley, climbed in an apparent attempt to establish his position. He had picked one of the worst possible places to do so, having erred on that part of the route that ran between the Luftwaffe airfields at Gilze-Rijen and Eindhoven. Intruder sorties to Gilze-Rijen and the earlier passage of the first wave had put the airfield flak units very much on the alert.

Brown and his bomb aimer, Sgt Stefan Oancia, clearly saw what happened next. Tracer came snapping up from Gilze-Rijen, Burpee's fuel tanks exploded and the blazing Lancaster crashed onto the airfield. A moment later its Upkeep exploded in an orange ball of fire, destroying several of the buildings there. Saying, 'Goddamn, must be either Burpee or Barlow,' Brown got as close to the ground as he could, flying down a road behind some trees.

Like 617's other pilots on this night, Brown depended on his bomb aimer's map-reading to pass information back to him and his navigator, Dudley Heal, who had earlier been so unhappy at the reduction of the bombing height to sixty feet. Brown and his flight engineer, Basil Feneron, had decided to divide the responsibility for the lookout through the bomber's windscreen, Brown taking the port side and Feneron the starboard.

High-tension wires were seen to twinkle in the moonlight some distance ahead, giving Brown a second or two in which to decide whether to fly over them or risk going underneath. Any attempt to climb at the last moment would result in a collision. Although the Gee navigation aid was available to all crews, with some later reporting

The opposition. A Messerschmitt Bf 110G night fighter, fitted with Lichtenstein radar. (Author's collection)

favourably on its reception a long way into Germany, Heal found it to be jammed. However, due to the clear night he could easily tell if they were off track.

Perhaps in anger at Burpee's fate, Brown's gunners strafed a train they met and on meeting more flak over Germany he ducked behind trees again, observing with relief and satisfaction that the shells hit the trees but missed the Lancaster. Advised of the Eder's destruction, Brown turned towards the Sorpe, encountering further flak from what remained of the Möhne's dam walls on the way.

By the time AJ-F reached the Sorpe, the mist had thickened and Brown circled before determining the dam's position. Several times they dived into the valley, each time facing the threat of collision with Langscheid's church steeple, but, despite what has previously been said, they did not use flares to mark the target. With the spotlights on, but the Upkeep not spinning, AJ-F dived in again and released its load, crumbling away more of the upper surface of the Sorpe, but still there was no breach.

Duty done, Brown turned for home, his rear gunner having a sharp exchange with one gun that remained active at the Möhne. He went low again, survived a barrage of flak from Hamm's by now thoroughly alert defenders, dumping his incendiaries on some barges and buildings that seemed important.

With its gunners anxiously scanning the dawn sky for fighters, AJ-F met yet another well-defended area at the Zuider Zee. The glare from searchlights seared into the cockpit and Brown, all but blinded, flew very fast at fifty feet on instruments. Both he and Feneron crouched down, the latter uncomfortably aware that his pilot's seat had armour plate but his had not. For a few seconds that must have seemed like a minute tracer soared up and wobbled towards them from both sides, hitting the starboard fuselage and the top of the cockpit. Then the coast shot by beneath, they were out over the North Sea and could draw breath again. Small wonder that Feneron kissed the Lincolnshire earth after the Lancaster touched down at Scampton.

The last of 617's Lancasters to take off, though not the last to return, was AJ-Y, flown by Anderson. North of the Ruhr he met heavy flak, which forced him off track. Consequently navigation became difficult and a faulty rear turret did not help matters either. Anderson was directed to the Sorpe as a result of the mixed fortunes suffered by McCarthy's wave, but mist in the valleys added further to his crew's navigation problems and he turned back at 0310 without bombing. Like Munro, Anderson's Lancaster returned with its Upkeep still on board, despite the orders given at briefing.

Bill Townsend, in AJ-O, was the last to attack any dam that night. He was directed to the Ennerpe and made four runs before dropping his Upkeep, which exploded short of the wall. A pronounced gyroscopic effect made reading the cockpit instruments difficult. Post-war research has indicated that he actually attacked the Bever dam, which was not a *Chastise* target, but whose lake was similar in shape to that of the Ennerpe and only five miles from it. In any case, neither of these dams was breached. On their way home, Townsend's crew passed over the Möhne – the last of 617's crews to do so – and he saw several villages under water, some with only their church steeples showing. It was dawn before he left Germany.

A Messerschmitt Bf 110 of IV/NJG 1 had been scrambled on its second sortie of the night to head off Townsend's Lancaster on his return, but despite good visibility no interception was made. Their intended victim planned to sneak out between Texel and Vlieland, but the rising sun silhouetted the Lancaster and the flak gave them a hot reception. In a strange parallel of Upkeep, shells were bounced off the water towards them, to skip over AJ-O as it flew fast and low. Townsend swung to starboard, back towards Germany, then headed out again over Vlieland at low level in a north-westerly direction. Unknowingly, his change of direction meant that he not only avoided the flak but also the pursuing night fighter, whose crew went home empty-handed for the second time that night.

A malfunctioning oil gauge led Townsend to come home on three engines, while oil from the front guns smeared the windscreen. It was full daylight when he finally carried out a bumpy landing at Scampton, before a massive audience that included Harris and Cochrane.

Gibson, dishevelled and sweaty, took part in the debriefing of those crews that had returned. Rice, still angry with himself over losing his bomb en route, was concerned about what his CO would say, but was relieved when Gibson commented that it was bad luck and could just as easily have happened to him. Munro's decision to turn back due to his smashed radio was also accepted and returning with his bomb was not held against him. However, Anderson and his crew were judged more harshly. Gibson felt that they had not tried hard enough and they were posted back to their previous unit.

After a series of diligently listed cross-country training exercises, the next entry in David Shannon's log book was equally matter-of-fact in tone: 'Operations – Möhne & Erer [*sic*] dams. Low level. One store. 9,000lbs.' For his part in this raid Shannon would receive the DSO, to which a Bar would be added later on, in addition to the DFC that he already held. He was not quite twenty-one and looked as if he should still have been at school.

A PRU Spitfire pilot, Flg-Off Gerry Fray of 542 Sqdn, now had the task of covering the Möhne and Sorpe, which meant he would take some of the most famous photographs of the war. When 150 miles from the target area he saw the sun glinting on the muddy froth that was still pouring from the Möhne. Two of his colleagues also flew over this part of Germany and on 19 May two further PRU sorties were flown over the Sorpe, in the vain hope of a final collapse.

At this time a famous Mosquito and its crew were also given the task of covering the flooding caused by *Chastise*. Flt Lt Charles Patterson and Flt Sgt Leigh Howard of the RAF Film Production Unit were detailed to fly through the Eder's breach, filming it while doing so! This would have been suicidal, so it was fortunate for them that they were taken off it to film a long-range Mosquito raid on the Zeiss optical works at Jena on 27 May. Although this crew repeatedly went to war with nothing more

MOHNE DAM

The Möhne dam photographed by a Spitfire of 542 Squadron the morning after the attack. Guy Gibson signed his name in the breach, and those of other surviving crew members, including Len Sumpter, appear on the exposed mud banks to the right. (Author's collection)

than cameras, they both survived. Leigh Howard's work would later reach a wider audience when he filmed the famous Operation *Jericho* raid the following February.

Once their debriefing was over, some of 617's hardier spirits organised an impromptu party. Everyone began congratulating everyone else, but the most important accolade was one that arrived from the Prime Minister:

> Please convey to the crews of the Lancasters of Number 617 Squadron who attacked the Möhne, Eder and Sorpe Dams my admiration and my congratulations on this outstanding and very gallant action. They have struck a blow which will have far-reaching effects.

Cochrane subsequently contributed an article to 5 Group's ORB and newsletter, stating, 'May saw a continuation of the Battle of the Ruhr and a new form of pressure by the destruction of the dams.' After a plea for greater bombing accuracy, he continued, 'Much depends upon training, and in this connection I would mention that the success which Number 617 Sqdn achieved against the dams was largely the result of solid hard work in training. Over a period of six weeks ending 14 May they

Right: The Sorpe dam, also photographed by 542 Squadron on the morning after *Chastise*. This was attacked by McCarthy and Brown but was not destroyed. On 15 October 1944, 9 Squadron's Lancasters dropped sixteen Tallboy bombs on this target, but despite five hits still failed to breach it! (NA)

Below: The Eder dam photographed the next morning, with the off-centre breach neatly silhouetted by the rising sun. Maudslay, Shannon and Knight had followed the curve of the lake, banking to the left before lining up at the last moment to make their bomb runs. (Imperial War Museum, neg. no. CH9750)

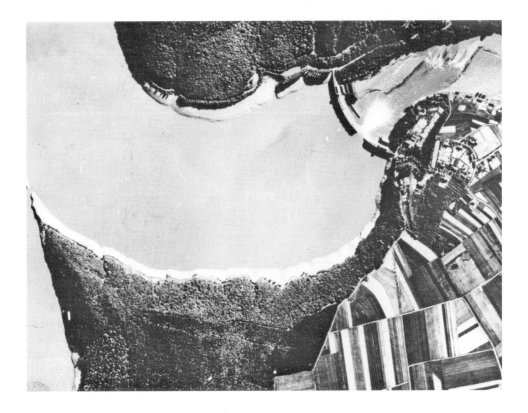

The Möhne the next morning. Note the single 20-mm flak emplacement in the tower roof and the artificial pine trees along what remains of the dam wall. (Mr D. Carpenter, via Imperial War Museum, neg. no. MH7526)

dropped 2,288 practice bombs … Continued and systematic training in squadrons is the key to success and to early victory in the Ruhr.'

Operation *Chastise* was over, but its repercussions would be felt for years to come. Of the nineteen aircraft that had taken part, eight had been brought down by various causes and fifty-three men were dead. Three others were by now prisoners, two of them in hospital. Gibson would have fifty-six letters to write, this time with the help of Sgt Heveron.

As the details of 617's casualties began to emerge Wallis became distraught and said: 'I would never have ordered it had I known.' Martin took him to one side, sat down with him and quietly explained that these men had all come from Bomber Command's Main Force, that sudden death was nothing new to them and that even if they had known how difficult things were going to be they would still have done their utmost to get to the dams.

All this was true enough, but a sense of guilt would remain with Wallis for the rest of his life. When interviewed by Trevor Philpott for a BBC documentary shown in 1966, he said, 'I had to ask Guy Gibson and his men to fly at sixty feet,' in a plaintive tone of voice that I can still recall today. The question in his mind still was, 'Did I do right in doing so?'

This leads to another question. Although *Chastise* was acclaimed in Bomber Command's camp as a great morale-booster, which it undoubtedly was, coming hard on the heels of the Allied victory in North Africa, what effect did it have on the German war effort at the time? Certainly it was not a winning blow, for the European war went on for another two years, being ended by a land campaign of the kind that Harris had wanted to avoid, especially as for a time he had to divert his heavy bomber force to support it instead of attacking German cities. To answer this it is now necessary to look at how the Germans reacted at the time and at how they would later assess the raid.

On 17 May the OKW reported: 'Weak British flying formations entered the area of the Reich last night and dropped a few bombs in specially planned locations. Two reservoirs were damaged and due to the resulting escape of water heavy losses were caused among the civilian population. Eight of the attacking planes were shot down.'

Although there was an admission that two dams had been severely damaged, far more lay behind this short statement than the High Command was prepared to admit.

How had such damage and casualties occurred? What procedures had been in place before the attack? Had these procedures been followed and if so why had there been insufficient warning? As a result of these enquiries, a report was submitted by the *Regierungspräsident* of the town of Arnsberg to the Ministry for Home Affairs.

On that night the warden of the Möhne, *Oberförster* Wilkening, had had a direct line to the exchange at the town of Soest and another to whoever was on duty at the dam. This line was tested each evening, including this one, and was found to be in order.

In accordance with procedure, by 0030 the *Regierungsdirektor*, I. Niewisch, had already gone to Arnsberg Town Hall when low-flying aircraft indicated a threat. The *Regierungspräsident* himself was in Berlin at the time – something he was probably glad of afterwards, when it seemed likely that heads would roll.

An air-raid warning had sounded at Günne half an hour before Gibson attacked the Möhne. Klemens Köhler, the engineer in charge, phoned his superiors in the towns of Niederensee and Neheim, downstream from the dam, to voice his fears of the effects of the water should a breach occur, especially while the lake was almost at its maximum capacity. The response from Neheim was, 'Don't tell us any fairy tales!' Having done what he could, he replaced the receiver and later complained that no warning was given to the valley's inhabitants. Like Justus Dillgardt just before the war, Köhler's warning would be fully vindicated, but it was too late now.

In Tower 1 – the nearest to the present-day car park and restaurant – was a twenty-three-year-old *Gefreiter* named Karl Schutte. Normally he had seven men under him, but tonight one was on leave and his detachment had been increased by an extra four. His gun, with the other two on the other tower and the dam wall, would turn out to be the first line of defence, for the flak detachments at Günne could not open fire on each aircraft until it had passed over the dam wall. He would be on the right and ahead of each Lancaster as it approached.

For a while it seemed as if official optimism was justified. Gibson's Upkeep exploded short of the dam due to the netting and Hopgood's attempt ended in tragedy near Ostonnen. The six 20mm guns at the Möhne had reacted vigorously to Gibson's attack, but things began to go wrong for the defenders when the two weapons on the towers were put out of action by bomb blast. One gun on the dam wall and the three near Günne continued throughout the remainder of the attack, putting up sporadic resistance against other aircraft even after the dam had been breached.

The Möhne's gunners certainly earned their pay that night, but, when they paused to draw breath, they must have wondered where their own fighters were. The answer was that due to a communication breakdown there was no reaction from a nearby Luftwaffe night fighter base at the town of Werl, which continued its night flying training programme despite Gibson's force remaining in the vicinity for half an hour. Other night fighters, as McCarthy saw on the way in, flew too high to see and intercept the bombers they knew were active. Blind despite their radar, those that were scrambled blundered around the sky. This time there would be no victory marks on their tail units.

Battles and lives are all too frequently lost for want of timely communications. A bomb explosion at the dam – possibly Hopgood's – cut Wilkening's line to the dam and apparently to Soest as well. After a fruitless attempt to call the exchange he then ran to a station of the Ruhr-Lippe railway and got through to Körbecke at around 0110. Most telephones around the Möhne were out of action for at least an hour, after which the flak battery commander was finally able to report news of the breach.

Perhaps someone on the dam had reacted more quickly, for news of the impending flood had already been passed on to *Regierungsdirektor* Niewisch at Arnsberg, some twenty minutes before Wilkening was able to get through to the Möhne and find out what was happening. Niewisch promptly ordered the police at the town of Neheim to be warned, then police stations in towns further downstream. At 0130 a second warning of the floods arrived at Arnsberg, but by now the danger had outpaced the warning system. Officials were unable to pass this on to Neheim as the lines were under water. The Neheim police received the first call before the floods arrived, but due to the air-raid warning that had already been sounded most people were in their shelters – just about the worst places for them to be. Consequently the police could not warn them in time.

As most of Günne was on high ground to the north of the Möhne, damage there was limited. The police and flak detachment on the dam were probably in the safest position of all, being close to but above what happened, and suffered no casualties. One piece of the powerhouse's turbine housing was later found 250 yards downstream from its original position.

The village of Himmelpforten, which lay in the valley below the dam, was all but wiped off the map by the wall of water. Most of the villagers escaped when the parish priest, Father Berkenkopf, rang a bell to warn them at the cost of his own life. Six did not, dying with their priest, who was still ringing the bell as his church was engulfed.

The water roared on at up to 30mph, sweeping away bridges, buildings and many of those who had not had the wit or the time to reach high ground. Neheim was devastated, as was the town of Wickede. The number of casualties quickly rose to four figures, a large number of whom were foreign conscript labourers. At the foot of the Wiedenberg, a tall hill near the Möhne, there had been a Ukrainian women's camp, half of whose inmates perished when their wooden huts were smashed against a concrete bridge.

The trail of destruction left behind in the Möhne and Ruhr valleys had to be seen to be believed. Near the town of Herdecke a railway viaduct which carried the Dortmund-Düsseldorf main line was put out of action when one of its centre piers collapsed, leaving both sets of track suspended in mid-air. Dahlhausen marshalling yard, the tenth largest of thirty in the Ruhr, was flooded, as were four other lines. A girder bridge at Frondenberg was swept away, accompanied by 500 metres of a nearby embankment.

It was not only communications that suffered. Eleven factories were destroyed and 114 damaged; pumping and power stations were all either demolished or put out of action and the number of dead was finally put at 1,294, of whom 476 were German; it was a far higher number of casualties than had been inflicted by any previous British raid. There was an elaborate series of funerals for them, but only a mass burial for the foreign workers. A substantial acreage of arable land was rendered useless and twenty-five bridges were swept away. Like a peacetime flood disaster, those who had survived sat on their roofs awaiting rescue while debris lapped around them. For the time being, chaos reigned.

The Eder was to suffer damage from all of the three Upkeeps that were aimed at it. Although Len Sumpter thought that his had caused a nine-foot breach, some German witnesses later said it exploded just short of the wall, damaging the parapet, a roadway across the top of the dam and a landing stage, all near Edersee village, which had been on the right of the attacking aircraft. Maudslay's bomb caused damage to the parapet on the dam's air side, resulting in horizontal fissures beyond the main V-shaped breach caused by Knight. This sequence of damage may indicate why the eventual breach at the Eder was much more angular in shape than the semi-circular one cut by Young and Maltby at the Möhne. There was also a marked diagonal step at each side of the breach, where loosened masonry had been gouged out by the water.

Nevertheless, the scenes of destruction were much the same. Karl Albrecht, the engineer in charge of the two power stations below the Eder, was lucky to escape with his life as water and debris began to fall through the roof of the one he was in. He hastily scrambled up the steps to the parapet of the dam, saw the breach widen and the Edersee's contents gush into the valley below. Again, the phone links were cut by the water, but not before the first words of a warning had reached Bad Wildungen post office, some five miles south-east of the dam, followed by a train-like roar in the distance. The postmaster acted on his own authority, contacting other villages in the Eder valley, beginning with Affoldern, the nearest to the dam. This undoubtedly saved many lives, but nothing could halt the high wall of water that had been unleashed.

At Affoldern the village church was destroyed and ten lives were lost – a substantial blow to so small a community. These ranged from a man of seventy-eight to a baby girl of nine months. One who survived was Heinz Baumann, a sixteen-year-old youth who for some reason had decided to go for a walk in the hills and so was almost on high ground when the water came without warning, in waves. It rose rapidly to his waist, but he managed to reach safety. His father survived by clinging to an apple tree. The villages of Bergheim, Giflitz and Hemfurth also suffered, losing eighteen people between them. Many of these were either elderly or very young.

Although the valley at the foot of the dam was steeper than that at the Möhne, further on it broadened out, allowing the flood to spread outwards over the next two days, aided by the larger capacity of the Eder lake. Heavy flooding again badly affected agricultural land as well as destroying a large stock of fish. Floods up to twenty feet deep inundated most villages between there and the town of Kassel, whose older parts were also affected, though the nearby Henschel aircraft factory was not. Fritzlar airfield's runway went under water and a bridge carrying the main Giessen-Frankfurt railway line was demolished. Other railway lines and bridges in the area suffered cuts or dislocation.

The two attacks by McCarthy and Brown at the Sorpe had little effect beyond destroying some seventy metres of the parapet, with structural damage to a pumping station and some houses in the vicinity. The Sorpe still stood, with no breach or any prospect of one.

German senior officers descended on the dams to view the damage, pausing only to congratulate the flak battery at the Möhne for their success in destroying one of the Lancasters. Karl Schutte had burnt his hands on his gun while reloading it – which indicates how hot it had become from prolonged firing – and he would receive the Iron Cross Second Class for his part in this action.

Still, however stout the defences at the Möhne had been, it did not alter the fact that the RAF had struck a heavy blow. Perhaps as an inducement to talk after seven days in solitary confinement at Werl, Fraser, Hopgood's bomb aimer, was told by an interrogating officer that the damage was equivalent to one hundred raids, which made him feel pretty good despite his current situation. However, there is no reason to believe that Fraser told his captors anything; Upkeep's details would be pieced together from other sources before long.

Someone who did give some answers, but not the sort the Germans wanted to hear, was Tony Burcher. Despite his back injury, his thirst had been so great that he had tried to crawl towards a ditch, only to be spotted by a member of the Hitler Youth. On asking a guard for water, he was told there was none! However, the smile was literally wiped from his face when some typically blunt Australian replies during an interrogation resulted in a blow from a rifle butt, knocking out several teeth. Having survived this and a prison hospital, he finished up in *Stalag Luft III*, where he acquired some false ones made from, of all things, toilet porcelain!

Albert Speer, Hitler's Armaments Minister, was advised of the news in the early hours of the morning and flew over the floods in a Fieseler Storch light aircraft to land at Werl. Sure that the primary object had been to destroy hydroelectric power, he demanded replacement motors from other factories to provide electricity, regardless of the consequences to production elsewhere. Quite apart from the loss of industrial power, the supply of domestic electricity as well as water had been cut off, although within two days this was being made good. Speer's genius for improving the Reich's war effort would now be tested to the full.

Another of his demands, which was quickly acceded to, was that from now on all the dams should be heavily defended, including those that had not been attacked this time. Ten thousand men were sent to them, at a time when the Eastern Front was absorbing some two-thirds of the *Wehrmacht* and a quarter of a million Axis troops had just surrendered in North Africa.

This meant that from now on each dam, regardless of its importance, would be crawling with flak detachments, guns and barrage balloons, at much cost to the defences elsewhere. Such an extreme reaction indicated how shaken the Germans were.

Not knowing what had happened to all of 617's aircraft, Speer expressed surprise that so few of them had attacked the Sorpe, as he considered it to be more vital to German war production than the Eder. The day after the raid he had inspected it and later said that the damage was slightly higher than the water. However, even if the two hits had been deep enough to allow some water to spill over the top, it is unlikely that this would have been enough to breach it. He could be thankful that this one had held.

A repeat attack on the dams while they were being repaired could be anticipated. Such an attack might not stop the breaches from being refilled, but could hinder progress on them, and it had now become vital to complete this job before the autumn rains came, otherwise the water would be lost. Hitler quickly approved a plan to send 7,000 workers to the area to assist in clearing up, followed by a further 20,000 as soon as possible. Such was the priority given to this that many of them were taken by the *Organization Todt* from work on the Atlantic Wall defences and shipped to Germany. Since the Wall was far from complete when six Allied divisions stormed it on D-Day a year later, it may be said that a good many Allied soldiers' lives were indirectly saved by *Chastise*.

German resilience frequently astonished the Allies. Speer, whom Churchill nicknamed 'the crafty expert', was not only resourceful when it came to establishing priorities and increasing production, but also none too choosy about where his forced labour came from. He had had no objection to workers being brought to Germany against their will, but was to claim that one of the effects of *Chastise* was to change that.

While on trial at Nuremberg after the war, Speer declared, 'This policy changed the following year [1943] when workers were transferred from building the Atlantic Wall to repairing the Möhne and Eder Dams destroyed by the RAF. I must say that the transfer of these fifty thousand workers [*sic*] from the west into Germany amounted to a catastrophe for us on the Atlantic Wall. It meant that more than one-third of all the workers engaged on the Atlantic Wall left because they too were afraid they might have to go to Germany. That is why we rescinded the order as quickly as possible, so that the French workers on the Atlantic Wall should have confidence in us.'

With his life hanging in the balance, it was not surprising that Speer should have sought to present his conduct in the best possible light, but all this was no comfort to the families of those forced labourers who had been in the path of the flood waters. The picture of disruption he conjured up contrasted with his comments under interrogation by the Americans in May 1945:

> The attack on the Eder Dam had no effects except some slight flood damage. The Möhne Dam attack would have had serious consequences only if the Sorpe Dam and two other small dams had been broken at the same time. The chief factor which prevented serious reduction in industrial water supplies to the Ruhr was the existence of a pumping system from the Rhine up the Ruhr valley designed to supply the whole district as far upstream as Essen. The pumping plants were silted up by the floodwave from the Möhne, but were quickly restored. Repairs to the Möhne Dam were then rushed through in time for catching the autumn rains. Restrictions on water consumption were imposed on the Ruhr industry during the summer, but otherwise the attacks had no effect except that of giving the Germans 'a big scare.'

The pumping system had come into use only a short time before *Chastise*; had it been possible to breach the dams a year before, the effects would have been far more serious. The system's use gives some insight into how the Germans recovered from the flooding, but while Speer might have chosen to minimise the effects of *Chastise*, those with the task of clearing up would have had different views on the subject. If the effect of breaching two dams was only marginal, why go to the trouble of rebuilding and heavily defending them afterwards? It would have been interesting, to say the least, to have seen the reaction of the local population if Speer had made his opinions known to them at the time. Quite apart from the blow to morale, he made no mention of the production time that had been lost. It was some scare.

Speer's report shook Hitler, who spoke of 'this disaster in the west' and took seriously the resulting delay in self-propelled gun production in the Ruhr, especially after recent losses in North Africa. Then another problem loomed up. 'If a dry year occurs, it will be catastrophic. If we encounter a year when the Ruhr has no water, can we survive?'

Hitler's anger at the Luftwaffe's handling of the affair was evident and Hermann Göring, whose influence with his *Führer* had declined since losing the Battle of Britain, would have had a hard time explaining why. General Josef Kammhuber, whose night fighter defensive line had so clearly failed, declared, 'The night fighter force could not come to grips with the attackers since it was an attack at the lowest level, and the targets could not be picked up by radar, hence they offered no prey for the night fighters.'

The feelings of the German High Command were understandable, but their initial fears were never realised. There were to be no follow-up attacks on the repair teams at the Möhne or the Eder; an error since, as Speer observed, delays would have occurred, prolonging the effects of the water shortages on both civilians and industry.

Within days barrage balloons had been emplaced on all three major dams: a classic instance of shutting the stable door. The task of Herr Wildbrett of Heinrich Butzer of Dortmund, the engineers appointed to rebuild the Möhne, was formidable but not insurmountable. The two bombs had blown a gap 240ft across and 200ft deep, roughly equidistant between the towers. 12,000 cubic metres of concrete had been washed away and due to damage a further 7,000 would have to be removed. The remaining water was some sixty feet deep and just covered the alluvial deposit that had built up behind the wall. A floating crane was used to place a temporary wall over the top of this deposit, to ten feet above the water's surface.

Although the work was scheduled to start as soon as possible after the raid, it did not begin until July. By October the breach at the Möhne had been refilled, in time for the autumn rains to refill the lake, although the installation of new sluice valves and safeguards continued until the beginning of August 1944. During this period the dam's towers were reduced to almost the same height as the parapet; the Germans had evidently realised their significance for sighting purposes.

At both dams, cyclopean rubble masonry was used to fill the breaches; it was the same material that had originally been used in their construction. Cement was used in the mortar and cracks were sealed using pressure grouting.

The tremendous outpouring of water at the Möhne had scoured out the ground at its foot on the air side, leaving a hole where the edge of the compensating basin had been. Fearing the dam's foundations might have been undermined, the Germans partly filled this with a large concrete block. The powerhouse that had been destroyed by Hopgood's bomb was not reinstated.

Due to favourable weather, by February 1944 the Möhnesee had risen to almost its full capacity, which was 213.5m deep. However, at the insistence of surviving members of the local population, the lake's level was reduced by ten metres, which meant that instead of a possible 131 million cubic metres, only 68 million were held, which reduced the static water pressure. Such was the continuing nature of Speer's scare.

Thirty-five large balloons were added to the defences, which by August 1944 had been beefed up by 88mm guns on the nearby hillsides, as well as quadruple 20mm weapons along the shoreline. To further deter low-flying aircraft, a number of 5-kilo explosive charges on wires were slung across the valley on the air side of the dam.

Even this was not enough; a special proximity-fused mine was developed by the *Kriegsmarine* to go off if an aircraft flew over it. To make sure, five rows of them were added to the lake, but they did not prove satisfactory as they were apt to be set off by 'changes in atmospheric conditions'. *Nebelwerfer* smokescreen apparatus was located up to 1,000 metres downsteam from the dam, its ammunition fitted with variable height settings. By the lake a further two towers were erected and cables were suspended horizontally from them. These in turn supported vertical cables across the width of the dam. The anti-torpedo netting was reinstated, with timber deflectors, which were held out from the dam wall by floats on the lake's surface.

As a precaution against 'rocket bombs' chain mail was suspended twenty-five feet out from the air side, its top being some fifty feet below the parapet, to deflect vertical bombs away from the foot of the dam. Two of the concrete anchor points for this can still be seen on the hillside at the south end of the dam today.

This formidable defensive array was manned by 2,500 men, most of whom would see little action until they fired once again at 617 in the spring of 1945. By then the squadron's target would be a different one. They could all have been better employed elsewhere, but such was the upheaval caused by the 'Wasser-Katastrophe' that it was out of the question. All this does not take into account the defences at the other Ruhr dams, which would also see little or no action.

By October the damage at the Eder had also been made good by Philipp Holzmann of Frankfurt, who had had the task of filling a breach 210ft across and 140ft deep. As the Eder's power installations had been sited on the hillsides, they had got off fairly lightly, although the compensating basin had been almost completely destroyed and its water control house heavily damaged. The Edersee too began to refill, although it would not reach full capacity again until after repairs were completed in 1947. There would be further problems with this dam nearly half a century later, as will be seen. Until the war's end both dams would have a temporary parapet and flood damage would remain visible for a mile downstream.

What was this strange new weapon that had caused such havoc? Nothing more than a few casing fragments would ever be found from the Upkeeps that had exploded, but that carried by Flt Lt Barlow, which now lay in the wreckage of his Lancaster at Haldern, would supply the answers.

Where new unexploded bombs were concerned, German procedure was to contact Air Inspectorate 13, a department of the RLM – the German Air Ministry. Photographs and sketches would be taken if possible, to provide a record in case of accidents. The bomb was to be investigated by day, but only by an officer or senior NCO specifically trained in such work. In the interests of safety and security outsiders would be excluded – this was no job for amateurs. As a precaution against delayed-action fuses, work was to begin after a week, although if the bomb had landed in an industrial plant the minimum delay would be three days. However, if the bomb was not embedded in the earth – and in this instance Barlow's Upkeep may have been on or near the surface – then it could be disposed of immediately.

Showing that cold courage demanded of bomb disposal men the world over, *Hauptmann* Heinz Schweitzer of the Luftwaffe rendered the Upkeep safe and its secrets were quickly revealed. Like their British opposite numbers, the Germans seemed unsure as to how to classify it, eventually describing it as a 'Rotations-Wasserbombe' (a rotating depth charge), which was as good a description as any. They underestimated its charge by 880lb, describing it as 2,600kg (5,720lb) and its overall weight as 3,900kg.

Curiously, despite the Air Ministry instruction that all live Upkeeps were to be dark green in colour, Barlow's Upkeep was a dark red oxide shade, with white letters and numbers on each end. All this was faithfully recorded by the Germans in two detailed drawings that later fell into British hands. A translated version of them, kept by the Royal Engineers, was used in 1997 in the recovery of inert weapons from Reculver.

There would be no repetition of *Chastise*, although that did not prevent the Germans from experimenting with their own version of Upkeep, once its secrets had been revealed. By July they knew enough to make some detailed drawings. Wallis in turn knew, from information supplied, he said, by MI5, that his brainchild's secrets had been found out by the Germans, though he wrongly thought that they had recovered Rice's Upkeep from the Zuider Zee.

Referred to as Kurt or Emil, the German bomb introduced a further refinement, being rocket-powered and small enough to be dropped from an FW 190 fighter, achieving a range of four kilometres, although it may be asked what use such a small weapon would have been. German scientists, as sceptical as some of their British opposite numbers had been about its characteristics, went back to basics and checked the data for themselves, resulting in an eighteen-month delay. This weapon was never used by the Luftwaffe, although fears of such an event led to increased defences on dams in the hills above Sheffield.

In April 1944 ten modified Lancasters would be put into storage by 617 at RAF Metheringham in Lincolnshire, along with a quantity of Upkeeps, but the weapon was never used again. The surviving bombs would later be dumped, minus their depth charge pistols, at sea, and the remaining Lancasters went to the scrap heap soon after the war. Sadly for posterity, these included Gibson's Lancaster, ED932/G, which unlike its crew survived until 1947. What a museum exhibit that would have been!

Cochrane's ambition to improve bombing accuracy within 5 Group has already been mentioned. One idea that had been pioneered during *Chastise* was subsequently adopted by Bomber Command's Main Force. This was to have a Master Bomber and his Deputy controlling future area attacks in the same way that Gibson had done over the dams.

So, what did the survivors think of it all? When interviewed for a Channel 4 *Secret History* television documentary that was shown on the 50th anniversary of *Chastise*, Joe McCarthy said that he considered the raid worthwhile, that the boost to morale was unmistakeable and that for a long time afterwards anyone from 617 could go into a pub without having to pay for a drink. Ken Brown acknowledged the morale effect, but was still bitter over the loss of his friends. Because of them he did not consider that it was worth it.

There was an echo of *Chastise* during the Gulf War in 1991, when the Americans considered breaching dams on the Tigris and Euphrates rivers if the ground troops taking part in Operation *Desert Storm* were attacked by Iraqi chemical weapons. General Colin Powell later said that if this had succeeded Baghdad would have been flooded with up to six feet of water, resulting in high civilian loss of life. It was fortunate for all concerned that when the ground attack started most Iraqis surrendered without firing a shot. So much for 'the mother of all battles'. As the Coalition's order of battle had included Panavia Tornadoes flown by 617 Sqdn, this could indeed have been a rerun of May 1943!

Although just two dams were breached, making the operation only a partial success, *Chastise* was politically timely, both for the government of the day and for Bomber Command. More importantly, it established Wallis' credentials as a bomb designer and paved the way for the two earthquake weapons that were to follow; weapons which no film maker has seen fit to celebrate but which would in the end prove to be far more devastating.

Highball

I turn green with envy when I see the Mosquito. The British knock together a beautiful wooden aircraft that every piano factory over there is building ... There is nothing the British do not have.

Reichsmarschall Hermann Göring

While the preparations for Upkeep's use had been going ahead, attention had also been paid to a second weapon that Wallis had designed. Capable of being carried by the de Havilland Mosquito light bomber, the Highball bomb was intended to be just under three feet in diameter and have a gross weight of 1,000lb, of which 545lb would be the charge. When this bomb had first been considered in November 1942, the Bristol Beaufort torpedo bomber had been looked on as a suitable carrier. However, by 1943 the Beaufort was seen to be underpowered and the Mosquito possessed a much better performance, particularly at low level.

On 1 April 1943 618 Sqdn was formed at RAF Skitten, a satellite of RAF Wick in the north-east of Scotland – a suitably remote place to experiment with a weapon whose success, like Upkeep, would depend on secrecy being maintained until the time came to use it. This would be a unique unit, as a proposal to form a second Highball squadron went no further, in part because Coastal Command's AOC, Air Marshal Sir John Slessor, felt it would not be ready until the following September. His opinion would turn out to be an understatement as far as 618 was concerned.

Initially under the joint leadership of Sqdn Ldrs C. F. Rose and G. H. Melville-Jackson, 618 came under Coastal Command's 18 Group and, like 617, had to make do with unmodified aircraft to begin with. Its first personnel were mainly drawn from 105 and 139 Sqdns at RAF Marham in Norfolk, who arrived with some of their Mosquitoes.

Training began with a warning of the perils of low flying. On 5 April DZ486, piloted by P/O Pavey and Sgt Stimson, was flying inland from the sea. After crossing the coast the crew disregarded a QDM, flew too low and hit a hill ten miles south-west of Durness, in Caithness. A shepherd witnessed the accident, but there was nothing he could do apart from testify at the inquiry. Both men died and their aircraft was burned out. Personnel from an RAF W/T station at Durness were given the unenviable job of clearing up afterwards. On 15 April Wg Cdr G. H. B. Hutchinson took command and some progress was made when the first modified Mosquito, DZ531/G, arrived from Brooklands.

The main type of Mosquito to be used by 618 would be the BIV light bomber, whose perspex nose carried no gun armament, although some experiments during the war and afterwards would also be conducted with the heavily armed FBVI fighter-bomber type. It was the BIV that had really brought the Mosquito to the public's attention in May 1942, when aircraft of 105 Sqdn had stoked up the fires in Cologne the morning after the first 1,000-bomber raid. It had also been this mark that had later mounted a spectacular though not wholly successful attack on the Gestapo headquarters in Oslo.

The Highball aircraft were taken from the de Havilland production line at Hatfield in Hertfordshire and flown to Brooklands, where they were modified by Brooklands Aviation, who still maintained a presence at the Flying Village, despite having moved most of their facilities to Sywell in Northamptonshire to repair damaged Wellingtons.

DK290, a Mosquito BIV, pictured before conversion to the Highball role. (RAF Museum, neg. no. P5393CC)

DK290 pictured in flight after conversion. Two trial Highballs can be seen in the modified bomb bay. The G suffix now added to the aircraft's serial number indicated that it had to be guarded at all times while on the ground, due to the nature of the equipment carried. (Imperial War Museum, neg. no. MH4583)

Two different versions of the Highball bomb are put through their paces on the Foxwarren test rig, *c.* 1943. (Author's collection)

This involved the removal of the bomb bay doors and the fitting of two sets of caliper arms, as two bombs were to be carried semi-internally in tandem. Unlike the Lancaster, there would not be sufficient space to fit a V8 or any other type of motor to spin the bombs, so, since the Mosquito's hydraulic system lacked the power to do so, a small wind-driven turbine was installed. It was also decided that 618's aircraft should be equipped with drop tanks of 42-gallon capacity, increasing their range by 200 miles.

DK290/G, a BIV used for AAEE trials, was fitted with a pair of dummy weapons at Heston airfield on the west side of London, not Brooklands or Boscombe Down as might have been expected. This aircraft's fabric outer surface was polished, giving a diving speed of 390mph ASI, although the test pilot who experienced this found that maximum force was necessary to hold it in the dive. Slightly less was needed when diving it without the bombs. This aircraft was also the subject of experiments with a ten-degree dihedral tailplane. These appear not to have given any additional benefit as there is no mention of any of 618's aircraft being so modified.

For some months Highball experiments had been carried out at the dispersed site at Foxwarren. Smooth and dimpled versions of Highball were spun on its test rig, and George Roake, a Vickers tinsmith, had good cause to remember one when he was interviewed in 1988:

We made a small one over in Foxwarren and they set up these sandbags. They released it and it was going to go along the workshop floor and into these sandbags, but it didn't. It went through them and finished up in the lake, which is part of Silvermere golf course. It was only about a year ago they found it when they were cleaning the lake out. People didn't know the story of it and they said that they had found a piece that was dumped in the lake. It was concrete-filled.

Above: Looking west along Reculver beach towards the disused church. A Highball can be seen lying on the shingle in the foreground. (A. Lane)

Left: One of the Reculver targets, made from chestnut palings on scaffolding. (A. Lane)

The idea of a bomb of this type was not new, for the RAE had carried out experiments during the First World War on smooth and dimpled weapons. These went no further, perhaps because, as in 1939, there was no aircraft able to deliver them. Possibly Wallis had read of this, although even today it is part of local legend that golf balls were at one time tested in the wind tunnel!

It was not only the bombs that had to be tested at Foxwarren, but also the equipment associated with them, such as the turbine. This too was not without its dangers, as recalled by Ted Petty, one of George Roake's colleagues:

> That brought to light this peculiar friendship and thoughtfulness of people like Sir George Edwards, because during the development of this we had to spin the air turbine up to test it … The first one we tested – it disintegrated and went out through the roof of the hangar. We phoned up Mr Edwards at about midnight and told him what had happened. His first words were, 'Are you blokes all right?' That was the measure of this sort of family and friendship that you always got from the management. He didn't worry about the job. His first thoughts were, 'Are the chaps all right?' It was a marvellous illustration of the attitude which has pertained all through the years.

During April 1943 twenty inert and eleven live Highballs were made available. There was also a larger 1,200lb version, 4ft in diameter, with a 750lb charge, four of which were intended to be carried in a Wellington, or six in a Warwick, with a view to attacks on Italian dams, merchant ships and canal locks. Trials of the larger bomb were initially delayed by a bearing failure on the Wellington that had been modified to carry it, and this weapon was later discarded. Perhaps this was as well, for by now the Wellington was nearing the end of its front-line career, at least in northern Europe, and the Warwick would be dogged by problems for another two years.

The plan was to try Highball off Reculver, concurrent with the Upkeep trials, then follow this up with mock attacks against a target ship, which would be the old French battleship *L'Amiral Courbet*, but, as might have been expected, things did not go as Wallis had hoped. The first problem was that by now 618's crews were even more of a mixed bag than at the beginning, as some had been posted in from Beaufighter squadrons of Coastal Command, making Mosquito conversion training necessary. Due to their differing levels of experience, it was considered desirable that each crew should drop at least two bombs before going into action, and they were to witness as many of the trials as possible.

These began on 13 April, when two Mosquitoes dropped Highballs at Reculver. In each instance the wooden casing broke up, and another dropped by the Wellington behaved in the same fashion. Three Highballs were then modified, being fitted with tightened bands and their recesses filled with aerated resin; a substance that was described as looking like Aero chocolate but coral red in colour. These were dropped a week later. None bounced and part of the casing still broke away. An eighteen-inch-wide steel plate was now fitted over the canister, and this worked better on 29 April, when one bounced a thousand yards in a one-foot swell. It was slightly dented, but there was no major damage.

As April turned to May trials began against the *Courbet* at Loch Striven in Argyllshire. The name ship of her class, she had been launched in 1913 as one of the French Navy's first dreadnoughts. By 1939 she had become a training ship and after the fall of France had languished in dock at Portsmouth, her AA guns providing a useful extra defence during Luftwaffe raids. Although her hull armour had been thinner than that fitted to British capital ships, unlike them it had been extended well down her sides as a precaution against underwater hits. She therefore posed a demanding test for Highball.

Now release gear problems began to emerge. Some bombs were released too close, breaking up on contact with the ship. Others fell off as aircraft approached, although this was ascribed by Vickers to the use of steel-cored cable, which stretched and was

A dented Highball after recovery, with a figure at the right giving scale. (A. Lane)

Recovering an inert Highball at Reculver. One of the chestnut paling targets can be seen over the bank in the background. (A. Lane)

Although much smaller than Upkeep, considerable effort was needed to roll a Highball into the back of a lorry. The Wren, presumably its driver, was evidently considered exempt from this task! (A. Lane)

Safely aboard at last. The officer with his back to the camera may be Vice-Admiral Renoulf and the civilian to his left is almost certainly Barnes Wallis. (A. Lane)

The French battleship *L'Amiral Courbet* at Loch Striven. (A. Lane)

Courbet under Highball 'attack'. By now, white stripes appear on funnels and hull as aiming marks. (A. Lane)

later replaced by rods. Like Upkeep, Highball was designed as an almost completely spherical depth charge, but unlike its larger brother it would retain that shape, being spun backwards to nearly 1,000rpm and released from the Mosquito at low level.

The bomb would bounce in the same manner as Upkeep, so avoiding the anti-torpedo nets placed round a capital ship's sides while it was at anchor. On striking the hull Highball would either roll down or around it, the Torpex filling being detonated by a hydrostatic pistol. Ideally, this would take place underneath the ship's keel, which, even if it had a double bottom, would be more thinly plated than the armoured anti-torpedo bulges on its sides. Also, a weapon which tore the bottom out of a ship would be more likely to sink it; experience had shown that a well-trained damage control party could patch up a hole in the side of a vessel by the use of collision mats and counterflooding to maintain an even keel. Clearly impressed by what he had seen so far, 618's diarist wrote, 'Incredible prospects lay ahead of the invention.'

So, provided the bugs could be dealt with, what uses might Highball be put to? Before 618's formation various options had been considered by the Ad Hoc Highball Sub-Committee, which from March 1943 had had the task of issuing fortnightly progress reports to the Chiefs of Staff. Of the five main ports used by the *Kriegsmarine*, only Trondheim in Norway and Kiel on the north-east German coast were within the Mosquito's range from Britain. Narvik and the *Tirpitz*'s lair at Altenfjord in Norway were beyond this, as was Gdynia in the Baltic.

Attacks on inland waterways in western Europe were also ruled out, as a high degree of accuracy would be necessary in the face of fierce opposition and only the simultaneous destruction of two or three lock gates would disrupt canal traffic over a sufficiently long period of time to make such attacks worthwhile. The ideas of flying along the canals, or at right-angles to them and rolling bombs over an embankment into the water, were rejected.

Of the five Biscay ports that had U-boat pens, only Brest was considered assailable by Highball. Direct hits on several pens would be necessary, which would not be possible unless a large force was used. Even then the attackers would be dependent on maintaining surprise until the last moment. Each port's defences were strong and it was doubtful if even a few aircraft could reach their targets. There were also two locks at Saint-Nazaire and one at La Pallice through which U-boats had to pass, but these presented the same problems as the canal ones. A plum target at Saint-Nazaire would have been the dry dock built for the ill-fated French liner *Normandie*, and big enough to accommodate the *Tirpitz* should she ever leave Norway. However, this had been wrecked in 1942 by a famous Commando raid that had featured the old and expendable destroyer HMS *Campbeltown*, her bows crammed with explosive.

As would be seen during the summer of 1944, the pens would offer stout resistance to even the six-ton Tallboy bomb and it was as well for 618 that no one saw fit to order them to attack these targets. The squadron would certainly have been slaughtered for little gain. Highball's use against beach obstacles in support of an amphibious landing was also considered, but it was pointed out that as both it and Upkeep had been designed as underwater weapons, neither would be any substitute for conventional bombs in raids against land defences.

There were two other potential targets, one of them the Rothensee Ship Lift in Germany. This unusual target, which was also considered for the Tallboy bomb, was sited on the Mittelland Canal, where its traffic either joined or crossed over the Elbe River. Shortly before the war the Mittelland Canal and the southern part of the Dortmund-Ems Canal had been developed to provide communication by water between the Ruhr and the Upper Elbe industries around Berlin and beyond. The Mittelland Canal now carried the bulk of the heavy traffic in fuel, iron and steel from the Ruhr to Berlin. It was therefore assessed as the most important waterway in Europe. Rothensee was the only construction of its type to be within Mosquito range, but any attack would be at long distance and would have to be made either under cloudy conditions by day, or by night in bright moonlight.

The other target was the Royal Italian Navy, the *Regia Marina*. Despite a successful Fleet Air Arm attack on its base at Taranto in November 1940, the remainder of the Italian Fleet still presented a threat to Allied operations in the Mediterranean, especially with the invasion of Sicily now in the offing. Its ships would be a useful asset to the Germans if they should decide to take them over. However, it was considered that even if Highball were to become operationally ready by May, it would not be possible to prepare the aircraft for overseas service, or to operate them from bases in North Africa.

The question of security was to act as a restraint on the use of Highball throughout the remainder of the war. As previously noted in Chapter 2, the Chiefs of Staff, especially the First Sea Lord, Admiral Sir Dudley Pound, were anxious that it should be used at around the same time as the dams attack. Things now moved rapidly, with every effort being made to get sixteen modified Mosquitoes ready during May.

Liaison between Rose and Longbottom had resulted in the former dropping twenty-three Highballs off Reculver during April. 618 trained extensively, covering low-level attacks and long-distance navigation, using as their target the depot ship *Bonaventure*, in Loch Cairnbawn. In the light of what subsequently happened, it is interesting to note that this ship had also been used as a target by the Royal Navy's midget submarines, known as X-craft.

As with 617, the need for security had been stressed from the start and erks heading south on leave trains from Thurso were wise enough to keep their opinions to themselves. These trains also serviced the Home Fleet at Scapa Flow and it would not have taken long to arouse any eavesdropping matelot's suspicions. In addition, the RAF's No.27 Embarkation Unit, dealing with postings to and from Russia, was based at Thurso. Apart from its own airmen in transit, on at least one occasion in 1944 it had to handle a party of eleven Soviet Air Force officers on their way home. Hutchinson's lectures ensured that there was no careless talk on the platform.

On approaching the target the height of the aircraft was to be between fifty and sixty feet, the ground speed to be 360mph, the bomb to be spun at 700rpm and the range to be 1,200yds. The bomb's pistols were to be set to a depth of twenty-seven feet, although this could be altered to forty if necessary.

A detachment from 618 Sqdn was sent to RAF Turnberry in Ayrshire, on the south-west coast of Scotland. This airfield, once home to an RFC training unit, had been reactivated early in 1942 and had housed 5 OTU, who had carried out torpedo training with Hampdens and Beauforts. It was from here that Rose attacked the *Courbet* with ten Highballs, five of them unsuccessful due to the release gear failures already described. During May he also found time to drop a further twenty-three bombs off Reculver. However, the result of all this activity was to show that there was still a long way to go before Highball could be accepted for operational use.

On 14 May the Chiefs of Staff finally agreed to use Upkeep without waiting any longer for Highball to be perfected. This gave the green light for *Chastise*, but even after the dams had been breached Admiral Pound remained concerned about Highball's security and wanted Upkeep not to be used again, or at least not for the time being. Since Flt Lt Barlow's bomb had been recovered intact by the Germans, the need for such excessive secrecy no longer existed, although few on the Allied side knew this at the time. The Highball Committee saw Upkeep as a one-shot weapon and subsequent events were to prove them right. In view of the Navy's objections, a projected attack on the *Tirpitz*, code-named Operation *Servant*, was postponed.

At this time Wg Cdr Hutchinson had flown down to Brooklands for a conference. News of 617's attack on the dams now came through, and the knowledge that his own squadron was still in training must have given him some mixed feelings. On the morning of 17 May, as the Ruhr's shocked civilians surveyed the flooded mess around them, Hutchinson prepared to take off from Brooklands in his Mosquito, DK493, to return to Scotland. What happened next was later described on a return visit to the airfield by Sir George Edwards, whose life nearly ended that day:

There were some spectacular crashes around here, because the CO of the squadron couldn't fly a Mosquito properly. When you took a Mosquito off you had to lead with left thumb on the throttles, because there was a built-in swing to port. I suppose one of the nearest stages of being blown up or killed that I was in – and there were a good many – we were going up to Scotland, where we did the trials against an old French battleship, and there was the pilot and navigator and I sat down in the bomb-aimer's window, which is in front. At the last minute it was decided to take another one for a reason that I can't remember, so I was hoiked out of that one and put in the navigator's seat on the second one. And the one that I was in the bomb-aimer's window of he was flying and didn't do his port-up and it went round like that and knocked the fin and rudder straight off a Warwick which was parked by the side and hit the Banking and went up in a ball of flame. They both got out, but I had been sitting in the bit that didn't any longer exist. That was fairly close. He did that two or three times, actually. We were bumping Mosquitoes off here – it was a pretty tiddly airfield to put Mosquitoes in and out of.

It was fortunate that this aircraft had not been bombed up. According to 618's ORB, DZ493's wing hit a vehicle on the perimeter track, then a lorry, a van and finally a barrage balloon cable. Hutchinson and his observer hurriedly scrambled clear of the burning wreck, with some slight injuries to add to his feelings of disappointment concerning 618. There was no mention of any other casualties and if the Mosquito did strike a Warwick as well then the latter was only damaged, as there is no record of one being written off in such circumstances.

Sir George's relief at avoiding a fiery death led him to be rather hard on Hutchinson's flying ability; an incompetent pilot would not have lasted long or risen to such high rank in any air force, especially in wartime. It should be said that although the Mosquito was popular with those who used it, it was not a vice-free design. The US 8th Air Force, who used some for photo-reconnaissance, nicknamed it 'a hollowed-out log with a built-in swing'. As both propellers rotated in the same direction problems could indeed occur while taxiing, followed by an undercarriage collapse, if the throttles were not carefully handled.

This drama led to another – on 20 May two more of 618's aircraft flew into Brooklands to be modified. One, DZ547, had been intended as a replacement for Hutchinson's Mosquito. While landing, it struck a Vickers flight van on the perimeter track and was damaged but later repaired. Fortunately, once again there were only a few slight injuries, to Sgt Coleman, a passenger in the Mosquito, and to two Vickers staff who had been in the van at the time. The pilot, Flg-Off E. H. Jeffreys, seems to have escaped without a scratch. On this date Hutchinson was granted sick leave for eleven days, which he would have been glad to accept, and an award to him of the DFC at this time must have been some consolation.

As Sir George had said, Brooklands and Mosquitoes did not really go together, and there are two more Mosquito stories that were told to me, though neither can be dated or verified. On one occasion one Mosquito reputedly crashed on top of another. The other tale, which seems more likely, is that of the Mosquito which slewed across the grass airfield before coming to a halt intact but a few feet short of the infamous Brooklands sewage farm. This smelly obstacle, originally provided by the site's landowner, Hugh Locke King, as a gift to Woking Borough Council before the race track was built, would remain a hazard to aircrew until after the war ended.

On his recovery Hutchinson joined Rose and Longbottom for further trials at Reculver during June. Although two bombs could be carried in each of the three Mosquitoes that were used, as yet no double drops had been carried out. Trials with a single bomb on 5 and 6 June showed that when flying at 360mph at a height of between thirty and fifty feet above water, effective attacks could be mounted at ranges of 1,000-1,400 yards when attacking a ship at between forty-five and sixty degrees of that vessel's fore and aft line. However, the bomb was still not running consistently, although a special bombsight that Wallis had designed showed promise. So far, all the trials had been in smooth sheltered water, but Wallis was of the opinion that the bomb would also work in sea conditions, though possibly with a shorter range.

As a preparation for *Servant*, forty live bombs had been stored for 618's use at RAF Sumburgh in the Shetlands, and this plan was now reconsidered. The *Tirpitz* still lay in Kaafjord, a tributary of Altenfjord, so any attacking force would have to fly on to Vaenga airfield in the Soviet Union afterwards. To do this would mean running the gauntlet of the Luftwaffe's fighter bases at Elvenes, Alta, Banak, Kirkenes and Petsamo, with an estimated minimum total of eighty single-engined fighters. As 618's aircraft carried no gun armament their only defence would be speed and surprise, especially as Alta and Banak were less than fifty miles from the target.

Two alternative routes were worked out. One ran parallel to and close in to the Norwegian coast, but at sea level to avoid registering on German radar screens until the last minute. The other route was further out but would be flown at 15,000 feet, 150 miles from the coast. Should this second course be adopted, 618 would then lose height, diving to sea level as they approached the fjord. At this point the two routes joined in a climb to 5,000ft after crossing the coast, to gain momentum for the final dive towards the target.

Should 618 fly at sea level all the way – a task requiring considerable concentration – two Royal Navy submarines, one positioned at sea off the mouth of the fjord, would be required to give navigational homing facilities.

Whichever route was used, fuel would be a critical factor. The Mosquitoes were to use their drop tanks first, then jettison them after 510 miles. The final climb and the attack would be done on a weak cruising mixture, covering a further 115 miles and allowing five minutes for the bomb runs. The last leg to Vaenga, just under 300 miles away, would be covered using the maximum weak mixture. The margin of fuel left over from all of this was assessed as '0 per cent'!

Had 618 been spotted by fighters and used up their last dregs in evasion, it is doubtful if any of the Mosquitoes would have reached Soviet territory. Those that survived the defences would have had to face a crash-landing in one of the most inhospitable areas of the world. As a last resort, Sweden might have been tried, but that would have meant internment, at least for a while, with the inevitable suspicion in some quarters that any crew opting for this would have chosen an easy way out of the war.

As far as fuel was concerned, flying across the sea at 15,000ft would be more economical, but this would largely be negated by the need to fly outside radar range for as long as possible, resulting in a saving of no more than thirty-five gallons. Once again, it was as well for 618 that this raid was never carried out. Neither was one on the port of Narvik, for the same reasons.

Quite apart from all this, there was the perennial problem of security. Any negotiations with the Russians to use Vaenga would have meant informing them of Highball first, which might have resulted in the weapon's details being leaked to the Germans before any attack was made.

618 continued to hone their skills, although by now the crews were beginning to ask themselves whether they would ever see action in this role. The range error had now been reduced to less than a hundred yards and the Wallis sight was found to be satisfactory. Premature releases had been found to be due to 'whip' in the fuselage when travelling at high speed, but modifications were in hand to correct this. Other problems were indicated by an elbowing action when the bomb was spun, leading to a change in the axis of rotation, so various driving wheels and balance positions were tried during the last week in June.

It was apparently at around this time, shortly before the Weybridge works took a week's holiday in August, that an admiral came to Burhill and, according to Reg Firman, a Vickers draughtsman, made a speech to assembled Vickers workers to the effect that there was something secret going on within the works. This may have been the talk recalled by Jack Froude earlier, at Burhill. Not surprisingly, Firman took a dim view of this, but whatever was said, it seems not to have been repeated elsewhere. Those already in the know would have said no more and for the rest the factory bombing of September 1940 was still a bitter memory. There was no point in bringing the enemy's attention back to what was currently going on in this part of Surrey.

Firman had done a variety of design work, but his speciality was bomb slips, at first for conventional weapons and now for spinning ones. It was in this connection that he was now summoned to the presence – something he rarely had to do.

> He was sitting at his desk and this admiral was sitting in another corner of the room. Wallis handed me one of my slips – the hooks had broken. He said to me in a casual sort of voice, 'How do you think that came to be broken in that manner?' I said, 'How it happened I don't know, but what has happened is that those hooks have been strained beyond their acceptance and they have broken.'
>
> He said, 'That's nonsense. What I want to know is why they have broken, and I'm telling you they have been broken by excessive internal vibration of the molecules.' The admiral looked at me with a little quiet smile, as if to say, 'You've got to put up with that.'

Firman had worked for Vickers since he was thirteen and this was not the first time he had encountered this sort of attitude from Wallis, nor was it the first time he had got round it:

> So I said, 'Well, if you think it was that, for this particular purpose that you're using the slip I can make those hooks much stronger and they should be able to put up with what you're saying.'

Wallis was not convinced. 'How is it that you can do that? In the ordinary way that slip is meant to hook onto a bomb, then you wind that bomb up into a slip housing and so you have to have a pulley, mounted between those two hooks.'

Firman had his answer ready. It was tactfully phrased, which was just as well.

> You're mounting my slip and using it to take a load. There's no pulley really required. So if you wished, I could make those hooks without the pulley and they would be so much stronger. He said, 'Well, you go away – the holiday's on – and bring me back six slips with strengthened hooks and no pulleys. We'll see what happens then.' Of course I knew damn well that that break was a standard stress break, which we got when we stressed the thing up to its maximum and it had to give in. High-frequency vibrations! Never heard of such a thing.'

There might be a holiday for the Vickers staff, but it was unlikely that Wallis would have taken one at this time – in spite of Gibson's recommendation, after *Chastise*, that he should do so. Firman now had to give up some of his own break and push whatever staff were available at Vickers' Dartford works to get on with the job.

> They didn't want to do it, but they had to. Everyone was afraid of Mr Wallis. I only had to mention his name and no one argued. So I went back to my home at Dartford, where they had to make these hooks, and told them that I wanted a slip without the pulley in it, so the hooks would be that much stronger, They worked all weekend, gave me six slips and I took them back to the office. Wallis never once asked for those slips. He knew high frequency vibrations had nothing to do with it, but he was trying to explain to the admiral what a grip he had over the technical details. Those slips were made for nothing and could never have done anything.

All of this looked like Wallis being difficult just for the sake of it, coupled with that 'quality at all costs' attitude that George Edwards had previously noted, but it was this attitude, this stubborn refusal to be thwarted by any problem, that had carried him this far.

So far the *Tirpitz* had been Highball's prime target and the reason for the protracted experiments with it, but now there was a further delay to the execution of Operation *Servant*. At a meeting between the Admiralty and the Air Ministry on 30 June it was decided that a midget submarine attack, code-named Operation *Source*, should go ahead and that 618 should continue to be held back, since an unsuccessful attack by them would not only reveal Highball but also result in the Germans reinforcing the fjord's defences, so making a hazardous underwater attack by the *Source* crews even more difficult. Further defects in the design of the bombs showed this to be a wise decision.

There was yet another reason behind the Admiralty's decision to hold back *Servant* in favour of *Source*, and that stemmed from the old problem of inter-Service rivalry. In May 1941 the Home Fleet had sunk the battleship *Bismarck* in the North Atlantic, but only after a long chase and the loss of the battlecruiser HMS *Hood*. Clearly Britannia no longer ruled the waves – a truth reinforced by the loss of two other capital ships off Malaya to Japanese air attacks. From the point of view of the admirals it was therefore desirable to regain some credibility by destroying the *Bismarck*'s sister ship, by whatever means. Some senior naval officers had never forgiven the RAF for absorbing the Royal Naval Air Service in 1918, not to mention keeping the Fleet Air Arm short of new equipment for most of the inter-war years, and were not likely to be happy at their rivals beating them at their own game.

So resentment lingered, and as Coastal Command had been under the Admiralty's operational control since 1941, their Lordships were well placed to ensure that this game would be played their way. Had 618 been a Fleet Air Arm squadron their attitudes might have been different.

By July 618 were up to standard in one respect, as they now had their full establishment of modified Mosquitoes, but where Highball was concerned success still eluded them. The bomb's inconsistent running was now thought to be due to the use of unseasoned or unsuitable wood in the casing. Subject to availability – like everything else in wartime – ash was to be used instead, as was an alternative outer casing of heavier gauge metal, without wood at all. Additionally, a new type of bomb pistol was being developed, to withstand an impact of 2,000G. This was essential, as a metal casing, whatever its strength, would not cushion a water impact as well as a wooden one. This was left to RAE at Farnborough to develop.

However, this process of gradual improvement made little impression on the Chiefs of Staff, who after consultation with Air Marshal Slessor agreed that there seemed no justification for maintaining this special unit at a time when the resources and manpower that had been allotted to it could be more profitably used elsewhere. 618 would be reduced to a cadre, the majority of its personnel being seconded to 236 and 248 Sqdns of Coastal Command, or to the PRU at RAF Benson in Oxfordshire.

This did not mean the end for Highball, for Slessor was of the opinion that it might be used for anti-submarine work in the Faeroe Channel, against U-boats coming out of the Baltic. Also, some trials flying would continue from Turnberry, where a number of the modified Mosquitoes would be stored.

For the moment 618 trained as before. Whether Hutchinson or any of his officers were aware of the opinions of those above them at this stage is not known, but, if so, little or nothing would have been said, for fear of impairing morale in a unit that despite its best efforts was still non-operational.

By August it was clear that the bomb's steel casing was strong enough to withstand a high-speed water impact, but wobble had become a problem. This was believed to be due to too high a rate of spin, but further experiments with ash or all-metal casings were expected to at last make consistent running possible. By the first week in August both types had been satisfactorily tried and the pistols they carried also worked correctly.

On 28 August five aircraft took part in an exercise that was described in the ORB as a dummy attack 'over' RAF Peterhead. DZ545/G, flown by Sgts H. Ellis and R. Donald, flew too low, struck a weathervane and crash-landed on the airfield. Aided by a prompt response from Peterhead's crash tender, both men scrambled from their blazing aircraft with nothing worse than superficial burns.

Perhaps Slessor's anti-submarine idea had been passed on to Hutchinson, for now there was a sudden flurry of activity at Skitten as thirty-five bombs were loaded and released in the Sinclairs Bay area, north of Wick. After this, nine aircraft were bombed up with live Highballs, but whatever the intention, it was 'eventually abandoned in the light of existing circumstances'. In making this comment, 618's diarist sounded as if he was unable to commit to paper all that he knew.

Having failed to sink the *Tirpitz* with conventional bombs, it was not surprising that the Fleet Air Arm should now show an interest in Highball as well, for in the Grumman Avenger they had an aircraft which could be adapted to carry it. Supplied to the FAA under lease-lend, the Avenger, known to the British as the Tarpon until 1944, was a large radial-engined torpedo bomber that had first seen action in the Pacific at the Battle of Midway in 1942.

At the beginning of 1943 two Tarpons, FN766 and FN795, had been delivered to the Fleet Air Arm and at some point were earmarked for Highball experimental use. During the following August FN795 was flown into Brooklands to be fitted with a mock-up Highball installation, from which production drawings were to be made. This included the same wind-driven turbine mechanism that was fitted to the Mosquitoes.

Longbottom carried out four checkout flights in FN795 from Brooklands on 19 August. Evidently the system worked, as film now in the archives of both Brooklands and the Imperial War Museum shows an Avenger dropping a Highball on what appears to be a coastal test range similar to Reculver, on an unknown date.

One of the two modified Avengers drops a test Highball. (Imperial War Museum)

This may have been FN795, as not only was it the first aircraft to be modified, but it subsequently went to the RN air station at Arbroath at the beginning of January 1944. Also, some rough sea trials of Highball were carried out during this month, but apparently not by 618's Mosquitoes. This sequence may therefore have been shot somewhere on the Scottish east coast.

A second Avenger, FN766, was also modified at Brough for this role, being flown from there to Brooklands the following December, but the Avenger's trials with Highball were delayed until 1944. These two aircraft seem later to have been stored at Wisley – along with a lot of 'white elephant' Warwicks – and went back to the Fleet Air Arm in September 1945. Two other Avengers, FN844 and FW544, were tested by AAEE in 1943-1944, but this was for conventional loads, not Highball.

Like so many initiatives associated with Highball, this one went no further, though why is not known. It was true that the modified Avenger could not have reached Norway from any British land base and at this time most of the Navy's carriers were fully employed elsewhere. Still, they had been made available on other occasions for conventional FAA strikes against Norwegian targets and would undoubtedly have been used for this purpose again if their Lordships had deemed such an attack viable. The most likely explanation is that the FAA had taken note of 618's struggles and had decided to rely on more conventional weapons.

On 5 September some steel all-welded Highballs were tried against the *Courbet*, but these deviated in direction, missing the recovery nets around the ship. All that was achieved was consistency of range. The trial had been particularly important as mass production of this type of Highball was about to begin and a critical report accused the Admiralty of 'lack of imagination' in failing to extend the nets to catch all the bombs. It also seemed that whoever had sanctioned the production of these weapons was unaware of 618's impending fate. At this time Slessor's anti-submarine idea was dropped, security again being the reason, as the bomb's surface bouncing would be observed if U-boat crews elected to fight back instead of crash-diving.

On 8 September another potential target melted away when Italy surrendered to the Allies and units of the Italian Fleet sailed to Malta on the 11th. En route the battleship *Roma* was the victim of German retaliation when she was sunk by an air-launched and radio-controlled FX1400 bomb – a weapon that Wallis would certainly have taken an interest in if he had known of its details at the time. There now seemed no alternative to cadre status and on 13 September the axe finally fell, with orders from Coastal Command to disband the squadron.

The sense of frustration was added to when *Source* took place during this month. At least two of the 12th Submarine Flotilla's X-craft penetrated Kaafjord and successfully laid explosive charges beneath the hull of the *Tirpitz*. Although they were spotted and sunk, with some members of their crews taken prisoner, the resulting series of explosions caused severe internal damage to the battleship, throwing two gun turrets out of line and smashing most of the diesel generators which supplied power to the armament when the ship's boilers were shut down. The *Tirpitz* was out of action for six months. Although they had not sunk her, the courage of the submariners earned the respect of their captors as well as two Victoria Crosses, whose recipients happily survived to wear them. Throughout all this the Turnberry trials detachment continued to fly, with yet another target, this time on land, now being considered.

As early as the previous April, Highball had been tried against what was described as an armoured wall at Ashley Walk bombing range in the New Forest. A witness, Henry Wills, later described how a Mosquito dropped 'dozens' of these weapons, two on each trip to the range, although film shows that they were released one at a time, using a small prefabricated hut as the target. 618's first double releases would not be recorded until 1944.

The sequence from which the next two shots are taken shows a Mosquito coming in from the left of the camera to drop one smooth-cased inert bomb, which hits with what looks like a massive explosion, but is actually a cloud of earth flying up. The

A Mosquito bounces its Highball towards the Ashley Walk hut. It is interesting to note that this BIV had been fitted with four-blade propellers; a modification that would not become standard for 618 until shortly before going to the Far East. (Imperial War Museum)

Moments later, the bomb strikes the hut's roof. A second Highball lies on the ground nearby. (Imperial War Museum)

Highball then bounces forward, accompanied by two smaller fountains of earth, hits the hut, knocking a piece off one roof corner, jumps backwards several yards onto the ground, then sits there for a few seconds as if thinking about what it has just hit. The camera shows clearly that the bomb is being spun forwards. It then moves forward towards the hut again, but fails to demolish it.

The use of Highball at Ashley Walk was to set a precedent for what was surely one of the strangest bomb trials ever to be carried out. At the beginning of October, Longbottom flew a Mosquito to RAF Angle in Pembrokeshire, on the south-western tip of Wales. Following its return from temporary loan to the Admiralty a month before, this rather remote airfield had become home to the Coastal Command Development Unit, which tested a variety of aircraft-mounted equipment. The CCDU appears not to have kept any record of this Highball trial, although that may have been due to its being directed against a land target rather than the RN submarines that they often co-operated with. It is likely that Angle was used to provide a convenient forward base for what was to follow.

The object of this exercise was to test the bomb's feasibility against some major communications targets – the railway tunnels in the German-held northern part of Italy. For this it had been decided that the bomb would be spun forwards at 900rpm and the Great Western Railway provided a suitable substitute target in the shape of the Maenclochog tunnel, near Haverfordwest. This tunnel was single-track, with a minimum height of just over 14ft and about 100yds long. Longbottom was to carry out the tests on 6 October. Just to make his task a little more interesting, there was undulating ground and a curve on the tunnel approach. Any delay in releasing the bomb could lead to the Mosquito hitting the ground above the tunnel mouth. Perhaps Longbottom consoled himself with the thought that at least there was no flak! Nevertheless, the results he obtained were spectacular.

His audience included one very surprised spectator, for whom the sight of a large ball being lobbed into the tunnel was the culmination of a string of mysterious events that had begun the previous evening. Mr Dewi Davies, a twenty-two-year-old GPO linesman, had been aware since the day before that something out of the ordinary was going on.

> The previous day I had been called back to the office in Haverfordwest and told I would have to provide a telephone on a train that would be arriving in Clyderwen at about 6 a.m. the next morning. There were no other details, except that I should be there early and carry out what work was instructed by the staff on the train. I was also told that I could take my Post Office van to my home in Efailwen so that I could be there early. This in itself was very unusual.

The plot thickened the next morning.

> I arrived at Clyderwen station to find the staff knew nothing except that the mail train had been delayed for a special train. When it arrived, the train, consisting of several coaches, one of which was an old Royal coach, was shunted into a siding.

The old Royal Train, once used by King George V, had been replaced by an armoured one in 1941. Evidently one of its redundant coaches had now been put to a rather different use.

Mr Davies recalled, 'The first person I met was the GWR head guard. I remember he was dressed in a tail-coat uniform.' At a time when clothes rationing had given most civilians an air of discreet shabbiness, perhaps this resplendent outfit had come with the coach. The guard's regalia was just one example among several, for the train contained a party led by a rear-admiral, consisting of several high-ranking Army and RAF officers, plus, strangely, one civilian, who was Barnes Wallis. Also, the accompanying Army guards were all commissioned. Perhaps someone on high had decided that if any Other Ranks were left to tediously patrol the train's corridors, they were likely to eavesdrop and gossip afterwards.

Although wondering what he had got himself into, for the moment Mr Davies curbed his curiosity and got on with his job.

> I connected the telephone, which was linked to the Narberth exchange. At the exchange our travelling supervisor had been there all night to deal himself with calls on this special line.

Curious indeed. About three hours after he had boarded the special train, Mr Davies was told to rejig the phone lines that travelled parallel with the railway line between the villages of Narberth and Maenclochog. He then travelled in his van to await the train at a point indicated to him on a map. This turned out to be about a mile south of Maenclochog.

The train halted south of the tunnel and the van was then used to transport cameras and other equipment, so that a film crew could record the coming event from a field on the other side of the valley. The Army had mounted a substantial guard around the site. Presumably not all of these men were officers, but they would have been reminded that any careless talk would have been severely punished. In any case, who would have believed a wild tale of giant black and white wooden balls being bounced through a tunnel?

Mr Davies made his way back to the train and after he had reconnected the phone line a call was put through to Angle. The reason for all this finally became clear when Longbottom's Mosquito made a dramatic entrance from stage left, releasing its forward-spinning cargo some one hundred yards from its target.

> It travelled very fast due to the spin, right into the mouth of the tunnel. Barnes Wallis jumped with joy. They dropped several of these wooden circular bombs – two or three entered the tunnel and one bounced onto a field above the entrance. I well remember Barnes Wallis looked a typical country gent, dressed in a tweed suit. He had the bottom part of his trousers tucked into his socks and wore very heavy shoes. He was exactly as Michael Redgrave depicted him in the film *The Dam Busters*.

A good description, but also an example of how the memory of a witness can be influenced by subsequent events.

> After the test, the Army officers collected every scrap of wood from the bombs and burnt every scrap of evidence. I was invited back to Clyderwen and had tea in the large old Royal coach with its round wooden tables and large comfortable seats. Afterwards, the rear-admiral gave me a £1 note, which was half a week's wages, and told me to 'forget all that you have seen'.

Mr Davies did not reveal the story until nearly fifty years later. His temporary phone system still had one final task to perform, for the GWR guard used it to call his head office at Paddington, saying, 'Delay the mail. We are now leaving.' This call further indicated the special train's importance and would have explained one of the delays that were the lot of the wartime railway traveller.

On the following day, Hutchinson went to Angle, presumably to confer with Longbottom, then on to Weybridge to see Wallis, with fingers crossed that 618 would stop rehearsing and finally go on stage. Once again he was to be disappointed, despite the spectacular footage shot of Longbottom's attacks, much of it in slow motion. A copy of this film is held today by Brooklands Museum, plus two release sequences by the Imperial War Museum. Although not as startling as the notorious occasion at Reculver when an early Highball veered off track and narrowly missed the cameraman, these shots still make extraordinary viewing.

Reports of the tunnel trials varied. 618's ORB said that out of twelve bombs dropped, four bounced through the tunnel, but another file now held at the National Archives states that only two got through, which would match the recollections of Mr Davies, with a further seven hitting the tunnel face.

It was estimated that if Highball had been used against the wider mouths of the Italian double-track tunnels, nine bombs out of twelve would have entered them. The debris disposed of at Maenclochog had shown that a wooden casing could withstand an impact speed of 200mph against the tunnel face, but would be damaged at higher speeds. An all-steel bomb would be better, being capable of taking an impact speed of 300mph. At 200mph a Highball would travel at least 200 yards into a tunnel, regardless of whether it was single or double-track. A self-destruct fuse with a one-minute delay would be satisfactory.

A subsequent plan to try out two bombs against a reinforced tunnel in North Wales was dropped in favour of the detonation of 500lb of Torpex in another GWR tunnel, this time a trackless, blocked and disused one in Derbyshire. In this instance the explosive had been packed into a pair of 250lb depth charges, to reproduce the effect of 500lb dropped in action. On this occasion Longbottom's services were not required, as the charges were placed in position by hand. After three explosions on 14 October and another the next day, Mr A. S. Quartermaine, the GWR's Chief Engineer, reported that if eight bombs entered a tunnel and four of them exploded inside it there was every reason to believe that rail traffic through it would be stopped for at least a month.

However, statistics may be used to prove whatever result is required. Someone else calculated that a tunnel attack would need sixteen aircraft per target to reach an expected 40 per cent of hits. Despite the promise shown in the tunnel experiments, the Admiralty remained concerned about Highball security and it was decided not to use it for this purpose, since the extent of any damage would be uncertain and the weapon would be compromised before it could be used against shipping, which their Lordships still saw as its primary role. The Italian tunnels would have been more difficult to reach than the Welsh one, and an attack on one would inevitably have led to a stiffening of defences at the others.

Although no one seems to have mentioned it, there was another limitation, in that the bomb would only have worked satisfactorily inside a tunnel of at least 300 yards in length. Any attack on a shorter one, especially if conducted at 300mph, could have resulted in the bomb bouncing all the way through and exploding harmlessly in the open air beyond the target. Track damage could have been quickly repaired, as past experience with conventional bombs had shown.

At this point in the story it is necessary to move forward a year, to a one-off operation by 8 Group, who used some of their Mosquito crews against this type of target. Seventeen aircraft were detailed to attack fourteen railway tunnels in the hilly and wooded Eifel region between France and Germany.

This time there were no security hang-ups, for the weapon used was the well-known 4,000lb 'cookie'. Fitted with a short delay fuse, this was a thin-cased high-capacity blast bomb, in service since 1941 and originally designed for area target use. Although it had represented a major advance over the earlier GP bombs, it was notorious for being unable to be dropped 'safe', and any crew crash-landing with one aboard would be very fortunate if it did not explode. Shaped like a giant steel dustbin, it was a very basic creation, unaerodynamic and the exact opposite of Highball. It was intended that the aircraft's forward momentum would lob the bomb, like a large stumpy torpedo, into the tunnel mouth.

At dawn on New Year's Day 1945, six aircraft from 128 Sqdn, five from 571 and six from 692 took off to attack targets in the Koblenz, Trier and Cologne areas. One of 128's Mosquitoes crashed on take-off, killing its crew, and 692 lost one to light flak in the Schulda area, but all the rest returned, reporting apparently successful actions. Flt Lt C. H. Burbidge of 692 described his own attack as follows:

Loading a 4,000-pound HC 'cookie' bomb into a Mosquito, probably of 692 Squadron, at RAF Graveley. (Imperial War Museum, neg. no. CH12621)

> The first aircraft clearly identified the target … A good run was made at 200 feet and the 4,000lb bomb was released approximately 400 yards from the tunnel mouth. Bomb was not actually seen to enter the tunnel, but on second run to observe results, much smoke was billowing out and the outline of the tunnel appeared very ragged.

One of 571's crews, for reasons known only to themselves, attacked their tunnel at right-angles, while another said of theirs, 'Tunnel erupted followed by partial collapse of cliff.'

The laconic report of Flt Lt T. H. Galloway DFC and Sgt J. S. Morell of 692 was indicative of what the Highball crews would have had to face:

> Aircraft found that the hill immediately behind the target made it difficult to get down low enough for release, as this hill had to be cleared on run out of target. Approach, too, owing to high ground, could only be made in a steep dive. Two attempts were made before the 4,000-pounder was released on a third run. It overshot to south of tunnel, in line with it, and smoke was afterwards seen in built-up area in Kochum, 400 yards south of tunnel mouth. Defences – nil.

All the tunnels except one were undefended, but the natural obstacles were not to be underestimated. Flak might be fatal, but the ground would kill every time.

Although this raid showed that tunnel attacks could be carried out – and by Pathfinder crews, who normally fought at much higher altitudes – it was inconclusive, despite the destruction of a tunnel near the town of Bitburg, and it may be asked how much effect it had on the German supply situation, which had become increasingly chaotic as the European war entered its final months. The fact that these tunnel attacks were not repeated indicates that they may not have been as decisive as had been hoped. In view of 5 Group's success at low-level marking during 1944, perhaps 8 Group's AOC, Air Vice-Marshal Donald Bennett, had decided that it was time to reclaim some of the limelight for his own command. Had 618 still been in Europe they too might have taken part in this attack. However, by then they were on the other side of the world and in the wrong place at the wrong time, as will be seen.

With hindsight, the Admiralty's rejection of tunnel bombing in 1943 was probably correct, even if it was taken for the wrong reasons. Some proof of this would become apparent in 1944, when the effects of Operation *Strangle* were assessed. This campaign of interdiction by Allied fighter-bombers against German communication routes in Italy made movement of supplies more difficult by day, but the Germans had already stockpiled much ammunition in dumps close to the front line and consequently it was available regardless of what was happening in the skies further north. The series of costly battles around the town of Cassino and its overlooking monastery not only showed that airpower had its limitations, but also that the Germans could still put up stubborn resistance, whatever their supply situation. *Strangle* therefore did not fulfil all the hopes which had been placed on it and it is doubtful whether the use of Highball would have made much difference.

Shipping remained at the top of the Admiralty's target list and as far as they were concerned there was only one ship that really mattered. Though damaged by *Source*, the *Tirpitz* remained afloat. The Allies knew she was not seaworthy, but while she continued to exist she was still a threat. After all this effort, Hutchinson, Longbottom and indeed Wallis must have wondered what else they could do to sell Highball to their elders and betters.

Someone who could view the immediate future with less frustration was Sqdn Ldr Rose, who had accompanied three crews and thirty ground staff on detachment to 248 Sqdn at RAF Predannack in Cornwall. This unit's C Flight was equipped with the Mosquito Mark XVIII, known as the 'Tsetse', which mounted a formidable semi-automatic six-pounder gun. Though at first alarming to fire, it was accurate and its recoil was excellently absorbed by the aircraft's wooden structure.

The Mark XVIIIs began patrols in October 1943, and while intended for shipping and anti-U-boat strikes, the gun had other applications, as Sqdn Ldr A. Phillips would demonstrate the following March when he intercepted one of ten Junkers 88s escorting a convoy off the Spanish coast. After four shells had been fired, one of them blew one of the German's engines clean out of the wing! For the 618 members this was action indeed and all the more welcome after the prolonged routine of trials flying.

On 4 November Rose, with Flt Sgt S. Cowley as his observer, spotted an armed trawler in the Bay of Biscay. It was not fishing and was probably acting as a lookout for the U-boat crews that frequented this area, so he attacked. However, Rose only fired two six-pounder rounds before being hit, either by a ricochet or return fire. The Mosquito was seen to ditch at high speed and then break up. Neither man survived.

Those who survived this return to the sharp end reaped the rewards – one DSO and three DFCs were awarded to 618's crews while on detachment – but for those who remained behind life could be just as dangerous. On 18 November two trials aircraft were hit by a flock of birds. Flt Sgt J. Massey and Flg-Off F. J. French, in DZ586/G, suffered considerable damage to their aircraft, but landed safely. DZ520/G, flown by Flg-Off K. H. N. Ellis and Flt Sgt R. W. Donald, was hit in the port wing. This aircraft also landed in one piece, but the crew turned out to be as lucky as their friends, for the full extent of the damage was not realised until the wing was later checked.

Highball trials continued, both at Reculver and against a concrete target on a bombing range at Porton, where it was bounced on a hard surface. Imperial War Museum film of this shows the bomb bouncing awkwardly, like a giant cheese with one edge flattened after impact. This was another short-lived initiative that came to nothing.

On 26 November the *Courbet* was attacked again, this time from different angles. Frustratingly, still more casing problems came to light. If the casing became deformed on impact, either by hitting the water or the ship's side, its underwater travel would be affected and it would be likely to sink vertically, exploding below the ship instead of adhering to the hull. As with Upkeep, the bomb's power would be reduced unless it was in contact with the hull when it exploded, so shock-absorbent padding needed to be fitted between the explosive canister and its outer cover.

A Mosquito drops a single Highball on the same unidentified coastal range as the previous
Avenger shot. (Imperial War Museum)

A Mosquito of 618 Squadron drops a Highball at Reculver on 21 January 1944. (Author's
collection)

Although the Wallis sight had previously been declared satisfactory, evidently its creator had had second thoughts, for at another conference at Burhill in December it was decided to fit a flying helmet with a ring aperture that would coincide with the wearer's eye. This new arrangement would dispense with the need for the observer to sight from the Mosquito's nose. An intriguing note in 618's ORB at this time says that Hutchinson would be using this on a target at Weybridge. No further details were given, but it is possible that George Roake at Foxwarren had the answer. When interviewed, he described a target in the Experimental Department as being a bridge-like affair, some ten feet across and as high as the workshop ceiling. It was this that the errant Silvermere bomb had been aimed at, the sandbags behind the target being intended as a backstop.

If Hutchinson made any resolutions at the beginning of 1944, one of them would have been that his squadron would come back together and justify its existence before this year was out. For the time being he had the task of sorting out supply problems regarding the necessary special equipment – a dull but unavoidable chore. This meant yet another flight to Brooklands. Afterwards, Hutchinson and his observer, Flg-Off E. J. French, were taking off from the grass airfield in DZ533/G, a trials Mosquito, on loan to Vickers, when the undercarriage collapsed. This time there was no fire or injuries, but as Hutchinson stepped out of the resulting mess he must by now have been convinced that something at Brooklands was out to get him. French, having already survived the birdstrike incident, had used up another of his nine lives.

618 Sqdn remained in cadre form, consisting now of four crews and a few ground staff. Experiments continued in a quest for that elusive perfection and despite Hutchinson's efforts supplies proved a headache as production of Highball had been taken off the priority list. This meant that its makers could only supply these bombs during their slack periods, which were few due to the invasion build-up.

It was at around this time that there was another change. The *Courbet*, having gallantly withstood everything the trials crews could throw at her, moved off down the west coast to perform her final service. Her fate was to be one of nine blockships sunk to form a Gooseberry breakwater off the Normandy town of Ouistreham, protecting Sword beach. Her replacement for the trials would be the veteran battleship HMS *Malaya*. As the *Courbet* settled slowly in fifteen feet of water on 9 June 1944, three days after D-Day, perhaps the few who were aware of her recent history reflected that in view of all the uncertainty associated with Highball, the old ship was now performing a better service than she had done for some time.

The Queen Elizabeth-class battleship HMS *Malaya*, before being relegated to the role of a Highball target ship. (Imperial War Museum, neg. no. A7734)

One of five ships of the Queen Elizabeth class, HMS *Malaya* had been completed just in time to see action at the Battle of Jutland in 1916. After early wartime service escorting convoys, during which she survived a torpedo attack by U-106, by the time the battleship arrived in Loch Striven she had been fitted with hydrophones to check the functioning of the bomb pistols. This was particularly important now, as double releases were tried for the first time during May.

Between 15 and 17 May, Longbottom, or 618's B Flight commander, Sqdn Ldr Melville-Jackson, acted as the trials pilots, with Hutchinson gaining further experience by doing the sighting in all instances. This culminated in six double releases by Longbottom on 17 May.

The sight that followed was unforgettable for those who were allowed to witness it. No one aboard the battleship, whether they were old salts or just in for the duration, had ever seen anything like it before. Dropping within a second of each other, two Highballs leapt from the Mosquito's bomb bay, to leave a series of splashes behind them as they rapidly leapfrogged over each other while bouncing across the loch's surface.

The double releases were filmed from several angles, including on board the ship. One amusing shot showed men at the ship's side quickly and instinctively scattering as a bomb hit the hull just below them. This was just an inert weapon. What would the real thing be like, and against what target? As usual, they were being given the mushroom treatment, but it had to be the *Tirpitz*. The rumours would have circulated from wardroom to mess deck, no doubt with the resident sea-lawyer moaning that he had not joined up to be used for target practice.

The crew's apprehension was justified, for it was during these three days that they received rather more than they might have expected. Not all the bombs were content

HMS *Malaya*'s hull after a Highball hit. The bomb can be seen inside, to the left of the hole. (A. Lane)

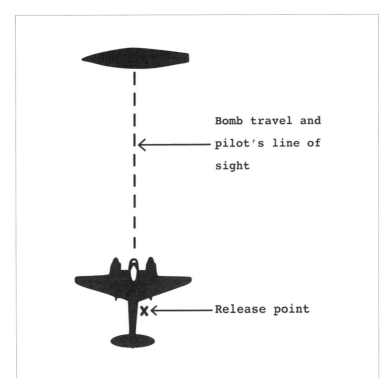

Firstly, if there was no crosswind, then the fore and aft line of the aircraft would coincide with the pilot's or observer's line of sight and a straightforward attack could be made, with a good chance of a hit. (S. Flower)

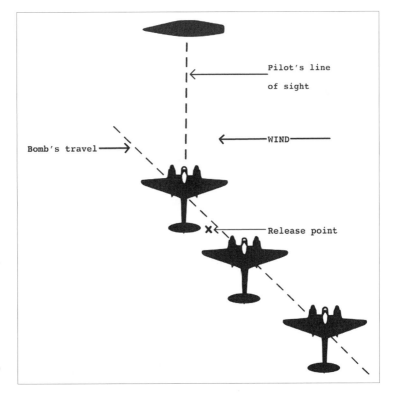

Secondly, if there was a crosswind and no allowance was made for it, a sighting would be taken on the target but the aircraft would be blown sideways by the wind. When released, the bomb would continue in the direction of the aircraft's sideways travel and therefore miss. (S. Flower)

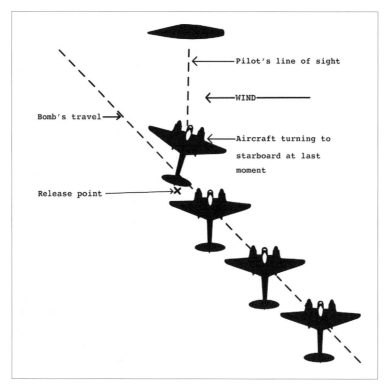

Pilot's line of sight

WIND

Bomb's travel →

Aircraft turning to starboard at last moment

Release point →✕

Thirdly, when the rangefinder was introduced it had been mounted on the fore and aft line of the aircraft. If approaching in a crosswind, the pilot therefore had to point the aircraft at the target until he reached the release point. He then had to yaw the nose into wind before releasing. This could cause the aircraft to skid, so leading the bomb to miss as it still travelled in the direction of the wind. (S. Flower)

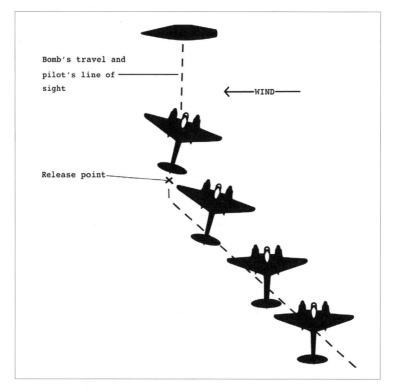

Bomb's travel and pilot's line of sight

WIND

Release point ✕

Finally, if the observer used the helmet sight, the pilot could turn more slowly to counteract the drift and the bomb would hit. (S. Flower)

to hit and then bounce off. With some satisfaction, 618's diarist wrote, 'The trials of the last three days, with double releases, were fairly successful from the technical aspect, and certainly very impressive. The target ship was holed by a release from Sqdn Ldr Longbottom, much to the consternation of senior naval officers witnessing the trials.'

Just in case their Lordships, or anyone else, should declare such a thing impossible, the hole was included in the film as well, with a rather worried-looking sailor putting his head through it. Despite this impact, *Malaya*'s hydrophone operators stayed at their posts throughout the attacks, their diligence being rewarded as most of the bombs hit, with their pistols heard to detonate before they sank.

On 20 May these results were discussed with Wallis at Burhill, where it was decided that the helmet sight would be used by the observer as a rangefinder. The pilot's role would be to judge the drift and drop the bombs on the observer's signal. The sight was to be used by the observer without reference to the fore and aft line of the aircraft, as experience had shown that there were four situations that could occur. These are illustrated by the drawings, which are not to scale.

It will now be appreciated not only how complex the trials had become, but also why the methods of aiming and release had taken so long to perfect. This was a particularly precise form of flying and carrying it out at low level while running up Altenfjord would have been very difficult, especially as the *Tirpitz*'s anchorage in Kaafjord would have necessitated a sharp 180-degree turn at the last moment while trying to sight on the battleship through the smokescreen that would have been generated. It would have been necessary to run the gauntlet of intense flak, much of it from the ship itself, and the strain on each Mosquito's two-man crew would have been considerable.

It was at this conference that Hutchinson proposed two further aircraft modifications. The first was that the original V-shaped bomber windscreens should be replaced by armoured fighter ones, so giving better protection and also avoiding distortion through the perspex while using the helmet sight. The second was that Merlin 25 engines should be fitted to boost low-level performance. Films of the trials were then shown to a highly impressed audience.

The idea of using Highball against land targets had still not been entirely discarded, for tests at Wisley airfield, a few miles south-east of Brooklands, were recommended. Built during the mid-war years as a dispersed site for Wellingtons and Warwicks produced at Brooklands, Wisley was larger than the factory airfield, it was conveniently close to Foxwarren and it also offered the opportunity to carry out further Highball checks without attracting too much attention from the rest of the Vickers work force. However, there was an unexpected drawback, as Sir George Edwards later recalled:

There was the famous story of Shorty Longbottom, who was killed in a Warwick – one of the test pilots. We had a bit of trouble loading the Highball into the Mosquitoes. With a bit of G on the jaws used to come open and the thing used to come out. At the end of the runway at Wisley there was a cottage and Shorty was coming in to land one day and when he pulled out – to flare out to land – the damn thing came unhooked and though it was inert there was a lot of it and it landed on this cottage and did it a power of no good. He went round and apologized to the people concerned and the cottage was rebuilt. And, blow me down, they'd only just got it rebuilt when he came round there again on the same mission and the thing came out again and hit the cottage again and knocked it down again! I think it's a wonderful example of British phlegm that this poor woman, who'd had her house knocked over twice – when Shorty went round the second time to go and see how they were doing and to apologize, when he came round the corner, all she could say was, 'Oh no, not you again!'

A double release. (Imperial War Museum)

The bombs leapfrog over one another, one losing part of its casing as it does so. (Imperial War Museum)

Reg Firman also recalled this incident, but said it occurred during 'bouncing bomb practice' at Wisley, which would indicate a botched intentional release rather than an accidental one.

> When you spin an object like that, it doesn't want to go out of that line – it wants to keep in that direct line. They used to fly at an object, then turn the machine away. It was held by two arms. If your machine went this way and your bomb went that way this arm got a colossal load on it and the load came off that one. The load got free – it pushed and strained till that axle came out and there was the bomb hanging on one axle, and of course that broke the slip. It got away and knocked the same place down because the bomb didn't turn with the aircraft. What they ought to have done was to drop the bomb and then wait until after the bomb had gone before they turned the aircraft away, but they turned the aircraft away while the bomb was pressing outwards.

Despite Firman's mention of an axle, such a device was never used to spin either Highball or Upkeep. It seems likely that he was referring to the circular metal plates on the end of the V-shaped arms. Anyway, this problem was solved by one of the staff at Burhill.

> In Wallis' office there was a young man called Nash – he brought to me a strain gauge with photographic apparatus on it – a tiny thing.

It was some two inches long. Firman had realised what the problem was, but with Wallis proof was necessary. So he asked Nash to fit the gauge to the aircraft and if possible to get himself inside it to photograph the results. For Nash this would have meant lying inside the modified bomb bay and taking his life in his hands, for, despite a cargo hatch on the aircraft's starboard side, there would have been little chance of survival in the event of a crash.

> The next time it flew he brought me a photograph of that strain gauge doing exactly what I'd said. He also brought parts of the aircraft that were connected to the member on which we put that strain gauge. I said, 'Now we've got proof of what's happening.' I gave it to the designers, who hadn't thought of anything like that before. Through this man Nash and through that strain gauge we were able to put the matter right.

Even Wallis would have been hard put to argue with that one. It was indicative of how much he owed to those who worked under him at Burhill.

As if past tribulations had not been enough, during August a further problem surfaced concerning the double-release technique. Analysis showed that the detonation of one bomb would almost inevitably countermine the other – meaning that the second one would prematurely detonate. If both were dropped simultaneously, each would interfere with the run of the other and it was possible that neither would reach the ship.

However, the trials also showed that a bomb distributor giving a gap of 0.3sec. was a satisfactory interval as far as surface running was concerned. Both bombs could be set for their optimum depths and even if one did countermine the other, it would still go off only slightly above the depth at which it was intended to explode. It was calculated that the two bombs going off together would achieve far greater damage than one at the optimum depth. This had been established by static tests involving two bombs placed eight feet apart.

The pistol tests against *Malaya* had also been conducted at varying distances to give a representative scale of impact. Thirty-two bombs had been dropped from 600 yards, with three bounces, to 1,700 yards, with seventeen. Some had also been dropped at a sixty-degree angle to the target, but the pistols had functioned satisfactorily in all cases. During this the sight had been modified to counter drift of the aircraft, but after a further six Highballs had been dropped it was found that all the hits from these were within fifty feet of each other, curing a previous tendency for bombs to deviate from the target's centre.

By now Highball had been established as a weapon of 1,280lb, carrying 600lb of Torpex, armed by a modified Mark XIV depth charge pistol and capable of bouncing to about 1,500 yards. Not the least of the problems surrounding it had been the hot and cold attitudes shown by authority, but Wallis and those around him had carried on anyway. Upkeep too had been a struggle, but one rewarded by some success. There was also the possibility that abandoning Highball would affect the chances of the earthquake bombs being accepted. A clue to the motivation of the Experimental Department was to be found in the family motto of its manager, which was 'Never Give Up'. Certainly George Edwards was not the man to do so. His feelings about Highball were mixed, but there were some quite affectionate memories.

It was a pretty lethal weapon, because it skittled along the top, and we fixed up some sighting things on each of the Japanese silhouettes – the silhouettes of the Japanese warships, so that you got yourself at precisely the right distance and pressed the tit and off she went, skittling along the top of the water and crashing through the side of the old ship. This old French dreadnought up in Loch Striven – that had a hell of a time. And I used to go tearing up and down the sides of these mountains with the lads … What I did during the war, that was good fun, actually, that was entertaining.

Now that the bomb was at last seen as a reliable weapon, during the last week in June 1944 618's fortunes took a turn for the better when the Chiefs of Staff, through Coastal Command, directed them to reform, as a matter of some urgency, with an attached PR Mosquito unit. Now they were to re-equip with a view to carrier-borne operations in the Pacific.

This change to yet another set of targets had been prompted by the official view that the *Tirpitz* had recently been damaged by another FAA raid and that by being tucked away in Kaafjord she was in a position which made a Highball attack difficult if not impossible. Since the Luftwaffe had learned Upkeep's secrets a year before, it is possible that they had anticipated such an attack – certainly, netting in the fjord ruled out torpedoes and the high ground around her left little space for pulling out after a fast low-level run. There were no other worthwhile naval targets left in Europe, so if Highball was to see action it would have to be against the Japanese.

The idea of carrier-borne operations had been suggested at the time of 618's formation and on 25 March 1944 a lightly loaded Mosquito FBVI had been successfully landed on HMS *Indefatigable*. Now 618's cover story was to be that they were a special minelaying unit – which was not too far from the truth – and their preparations were given the code-name *Oxtail*.

The first task was to prepare the Mosquitoes for their new role. 618's aircraft, which were at RAF Wick or in store at 27 MU at Shawbury, were to be flown to either Airspeed at Portsmouth via RAF Thorney Island, or to Marshalls of Cambridge. Airspeed, who had to their credit the Oxford advanced trainer, had been founded by Nevil Shute Norway in Yorkshire before moving south prewar. Marshalls had been set up in 1909 as part of the infant British motor industry, but had from 1937 trained RAF aircrew at Cambridge before joining Lord Nuffield's Civilian Repair Organisation two years later to repair and modify aircraft.

Once secret equipment had been removed, deliveries were to be made by the squadron pilots, the first three going to Cambridge. These two contractors would, in conjunction with Vickers, install Hutchinson's modifications, together with four-bladed de Havilland propellers, arrester hooks and a new type of bomb-spinning turbine. Trevor Westbrook of MAP – who had once worked at Weybridge and crossed swords with Wallis over the Wellington – would liaise between the Air Ministry and de Havillands.

Of the thirty aircraft available, twenty-nine would be modified, the thirtieth being kept as a spare. To provide photographic cover, three PR XVIs would be provided by de Havillands. These would be modified in a similar way. One hundred and fifty Highballs would also be required. During July the unit began to reassemble at RAF Wick.

It was anticipated that this programme would take five months to carry out, which may seem a long time, but it should be remembered that both skilled labour and aircraft factory space were then at a premium.

Another task to be carried out was the training of 618's crews in deck landings. Just in case Fleet Air Arm aircrew should speculate on the real reason for all of this, a second cover story given out was that 'a number of Coastal Command pilots were being trained in carrier landings as an additional safeguard in the event of forced descent when operating over sea.'

During August the squadron moved to RAF Beccles in Suffolk. Built in 1943, this airfield had been intended for the USAAF, but had not been used as such and after coming under Bomber Command had gone to Coastal Command's 16 Group. It had been chosen as the 'nearest' airfield to what was described in a later report as the only Highball range in the UK. By then it probably was – the writer clearly knew nothing of the earlier trials at Chesil Beach and Reculver. This range had been laid out by MAP at Wells-next-the-Sea on the Norfolk coast. Its use would involve a good deal of flying between the villages of Burnham Overy and Stiffkey. RAF Langham was closer, being six miles away, but this housed ASR Warwicks and was not available. Other Allied aircrew were briefed to either avoid this area altogether, or to fly over it at not less than 5,000 feet. Attached to 618 Sqdn were a Royal Navy chief petty officer, a shipwright and four able seamen, the purpose of the latter being to recover the inert Highballs after dropping.

Training had been scheduled to begin on 21 August, but, regarding the recovery of the inert bombs, the daylight tides were not suitable then and an initial lack of modified BIVs led to ten FBVI armed fighter-bombers being used as a stop-gap. Although these aircraft could not drop Highballs, they proved invaluable for the first stage of training. The special rangefinding sight could be fitted to them by means of a bracket, and a Sashalite circuit was installed, giving a light flash to indicate the immediate release of a bomb. The training was divided into four stages:

1. Sashalite attacks on a dummy target.
2. Dropping of inert Highballs on the Wells range.
3. Tactical training.
4. Dropping of inert Highballs against HMS *Malaya*.

Hutchinson devised dummy targets by putting up two vertical white boards, 20ft high, at one end of the long runway at Beccles. Six hundred feet apart, these represented a capital ship's broadside to an aircraft flying low along the runway's length. The sight would be used by the observer, the pilot releasing the weapon on his instruction. This would be indicated by the flash of the Sashalite bulb.

The release point depended on the airspeed, the water conditions and the length of the target. These were marked beside the runway by walking along it, holding a sight, until the two white boards exactly coincided with the two vertical lines on the sight's rangefinder panels. Marks, which were not too obvious, were made beside the runway, corresponding to the actual settings on the sight.

The crews then carried out their attacks on the dummy target, using rangefinder settings whose appropriate mark by the runway was known only to a recording officer. This individual stood sufficiently far back from the runway to prevent each pilot from taking matters into his own hands and pressing the release before the observer said so. The number of 'light' attacks made during each aircraft's flight depended on the number of bulbs carried. The distance of each release before and after the correct mark was recorded and subsequently analysed.

By 13 September all the crews had achieved a range error of plus or minus fifty yards. To prevent accidents, only two crews flew at once, with instructions to stop diving as soon as they were ordered to by VHF R/T, or if they lost sight of each other, or lost VHF contact with Flying Control.

The Wells range ran east to west, with a target, similar to that on the airfield, at each end of it. These were 1,600yds apart, so the range could be used in either direction according to the sun and wind conditions. An observation tower was sited on top of the sand dunes on the landward side of the range and on its seaward side distinctive posts were erected on lines of sight from the tower, passing through imaginary points at 100-yard intervals down the range's centre-line. As the tower was 50ft above the horizon, the height of each release could be judged fairly accurately.

Dropping could only take place up to two hours before and after high tide. This was not always in daylight, or in good weather. However, using eight aircraft for up to forty drops a time, twenty crews each satisfactorily carried out two single drops and one double in ten days.

It was determined that they had to fly at no higher than 45ft, with a groundspeed of 360mph at the moment of release. If possible, 25ft and 380mph would be even better. Mosquitoes fitted with Merlin 25s had to be trimmed nose heavy, then dived steeply from 3,000ft at full boost of +18, with their propellers in fully-fine pitch.

Another restriction was the slow procedure that had to be adopted for the recovery of the Highballs. A caterpillar tractor was needed, with a towbar that could be inserted through the bomb's hollow centre. The bombs had to be moved onto the beach, as near as possible to a road, then hoisted into three-ton lorries, each of which would carry six of them at no more than 20mph back to Beccles, which was sixty miles away. They then had to be washed, examined and checked for static balance.

Little thought was given to the comfort or convenience of the range personnel. They were poorly protected from wind and cold, the tower lacked a phone line to the airfield, and there was no accommodation provided on the range.

The third stage, that of tactical training, had come about due to a Admiralty and Air Staff decision that three aircraft, each armed with two Highballs, would ensure worthwhile damage to a target without unnecessary risk of 'overhitting' it. Practice was therefore carried out by sub-sections of three Mosquitoes, getting down to dropping height at the correct range and releasing all six Highballs in the shortest possible time. The Sashalite attacks showed that this could be accomplished in ten seconds, leading to a hope that it could be verified by formations of three aircraft carrying out actual drops against *Malaya*. So far, so good, but it will shortly be seen that, once again, things did not go according to plan.

Access to this part of East Anglia was restricted and lists had to be compiled of the favoured few who were allocated special passes. The only other naval staff were Lieutenant Commander 'Tubby' Lane and Lieutenant Eric 'Winkle' Brown, both of whom had by now landed two MAP trials Mosquitoes on carriers. Brown, who later rose to captain, would become well known as a post-war test pilot. Just three civilians were allowed in; Wallis, A. D. Grant and H. Jeffree, both of whom had previously been involved with Upkeep. On 20 September Wallis visited 618, giving an illustrated talk that was of considerable interest. Although there was no impending operation this time, he may have experienced the same 'Father Christmas' feeling he had had when briefing 617 a year before.

During August an attempt was made to acquire *Malaya* for inert Highball practice. This time recovery of the bombs would be out of the question, as the ship would have to be moored in at least thirty-five feet of water. The anchorage would have to be open enough to allow three Mosquitoes to simultaneously carry out high-speed manoeuvres over it, but be so sheltered that the waves were no more than three feet high.

Dornoch Firth was considered suitable, but their Lordships, fearing a U-boat attack, were not prepared to risk a capital ship and could only offer a light cruiser. This was unsuitable due to its light construction and low freeboard, quite apart from the possibilities of damage and crew casualties should a Highball pass through it. The Admiralty's suggestion of sighting on the cruiser while lobbing the bombs at a battle practice target behind it was, not surprisingly, viewed as in no way meeting the RAF's requirements for realistic training. Prolonged official correspondence was not likely to improve matters, so it was suggested that the Vice-Chief of the Air Staff might like to confer with his naval opposite number. This behind-the-scenes effort was assisted by Vice-Admiral Renouf, and it would succeed shortly.

There was also the question of how to get the squadron out to the Far East. A proposal to fly them out to India or Ceylon to embark there was rejected on the grounds that it would be far easier if the aircraft, their crews and other associated stores were kept together. This therefore meant carrier loading trials, for which only the King George V Dock in Glasgow could be used, due to the Mosquito's wingspan. Then there was the need for tropicalisation – particularly important for a wooden aircraft.

As with *Chastise*, requests for training and further modifications piled up. There was a requirement for 618's PR crews to keep their hands in by a training exercise over Scapa Flow, for which the Admiralty gave permission. Once their aircraft were available they were to be fitted with two stereoscopic vertical cameras at RAF Benson. Then there was the question of their paddle-blade propellers, which were seen as giving good performance at high altitude but not when leaving a carrier's deck. However, investigation showed that an aircraft fitted with them would 'unstick' a hundred yards sooner than those fitted with the earlier narrow pointed type. It was decided to use narrow ones, but make them four-bladed.

Could the Mosquitoes be modified to accept 100-gallon drop tanks, just in case they had to operate from a land base instead? No, that was a major task and would take too long. Could another compass be fitted on the dashboard top? No, the space for it was taken up by the windscreen wiper motor. Could a radio altimeter be fitted into the bomb bay? No, they were too bulky for this. Were there enough tropicalisation sets available for the BIVs? Yes, but as they were now out of production they had been in store for a long while and might have suffered. All right, send the gear with the squadron, check it out en route, fit it if necessary and hope that any deficiencies could be made good by local resources at the other end. Camouflage? Adapt them on the spot to whatever local scheme was deemed suitable.

Who would balance the Highballs? During September some of 618's armourers would be so employed at 28 MU at Buxton, using a similar rig to that at Foxwarren. The Naval Intelligence Division would supply details regarding the differing lengths of the surviving Japanese carriers, battleships and cruisers. Would a large Royal Navy fleet carrier be made available? No, the one that had been considered was unsuitable for tropical use without modifying its ventilation system. So, how would Hutchinson brief the squadron if it was spread over two or three smaller vessels? Use a helicopter – they were beginning to be available now – or some light FAA aircraft. What of the Japanese fighters? Most at sea level were slower than the Mosquito, but a new one was described as capable of over 400mph. Anyway, 150-octane fuel would boost speed at sea level from 340 to 365mph, with no appreciable reduction in the squadron's radius of action.

Conversion of 618's crews to carrier operations was not completed until 29 August, using Fairey Barracudas supplied by HMS *Rajah*. It had been their intention to concurrently practise dummy deck landings at Beccles, but for this a naval batsman had been needed. Only one had been belatedly supplied on 28 August, at which point this type of training had immediately begun. To give them some idea of what to aim at, scale models of Japanese warships were also provided.

Due to a tendency to crash on take-off or to spin inverted into the sea when making torpedo attacks, the Barracuda had never been popular with FAA pilots, so no one was particularly surprised when six of them were damaged in accidents and one was ditched in the sea off Troon by Flt Lt Maclean. Matters were not helped by an initial lack of modified Mosquitoes, but once they were obtained definite progress was made when three pilots successfully landed them on HMS *Implacable* at Scapa Flow.

By 2 September Mosquito DZ537/G had been modified at Marshalls and was ready to fly to Renfrew airfield for the carrier loading trials. Three days later this aircraft was towed on its own undercarriage from Renfrew by an Allan tractor, put onto a barge by shore cranes and taken out into the Clyde, to the Tail of Bank, near Gourock. The carrier's cranes then hoisted it aboard. Success, but in future the others would go direct from the King George V Dock to the carrier.

On 7 September there were further trials against *Malaya*: four Highballs were dropped by Hutchinson, four by Melville-Jackson and four by Flt Lt Hopwood. Interestingly, the ship had been slightly listed so the bombs would strike her armour plating, although it is not known whether this was done to check their behaviour against it or to stop further damage from being inflicted!

During September there was an attempt to carry through the fourth stage of training – that of using Highball in open water. It was still felt that three crews attacking simultaneously was the right number, provided a target's anchorage had been checked out first by a PR aircraft.

To find out, three crews were sent north to RAF Dallachy, Scotland, to attack *Malaya*, which, with the agreement of the Commander-in-Chief of Rosyth naval base, would be anchored fifteen miles off the Scottish east coast, between the towns of Montrose and Dundee, towards the end of this month. This transit flight was not without incident; one of the three Mosquitoes had to force-land at RAF Thornaby, near Middlesbrough, on one engine, having first jettisoned its two bombs into the sea.

The plan was for all twenty-four crews to undergo this, six at a time, each detachment lasting fourteen days. However, bad weather led to hold-ups in this schedule. On 28 September the Dallachy detachment, directed by Vice-Admiral Renouf from *Malaya* by VHF R/T, dropped ten bombs, of which only one hit. This disappointing result was put down to adverse conditions, the waves being some fifteen feet high at the time.

As there was no prospect of improvement it was reluctantly agreed to return *Malaya* to Loch Striven and be content with single drops there. The topography meant that only one Mosquito could safely attack at a time, but twenty-three Highball crews would carry out at least four single drops there. The detachments now went to Turnberry instead, and as if to make up for the lack of success at sea, two more of Longbottom's bombs passed through unarmoured parts of *Malaya*'s hull. One lodged in the wardroom flat and the other in the admiral's pantry. All of this spelled further consternation for their Lordships, so it was as well that the bombs were inert.

During the first two weeks of October, 618's crews were constantly in the air, practising deck landings on a marked strip at Beccles, ferrying aircraft for modification or going in rotation to Turnberry for final attack practices until weapon training was completed on 12 October. Like the *Chastise* Lancasters, the modified Mosquitoes were by now very different from the standard BIV, so much so that they were referred to as the 'Mark IV Special'. Their new engines had been further boosted by the improved diet of 150-octane fuel, its supply augmented by provision for a pair of 50-gallon drop tanks under the wings. The three PR XVIs that were to accompany them had been modified in the same way.

With all this came other limitations. The aircraft were not to be relied on to make more than one deck landing and if they did so during training they would need to be checked by a de Havilland engineer. The maximum permissible diving speed was to be 410mph IAS.

During this month two incidents served as a further reminder of the dangers that 618's crews all faced. On 3 October DZ578/G was written off after it swung on take-off from Beccles, causing the undercarriage to collapse. Much worse came on 11 October when DZ543/G, flown by W/O A. R. W. Milne and Flt Sgt E. A. Stubbs in transit to Turnberry, rose up through cloud, lost control and crashed on the reverse slope of a moorland hill at Bransdale in Yorkshire's North Riding. The crew did not survive and an inert Highball that they had carried was removed in great secrecy by the RAF Service Police. Indeed, the security that surrounded this incident was such that there was no mention of it in the ORB of RAF Wombleton, whose RCAF personnel provided a crash guard after being alerted by the local police.

At last the results were satisfactory all round and the squadron was judged fit for operations. By now it had been decided that 618 was to be transported by two small escort carriers, HMS *Striker* and HMS *Fencer*. The squadron would be split into its A and B Flights, its headquarters and the PRU contingent, whose three Mosquitoes had been completed by RAF Benson and had been delivered by 8 October. The aircraft would fly to Renfrew, be housed safe from curious eyes in two T2 hangars provided by the Airwork General Trading Company, then be towed to the King George V Dock and put onto the carriers by Number 8 Embarkation Unit. Again, the Highballs were to be serviced by 28 MU.

On 10 October Coastal Command headquarters had had the idea of staging a mass mock attack, code-named Fancy Dress, on the Home Fleet at Scapa Flow, including *Malaya*, which would have been the principal target ship. However, it was abandoned on 15 October due to lack of time before embarkation. Installation of the US-made fluxgate compass in the Mosquitoes was proving 'difficult and lengthy', quite apart from the need for carburettor modifications for the 150-octane fuel, all of which meant that not enough aircraft would have been available for a worthwhile exercise.

With some pleasure 618's diarist noted, 'By the end of the month the squadron was completely confident of its ability to fulfil the operational task it had been allotted.' To do this it had twenty-four Highball crews for twenty-five BIVs, as well as five PR crews for the three PR XVIs. Two other BIVs had been retained for trials by MAP. Only the PR crews had deck-landed a Mosquito, but as the remainder had satisfactorily completed their Barracuda training this was not considered a problem. Also available were three months' supplies and sufficient Highballs for, it was considered, two abortive attacks, as well as one successful one.

After *Chastise*, much interest had been shown in both types of bouncing bomb by the Americans and information had been passed to General H. 'Hap' Arnold of the USAAF. In October 1944 Arnold, clearly not one to do things by halves, made the astonishing suggestion that the giant Boeing B-29 Superfortress be adapted for this role. He was tactfully informed by Portal that smaller aircraft would be more suitable, as the Brooklands-modified Avengers had shown.

Two months later arrangements were made for a Douglas A-26 Invader to be shipped to Britain for Highball modifications. A fast twin-engined light bomber in the same class as the Mosquito, the A-26's speed and flight characteristics had been judged suitable. Although further details of its destination are unknown, it is likely that it too went to Brooklands.

Early in 1945 the modified A-26 was tried out by the Army Air Forces Proving Ground Command, with similar results to those obtained by the Mosquito. Sadly, the tests ended in a fatal crash when a bomb ricocheted from the sea and struck the A-26's tail. The following May Lieutenant-General Ira C. Eaker expressed his thanks for the RAF's co-operation, but stated that he did not feel the USAAF had a need for this type of weapon. In view of what happened to 618 during 1945, the loss of the A-26 may have been one factor in determining their fate.

Towards the end of October 618 sailed for Australia. Due to lack of space below, their aircraft remained on deck, covered to conceal their modifications. Mail was censored, the squadron was to have no shore leave en route, and preferably none for the sailors either. In spite of this, Gp Capt. Keary, formerly the CO of Beccles, who now accompanied 618, commented that the crews were enjoying the rest.

They reached Melbourne two days before Christmas 1944. Offloading began just before the New Year, with the aircraft being based at Narromine in New South Wales. While they embarked on another programme of navigation practice and low-level formation flying, there was further debate concerning how and indeed if they should

be used. Two months of discussion with the British Pacific Fleet at the beginning of
1945 resulted only in no decision being made.

The Imperial Japanese Navy had been in decline ever since its heavy carrier losses
at Midway and one argument against the use of 618 was that by now there were few
Japanese surface units left that were worth attacking with Highball. Seven of their
battleships had been sunk and of the four that remained the most important was the
Yamato, a 72,200-ton monster that dwarfed even the *Tirpitz*, with hull armour over
16ins thick. While the planners argued, in April this ship also succumbed to American
air power, although she did not finally capsize until after enduring three hours of
bombing and torpedo attacks, taking far more punishment than that which had been
allowed for in her construction. Again, in this case it is doubtful whether Highball
would have made much impression.

From the Allied point of view suicide attacks were more of a problem now and as
carriers were often singled out 618 might well have found themselves at the receiving
end of a Kamikaze strike before they left the deck. This last-ditch land-based defence
of Japan was one that could only be countered by patrolling carrier fighters or intense
anti-aircraft fire. It was a battle in which Highball had no part to play. Three other
Japanese capital ships also went to the bottom in July, again sunk by conventional
air attacks.

It should also be said that the British Pacific Fleet, like the Fourteenth Army in
Burma, was something of a forgotten force, its exploits often overshadowed by those
of the US Navy, whose Chief of Operations, Admiral Ernest J. King, had said, 'I served
under the British in the last war and I'm damned if I'll serve under them again.'

There was no question of such a situation recurring, as by now Britain was very
much the junior partner and compelled to bow to her ally's wishes. Nevertheless, there
was some suspicion among senior American officers that Britain's prime concern was
to recover her Empire's Far Eastern possessions. Since the USA had once fought to be
free from that Empire, and was looking to extend her own influence around the world,
it had been difficult to get the Americans to accept even a small British force back
into an area from which they had been so ignominiously expelled in 1942. Also, after
the fall of Singapore there was a growing body of opinion in some of Britain's other
dominions that they had been left out on a limb. Consequently Australia had begun
to look to America for help, rather than the 'Mother Country'.

Growing criticism of Britain's past efforts and suspicion of her future intentions in
the Pacific was added to by Admiral King, who declared his intention to conduct a
naval campaign 'without reference to the British.' Control over the British Pacific Fleet
was clearly not enough for King; as far as he was concerned it would have been better
if they were completely out of the picture. Some of his colleagues, with less emotion
and more reason, expressed concern about the Royal Navy's ability to maintain an
adequate fleet supply train. In the event, the 'Forgotten Fleet' provided the Americans
with a useful task force whose carriers, with their armoured decks, proved better
able to stand up to Kamikaze hits than their US Navy counterparts. However, before
British sailors could prove themselves in action in this area their senior officers had to
fight an equally important battle across the conference table.

One consequence of all this was that once again there was no room in the scheme
of things for 618, even when the naval battle finally reached Japanese home waters in
July. It was now that the axe fell for the second and last time, when the Air Ministry
instructed that they were to be disbanded. The squadron was posted to India and on
14 July, as an attempt to boost whatever morale was left, an appreciative telegram
was read out to all ranks, stressing that valuable knowledge had been gained. Highball
would be kept in reserve and once again the need for continuing secrecy was pointed
out. It was maintained until 1962, when details of Highball and Upkeep were
released.

There now remained the question of what to do with the remaining Highballs,
which led to a strange sequence of events. Special equipment for their local destruction

A post-war reunion at the Brooklands racetrack Clubhouse, which by now was occupied by Vickers. The window of the office used by Wallis after the war can be seen in the top left-hand corner. Also visible is Tallboy Small, one of the twelve made to test the earthquake bomb's characteristics. Identifiable in this group are Barnes Wallis (left), Group Captain Wynter-Morgan, former Deputy Director of the Armament Development of MAP (second from left), and Lieutenant-Commander Lane (fourth from left), the retired RNVR officer whose son provided this and other photographs relating to the Wallis bombs. (A. Lane)

had been provided, but for some reason this was disposed of first, by shipping it out from Sydney and dumping it in the Pacific. This 'tragic performance' was witnessed by 618's armament and security officers. It was then decided to destroy the remaining 125 Highballs by static explosion at the Royal Australian Navy Arms Depot at Auburn. 618's diarist said, 'Violent explosions caused a certain amount of discomfort to housewives within a large radius of the point of demolition; otherwise, destruction was completed satisfactorily'. It would be interesting to know what cover story was given out this time.

Even this was not quite the end of the story, for Wallis had continued to work on Highball whenever his other commitments permitted and a Mosquito FBVI, PZ281, was the subject of further experiments during 1945, in which a Mark II version of the weapon was tried in conjunction with other bombs and rockets.

Assuming it could have flown satisfactorily with all this extra weight, this aircraft could indeed have been a potent fighter-bomber, which might have been equalled only by *Card*, a code-name for a crate of two or four bombs, to be fitted beneath a de Havilland Sea Hornet. This twin-engined single-seater, the Mosquito's successor, had come too late for the war, but would prove to be the fastest piston-engined fighter ever to see British service. The crate could have been fitted to a variety of aircraft types, but it went no further and like everything else connected with the Highball project it represented a great deal of effort for no real gain.

Looking back over the long saga of Highball, the overall impression is that the Chiefs of Staff had been presented with a strange, initially unreliable new toy and had been hard put to know what to do with it. The success of *Chastise* had provided impetus for Highball's development, but as things turned out its fortunes rose and fell with those of Upkeep. In time a feeling grew that Upkeep had had its day and that the circumstances that had justified its use would not occur again. The elimination of naval targets, especially the *Tirpitz*, by other means called Highball's future into question and Wallis must have been very persuasive to keep it going at all.

Today, what happened is illustrated by a series of film clips, now held by, among others, Brooklands Museum, showing the Reculver trials, the hole punched by one bomb through HMS *Malaya* and the Welsh tunnel tests. During the early 1990s an inert Highball, recovered from the sea off Portland, went on display at a local museum there. At Loch Striven, no trace remains of HMS *Malaya*, consigned to the scrapyard soon after the war's end, but no doubt some of the inert bombs are still there, waiting to be recovered. A well-known golf course at Turnberry has now been restored on the former airfield, its twelfth hole a monument to the airmen who once trained there. Highball remains a story of what might have been.

5

Enter Tallboy

If there was such a thing as a 'beautiful' bomb, then Tallboy deserves that title!
Tom Bennett, 617 Sqdn navigator, writing in 1994

In the heat of the moment when the Möhne had been breached, Harris had informed Wallis that he could now sell him a pink elephant. Wallis went from being looked on as an eccentric to the hero of the hour and in 617 Sqdn he now had a unit capable of accurately delivering any future special weapons.

Of equal importance was the fact that, thanks to Roy Dobson, Roy Chadwick and their staff at Avro, the experience of modifying the Lancaster for *Chastise* had shown just how adaptable it could be. It had originally been intended to carry a 4,000lb bomb load, but, incredible as it now seems, it had been stressed for catapult launching should airfield runways be cratered by bombing. Since the Battle of Britain, few RAF airfields had been heavily attacked, but the result of this extra engineering was that the Lancaster had proved capable of carrying up to 14,000lbs. Chadwick's masterpiece might not be the size of the late-lamented Victory Bomber, but its ability to carry ever-increasing loads was not in doubt. In the last interview before his death in 1984, Harris described it as 'the camel's back that never broke.' Perhaps in time it might be adapted to carry the ten-ton bomb Wallis had originally proposed.

However, the setbacks that followed after *Chastise* would cause the euphoria to fade and in the months that followed 617's fortunes would sink to a low ebb. They had gone on to mount some dummy attacks against British dams, which had had their defences reinforced in case the Germans retaliated in kind. It was not yet appreciated that the Luftwaffe did not possess the means to do so.

On 11 July 1943 there was what turned out to be a particularly significant conference at the Ministry of Aircraft Production. Taking part were Wallis, Gibson and a 5 Group representative, to discuss further trials of Upkeep and a new special 12,000lb bomb that Wallis had designed – although, as will be seen, a good deal of that work was carried out by those below him, on the Burhill squash court.

The use of Upkeep against land targets had been considered, and trials had shown that it would travel in a straight line for a distance of about 700 yards when dropped from 200ft onto level ground. Further trials were now taking place to see if Upkeep, on striking the base of a solid obstruction, such as a viaduct, would remain in place long enough to destroy it. The 12,000-pounder had been designed with the Rothensee Ship Lift in mind, although that target was not debated on this occasion. An alternative that was discussed was a 12,000lb HC bomb. This thin-cased cylindrical weapon was not a Wallis design and was made of three 4,000lb sections bolted together. It had been tried at the Shoeburyness range, but unfortunately one of the sections had broken away, leaving a crater to be caused by the other two. Still, it might be used against canal banks.

On the assumption that both these weapons would be available in the future, targets such as the railway viaducts at Altenbeken and Bielefeld in north-west Germany were looked at. Destroying them would disrupt most of the rail traffic moving north and east from the Ruhr, leaving only one line, which was seen as inadequate, in the Osnabrück area. Breaching the Dortmund-Ems Canal, south of its junction with the

Mittelland Canal, would stop all inland waterway traffic in the Ruhr. In time, all these targets would be attacked using the Wallis earthquake bombs.

On 5 August 617 Sqdn had carried out a low-level practice, using a forward-spinning trials Upkeep against a simulated viaduct target at Ashley Walk range. While approaching in bad weather at 60ft, Flt Lt W. H. Kellaway's Lancaster was struck by a gust of wind, causing it to fly into the ground, injuring Kellaway and five of his crew. Kellaway, who had somehow survived previous tours on Fairey Battles and Short Stirlings, must have thought this idea a particularly suicidal one. Not surprisingly, 5 Group decided that to use Upkeep against viaducts was not practical, and this idea was not pursued any further.

The squadron subsequently altered some of its surviving Upkeep Lancasters back to their original standard, but kept ten in reserve in case another dams attack should be deemed necessary. New crews had arrived to fill the depleted ranks and Gibson was sent off to do a flag-waving tour of America and Canada, before being shunted into a staff job and told to write his memoirs. During August 617 moved to RAF Coningsby, also in Lincolnshire.

The squadron's re-equipping had in part come about because Group Captain Operations at Bomber Command, Nigel Marwood-Elton, suggested on 18 August that 617 give up most of their Upkeep aircraft and re-equip with standard BIIIs. The normal type of bomb doors, which followed the line of the Lancaster's lower fuselage, would not be able to close around the new weapon, but if fitted with 'blown' ones, these aircraft would be able to carry either of the 12,000-pounders that had been under discussion.

As to their use, Marwood-Elton also put forward the Rothensee Ship Lift as the target for their next major operation. If it was decided that it should be against rail communications in Italy, then one flight of Upkeep aircraft could be retained to attack a dam five miles west of the town of Modane, thereby severing a rail link between Turin and Lyons. Also under consideration at this time was the Bissorte reservoir in northern Italy. With regard to the canal attack proposal, Marwood-Elton commented that such an attack by a small force was unsound: 'I consider that the casualties incurred on operations of this type are not commensurate with the results likely to be achieved.'

His sound advice was ignored. On the night of 15/16 September 617 Sqdn lost five aircraft and thirty-three men in an attempt to breach the Dortmund-Ems Canal. They included Gibson's successor, Sqdn Ldr George Holden, and Flt Lt Les Knight, skipper of one of the crews that attacked the Eder. Mick Martin, a survivor if ever there was one, found himself promoted to squadron leader and suddenly in command.

These losses, coming in the wake of the *Chastise* ones, now made it clear that low-level attacks by heavy bombers were not viable and raised a question as to whether a specialist unit was still needed. Despite the success of *Chastise*, there were those within Bomber Command who considered it to have been a one-off affair that had been excessively rewarded and that 617 should now 'come back to the real war' by becoming a Main Force squadron.

Aware of the drop in the unit's morale, Scampton's station commander, Gp Capt. J. N. H. Whitworth, put forward a list of targets, from dams in Italy to a ball-bearing plant in the Paris area – a small target but a vital one in the wake of the costly USAAF attacks on its sister plants at Schweinfurt in central Germany. The Bissorte proposal led to a dam model being blown up again, but this trial was dismissed as not valid, for the model had been rebuilt on an old base, leaving a weakness between its old and new areas.

While all this was being debated 617 had been retraining as a high-altitude specialist unit. In December 1943 attacks by them on *Noball* sites were considered – this being the codeword for the strange concrete constructions that were now appearing in northern France in connection with the German V-weapons projects. Prominent among them were the 'ski sites', so named because of their distinctive long and curved appearance from the air, and intended to house V-1 flying bombs. However, Harris, sensing another set of panacea targets, was not eager to commit 617 to this battle, feeling that such employment would be the thin edge of the wedge as far as his command was concerned. Let the 2nd Tactical Air Force's bombers destroy these concrete objects, if they could. As far as he was concerned, Bomber Command was there for the sole purpose of attacking German cities.

Despite his opposition, 617 attacked some ski sites by night during December and January 1944, but the results were not conclusive and the Germans ceased work on them in favour of less obvious 'modified' V-weapon sites, whose firing ramps would come to life the following June. It was also during January that 617 moved a short distance from Coningsby to RAF Woodhall Spa, which would be their final wartime home.

All the debate over targets and how to attack them would have come to nothing without an appropriate weapon. It was probably as a result of the July MAP conference that the Wallis earthquake bomb project had been revived by Bomber Command, who put forward their requirements for a special 12,000lb bomb, to be code-named Tallboy, at the end of that month. However, by the following October it seemed that this new weapon was not likely to be available before the following February. 617 would have to make do with more conventional bombs for the time being.

It had been time for Spud Boorer and his colleague Ernie Marshall to go back to the Burhill squash court drawing board, having gained from their Upkeep experience.

> After this bomb exercise more interest was taken in Wallis' activity and his big ten-ton bombs were revived for attacking other targets, like submarine pens, viaducts and eventually of course the *Tirpitz*. These were drawn on the same drawing board, because the Lancaster had the capability of lifting ten tons – it had a bomb bay big enough to lift it. So we got down again with Eric Allwright as section leader, Ernie and I, to drawing up the casings of these bombs in solid steel. Two-inch diameter small ones were built in various dimensions, to give us the dimensions, so that when they were fired by a mortar into various substances – chalk and gypsum and things like that – we could see the deformation and see where to put the strength. It was quite scientifically done.

Eric Allwright witnessed the gypsum mine tests.

> The idea was to learn what happened to a projectile flung into the ground, because there was little known about that. Actually, they weren't dropped – they were fired from a gun … Presumably the geologists advised Wallis that the soil into which they should be fired was something like gypsum. It's calcium sulphate, I believe – mined, from which plaster is made.
>
> So I went there with one or two others, because Wallis had a man called Grant as his project man working for him on these things. We all had other responsibilities for wing and fuselage design and all the rest of it, when this bomb thing came in. So I went down to this gypsum mine with these other chaps, and there we saw the firing of these projectiles down in the mine. These were the two-inch ones. That gave everybody enough confidence to make a 4,000lb one as a specimen to prove the ballistics of it. This 4,000-pounder had no ordnance at all, as it never went into service and had no explosive in it. That was to prove the behaviour of the bomb when dropped.

Whatever the bomb's size, it was still Spud Boorer and his colleagues who would draw it.

> We designed up those. English Steel made the casings for us and 'Father' Brown did the light alloy tail cone, because we didn't want to throw any weight away on the tailend. The fins on the back were given an angle of incidence to spin the bomb, because it had to hit the ground at about the speed of Mach 2.

The tails would be modified in this manner after the first tests of the 4,000-pounder. Apart from improving accuracy, this high-speed spin would also assist the bomb's penetration, so helping to bring about the earthquake effect that Wallis was seeking.

Cecil Brown, another member of the Drawing Office staff and nicknamed after G. K. Chesterton's priest turned sleuth, had previously done the bomb beam drawings for the Wellington as well as working on the ten-ton bomb before Upkeep.

> With the big one designed, we then designed a 12,000-pounder. The big one was called Grand Slam; the 12,000-pounder was called Tallboy. It was exact scale.

The explosive filling, which will be described later, would be the same for both types of bomb.

> There were three detonators in it, in the tail-end casing. This was the sort of thing that a young aeronautical engineer like myself found out when you got into doing things like bombs, because one of the jobs I did was the cap that went onto the bomb. It was hollowed out – you filled it up and then you laid a cap on the top. The three detonators went into the cap.

Three exploder pockets were designed, to take the detonators and pistols. Like Upkeep, three were used in case one failed with the shock of impact. As with any bomb designed for penetration, the arming arrangements could not be in the nose. In this case, the pistols were placed at the rear of the steel casing that held the bomb's filling, covered by the tail unit but accessible via two circular inspection plates, through which the tail could also be bolted on. Although made from aluminium, the tail, which took the form of a tapering cylinder, was quite robust in construction. Being light, it would cause the bomb to fall nose first, its streamlined shape and pointed nose assisting penetration.

> All that was easy, but you didn't draw these things up full-size. Of course, you suddenly thought when you were working away there, 'You can't lift that up and put that on top.' So you then had to design studs and that to screw on – like heavy machinery people do – and cranes to lift it on, so you had to learn a lot about heavy engineering. This was fun.

Hopefully the Farnborough Upkeep rope problem would be avoided this time. Still, it was one thing to design the bomb, but another to produce them at a time when the steel-makers were fully employed elsewhere. The estimate of Tallboy not being ready until the following February came about despite Bomber Command's request for the new bomb being approved just four days after it had been made, resulting in an initial order of sixty bombs.

There was still the question of what targets to employ Tallboy on, and how to do so. On 9 January 1944 Wallis, Cochrane, Air Commodore Sam Patch, who was Director of Armament Research at the Air Ministry, and two other senior RAF officers met at Burhill. The concrete pens protecting E- and U-boats were obvious candidates since they had so far resisted other attacks on them. The report that Wallis later wrote was based on the assumption of the pens having reinforced concrete roofs of either eleven feet or twenty feet – in the second instance, the first layer being four to six feet and an air space in between four and six feet, then a bottom layer of eleven feet:

> Questioned on the best methods of attacking these targets, I said that in my opinion the most successful method would be to attack the roof, as this not only offers the best target, but experiments carried out at the Road Research Laboratory on piers of viaducts, which are similar in height and dimensions to the dividing walls of the piers, showed that whereas single unsupported piers could be readily destroyed by near misses, the same piers when heavily loaded by the roofs were singularly resistant, and the largest charges which we could lay alongside were scarcely sufficient to do any material damage.

Secondly, that once the roof was destroyed the walls themselves would become unstable and an explosion taking place at a considerable depth near the foundation might then cause the collapse of several walls simultaneously once the roof had been destroyed.

Thirdly, that the proportions of the roof as given show that the thickness of the arched outer cover could not be more than a few feet and this would readily be penetrated by Tallboy Medium when dropped from a height of 14-18,000 feet.

The comment 'as given' indicated that Wallis had received some inside information, although from what source was not stated.

I estimate the penetration into solid reinforced concrete of Tallboy Medium at about eight feet, so that the store should be partially buried in the upper surface of the Jack arches. The explosion taking place in the enclosed air space between the false and the outer roof would thus cause extensive damage.

It would later be found that the Germans had arranged these layers differently, but his estimate of the overall thickness would be close to the mark and he had correctly foreseen the use of an air space as a bomb-trap.

As with Upkeep, Wallis based his statements on the calculations he had reached, which would be modified by trials experience, but at best he could only estimate what 617 would be up against where the pens were concerned. The real test for Tallboy would come in action.

On 12 February 617 were ordered to pass a Lancaster, DV405 'J', to the AAEE at Boscombe Down for Tallboy modifications. This entailed fitting the blown bomb bay doors that Marwood-Elton had suggested. By the end of this month twenty aircraft had been modified, with one more available for training.

There was also the question of manufacture. An order was placed for 325 Tallboys, of which 200 were to be made in the UK and the remainder in America, but to avoid the weapon breaking up on impact there was a need for a special chrome molybdenum steel casing, 21ft in length, with a maximum diameter of 3ft 2in, of which the bomb body, containing the explosive, made up the first 10ft 4in. A costly undertaking.

When Tallboy was filled the total weight was 11,800lbs, despite it being classed as a 12,000-pounder. Of this, 5,200lb was the Torpex charge, with, at first, a one-inch cushioning layer of TNT inside the nose. The thickness of this layer would be subject to change during the trials to come.

RDX, which was more sensitive than TNT, was used for the gaine – a booster charge between the detonators and the main explosive filling. These could not function until after the extraction of arming wires as the bomb left the aircraft.

Two types of pistol were to be made available. They were simple and similar to those used on the RAF's 4lb incendiary bombs. The Number 58 would be a direct-impact type, whose striker would hit the detonator when the bomb struck the ground. If desired, detonation could delayed by up to eleven seconds. The Number 47 was an alternative, giving a delay of thirty minutes or one hour, depending on the thickness of a celluloid disc. In this instance, when the bomb left the aircraft, a cable pulley would wind in the pistol-arming screw. This would crush an acetone-filled ampoule, releasing its contents. The acetone would then soften the disc, causing it to give way at the desired time. This would then release a striker to hit the detonator.

All this had to go ahead at a time when the build-up for D-Day was gathering momentum and Britain's capacity to manufacture steel was needed as never before. Once again security problems arose, and it is said that a Scots foundry employed on Tallboy casing production believed they were making midget submarines, although it is not clear whether this was an official cover story. Those concerned later said they had no idea what the purpose of these strange objects could have been, until Paul Brickhill's book was published a few years after the war.

Someone involved in the filling of Tallboy cases was Clive Marler, who since 1941 had worked at a dispersed complex at Swynnerton in Staffordshire. One of ten filling factories, this ROF, known as Site 55, was situated between the villages of Swynnerton and Coldmeece, south-west of Stoke-on-Trent. He was no stranger to such employment, for his father and aunt had previously worked at Woolwich Arsenal in south-east London and at Brunner Monds (later part of ICI) at Silvertown in the East End – site of an infamous explosion in 1917.

Being in a reserved War Office occupation, he had been moved up to this site, which was less vulnerable to bombing than Woolwich, and his experience had led to him being called on to work with 9th Bomb Disposal Company of the Royal Engineers at Birmingham, although he had not had to dispose of any bombs himself.

> We did the filling of HC and MC bombs, Tallboy, but not Grand Slam. We also made and filled detonators as well as the Torpex side cargoes for the midget submarines. Staff totalled 23,000, with a high proportion of girls, mainly drawn from Stoke and to the north, as far as Cheadle. Later this included 2,500 airmen from the USAAF – they kept the girls from the Potteries happy! The site was serviced by coaches and also had a special branch line, to an eight-platform rail terminus, with trains in at each shift change, with three shifts per day. There was an internal rail system, for goods and to the magazines. It took two days to fill each Tallboy, though I don't know how many we did.

This source of supply was particularly important, as it took place at a time before American manufacture had really begun. Handling such a weapon was demanding and dangerous, but hazards were something that the staff had become used to.

> There were accidents, as TNT built up due to spillage on the asphalt floor. The explosive turned to black when people walked over it, so it wasn't noticed. We only found it because the shop stopped when it was time to install new machinery. Oxyacetylene gear was brought in to cut off the legs of what was in there and the sparks caused an explosion. Two men didn't go home that night.
>
> We also disposed of surplus explosive by burning it in a destructor furnace on the north-eastern edge, until two men got careless and threw in a piece the size of a head. They were both killed.

As if all this was not enough, the site was also used for the development of 20mm cannon, with a range to test them on.

> I had experience of both the Hispano and the Oerlikon. A drunken colleague shot a 20mm gun on the range and killed some cows. The farmer was irate!

For obvious reasons the site operated under blackout conditions. Sabotage was also considered a possibility and the perimeter was protected by barbed wire, patrolled by the site's own police force. However, the Luftwaffe proved the least of anyone's problems. Site 55 was protected by anti-aircraft units, but it seems their only victim was a Lancaster which returned from a raid either damaged or lost. Straying into a forbidden area, it was shot down.

An explosion at an underground storage dump at Fauld, which was felt by staff at Swynnerton despite being twenty-five miles from it, served to remind everyone of the dangers. It was put down to sabotage by Italian POWs employed as labourers there, but Clive Marler was of the opinion that it had been due to the fitting of detonators into Army 4.2in mortar bombs – a fact he had tried to draw attention to, but had been ignored. In spite of all this he survived, being one of the last to leave. In 1946 Site 55 closed, but the Coldmeece range continued in use until March 1993.

By April 1944 the picture regarding Tallboy's future availability and employment was becoming clearer. Production had risen to fifteen a week and Wallis now considered that the effect of one Tallboy hit on a pen would only be local, but that up to five could be expected to cause complete destruction. To achieve the correct penetration, he was concerned that the bomb's pistols should carry a delay of 0.01 seconds, but this was not yet available, the best to hand being a delay of 0.025 seconds. One giving 0.091 seconds had also been developed, but was not yet in production. The only suitable concrete target was one at Ashley Walk. It was not an easy one to hit, but then no operational target would be either.

As already stated, the 4,000lb weapon had had to be scaled down from the ten-tonner. It became known as Tallboy Small, to distinguish it from the six-ton Tallboy Medium and the ten-ton Tallboy Large, which would later become Grand Slam. Twelve 4,000-pounders were made and the first were tried in December 1943 by the AAEE, operating from Boscombe Down but using the range at Orford Ness on the East Anglian coast.

Incomplete data resulted in further trials during April 1944. The first 4,000-pounders dropped had penetrated to their estimated depth but had broken up in doing so. This trial would be repeated using bombs made of tougher steel, called Hykro.

The first trials had also shown that the 4,000-pounders oscillated after falling for 15,000 feet. This was corrected by a modified tail, on which the fins were set at five degrees to the axis of rotation, giving a spin to the bomb which it was considered would rectify this instability, and, as already noted, assist with penetration. The modified 4,000-pounder was then dropped from 18,000ft by a Lancaster flying at 190mph.

The offset fins worked, for the bomb now gave a more consistent performance. Each one drifted to port, by ninety feet on average, with a terminal velocity of 3,300ft per second. Although not desirable, this drift could at least be allowed for and was better than the unpredictable oscillation of the previous unmodified bombs.

Scaling this up for the six-tonner would result in 3,800ft per second, although it was later amended to 4,060ft when the full series of trials had been completed. The drift to port was thought to be due to the fins spinning and was considered likely to be less for a larger-sized bomb. Something else which bomb aimers would have to allow for when using Tallboy was the earth's rotation, which when bombing from 18,000ft could add an additional error of ten yards to the east.

Air Commodore Pat Huskinson has already been mentioned as an early convert to the Wallis cause. Although he did not recover his sight after his flat had been bombed, Huskinson, rather like the legless fighter pilot Douglas Bader, decided that he was not going to be beaten by a handicap, and went back to bomb testing. His determination and sense of humour were indicated by the title of his autobiography – *Vision Ahead*.

At a range at Shoeburyness on the Essex coast Huskinson put Tallboy prototypes through a variety of tests, including deliberately rough use on bomb trolleys and extremes of heat and cold before filling one with RDX, standing it on its nose and exploding it. A slow-motion camera showed the bomb swelling to nearly twice its size before the casing burst, while instruments spread across hundreds of yards bore witness to its blast effects.

While they were awaiting the Hykro version, a trial installation of the 12,000-pounder was made by the AAEE in the prototype Tallboy aircraft. This bomb's tail unit had the offset fins and when it was dropped on the Crichel Down range, on Salisbury Plain, from 16,000ft it appeared to be quite stable. The bomb had been a dummy and when it was recovered – intact – it had penetrated thirty-five feet of earth, then travelled horizontally for a further twenty-four feet.

Some potential targets recurred time and again when these weapons were being considered, the Rothensee Ship Lift being one. As far back as July 1943 Wallis had stated that this could not be destroyed due to its massive construction, but thought the two underground chambers that housed floats for it could be put out of action if Tallboy could be dropped from 22,000ft within fifty yards of either one. When doubt was expressed as to whether a Tallboy-equipped Lancaster could reach this height, Wallis said that a reduction to 19,000ft would reduce penetration from 120ft to 104ft, but this would have little effect on the final result if the bombs landed in the right place.

At an Air Ministry meeting on 22 March 1944, which included Cochrane among thirteen RAF officers, Rothensee was debated again, as was the possible use of Tallboy on coastal gun batteries, with D-Day in mind, but in the event neither of these ideas came to anything. Wallis stated that by now Tallboy's development was complete, and hoped it would penetrate five feet of concrete, although without trials he could not be sure that it would do so without breaking up. Also, he was unsure whether it would not break up after going down through sixty feet of earth, as it tended to turn at the end of its penetration. Another attack on the Sorpe was debated, but considered not worthwhile until after D-Day.

By now twenty-five Tallboy bodies had been cast. Filling was due to take place within the next three weeks. Tail production had initially got ahead of this, as they had been produced at thirty a month, although they were now being delayed by the need to offset the fins. Live trials, which were due in two to three weeks, would determine the cratering effect, as well as use against the Ashley Walk concrete target. The bomb's pistol had proved satisfactory, with sixty due to be ready shortly and others on order.

A report by the Ministry of Home Security's Research and Experiments Department stated that Tallboy should be seen as a deep penetration and cratering weapon – the crater being used to undercut bridge piers, for example. Despite what Wallis had said about the pens, it was thought that in some instances a near miss would be better, for the bomb's delay fuse would then go off beneath the surface at the side of the target. The resulting shockwave would then knock away the foundations, so undermining the target and causing it to collapse. The report agreed with Wallis in saying that a 0.01 -second delay should be used for concrete but pointed out that, 'It was not designed for this purpose and the results of using it in this way may be disappointing.'

In April the Ashley Walk trials were carried out with the Stabilised Automatic Bomb Sight Mark IIA, which 617 would be using on operations in the future. Sqdn Ldr R. G. Whitehead of the Air Ministry's Directorate of Bombing Operations witnessed the trials and part of what follows is based on a report made by him shortly afterwards.

The four specially made fins, each held in place by a locking bolt, were aero-foil in section and numbered to fit in the same place on each bomb, with a corresponding number on the tail itself. Wallis had evidently briefed Whitehead, for the latter commented that offsetting the fins at five degrees to the main axis of the bomb would cause it to rotate in flight 'and so help it through the near-sonic band where I understand the most dangerous oscillation is likely to occur'.

Perhaps, in addition to accuracy, speed and penetration, Wallis had the then-new phenomenon of 'compressibility' in mind. This was the term used for successive shock waves of air building up in front of a fighter's wings during a high-speed dive, causing buffeting which could lead to sudden structural failure. Supersonic flight was very much an unknown quantity in the early 1940s and this problem would not be solved until swept wings became the norm a decade later.

Special jigs had been made to ensure the correct fin alignment. This entailed placing the bomb in a purpose-designed cradle, which had four rollers to rotate it. The alignment of the fins was adjusted by wires set to the correct angle. According to an unnamed Vickers chief mechanic, it took two skilled men one day to fit and adjust two tails.

The transport and handling of the bomb would also require special equipment to be designed or adapted by Vickers. A type of crane known as the Lorraine proved suitable for getting the bomb from the dump onto its trolley, which was the type used for the 8,000lb and 12,000lb HC bombs, though it was now fitted with four upright pillars. After the trolley had been taken by tractor to the Lancaster's dispersal pan, the platform on which the weapon lay was raised by four 4,000lb bomb winches, one attached to each of the pillars.

The trolley had to be correctly aligned beneath the aircraft, as a peg fitted to the carrier in its bomb bay had to fit a hole in the bomb's body, with just one-eighth of an inch clearance between the two. This fitting had been necessary to stop the bomb rotating before release. A corporal who had been specially trained said that it would take skilled men half an hour to complete loading and added, rather obviously, that perfect teamwork would be essential.

To ensure accuracy a new method of bomb release was necessary, and that meant a new bomb-slip for Reg Firman when he was not grappling with Highball's problems.

> Pierson came to me one day – he was our Chief Designer. 'That new slip you were designing – would that carry ten tons?' I said, 'No, that would be its maximum breaking strength.' He said, 'That's the breaking strength of the machine anyway, but we've got to carry it.' They knew it was going onto a Lancaster.

Clearly Pierson and Wallis had looked ahead to a time when the ten-ton bomb would be a reality. In the meantime Firman's slip would serve equally well for Tallboy. Despite the availability of new and stronger materials, it was clear that it would not be sufficient to simply scale up an existing design.

> This one was a new duralumin which had come out. I made a new slip, exactly the same, out of it, and it broke everywhere except where it should have done so! But I found a position where I could use the strength of it rather than the weakness – I redesigned the slip and made the load-carrying different.

Eric Allwright, still a section leader in the Vickers Drawing Office at Burhill, had a contribution to make to this as well.

> The 12,000lb bomb went into ordinary Lancs, structurally, but going on from that they were suspended from the aeroplane in an unusual way. The reason is this. If you imagine that you're going to have a very, very accurate bomb dropped, timing is all-important – even parts of a second, when you release the thing. If you get a second hold-up, you travel too far. So the way it was selected – I don't know who did it, it might have been Basil Stephenson or Avros – the final system was to suspend the bomb by a chain round its middle. The two halves of the chain were joined together by the bomb-slip, and then it was crutched up – pulled up against the front and back supports, winched up, and then the bomb-slip was set, so that when the bomb-slip was fired, these two half-chains came out and you had immediate release. The chain was manufactured with big links about three inches long. It was a unique suspension system to make sure that the bomb dropped accurately.

So what was the method used with conventional bombs, and why was this redesign considered necessary?

> They used to have a hook on the top of the bomb, and a bomb-slip above with a hook on it. Then the bomb wasn't symmetrical to anything. This method, however, worked very well and was also employed for the 22,000lb bomb.

To fit a hook – or, to be more correct, a suspension lug – to the outside of the bomb's casing would have caused drag and resistance, affecting the airflow over it. Also, the lug would have sheered off on impact, damaging the casing. This could have led to the bomb breaking up, with only partial detonation of its contents, or could have affected its path of penetration and therefore its accuracy. There was therefore no alternative to a chain, especially as this method appeared to give prompt release while preserving the smooth symmetrical outer surface of the bomb. However, it was to lead to release problems, which would never be satisfactorily solved.

Once loaded, the Tallboy, despite its size, did not entirely fill the Lancaster's cavernous bomb bay. Crutches were used to hold the weapon firmly in place, in addition to the carrier peg. The fusing links were fed through three holes in the tail to the three tail pistols in the bomb. At first, a delay of eleven seconds was used, to allow the bomb to achieve its maximum penetration and come to rest before exploding. It was hoped that this delay would establish whether the bomb would break up at the bottom of its travel, as experience with the 4,000lb version had indicated.

So, having got it in, was it going to work when dropped? Eric Allwright again:

Among the worries that Wallis had – he was fighting the Establishment, bomb designers, explosive experts, the RAF – they didn't want to play around with these new fangled ideas. They wanted to carry on where they were. But one of the worries put up by Fort Halstead – the Armament Design Section of the Ministry in those days, in Kent – they didn't think it possible to explode such a large quantity of explosive at once. In other words, a lot of it would burn rather than explode. In the end we put in these three fuses, which were designed and supplied by Fort Halstead – we never saw these explosive bombs, of course. They were screwed in the end-caps. Actually, it worked every time. Their fears were justified, but groundless in the end – it did explode rather than just burn.

The first Ashley Walk trial, which took place on 18 April, had been scheduled for 0900, but had been put back to 1800 by unsuitable flying weather. The Lancaster first dropped four small practice bombs to check accuracy, then made two dummy runs before dropping the Tallboy at an airspeed of 169mph from 18,000ft, which AAEE had been given to understand would be the operational height.

The Tallboy was seen to oscillate slightly at high level just after leaving the aircraft, but when seen again at 3,000ft it was falling very steadily and rotating slowly. It hit one hundred yards from the target, on the edge of a pine wood, throwing up a fountain of earth. Seconds later the observers heard the whine of it falling – a sound which grew until the apparent impact. Immediately after this the shock of the impact was felt, shaking a concrete apron on which the observers stood. Then a cloud of earth was thrown up from the wood 'and immediately afterwards a mushroom of fire appeared to boil up from the crater'.

It had taken thirty-seven seconds to fall, impacting at just over 1,000ft per second. The delay was thought to have been only five seconds instead of the eleven that had been set, but even so this would have given ample time for penetration. Wallis was concerned that the bomb appeared to have broken up on impact, and that the flames were caused by its Torpex filling burning on the ground, instead of all of it instantaneously exploding. However, when all this had died down they went to the crater and 'we found that his fears were groundless'.

The crater was almost exactly circular, measuring 92ft from rim to rim. Its deepest part was between twenty and thirty feet, while two mounds of loam clay, some of it blackened, stood up from the crater bottom. This was considered significant as this type of clay was usually found in this area at forty feet below the surface. It was estimated that the bomb had penetrated to sixty feet and caused a partial camouflet – an explosion below ground level. Other clay had been forced up inside the crater, while some earth had fallen back into it.

Not surprisingly, the trial was considered successful. Whitehead commented, 'It appeared to me that the performance of the bomb was most impressive. Apart from the size of the crater I think that this earth shock effect may have distinct possibilities against rigid constructions. An interesting feature of the trial was that the surrounding trees close to the crater were still standing, but had had their tops blown away, indicating that such of the force as was not absorbed by the earth had gone more or less directly upwards.'

A second Tallboy, also with eleven seconds' delay, was dropped on the same date, apparently with similar results to the first.

These were followed up on 24 and 25 April by a further six Tallboys, also at Ashley Walk, but this time aimed at a raised concrete platform, 100 square feet and 8 feet thick, by 617's Bombing Leader, Flt Lt Keith Astbury, DFC RAAF. Wallis felt that a direct hit would penetrate this target and if a near miss was obtained it 'was expected that the concrete would be severely disrupted'. All six bombs were dropped from 18,000ft in good weather, with the following results:

Number	Crater diameter	Crater depth	Distance from AP
1	80ft (sand)	11ft 8ins	106yds
2	75ft (clay)	10ft 8ins	302yds
3	66ft (clay)	21ft	150yds
4	84ft (sand)	19ft 3ins	107yds
5	89ft (sand)	18ft	84yds
6	80ft (clay)	17ft	83yds

This averaged out to a diameter of 84ft in sand and 73ft in clay, with the same depth of 16ft for both. The first two bombs had been delayed for 0.05 seconds and the rest for 0.025 seconds. With regard to aim, the second one was probably an aberration, since the distance from the AP narrowed as Astbury gained experience.

However, it was also apparent that in all cases only half the charge had gone off. Although the last one had landed the closest to the AP, explosions had continued for some twenty minutes after the initial detonation. The earth shock was considerable, being felt 2,000 yards away and causing the concrete platform to move one-eighth of an inch. Someone cautiously stated, 'It is likely that a near miss will cause considerable movement.'

Two days later Wallis, Astbury, representatives of the Ministry of Home Security, production and explosives experts all met to discuss the results. A Home Security representative thought the partial detonation might have been caused by a break-up of the casing or by a failure of the explosive to adequately ignite. Despite the burning Torpex on 18 April, the two bombs dropped then, each with a delay of eleven seconds, were both assessed as having satisfactorily and completely detonated.

Wallis did not think a break-up of the casing was likely, and considered the failure might be due to the shorter delay used – that due to the high velocity achieved the bomb's contents would be compressed by up to three inches when it struck the ground. As the pistols were in the top of the bomb they would then be only partially immersed in the explosive, leading to inefficient operation. With the previous longer delay fuse, the bomb had come to rest before going off, giving the contents time to re-establish themselves in their former position.

Something else that might have affected the detonation was the fact that the cushion of TNT in the noses of the last six bombs dropped was four and a half inches, as opposed to the nine-inch cushion fitted to the first two. As it was intended that Tallboy would strike nose first, this had clearly been fitted with an eye to the known sensitivity of Torpex.

Astbury had replaced Bob Hay after the latter's death in action the previous January. 'The unique Aspro', as he was known, stood out as a character in a squadron that had plenty of them. His off-duty antics had become legendary, but he was also a highly professional airman.

He said that due to lack of knowledge of how Tallboy would perform the aiming error with it had been worse than with conventional weapons. While dropping the six bombs it had also become apparent to him that the bomb's trail angle – the attitude it had adopted while falling – had been wrongly estimated and he had tried to compensate for this in the air. It was clear from the figures listed above that he had begun to reduce the aiming error, but as usual there would be no substitute for experience. Astbury agreed that the partial charge detonations warranted immediate investigation, with further trials being necessary.

The idea of attacking coastal gun positions was considered again, but deferred once more. It was considered that if Tallboy and 617 were ready in time they should be used in conjunction with Main Force at the time of the invasion, but as things turned out the squadron would be needed elsewhere when that day dawned.

Tallboy weekly production had for some unstated reason dropped back to ten, but after three months an increase to sixty a week had been planned, with an estimated fifty to be ready by the end of May. No increase in the current order of 375 was recommended, and the modification of Tallboy aircraft in 5 Group was by now nearly complete.

As the question of the Sorpe came up again during May, on the 6th Wallis, reluctant to admit defeat where this dam was concerned, advocated an unusual and very different method from that which had been tried with Upkeep. This time aircraft should attack at right-angles to the dam, aiming for the air side. His reasoning was that as the dam consisted of earth over a concrete core, the material on the air side would be dry. If this earth was eroded and the concrete core cracked, the leak that followed would then erode the non-watertight material, leading to a rapid collapse. Some six hits sixty feet from the crest ought to do it. Five months later, once the supply of Tallboys had improved, this method would be tried – but not by 617.

On 11 May, to provide more fusing data in order to establish which types to use against different targets, two more Tallboys were dropped, the first with a direct-impact pistol and the second with a delay of 0.1 second. Both worked correctly, but their craters were not as large as had been expected.

Attention was now paid to the make-up of the bomb's filling. So far, those Tallboys that had been dropped had had 5 per cent beeswax mixed in with their Torpex to desensitize it, so preventing spontaneous ignition on impact. It was now thought that this was the reason for them not giving complete detonation. A charge that consisted entirely of Torpex, being more sensitive, would give a wider crater, but any bombs so filled could not then be used against hard targets, such as the U-boat pens. It was felt that these could only be destroyed if the bomb penetrated them.

During this month a target list of E and U-boat pens was drawn up, as follows:

E/R-boat pens		U-boat pens	
Boulogne	Le Havre	Bergen	Lorient (Keroman)
Bruges	Ostend	Bordeaux	Lorient (Port Geydon)
Cherbourg	Rotterdam	Brest	St Nazaire
Dunkirk		Hamburg	Trondheim
Heligoland		Kiel	
Ijmuiden		La Pallice	

Clearly there would be plenty of targets for the new bomb once it entered service. While all this was being digested, it was also during this month that questions surfaced concerning the possible re-employment of Upkeep. Wallis, having learned from *Chastise*, did not recommend a further attack with this weapon at the Sorpe. Another target considered once again was the Bissorte dam. This time the debate went as high as Air Chief Marshal Sir Arthur Tedder, Deputy Commander of SHAEF, who ruled it out on the grounds of prohibitive civilian casualties. The option to use this weapon again was however kept open, as Tedder directed that the Upkeep aircraft still held by 617 should be kept available until further notice.

By the last week in May Tallboy production had climbed back to fifteen a week, with thirty-seven available at 233 MU at Market Stainton in Lincolnshire for issue to 617. The hardware now looked promising enough, but what of the men who were to take it into action?

The fortunes of 617 Sqdn had begun to rise again when Wg Cdr Leonard Cheshire took up the post of commanding officer in November 1943. This was no criticism of Mick Martin, who had taken over the reins at a difficult time after the Dortmund-Ems Canal fiasco. Against Martin's will, like Gibson he was taken off operations

Wing Commander Leonard Cheshire. (Imperial
War Museum, neg. no. CH12667)

and 'proceeded to 100 Group Headquarters on temporary duty.' Whatever this
was intended to be, Martin soon flew again, this time in an intruder Mosquito. His
successor was to consider him the best bomber pilot that the RAF had ever had.

Cheshire had previously served with 4 Group, the unglamorous workhorse of
Bomber Command, with three tours on Whitleys and Halifaxes. By 1943, at twenty-
six he had become the youngest Group Captain in the RAF and was in command
of a training unit at Marston Moor, near York. Like Gibson, Cheshire had earned a
rest, but after a few months he wanted to get back onto operations and caused some
surprise by asking to be demoted to Wg Cdr in order to do so.

It is necessary at this point to describe the controversy that developed between some
Bomber Command units, in order to give a background to the operations conducted by
617 and later by 9 Sqdn during the last year of the European war. Mention has already
been made of the friction that had developed between 5 Group and the remainder of
the Command. As far as Donald Bennett's 8 Group was concerned, this would grow
worse during the last year of the war, not helped by some criticism of Cheshire's role in
a raid on Mailly-le-Camp tank park in France on the night of 3-4 May 1944.

During 1943 Cochrane had initiated experiments involving a timed run to the target
from a fixed point. This technique had first been used by 5 Group during June against
the Zeppelin factory at Friedrichshafen, which had been producing radar parts, resulting
in accurate bombing. This raid had also seen the first use of a Master Bomber and his
Deputy by the Main Force – a follow-up of Gibson's role during *Chastise*. They had
also been used by 5 Group on the famous Peenemünde V-weapon test site raid, although
with limited success on that occasion. During training Cochrane himself had set an
example at Wainfleet range by dropping bombs within thirty yards of the target.

Mailly-le-Camp was important, being not only a tank training area but also the
depot for the 21st Panzer Division, which would be one of the first units to go into
action once the Allies came ashore. This raid had stemmed from an attack in the
spring of 1944 by 144 Lancasters of 5 Group on an aircraft factory at Toulouse, using
Cochrane's low-level marking technique. The target had been successfully hit.

It will be recalled that Harris had opposed the creation of the PFF in 1942,
preferring Groups to conduct their own experiments. This result therefore agreed with
his own thinking and it impressed him, leading him to give Cochrane more of a chance
to use 5 Group in a semi-independent role. 617's prowess on precision night raids
against small but vital factory targets had also been noted. As a result of this, and a
memorandum written by Woodhall Spa's Station Commander on 617's future role as

a precision bombing squadron, two Mosquitoes were allocated to them for marking purposes during March. The squadron was indeed developing a character all its own and Lancaster crews from other units were beginning to seek a posting to it.

Harris had been inclined to look on the successes of 8 Group as limited and at Friedrichshafen a precedent had been set when four Pathfinder Lancasters had accompanied 5 Group. Now, to Bennett's fury, Harris reassigned three of his squadrons to Cochrane. 83 and 97 Sqdns, flying Lancasters, would be sent to RAF Coningsby in Lincolnshire, while 627 Sqdn's Mosquitoes joined 617 at nearby Woodhall Spa in April, at just one day's notice.

The consequence of this was that 5 Group now had three squadrons within it who had brought a 'them and us' attitude with them. In 627's case this was not helped when they discovered that 617's officers had completely filled the No.1 Officers' Mess, the palatial Petwood Hotel, in the nearby village, leaving the rather rundown No.2 Mess, at Tattershall Thorpe on the airfield's communal site, for 627's commissioned ranks. For three days the newly-arrived officers added to the Petwood's congestion until their quarters had been hastily spruced up for them. Then, after having been given a glimpse of how the other half lived, it was time to move out into the woods, to the delights of the coke stove and the Maycrete hut.

This accommodation problem had been unavoidable and made no difference to the NCOs of both squadrons, who would live out there anyway, but it added to 627's resentment. Their feelings were vented on Gibson when, on a return visit to his friends, he unwisely entered 627's territory and announced who he was. A typically blunt Australian voice replied, 'So what?' and in the scuffle that followed 'The Boy Emperor' was 'debagged'!

The crews of these three units remained fiercely loyal to their former AOC and disliked what they viewed as 5 Group's stricter regime. In addition 83 and 97 were not overjoyed when they found they were expected to act as a flare force for 617, although it should also be said that despite their feelings all three squadrons supported 5 Group in a highly professional manner.

This attitude lingered on for years to come. A former member of 627 Sqdn, whom I met by chance at the National Archives while researching this story, said that Bennett dubbed 5 Group 'The Lincolnshire Poachers' and that he never spoke to Cochrane again! However, Bennett did not use this phrase in his outspoken autobiography, dismissed stories of a feud as gossip and claimed to have remained a friend of Cochrane's. It must have been a rather strained friendship, during the rest of the war and after it.

With the change of Group also came further alterations to the conditions under which 83 and 97 would have to operate. With 617's experiences during *Chastise* in mind, it was decided to fit these two squadrons with VHF R/T sets. For now, the rest of 5 Group's squadrons would be controlled by W/T. So TR1143 sets were fitted, only to suffer severe interference from H2S due to the base of the set's aerial protruding through the aircraft skin near the radar set. This was cured by mounting the aerial outside the skin. In June this process would be taken to its logical conclusion by fitting all of 5 Group's aircraft with VHF sets, followed by *Loran*, a new radar aid. Once again Cochrane had used his influence with Harris to move his Group one jump ahead of everybody else.

The addition of the two Mosquitoes to 617's establishment meant that members of two crews had to be 'put up for disposal' due to the need to convert their pilots and bomb aimers onto these aircraft. Len Sumpter, by now a Flying Officer, and his skipper Dave Shannon, along with Flt Lt Kearns and his bomb aimer Flg-Off Barclay, were recalled from leave to 1655 MTU to convert onto an aircraft that would prove to be far faster and more responsive to control movements than a Lancaster. The course was a brief one, lasting just one day! Joining them in this role came Flt Lt Gerry Fawke and Flg-Off Tom Bennett, of whom more will be heard later on. Len Sumpter, whose new 'Nav B' status reflected his dual responsibilities of navigation and bomb aiming, received a DFC the following month.

An accurate attack on an aircraft repair plant at Tours was further proof of what 5 Group's marking could do, but shortly afterwards came the Mailly-le-Camp raid. On this occasion Cheshire flew a Mosquito as the Marker Leader, leading three others, with 1 Group's Special Duties Flight also involved. 97 were to act as target illuminators.

Cheshire's low-level marking was accurate, but the Main Force Controller, Wg Cdr Deane of 83, found it difficult to order 5 Group in to bomb as a wrongly tuned transmitter caused his orders to be drowned out by an American Forces Network broadcast. Only a few of 5 Group's Lancasters responded and during this confusion 1 Group's aircraft had been arriving at their holding point, which had been marked by yellow TIs. Night fighters were arriving as well, leading to angry exchanges over the R/T as Deane's deputy, Sqdn Ldr Sparks of 83, had ordered them to maintain their orbits while the matter was sorted out. Some crews survived by disobeying orders and moving away from the TIs, but relief did not come until Flg-Off Edwards of 97 marked the second AP. Sparks then ordered 1 Group in and the tank training area was deluged with bombs.

The attack had been in bright moonlight and the delay resulted in forty-three Lancasters, most of them from 1 Group, being picked off by the fighters, either in the target area or on their way home. None of this had been the fault of Cheshire, but his move to 5 Group – and to the most 'glamorous' squadron in 'Cocky's Private Air Force' – did not help matters.

From Bennett's point of view, what was more serious was that those squadrons that were still under his command had been left out of this attack and that, with the approval of Harris, Cochrane's ideas were taking root. Bennett, who had seen his crews as the mould-breakers where tactics were concerned, felt that his clothes were being stolen by 5 Group. However, his argument was weakened by the fact that those aircraft that had bombed at Mailly-le-Camp had done so with a high degree of accuracy. German tank crew casualties had been high – including veterans who would be missed in the forthcoming battle in Normandy. The only French civilian losses had been caused not by bombing, but by a crashing Lancaster.

Cochrane's low-level marking was anathema to 8 Group, who argued with some justification that such methods could not be used over a cloud-covered target. Nor could they be used in conjunction with a large force, whose bombs were bound to obliterate the small number of markers used. Thirdly, the Luftwaffe night fighter threat was such that a large force could not be kept waiting while Cheshire and his pilots readjusted their marking. Not that Cheshire had needed to in this instance, but whatever method he used, his aim could not be correct every time. Cheshire might well be skilled enough to mark for one of 617's small-scale raids, but as far as Bennett and his men were concerned, high-level sky marking, to be performed by them, was the only answer for the Main Force.

Just to add to all the bad feeling, Cheshire had once considered joining 8 Group, but Bennett had said he would only be prepared to accept him if his flying was up to the required standard – which surely his previous tours ought to have proved! Not surprisingly, Cheshire had said that if that was the case he would see if he could find somewhere else to go. That somewhere had turned out to be Cochrane's side of the fence, although it was indicative of Cheshire's character that instead of criticising Bennett, he later described his own attitude as 'rather ungracious'. More fat had been added to the fire when Cheshire had expressed some dissatisfaction with 8 Group's marking at the time of the ski site raids, leading to an idea that 617 should do their own.

Still, whatever 8 Group and the three reassigned squadrons may have thought, 617's CO had plenty of supporters in his new command. 'Chesh', as he became known while in charge of 617, was a natural leader, a VR officer who lacked the stiffness of some regulars, and was without doubt the most popular of all 617's wartime commanding officers. He took an active interest in every man in his unit and, although sometimes critical, never descended to sarcasm or to the displays of temper that Gibson had been prone to. What becomes apparent, especially from reading Tom Bennett's book

617 Squadron; The Dambusters At War is that Cheshire had the gift of motivating everyone under him and making them feel that they were an essential part of the unit. This book gives a good account of what it was like to be part of such a squadron at this time.

So, 617's morale was improved and the bomb trials had been encouraging, but how would Tallboy fare in action? Bearing in mind what he had asked Gibson to do, and his all too recent memory of the *Chastise* losses, what demands would Wallis make of Cheshire? Would Cheshire establish the same rapport with him that Gibson had done?

Some of the answers had come on 4 March when Cheshire had flown down to Brooklands, to see Wallis at Burhill. Could the Tallboy be dropped from 20,000ft? This was a month before the live Ashley Walk trials, but, based on his long experience as a bomber pilot and reports of the Boscombe Down trials to date, Cheshire said the aircraft would be inclined to 'waffle' at that height. Would 18,000ft be sufficient?

Wallis did not think so, saying that while AAEE had had problems, these would be overcome if the aircraft flew at full boost during the bomb run. This gave extra speed and therefore the necessary stability for bombing. The bomb would curve when travelling through the ground before exploding, but this was an advantage as it could be dropped slightly short, then move forward of its own accord to detonate directly beneath the target. Wallis stressed the need for Cheshire's crews to speed up on bombing, claiming that Boscombe Down's pilots had not realised the need for it. This complication would have to borne in mind when aiming the monster.

The picture would become clearer in the wake of the Ashley Walk trials. On 17 April Wallis wrote to Cheshire, first to congratulate him on the award of a second Bar to his DSO, then going on to say that he was confident about the future potency of Tallboy. The following day's trials would prove him right.

What would they use to aim it with? The answer to this question came in the form of the Stabilised Automatic Bomb Sight – a complicated device whose operation required a great deal of team work.

First, drifts would be taken by the gunners to help the navigator in calculating the precise wind speed and direction. The navigator and the bomb aimer would then work out various instrument corrections. Altimeters work from barometric pressure, which changes constantly, so it was necessary to work out ground-level pressures over the target, correcting altimeters by pressure lapse rates, with temperatures as a further complication. Apart from altimeter inaccuracy, airspeed indicators could read falsely depending on the height and attitude of the aircraft, so this also had to be allowed for.

When it was all set on the SABS, the pilot had to hold his exact course for several miles while the engineer manipulated the throttles to maintain a constant speed. This need to fly straight and level at the critical stage ruled out any evasive action, leaving the Lancaster vulnerable to flak and fighter attacks during the bomb run, whether by night or day.

As soon as the bomb aimer had the sight's cross-wires on the target he clicked a switch and the SABS used its gyroscopes to track the target, passing corrections to the pilot by means of an indicator in the cockpit. One thing the bomb aimer did not have to do was to press the bomb release, for the SABS did that, informing the pilot by switching off a red light in the cockpit. In July 1943 it was anticipated that the average error with this sight would be 130-150 yards. It could, if necessary, cope with a Lancaster banking at up to fifty degrees.

The SABS was therefore a remarkable if demanding piece of kit and arguably superior to area bombing sights, such as the Main Force's Mark XIV. It was just one example of the progress made in Bomber Command since its outdated equipment of 1939 and, looked at with modern eyes, it was clearly a step nearer to the computerised weapons systems that would be fitted to the later generations of jet aircraft.

This was the way forward and to show that to everyone came Wg Cdr D. S. Richardson, 5 Group's Armament Officer, whose obsession with his subject was such that he earned the nickname 'Talking Bomb.' Formerly an instructor at No.1 Air

Armament School at Manby on the Lincolnshire coast, Richardson had previously coached 106 Sqdn on this sight, but as a decision had been made to no longer teach it at Manby his expertise was now available to 617.

As with the other Wallis bombs, there was also the need for security. However, the person who decided that the first Tallboys should arrive at Woodhall Spa by night at the start of June had not considered the difficulty a driver would have finding his way round an unfamiliar and blacked-out airfield in the Lincolnshire countryside. Bomber bases were huge, with dispersals up to two miles from the living quarters. Bomb dumps, for obvious reasons, were sited well away from everything else.

The consequence was that the first arrivals, unable to see the parked Lancasters, blundered into 627 Sqdn's dispersal instead. 627's equally mystified erks wondered why they wanted to know where the dump was. So they looked into the backs of the lorries and all was revealed.

Realising they had come to a Mosquito unit, the drivers then asked how anyone could get a Tallboy onto one of those, to be airily told, 'Oh, you'd be surprised what we can carry!' Having had their little joke, the erks then phoned the airfield's watch office, announced that the drivers had arrived and obtained permission for them to proceed.

Perhaps the official who failed to give the drivers enough information was the same one who also decided on a particularly inane cover story. Cheshire had been rather suspicious one evening when two Tallboys had arrived in a large lorry, whose driver had first claimed they were new boilers for the cookhouse, but then said that he had been told to deliver them to the bomb dump!

Cheshire followed these strange items of cargo and found the dump almost full of their brethren, camouflaged under tarpaulins. An armament officer apologetically explained that they had been coming in at night for a week, but that he had been told to keep quiet about them: a story that amused Cochrane when Cheshire passed it on to him. The new arrivals were safely offloaded and placed under special guard.

The first use of Tallboy was delayed by a spoof operation mounted on the morning of D-Day by 617, with the Stirling crews of 218 Sqdn, using Window to fool the

Gently does it. Armourers guide a Tallboy from the bomb dump onto its trolley. (Imperial War Museum, neg. no. CH15363)

Germans into thinking an invasion force was headed towards the Pas de Calais. This was successful, drawing off E-boats to chase it while the real one arrived off Normandy. Three nights after this, 617 took their Tallboys into action for the first time on another raid intended to assist the build-up of the invasion forces.

8-9 June 1944
Targets The railway tunnel and bridge at Saumur, France.
Weather Cloudy over the Continent, but moonlight over the targets.

Force 4 Lancasters of 83 Sqdn to provide a flare force for both targets and also to bomb the Saumur railway bridge:

JA705 'M' Flt Lt C. P. Macdonald	ND333 'W' Flg-Off A. Drinkall
ND442 'O' Flt Lt D. H. Pidding	ND930 'Q' W/O C. Erritt

25 Lancasters of 617 Sqdn:

LM482 'W' Sqdn Ldr L. Munro	DV385 'A' Flg-Off R. E. Knights
LM492 'Q' Sqdn Ldr J. C. McCarthy	ME561 'R' Lt H. C. Knilans USAAF
ME560 'H' Flt Lt B. W. Clayton	ME562 'Z' Flg-Off N. R. Ross
EE131 'B' Flt Lt J. A. Edward	ME554 Flg-Off R. M. Stanford
DV246 'U' Flt Lt R. S. D. Kearns	ME559 'Y' Flg-Off G. S. Stout
DV391 'O' Flt Lt A. F. Poore	DV393 'T' Flg-Off E. Willsher
ME557 'C' Flt Lt W. Reid	EE146 'K' P/O T. A. Carey
LM485 'N' Flt Lt D. J. B. Wilson	ND472 P/O J. Castagnola
JB139 'V' Flg-Off D. H. Cheney	ED631 P/O F. Levy
ME555 'C' Flg-Off W. A. Duffy	JB370 P/O I. A. Ross
DV380 'X' Flg-Off A. W. Fearn	ED909 P/O J. A. Sanders
DV403 'G' Flg-Off M. Hamilton	ED933 P/O F. H. A. Watts
DV402 'P' Flg-Off A. E. Kell	

Some of these aircraft were ex-*Chastise* ones, partly returned to their original standard, but which are said to have flown without bomb doors. Others were more recent arrivals and had been modified with the blown doors. Three more aircraft were not included as there was no time to bomb them up. By now the squadron had changed its code letters from AJ to KC, although the stored Type 464s are known to have retained their old letters for a time.

Three 617 Sqdn Mosquitoes as marker aircraft:
NS993 'N' Wg Cdr G. L. Cheshire and Flg-Off P. Kelly
DZ418   Sqdn Ldr D. Shannon and Flg-Off L. J. Sumpter
DZ421   Flt Lt G. A. Fawke and Flg-Off T. A. Bennett

Although a few Mosquitoes had been issued to 617, from now on there would be some instances in which these aircraft were borrowed from 627 Sqdn.

Bomb Loads
83 Sqdn – Five 1,000lb GP bombs and nine clusters of 7in flares per aircraft.
617 Sqdn – Nineteen of their Lancasters carried one Tallboy each, with 0.025 seconds delay. The other six carried eight 1,000lb MC bombs and six clusters of 7in flares each. With the possible exception of Fawke, each Mosquito carried four red spot fires.

In addition to this raid, 483 Main Force aircraft would also attack five other French railway targets.

The German forces in Normandy had been caught on the hop on the morning of D-Day and their High Command had at first considered the landings to be a diversion. When they

A de Havilland Mosquito FBVI, of the type flown by 617 Squadron from the Saumur raid onwards as a marker aircraft. (Imperial War Museum, neg. no. CH12404)

had finally accepted them as the real thing, reinforcements had been hastily summoned and Ultra had indicated that the Germans were preparing to counterattack.

The *Wehrmacht* had few transporter vehicles as the Germans preferred to carry out the long-distance movement of tanks and other vehicles by rail. Consequently the destruction of a railway bridge and the blocking of the adjacent 1,130-yard long Tunnel de Nantilly near the town of Saumur would severely hamper the traffic flow from south-western France, including an armoured division on its way to the new battlefront.

This operation had come about in a hasty manner as the squadron had first been stood down at 1745 following discussion by the Air Staff. It had then been reinstated by Harris on his own initiative. His earlier fears concerning Bomber Command's change of employment had been realised and he had resented being ordered to use his crews as a tactical force in support of the invasion, but nevertheless he was determined to give the best support he could.

Before detailing the plan it is necessary to show how recent changes in 617 had affected those who were to fly the Mosquitoes. Their task was to be low-level marking, using red spot fires. As previously noted, the three Mosquito 'observers', as they were normally described, were actually bomb aimers, still wearing their original 'B' brevet but now with additional navigational duties.

The red spot fire had come about as a result of some adverse comments on the efficiency of TIs, which spread over 200 yards on impact. Gibson had been sent to 8 Group to check it out, which would have been a welcome change from his usual desk-bound routine. First used at Peenemünde, the spot fire burst at 3,000ft and burned on the ground with a vivid crimson flame for some ten minutes. This had the advantages of being easy to recognise and difficult for the Germans to simulate as it cascaded to the ground in an unmistakeable manner, earning it the nickname 'Christmas Tree Marker'.

There were two APs, labelled A and B. A was at the south-western entrance to the tunnel, where the double-tracked line ran in a cutting, while B was the fourteen-span girder railway bridge crossing a road and the Loire river at the tunnel's north-eastern entrance.

H-Hour was to be 0200. The primary task of the 83 Sqdn crews would be to drop clusters of flares by H2S to provide illumination for Cheshire, who would then dive and drop his spot fires onto A. The nineteen Tallboy aircraft would then bomb this on an easterly heading from below cloud at 160 mph IAS. B was then to be marked by a second Mosquito in the same way, following which the rest of 617's aircraft, with the four from 83, would attack the bridge with their 1,000-pounders.

Just to make things a little more uncertain, at the time of this raid a Bomber Command report on Tallboy's ballistics was not yet available and the bomb's terminal velocity was thought to be 3,800ft per second, although the trials so far had indicated 2,830ft. To give the necessary additional correction the true air speed had to be set on the SABS drum and then reduced by one turn of the air speed knob. This may have seemed hit and miss but it proved an accurate method – perhaps surprisingly so for the true speed, as already stated, turned out to be 4,060ft per second.

Due to its D-Day spoof commitment, which had required a very different type of flying, 617 had not carried out any recent range practice, so their expectation was 60 per cent hits within 100 yards. The wind had been forecast at 23mph, but the SABS indicated it to be 25-30mph.

On arrival 83's crews found there was a lack of a good H2S response, which may have been due to the target being part of the ground rather than above it, though the bridge could be clearly seen in the moonlight. As the tunnel area lacked any features that would have assisted the H2S sets of the 83 Sqdn crews, flares from the first two fell mainly to the south and east. This led to demands from the Controller (presumably Cheshire) at 0200 for more marking to the north and west.

Six minutes later the other two crews complied, but Flg-Off Tom Bennett, watching events with the other Mosquito crews, considered that only the last two or three flares in each stick would be useful to them. After this the Controller's transmitter was described by the flare force as very bad – shades of Mailly-le-Camp – but this time there were no night fighters at the target. It was just as well, for the four 83 Sqdn aircraft had to circle while 617 bombed the tunnel before the bridge was marked. The flare force could then drop the remainder of their loads onto it.

However, some of the last flares provided sufficient illumination for Cheshire, and Tom Bennett watched as he dropped his four spot fires in a dive to 500ft: 'Leonard Cheshire found the tunnel mouth and laid his spot fires perfectly on the aiming point. Flt Lt Fawke's detail was to mark the other end of the tunnel, where it emerged on to a bridge across the Loire.'

Cheshire's markers were estimated as being forty yards short of the tunnel mouth, but were actually 100 yards south of AP A and in the cutting. He then passed his estimate to the Tallboy force and ordered them in at 0208, with the first bomb falling three minutes later. Half a century later, the memory of what followed remained vivid in Tom Bennett's mind:

> I recall my admiration at the accuracy of Chesh's red spot fires, as we came round to assess them. I felt they could not have been positioned more accurately if they had been wheeled there in a barrow!
>
> Chesh gave the order to commence bombing to the approaching Lancasters. I was still in my euphoric state about the marking when the first Tallboy crashed down. It was so near the markers that the glow of the red spot fires was vividly reflected in the debris thrown up. My initial reaction was 'What silly bugger has 'doused' the markers!' Then a more realistic appraisal turned my thoughts to admiring the accuracy of that bomb from some 13,000 feet above!

Initially the Tallboys did indeed fall accurately by the spot fires; Edward too would later make the same comment about the first one. It was perhaps as well that the reds were spread over 100 yards, for they became visible again as the smoke from the first bomb cleared, but inevitably disappeared and reappeared several times as the other Tallboys went down. Eighteen aircraft made several runs at between 8,000ft and 10,500ft on a variety of headings and altitudes, bombing only when they could clearly see the spot fires. The nineteenth, flown by Wilson, made seven runs but still could not see them, so waited for AP B to be marked and bombed that instead.

As Shannon's Mosquito had returned earlier when its port engine had started overspeeding, it was Fawke who marked AP B some thirty minutes after the tunnel attack had begun, dropping three spot fires, accompanied by a Wanganui flare. Wilson claimed that his Tallboy fell 100 yards from these, accompanied by a total of sixty-three 1,000-pounders from 617's six remaining aircraft and three of 83's – Flg-Off Drinkall's crew failed to bomb due to a defective sight. Sanders used his H2S and his flares as well, but seems to have been the only one of 617's crews to do so as Cheshire had not called for 83's illumination to be backed up. Fawke was unable to observe the bridge bombing as by then his fuel was running low.

Crews later reported some slight flak and fighter activity, but no aircraft had been lost. The bombing had not appeared particularly spectacular at the time, for due to their delay fuses the Tallboys did not go off on impact with a bright flash like the cookies and blockbusters used by the Main Force, but had shown only momentary red pinpoints of light as they burst beneath the surface. 617's crews were confident that the attack had been a success, but 83's diarist was more cautious, saying only that, 'Reports tend to show this was a good prang.'

Next morning's PRU coverage showed just how good it had been. With the exception of one Tallboy which had fallen 680yds from AP A, the craters were very close, each an average of 84ft in diameter and up to 30ft deep. The mean point of impact was south of the tunnel mouth, the other seventeen craters being an average of 134yds from the AP and 96yds from the MPI. Two Tallboys had fallen in the cutting, three were very close to it, four more were to the south-east and three to the north-west. One which landed 143yds from the AP had done some other useful damage by blowing the roof from a power station. Wilson's bomb had fallen 170yds from the north-eastern AP and had not done any railway damage. The 1,000-pounders had fallen around the bridge without demolishing it.

However, the one that really counted was the Tallboy that had struck the top of the tunnel itself, just eighteen yards from the AP and the nearest one to it. This bomb had penetrated an estimated fifteen feet into twenty-six feet of yellow sand, over an eighteen-foot-thick masonry lining. Although this natural and man-made protection sounded formidable enough, the bomb had struck what was rated as a fairly thin part of the tunnel roof, for the rest of the ground above it sloped markedly, being up to forty feet thick at the north-eastern end.

The luck was added to when it later emerged that a train with at least one ammunition wagon had been passing through the tunnel at the time. By an astonishing coincidence this wagon had apparently been under the bomb when it went off. The resulting massive explosion had blown the roof away, cracked the masonry for sixty-five feet from the point of detonation and completely blocked the tunnel. Eight months after the attack, one distorted wheel and axle from the wagon were still buried in the floor. The bomb aimer involved would have received an immediate decoration, but unfortunately it was never possible to establish who had been responsible.

The Germans worked night and day throughout the next six weeks in an attempt to clear the blockage, excavating from above the tunnel as well as below, and widening the crater to prevent any more sand slipping into the tunnel. Some 16,000 cubic metres of debris had to be removed – a long job as it could only be done from one side. This was not helped by the craters in the cutting severing both sets of track, so making it impossible to bring up earth-moving equipment from the south-western side. In addition, these two craters would have caused more problems than smaller ones, as there would have been heavy subsidence after filling them in and the earth put back would have to be thoroughly compact before trains could run over the top of it afterwards. Railway experts had estimated that a Tallboy crater would take between seven and ten days to fill in.

By 23 June one of the lines in the cutting had been reinstated and the other soon followed, but this was of little use until the tunnel itself was cleared. The repair work had been monitored by further PRU sorties, leading American tactical bombers to attack the bridge again on 22 June, blocking the tunnel at its north-eastern end. The Germans shored this up with timber, which they had also used to cover the roof hole, then for some reason they decided to demolish the timber at the northern end by

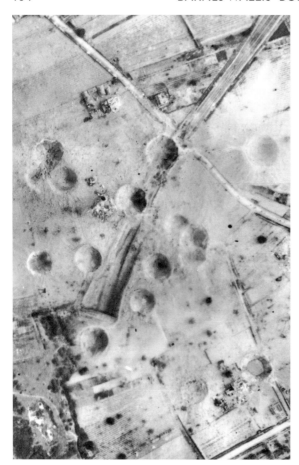

The Saumur railway tunnel in Normandy, photographed in June 1944 after the first operational use of the Tallboy bomb. (Imperial War Museum, neg. no. CL80)

exploding a charge, which also had the effect of bringing down the roof timber near the south-western end! It was no wonder that they did not finally clear the tunnel until just before the Allies took over the area, and by then only one track was in use through it. It is interesting to see that the double track in the cutting today still narrows to a single track at the south-western entrance.

A report compiled in February 1945 said the Tallboy's delay had been 0.0025 seconds – probably a typing error as it conflicts with records elsewhere. It also estimated that it hit at 800ft per second and considered that a delay of eleven seconds might have been better, as it would have allowed the bomb to penetrate and explode below the railway line in the tunnel. However, in this instance it would have had to pass through the ammunition wagon in order to do so, which clearly would not have been possible. If the bomb had had a clear passage through into the tunnel floor, it would certainly have taken the Germans longer to clear it, but from the Allied point of view the actual damage was satisfactory enough.

The consequence of all this was that the armoured division did not get through to the Normandy front in time to play any significant role in the planned attack. The battle fought in the close countryside over the next two months proved tough for both sides, but it was the Germans who gave ground, allowing the Allies to push forward into France.

On 26 June the Bomber Command Tallboy report finally became available. It stated that during trials Tallboy had shown a systematic error of thirty yards to port when dropped from 18,000ft. This was considered to be due to the rotation of the bomb during its fall and if so appeared to indicate the benefits conferred by offsetting the bomb's fins. However, something else to consider was the fact that at 3,800ft per second Tallboy's terminal velocity was outside the range of velocities for which the SABS Mark IIA could be adjusted. The error introduced by this when setting the maximum velocity on the sight and bombing from 18,000ft would be an overshoot of some thirty yards. Saumur had not proved a reliable test as due to cloud it had been impossible to bomb from this altitude that night, quite apart from the crews' lack of consistency in bombing altitudes and headings.

Still, despite all the statistics and speculation, 617 were satisfied and fully deserved the congratulations given them by Cochrane. So too did Woodhall Spa's Armament Section, which was singled out for particular praise by Harris. Once again the squadron's skill, with a certain amount of luck, had vindicated the bombing theories of Wallis. Had the two targets been attacked with only 1,000-pounders the raid would have been far less successful. Shallower craters on the track would have slowed down German troop movements, but would not have stopped them altogether.

The amazing photographs brought back from Saumur led to some euphoria at High Wycombe, with an increased demand for Tallboy. Air Commodore S. O. Bufton, Director of Bombing Operations, was faced with a call for no less than 3,000 of them, to be delivered at 500 a month, as soon as possible! Once he had recovered his composure, Bufton met Air Marshal Sir Robert Saundby, Bomber Command's Deputy Commander-in-Chief, on 13 June. With some tact and understatement Bufton informed Saundby that this large order could not definitely be confirmed, but that calls for Tallboy were likely to increase, with new uses being found for it. There was also the possibility of a second squadron using this weapon, with a consequent need for blown bomb doors and other parts.

Something else that would also be required was increased production of the SABS sight. The Directorate of Armament Research had recently asked for twenty a month, but at the moment only half that number were being produced. Should these not be available, the second squadron would have to make do with the Mark XIV sight. With an eye to breaking down Cochrane's independent outlook, Bufton suggested that one specialist squadron should be formed in each Group in the future. However, Cochrane was to get his way once again, for the next squadron to drop Tallboy would be another 5 Group one.

Loading a Tallboy into a Lancaster. Judging by the 'dressed' propellers, this aircraft has been specially prepared for the occasion. (Imperial War Museum, neg. no. CH13954)

In view of all this, it was as well that in addition to the 350 Tallboys already on order, the Ministry of Aircraft Production had, in order to keep the factories going, now doubled that order. Even so, some time was going to elapse before supply could meet the demands that would now be made.

It was now time for 617 to try out Tallboy on a much harder surface.

14 June 1944
Target The E-boat pens at Le Havre.
Weather Clear over target, with slight ground haze.

Force 22 Lancasters of 617 Sqdn:

LM492 'Q' Sqdn Ldr J. C. McCarthy	JB139 'V' Flg-Off D. H. Cheney
LM482 'W' Sqdn Ldr L. Munro	ME555 'C' Flg-Off W. A. Duffy
ME560 'H' Flt Lt B. W. Clayton	DV403 'G' Flg-Off M. Hamilton
EE146 'K' Flt Lt J. A. Edward	DV402 'P' Flg-Off A. E. Kell
DV380 'X' Flt Lt A. W. Fearn	DV385 'A' Flg-Off R. E. Knights
ED763 'D' Flt Lt C. J. G. Howard	ME561 'R' Lt H. C. Knilans USAAF
DV246 'U' Flt Lt R. S. Kearns	ME562 'Z' Flg-Off N. R. Ross
DV391 'O' Flt Lt A. F. Poore	ME543 'F' Flg-Off R. M. Stanford
ME557 'C' Flt Lt W. Reid	ME559 'Y' Flg-Off G. S. Stout
EE131 'B' Flt Lt J. E. R. Williams	DV393 'T' Flg-Off E. Willsher
LM485 'N' Flt Lt D. J. B. Wilson	LM489 'L' P/O J. Gingles

On this raid most of 617 Sqdn's Lancasters carried one or two passengers from other crews in addition to their own.

Three 617 Sqdn Mosquitoes as marker aircraft:
NS993 'N' Wg Cdr G. L. Cheshire and Flg-Off P. Kelly
DZ484   Sqdn Ldr D. Shannon and Flg-Off L. J. Sumpter
DZ418   Flt Lt G. A. Fawke and Flg-Off T. A. Bennett

The importance of this target was underlined by the large number of Main Force aircraft that took part in a two-wave attack. The first wave, which included 617, consisted of 221 Lancasters and 5 Mosquitoes of 1, 3, 5 ad 8 Groups. The second wave of 114 Lancasters and 5 Mosquitoes bombed at dusk. These totals included 15 Mosquitoes of 105 and 109 Sqdns, for further marking. Five aircraft from each of these units accompanied the first wave.

Escort 123 Spitfire IXs of 11 Group:

33 Sqdn RAF	308 Sqdn (Polish)	411 Sqdn RCAF
127 Sqdn RAF	317 Sqdn (Polish)	412 Sqdn RCAF
222 Sqdn RAF	331 Sqdn (Norwegian)	441 Sqdn RCAF
302 Sqdn (Polish)	332 Sqdn (Norwegian)	443 Sqdn RCAF

Bomb Loads Each 617 Sqdn Lancaster carried one Tallboy, with a 0.5-second delay. Four red spot fires were carried by each of the three Mosquitoes.

This raid was an experimental evening one ordered by Harris and as such was the first daylight attack to be carried out by him since 2 Group's tactical bombers had left Bomber Command at the end of May 1943. It was also a test for Tallboy against the very type of target that Harris had previously attacked without success. He had not forgotten the Admiralty's requests for attacks on the U-boat pens. At that time their roofs had been sixteen feet thick and in his words, 'When bombs exploded on the roofs of these shelters they made no more than a slight indentation in the surface.' This had certainly been true of conventional weapons, which in addition had led to French civilian casualties.

German E-boats (known as *Schnellboote* or S-boats to the *Kriegsmarine*) had first proved their worth in the Norwegian campaign of 1940. They had been the scourge of Allied shipping in the Channel and the southern part of the North Sea ever since. Well armed and powered by diesel engines, whose fuel was safer than the high-octane petrol used by British MTBs, they were capable of over 35 knots. It had been partly with this threat in mind that the spoof convoy operation had been staged on the morning of D-Day. Now there was a need to protect the Allied naval supply line to Normandy, which was only thirty miles away from Le Havre.

The E-boat flotilla was berthed in concrete pens similar to those used elsewhere for U-boats, but here the pen roofs were estimated as being eight to ten feet thick. Apart from any damage caused by the Tallboys, it was hoped that a tidal wave would be created, smashing the E-boats against the docks and concrete pillars.

The flight across the Channel in the summer evening light was fairly uneventful and aerial opposition was neglible. Indeed, it seemed as if some German aircrews had been ordered to attack rather than defend, as two of 443 Sqdn's Spitfires shot down two out of four Dornier Do 217s that were seen going the other way. According to one account, some anxiety was caused when an Australian Main Force pilot's voice was heard over the R/T nattering to his crew about their height, speed and other operational details, but if the Germans heard they lacked the means to take advantage of it in time. The only enemy aircraft seen in the target area was a Messerschmitt Me 410, which was claimed as damaged by three of 332 Sqdn's pilots.

By now it was becoming apparent that the main threat to heavy bombers by day was not the Luftwaffe, which was on the decline, but radar-guided flak. To combat this the 'gaggle' formation had been developed, in which a squadron flew in line abreast or astern but at different heights, offering a dispersed target for the defenders but still able to be controlled and bomb with a reasonable chance of accuracy with, it was hoped, less chance of being hit by 'friendly' bombs from above.

This formation also took account of the need for SABS-equipped aircraft to fly a precise course and speed during the final run-up to the target. It would become the norm for Bomber Command squadrons in the last months of the European war, for more daylight operations would be carried out by them from now on.

Such a precaution was needed, for the port was well defended and a heavy barrage of both heavy and light flak claimed a Lancaster of 15 Sqdn. Several other aircraft were hit as well, some coming home on three engines, and though 617 lost no aircraft this time, they had their share of narrow escapes. Knights' Lancaster was rated Category AC (repairable beyond unit capacity) on his return, while Sgt Alf 'Bing' Crosby, 'Nicky' Knilans' mid-upper gunner, suffered a leg wound from the light flak. For Poore's crew it was a case of 'defend me from my friends' as a 4,000lb cookie and several 1,000lb bombs dropped from a 460 Sqdn aircraft above were avoided only by him putting his Lancaster into a steep turn.

Like all E and U-boat pens, the target was a distinctive rectangular building at the water's edge. The attack was timed for 2230, the intention being to catch the E-boats after they had been fully manned and armed, but before they could leave harbour for a night attack.

There were two APs, a northern and a southern one. Although the sky had darkened visibility was assessed as clear. Followed by Shannon and Fawke, Cheshire dived to 7,000ft to release his spot fires midway between the two APs. 105 and 109 Sqdns followed this up with 250lb markers. The first Main Force stick of bombs fell right against the northern AP and Munro's Tallboy fell onto the southern one.

With the desired tidal wave effect in mind, it was intended that half the Tallboys should fall onto the pens and the other half in the harbour. Several crews reported seeing up to four direct hits on the pens, two of them being claimed by Kearns and Cheney's crews. Several Tallboys exploded in the water and smoke quickly covered the pens, while 1 Group's Lancasters plastered the nearby jetties. Some 1,230 tons of bombs fell onto the harbour and its surroundings. High above the first wave, the Spitfire pilots had an unforgettable view of the heaviest raid they had so far witnessed. 222 Sqdn's diarist rated it, 'A most amazing sight,' while 411 Sqdn commented, 'It was a noteworthy effort because this was the first time British night bombers were used in daylight ... Intense flak encountered at first but gradually petered out. Pilots reported bombing successful and a good job done to wipe out the E-boat menace to Channel transportation.'

One 500lb or 1,000lb bomb had hit the pens' roof, but left only blast marks to indicate its arrival. In contrast, a Tallboy had blown a 16ft-diameter hole in the north-west corner, displacing an area some twenty-four feet square and its supporting walls. A report later stated this was consistent with the bomb penetrating several feet and causing 'a substantial spall on the underside of the roof by its impact, the subsequent explosion blasting the loosened material down into the pen.' Considerable damage was visible along the whole length of the structure.

This was not bad considering that Wallis had not designed Tallboy with concrete in mind, but the same report added a word of caution after noting a third Tallboy hit on the more easterly block of the pens. Although of the same diameter, this crater had not gone completely through the roof and the bomb was considered to have not functioned correctly.

> The pens are known to be subdivided internally by substantial reinforced concrete walls. Unless the bombs can get right through the roof before exploding, which appears unlikely from the evidence of this attack, internal damage will be limited to the subdivision hit and may even be localised to a comparatively small portion of this. The absolute minimum requirement for 'destruction' if the objective would be one hit on each subdivision, of which there are probably eight or ten at Le Havre. Totally to destroy the contents of the pens might well require three times this number of hits – a total of twenty-five to thirty.

Clearly other E and U-boat pens would be a tough nut to crack whatever bombs were used – and the U-boat pen roofs would turn out to be thicker than those at Le Havre. It also seems that the idea of undermining the target by a near miss had been considered impracticable in this instance. However, what mattered was that most of the E-boats had been sunk and their threat had been almost completely removed. A floating dock had also gone down and substantial damage had been done to quayside buildings. Large fires were still burning the next morning.

Despite this, not all the bombs had landed where they should have. French civilians, who had suffered seventy-six dead and 150 injured, referred to the impact of the Tallboys as 'ravages considerables', although it is likely that some of this was also due to the Main Force bombing. None of it would stop the same type of force being used against a similar target the following day.

15 June 1944
Target The E-boat pens at Boulogne.
Weather Cloud down to 8,000ft over target.

Force 22 Lancasters of 617 Sqdn:

LM492	'Q'	Sqdn Ldr J. C. McCarthy		JB139	'V'	Flg-Off D. H. Cheney
LM482	'W'	Sqdn Ldr L. Munro		ME555	'C'	Flg-Off W. A. Duffy
ME560	'H'	Flt Lt B. W. Clayton		LM489	'L'	Flg-Off J. Gingles
EE146	'K'	Flt Lt J. A. Edward		DV403	'G'	Flg-Off M. L. Hamilton
DV390	'X'	Flt Lt A. W. Fearn		DV402	'P'	Flg-Off A. E. Kell
ED763	'D'	Flt Lt C. J. G. Howard		DV385	'A'	Flg-Off R. E. Knights
DV246	'U'	Flt Lt R. S. D. Kearns		ME561	'R'	Lt H. C. Knilans USAAF
DV391	'O'	Flt Lt A. F. Poore		ME562	'Z'	Flg-Off N. R. Ross
ME557	'S'	Flt Lt W. Reid		ME543	'F'	Flg-Off R. M. Stanford
EE131	'B'	Flt Lt J. E. R. Williams		ME559	'Y'	Flg-Off G. S. Stout
LM485	'N'	Flt Lt D. J. B. Wilson		DV393	'T'	Flg-Off E. Willsher

All of 617's aircraft on this raid carried one or two extra squadron members as passengers.

One 617 Sqdn Mosquito as a marker aircraft:
NS993 'N' Wg Cdr G. L. Cheshire and Flg-Off P. Kelly
5 Mosquitoes of 105 Sqdn and 6 from 109 also acted as marker aircraft. The total force consisted of 297 aircraft, comprising 155 Lancasters, 130 Halifaxes and 12 Mosquitoes of 1, 4, 5, 6 and 8 Groups.

Escort Spitfire IXs of 11 Group:

33 Sqdn RAF	302 Sqdn (Polish)
66 Sqdn RAF	308 Sqdn (Polish)
74 Sqdn RAF	332 Sqdn (Norwegian)
229 Sqdn RAF	349 Sqdn (Belgian)
274 Sqdn RAF	

Bomb Loads Each 617 Sqdn Lancaster carried one Tallboy, with a 0.5-second delay. Window was also carried by them. Cheshire's Mosquito carried two red spot fires and two 500lb MC bombs.

This raid had the objective of attacking both the pens and a number of light naval vessels that were now gathering in Boulogne harbour. 617 were to bomb the pens while the Main Force attacked nearby harbour installations.

Situated between the port's Bassin Loubert and the Avant-Port, the pens were similar to those at Le Havre, being of reinforced concrete with an overall roof that was up to eleven feet thick. There were six of them, housing up to fourteen E-boats. The AP was the centre of the roof.

617's planned bombing heights should have been between 15,000 and 18,000ft, and as they crossed the Thames estuary the weather was good. However, the first indication that things would not go according to plan came when they met heavy cloud up to 13,000ft over the French coast. As previously noted, the accuracy of the SABS depended on keeping the sights on the target, which was impossible if it could not be seen.

The squadron circled Boulogne, but were still unable to see the pens through the cloud. Mindful of his AOC's orders that these bombs were not to be wasted, Cheshire reluctantly broke radio silence, ordering everyone back to base. They were on their way back over Kent when they had a call to say that the weather was now clear over the pens to a height of 8,000ft, which was assessed as the minimum height from which to drop a Tallboy to build up sufficient velocity to penetrate the concrete roof. Cheshire's own part in the proceedings had to be altered when he saw what the Oboe Mosquitoes of 8 Group had done.

> We arrived over the primary (E-boat pens) Boulogne 1 minute before H-Hour and saw the red TI Oboe markers dropped by PFF for the No.1 Group attack – these appeared accurate. Weather did not permit of 617 Sqdn carrying out a visual bombing attack and it was impracticable to drop red spot fires in view of the colour of No.1 Group TIs, so returned to base at 2245, dropping bombs on a light flak position on the way out of the target area.

This referred to his aircraft's two 500-pounders and not that of the Tallboy force behind him. As at Le Havre, an Australian voice was heard over the air and although one of 617's crew members was initially thought to be the culprit he was later cleared of the blame. The bad weather meant that those aircraft of 617 that did bomb had to do so individually. Munro, who led them, assessed his bomb as falling some 150 yards south-east of the target. Clayton ran up to the target at 16,500ft but could not see it due to smoke. He then turned back out to sea and, after orbiting two or three times while diving to 8,000ft, came in again but received Cheshire's recall signal and turned back. He said afterwards that the conditions had not been suitable for visual bombing.

As Cheshire gave the order to return, a heavy explosion 1,000 yards east of the pens was seen by several crews. Wilson saw an R-boat blown out of the water by a Main Force bomb. Heavy flak brought down a 425 Sqdn Halifax and would come near to destroying one of 617's crews as well.

Flt Lt Malcolm 'Mac' Hamilton's crew had already done over twenty operations with 619 Sqdn before joining 617. On this date they were carrying an eighth man in the front turret – W/O Tom McLean, a very experienced gunner who had assisted in the destruction of several night fighters, and whose services Hamilton was glad to have. Hamilton's crew, the fifth of 617's aircraft to attack, followed Cheshire in a dive from 20,000ft to 8,000ft, beginning their bomb run twelve miles from the AP.

By now the gunners were flinging up a furious barrage. One shell burst beneath the Lancaster, smashing the hydraulics and cutting off the rear and mid-upper gunners from the rest of the crew. It also damaged the starboard flap. A second shell then struck one of the open bomb bay doors and tore off an engine nacelle, while a third caused the starboard wheel to drop. A fourth went clean through the starboard inner wing tank without exploding, but released four hundred gallons of fuel, which drenched the fuselage and the rear gunner. Tail damage also made the bomber difficult to fly straight and level.

Flg-Off Roland Duck, Hamilton's bomb aimer, who had somehow to concentrate on his duties in the face of all this, shouted, 'Bomb gone!' then asked his skipper to keep on course for a picture. As the aircraft's camera recorded the Tallboy's impact, another shell exploded, this time in the nose. Duck was blown part of the way up the steps into the cockpit as the nose perspex dissolved into fragments, letting in a tremendous draught which blew the navigator's charts into the air, accompanied by a sudden silver blizzard of Window.

Hamilton's intercom had now gone completely and when he looked down below his seat he could see the open air. Miraculously, McLean had survived without a scratch, but Duck had been hit in both legs by shrapnel and was bleeding badly. He felt only numbness until Flt Sgt Len Rooke, the flight engineer, tried to inject morphine. The sudden pain caused Duck's legs to thrash the air around him, kicking the controls and putting both the Lancaster's starboard engines out of action, so sending it into a violent dive. Hamilton knocked his legs away and got the aircraft back onto an even keel after restarting the engines.

By now they were running low on fuel, the nose damage had affected the 'feel' of the aircraft and, to add to Hamilton's troubles, the bomb doors could not be closed, leaving the two parts of the chain which had held the Tallboy hanging down to cause further drag. Although the W/T set still worked, allowing messages to be sent concerning their position, ditching was a possibility and their flight back across the Channel was a tense one, made even more so by some mysterious aircraft, one of which seemed to be on fire, overtaking them en route, but ignoring them and heading on towards London.

The stricken Lancaster was directed to the fighter base at RAF West Malling in Kent, but although the east-west runway there was lit, Hamilton was directed to land on the grass a hundred yards north of it. Just to make the landing even more interesting, there was no indication that his undercarriage had locked down, in which case it would fold up as soon as they touched the surface. An emergency CO_2 bottle was therefore used, which also gave them fifteen degrees of flap – half the usual amount.

At 2330 Hamilton came down on the grass, with his crew in crash positions behind the main spar and West Malling's crash crew in close attendance. After all that, he pulled off a smooth landing and the bomber stayed on its wheels, although West Mailing's erks were shocked when they saw the state of it. Duck was taken away in the ambulance and an officer explained to Hamilton that the runway had been needed for West Malling's fighters, who had been taking off to intercept the strange new aircraft that the crew had seen while coming back across the Channel.

The wounded bomb aimer was to see more of these as they passed over the hospital at East Grinstead in which he lay. His souvenir of this occasion was a NAAFI pint mug, containing twenty-seven pieces of shrapnel extracted from his legs. It had been a close call indeed, especially when gangrene made its appearance later on and amputation was considered. Roland Duck was spared this, thanks to the efforts of a top orthopaedic surgeon at Rauceby Hospital, a few miles from Woodhall Spa, Although he would later fly again, his days with Hamilton's crew were over. After several bone grafts, he would also be left with a permanent limp.

Over Boulogne at least seven more of 617's aircraft were hit by flak and Howard experienced the first of a string of release problems that were to dog the Tallboy aircraft for some time to come. His bomb hung-up on the first run and on making a second he released it manually. Afterwards, no trace of an armament or electrical fault was found. Someone else who may have suffered from the same problem was McCarthy, who commented afterwards, 'While on bombing run, thrown off course by heavy flak. Whilst again on bombing run, bomb was found to have been lost, but it is not known when.'

No allowances were made by Main Force aircraft for 617 and Knilans had to dive steeply to port to avoid several 1,000-pounders dumped blindly through the cloud. One of these narrowly missed his rear gunner's turret.

The bombing appeared concentrated, with several fires, but some sticks of Main Force bombs fell well out to sea. Poore's aircraft was hit repeatedly by flak, made a second run but was then ordered to return. Despite the weather Stout bombed from 18,500ft, observing, 'Difficult to assess results of bombing owing to cloud. Some bombs seen to fall close to red markers that were on the edge of the E-boat pens. Difficulties were accentuated by lack of daylight. In my opinion, an earlier attack would have been more successful.'

Including McCarthy's accidental release, twelve of 617's aircraft bombed from a variety of heights. The other ten brought their Tallboys back. A bomb plot compiled later showed an average error of 875 yards as far as eight of the Tallboys were concerned, the nearest to the pens probably falling in the water some seventy yards from them. The accompanying photograph indicates that damage to the pens was caused by this one. As at Le Havre, destruction had been caused by a tidal wave, which by undermining part of the front of the structure might well have achieved more than a direct hit on the roof would have done.

According to one account, over 130 E-boats had been sunk, along with thirteen other vessels wrecked or badly damaged. Oil storage tanks had also been burnt out – these may have been the cause of the large explosion that several crews witnessed. Much damage had been inflicted on the port, a large building having been destroyed by a Tallboy that had landed ninety-eight feet from it. From the French point of view this was the worst raid of the war on Boulogne, with heavy damage in the areas surrounding the port and the deaths of some 200 civilians.

This was not known to the 8 Group squadrons, who received a congratulatory signal from Bennett.

> The attacks on Le Havre and Boulogne succeeded in virtually destroying the entire German Naval Forces in these harbours. The proportion sunk, at least sixty, being remarkably high. For security reasons, not too much was made of this latest of air/sea victories, but crews can be satisfied that their efforts have altered the entire aspect of the naval war in the Channel.

Harris praised 617: 'If the Navy had done what you have done it would be a major naval victory.'

The result of these two raids was that the remnants of the French-based E-boat flotillas were forced to pull back to the Dutch port of Ijmuiden. In due course this too would receive the attention of 617.

The Boulogne E-boat pens after the Tallboy attack. The roof was up to eleven feet thick. (Imperial War Museum, neg. no. CL1225)

So far, this new wonder weapon seemed likely to sweep all before it, but what about other concrete buildings? On 17 June a Ministry of Home Security report made a plea for caution:

> It should never be forgotten that the purpose for which the Tallboy bombs were designed was to achieve deep penetration, followed by maximum cratering and earthshock effect. With this end in mind, the design envisages a high striking velocity, combined with the highest charge-weight ratio compatible with reasonable impact strength. It does not follow that the bomb should not be used to produce other effects (eg by direct hits on large and substantial buildings), but nevertheless the fact that Tallboy is primarily a cratering bomb should be borne in mind, particularly if there are not enough bombs available to deal with all the targets for which their use may be proposed.

The same report also commented that with regard to area attacks Tallboy had less effect than the 12,000lb or even the 8,000lb MC bomb, and that therefore it should not be used for such raids. This was as well, for Tallboy production was slow to start with and 617's limited stock might have been squandered to no great purpose. It also recommended that long-delay fuses should be used, which created a greater depth of explosion, so making repairs more difficult. If the bomb was to be used against concrete, a short type of, say, 0.01 seconds, could be used, but as Tallboy had not been designed for this purpose the results might prove disappointing.

One threat had been eliminated from this area, but another was now making itself known. As 229 Sqdn's Spitfires landed at RAF Detling in Kent, they witnessed an incident that showed that a new chapter in the air war had begun. A strange spluttering noise was heard from the sky, accompanied by a small black aircraft with a sheet of flame trailing out behind it. Maintaining a straight and level course, this sinister object flew on across the Kentish sky towards London. It was one of the strange aircraft that Hamilton's crew had seen while limping back over the Channel that evening.

Within the last three days the first of Hitler's 'revenge' weapons had made its debut. The bombing by 617 and other units of the Noball sites had brought about a delay in their deployment, but had not stopped them altogether. This was a V-1 flying bomb – probably the one that on this day skimmed over the roof of the National Liberal Club and the War Office to open a heavy attack on London. It was therefore hardly surprising that the next group of Tallboy targets would be a series of massive concrete bunkers in the Pas de Calais area.

6

Revenge Weapons

The moment might very quickly come for us to use a weapon with which we ourselves could not be attacked.

Adolf Hitler, Danzig, September 1939

On 16 June 1944 the Home Secretary, Herbert Morrison, announced a new German weapon and the *Evening Standard*'s headlines proclaimed, 'Pilotless Planes Now Raid Britain' … 'Counter-measures are vigorous.'

11 Group's fighters were now going into action over the Channel, shooting down the bombs or learning to turn them over with their wing tips. However, the best way to combat this new menace was to destroy it on the ground, either on its launching sites or in the buildings that had been erected for V-weapon use. It would be some time before the Anglo-Canadian 21st Army Group could move up to liberate this part of northern France, so in the meantime Tallboy would face a new test.

617 were ready, but the weather was not. Tom Bennett later said, 'Frustrated aircrews stood by in their flight offices throughout the day, waiting for the opportunity to open the campaign against these sites. Armourers had to lower Tallboys onto bomb-cradles, to ease the strain on the main spars of the aircraft, and be instantly ready to restore them to the bomb bays, should the word come through. Several times the alert was given, only to be scrubbed when later met information was provided. This stand-by lasted four days and precluded the usual bombing practice that lulls afforded the squadron crews.'

19 June 1944
Target The V-2 liquid oxygen plant at Watten.
Weather Cirrus on approach to target, then a patch of ten-tenths' cloud over it.

Force 18 Lancasters of 617 Sqdn:

LM482 'W' Sqdn Ldr J. C. McCarthy		ME555 'C' Flg-Off W. A. Duffy	
ME560 'H' Flt Lt B. W. Clayton		DV403 'G' Flg-Off M. Hamilton	
EE146 'K' Flt Lt J. A. Edward		DV402 'P' Flg-Off A. E. Kell	
ED763 'D' Flt Lt C. J. G. Howard		DV385 'A' Flg-Off R. E. Knights	
DV391 'O' Flt Lt A. F. Poore		ME561 'R' Lt H. C. Knilans USAAF	
ME557 'C' Flt Lt W. Reid		ME554 Flg-Off N. R. Ross	
EE131 'B' Flt Lt J. E. R. Williams		ME559 Flg-Off G. S. Stout	
DV380 'X' Flt Lt D. J. B. Wilson		DV393 'T' Flg-Off E. Willsher	
JB139 'V' Flg-Off D. H. Cheney		LM489 'L' P/O J. Gingles	

Two 617 Sqdn Mosquitoes as marker aircraft:
NS993 'N' Wg Cdr G. L. Cheshire and Flg-Off P. Kelly
DZ421   Sqdn Ldr D. J. Shannon and Flg-Off L. J. Sumpter

3 Mosquitoes of 105 Sqdn and 6 from 109 also acted as markers. 9 Sqdn's Lancasters, with conventional bombs, had also been ordered to attack Watten, but for some reason they were recalled an hour after take-off.

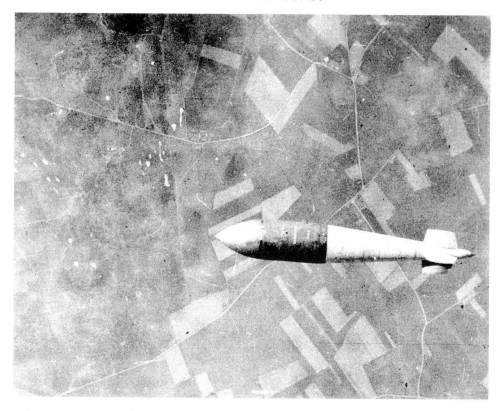

A Tallboy just after release over a Continental target. This was reputedly taken on 19 June, which if correct means it was during the first of 617's attacks on Watten. (Imperial War Museum, neg. no. CH15380)

Escort 47 AEAF Spitfire IXs:
   33 Sqdn RAF   80 Sqdn RAF
   74 Sqdn RAF   127 Sqdn RAF

Bomb Loads Each Lancaster carried one Tallboy, with an 11-second delay. The Mosquitoes carried two red spot fires and two 500lb bombs each.

The planning of launching bunkers for the V-1 and the V-2 long-range rocket had begun in the autumn of 1942. In the last week of December officers and engineers from the V-weapons test site at Peenemünde had toured north-eastern France looking for suitable sites. One was in a quarry near Wizernes and the other in a wood, the Forêt d'Eperlecques, near the village of Watten. Both were in the Pas de Calais.

During 1943 some 6,000 *Organization Todt* labourers began work in the forest near Watten, the site's German cover name being the 'North Western Power Plant'. The locals apparently believed that it would be a power station, which makes them seem gullible now, but who amongst them at that time would have credited the idea of a giant bombproof building to fire supersonic rockets from? Even science fiction had hardly gone that far.

The original German plan was that after completion the site would fire up to thirty-six V-2s a day at London. A railway line would run through the building from east to west, through a hall that was originally intended to be 82ft high, although this was later raised by ten feet to be above the water table. Liquid oxygen, which was part of the rocket's fuel, would be manufactured on the north side and completed V-2s fired after emerging from the south side.

Protection to the hall would be given by a massive door, over 7 feet thick and filled with 215 tons of concrete. Air spaces were included in the roof to trap bombs and contain the blast from them; a technique similar to that used on the U-boat pens. This will be described in more detail later.

Briefed to be on the alert for just this sort of activity, the PRU began coverage in May 1943. Near Watten excavations were noted at the base of a hill, with the spoil being removed by a network of light railways. A building measuring 460ft by 330ft was under construction, being serviced by a line that branched off the main railway between Calais and St Omer. Its purpose was as yet unknown to the Allies, but in the wake of the Peenemünde attack it was thought likely to be intended for secret weapon use.

Sir Malcolm McAlpine, of the famous civil engineering firm, had been asked for his advice, which was succinct; bomb the construction after the concrete had been poured but before it had had time to set. The US 8th Air Force had done so, and on seeing the damage photographs afterwards Sir Malcolm had commented that the Germans would be better off starting again elsewhere. Faced with a rigid mess of steel reinforcing rods and cement, the *Organization Todt* engineer in charge came to the same conclusion in August 1943.

This did not mean that Watten would be given up completely. By January 1944 the site had been cleared, with the exception of the original liquid oxygen plant, which had been abandoned after only its first two storeys had been completed. New stronger buildings had been erected on the southern part of the foundations of the earlier structures. The Germans had decided to give the site over entirely to the manufacture of liquid oxygen, which would fuel V-2s for launching elsewhere. Fifteen-ton railway wagons would be used, supplying up to three V-2s each.

As further protection against bombing a new construction technique, called *Verbunkerung*, was now in use at several V-weapon sites in this area. The idea was to give the Allies as little to bomb as possible, so at Watten the Germans cast the new building's roof first, then jacked it up and continued building underneath; no mean feat as some of the roof sections weighed 3,000 tons. Nearby was a supply dump that held parts for this and other V-weapon sites.

The target, vaguely described in 617's ORB as 'a constructional works' was on the south-eastern fringe of the forest, one mile from Watten and six from St Omer. Despite the cloud over it, 617 attacked as intended in the early evening, their gaggle spread between 15,500-18,000ft to meet heavy flak. Cheshire and Shannon marked it with their loads, but the spot fires failed to ignite so the bomber force, led by McCarthy, marked it visually, although according to 105 Sqdn the bombing was done on the glow of their TIs, which were accurately dropped. Two of the Mosquitoes, one each from 105 and 109, failed to mark due to technical problems.

The Lancaster crews did not see the results, although Shannon, flying at low level, reported several hits on and around the construction site. They did not expect the Tallboys to penetrate this roof, although there was a report that one had left blast marks there when it was thought to have broken up after impact.

617 were lucky to make any impression on the target at all, for during this attack a whole crop of release problems came to light. Wilson released his bomb manually after a hang-up, Ross blamed an overshoot due to a need to do the same on his second run and Howard brought his back, unable to release it at all. Particularly alarming was the experience of Knilans, whose bomb failed to release when required, then fell away on its own twenty seconds after all the switches had been returned to 'safe'.

Reg Firman, the Vickers representative at Woodhall Spa, who, as we have seen, was answerable directly to Wallis, now faced a frustrating task. Of the four aircraft he checked, in only one case could a definite fault be found. Howard's Lancaster was also looked over by two staff from Boscombe Down, who could only suggest that some maladjustment of the linkage had been caused by an undersize bomb, causing friction at the release hooks.

Apart from all this, 617's bombing had not been up to the standard previously set. Tom Bennett later attributed this to their not being able to practise and the tedium of the last few days. Watten still stood and the MPI error was 160 yards. The nearest ones to the main building had gone off 75ft and 100ft away from it, but there was no visual structural damage. One obliterated a flak position south of the forest and three others blocked railway lines in the area, but two of these were made good during the following fortnight. There was definitely unfinished business here, but it would be over a month before 617 would return.

On 20 June, seventeen Lancasters and three Mosquitoes of 617, with escort, went to the V-2 launching bunker at Wizernes with Tallboys. They were unable to bomb due to ten-tenths' cloud over the target and were recalled just before reaching the French coast near Gravelines. All aircraft returned safely, although two of 332 Sqdn's Spitfires livened up the proceedings by shooting down a V-1 on the way back.

Wizernes had been earmarked for V-2 storage and launching at the same time as Watten, and following the damage due by the 8th Air Force to that site it became even more important. Situated in a quarry alongside a main road and railway near the village from which it took its name, the usual spur line and sidings had already been constructed.

The plan, which had been agreed in September 1943 by Hitler, Speer and Xavier Dorsch, chief engineer of the *Organization Todt*, was to use an adaptation of the *Verbunkerung* technique to build a one-million-ton concrete dome, then a network of tunnels, over four miles in total, in the hillside beneath it. These would lead to two giant doors, each high enough to pass a V-2 through after it had been erected ready for launching.

Starting in November 1943, a tunnel, level with the floor of the existing quarry, was driven into its face. Just over 4m wide and 5m high, it housed a standard gauge line and was concrete-lined for 150 metres in from its entrance. By the time of the site's capture a pilot tunnel had been driven onward from this, as had eight side galleries, one of which housed a 600hp diesel generator for lighting. The others were intended as offices, workshops, or storage for the construction plant.

Some earth had been removed from beneath the three-metre-thick dome, which was 50m in diameter. There was another concrete-lined tunnel in the cliff face, although this would later be rendered inaccessible by bombing. As if all this was not enough, there was a nine-metre square concrete strongpoint on top of the quarry, possibly intended as an observation and defence point.

It may now be said that Wizernes was a prototype for the post-war nuclear ballistic missile silos, and the Americans would certainly have seen it as such. Rockets were to be brought to the site on railway wagons, which would enter the quarry and the tunnels. They would be assembled, fuelled, then made ready in what was thought to be complete safety beneath the dome and a hundred-foot high chalk hill. Then they would be trundled back out through the doorways to be fired at London and other targets, at an intended rate of fifty a day. The rocket would be vulnerable to return fire only for the short period that it stood outside before firing.

If the V-1 was a heart-stopping weapon, the V-2 was a frighteningly advanced design. With a range of 260 kilometres, the first would be launched from Holland to fall on Chiswick, in west London, the following September. Those on the receiving end would have cause to be thankful for the fact that over half would blow up en route and that the rest would bury themselves in the ground without the same blast effect as the V-1.

However, once it was safely launched the V-2 would prove to be unstoppable. Radar stations could track it just after it had left the ground, but as it travelled through the stratosphere at supersonic speed it could not be seen or heard, making interception impossible. The V-2's arrival would be announced by a loud double bang, followed by a noise in the sky like a faraway express train. The only answer was to bomb any site thought to be connected with it, which Wizernes certainly was. Raids on it began in March 1944, but construction continued.

It was during June that a letter was sent from Bomber Command to 5 Group:

For your information it has been ascertained that the Tallboy bomb should come to rest in about 0.125 of a second when dropped from about 18,000 feet into average soil. For maximum crater and earth shock effect, the bomb should not only be allowed to come to rest but should also remain there for sufficient time to allow the debris from the entry hole to fall back and cause a good tamping effect. Furthermore, at the end of its passage the bomb is apt to turn in the vertical plane and time is required for the debris on the radius of this turn to cavitate and give more effective tamping. Eleven seconds' fusing is therefore recommended on dry targets to obtain maximum possible confinement of the charge.

The letter went on to recommend 0.5 seconds for maximum disturbance under water fifty feet deep and 0.1 seconds for maximum damage on a very hard target. This was to prove significant later.

As a further refinement, fitting a modified Tallboy tail unit with a No.47 pistol would give a half-hour delay. A No.58 was normally used to arm the bomb, but the fitting of a No.47 as well would not affect this. The modified tails would be supplied by the aviation company Short Brothers of Rochester in Kent, starting from the middle of July.

On 21 June Wizernes was again the target for 617, but this raid was cancelled an hour before take-off. The reason was not given but was probably bad weather.

It was on 22 June that a new aircraft type came to Woodhall Spa. Cheshire had made use of the old boy net, resulting in the arrival of two North American Mustang IIIs. Once the erks had assembled one of them, he would use it as a marker aircraft in addition to 617's Mosquitoes.

On this day 617 headed for Wizernes, but again due to cloud cover they were recalled en route.

24 June 1944
Target The V-2 launching bunker at Wizernes.
Weather Clear weather and excellent visibility at target.

Force 16 Lancasters of 617 Sqdn:

ME559 'Y'	Sqdn Ldr J. C. McCarthy		DV380 'X'	Flt Lt D. J. B. Wilson
LM482 'W'	Sqdn Ldr J. L. Munro		JB139 'V'	Flg-Off D. H. Cheney
ME560 'H'	Flt Lt B. W. Clayton		DV402 'P'	Flg-Off A. E. Kell
DV403 'G'	Flt Lt J. A. Edward		DV385 'A'	Flg-Off R. E. Knight
ED763 'D'	Flt Lt C. J. G. Howard		ME561 'R'	Flg-Off N. R. Ross
DV391 'O'	Flt Lt A. F. Poore		ME554	Flg-Off R. M. Stanford
EE131 'B'	Flt Lt J. E. R. Williams		DV393 'T'	Flg-Off E. Willsher
ME557 'C'	Flt Lt W. Reid		LM489 'L'	P/O J. Gingles

Two 617 Sqdn Mosquitoes as marker aircraft:
NS993 'N' Wg Cdr G. L. Cheshire and Flg-Off P. Kelly
DZ415 Flt Lt G. E. Fawke and (probably) Flg-Off T. A. Bennett

617 were part of 321 aircraft of 1, 4, 5, 6 and 8 Groups to three V-weapons sites, all of which were accurately bombed for the total loss of five Lancasters. They were the only squadron to attack Wizernes on this date.

Escort Spitfire VIIs and IXs covered all three raids:

74 Sqdn RAF	131 Sqdn RAF	329 Sqdn (Free French)
80 Sqdn RAF	229 Sqdn RAF	340 Sqdn (Free French)
124 Sqdn RAF	274 Sqdn RAF	341 Sqdn (Free French)
127 Sqdn RAF		616 Sqdn R Aux AF

Bomb Loads Each 617 Sqdn Lancaster carried one Tallboy, with an 11-second delay. Both Mosquitoes carried four smoke bombs and two red spot fires each.

This time the weather co-operated, at least at Wizernes, but as Cheshire dived his load failed to release, so Fawke dropped his smoke bombs as an area marker instead. His Mosquito was hit several times by flak, as were four Lancasters, one of them flown by Munro.

One of them did not come back. Flt Lt Edward's port wing caught fire and his aircraft began to lose height, slowly at first, but then went out of control and blew up before it hit the ground at the village of Leulinghem, near St Omer. Edward had carried a mid-under gunner as well, which made eight men in all, four of whom jumped and were taken prisoner, though one died from his injuries soon afterwards. This was 617's first loss since a raid on Munich the previous April and it was keenly felt. It appeared that Edward's crew dropped their bomb as sixteen hits were reported.

The bombing was concentrated, although smoke quickly obscured the site, forcing Kell to do two runs and Poore three. Howard said four bombs, including his own, burst within 100 yards of the AP and Reid claimed three went off fifty yards from the mouth of one of the tunnels. He also said that just before they dropped their own bomb another had penetrated the ground above the tunnel mouth, causing the ground to lift and erupt.

The mean point of impact was 188 yards from the AP and the average radial error of the Tallboys was 241 yards. The three nearest to the target were probably those dropped by Cheney, Howard and Wilson. Damage had been caused to the domed roof and to installations on it. A hit at the top had caused a big landslide, completely blocking the railway track and the southern tunnel entrance, while other bombs had destroyed secondary installations in the vicinity. Impressive though this all looked, none of it was decisive and work at Wizernes continued.

25 June 1944
Target The V-1 launching bunker at Siracourt.
Weather Clear.

Force 17 Lancasters of 617 Sqdn:

ME559 'Y' Sqdn Ldr J. C. McCarthy		EE146 'K' Flg-Off T. A. Carey
LM482 'W' Sqdn Ldr J. L. Munro		DV402 'P' Flg-Off A. E. Kell
ME560 'H' Flt Lt B. W. Clayton		DV385 'A' Flg-Off R. E. Knights
ED763 'D' Flt Lt C. J. G. Howard		JB139 'V' Flg-Off W. R. Lee
ME554 Flt Lt R. S. D. Kearns		ME561 'R' Flg-Off N. R. Ross
DV380 'X' Flt Lt A. F. Poore		ME555 'C' Flg-Off R. M. Stanford
ME557 'C' Flt Lt W. Reid		DV393 'T' Flg-Off E. Willsher
EE131 'B' Flt Lt J. E. R. Williams		LM489 'L' P/O J. Gingles
LM485 'N' Flt Lt D. J. B. Wilson		

Two Mosquitoes and one Mustang of 617 Sqdn as marker aircraft:
Either HB825 or HB837 Wg Cdr G. L. Cheshire.
NT205 'L' Sqdn Ldr D. J. Shannon and Flg-Off L. J. Sumpter
NT202 'N' Flt Lt G. E. Fawke and Flg-Off T. A. Bennett

This was part of a force of 323 aircraft of 1,4,6 and 8 Groups that accurately attacked three V-weapons sites. Three 4 Group Halifaxes were lost.

Escort Spitfire IXs covered all three raids:

33 Sqdn RAF	222 Sqdn RAF
74 Sqdn RAF	331 Sqdn (Norwegian)
127 Sqdn RAF	332 Sqdn (Norwegian)

Bomb Loads Each 617 Sqdn Lancaster carried one Tallboy, with an 11-second delay. The Mustang carried two red spot fires under its wings, while the two Mosquitoes carried four smoke bombs and two red spot fires each.

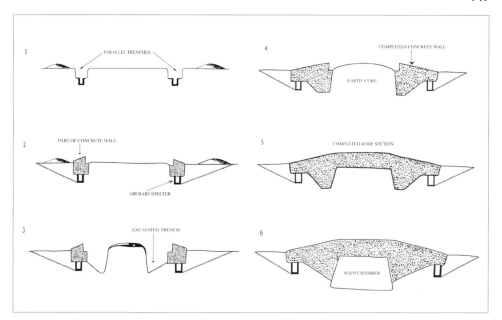

The *Verbunkerung* process as applied to the Siracourt bunker, shown in its six stages. (Julie Anne Hudson)

Three miles west-south-west of St Pol-sur-Ternoise in the Pas de Calais, this long low rectangular concrete building had been designed from the outset as a launching bunker, again using the *Verbunkerung* method of building. Two long parallel trenches would be dug, which although not especially conspicuous, were nevertheless picked up by the alert PRU interpreters at Medmenham. These would later serve as air-raid shelters for the workforce. The concrete walls of the building would be added and further trenches excavated in the ground to provide space in which to thicken them. The roof would then be built, after which the interior would be dug out.

All this showed that while the Germans now acknowledged that the site would be spotted and attacked, the initial stages of building would give very little to bomb, so ruling out the USAAF's technique of bombing wet concrete that had caused so many problems at Watten in 1943. The Siracourt bunker's roof could be built in stages, for the same reason. Once completed it would give overhead protection while the interior was being excavated and equipped. It would also emerge later that the Germans had given thought to protecting it from the sides as well.

The structure was 180m long and 15m wide, making it a long, narrow target that would be difficult to hit. Even if it was, the roof was 3.5m thick, which its builders judged to be bombproof.

Railway wagons would transport V-1s to the south end of the building. After preparation beneath the roof, they would be brought wingless through a side doorway onto a firing ramp mounted on earth, aimed slightly west of magnetic north. Since the doorway was a potential weakness if a bomb landed alongside, an I-section girder had been fitted inside the roof at this point, from which it was intended to hang a sliding steel door. Four-metre-thick wing walls and a concrete roof would have given additional protection to the doorway, but as things turned out these were never built. Bringing the bombs out without their wings meant that the doorway's width could be kept to a minimum of just over seven metres. Should any blast enter, it would be further limited by an internal wall.

Once their wings had been fitted the V-1s could be fired at London, which was just 130 miles away. The intended rate of fire was two an hour. Although the ramp could be bombed, any damaged parts could just as easily be replaced.

As previously mentioned, the discovery of the ski sites during the autumn of 1943 had led to their bombing by the Allies, causing them to be abandoned by the Germans in favour of what were dubbed 'modified' sites. These were less obvious ramps concealed in woodland, from which the V-1s were now being fired.

It had also been during October 1943 that new railway spur lines, as well as the parallel trenches, had attracted the eyes of the PRU's interpreters to Siracourt. They also noted a stores dump, a light railway and a standard gauge track bed being laid. As Siracourt's construction had been started a month before PRU coverage of the ski sites began it was assumed to be related to them, although as far as 617 were concerned it was simply a 'construction works'.

The building's narrow width and low height ruled out any involvement with the V-2, quite apart from the fact that the nearby lanes were unsuited to the heavy traffic that the rocket would have needed to bring it to this site. Further proof of this came after liberation, when it was also found that the bunker lacked the handling facilities, such as beams in the roof, which would have been necessary.

During April and May 1944, conventional bombing had resulted in much cratering of the surrounding landscape, but further PRU coverage showed that the work had continued. Not only was the bunker hardly touched, the houses in the nearby village still stood despite numerous impacts around them.

Cheshire's new marker aircraft, one of the two Mustangs passed to the squadron a few days before, turned out to be something of a mixed blessing for both him and 617's erks. The fighter had arrived in a packing case, with the need to have grease cleaned off before it could be assembled and the two spot fires fitted to the racks beneath its wings.

For Cheshire it meant flying a single-engined aircraft for the first time in three years and such was the pressure that there was no time even for a local 'circuit and bump'. His first flight in it would be an operational one, taking off nearly an hour after the Lancasters had left Woodhall Spa, although the fighter's speed was such that he caught them up on the way.

This was an early morning attack and Cheshire dived the Mustang from 7,000ft to 500ft through accurate heavy flak to drop his spot fires, followed by Shannon. This was evidently considered enough as Fawke's load was not required. The AP was easily identified and Willsher was the first to bomb, his Tallboy falling about fifty yards south of it.

Munro did not observe his own bomb, but saw the impact of several others: '[I] saw the two slit trenches very clearly and two direct hits on them.' He also saw three hits 'on the southern end. A large explosion occurred at the south-east end of the trenches at 0905.' This was Willsher's bomb.

Clayton saw twelve bombs burst close to the AP – four of them very close – and later commented, 'From what we saw, the concentration should have been even better than on the last two attacks.' Some crews saw three bombs falling at the same time, two of which were direct hits and the third a slight undershoot.

Lee was hit by flak, then his bomb hung-up despite three runs, so, rather than risk it fall off on landing, he jettisoned it over the Channel on his return. Reid and Howard both had the same thing happen, so each released his bomb on his second run. Howard's aircraft was by now becoming something of a persistent offender in this respect. Reg Firman later examined Reid's and Lee's aircraft, but the cause was described as remaining obscure.

When the smoke had cleared there appeared to have been one direct hit which had penetrated the sixteen-foot-thick roof and caused a large explosion, one hit by the western wall of the building, blowing the wall in and one very near miss, with the rim of the crater up against the western wall. Several bombs had also fallen on the eastern side of the building.

617 turned for home, confident that another job had been well done. Cheshire's on-the-job training continued on the way home, as he ranged up alongside Fawke's Mosquito to calibrate some instruments against checks supplied to him by its pilot. All this was in readiness for his first landing in his new aircraft.

The Tallboy damage at the side of the bunker, photographed in 1996. (S. Flower)

The story that Cheshire had to land his Mustang in the dark is not supported by the ORB, which shows him as being the first to reach home – safely – at 1018. The rest of the squadron followed him some twenty-five minutes later. After landing the aircraft were quickly made ready for another operation 'which did not materialize'. 617 were stood down until the following day, though as things turned out there would be no more operations for them until the first week in July.

In January 1945 the British Bombing Research Mission sent out a party to check on a number of the targets that had been hit by the earthquake and other bombs. They reported that Siracourt was still being built when it was attacked, that the earth beneath the roof had not yet been fully excavated and that only two Tallboys had fallen close enough to have any effect on the main structure. One had struck the roof, while damage caused by the other had been confined to disrupting a burster slab on the target's northern side.

These slabs ran parallel with the building's outer walls, acting as blast walls on each side, tapering from twelve feet in thickness at the bottom to nine feet at the top. They were not continuous, but ran in lengths of fifty to sixty feet. Since their foundations were as deep as the walls were high, it appeared that the Germans had anticipated not only blast at ground level, but also the undermining effect a near miss from a large bomb would have.

The hit on the roof had blasted an oval crater, 34ft by 29ft, leaving a perforation hole, 4ft by 2ft, in the ceiling below. The Tallboy had penetrated only half way through the roof, leaving its explosion to break up the remaining eight feet of concrete. Its nose, propelled forward by the explosion, forced its way into the interior and a fragment of it was later found. An absence of fragmentation on the interior walls clearly showed that the Tallboy had not gone off inside the structure.

Despite this roof hit the report commented, 'Clearly the building itself is practically untouched and has suffered no loss of usefulness whatsoever … It is clear that the bomb was at about the limiting distance for appreciable interior damage. The operational effects of it cannot have been serious, even if the structure had been in full use.'

Like other V-weapon constructions, the Siracourt bunker survives to this day, derelict in a field and still showing signs of Tallboy damage. From a 1996 visit, I can confirm the hit at the side of the building, close to the ramp doorway, but although a Tallboy did penetrate the 16ft-thick-roof, leaving a crater that was later photographed from both the ground and the air, this was expertly repaired by the French after the war. Why they should do so remains a mystery. Today the only obvious, and minor, damage on the roof is to one of three large concrete blocks on it. The area around the field in which the bunker lies has since been built up and no trace of the craters, railway lines or ramp can now be seen.

Although the bunker survived, the results achieved by Tallboy at the time certainly impressed two American Eighth Air Force headquarters officers who inspected the site, after liberation, on 28 September, confirming the hit on the roof. Both were bomb and fuse specialists, but they had never seen Tallboy craters before. In civilian life one was an architect and the other a structural engineer, so they fully appreciated what had occurred. The bomb had landed almost exactly on the centre of the long vault below. Had it landed over the thick foundation wall there might have been nothing more than a deep crater.

Siracourt was again the target on 31 July 1944, but this time by four B-24 Liberator Groups of the 8th Air Force's 2nd Bombardment Division. Someone above them had not yet grasped that a large number of smaller GP bombs were no substitute for Tallboy hits. No less than 212 tons of bombs were dropped, but most fell in the fields around the north side of the building and nothing vital was hit. It was still not the end of the matter, for 617 would return at the beginning of August.

Cheshire's Mustang had proved itself on this raid, although that did not prevent 5 Group's Chief Engineer from moaning about the serviceability problems that it caused. Could a Spitfire not be used instead? His complaint fell on deaf ears, for 5 Group had other problems, one of them being that despite an increased output of seventeen Tallboys a week, by 26 June the stock of filled bombs had fallen to four. Not until the end of August would the supply situation improve sufficiently for 9 Sqdn to change their role.

4 July 1944
Target The V-1 storage dump at St Leu d'Esserent.
Weather Clear weather, with good visibility.

Force 17 Lancasters of 617 Sqdn:

LM492 'Q' Sqdn Ldr J. C. McCarthy	ME561 'R' Lt H. C. Knilans USAAF
LM482 'W' Sqdn Ldr J. L. Munro	JB139 'V' Flg-Off W. R. Lee
ME557 'S' Flt Lt C. J. G. Howard	ME559 'Y' Flg-Off G. S. Stout
DV391 'O' Flt Lt A. F. Poore	ED763 'D' Flg-Off F. H. A. Watts
ME562 'Z' Flt Lt H. J. Pryor	DV393 'T' Flg-Off E. Willsher
EE131 'B' Flt Lt J. E. R. Williams	LM489 'L' P/O J. Gingles
LM485 'N' Flt Lt D. J. B. Wilson	ME560 'H' P/O I. S. Ross
ME555 'C' Flg-Off W. A. Duffy	DV385 'A' P/O J. A. Sanders
DV402 'P' Flg-Off A. E. Kell	

One 617 Sqdn Mosquito and one Mustang as marker aircraft:
Either HB825 or HB837 Wg Cdr G. L. Cheshire.
NT205 'L' Flt Lt G. E. Fawke and Flg-Off T. A. Bennett

In addition to this raid there was a Main Force one by 4, 6 and 8 Groups on three V-weapon launching sites. There was some cloud but at least two of the attacks were rated as accurate, with no aircraft losses by these three Groups on this date. Immediately after this attack there was another on St Leu d'Esserent by 231 Lancasters and fifteen Mosquitoes of 5 Group, with some PFF assistance. This was classed as a night raid, with thirteen Lancasters being lost to night fighter attacks. Also during the night 1, 6 and 8 Groups attacked two French railway yards, losing fifteen Lancasters.

Escort Support was given to all these raids by 100 Group's *Serrate*-equipped Mosquitoes, with ECM support by *Mandrel* aircraft and 8 *Airborne Cigar* Lancasters of 1 Group's 101 Sqdn. One of 100 Group's Halifaxes was lost.

Bomb Loads Each 617 Sqdn Lancaster carried one Tallboy, with an ll-second delay. Cheshire's Mustang carried two red spot fires. Fawke's Mosquito probably had a similar load, but this time he was not called on to mark the target.

This target was a series of large caves in the Creil area, twenty-six miles north-east of Paris, with three entrances, two on the south-western side, near the town from which it took its name, and one on the north side near Thiverny. The area consisted of flat-topped downland, up to eighty-five metres at its summit, with steep slopes that descended to the river Oise and its tributary, the Therain. A main road and railway ran along the foot of the slope, on the south side of the target, with a marshalling yard on its south-eastern side.

The caves had been used pre-war by French farmers to grow mushrooms in, but now housed V-1s, whose owners had made good use of natural and artificial protection for them. The roof was some twenty-five feet thick, consisting of ten feet of clay over fifteen feet of limestone. The caves had been enlarged and reinforced by linings of concrete up to five feet thick, their entrances being fitted with steel doors.

617's raid would be a night one, immediately preceding a three-wave attack on the same target by 5 Group, who would deploy their force against two APs to the east and west of the target, with Pathfinder assistance. Most aircraft were to attack the eastern AP with 1,000lb bombs to cut the communications to the site, with 617 going for the western one.

The plan was that marking was to be carried out after 97 had dropped flares, the marking being by the Controller, or his Deputy, with two red spot fires. If this was accurate 627 Sqdn's Mosquitoes were to back it up with green and red TIs, followed by more spot fires. If the markers were inaccurate they were to be cancelled by a yellow marker by the Controller, his deputy or a Main Force aircraft, then remarking was to be carried out. One of 627's crews was also to film the attack; a role they would frequently carry out with 617 during the daylight raids to come.

100 Group's support was needed, for there was much night fighter and searchlight activity from the French coast onwards. TIs, followed by flares, were accurately dropped by some of the eleven of 627's Mosquitoes that took part. Cheshire then marked his AP in a dive to 500ft, but did not see what he had dropped and anyway was unable to communicate as his VHF radio was out of action. However, his marking was judged accurate by 617's crews, so much so that Fawke did not back it up.

Sanders was unable to bomb due to failed switchgear. He was also attacked by a Ju 88, but combined fire from his rear and mid-upper gunners brought it down. Only eight Tallboys were dropped as Cheshire's two spot fires were obscured during the attack, possibly by Knilans, who said his bomb burst on them. However, this may have been due to the Main Force marking at the other AP, which spread over some 600 yards, leading three of 617's crews to take their AP's position from it. The remainder, no longer able to identify their AP, brought their bombs back.

At the eastern AP, 97 Sqdn sent eleven Lancasters, who illuminated it in three waves with clusters of flares. Wg Cdr J. A. Ingham, 97's CO and Controller on this night, handed over to his deputy, Sqdn Ldr H. B. Locke, after his aircraft sustained damage in its port wing from a night fighter's attack. There was some intense heavy flak over the target, but it was not as bad as had been anticipated.

Although there was a tendency for the initial marking to drift to the north-north-east, Locke assessed it as accurate and backed it up with red TIs from 627. These formed a concentration to the east of the MP. Yellow and green TIs were also dropped by Mosquitoes of 105 and 109 Sqdns, the greens falling some distance to the north of the reds. 97 then backed these up, with the 600-yard spread of markers noted above. Locke then ordered in the Main Force, who could hardly miss such a well-marked target. 'Some accurate bombing then ensued. The whole attack went smoothly and according to plan, though no spectacular results were seen.'

The fighter attacks continued over the target and did not abate until some twenty miles off the French coast, by which time thirteen Lancasters had been shot down.

All of these came from 5 Group and had been involved in the St Leu d'Esserent raid. Several of 97's aircraft were attacked and some sustained damage, though all returned safely, one of them shooting down a Messerschmitt 410.

Both attacks were successful, burying the V-1s under tons of earth and limestone. A 105 Sqdn pilot had seen one of 617's Tallboys score a direct hit on a cave entrance, causing a large subsidence. A near miss had also helped to render this entrance useless and the railway line had been destroyed.

5 Group raided this site again on the night of 7/8 July and it would receive a further visit on 15 August. Later PRU coverage revealed three concentrations of Tallboy craters at three main entrances to the caves, as well as two more craters over them. Roadways into the site had also been blocked by Main Force bombing, despite an attempt by the Germans to clear a path down the hill on the north side.

After the area had been liberated Harris visited it and saw the mess for himself. On asking a small boy what the smell was, he received the reply that eight hundred Germans had been trapped in the caves. What they had probably thought a refuge had become their mass grave.

6 July 1944
Target The V-3 long-range gun site at Marquise/Mimoyecques.
Weather Good, with excellent visibility.

Force 17 Lancasters of 617 Sqdn:

LM482 'W' Sqdn Ldr J. L. Munro		JB139 'V' Flg-Off W. R. Lee
DV380 'X' Flt Lt A. W. Fearn		EE131 'B' Flg-Off E. M. Stanford
ED763 'D' Flt Lt C. J. G. Howard		ME559 'Y' Flg-Off G. S. Stout
DV391 'Q' Flt Lt A. F. Poore		ME557 'S' Flg-Off F. H. A. Watts
DV385 'A' Flt Lt H. J. Pryor		DV393 'T' Flg-Off E. Willsher
LM485 'N' Flt Lt D. J. B. Wilson		EE146 'K' P/O J. Gingles
ME555 'C' Flg-Off W. A. Duffy		LM560 'H' P/O I. S. Ross
DV402 'P' Flg-Off A. E. Kell		ME562 'Z' P/O N. R. Ross
ME561 'R' Lt H. C. Knilans USAAF		

One 617 Sqdn Mosquito, this time apparently for flak suppression:
NT205 'L' Flt Lt G. E. Fawke and Flg-Off T. A. Bennett

One 617 Sqdn Mustang as a marker aircraft:
Either HB825 or HB837 Wg Cdr G. L. Cheshire.

This afternoon raid was preceded by a morning Main Force attack on four V-weapon sites, one of which was Mimoyecques. These four raids involved a total of 532 aircraft. Five Halifaxes and one Lancaster were lost.

Escort 35 Spitfire IXs of 11 Group's Czech Wing as escort to Mimoyecques, while 24 Free French Spitfire IXs swept the Lille-Peronne area:

310 Sqdn (Czech)	340 Sqdn (Free French)
312 Sqdn (Czech)	341 Sqdn (Free French)
313 Sqdn (Czech)	

Bomb Loads Each 617 Sqdn Lancaster carried one Tallboy, with an 11-second delay. Fawke's Mosquito carried two 500lb MC bombs and Cheshire's Mustang two red TIs.

The target was the sole V-3 long-range gun site – a weapon now almost forgotten as it never went into action. In May 1943 Speer had revealed to Hitler details of an experimental long-range gun. This was not a new idea, as Parisians had been shelled by 'Big Bertha' during the First World War. However, the V-3, it was claimed, would not suffer from the same violent explosions and consequent rapid barrel wear. It was to have a smooth-bored barrel 400ft long, featuring a series of branches in which small charges would be fired electrically in sequence to gradually accelerate a six-inch finned shell. Firing tests were not conclusive, but, like all futuristic-looking weapons, the project appealed to Hitler and he ordered maximum support to be given to it.

As with the other V-weapon sites, it was railway construction that led to the PRU discovering this one in September 1943. Their attention had been drawn to the building of two new parallel railway tunnels, each approximately 2,000ft long, running south-west to north-east a mile apart at stone quarries on high ground in the Pas de Calais.

This site was near the village of Marquise, nine miles north-east of Boulogne, ten miles south-west of Calais and ninety-five miles from London. The spur line that ran into the workings came from the main railway to Boulogne, which snaked through the countryside in a south-westerly direction from Calais. One of these had been built on a large spoil heap, which was additional evidence of the extensive work going on there. Buildings, transporters and conveyors were all in evidence, as were two railway turntables that had been ineffectively camouflaged. Those who were building it were billeted in the villages of Wadenthun and La Rocherie, some two miles north and north-east of the site. The ground over the tunnels was chalk and limestone, with a narrow belt of clay. Although the ground rose, so did the tunnels, giving a maximum thickness above them of forty feet.

Further coverage during October showed evidence of shafts being sunk from the hilltop, despite attempts to hide them with false haystacks. In November the US Ninth Air Force bombed the site, causing the western tunnel to be abandoned, but work on the eastern one continued despite two Main Force raids during March 1944.

By May firing tests of the finned shells had established a range of fifty miles and the Germans hoped to have the site working by July, with a possible rate of fire of twenty-five shells every five minutes. In addition to the long inclined gun shafts, a deep and elaborate network of tunnels in three layers had been provided, over half of which had been lined with concrete. The top layer's tunnels were 200ft across and around 100ft below ground.

For protection against bombing, an enormous 18ft-thick slab of concrete had also been cast to cover three of the five gun shafts on the hilltop. Stored in another nearby quarry were a quantity of eight-inch-thick steel plates, which were intended to cover the gun slots, each plate having five one-foot holes for the barrels. These were all that would appear above ground; an arrangement that the Germans anticipated would give the guns and their detachments immunity from bombing. Further steel doors and plating were held in the supply dump at Watten, but as things turned out these would never be delivered.

H-Hour was 1530, making this an afternoon attack for 617. Cheshire dived to 800ft to accurately drop his TIs, only to find these did not show up well in daylight despite weather conditions that Pryor later described as 'perfect'.

Fawke dropped his bombs on a gun battery, but this was not enough to stop heavy flak from meeting the Lancasters as Munro led them in. Three were hit, wounding three members of Lee's crew and causing some damage to all four of his engines. Not surprisingly, Lee had trouble identifying the target and jettisoned his Tallboy into the Channel on the way home. Knilans, suffering from an unserviceable bombsight, returned with his load, while Watts and Gingles, unable to identify the AP, did not bomb either, on Cheshire's orders.

Of the thirteen crews who did, Kell had an engine cut out, so made two runs before dropping his Tallboy. Ian Ross saw one TI about fifty yards south of the AP, while Munro considered Cheshire's marking 'a good indicator'. Howard saw one hit on a corner of the target, while Duffy claimed his crew's bomb was a direct hit.

The damage was later assessed as one direct hit against a corner of 'the main construction' – meaning the concrete slab over the ends of the barrels – blasting a crater 35ft across and 100ft in diameter. It was later found that this bomb had also blown a cavity beneath the slab, causing part of it to collapse inwards.

It has since been claimed that one Tallboy – probably this one – actually went down a shaft and exploded at the bottom. However, there was what has been described as a release of gas and a breach of the water table at the site, entombing some 2,000 Germans and other workers. One man, a Pole, escaped as he was climbing a shaft at the time. He survived the war and later returned after the site had been opened to the public.

Another four Tallboys were within sixty yards of the AP, one being a near miss at the north end of the slab. All this led to the collapse of one of the gun shafts and some of the upper level of tunnels.

Time had run out for the Germans as far as this site was concerned and they abandoned it. One of their civil engineers made an apologetic report to the Reich Research Council: 'The installations were not designed to withstand bombs such as these.'

In March 1999 Tom Bennett returned to this site to be interviewed by the BBC: They were obviously staggered by the labyrinth of underground workings, and it was almost 2 p. m. before they had concluded their 'shooting' underground. The farmer and his wife who own the land took us for a most wonderful lunch in a local village and then we adjourned to the top of the small hill into which the workings were bored, where they were flabbergasted by the size of the Tallboy craters, particularly the one that wrought such havoc. It pierced the workings at their most vulnerable point, burrowing down past the breeches of the 'London gun', to penetrate a further five metres of concrete before detonating and causing the most awesome implosion. A water bed was reached, which flooded the lower workings and excavations into which the workers had sought shelter. The estimate is that there could be up to 3,000 dead down there (700 or so Ruhr miners and forced labour workers). These lower workings have been permanently sealed.

This raid was to be Cheshire's last as far as Cochrane was concerned. He had now officially done 100 raids – although the actual number may have been higher – and despite his protests Cochrane felt that this was a good number at which to stop. Cheshire resumed his previous rank of group captain and went off to a Senior Commander's Course at RAF Cranwell. He was awarded the VC two months later – not for any one heroic deed but for sustained effort over the last four years. 617 were not alone in considering that that was the hardest way to win it. On 12 July he was replaced by Wg Cdr James 'Willie' Tait, DSO and Bar, DFC, a taciturn twenty-six-year-old Welshman of whom it was said that when he opened his mouth it was usually to stick a large pipe into it. He too had done a hundred operations and had previously served with 4 Group.

Three other pilots and their crews – Shannon, McCarthy and Munro – were given the same glad tidings as their former CO. Their protests were treated in the same manner and they too went off for an enforced rest, in Len Sumpter's case to an OTU, though he would be back with 617 during the final months of the European war.

The uncompleted V-3 site – and a couple of others given a 'rocket gun' tag at the time – were liberated on 2 September by a battalion of Le Regiment de la Chaudiere of the 3rd Canadian Infantry Division, who reached it after a hard advance that had included battling through D-Day, Carpiquet airfield and the rubble of Caen. Their quartermaster found the tunnels useful for storage before the unit moved on a couple of days later.

Wallis was among the many fascinated scientists and engineers who later went underground to see how the handiwork of the Germans had stood up to his own. In November 1944 Colonel T. R. B. Sanders led a mission to survey the V-weapon sites and pointed out in his report that the V-3 site, although damaged, could still be completed and used. On reading this Churchill commented that, 'The installations might well have launched the most devastating attack of all on London'.

It was therefore decided to blow up what remained, which the Royal Engineers did during May 1945, using surplus 500lb bombs and, ironically, German plastic explosive.

A total charge weight of some thirty-six tons, roughly equivalent to ten Tallboys, was used to collapse the tunnel entrances. None of this deterred the locals from later reopening the upper level and putting together an interesting underground museum, whose huge tunnels, surprisingly cool on a summer's day, have to be seen to be believed. The top of the hill between the east and west tunnels is an overgrown heavily cratered landscape. Anyone exploring it should be advised that at weekends 'the hills are alive' with dogs and French sportsmen, who are apt to shoot at anything moving!

The V-3's ghost was to surface again many years later as the result of a further report being written on it by Major Robert Turp in 1945. Parts had been found in a factory, some of which were bolted together and test-fired. Low internal pressure in the barrel sustained the shell's momentum and the weapon worked without blowing up. It was therefore thought possible that the Marquise/Mimoyecques installation would have worked as intended.

A copy of Turp's report found its way into the Imperial War Museum, where it was studied by Dr Gerald Bull, a Canadian artillery expert who at the end of the 1980s was involved in the notorious Iraqi 'super-gun' affair. Noting that the multiple-charge gun might have worked, Bull bore this in mind when designing his own weapon. His work was to cost him his life in March 1990 when he was shot outside his Belgian flat's front door just before gun barrel parts, supposedly components for an oil pipeline, were intercepted en route to Iraq. It is hardly surprising that no one else has seen fit to revive this type of weapon.

17 July 1944
Target The V-2 launching bunker at Wizernes.
Weather Over target two-tenths' stratocumulus, base at 3,000ft.

Force 16 Lancasters of 617 Sqdn:

DV380 'X' Flt Lt A. W. Fearn	DV402 'P' Flg-Off A. E. Kell
LM485 'N' Flt Lt H. J. Pryor	DV385 'A' Flg-Off R. E. Knights
LM482 'W' Flg-Off D. H. Cheney	ME561 'R' Lt H. C. Knilans USAAF
ME555 'C' Flg-Off W. A. Duffy	ME562 'Z' Flg-Off J. A. Sanders
LM489 'L' Flg-Off J. Gingles	ME544 'F' Flg-Off R. M. Stanford
EE146 'K' Flg-Off M. Hamilton	ME559 'V' Flg-Off G. S. Stout
LM492 'Q' Flg-Off W. R. Lee	DV246 'U' Flg-Off F. H. A. Watts
ED763 'D' Flg-Off D. Levy	DV393 'T' Flg-Off E. Willsher

Flt Lt Bill Reid's crew had also been detailed but were unable to take part due to engine trouble.

One 617 Sqdn Mosquito and one Mustang as marker aircraft:
Either HB825 or HB837 Wg Cdr J. B. Tait.
NT202 'N' Flt Lt G. E. Fawke and Flg-Off T. A. Bennett

Including 617, attacks were mounted on three V-weapon sites by 132 aircraft, the other two being in the Dieppe area. There were no aircraft losses.

Escort 24 Spitfire IXs of 11 Group's Detling Wing escorted 617, while 3 Free French squadrons covered the other two attacks, as follows:

118 Sqdn RAF	329 Sqdn (Free French)
504 Sqdn RAF	340 Sqdn (Free French)
329 Sqdn (Free French)	

One Spitfire was lost to flak but the pilot was saved. Two other fighters were damaged.

Bomb Loads Each Lancaster carried one Tallboy, with an 11-second delay. Tait's Mustang carried two red spot fires and Fawke's Mosquito at least two more.

Although damaged, Wizernes was not yet definitely out of the running, and with the V-weapon campaign hotting up further visits were deemed necessary. Since the last raid construction had continued, with a giant octagonal chamber, 117ft in diameter, being fitted out beneath the overhead dome. Concreting of the tunnels had begun, including the chamber walls to a height of 40ft. It was planned to fit the two V-2 tunnel entrances with 55ft high doors, which were later found in the supply dump at Watten. The dome itself was wrongly thought by the Allies to be the firing point.

The Detling Wing rendezvoused with the Lancasters and headed out over the Channel on what turned out to be an uneventful flight to the 'constructional works'. From the fighters' point of view it was as well, for 504 considered 617 'straggled alarmingly', which would have made protection from fighter attack difficult and 118 said, 'The chief feature was the amount of sky covered by the sixteen bombers – they were everywhere.'

At 1228 Tait made his reputation with 617 by diving to 500ft to drop his spot fires by the edge of the dome, backed up by Fawke who dropped two more. Tait climbed to 4,000ft, then, realising that some haze and convection cloud over the target was making accurate observation difficult, he dived again to circle the fires, hoping the light would reflect from his wings, and called, 'Try bombing me!'

The raid was highly successful. Knights claimed a direct hit on the north-west edge of the dome, which Fearns also saw. Willsher's bomb fell close to one of the tunnels and that of Knilans on the railway track fifty yards from a tunnel entrance.

Those of Duffy, Hamilton, Levy and Stout were also very close. One of these caused part of a chalk cliff to collapse, undermining the dome, with part of the resulting landslide also blocking four tunnel entrances, including the two intended for the erected V-2s. The bomb that apparently burst at the side of the dome actually went off beneath it. The dome, all 10,000 tons of it, was knocked askew.

In spite of Tait sticking his neck out, two aircraft still could not identify the target, so they bombed its estimated position. His Mustang returned home with some light flak damage. Fortunately for him it did not include the Merlin's coolant tank – one bullet through that would have led to a leak that would have caused his engine to overheat and seize up. That would have left him with the choice of a forced landing in the Allied beachhead, if he could have made it, or attempting to glide across the Channel. Perhaps because of this, it has been said that Tait did not like the Mustang, preferring the security of the Mosquito's twin engines. There was also the advantage of a second crewman to share the workload.

One witness of German pre-war rocket experiments had been *Oberst* Walter Dornberger, who had appointed a young enthusiast, Wernher von Braun, to the research team, thus beginning an association with rockets and spacecraft that would culminate in the successful Apollo Moon shots a quarter of a century later. By the time of this raid Dornberger was a *Generalleutnant*, whose staff reported that, 'Although the construction itself has not been hit by the new six-ton bombs, the whole area around has been so churned up that it is unapproachable and the bunker is jeopardised from underneath.'

There was no choice but to cease work and abandon the site, but this was not the end as far as the V-2s were concerned. They were pulled back to The Hague in Holland, from where in September the Germans would begin firing them from mobile launchers. These would be less conspicuous and therefore much more difficult for Allied bombers to destroy.

By 20 July the Germans also had full details of Tallboy's size, filling and fusing arrangements. After examining an unexploded specimen, a detailed drawing would now be circulated to their bomb disposal teams. It is not known from which raid this bomb was recovered.

On the night of 20-21 July, just to make sure, another Wizernes attack was planned, this time at night, with 1 Group attacking at 2100 and 617 four hours later. However, although eight crews of 83 Sqdn illuminated the quarry, fifteen Lancasters of 617 and two Mosquitoes, the latter flown by Tait and Fawke, were turned back as cloud

An oblique shot of the lunar landscape left at the Wizernes V-weapon site in the Pas de Calais after repeated attacks by Tallboy and other weapons. The enormous concrete dome, undermined by Tallboys which burst around it, can be seen in the left background. (Imperial War Museum, neg. no. C5636)

over the target prevented visual observation. It was as well, as this raid was no longer necessary.

It took some time for the significance of this site to sink in, even after V-2s had started coming over. RAF Intelligence officers visited the site at the beginning of October, but despite taking their time scrambling over the unfinished workings they reported that as yet they had no opinion on what the Germans had intended to use them for. A copy of their findings was passed to Lord Cherwell, who, after once dismissing the V-2 as 'a mare's nest', must by now have had ample cause to eat his words.

As at Marquise/Mimoyecques, sealing the railway tunnel did not prove permanent and an interesting museum was opened there in 1997, covering not only the war years but also the conquest of space – a reminder that the Saturn V rocket that put two Apollo astronauts on the Moon in 1969 was a descendant of the V-2. The displays include a V-1 from London's Science Museum and a V-2 from the Smithsonian Institute in Washington.

On 24 July 617 were briefed for a return to Watten, but take-off was put back until 0715 the next day. The route out would be via the North Foreland and the return via Orfordness.

25 July 1944
Target The V-2 liquid oxygen plant at Watten.
Weather Excellent visibility.

Force 16 Lancasters of 617 Sqdn:

DV380	'X'	Flt Lt A. W. Fearn	DV385	'A'	Flg-Off R. E. Knights
ED763	'D'	Flt Lt C. J. G. Howard	ME561	'R'	Lt H. C. Knilans USAAF
DV391	'O'	Flt Lt A. F. Poore	DV402	'P'	Flg-Off F. Levy
ME557	'S'	Flt Lt W. Reid	ME555	'C'	Flg-Off I. S. Ross
LM489	'L'	Flt Lt J. E. R. Williams	ME562	'Z'	Flg-Off J. Sanders
LM482	'W'	Flg-Off T. A. Carey	ME554	'F'	Flg-Off R. M. Stanford
DV393	'T'	Flg-Off D. H. Cheney	ME559	'Y'	Flg-Off G. S. Stout
LM485	'N'	Flg-Off M. Hamilton	LM482	'Q'	Flg-Off F. H. A. Watts

One 617 Sqdn Mosquito and one Mustang as marker aircraft:
HB837 'N' WgCdr J. B. Tait
NT205 'L' Flt Lt G. E. Fawke and Flg-Off T. A. Bennett

75 Main Force aircraft raided two other V-weapons sites in the Dieppe area, without loss.

Escort Seven 11 Group Spitfire IX squadrons to cover all three raids:

33 Sqdn RAF	124 Sqdn RAF	349 Sqdn (Free French)
80 Sqdn RAF	274 Sqdn RAF	485 Sqdn RNZAF
504 Sqdn R Aux AF		

Bomb Loads Each 617 Sqdn Lancaster carried one Tallboy. For the first time No.47 pistol was fitted, giving a half-hour delay. Tait's Mustang and Fawke's Mosquito carried two red spot fires each.

A week before this attack Hitler had ordered work on the giant bunkers to cease in favour of the mobile launching sites, so from 19 July the three liquid oxygen compressors and other machinery that had already been installed in the newer building on the site's south side were removed. Others that had been planned for it had not been added due to the fear of further Tallboy attacks.

Tait arrived over the target at around 0900 and decided that as the visibility was excellent no marking was necessary. With one exception all aircraft bombed on the first run. Heavy predicted flak hit at least three bombers, one of them flown by Cheney, whose Lancaster dived away from the formation, the mid-upper gunner bailing out to become a POW. This was probably due to a misunderstanding, as the intercom had been smashed. Cheney came home after releasing his Tallboy manually some seven miles south-south-east of the AP; it may have been the one that Carey saw fall into some woods. Fearn's aircraft also dropped its bomb manually after the release cable was severed by flak.

Poore and Hamilton claimed direct hits, while the Tallboys of Knilans and Sanders both fell at the north side of the building. Watts saw three hit very close to the AP before it became covered in smoke, and Stout reported no less than ten around it. A large dust column rose to 5,000ft, completely obscuring the target. One hit on the northern edge of the main building blew a large chunk of concrete down onto a subsidiary building below.

Harris, who could not yet have known what was going on within the building, congratulated 617 when he saw the bombing photographs, but despite several near misses the bunker remained standing. Dornberger now ordered Watten to be abandoned, although for a while minor work would carry on for deception purposes. Although 617 had carried out this task as briefed, without loss to themselves, as a result of Hitler's decision this raid had not really been necessary.

During August 1944 Watten was also on the receiving end of three radio-controlled 'war weary' B-17s, which, after being filled with Torpex explosive, were dived onto it, but these caused little damage. After the Canadian 1st Army had liberated the area the Americans also used the building to test the rocket-propelled Disney bomb, but this too had little effect on the massive structure.

As mentioned earlier, the British Bombing Research Mission's 1945 report stated that the advice to bomb this site while it was being built in 1943 had been correct. The USAAF raid on it had so damaged the original liquid oxygen plant on the site's north side that it had been abandoned. Later two Tallboys had hit the other building's roof, leaving craters some nine feet deep but causing only minor internal damage.

Today the site, referred to as Eperlecques after the wooded hillside on which it stands, has been developed as a museum. The forest has grown back, but the ground was heavily cratered and despite some landscaping it remains uneven. Disney and Tallboy damage to the building is still visible. It was apparently also subject to post-war tests using the Grand Slam bomb, although no details of these have come to light.

In 1944, to sum up what had been learned from these attacks so far, as well as what might be achieved in the future, an Armament Research report on 30 July stated

Tallboy damage to the roof at Watten, photographed in 1996. It is possible that this also includes damage inflicted by Grand Slams during post-war tests. (S. Flower)

that the most serious damage to a concrete structure would occur by a near miss, not a direct hit. If a near-miss crater did not overlap with the building it could fail to cause serious damage. Caves could be damaged by subsidence caused by a direct hit. Buildings were not likely to be seriously damaged if the bomb went off more than seventy yards away. The cratering of roads or railways would involve the dumping of 5,000 tons of soil to fill a Tallboy crater, which in open ground could be up to 135ft in diameter and up to 35ft deep. Small vessels could be capsized and larger ones sunk by staving in their plates against quay-sides. Wallis had had the chance to defend his roof-destroying idea when Air Commodore C. N. H. Bilney of Bomber Command had written to him on 18 July with photographs of Le Havre after the attack, commenting that he thought the roof damage was due to E-boat torpedo warheads going off. No one who knew Wallis would have been surprised at the reasoned and forceful arguments that he used in reply. As might have been expected, he disagreed, stating that this was conclusive evidence that the damage was due to Tallboy. He considered that the warheads had been stacked on the quayside, on the other side of a pen dividing wall that had been four feet thick where it joined the roof, but had widened to perhaps as much as sixteen feet lower down.

> We know from a series of elaborate experiments carried out at the Road Research Laboratory at a time when an attempt to destroy a number of important viaducts leading out of the Ruhr district was contemplated by bowling Upkeep along the ground, that vertical piers of this kind are exceedingly hard to destroy. We proved that it would require no less than three tons of Torpex placed in contact with the foot of a pier to demolish a pier eight feet high and twelve feet thick when the charge was situated above ground, and therefore had no tamping other than that given by the charge case.

Experiments had also shown that where heavy targets were concerned multiple explosions were not as effective as a single equivalent charge would be. It was also impossible to make the effects of several charges 'build up'. 'Experience confirms the point that one charge rather tends to interfere with another, and no cumulative effect is obtained.'

Wallis felt that two of the piers might have been demolished by Tallboys bursting under water, which would have provided very effective tamping. Certainly photographs taken at low tide showed that two of the dividing walls, each up to 16ft thick, had completely disappeared. Also, a gun emplacement had taken a direct hit, resulting in a complete circular penetration of the roof. The Tallboy that had done this had gone straight through the roof, been slightly deflected into one of the pens below and then exploded, bringing down the intervening walls. This had led to the roof sagging and finally collapsing. Possibly some of the warheads had gone off when masonry fell on them. Wallis had consulted Sir W. Halcrow & Partners – a company experienced in ferroconcrete structures, who, not surprisingly, had agreed with him.

It therefore seemed as if his theory of bringing down the internal walls was correct, but until Le Havre fell into Allied hands and the pens could be examined it would not be possible to say otherwise. Had anyone tackled Wallis at this point on the subject of the V-weapon sites he would probably have replied that the same principles applied.

31 July 1944
Target The V-1 store at Rilly-la-Montagne.
Weather No cloud but slight haze over target.

Force 16 Lancasters of 617 Sqdn:

DV380	'X' Flt Lt A. W. Fearn	DV385 'A'	Flg-Off R. E. Knights
ED763	'D' Flt Lt C. J. G. Howard	ME561 'R'	Lt H. C. Knilans USAAF
DV391	'O' Flt Lt A. F. Poore	DV402 'P'	Flg-Off E. Levy
ME557	'S' Flt Lt W. Reid	LM489 'L'	Flg-Off I. S. Ross
EE131	'B' Flt Lt J. E. R. Williams	ME562 'Z'	Flg-Off J. A. Sanders
DV246	'U' Flg-Off T. A. Carey	ME554 'F'	Flg-Off R. M. Stanford
JB139	'V' Flg-Off D. H. Cheney	ME559 'Y'	Flg-Off G. S. Stout
LM485	'N' Flg-Off M. Hamilton	LM492 'Q'	Flg-Off E. Willsher

Two 617 Sqdn Mosquitoes as marker aircraft:
NS993 'N' Wg Cdr J. B. Tait and Sqdn Ldr D. R. Walker
NT205 'L' Flg-Off W. A. Duffy and Flg-Off D. A. Bell

Three other marker aircraft took part – two from 105 Sqdn and one from 109. One 627 Sqdn Mosquito was detailed as a PR aircraft.

A total of 103 aircraft from 5 and 8 Groups attacked both ends of the Rilly-la-Montagne railway tunnel, losing two Lancasters.

Escort 102 Spitfire IXs:

80 Sqdn RAF	274 Sqdn RAF	341 Sqdn (Free French)
118 Sqdn RAF	329 Sqdn (Free French)	485 Sqdn RNZAF
124 Sqdn RAF	340 Sqdn (Free French)	504 Sqdn R Aux AF

Bomb Loads Each 617 Sqdn Lancaster carried one Tallboy, with a half-hour delay. Tait and Duffy's Mosquitoes carried two red spot fires each.

This time 617 were part of a Main Force raid and protested when they were told that they would be flying at 12,000ft, while the others would be at 18,000ft. Complaints about the danger of bombs falling from above were ignored and the plan stood. Another experiment – that of Oboe aircraft leading formations – was now being tried, though due to the high performance of their Mosquitoes 105 Sqdn was to experience some difficulty in maintaining a low enough speed to enable the heavy bombers to keep a tight formation on them.

The three 8 Group Mosquitoes each carried four Long Burning red TIs, which they were to drop at six, five and four minutes before H-Hour. The Oboe aircraft were to drop their TIs at a point midway between the two tunnel entrances at these three specified times. 617's two Mosquitoes should have dropped white smoke markers at the tunnel entrances, but, as seen above, for some reason they carried red spot fires instead.

Immediately behind the Oboe aircraft would be six Lancasters of 83 Sqdn, in two vics of three, one at 15,000ft and the other at 18,000ft. To indicate their status, these six Lancasters would carry white stripes on their fins. Their brief was 'to destroy enemy communications and storage installations.' The target was a V-1 store in a railway tunnel some seven miles south of the city of Rheims, the marking points and APs being the north and south entrances to it. 617 would bomb both of them.

The formation met its escort at the French coast and flew to the target without incident, although the forecast winds proved inaccurate and things did not go entirely according to plan. For a time the R/T VHF channel was jammed by a 467 Sqdn aircraft which had left its set on transmit due to a defect, although this did not affect control at the target as by then the offending aircraft had switched to another frequency.

The bombers arrived two minutes ahead of the designated H-Hour, possibly due to the inaccurate winds. This was despite Flt Lt T. V. Vernon of 83 lowering his flaps and reducing speed to around 120 knots. The special fin markings were evidently disregarded as Flt Lt A. Drinkall, also of 83, found that 'Main Force' aircraft kept flying ahead of him, ignoring green Very lights that he fired. What happened to Knilans and Reid over the target indicated that 617 were anxious to get there ahead of everyone else, which due to their low bombing height was understandable. They met no fighters, but intermittent flak en route to the target became more intense over it.

The three other Mosquitoes marked the target – evidently satisfactorily as neither Tait nor Duffy's services were required, although Duffy made one run over it. Despite its early arrival the formation achieved a good bombing concentration, attacking both ends of the tunnel with what was considered equal success.

It was not achieved without cost. One of 9 Sqdn's Lancasters crashed at Puisieulx near Rheims and although 83 had been briefed to fly at 15,000ft, well above 617's briefed bombing altitude, another of their pilots, Flt Lt R. E. H. Foote, saw a 12,000lb bomb fall some 200 yards from his starboard wing. He did not say that it was a Tallboy, so it might have been a Main Force HC weapon, but if not then at least one of 617's pilots had decided to better his chances by climbing. Perhaps this pilot was also responsible for what nearly happened to Knilans, who had to swing his aircraft sharply to one side when his flight engineer saw another of 617's Lancasters above them with its bomb doors open. His bomb aimer found the AP again and dropped the Tallboy, but Knilans' starboard outer engine then began overheating, forcing him to feather it.

At least he fared better than Bill Reid's crew, who were flying behind them and whose fate Knilans' rear gunner witnessed. Reid dropped his bomb and was about to turn away when his bomb aimer asked him to hold his course for another twenty-eight seconds until their aiming point picture had been taken. As Reid reluctantly complied, he heard and felt what he most feared – a bang behind him as a Main Force bomb dropped from above hit the Lancaster.

Prepare to bail out.
Reid wore a harness with chest clips, as opposed to the permanently attached parachute that many pilots sat on. As his flight engineer handed his chute to him, another bomb struck them, the two hits causing damage to one of the port engines as well as the fuselage. High above, 118 Sqdn's Spitfire pilots watched as the Lancaster began to spin down in two pieces.

Bail out!
As Reid unstrapped himself and struggled to open the crash exit overhead, the aircraft's nose seemed to break away, leaving him to tumble through empty air. He pulled his ripcord but kept a tight grip on the lines, being uncertain as to whether he

had properly locked the chute to his harness. Landing in a tree, he slid down it, with injuries to his face and one hand.

The ground must have seemed welcoming indeed, but there was no time to linger. Training asserted itself and after pausing long enough to apply his field dressing to his cut face, Reid headed south towards Paris. He carried a silk escape map, the capital was only thirty miles away and he was confident of his ability to speak French, but his attempt at evasion was cut short when three German soldiers challenged him.

Reid was taken to a flak site and attended to by a doctor, where he met up with Flg-Off Dave Luker, his wireless-operator, who had also been thrown out of the Lancaster, used his parachute and come to on the ground with a German standing over him. The other five crew members did not survive. On their way to a POW camp, Reid's crimson VC ribbon attracted some attention from his captors. He had received it while previously serving with 61 Sqdn, after completing an operation to Dusseldorf and bringing back his damaged Lancaster despite being injured by fighter attacks.

617 had been determined to bomb before the target disappeared under smoke and before the Main Force arrived. Despite his other problems, Knilans saw three Tallboys fall within 100 yards of the northern AP and Levy noted a cloud of dust very close to the southern tunnel entrance. Main Force bombs cut the track on both sides of the tunnel, while those Tallboys that fell apparently caved in the entrances. Four crews brought their loads back. Carey and Williams identified the target too late to make a good run. Ross could not get it in his sights and Knights did not consider his bombing run good enough to release his Tallboy.

The crews felt the attack had been successful. The northern entrance was later assessed as having been hit, the cutting leading to it having been blocked by craters and earth falls. At the southern entrance there was no apparent damage to the tunnel portal, but the track in the cutting was completely blocked by craters, at least one of them caused by a Tallboy.

On 1 August 617 returned to the Siracourt bunker, but ten-tenths' cloud at 6,000ft over the target forced them to return without bombing. This was perhaps as well; it was doubtful whether they could have inflicted any further worthwhile damage, and it would not be long before the Germans withdrew from this area.

It has since been pointed out that the attacks on the bunkers did not stop the flow of V-1s falling onto south-eastern England, nor did they prevent the first use of the V-2 the following month. There is also a case for claiming that the 21st Army Group's advance towards the Pas de Calais would have compelled Hitler to give up the V-weapon sites in a general withdrawal, as did indeed occur, and that this would have happened whether or not they had been bombed. Certainly news that the enemy had been cleared out of the Pas de Calais came as a welcome relief, albeit a temporary one, for the V-weapon offensive would continue. Perhaps in anticipation of what would happen, the Germans had modified Heinkel 111s to fire V-1s from over the North Sea.

At the time of the V-weapon site attacks full details of these new threats were not available, but what was known was sufficiently ominous to justify taking every possible step to overcome them before they could fully develop. Attack, with whatever was available, was still the best form of defence.

While they did not achieve complete obliteration, what Wallis' bombs did do was to make certain that none of these sites, which had absorbed so much German effort, expense and manpower, ever fired one flying bomb, rocket or long-range shell. Also, by attacking the V-1 storage areas, in conjunction with other air attacks on the transportation system, the flow of these weapons to their 'modified' launching sites was seriously disrupted. Had Tallboy not been available in time the loss of life in London and elsewhere could have been far higher.

7

The U-Boat Pens

A new chapter opened during August 1944, when 9 Sqdn co-operated with 617 for the first time in a raid that damaged a railway bridge near Etaples. By now a delay in the filling of British Tallboys was being felt and the planned American production of them was only just beginning, so 1,000lb bombs were used by both squadrons. However, 617's marking techniques, using the Mustang and a Mosquito, remained the same.

In August thirty-six bombs would be listed as available, including six from production sub-contracted to the Smith Corporation of Milwaukee in the USA, During the last three months of 1944 this would rise from fifty to ninety-five in the UK, supplemented by an even more dramatic rise in American production; from sixty to over twice that number by the end of the year, but these would have to face a slow and still dangerous passage across the Atlantic.

On 1 July a proposal had been put forward, apparently by Harris, for a second 5 Group squadron to be equipped with Tallboy. The one he had in mind was 9 Sqdn. This unit, under Wg Cdr Jim Bazin at RAF Bardney in Lincolnshire, had earned itself a good reputation in bombing and navigation. His idea was supported by Air Commodore Bufton, who had mentioned such an idea to Saundby in June, though with some doubts as to whether Tallboy could be accurately aimed with the Mark XIV sight. This was used by 9, but was intended for the area bombing of cities.

The events of this month would show that there were scarcely enough Tallboys for 617 Sqdn's requirements so for now 9 Sqdn would have to use smaller bombs, perhaps in the hope that 617 Sqdn's attacks would have softened up the target for them. At present all Tallboys would go to 617 Sqdn, although one step that could be taken was to provide blown bomb doors for 9 Sqdn's aircraft.

Churchill would later admit that, 'The only thing that really frightened me during the war was the U-boat peril.' He had never forgotten the dire straits that Britain had found herself in at the height of the First World War, when prefabricated U-boats, assembled in the shipyards at Bruges, had turned the shipping lanes off Britain's south-western approaches into a graveyard.

In April 1917 it had been admitted by Field-Marshal Sir Douglas Haig that Britain had lost command of the sea. However reluctant the Admiralty might have been to agree, they had been well aware of the submarine threat. The Flanders U-boat flotillas had had shelters at Bruges, whose six-foot-thick roofs had protected them against the aerial bombs of the time. This was the German reply to the British naval blockade, and it had become a question of who would go under first. At one point there had been just six weeks of corn supplies left in the UK. On 23 April 1918 a naval raid had been made on the German-held base at Zeebrugge, but it had not been enough to stem the U-boat attacks. The fitting of the Asdic underwater detection system, later rechristened Sonar, to British warships came too late to have much effect before the Armistice.

By 1937, with 1914-1918 a memory safely consigned to the past, the Admiralty had confidently declared, 'The submarine should never again be able to present us with the problem we were faced with in 1917'. Three years later, German submariners had gained something their fathers could only have dreamt of – access to the Atlantic from French ports in the Bay of Biscay. According to Admiral Karl Dönitz, in charge of the *Kriegsmarine*'s U-boat arm, Lorient's facilities were superior to those in the overburdened German dockyards and each crew could save a week's patrol by not having to make a 450-mile journey to the Atlantic.

Himself a U-boat skipper in the previous conflict, Dönitz had become embittered by the destruction of Germany's submarine force after 1918. The British blockade, which had inflicted severe hardship on German civilians in the First World War's final months, was another memory that still rankled. From his point of view Britain's claim to rule the waves was one that deserved to be challenged again, and the Anglo-German Naval Treaty of 1935, giving the two countries parity in submarines, had provided an opportunity to do so. As Hitler rebuilt the *Kriegsmarine* it was hardly surprising that Dönitz became a loyal follower of Nazism. Early successes against the Royal Navy, such as the sinking of the battleship HMS *Royal Oak* in the supposedly safe anchorage of Scapa Flow, had clearly shown that his U-boats could deliver the goods, while the Battle of Britain had shown that Göring's Luftwaffe could not.

In October 1940, in response to a question by Hitler as to what protection the U-boats should have in their new Biscay bases, Dönitz, thinking back to Bruges a generation before, said that concrete should be used whether they were in dry dock or afloat. This should also apply to their workshops.

Hitler gave this task to an *Organization Todt* architect and work quickly began at five French ports – Lorient, La Pallice, Brest, St Nazaire and Bordeaux. The foundation work was carried out behind caissons that kept the sea out but were vulnerable to attack. Nevertheless, Bomber Command, with the Air Ministry's backing, had decided its attacks on German industrial centres were more important. As the Command lacked large and effective bombs in the early war years, there was some excuse for their attitude; any attempt to disrupt the construction might have delayed it for a while but would not have stopped it altogether. However, in a classic instance of slamming the stable door, they later bombed the pens only after they had been roofed with sixteen feet of concrete. This hardly scratched the pens, but destroyed everything around them. In August 1942 Dönitz could declare that, 'The aeroplane can no more eliminate the submarine than a crow can fight a mole.'

During that summer the U-boats at last began to take significant losses, due in part to another product first developed by Vickers at Brooklands – the Leigh Light, which, in conjunction with ASV radar and improved depth charges, enabled attacks to be carried out on the surface of the Bay of Biscay at night. P/O S. J. Pooley, the young scientist who had invented Torpex, was the navigator of the first Wellington to make such an attack. However, further bombing of the pens at the start of 1943 caused only slight roof damage. PRU coverage, Ultra intercepts and the reports of agents all confirmed this.

Another development was the Schnorchel, an air pipe which could be extended to the surface and retracted at will, with a ballcock valve, like those in toilet cisterns, to prevent flooding in heavy seas. Now a U-boat could remain submerged almost indefinitely, travelling on her diesels, without the need to surface to recharge her batteries or indeed to use much current from them at all. Ultra informed the Allies of this device in 1943 and it was in use by February 1944.

The need to curb U-boat manufacture had been one reason for the port of Hamburg being selected for a series of firestorm raids in the summer of 1943, resulting in at least a month's lost production at the Blohm und Voss shipyards there. This was to have further consequences for Hamburg – and for 5 Group's two precision squadrons – during 1945.

Although the E-boats had left the Channel, there was still the possibility of U-boat attacks on the Atlantic convoys, or on supply ships crossing to the British *Mulberry* harbour at Arromanches and the American-held port of Cherbourg. For now these were the only Continental ports available to the Allies. The threat was made clear in a signal by Dönitz:

Every vessel taking part in the landing, even if it has but a handful of men or a solitary tank onboard, is a target of the utmost importance which must be attacked regardless of risk. Every effort will be made to close the enemy invasion fleet regardless of danger from shallow water, possible minefelds or anything else. Every man and weapon destroyed before reaching the beaches lessens the enemy's chances of ultimate success. Every boat that inflicts losses on the enemy while he is landing has fulfilled its primary function, even though it perishes in so doing.

This was not unlike the suicidal tactics that would be adopted by the Japanese in the final months of the Pacific war. By now both the remaining U-boats and their crews were clearly considered expendable. Nine days after D-day, despite the naval screen that had been set up in the Western Approaches, the U-boats began to score, sinking two Royal Navy frigates and a landirig craft. Dönitz was not going to see his country and his navy humiliated for a second time, at least not without a fight to the bitter end.

5 August 1944
Target The U-boat pens at Brest.
Weather Excellent, with good visibility.

Force 15 Lancasters of 617 Sqdn:

DV380 'X' Flt Lt A. F. Fearn	DV402 'F' Flg-Off A. E. Kell
ED763 'D' Flt Lt C. J. G. Howard	DV385 'A' Flg-Off R. E. Knights
ME554 'F' Flt Lt T. C. Iveson	ME561 'R' Lt H. C. Knilans USAAF
LM485 'N' Flt Lt D. J. Oram	DV426 'U' Flg-Off F. Levy
DV391 'O' Flt Lt A. F. Poore	ME562 'Z' Flg-Off J. A. Sanders
EE131 'B' Flt Lt J. E. R. Williams	ME559 'Y' Flg-Off G. S. Stout
JB139 'V' Flg-Off D. H. Cheney	LM492 'Q' Flg-Off E. Willsher
LM489 'L' Flg-Off J. Gingles	

Two 617 Sqdn Mosquitoes as marker aircraft:
NS993 'N' Wg Cdr J. B. Tait and Sqdn Ldr D. R. Walker
NT205 'L' Flt Lt G. E. Fawke and Flg-Off T. A. Bennett

One 627 Sqdn Mosquito as a camera aircraft:
KB195 'B' Sqdn Ldr R. G. Churcher and Flg-Off P. G. Herbert

Escort 23 AEAF Spitfire IXs:
64 Sqdn RAF   126 Sqdn RAF

Bomb Loads Each Lancaster carried one Tallboy, with an 11-second delay. Tait's Mosquito carried four 100lb smoke markers, while Fawke's carried at least two more. One of these two crews, probably Fawke, was to drop smoke markers at a particular map reference, then join in the main attack. The Lancasters also carried Window.

Since 1941 Brest had been the base for the 1st and 9th U-Boat Flotillas. Early that year, construction of the pens had begun on the south-western edge of the town, on the site of a former seaplane station, and in front of a French naval training school. By 1942 they were ready, following what became a standard pattern; 'wet' and 'dry' pens for berthing and dry-docking, each with quays and overhead cranes for servicing, while workshops were constructed at the rear, this area being divided from the pens by a railway which ran in a passage through the building behind them. Each end of the passage was protected from outside bomb blast by massive steel doors. Dangerous stores were kept some distance away, oil was brought to the site by pipes from tanks dug into a hill to the west of the pens. Torpedoes and ammunition were stored in tunnels cut into the cliffs behind the shelter.

Of the five Biscay U-boat bases Lorient covered the biggest acreage, but at 52,000 square metres the Brest pen was the largest of all these buildings. The original roof slab was up to 14ft thick, but before the Tallboy attacks began it had been increased by a second layer to 19ft above the pens, though not over the rear services area. The internal pen walls varied between 4ft and 8ft in thickness.

At each base priority for roof reinforcement had always been given to the dry-dock pens. To further increase protection a *Fangrost* concrete bomb-trap was then added. This consisted of concrete support walls some 2m high by 1.5m wide, laid on the shelter roof to run parallel with the dividing walls of the pens below. Across these support walls were laid concrete beams, about 1.5 square metres and in the shape of an inverted U, about 0.3m apart.

It was intended that the beams would set off the bombs, so that their explosions would be contained in the chamber beneath. After the war proof that the beams worked came to light when an American 500lb bomb was found wedged between them, its casing deformed but not cracked. At Brest this system had not been completed before 617 came on the scene.

The five 'wet' pens, A to E, were set 45m forward from the other ten 'dry' ones, giving further space for workshops between the back of them and the railway passage. Flak positions, housed in yet more concrete structures, shaped like truncated pyramids, were mounted on the roof. This would be Tallboy's next test.

The bombers' route out was over Sidmouth and their escort flew to join them from RAF Harrowbeer in south Devon. All pressed on except Gingles, who had been forced to turn back just south of Bristol when his starboard outer engine failed. H-Hour would be 1100, with the escort accompanying them to and from the South Coast.

The target, roughly rectangular and as distinctive as the E-boat pens had been, was clearly identified in excellent visibility. There were no fighters, but accurate and intense heavy flak. Tait dived to drop his markers from 4,500ft, but Fawke's were not required, probably due to the good weather. Both would consider the bombing to be extremely well concentrated. The 627 Sqdn crew, who filmed the attack for six minutes from 14,000ft, later stated, 'Bombing started punctually and was accurate. One hit was seen on the south-west corner of the pens.'

All fourteen Tallboys were released, of which three fell in the water near the southern end of the pens and six hit the roof. According to Ultra information received afterwards, four of these penetrated the pens, although a US Strategic Bombing Survey report later said five. Large holes were smashed through 18ft of concrete above Berth E and Dock 3. Two other craters were 8ft in depth.

Two U-boats suffered battery damage and were out of action for five days, while a breakwater to the west of the pens was breached in two places. The Ultra comment that 'bombs seem only to be effective if roof is breached' was true, if rather obvious. 617 had been fortunate in that the Tallboys struck areas of the roof that had not yet been given the *Fangrost* treatment.

Flak hit three aircraft and <u>again it was Knilans' rear gunner who saw what happened next.</u> The demands of the SABS had forced Flg-Off Don Cheney's crew to fly straight and level at 18,000ft for seventeen miles, much of it through a heavy barrage. Just after bombing his Lancaster was struck by a shell in the bomb bay, wounding the navigator and wireless-operator.

Cheney asked for a new course and P/O R. Welch, the navigator, unable to speak due to facial injuries, passed it forward. Then the engineer and bomb aimer gave both men first aid. As Cheney turned to port to follow the course Welch had given him the starboard outer engine failed and caught fire. It was feathered and the fire seemed to go out. Cheney began to descend as splinters had torn the oxygen masks of both the wounded men. He then saw a fire in the starboard wing.

Bail out.
Cheney's flight engineer clipped his chute on for him. The aircraft's nose hatch, usually seen as the safest emergency exit, jammed despite help from the navigator and flight

engineer to open it. They managed to prise it open just sufficiently for Welch to jump first, followed by Flt Sgt J. Rosher, the flight engineer, and Flt Sgt A. Curtis, the bomb aimer. Both the gunners went out from further aft.

Flt Sgt Reginald Pool, the wireless-operator, was unable to move, so after Cheney had put the Lancaster into a climb he went back to attend to him, clipping on Pool's parachute in between trying to keep whatever control he still had. He dragged Pool to the nose hatch and as he went out Pool was able to pull his own ripcord.

Cheney went back up into the cockpit to get the Lancaster straight and level for his own jump, but then the flames broke through the starboard side of the fuselage, burning his face and one knee. Unable now to return to the nose, he scrambled out through the crash exit above him, then shot back along the top of the fuselage, missing both the mid-upper turret and the tail before pulling his ripcord.

The aircraft spun down into Douarnenez Bay, near Ste Anne-la-Palud. Pool, Welch and P/O W. N. Watt, the rear gunner, did not survive – the latter having also been wounded. Curtis swam ashore and was taken prisoner but freed by the Americans a month later. Cheney, Rosher and W/O K. R. Porter, the mid-upper gunner, all evaded capture due to the Resistance – in Cheney's case by the crew of a boat which fished him out of the sea while others held off the Germans with machine-gun fire.

The remainder of 617 Sqdn's formation flew home safely, although the escort took it upon themselves to carry out some ground attacks for want of aerial opposition. 64 Sqdn sent four Spitfires to strafe German vehicles, another four against a Freya radar site and the rest took on an armed trawler, seriously damaging it. Flak claimed Flt Lt H. J. Meharry and Flg-Off A. Thorpe, the latter bailing out over the Channel. He was later picked up by an ASR Walrus amphibian, but Meharry was posted missing. 126, less one pilot who turned back early with engine trouble, strafed the same Freya site without loss to themselves.

The three fugitives were hidden at the port commandant's house in Douarnenez before being passed to the Americans at the end of the month. Cheney returned briefly to 617, but this had been his thirty-eighth operation and he did not fly with them again, returning to his native Canada. The DFC he was awarded at the beginning of 1945 was a well-earned one.

The pens were not the only objectives under scrutiny at this time. Some targets, such as Rothensee and the Sorpe, seemed to be a perennial topic for discussion. Based on the experience gained in this attack on Brest, Wallis felt that as the concrete apron round the ship lift was no greater than 12ft thick it was probable that Tallboy would penetrate it and burst underneath, although admittedly this could not be done if premature detonation occurred, as had apparently been the case at Brest. Even so, it might jam the lift and he considered a Tallboy attack to have a reasonable chance of success.

With regard to the Sorpe, Wallis remained reluctant to admit defeat and still considered the air side method of attack that he had advocated the previous May to be a viable one.

6 August 1944
Target The U-boat pens at Lorient.
Weather Good.

Force 12 Lancasters of 617 Sqdn:

DV402 'F' Flt Lt A. F. Fearn	DV246 'U' Flg-Off A. E. Kell
ED763 'D' Flt Lt C. J. G. Howard	? Flg-Off R. E. Knights
ME554 'F' Flt Lt T. C. Iveson	ME561 'R' Lt H. C. Knilans USAAF
LM485 'N' Flt Lt D. J. Oram	ME562 'Z' Flg-Off J. A. Sanders
PD238 'H' Flg-Off T. A. Carey	ME559 'Y' Flg-Off G. S. Stout
LM489 'L' Flg-Off J. Gingles	LM492 'Q' Flg-Off E. Willsher

Two other Lancasters that had been detailed were grounded due to technical trouble. 617's ORB incorrectly states that LM492 was flown by both Knights and

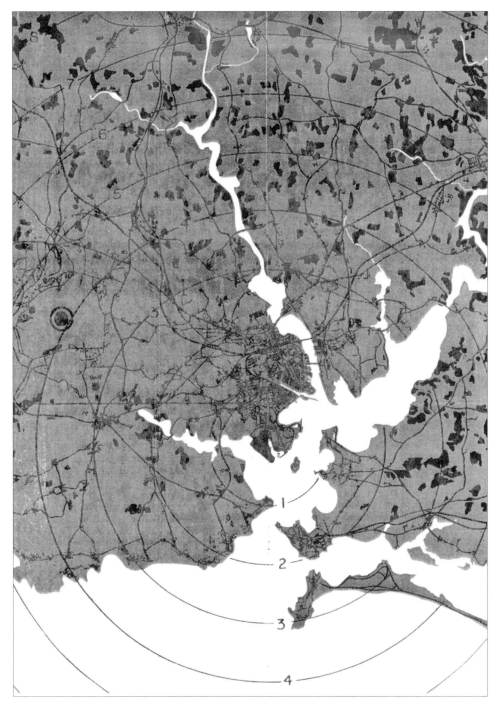

An RAF target map of the Keroman pens at Lorient, with north at the top of the diagram. The numbers 1 and 2, just visible in the centre, refer to the long and large harbour basins. (H. F. C. Parsons)

Willsher. As this Lancaster was Willsher's normal mount, Knights possibly flew DV385, which he had previously used on several occasions.

Two 617 Sqdn Mosquitoes as marker aircraft:
NS993 'N' Wg Cdr J. B. Tait and Flt Sgt L. E. Gosling
NT205 'L' Flt Lt G. E. Fawke and Flg-Off T. A. Bennett
Due to Lorient's heavy defences Window was to be used and these two aircraft were ordered not to descend below 8,000ft while marking the target.

One 627 Sqdn Mosquito as a camera aircraft:
KB215 'H' Flt Lt I. H. Hanlon and Flt Lt K. G. Tice

This was to be an evening attack, controlled by 617. Since 9 Sqdn were practising at Wainfleet range on this date, sixteen Lancasters of 106 Sqdn were detailed to follow 617, each carrying thirteen 1,000lb GP bombs. As a result of the Allied breakout from Normandy, the US 4th Armoured Division was due to attack the town the next day.

Escort Seventeen 10 Group Spitfires:
131 Sqdn RAF   611 Sqdn R Aux AF
It had been planned to have 64 and 126 Sqdns from RAF Harrowbeer as rear escort, but in the event they were reassigned to two fighter sweeps instead. According to 106 Sqdn's ORB some Mosquitoes were also employed as escort, but no details of these are available.

Bomb Loads Each 617 Sqdn Lancaster carried one Tallboy, with an 11-second delay. Tait's load was two red TIs and Fawke probably carried the same.

The Germans had greatly enlarged the facilities at Lorient since its capture in 1940, adapting existing facilities on the Scarff River and building a completely new base on the Keroman foreland. Initially two large 'Dombunkers' – 'Dom' being the German word for cathedral – were built alongside a slipway at the civilian shipyard. These buildings were given curved roofs to deflect any bombs away from them, although they fell into disuse later on.

Then the pens Keroman I and II were built nearby, facing each other, with space for twelve U-boats between them. These pens were served by a protected slipway and a unique transporter system to haul the U-boats onto dry land. Later the larger Keroman III pen was added. This faced out towards the sea, with a further seven pens, five of which could accommodate two boats at once. Its roof was up to 740m thick, on top of which construction of the *Fangrost* system was started but never completed.

The consequence of all this activity was that by 1944 Lorient had become the largest of all the French U-boat bases, although there had been insufficient time to carry out planned further bunker extensions, or to add a second layer to the roofs of the shore facilities. It was extremely well defended, with two hundred weapons ranging in calibre from 20mm to 128mm.

The first base of its kind to see service in the Battle of the Atlantic, Lorient housed the 2nd and 10th U-Boat Flotillas, with ample space to service other visitors if required; the pens' customers had at one time included some Japanese I-class submarines. At least one of these had been a large blockade runner, bringing gold bullion, tin, wolfram and rubber from Malaya in exchange for German weapon plans and other related items. Well-known U-boat captains such as Otto Kretschmer, Günther Prien and Joachim Schepke had all sailed on their last voyages from Lorient in early 1941. Always the fighting submariner at heart, and the kind of commander to meet his men on the dockside when they returned from a successful patrol, Dönitz had also had his headquarters there until 1942, when the Saint-Nazaire Commando raid and air attacks had led Hitler to order him back to Paris.

It was a measure of Allied concern that X Troop of 10 (Inter-Allied) Commando had once been detailed to parachute into France near the Blavet River, paddle down it in rubber dinghies and destroy the Lorient pens with explosive. X Troop had been made up of German Jews, operating under British cover names while led by British officers. This operation, worthy of Alistair Maclean, had been given the strange code-name of *Coughdrop*. At the last minute it had been cancelled, which was as well for all involved, for even if they had reached the pens they could never have carried enough explosive to have demolished them.

617's route out was over Sidmouth, with 106 following behind, less one who returned early due to engine failure. The escort, with strict instructions not to attack ground targets, joined them from Bolt Head. Although the Lancasters arrived later than their H-Hour of 2000, good visibility enabled them to easily identify the Keroman pen complex from the start of their bombing run over the Isle de Croix. Once again there were no fighters, so the escorting Spitfires had a grandstand view of what happened below. Heavy flak hit four bombers from 617 and several from 106, but this time there were no losses.

While the 627 Sqdn Mosquito filmed the raid, Tait dropped his two TIs at 2023 from 8,000ft, backed up by Fawke, and the Tallboys fell in a quick salvo, covering the peninsula with smoke. There had been two APs: the 'southern pen' – Keroman III; and the 'northern pen' – Keromans I and II. All of 617's crews bombed except Carey, who due to an electrical failure jettisoned his Tallboy out to sea. 106 then followed with their own attack, bombing from 15,000-19,000ft.

The bombing had appeared concentrated, but PRU coverage later on showed that three Tallboys had hit the roofs without penetrating them. Keroman III suffered some internal crumbling, but this pen had had the thickest roof and only a small area inside had been affected. Three pens had been hit on the rear and thinner part of their roof, forcing it up while also tilting it forward. It was thought that they had been put out of action due to ammunition exploding inside.

106 Sqdn's bombing had appeared to be east of the complex, but even if all their loads had been on target they could not have inflicted any more worthwhile damage. However, their attack would have had some nuisance value as 10 per cent of their bombs were fused to go off between six to thirty-six hours after the attack.

On 7 August, 9 and 617 went to the Lorient pens again, but were recalled within half a minute of bombing as attacking American troops were believed to be in the vicinity of the target area. 617 returned with their Tallboys, while 64 Sqdn, who with 126 formed the escort, commented, 'On reaching the target the Lancasters turned about and jettisoned their bombs in the sea, Lorient presumably having been captured by the Americans.' Not yet. This was 9 Sqdn dumping their loads, for 617 returned with theirs.

Lorient was still in German hands, but the U-boats would not remain there for much longer. On 19 August, U-123 and U-129, seen as unseaworthy, were blown up. U-188 and UIT-21, formerly of the Italian Navy, would suffer the same fate at Bordeaux the next day. Mindful of the way that the Germans had resisted at other French ports while demolishing their facilities, the Americans wisely chose to bypass this one. Lorient was surrounded and laid siege to by three 'resting' American infantry divisions in turn, but its trapped garrison refused to surrender until shortly after VE Day in May 1945. After the war the pens would continue to be used by the French Navy.

9 August 1944
Target The U-boat pens at La Pallice.
Weather Cloud but a clear patch over the target.

Force 12 Lancasters of 617 Sqdn:

DV380 'P' Flt Lt A. W. Fearn	PD233 'G' Flg-Off M. Hamilton
ED763 'D' Flt Lt C. J. G. Howard	LM492 'W' Flg-Off A. E. Kell
ME554 'F' Flt Lt T. C. Iveson	LM482 'Q' Flg-Off R. E. Knights
DV391 'O' Flt Lt D. J. Oram	ME555 'C' Flg-Off I. S. Ross

ME561 'R' Flt Lt H. J. Pryor   ME562 'K' Flg-Off J. A. Sanders
PD238 'H' Flg-Off J. Gingles   DV246 'U' Flg-Off F. H. A. Watts

One 617 Sqdn Mosquito as marker aircraft:
  NT205 'L' Wg Cdr J. B. Tait and Flt Sgt L. E. Gosling

One 627 Sqdn Mosquito as film aircraft:
  KB195 'B' Flt Lt I. H. Hanlon and Flt Lt K. G. Tice

Seventeen other Lancasters of 9 Sqdn were to attack the oil storage tanks at La Pallice with 1,000lb GP bombs, immediately after 617.

Escort 12 Mustang IIIs and 44 Spitfire IXs of the AEAF:
  64 Sqdn RAF   126 Sqdn RAF   611 Sqdn R Aux AF
  65 Sqdn RAF   131 Sqdn RAF

Bomb Loads Each 617 Sqdn Lancaster carried one Tallboy, with a 0.5-second delay. Tait's Mosquito carried two 120lb smoke markers.

Since 1941 La Pallice had been the home of the 3rd U-Boat Flotilla. The base was built on the eastern side of the basin of La Pallice, just to the west of the old port of La Rochelle, and linked to the sea by two parallel locks. The shelter complex, some 35,000 square metres in size, had a roof of 7.30m above Pens 1 to 5 and 6.50m above Pens 6 to 10. Again, work on the *Fangrost* had begun, but it was nowhere near completion.

The route out was over Bridport and H-Hour was 0800. Despite cloud on the approach, it was decided that Tait's markers were not required. The Tallboys went down in three minutes, the first one falling just short, in the water. Hamilton's was the second and he claimed a direct hit. Iveson said he saw one hit in the centre of the target, with a big orange flash, which was confirmed by one of 9 Sqdn's pilots. Pryor's bomb hit the north-east corner of the pen. Flak hit Fearn's Lancaster, forcing him to come home on three engines. Withdrawal cover was given by 64 and 126 Sqdns, whose Spitfires' short range had been boosted by the fitting of 90-gallon drop tanks at short notice.

9 Sqdn's sticks were scattered, some overshooting into the water, due to a 'spread' of winds found by them at different heights and distances from the target. At this distance Gee was inaccurate by up to two miles. Fires were started just to the east of the AP, followed by a huge column of dark brown smoke, but the oil tanks were not hit.

As far as 9 were concerned, a tendency for their navigators to slacken off while on daylight operations had been noted, leading to Bardney's station commander giving them and their bomb aimers a lecture on the need for accuracy. This quickly led to a marked improvement, which would have benefits for other raids later on.

One Tallboy hit the twenty-foot-thick pen roof, blasting a crater five feet deep. Another landed over Pen 10, penetrating nine feet of the second roof layer and going off above the eleven feet of concrete below, where its nose was later found. The roof cracked inwards and bulged slightly. Altogether there were six hits on it, dislodging large pieces of concrete from the south-east corner and tearing up a large part of the centre. Nevertheless, there was no U-boat damage and little effect on the repair shops. As at Brest, there had not been enough *Fangrost* to make much of a difference to the performance of the Tallboys, but the two original roof layers had proved sufficient.

Cochrane was delighted by what at first appeared to be impressive results: 'In the attack on La Pallice 617 Sqdn broke all records by obtaining six or seven hits on the pens.'

Indeed they had, but it became clear that the damage was not decisive and 617 returned to La Pallice on 11 August with 2,000lb AP bombs. This turned out to be futile and it was evident that at present, even with only one squadron using them, the

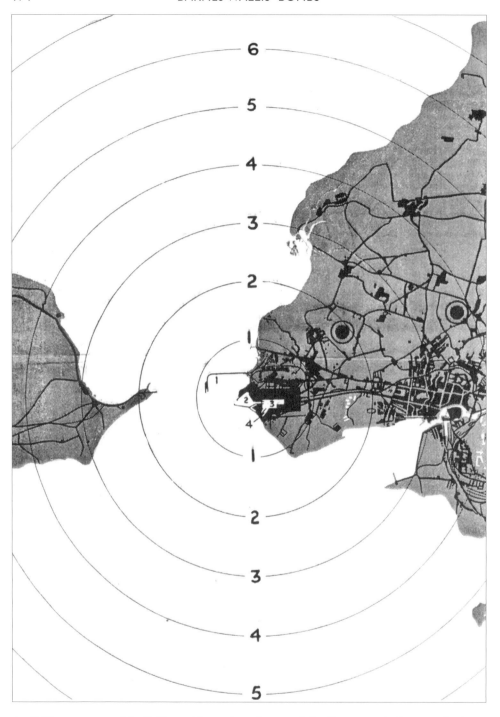

An RAF target map of La Pallice, with north at the top of the diagram. 1 is the outer harbour, 2 the inner port, 3 the wet dock, and 4 the dry docks. The pens were situated on the east side of the harbour basin. (H. F. C. Parsons)

stock of Tallboys was being expended far more rapidly than they could be replaced. For the time being the squadron would have to make do with whatever else was available.

12 August 1944
Target The U-boat pens at Brest.
Weather Very good visibility.

Force Ten Lancasters of 617 Sqn:

DV380 'P' Wg Cdr J. B. Tait	PD233 'G' Flg-Off M. Hamilton
PD238 'H' Sqdn Ldr J. V. Cockshott	ME561 'R' Flg-Off A. E. Kell
LM485 'N' Flt Lt H. J. Pryor	ME555 'C' Flg-Off I. S. Ross
DV391 'O' Flt Lt D. J. Oram	ME562 'K' Flg-Off J. A. Sanders
LM489 'A' Flg-Off J. Gingles	DV246 'U' Flg-Off F. H. A. Watts

Two Mosquitoes of 617 and 627 as camera aircraft:
  NT205 'L' Flt Lt G. E. Fawke and Flg-Off T. A. Bennett
  KB215 'H' Sqdn Ldr N. W. Mackenzie and P/O A. Denholm

Sixty-eight Lancasters and two Mosquitoes of 1 and 5 Groups attacked pens at Bordeaux and La Pallice as well as Brest, without loss.

Escort Two AEAF Spitfire squadrons provided general cover, eight Mosquitoes of 100 Group also taking part in the Bordeaux raid:
  64 Sqdn RAF   126 Sqdn RAF   515 Sqdn RAF

Bomb Loads As many aircraft as possible were to carry one Tallboy, with a 0.5-second delay, which indicated the bomb shortage at this time. The others would have carried 2,000lb AP bombs, but supplies proved better than expected, allowing sufficient Tallboys to be made available for all ten aircraft.

This was a morning raid, with H-Hour at 0900, although the squadron was three-quarters of an hour late. Cockshott returned early due to engine trouble, bringing his bomb back. So did Watts, due to an unserviceable SABS.

For the first time Tait flew a Lancaster with this unit, taking Fearn's place as skipper of his crew. Heavy flak hit his aircraft and three others, but three direct hits were made, piercing the main roof, damaging an outer wall, and breaking off a large piece of overhanging concrete at the west side. One roof crater was 54ft across.

Tait's bomb hit close to the centre and all the others were on target except for one which fell in the water about 100 yards from the front of the pens. Even this had its effect, for one U-boat was believed to be hit and the tanker *Rade* was down by the stern. Another one, the *Wat Kross*, had capsized, blocking half the harbour. There were possibly two more hits that did not penetrate.

13 August 1944
Target The U-boat pens and shipping at Brest.
Weather Fair with good visibility.

Force 13 Lancasters of 617 Sqn:

EE146 'D' Wg Cdr J. B. Tait	LM482 'Q' Flg-Off R. E. Knights
PD238 'H' Sqdn Ldr J. V. Cockshott	LM492 'W' Flg-Off W. R. Lee
ED763 'Z' Flt Lt C. J. G. Howard	ME555 'C' Flg-Off I. S. Ross
DV391 'O' Flt Lt D. J. Oram	ME562 'K' Flg-Off J. A. Sanders
LM485 'N' Flt Lt H. J. Pryor	DV246 'U' Flg-Off F. H. A. Watts
LM489 'A' Flt Lt J. E. R. Williams	ME561 'R' Flg-Off E. Willsher
PD233 'G' Flg-Off M. Hamilton	

Two Mosquitoes of 617 and 627 as camera aircraft:
  NT202 'N' Flt Lt G. E. Fawke and Flg-Off T. A. Bennett
  KB215 'H' Flt Lt I. H. Hanlon and Flt Lt K. G. Tice

A further fourteen Lancasters of 9 Sqdn also attacked Brest, using 1,000lb AP bombs.

Escort 13 Spitfire IXs of 611 Sqdn R Aux AF

Bomb Loads Tait, Hamilton, Knights, Watts and Williams all carried Tallboys, with a
0.5-second delay. The rest of 617 all carried 1,000lb bombs.

This morning raid was aimed not only at the pens but also at two old French warships,
the battleship *Clemenceau* and the cruiser *Gueydon*, with which the Germans had
planned to block the harbour before finally ceding it to the Allies. The minimal
fighter escort showed clearly that as far as this area was concerned the Luftwaffe was
something that few bomber crews were likely to meet again.

617 estimated three Tallboy hits on the pens, with another falling wide. Eight
aircraft of 617 and three from 9 straddled the *Gueydon* with four sticks of 1,000-
pounders – the rest overshot. Hits were claimed on both blockships. 9 Sqdn's primary
target, a tanker, was left blazing and down at the stern. Flt Lt E. H. M. Relton of 9
Sqdn and his crew were lost to flak.

Information obtained via Ultra later indicated that once again little internal damage
had been done to the pens, though it was now believed that two near misses had
undermined the north wall. Once ground inspection became possible, a US Strategic
Bombing Survey report would confirm these and add one hit. These two would have
been due to Hamilton and Knights, who both claimed that their Tallboys fell at the
northern edge – close, but not close enough to bring the building down.

Tait had concentrated on the western part of the pens, while the Tallboys of Watts
and Williams were said to have fallen south-east of the AP or in the centre. No one
seemed prepared to put their hand up for the one which fell 500 yards north-east of
the target! PRU coverage indicated one more hit on the roof, but both the pens and
the two blockships were still in evidence. The tanker had indeed gone down by the
stern and was now resting on the bottom of the harbour.

On 14 August twenty-seven Lancasters of 9 and 617, with their usual Mosquito
attendants and fighter escort, were part of a 159-strong 5 Group raid which attacked
the *Clemenceau* and *Gueydon* again, together with a supply ship. All the Lancasters
carried either 1,000lb or 2,000lb AP bombs.

By now Brest's landward side had been fully occupied by the US VIII Corps, but
still the port's stubborn garrison held out and the flak was as heavy as ever. Two of
5 Group's Lancasters were lost and several of 617's aircraft were hit, wounding one
pilot and killing a bomb aimer. One of 9 Sqdn's pilots was also slightly wounded and
his wireless-operator killed, necessitating a forced landing at Exeter.

Although not all the bombing on 14 August was accurate, 97 Sqdn afterwards reported
that 'Photographic evidence later showed no sign of the vessels on the surface … An
extraordinary display of precision bombing.' It certainly was, but the pens still stood.

By the middle of August eight serviceable U-boats had left Brest, leading to the
disbanding of the 9th U-Boat Flotilla. The 1st Flotilla met the same fate when another
boat that had been patched up left on 3 September, leaving behind one other mine-
damaged one. Both Dönitz and Hitler had ordered the French ports to be defended
to the last man, each of their commanders having taken an oath to do so. In this
instance the defenders were led by the redoubtable German paratroop commander
Generalleutnant Bernhard-Herrmann Ramcke, so it was not surprising that Brest
held out against the Americans until 18 September. The surrender came only after a
fierce month-long battle that wrecked just about every building in the town except
the pens!

The U-boat pens at Brest, still intact despite several direct hits by Tallboys. (Imperial War Museum, neg. no. CL1221)

A close-up of the roof of the Brest pens. At least six Tallboy hits can be seen, but only three appear to have penetrated. (Imperial War Museum, neg. no. CL1223)

Once the bullets had stopped flying, the US Strategic Bombing Survey then went over them, reporting that Tallboys had scored a total of nine direct hits on the roof, but being unable to distinguish between the damage caused by the differently fused bombs. However, it was evident that all of them had partly penetrated the roof and come to rest before exploding. Of these, two had been above walls, causing little scabbing, but two others had blown scab holes similar in size to the craters, which were 9m across and 3m deep. In the other five instances the craters and scab holes joined up to form holes some 5m across. Damage done inside had been slight as in each case the blast had spent itself while tearing through the concrete. None of these bombs had struck the *Fangrost*, so a test of its strength against Tallboy was never established.

The two Tallboy near misses outside had produced craters 30m across but they had not resulted in any blast, shock, or fragmentation damage to the outside walls. Contrary to what Ultra had said after the raid of 13 August, there was no mention of any undermining. German casualties at the pens had been light, with four killed, three of them on the roof and one inside one of the pens.

Nevertheless, once the French Navy occupied the pens after the war, they found that a good deal of concrete had been brought down inside them, partly blocking access to those pens just under the craters and allowing rain into the workshops through cracks in the roof. Fallen chunks also partly blocked the drainage system. As if this mess had not been enough, the Germans, defiant to the last, had added to it by dumping everything from grenades to vehicles inside. Following clearance, the pens would be used by ships and diesel-powered submarines of the French Navy.

On 16 August La Pallice was again the target for fourteen Lancasters from 9 and eleven of 617, four of the latter carrying Tallboys. The bombers were twenty minutes late and so failed to meet their escort. They ran up to the target through thick flak, which damaged Fearn's aircraft for the fourth time running. Tait dropped six 2,000lb AP bombs on what he took to be the AP, seen through a gap in the clouds, but to his chagrin the real AP was identified a few seconds later through another gap. Only one of 9 Sqdn's aircraft bombed before the raid was called off due to the cloud. No Tallboys were expended this time.

18 August 1944
Target The U-boat pens at La Pallice.
Weather Good.

Force 11 Lancasters of 617 Sqdn:

EE146 'D' Wg Cdr J. B. Tait	PD238 'H' Lt H. C. Knilans USAAF
PD233 'G' Flt Lt A. W. Fearn	PB415 'S' Flg-Off R. E. Knights
ED763 'Z' Flt Lt C. J. G. Howard	PB416 'V' Flg-Off F. Levy
EE131 'B' Flt Lt D. J. Oram	LM489 'A' Flg-Off I. S. Ross
LM485 'N' Flt Lt H. J. Pryor	DV402 'X' Flg-Off E. H. A. Watts
ME555 'C' Flg-Off D. W. Carey	

One 617 Sqdn Mosquito as a camera aircraft:
   NT205 'L' Flt Lt G. E. Fawke and Flg-Off T. A. Bennett

A further 14 Lancasters of 9 Sqdn also attacked the pens with conventional bombs.

Escort No details available.

Bomb Loads Tait, Howard, Knilans, Oram, Pryor and Watts each carried one Tallboy, with a 0.5-second delay. The remainder carried six 2,000lb AP bombs each.

Five of 9 Sqdn's aircraft were detailed to act as windfinders. These would pass their findings to their leader, who after averaging them out would then broadcast this to the whole force. Wg Cdr Jim Bazin, 9's CO, later claimed he had difficulty following 617's formation and alleged that they did not adhere to the planned turning points. Nevertheless, the raid was apparently successful.

Once again 617 faced a hot reception. Fearn was hit for the fifth time just as he released his load, and took violent evasive action. Despite extensive damage he reached home. Oram lost an engine over the target, but still bombed it.

The first bombs seemed to be concentrated on the eastern side of the pens, but then smoke soon covered all of them. Tait saw one Tallboy burst on the south-west corner of the pens and another slightly overshoot to the north. Levy saw one land on the dockside two hundred yards away, while Pryor saw one hit dead centre, with another at the north-west corner.

As far as the Tallboys were concerned, PRU coverage showed at least one and possibly two hits on the roof of the pens, with one very near miss, Some of 9 Sqdn's bombs had also hit it, but neither the 2,000-pounders nor the Tallboys appeared to have penetrated. It seems that in all the raids on this target just four Tallboys went through the roof.

The rapid American advance resulted in La Pallice becoming increasingly isolated and, helped on its way by the air-raids, the 3rd U-Boat Flotilla withdrew to Norway, less one boat, U-766, which was unseaworthy and partly destroyed. Like Lorient, the port was besieged and did not surrender until May 1945. The pens were taken over by the French Navy, but now are no longer used by them. A Tallboy bomb nose, almost certainly the one found between the two roof layers after the attack of 9 August, was later displayed in a French Navy office there. In the 1980s the pens briefly reverted to their original use when they were featured in the German film *Das Boot*.

Information on the limitations of Tallboy against concrete had by now reached 5 Group, for on 22 August they passed a signal to both Bardney and Woodhall Spa:'For use against heavy concrete structures such as submarine pens, it has been decided to revert to 11 seconds' delay fusing.' The reference to Bardney was in anticipation of 9 Sqdn's imminent change to a Tallboy-carrying role.

This could be claimed to be an echo of what had been said after the Ashley Walk trials, but with hindsight, it may be doubted whether any fusing changes would have had much effect against such solid constructions. The idea that Wallis had put forward the previous spring – that of destroying the target's roof, then undermining its now unsupported walls by near misses – had seemed sound at the time, but in each instance the best that had been achieved was to punch holes through the roof. Even though more than one hit had occurred on top of each pen building, accompanied by some near misses, this damage had not been sufficient to cause the walls to collapse.

Even if only near misses had been tried, it would have proved extremely difficult to drop Tallboy at the right distance from the target in the face of heavy defensive fire. Too close and the result would be another roof hole; too far away and it would crater the ground without undermining the wall.

24 August 1944
Target The E/R-boat pens at Ijmuiden.
Weather No cloud but slight haze over target.

Force 8 Lancasters of 617 Sqdn:

EE146 'D' Wg Cdr J. B. Tait	LM489 'A' Flg-Off D. H. Carey
ED763 'Z' Flt Lt C. J. G. Howard	PB416 'V' Flg-Off F. Levy
PD238 'H' Flt Lt T. C. Iveson	EE131 'B' Flg-Off I. S. Ross
PD233 'G' Flt Lt H. J. Pryor	PB415 'S' Flg-Off F. H. A. Watts

Two Mosquitoes of 617 and 627 as camera aircraft:
  NT205 'L' Flt Lt G. E. Fawke and Flg-Off T. A. Bennett
  KB215 'H' Flg-Off M. D. Gribbin and Flg-Off P. G. Herbert

14 Lancasters of 9 Sqdn also took part in this early afternoon attack, using 1,000lb bombs.

Escort Twenty-two 12 Group Spitfire IXs:
  229 Sqdn RAF   312 Sqdn (Czech)

Bomb Loads Each 617 Sqdn Lancaster carried one Tallboy, with an 11-second delay.

The pens at Ijmuiden docks had been constructed along similar lines to those at Boulogne and Le Havre, but this time there were two different sets of buildings, known as the old and new pens.

Built around the area known as the Haring Haven (Herring Harbour), the old pens, of which there were twelve, were intended for R-Boats – minesweepers – as well as E-boats, and were located at the harbour's south end. These were 480ft by 210ft, with walls two metres thick between the pens. The roof was eight to ten feet thick, being supported and reinforced by prefabricated concrete pilings. This method would also be used at the Farge U-boat shelter in north-western Germany, which would be attacked seven months later. The new pens, at the north-western end of the harbour, were exclusively for the use of E-boats, but as they would not be attacked until the following February their details may be omitted for the moment.

In May Ijmuiden's defences had been assessed as sixty-four light guns. Since the summer the Admiralty had been pressing for an attack on them, being well aware of the significance they would have once the Allies had pushed the Germans out of France and Belgium. Further ports would be needed to supply Allied troops as they moved forward into Holland, and a threat was posed by Ijmuiden's E-boats, which hid in the pens by day, operating at night.

229's Spitfires met one of the Lancaster squadrons over Happisburgh, on the Norfolk coast between Cromer and Great Yarmouth, then continued at 16,000ft to meet the other at a second rendezvous point south-west of Ijmuiden. Arriving over the target at 1350, 229 orbited for ten minutes until 312 joined them. Fifteen minutes later the Lancaster formation approached.

At 1407 Tait informed Group and then both squadrons that H-Hour had been postponed by six minutes. The reason was not given but it was possibly due to the need to find a bombing wind. A 9 Sqn aircraft that had been detailed as a windfinder for the whole force sent its message to them at 1421, receiving a prompt acknowledgement. A few minutes later the bombers reached Ijmuiden and their Tallboys went down in less than five minutes, while 627's Mosquito filmed from 9,000ft.

Orbiting clockwise, 229 rated the flak as 'very slight and inaccurate, amounting to only about one dozen bursts of heavy gunfire.' Bardney's diarist, writing on behalf of 9 Sqn, commented, 'The opposition from flak was surprisingly meagre, only two heavy guns being reported. Fighter escort was provided, but their task was a sinecure.'

Both bomber squadrons assessed this as a very successful operation, with several direct hits being claimed. Tait felt his own bomb probably fell on the northern edge of the pens. Several crews said they saw a hit in the centre and one at the north-western edge. Levy had probably the best view of all, saying the first Tallboy fell at the south-eastern corner, the next two in the dock about 100 yards from the pen mouth and the fourth was a direct hit which sparked off a huge explosion. He also confirmed the direct hit in the centre. Most of 9 Sqn's bombs also fell in the target area, creating a mass of smoke, although there were no fires. The bombers were then escorted back to within fifteen minutes of the English coast. Again there had been no fighter opposition.

Analysis of the strike photographs indicated that the damage was one direct hit and five near misses, three on the landward and two on the seaward side of the target. One hit in the south-western area of the pen had blown out a large portion on the south side. Another very near miss by the south-eastern corner did not penetrate.

A report compiled after liberation stated that there had in fact been one hit and one near miss. However, these had been sufficient to cause 3,465 square feet of the roof to break away, along with a substantial part of the rear and internal dividing walls. The roof's collapse had been due to these two, although it was apparently assisted by the other near misses undermining the foundations.

As the new pens had not been affected by this attack it seemed likely that further visits to Ijmuiden would be necessary, but for now there were other targets.

Although the *Clemenceau* and *Gueydon* had been disposed of at Brest, there was still the danger of the Germans denying the Allies use of this port with other blockships, so on 26 August, 9 and 617 Sqdns were again briefed to attack shipping there. At the last minute this was postponed until the following day, when both squadrons successfully attacked two ships in the harbour with conventional bombs.

A second Bar to Tait's DSO was awarded during this month and on 9 September news of Cheshire's VC award reached the squadron. However, while 617 Sqdn might have thought well of themselves, there were others who did not. Either 5 Group's signal on 22 August ordering the reversion to 11 seconds' Tallboy fusing had been repeated to Bomber Command, or there had been a query by 5 Group's Armament Officer, Wg Cdr Richardson, who, it will be recalled, had been christened 'Talking Bomb' when

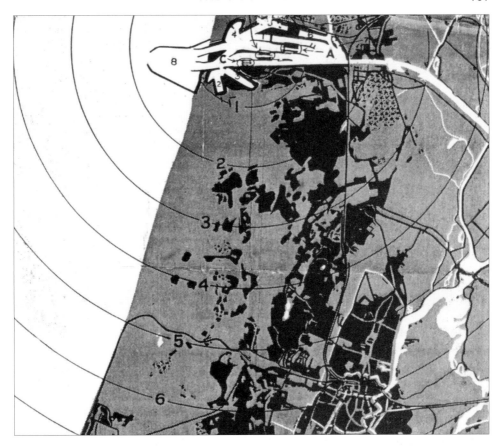

An RAF target map of Ijmuiden harbour, with north at the top of the diagram. Number 2 indicates the Herring Harbour, where the old pens were located (H. F. C. Parsons)

his obsession with this subject became apparent to 617. Anyway, the day after the Ijmuiden raid Air Commodore C. N. H. Bilney, who was on the Bomber Command staff at High Wycombe, penned a frank letter to Richardson on this question.

It was, Bilney said, well known from model tests that Tallboy was likely to be defeated by eleven feet of reinforced concrete and that a cast bomb of this type was likely to break up if pitted against a target of such strength. (This appeared to conflict with the Road Research Laboratory data on which Wallis had based his theory of attacking the roofs first.) It was also well known that Torpex, whether in 'straight' or 'desensitized' form, would self-initiate on impact due either to shock or to nipping of the charge during the fracture of the case. High Wycombe had therefore said that the delay was to be 0.01 seconds, so the bomb could detonate before it bounced back or broke up. 'These instructions have, of course, been completely ignored by your Group.' This was true, as any Tallboy used on the pens had carried either a delay of 0.5 seconds or 11 seconds, although pistol types had been subject to availability, like everything else.

Bilney's exasperated tone was aimed at 'Cocky's Private Air Force' and as such implied criticism of Cochrane rather than Richardson. The letter also suggested that the power of Tallboy had not been used to its fullest extent by 5 Group. Although Bilney did not point it out, the 0.01 setting had been that put forward by Wallis some three months before Tallboy had seen action. It therefore seemed that Wallis would have been proved right if his recommended delay setting had been adhered to, although his idea of destroying the roof to weaken the pen walls had not worked out.

Bilney went on to say that on small targets such as rocket sites the chances of a direct hit were small, and the aim of the attack was to cause earth subsidence by near misses.

Delay fusing was therefore justified in such instances. He considered that the Brest pen roof would not have been perforated unless some preliminary hits had softened it up, allowing subsequent hits to penetrate. The use of 0.01 seconds in all instances would mean the loss of the near miss effect (meaning that this fuse setting would not have been appropriate for the V-weapon sites, and implying that two types of fuse setting should have been used at the pens, the first for the roof and the second for the walls). He felt there was nothing to worry about as far as fusing was concerned. All this was said before the damage at the pens could be subjected to Allied scrutiny on the ground.

The wrong choice of AP at the pens, the sensitivity of Torpex and 5 Group's disregard of fusing instructions will shed some light on why the pen raids were not as devastating as might have been expected and why it was necessary to attack some of them more than once. In fairness to those at the sharp end, it was one thing for High Wycombe to icily point out how things ought to be done; it was quite another to carry them out while being faced with cloud and flak at high altitude.

What mattered was that, however fused or aimed, Tallboy had been able to inflict damage on the Biscay pens to the point where the U-boats had been driven back from the Atlantic coast, with a consequent saving of Allied lives at sea. To hold the Allied ground advance solely responsible for this departure would be to ignore the fact that some of these ports remained in German hands until the war's end. After the failed attempt on Hitler's life, everyone who had supported him was watching their backs, so their reluctance to surrender was understandable but futile; the troops in question would remain bottled up until VE Day. The Americans had plenty of infantry divisions to guard against any breakout and with the U-boats gone the Biscay ports no longer had any significance. Their retreat had left the pens empty and useless. Only Tallboy had been able to accomplish it.

If anyone had anything further to say concerning Tallboy's performance, use and abuse, there would now be another target which seemed likely to settle the matter, this time with two squadrons to attack it. The availability of Tallboys had improved as American production had got into its stride, so the previous July's proposal that 9 Sqdn should also carry them in future could now go ahead. For both units their next operation would be their most important one to date. It was for this that 9 had intensively practised on the Wainfleet and Epperstone bombing ranges throughout the fortnight following the Ijmuiden raid. They were still equipped with the Mark XIV sight, although the RAE had assisted in improving it.

As their number indicated, 9 were one of the RAF's first units, with a proud history that dated back to the days of the Royal Flying Corps. They could trace their line back to a Headquarters Flight of the RFC that had been formed in April 1914, in which airborne wireless experiments had been carried out. On the outbreak of the First World War in the following August the wireless flight had joined 4 Sqdn, but had become 9 Sqdn in December. Its detached wireless flights had subsequently been sent to other squadrons, leading to disbandment and then reformation on 1 April 1915 at Brooklands under Major Hugh Dowding, later of Battle of Britain fame. It had gone on to use several aircraft with Brooklands connections, from the Avro 504 biplane to the Vickers Vimy, Virginia and Wellington bombers, before re-equipping with Lancasters in September 1942.

9 Sqdn's technique would be that of vector bombing, by which a marker was dropped on a selected point some hundreds of yards upwind of the target area and was attacked by the crews with a pre-selected false wind on the bombsight. This would displace the mean point of impact of the bombing from the marker onto the target, which would be correct if just one marker was accurately dropped.

That meant knowing the wind speed and direction at the target, so the squadron was provided with a new windfinding attachment to add to the Air Position Indicator. They were apparently the guinea pigs to determine its best method of use on operations, for at this time there were just five APIs of this type available for the whole of Bomber Command. This indicated that there had been some more string pulling by

Cochrane to make sure that his men got them first, although others would be made available to 8 Group later on.

As 9 Sqdn now shared 617 Sqdn's special status, their crews could now volunteer for a second tour of operations after completing their first. In this 9 Sqdn had now fallen into line with 8 Group's practice – although the Pathfinders would not have been impressed to hear it – and it was expected that this would increase the squadron's bombing standards. They might lack 617's SABS sight, but they did not see this as a handicap. Certainly their experience was second to none.

Wg Cdr Jim Bazin, 9's CO, had, unusually for a bomber pilot, begun his career on Gladiator biplanes and Hurricane fighters with 607 Sqdn, an Auxiliary Air Force unit from Tyneside. He had seen action both in France and during the Battle of Britain, at the end of which his DFC award had been for ten enemy aircraft destroyed. By 1944 he would have been one of very few pre-war Auxiliaries still on operations. Bazin was, in the words of one man who flew with him, 'a very quiet person', but clearly an effective leader.

On 29 August an order had gone out that the next twelve Tallboys to be filled were to go to 9 Sqdn, who were introduced to them on the 31st, two of 617's armourers having gone over there to help smooth the path. Bardney's diarist stated that one was 'drop-tested' by them on this date, possibly with regard to the release problems that 617 had earlier experienced.

Corporal Frank Hawkins, an armourer who had joined 9 Sqdn the previous spring after previously handling small practice bombs at 15 OTU at Harwell, now found himself confronted with much larger weapons – first the 4,000lb cookie and then something three times its size:

> In the summer of 1944 the squadron added a new dimension to its arsenal in the shape of the enormous 12,000lb Tallboy. Mounted on special trolleys, these monsters required even more skilful manoeuvring by the drivers to get the bomb positioned as near as possible under the aircraft, helped by an armourer who steered the rear wheels of the trolley. The greater the accuracy in lining up the bomb the speedier the bombing-up process was, for there was little room to spare.
>
> It required four winches to lift each Tallboy from its cradle, each armourer cranking at the same time in order to keep an even keel; one armourer working too hard produced all sorts of problems, so it was a question of gradually inching up in unison until we were within a foot of the Lanc's bomb bay floor.
>
> At this stage a fifth armourer would shout instruction – in the best armourer tradition – to the men on the winches so that a special recess in the bomb would slot into a spring-loaded dowel attached to the machine's bomb bay floor. The moment of joy came when the two engaged with a distinct 'clonk', though it could mean some heaving and pushing before the closely toleranced dowel went home. Next step was to attach the sling that held the Tallboy in position. This comprised a series of jointed steel bars, slung crab-like around the centre belly of the bomb and secured with an electric release unit. With good teamwork the operation took around twenty eventful minutes.

Cases did occur at Bardney of Tallboys falling out of aircraft after they had been bombed-up, but there were no fatal accidents. During the winter to come, Corporal Hawkins would experience an anxious moment when, due to the icy conditions, a Tallboy slipped, its tail going up through the bomb bay floor of one aircraft. This recurred three times that morning and although a catastrophe was avoided, it illustrated one of the dangers the erks had to face.

> Another difficulty was the flapping of the suspension sling in the bomb bay after the Tallboy had been released and one day I found our armament officer in deep conversation with Barnes Wallis himself, discussing the pros and cons of the subject out at dispersal. Soon after his visit we found Bowden cables and toggles running from inside the aircraft to each sling being fitted, enabling the aircrew to pull them

up out of the way – a simple but effective means of overcoming what threatened to be a serious problem. Eventful days, I must say.

They certainly were. On 8 September seventeen of 9's crews, with nineteen from 617, attended a secret lecture by Cochrane. The next day an American-designed Lorraine crane, working almost at the limit of its capacity, went into action in the Bardney bomb dump, hauling the new monsters onto their cradles. The crews were on standby for a secret operation and inevitably rumours crept round both their bases.

Cochrane subsequently discovered that despite a stern order that what had been said should go no further, some crew members had talked to others who would not be involved in this operation and it was not long before rumours spread to other 5 Group units. In their newsletter, *V Group News*, itself a classified document at the time, he stated, 'A number of individuals are about to face the consequences of their folly and I cannot, at present, refer in more detail to this episode. But it shows that there are still those who fail to realise their responsibilities.'

He also said that captured German records named seventeen 5 Group POWs who had said more than they should have during interrogation. They too would face the consequences once they returned to British soil. The only safe course was to stick to name, rank and number. The Germans would respect anyone who kept to that, but would seek to obtain further information from any POW who lacked the sense to keep his mouth shut. Gibson would certainly have approved of Cochrane's action and for some of 617's old hands it felt like *Chastise* again. It was fortunate for those involved that this time nothing of what was said reached the Germans.

So what target warranted this kind of security? A further piece of the puzzle was added during the next two days. Reg Firman, the Vickers representative and, it will be recalled, bomb slip designer, had been called in to investigate earlier reports of bomb release malfunctions, visiting both Bardney and Woodhall Spa in the course of witnessing timing tests on release of a Tallboy from a Lancaster. The testing instruments were accurate to one microsecond, and their figures showed that there were 18-25 milliseconds from the moment the slip was energised to the bomb beginning to fall. There was therefore no reason why the slips should not work correctly, but Firman was aware that the problem might still recur.

Someone who would not be going on this next raid was P/O Gordon Maguire, 9 Sqdn's Armament Officer, who although not aircrew was one of the unit's characters. Gordon Maguire had first seen action as a 'winged bullet' gunner on Fairey Battles with 88 Sqdn during the start of the Phoney War, at a time when there was as yet no regular air gunner's trade or brevet and a temporary metal sleeve badge had been issued instead. He had later flown an unofficial thirteen operations in W4964 'J-Johnnie', a famous veteran Lancaster, testing an undergun installation he had designed.

We had several Tallboys drop off Lancasters while they were on dispersal at Bardney. There was no one near the aircraft at the time. I checked the release unit for machinery aberrations – it was only a matter of a few thousandths of an inch. They had to be allowed to rest after each op. The Tallboy release unit was a good one, but we had problems with the No.1 Mark 1. It was difficult to get Vickers to agree that there were people who knew bombs better than they did. That was why after the war, when the Blue Steel standoff missile came along for the V-force, we used an American-made release unit.

Given the attitude that Reg Firman had had to face, it seemed likely to be a case of for 'Vickers', read 'Wallis'. Anyway, all seemed well. Looking at what was coming up now, it would have to be. The Bardney tests ended at noon on 11 September, as the test aircraft was needed for an operation. Although Firman did not yet know it, the target would be a well-known German battleship lurking in a remote Norwegian fjord. What other bombs had failed to destroy and Highball had not been allowed to attack, Tallboy now would.

8

A Hell of a Bomb

The destruction or even crippling at sea of the *Tirpitz* is the greatest event at sea at the present time. No other target is comparable to it. If she were only crippled it would be difficult to take her back to Germany. The entire naval situation throughout the world would be altered ... The whole strategy at this moment turns on this ship, which is holding four times the number of British ships paralysed, to say nothing of two new American battleships retained in the Atlantic. I regard the matter as being of the highest urgency and importance.

Winston Churchill to Chiefs of Staff, January 1942

The ship to which Churchill referred was indeed a formidable one. Launched on 1 April 1939, by the granddaughter of the admiral after whom she was named, she weighed 52,600 tons, was 118ft wide and 820ft long, mounted eight 15-inch guns and a massive array of secondary armament which included seventy 20mm anti-aircraft guns. Her crew consisted of 2,350 men and her maximum speed was 29 knots. A system of compartments fitted inside her had led to the claim that she was unsinkable – but then that had also been said of the *Titanic*.

Since the outbreak of war the *Tirpitz*, like her sister ship the *Bismarck*, had been a potential threat to what control of the sea Britain still had. She had not sunk a single ship, nor ever would, but by acting as a fleet-in-being she had helped to dictate the shape and progress of the naval war, not only in Arctic waters but around the world, holding back ships of the Royal Navy that were badly needed for the Pacific campaign.

The *Tirpitz*'s hiding place in northern Norway, 1,000 miles from the nearest RAF airfield, meant that Bomber Command could not fly there, attack her and return home. Her apparent reluctance to come out and fight made it impossible for the Home Fleet to destroy her as they had the *Bismarck*. In 1940 they had sent the veteran battleship HMS *Warspite* into the confines of the Narvik fjords. She had returned safely after causing eight German destroyers to be sunk or scuttled, but such a bold course of action could not be risked against a capital ship. Heavy underwater defences ruled out an attack by submarine.

The influence the *Tirpitz* could exert on events, just by sitting still, had been shown by the loss of most of the ships of the British convoy PQ17 in July 1942, while en route to the Russian port of Archangel. As the result of an unconfirmed rumour that the *Tirpitz* had put to sea the convoy's escort had been withdrawn, accompanied by the now notorious signal that the convoy was to disperse. The fleeing merchantmen had been easy targets for the Luftwaffe and the U-boats, who between them sank twenty-one ships out of thirty-five. The battleship had indeed sailed, but had turned round and gone home again when her captain's superiors, fearing a clash with the Home Fleet, called off her part in the attack. It was an episode from which the admirals on both sides had emerged with no credit.

Grossadmiral Erich Raeder, the last of the *Kriegsmarine*'s battleship men, had resigned his command in January 1943 in protest at Hitler's plans to pay off the last remaining heavy German surface units. His replacement had been Karl Dönitz, the submariner. Although the *Tirpitz*'s future had therefore seemed bleak, Dönitz had

The *Tirpitz* at Asenfjord, near Trondheim, her huge size illustrated by the passing motorboat. A double torpedo boom is visible on the left. Camouflage nets cover the bows and stern, while white sheets mask the main armament's gun barrels. (Imperial War Museum, neg. no. C2356A)

ruled out taking her back to Germany for scrapping. While en route she would have presented a tempting target. Putting her into a breaker's yard would have tied up labour that could have been more profitably used elsewhere and would have done the *Kriegsmarine*'s morale no good.

Although Dönitz agreed to paying off some of the surviving German cruisers, he told Hitler that he believed the *Tirpitz*, along with the battlecruiser *Scharnhorst* and the pocket battleship *Lützow*, still had a part to play. If they remained in the far north of Norway they could still pose a threat to the Allied convoys and therefore help to relive pressure on the Eastern Front, as well as assisting in the defence of Norway. Believing the British would mount an invasion there, Hitler agreed and the remaining capital ships were reprieved.

Churchill continued to press for action to eradicate this menace and, as we have seen, *Tirpitz* had been repeatedly attacked by a variety of methods, from the 1942 Halifax mining fiasco to the success of the *Source* midget submariners. During 1943 she had at last gone to sea to bombard a surface target – the Anglo-Norwegian weather station on the island of Spitzbergen. This had been a surprise to the Royal Navy's Intelligence as there had been no prior warning of it. In the interests of shoring up morale, her crew had been lavishly decorated for what had been a minor operation compared with the record of the *Scharnhorst*, whose crew were not impressed and said so. One of them later commented, '*Tirpitz* had a hangdog look about her.' Her crew were in general younger than those on the *Scharnhorst*, and lacking in the discipline that comes from experience.

Although the *Tirpitz* would never have the notoriety of the *Bismarck*, she had acquired what at the time had seemed like the ultimate accolade – a slighting reference on the BBC's *ITMA* radio show. When comedian Tommy Handley had been playing in his bath with his toy navy, he had, he said, torpedoed the *Tirpitz* with his big toe. Those charged with the job of sinking her no doubt wished it would be so easy.

The *Source* attack had put the *Tirpitz* out of action for several months while the gaping holes in her hull were repaired. This had to be carried out on site, as Dönitz had considered a long tow to Kiel or Wilhelmshaven too risky. *Lützow* returned to Germany and on Boxing Day 1943 *Scharnhorst* was sunk by the Home Fleet during the Battle of North Cape, when she attacked a British convoy.

So as 1944 dawned the *Tirpitz* was alone, but not forgotten. A Russian air attack in February was unsuccessful and in March, her repairs complete, she at last sailed for exercises, moving from her anchorage at Altenfjord to nearby Kaafjord. Here a PR Spitfire of 542 Sqdn found her and on 3 April Operation *Tungsten* was mounted. This consisted of FAA Barracudas, carrying up to 1,600lb of bombs each, escorted by American-built Corsairs, Hellcats and Wildcats from the carriers HMS *Furious* and *Victorious*.

Two Barracudas were lost in the attacks that followed. The pilots dived to below their ordered height of 3,000ft, so that most of their bombs did not have sufficient momentum to penetrate deep into the ship. There was a story afterwards that one did, but failed to go off. This caused some relief to the Germans, for on examination it was found to carry more sand than explosive! Fourteen hits caused many casualties and serious damage, but it was all above the battleship's armoured deck and she remained seaworthy, albeit out of action for another three months.

The carrier force returned in some triumph to Scapa Flow, but as far as the Admiralty was concerned it was still not the end of the matter. The *Tirpitz*'s last batch of repairs had been completed ahead of schedule. She would remain a threat until sunk, and if their own aircrew could not do the job then perhaps Harris – long known as no lover of battleships – could do it for them.

Harris' relations with their Lordships had long been robust. A keen amateur yachtsman before the war, his contempt for the Royal Navy knew no bounds. He is alleged to have said that if you were going to sea there were three things you should never take with you: a fish, a bicycle and a naval officer.

On rising to Air rank pre-war, Harris had been involved in planning for the next conflict.   He had started one of his own by repeatedly clashing with Admiral Sir Tom Philips, one of the Royal Navy's battleship champions. Once Philips had tried to assure Harris that if Italy entered the next war on Germany's side, the Royal Navy would still have free use of the Mediterranean, regardless of the strength of the Italian Air Force.

Harris had not been won over: 'One day, Tom, you will be standing on your bridge and your ship will be smashed to pieces by bombers and torpedo aircraft. As she sinks, your last words will be, "That was a whopping great mine we hit!"'

Tragically, his words turned out to be all too true. Off Malaya in December 1941, Philips and over half the men under him would be lost in the manner that Harris had described.

Whitehall warriors have long memories and while none of them would have thanked Harris for being right, or for his apparent attitude that only Bomber Command could win the war, it had to be admitted that so far the Fleet Air Arm had not sunk the *Tirpitz*, despite another eight raids by them on her, only one of which had scored any further hits. His task was to succeed where the Navy had failed, which would mean diverting two of the best squadrons in 5 Group from his attacks on Germany. So be it. That was no great hardship. His Main Force could manage without 9 and 617 for the time being. He had made a name for himself in part by frequently sounding off about the vulnerability of capital ships to air attack. Here was a chance to prove how right he was. The idea of rubbing their Lordships' noses in it was one that suited Harris very well.

Sub-Lieutenant John Lorimer, one of the surviving *Source* midget submarine crew members, said later, '*Tirpitz* had, I think I'm right in saying, a sixteen-inch armoured deck and it would take a hell of a bomb to go through that.'

Indeed, and at the time there was nothing better than Tallboy.

The first move in this latest bid to sink Germany's last capital ship was made by 192 Sqdn, an Elint unit that was part of 100 Group. Five of their Halifaxes were sent to

Lossiemouth on what was described as a 'special detachment' on 31 August. Their task was to plot the German coastal radar, looking for gaps in it, and the next day four of them covered the area from Kristiansand to the Lofoten Islands.

During the first three days of September, 192's crews flew a total of seven sorties, being in the air for up to nine hours at a time. The German radar stations provided overlapping cover on aircraft approaching the coast at 5,000ft and above. Due to the curvature of the earth they were less effective against low flyers and the Elint crews discovered a gap in their cover over central Norway, through which aircraft flying at 1,500ft and below could pass unobserved. Window had proved a valuable counter-measure, but in this instance any attempt to jam the radar would alert the defences long before the bombers reached their target. A stealthy approach would be better than one that swamped the screens.

Even if surprise was achieved, the task that now confronted 9 and 617 Sqdns was a formidable one. Kaafjord was a narrow and steep-sided inlet: factors that had eventually ruled out the use of Highball. Like *Chastise*, the operation was dependent on the weather, with less than three-tenths' cloud on only three days in September. Thirty-eight heavy and twenty-two light AA guns were stationed on shore, with efficient radar guidance. The anchorage's defences were reinforced by those of the battleship, with torpedo nets and smoke canisters around it. It was this last measure that made surprise essential, as the screen would take only ten minutes to become fully effective. As yet there were no guided weapons able to 'see' through the fog that would be created and for all its wonders the SABS could not do so either.

However, there was reason to believe that aircraft approaching from the landward side would not be detected until a quarter of an hour before they reached the fjord. Certainly the east would be the last direction from which the defenders would expect the RAF to attack, but that meant using Russian facilities.

Yagodnik, a Russian naval airfield ten miles south of Archangel, was the nearest base from which the two squadrons could operate, and approval to do so had been obtained following negotiations with the Russians. As it was 2,100 miles away from Lossiemouth, it was decided that extra tanks would have to be fitted into some of the Lancasters' fuselages. This would not only mean an increased fire risk within the fuselage, but also the removal of the mid-upper turrets, although their gunners could still be carried at the discretion of each squadron CO.

Extra fuel would be carried in a long-range Wellington tank and a Mosquito drop tank, which together gave an additional 250 gallons. Curiously, this modification was not deemed necessary for the Tallboy-carrying aircraft, which would carry their maximum of 2,154 gallons in their wing tanks. There would, however, be a second force carrying a new weapon – the Johnny Walker mine. These aircraft would be stuffed to the gills with 100-octane fuel. The thoughts of those who flew in them can be imagined.

Since two different types of bomb load were to be carried, the detachment would be split into Force A and Force B. Force A was to be twelve Tallboy-carrying aircraft from each squadron, with a further six JW mine carriers from each in Force B. As things turned out, thirty-eight Lancasters would be made available at the start of the operation; eighteen from 9 and twenty from 617. A 463 Sqdn Lancaster would film the raid. Support would be provided by two Liberators from 511 Sqdn at RAF Lyneham, which would carry ground crews and spares. Advanced bases at Lossiemouth, Kinloss and Milltown, all in north-eastern Scotland, would be made available.

Despite the previous failed attempt to mine the ship, it was decided that the Johnny Walker would be tried. This 500lb spherical weapon, which carried ninety pounds of Torpex, had not been used in action before. It was an oscillating mine, powered by a hydrogen reservoir which made it capable of moving sideways in the water as well as up and down, the idea being that it would continue to do so until it came up under a target. When released from the aircraft the mine's parachute opened by a static line, and the fuse's safety pin would be withdrawn on contact with the water. This also released the parachute and in so doing pulled a flexible wire, arming the fuse and a self-destruct device, which would go off once the hydrogen was expended. The JW mines were to be dropped on the north side of the fjord, in an area that would not be affected by the smokescreen. Like Tallboy, it was enveloped by security, to such an extent that some crew members wrongly thought that it too had been designed by Wallis.

By 8 September all aircraft were ready, except the one used for the Bardney Tallboy release tests, but the operation was temporarily shelved due to the weather. On this day the two Liberators arrived at Bardney – their pilots were told what was going on but for the moment the rest of their crews were not. A briefing also took place at Woodhall Spa on this day, featuring a large floor display that included the surrounding mountains and a model of the *Tirpitz*. Over the next two days the crews became familiar with the target and the terrain around it. The operation was code-named *Paravane*.

Navigation would be critical on such a long flight and while it was correctly anticipated that Gee would be available as an aid until 1,000 miles from Yagodnik, from that point the crews would be very much on their own. Perhaps with McCarthy's *Chastise* experience in mind, the instrument fitters took particular care in checking all the aircraft compasses, eliminating as much deviation as possible.

At Bardney Tallboys were being loaded aboard 9 Sqdn's Lancasters for the first time, being supervised by a Mr Chisholm, who was a Vickers representative. P/O Maguire, the armament officer, was approached by one of his corporals regarding the fitting of one into Flg-Off Lake's aircraft, EE136 'R'.

Mr Chisholm doesn't think it's right, sir.
Okay, take it off and Mr Chisholm can put it back on.

This time the spigot audibly locked into the corresponding hole in the bomb. However, this bomb would not reach the *Tirpitz*.

On 11 September both squadrons took off. The forecast was good and it was intended that they would reach Yagodnik in daylight on 12 September, assisted by

A painting of a Tallboy going aboard W4964 'J-Johnnie', a Lancaster that would complete 106 operations with 9 Squadron. Flown by Flight Lieutenant Doug Melrose, this veteran would take part in the first of three Tallboy operations against the *Tirpitz*. (J. Young)

radio beacons there and at Murmansk. The total of thirty-eight Lancasters consisted of twelve Tallboy aircraft from 9 Sqdn and fourteen from 617, with each unit contributing a further six JW mine carriers. On the next day the Film Unit aircraft would follow. The decision had been taken to fly direct to Yagodnik. However, despite their long range, the two Liberators paused at Lossiemouth to refuel; a move that put them behind those they were to support, which would cause problems later on.

The first to drop out was Flg-Off Lake, after his Tallboy slipped backwards in the bomb bay. His wireless-operator saw that the toggles used for raising the bomb sling were in the wrong position and a check by the bomb aimer revealed that the Tallboy had slid backwards, so that the tail was now piercing the well of the bomb bay. The bomb was forcing the doors open by a foot, leaving only its nose to be supported by the sling.

Lake had no choice but to return to Bardney after dumping the Tallboy over the North Sea, which he did by climbing to 10,000ft and, after all electrical and mechanical methods had failed, diving and pulling up sharply. The Tallboy then fell away with no further damage. Perhaps it was an omen that his aircraft, EE136 'R', carried the title 'Spirit of Russia'!

P/O Maguire was to realise later that the spigot on Lake's aircraft had not gone deep enough into the bomb, although he said that it had been a while before the armament staff worked that out. Lake was not put off flying by this or other incidents; after the war he became a senior BOAC airline captain.

Using the Elint information that 192 Sqdn had provided, the rest of the force flew on across the North Sea, for much of the way at no more than 400ft, then crossing the central Norwegian coast via the gap in the radar chain. Well aware of the Luftwaffe's eavesdroppers, they also maintained R/T and W/T silence throughout the flight.

As the Norwegian mountains approached, they climbed to 8,000ft. Confident that the Swedish Air Force would be unable to intercept them, they flew across that country's neutral airspace and over Finland, where the defences forced them to take evasive action. One of 617's aircraft, flown by Flg-Off Bill Carey, was hit and there was some return fire from the gunners. Some Swedish flak had also been directed at one of 9 Sqdn's Lancasters, but with little damage if any.

The weather forecast had been correct to begin with, but on the Finnish-Russian border the crews met a low-pressure system that the British meteorologists had not accurately positioned. The winds were therefore stronger than had been forecast, with a considerable lowering of the cloudbase, which was persistent and solid, accompanied by rain all the way from the border to Archangel.

It was later found that Russian meteorologists had correctly predicted this a week before, but their forecasts had not been available in the UK before the crews had taken off. Another late signal was one going the other way, informing the Russians that their guests were en route – it was not received at Yagodnik until a few hours before the bombers were due to arrive.

The ground became difficult to see, the maps lacked detail, there were few landmarks and attempts by the wireless-operators to raise the Yagodnik radio beacon were frustrated by language as well as navigational difficulties. The ground station call sign at Yagodnik had been given as 8BP when it should have been 8WP. The Russian 'W' was the equivalent of the English 'B', but not as far as Morse was concerned! However, radio altimeters did prove useful, obtaining a QFE for Yagodnik that was particularly valuable due to the low cloudbase.

Someone with an additional problem was Flg-Off Adams of 9 Sqdn, who had kept going despite having to feather his starboard outer engine due to a coolant leak. This had occurred while he was approaching the Norwegian coast, at which point he could have turned back, but he retained his bomb load and carried on, flying at 300ft in bad weather for two hours.

This excerpt from the report of Flg-Off Ian Ross of 617 sums up the experience.

Set course 1912 base, 11th September. Navigation very good, always in centre of stream until nav lights switched off on approaching enemy coast. No pinpoint obtained due to cloud, but a fix was obtained some distance inland on a large lake, found to be eight miles south of track; correction given and track regained. Further pinpoints were obtained until ten-tenths' cloud cover, just before Gulf of Omega. We were then dead on track. Descending in the Gulf to about base we flew inland, pinpointing occasionally. ETA found us circling various small islands. Several aircraft were circling in the same area, all using VHF. No QDMs were available and aircraft were using VHF with total disregard for others. Aircraft could be heard trying to land at the airfield. These aircraft were requested to fire Very cartridges but apparently ignored requests. After searching each islet and island in the vicinity, we circled a port, but were unable to pinpoint it definitely.

This turned out to be Molotovsk, which was not shown on their maps. It says much for the crews that most of them found Yagodnik airfield, which turned out to be twenty miles south-east of Archangel, on an island in the Dvina River, and landed safely on the grassy surface. However, ten aircraft, six from 9 and four from 617, did not.

Lieutenant Nicky Knilans landed in a field, careered through a barbed wire fence, then across mud and grass until the Lancaster finally stopped. Using his brakes on such an unprepared surface would have wiped off the aircraft's undercarriage. Shortly afterwards Sqdn Ldr Tony Iveson landed safely in the same field.

The fun really began after Tait arrived in an ancient Soviet biplane, followed by a Li-2 transport that brought just enough fuel to carry the two crews the last sixty miles to Yagodnik. Iveson took off first – not too difficult as he was flying light, having jettisoned his mines before landing.

Knilans, however, still had his Tallboy on board. Seeing a forest looming up, he shoved his throttles through the 'gate' and the Lancaster lurched off the ground, bending its propellers as it cut a swathe through the trees, but not sustaining enough damage to bring it down. A branch smashed through the windscreen and into the cockpit beside Knilans, who then flew on with one hand over his face, peering out from between two fingers. He reached Yagodnik on three engines, one having overheated due to a damaged radiator.

Ross and his crew circled several ships at Molotovsk harbour while vainly trying to attract their attention with an Aldis lamp. By now they had been searching for the airfield for well over two hours, so they looked for an alternative place. Ross saw a wooden road and tried to land on it, which showed how desperate his situation had become. His first run was too far to the right and his second was foiled by a lorry-load of troops who had stopped on it and were gazing up at him! With just thirty gallons left, Ross ordered his crew to their crash stations, then gritted his teeth and put the Lancaster down in a marshy area at 115mph.

The crew operated the engine fire extinguishers, then scrambled out unhurt. The bombsight was wrecked – although whether this was done in the crash or as a security measure Ross did not make clear. Something that definitely came under the latter heading was the detonation of the aircraft's IFF set, but they did not destroy the aircraft due to the proximity of the bomb's remains.

The crew then met some Red Army soldiers who came along a railway embankment towards them. Despite the lack of a common language, Ross found out that there was an American ship in the harbour, subsequently meeting a US Navy lieutenant and some British sailors who were also there. The naval headquarters in Archangel was then contacted and the rest of his crew were brought to the town, to be quizzed by immigration officials who wanted all their details.

It must have been obvious who the 'Angliski' were and what their purpose was, but in the Soviet Union everyone was both suspicious and apprehensive, from Stalin downwards. Security in the Murmansk area was tight; British sailors had in the past been warned that if they attempted to fraternize with the local population their next appointment would be with a Red Army firing squad. Nor was any gratitude shown for the supplies they brought in.

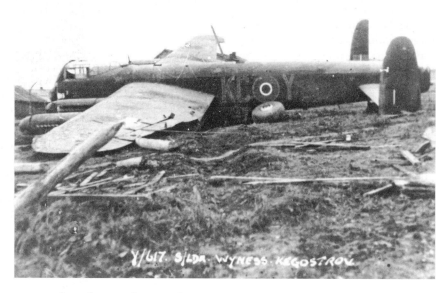

ME559, flown by Squadron Leader D. R. C. Wyness of 617 Squadron, on Kegostrov airfield. (NA)

An unforgettable moment in any pilot's career. LAC Ray Harris on the point of promotion after receiving his 'wings' at Calgary in March 1943. He was seventeen then, having put forward his age to join up. (R. Harris)

Sqdn Ldr D. R. C. 'Duke' Wyness found what looked like a fighter airfield, made a circuit and landed as close to the near boundary as possible, being unable to see the far one due to the bad weather. His touchdown was normal but he was obliged to swerve to avoid a white horse! Braking had no effect due to the wet surface and the Lancaster skidded on until it hit the opposite boundary fence, causing the port wheel to collapse. Welcome to Mother Russia.

Six of 9 Sqdn's crews – Flt Lt Camsell, Flt Lt Morrison, Flg-Offs Harris, Keeley, Laws and Tweddle – all had similar hair-raising experiences. To quote from the report submitted by Ray Harris:

> I have the honour to report that when attempting to land Lancaster aircraft WS.E at Keg Island [sic] landing field, I had to apply my brakes very hard to avoid crashing into a ditch, also a sentries' hut. In doing so the aircraft, although nearly at a standstill, tipped up onto its nose, doing damage to same.
>
> At the time of landing visibility was very bad due to rain and low cloud, therefore I had difficulty in finding the longest landing path. There were no signals on the airfield and I estimate the length of my path was 700 yards with a crosswind. The end of my landing run ended up in a ploughed-up potato patch, which in my opinion helped considerably to tip up the aircraft.

Flt Sgt 'Jimmy' Parsons, his bomb aimer, who was in the Lancaster's nose trying to see the ground ahead, came closer to it than he would have liked:

> The cloudbase was less than a thousand feet and we were so low that we almost flew between the masts of a ship! We weren't told there were several airfields in the Archangel area, and when we saw this fighter base we followed another aircraft in. We saw soldiers patrolling the perimeter, but they ran for it when they saw us. Flares were fired to tell us we were landing downwind, but by then we had to come in. We avoided a hangar by turning to the left, towards a cabbage patch, but we hit a ditch before that, and finished up standing on our nose.

The nose hatch could not be used and the rear door was out of the question as well, so one by one the crew emerged through the pilot's crash exit in the canopy roof, to find that they had actually come down at Vorskovo airfield. The local population, who lacked any mechanical assistance but had plenty of manpower, built a haystack underneath the aircraft, then sat on top of the fuselage, tipping the bomber down onto the hay. They then pulled the stack to pieces until the Lancaster sat on its own wheels again! It was a crude but effective method.

Unable to locate their destination due to the low cloudbase, Laws landed on an airstrip at Vestcova. Flt Sgt Ted Harrison, his flight engineer, would bear the results of this landing for the rest of his life:

> We overshot the wooden strip at a place much too short for a bombed-up Lanc, and wet. The harder the brakes were squeezed the faster we went. There looked to be a fine overshoot area, but what we hadn't seen was a ditch some twelve feet wide right across the end of the runway. Our wheels dropped into this (I still have a bent nose) and the aircraft's back was broken.

This ditch had been part of the airfield's drainage system. The impact with it also damaged the starboard wing.

> I suppose we were all lucky to walk away from it. I believe the Johnny Walker bombs were not fused. Damage was considerable and I remember one of the fuel tanks was split. Fortunately there was not a lot of fuel left as we had been on four reds for the last ten minutes before the crash. I believe most of the secret stuff was wrecked. I

PD211, Flight Lieutenant G. C. Camsell's Lancaster, after its crash-landing at Belomorsk airfield. (NA)

came away with the cockpit clock, which is now in Grantham Town Hall Museum. I also grabbed the first-aid kit, which has since been lost.

Eventually a Russian soldier turned up with a rifle and we were all flashing the special tags we were issued for the trip, with a Union Jack on one side and a chunk of Russian on the other.

This chit had been issued with the best of intentions, but it was of dubious value in a country where the average soldier was likely to be poorly educated if not illiterate. However, in this instance it did the trick.

We were taken to a shed, which was the only building on the strip. The first thing I saw was an old Ruston Hornsby oil engine connected to an antiquated generator for the strip lighting. There was a huge pot-bellied stove, glowing hot. We eventually convinced the soldier that after eleven and a half hours in the air we were a bit peckish, and with that he produced the biggest frying pan I have ever seen and into it he slapped a great lump of what looked like axle grease and then chopped some green potatoes and two or three fish heads and fried it all up together.

I thought if we would get the dreaded Delhi Belly this would be the time. We ate and it was delicious. As far as I remember none of us had any after-effects.

On 12 September they were flown by a Russian pilot to Yagodnik. The aircraft used was described in Ted Harrison's logbook as a 'U2' (a strange pre-echo of Gary Powers!), but was probably a two-seat Sukhoi Su-2 bomber.

This guy could only take one passenger at a time, but we were eventually all together at Yagodnik. Stan Laws and I came home in J with Doug Melrose. The rest of the crew were split up on other Lancs.

I have no idea what happened to the JW bombs as none of us returned to Vestcova. I believe all the Lancs that crashed were written off. Flaps and ailerons were removed from our aircraft, but I was not aware of this until I saw the photographs.

Morrison landed on the first apparently suitable field after a dummy run to check for bumps or ruts. Part of it turned out to be a marsh, which broke off the port wheel and spun the Lancaster round through ninety degrees.

Camsell, for lack of anything else, came down on an airstrip at the town of Belomorsk. His starboard engines, flying on the fumes, failed momentarily at 100ft, then packed up completely at fifty. Forty yards from the runway's end he hit a mound of mud, breaking off the undercarriage.

In such a situation any bomber captain's first concern had to be for the safety of his crew. Faced with a crash-landing in a marsh, for using his undercarriage on such a surface would be to invite disaster, Keeley reluctantly jettisoned his JW mines in a river before coming down just ten miles north of Yagodnik. His crew left the aircraft, clutching their parachutes and some Very cartridges, to trudge a long way through the swampy countryside before lighting a fire to attract the attention of a Russian aircraft that flew overhead.

Tweddle's crew joined that of Ray Harris at Vorskovo, in their case apparently without damage, as they were subsequently able to fly on to Yagodnik. Ray Harris later followed them, although his aircraft would not be ready in time to take part in the attack.

As soon as they could, Tait and Bazin took stock of their depleted force. 'N' and 'W', two of 9 Sqdn's aircraft which had safely landed at Yagodnik, were both in need of an engine change – 'W' had been brought in on three engines by Flg Off Adams. Of the ten that had 'landed away', Iveson, Knilans, Harris and Tweddle had finally reached Yagodnik, but two of their aircraft were damaged. The other six had to be declared Category E and abandoned, as follows:

PD211 'M' Flt Lt G. C. Camsell	Belomorsk airfield		9
NF938 'H' Flg-Off A. L. Keeley	Talagi (marshland)		9
NF985 'D' Flg-Off S. Laws	Vestcova airfield		9
LL884 'Q' Flt Lt A. M. Morrison	Chubalo-Navolsk		9
EE131 'B' Flg-Off I. S. Ross	Molotovsk (marshland)		617
ME559 'Y' Sqdn Ldr D. R. C. Wyness	Kegostrov airfield		617

More serious was the fact that three Tallboys and forty-eight JW mines had gone astray on what was politely termed 'friendly' soil. There had been no Russian casualties, but the total bomb load carried by the force was now substantially reduced. The bombs consisted of the two that had been carried by Camsell and Ross, with a third that had been jettisoned onto an island at Archangel by the crew of 'N' of 9 Sqdn, probably due to the engine trouble previously noted. The mines were scattered at Kegostrov, Chubalo-Navolsk, at Vestcova and in the Talagi area. All these, with some other items of aircraft equipment, would have to be safely and securely disposed of.

The Tallboy pistols and detonators were removed, being returned to the UK afterwards. The Russians were advised on how to unload those mines that had not been jettisoned and to destroy them without removing the fuses. The fate of the Tallboys is unknown. Remarkably, the Russians later repaired and used two of the Lancasters. One was ME559, which was flown by 16 Sqdn of their White Sea Air Fleet. The identity of the other is not known.

Another late arrival was the 463 Sqdn Film Unit Lancaster, which took off on the evening of 12 September from Bardney and landed at Kegostrov airfield the following day, after nearly thirteen hours in the air. It finally reached Yagodnik on 14 September. Although Flt Lt Bruce Buckham arrived later than everyone else, his report described what they had all had to face:

Nav skill in appalling weather conditions was responsible for the greater percentage of aircraft landing at Yagodnik. Absolutely no facilities, as beacon u/s and Liberators landed after Main Force – hence no W/T or R/T. Area maps inaccurate. Pinpoints no value.

Despite all this, 325 men had safely arrived without a scratch. Although Tait was in charge in the air, on the ground the detachment was commanded by Bardney's Station Commander, Gp Capt. C. C. McMullen.

It had been correctly anticipated that the facilities at Yagodnik would leave something to be desired. The approach to the airfield was good, but its surface consisted of grass and sandy soil, the latter with a fair number of potholes in it. Accommodation was overcrowded, with 290 men crammed into quarters intended for 180. The erks had to make do with three underground huts, while the officers and senior NCOs did somewhat better, being housed on the steamer *Ivan Kalyev*, which was decorated with a banner proclaiming; 'Welcome To The Glorious Flyers Of The Royal Air Force.'

The beds turned out to be alive, although their bugs were said to have bitten everyone except Tait! They were beaten back by aerosol insecticide that the crews had brought with them – this was one problem that had been foreseen! Tait claimed that vodka was the secret of survival in such a climate and Knilans' rear gunner found out how powerful it was after swiftly downing a glass of it in mistake for water. He recovered, eventually. Mealtimes were prolonged, with food that was good at first but later deteriorated despite being supplemented by supplies carried in the Liberators.

After finding somewhere to park the few items of kit they had been allowed to bring with them, the erks settled down in a strange and remote country amid square-faced brown-uniformed men whose attitudes varied from friendliness to curiosity. Co-operation was generally good, any grumbling being stifled by language barriers. The crews had been warned not to brag about the operations that they had done, in case the Russians tried to top anything they said.

Ray Harris remembered Yagodnik as, 'A Soviet naval training station. The Russians used to sit in a circle for lectures, then spit into a hole in the centre of the hut during them!'

The base had a few blister hangars, none of which were large enough to take a Lancaster. The bombers were dispersed over a mile, for although the Eastern Front had moved on, turning Yagodnik from an operational airfield to a ferry base, a Luftwaffe attack could not be ruled out. This did not materialise, so the only gunfire heard came from Russian pilots practising nearby against towed drogues, at what to their guests seemed an alarmingly low height. Because of the airfield's use as a base for Lease-Lend aircraft, the erks found themselves among Bostons, Hurricanes and Kittyhawks as well as Ilyushin Il-2 *Shturmovik* ground attack aircraft.

As far as 9 Sqdn were concerned, they had begun with eighteen aircraft, lost one when Lake turned back and abandoned four. That flown by Ray Harris had damaged its undercarriage and nose on landing. This left twelve Lancasters, nine of them with Tallboys and three with JW mines. Of these twelve, the two that needed engine changes would not be ready on the day, so 9 were finally whittled down to ten aircraft, eight of them with Tallboys and two with JW mines.

617 were not so badly off, for of their original twenty Lancasters, sixteen were currently available. Those flown by Ross and Wyness had been written off, while Carey's aircraft had its Swedish flak holes to be made good. After his treetop take-off, Knilans' aircraft required new nose perspex, a front turret panel, engine cowlings and spinners for both inner engines. Repairs were also needed to the starboard tailplane, starboard wingtip, starboard bomb door and one of the port undercarriage doors. All this had to be done on the night before the operation, with Russian assistance, using some parts from Flg-Off Adams' grounded 9 Sqdn Lancaster, which was still awaiting a new engine. It is indicative of the conditions that prevailed at Yagodnik that due to the lack of a suitable crane the spare engine carried in one of the Liberators could only be extracted from it by using a ramp of trees with blankets on them, so allowing the Merlin to be slid down.

In these circumstances, it was as well that the loss of six aircraft allowed them to be raided for more spares. It also turned out that there were not enough erks for the remainder – which begged the question of what would have happened if there had been any more damaged ones. A postponement of the raid gave just enough time for Knilans' aircraft to be made ready. This allowed 617 to field seventeen Lancasters on 15 September. By then some of the men who tended them had worked continuously for two days.

This meant that sorting out the eighteenth one in time was out of the question. Despite having reached Yagodnik with the rest, Bill Carey's flak-damaged Lancaster would be left behind on the day. However, it would play an indirect part, for his JW mines would be transferred to Iveson's aircraft, replacing those that Iveson had previously jettisoned. It was typical of the spirit prevailing within 617 that lack of aircraft did not stop Carey and Wyness from flying as second pilots with other crews during the raid.

Consequently the numbers of aircraft taking part in the attack had to be revised, although, as before, all the Tallboy aircraft, regardless of squadron, would become Force A and the rest Force B. A briefing for the crews followed, but the attack was postponed due to bad weather. On 12 September a PR Mosquito of 540 Sqdn took off from RAF Benson in Oxfordshire and also landed at Yagodnik, much to the surprise of the harassed erks, who had not been told it was coming and had no spares available for it. Luckily it was not yet in need of any. The Russians took an interest in this neat streamlined deep blue aircraft and clearly admired it. Yet another problem was the lack of facilities to swiftly turn round those bombers that were serviceable – it took eighteen hours to refuel twenty-six of them. The 97-octane Russian fuel, at a time when 100-octane was the norm, resulted in mag drop when the bombers' engines were run up, causing the problems of cruising at low rpm to be debated.

So, the stage was set and, after some last-minute cast changes, the drama would go ahead as soon as the weather curtain lifted. In the meantime the crews were treated to a monotonous diet of Russian war films and a football match, which they lost. Sqdn Ldr E. S. Harman of the ground staff later described it as 'a diplomatic defeat that was fruitful.'

Two days of wet weather gave the erks some time for repairs while denying them any comfort. Then the Mosquito went on a weather reconnaissance, which was routed some distance from Kaafjord to avoid arousing suspicion. It was off again at 0210 on 15 September and delivered a favourable report at 0600. Half an hour later the crews were taking off, with H-Hour set at 1100 (like all the other times quoted in this chapter, this was GMT, the local time being two hours ahead).

15 September 1944
Target The battleship *Tirpitz*, at Kaafjord.
Weather Good, but two-tenths' stratocumulus at 4,000-5,000ft over the target area.

Force 10 Lancasters of 9 Sqdn:

LM715	'O'	Wg Cdr J. M. Bazin	LM713 'Z'	Flg-Off D. Macintosh
LL845	'L'	Sqdn Ldr H. R. Pooley	LL901 'V'	Flg-Off C. B. Scott
W4964	'J'	Flt Lt J. D. Melrose	NF925	Flg-Off J. E. Stowell
LM548	'C'	Flg-Off J. J. Dunne	PB289 'B'	Flg-Off B. Taylor
LM448	'T'	Flg-Off A. J. Jones	LL914 'U'	Flg-Off W. D. Tweddle

17 Lancasters of 617 Sqdn:

EE146	'D'	Wg Cdr J. B. Tait	ME561 'R'	Flg-Off G. S. Stout
PD238	'H'	Sqdn Ldr J. V. Cockshott	PB415 'S'	Flg-Off J. Castagnola
DV405	'J'	Sqdn Ldr G. E. Fawke	LM489 'A'	Flg-Off J. Gingles
PD233	'G'	Flt Lt M. Hamilton	LM482 'Q'	Flg-Off A. E. Kell
NF923	'M'	Flt Lt C. J. G. Howard	LM492 'W'	Lt H. E. Knilans USAAF
ME554	'F'	Flt Lt T. T. Iveson	PB416 'V'	Flg-Off F. Levy
DV391	'O'	Flt Lt R. E. Knights	ME562 'K'	Flg-Off J. A. Sanders
ED763	'Z'	Flt Lt D. J. Oram	LM483 'N'	Flg-Off F. H. A. Watts
DV246	'U'	Flt Lt H. J. Pryor		

Escort None.

Bomb Loads 9 Sqdn – a total of 24 JW mines was carried by Macintosh and Stowell. The remainder carried one Tallboy each, with a 0.07-second delay.
617 Sqdn – a total of 48 JW mines was carried by Iveson, Levy, Sanders and Watts.
The others carried one Tallboy each, with the same delay as 9 Sqdn. For marking purposes, one red TI, one 120lb smoke bomb and one marine marker were also carried by Tait, Cockshott and Fawke.

One 463 Sqdn Lancaster as camera aircraft:
LM587 'L' Flt Lt B. A. Buckham

In addition to its normal seven-man crew, this aircraft carried two media representatives – W. E. West of the Associated Press and Guy Byams of the BBC. There were also two Bomber Command Film Unit camera operators, Flt Lt Loftus and P/O Kimberley.

One 540 Sqdn Mosquito as a follow-up PR aircraft:
MM397'W' Flt Lt G. Watson and W/O J. McArthur

The *Paravane* force was now down to twenty-seven Lancasters, twenty-one of which carried Tallboys and six JW mines.

The plan was for Force A's four waves of five Tallboy-carrying aircraft to attack in line abreast, with a distance of a few hundred yards between waves, at altitudes between 14,000ft and 18,000ft. There was a need for two clearly identifiable landmarks close to the target at which the bomb aimers could aim, using false settings on their sights.

The Tallboy crews would attack first and it was essential that they were able to do so visually. Due to the nature of their loads, the JW aircraft's bomb aimers were not dependent on a visual sighting. The direction of attack would be from the south, along the fore-and-aft axis of the ship. It was hoped that an attack from this direction would achieve surprise. H-Hour had been set early to give the crews the chance of returning to Yagodnik in daylight.

To ensure bombing accuracy as far as possible, the five aircraft in each wave would have slightly converging headings; another virtue of the gaggle, apart from offering a number of dispersed targets to the flak, was that the differing heights would allow this without collision, although the risk of being hit by a Tallboy from above was one that had to be accepted. The intention was to cover a square of 750 yards, with the target at its centre.

The JW mine carriers of Force B would bomb from between 10,000ft and 12,000ft, attacking from south-east to north-west, with four aircraft in the first wave and three in the second, which would be immediately behind.

On reaching a point 140 miles south of the target, three 9 Sqdn crews – Dunne, Pooley and Scott – were to fly three minutes ahead of everyone else to find the wind sixty miles from the target. They would then fall in behind Force A. Also at this point Force B was to diverge from Force A and fly ten miles to starboard of them, to sort out their correct heading across Kaafjord.

Radio silence was to be maintained en route and to avoid German radar all aircraft were to fly below 1,000ft until they reached the Finnish border, where Force A were to climb to 2,000ft above their bombing heights. Force B and the windfinders were to climb to 16,000ft. At sixty miles from the target Force A were to dive 2,000ft to increase speed and Force B were to lose 4,000ft, to keep slightly ahead of them.

On reaching a rendezvous point all aircraft were to set course for Kaafjord at their respective bombing heights, the windfinders flying three minutes ahead of the rest of the force. These three aircraft were to climb to 15,000ft and orbit over any well-defined landmark on the way, continuing to do so until they had passed the wind speed and direction on by VHF. They would then join Force A's last wave at the lowest bombing height.

9 Sqdn's Mark XIV sight was controlled by a computer box, into which was fed the bomber's compass course and airspeed. If the wind velocity and direction fed into the box were both spot-on the bombsight would also be correct and so it was vital that an accurate wind was found. For this reason three of their aircraft had been designated as windfinders. Since Tallboy's terminal velocity had been determined the previous June as 3,800ft per second, this had to be set on the Mark XIV by positioning its pointer one-third of the way between the 2,800foot mark and infinity. All the sight's other settings could be made in the usual manner. In contrast, 617's SABS sight could be adjusted during the bomb run and if it was correct on release the bomb would not over or undershoot the target.

A debate had begun, and no doubt still continues, over which sight was the better. Gordon Maguire commented:

> The Mark XIV sight was designed by Professor Blackett at Farnborough, but was made in America, which surprised USAAF bombardiers. These were of light alloy – better than British brass. The problem with it was a gyroscopic one. Those on the Mark XIV were the suction type, made by Sperrys. If the aircraft was steady the roll gyroscope was just sitting there with nothing to do, which would put it out if you had to take evasive action. The American Norden sight, which had polished bearings, suffered in the same way. The Barden Bearing Company, which was also over here, helped both the Mark XIV and the SABS to work.

This modification apparently worked, as it was his opinion that afterwards you could take evasive action with the Mark XIV, but not with the SABS. Whatever the truth of this, it was clearly part of 9's proud claim to be more accurate than 617. The rivalry between the two units was summed up by Ray Harris, who said to me, '617 may shoot the line, but they get the gen from number 9!'

Cochrane's strict instruction that Tallboys were not to be wasted still had to be followed. If there was little cloud and the smokescreen had only just started, then Force A was to immediately carry out individual bombing runs, aiming visually. If cloud or smoke completely obscured the *Tirpitz*, Force A would return to Yagodnik without bombing. Force B's mines were to be dropped irrespective of whether the target was covered or not. Bearing in mind that whatever happened the ship was unlikely to be fully visible, in either of the above eventualities the loads were to be aimed at one of two indirect APs, with false settings on the sights. Should these APs also be covered, then Force B were not to bomb either, and were to return to Scotland with their mines.

To add to the stealthy approach that would be necessary, W/T silence was to be maintained, but a listening watch was to be carried out at quarter to and quarter past each hour. This would become continuous at twenty minutes to H-Hour, but there would still be no W/T transmissions for a further fourteen minutes. All VHF sets were to be turned on at ten minutes before H-Hour to listen for the windfinders and Tait's instructions. It would be up to him to send a coded message to Lossiemouth after the attack, using one of the following code groups:

ZPR	Target sunk
FUG	Target hit by one Tallboy
BXY	Target hit by several Tallboys
CMB	No JW mines in water near target
AYF	Few JW mines in water near target
DRQ	Many JW mines in water near target
BAM	Target not in fjord

YWD	Target obscured by cloud
VLR	Target obscured by smoke
GQR	Results unobserved
BYG	Target attacked by indirect method by Force B
MIT	No attack made by Force A
HYC	No attack made by Force A or B

All of this showed that while *Paravane* was a totally different operation from *Chastise*, the planning for its execution was no less demanding, especially as it had been influenced by aircraft serviceability, which in turn had been affected by the primitive conditions at Yagodnik.

Buckham described the take-off as 'sticky', but all aircraft formed up behind Tait on time, climbing or diving to their various heights en route as briefed. The weather on the 600-mile flight to the fjord was good, but surprise may have been lost when the two squadrons inadvertently flew over a large Finnish airbase. Although its runway lights were on, they saw no aircraft. Indeed, throughout this operation there would be a welcome lack of fighter opposition. Force A dived as briefed, but also altered course on their final run-up when they realized they were several miles west of track.

Apart from some light cloud in the target area, the weather was good, which may have been why neither Tait nor his two flight commanders used their smoke markers to highlight the rendezvous point, as had originally been planned. As anticipated, the unusual direction of the bombers' approach had surprised the Germans, but belated word of their impending attack had been passed on. It probably came from a medium flak battery which they flew over on their approach, for as Kaafjord came into sight they saw that the smokescreen, which was mounted on the surrounding hills as well as the shoreline, had started. Intense flak came up through it from the *Tirpitz* and from two other ships nearby, although until the smoke fully deployed the gun flashes would give the target's position away.

As the smoke billowed over the water it all but obliterated the *Tirpitz*. Tait's bomb aimer, Flg-Off W. A. Daniel, reported his sights on the foremast and after he released his Tallboy so did almost everyone else, bombing into the smoke while using the gun flashes for reference.

The Film Unit Lancaster circled at between 10,000ft and 13,000ft, shooting 400ft of film. Buckham later reported:

> *Tirpitz* was located visually to be on the north side of the fjord, which was confirmed by the leader over VHF. The bombing of the lead aircraft and the following two appeared to be very accurate and was followed by an explosion some seconds later – soon after this, clouds of billowing black smoke appeared through the smokescreen.
>
> The Johnny Walker aircraft then came in, but by that time the smokescreen was extremely effective and *Tirpitz* was screened from view. As far as I could see, the Johnny Walker bombs fell in the centre of the smokescreen. We continued to circle the target area, but no further explosions were observed.

Force B's aircraft were slightly late and so Force A were ordered to support them by going round again, which gave Flg-Off Jimmy Castagnola's crew a chance to resolve a hang-up that had occurred on the first time round.

The flak was very inaccurate as far as height was concerned, most of it bursting below the bombers. However, several of 617's aircraft were hit and Knilans flew back on three engines when his starboard outer began to overheat – perhaps a problem not completely corrected after his earlier skimming of the treetops. Oram's tail was damaged by flak, rendering his elevator and rudder controls useless, but somehow he managed to return to Yagodnik. 9 Sqdn fared better, with two aircraft slightly damaged.

Flg-Off Roy Harvey, a navigator with Sqdn Ldr A. G. Williams' crew of 9 Sqdn, was not on this raid, but his memories would have been echoed by others who were:

> The navigator's position was just above the bomb release mechanism. On the run up the bomb aimer would give the pilot his instructions. Everything would be quiet except for the sound of the engines and his, 'left, left, steady, right, steady, steady' and just as he said 'bomb gone', there would be a clang from under my bench and the aircraft would jump in the air as the bomb dropped away. I nearly had kittens the first time!'

Fifteen Tallboys fell into the fjord, six from 9 Sqdn and the other nine from 617. Cockshott, Gingles and Knight could not locate the ship, so brought their bombs back, while Hamilton's Tallboy hung-up on three runs and then, frustratingly, finally dropped away four miles south of the fjord.

Buckham's observations during the attack were confirmed by several of 617's crews. Tait's bomb was thought to have been a hit or a very near miss. Fawke and Pryor said they had hit the ship, near misses also being claimed by Kell, Knilans, Oram and Stout. Several crews also reported seeing a large red flash amid the smoke.

Once the attack had ended, Buckham then headed out over the North Sea at low level in poor weather, made landfall at Aberdeen and continued on to his base at Waddington, which he reached at 2235. His crew had been in the air for 15 hours and 30 minutes, which he claimed at the time to have been the longest Lancaster flight on record.

Flt Lt Doug Melrose of 9 Sqdn claimed a near miss, but two of his fellow pilots were not so happy. Scott's bomb refused to release in spite of four runs over the target and his ORB report expressed his frustration in a few words: 'It eventually fell off through the bomb doors.' Dunne's bomb could not be released either electrically or manually, leaving him no choice but to fly back with it. However, Force B had no release problem; a total of seventy-two JW mines was dropped by two aircraft from 9 and four from 617.

At 1410 the PR Mosquito took off and returned four hours later, the crew's attempt to photograph the *Tirpitz* having been thwarted by smoke and low cloud over the whole of the fjord, though the pilot glimpsed the ship through a gap in the clouds while at 9,000ft.

Had they hit her? Certainly she was still afloat, and the strike photographs were inconclusive, so the interpreters would later base their report on a comparison with shots taken during a PRU sortie on 12 July. At the start of the raid smoke had come from the spit of land immediately south of the *Tirpitz*'s berth, while apparently also issuing from points on her deck and superstructure. This had spread in a northerly direction, quickly covering everything except part of her port side and stern.

The smoke's streaky but widespread coverage was such that the interpreters were reluctant even to positively identify the *Tirpitz*, although her two accompanying flak ships, the supply vessel Nordmark and a whale factory ship, the CV Larsen, were positively confirmed, the latter two still at the berths they had occupied the previous July. It was therefore a reasonable assumption that the vessel that had gone under the smoke must have been the battleship. So, had she suffered any damage? Had the Tallboys dropped by Tait and Melrose landed near her? Trying to conceal their impatience and frustration, the leading crews would claim that the smokescreen had not been in operation when they attacked and they were reasonably sure that the ship was in her usual position on the east side of Kaafjord.

At first the Germans said that only three smaller vessels had been sunk, but four days after the attack they admitted that the *Tirpitz* had been hit forward by a heavy bomb, which had gone through the deck and emerged below the waterline on the starboard side before exploding. This might have come from either Tait or Melrose, but in any case it would mean another nine months of repairs.

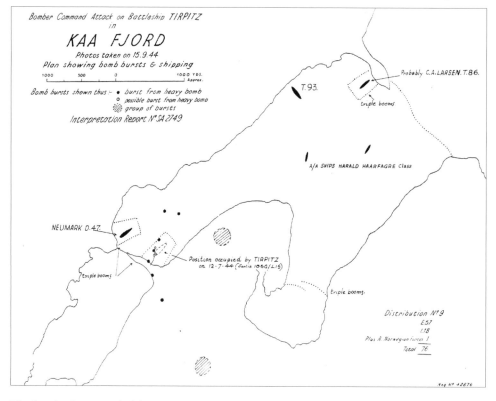

The bomb plot compiled for Operation *Paravane*. If it was correct, then most of the Tallboys were a long way off target. (NA)

Apart from Tait's W/T signal at the time of the attack, any other communications had to be sent via Capt. Walker, the Senior British Naval Officer at Archangel – a long-winded process taking up to six hours, but which had to be adopted for security reasons. Messages had to be carried 'by officer only' to Archangel.

Although pleased, Cochrane was aware that the job had not been fully completed. 'Well done. Do you consider any further attack with remaining bombs will achieve useful results? If so, make use of present spell of fine weather and use discretion as to number of aircraft to be employed on this operation. Film aircraft landed safely.'

Clearly Cochrane did not yet realise the problems the weather had posed, or that the British meteorologists had slipped up at the start. McMullen replied that due to a possible redistribution of the enemy's fighter force and that since the weather in the target area was unlikely to be fit for the next forty-eight hours, he would now return to the UK by 17 September. Cochrane agreed and ordered the detachment home.

On 16 July the PRU crew tried again to obtain coverage, but low cloud interfered once more and going below it resulted in flak damage, which gave the erks another eight days of toil before the Mosquito could be air-tested and flown back to Lossiemouth. No matter how many bombs had hit or near-missed, there was still a feeling of unfinished business. A total of seventeen Tallboys had been expended during *Paravane*, but despite everyone's best efforts the *Tirpitz* had not sunk.

There was now a need to fly back to civilisation and away from the reproachful gaze of their disappointed hosts. It was decided that it was not possible to bring home the five remaining Tallboys and they were left behind at Yagodnik. It was no longer a question of security; by now the Germans and Russians knew perfectly well what form this bomb took. The Lancaster crews made their way home during the four days after the attack, bringing out the crews of the crashed ones. The ground crews followed a week later.

Flg-Off Ray Harris and his crew returned on 19 September in Lancaster 'N', carrying his friend Flg-Off Keeley and two of his crew. They had taken a Tallboy out, but it was one of the five to be dumped on the airfield, to the horror of the Russians, who, the pilot said, 'ran like mad when it hit the deck!' For some reason they were detailed to bring twelve JW mines back. Once its nose repairs were complete, their own aircraft, 'E', was returned by another crew.

The feelings of Ray Harris and his crew can be imagined when they were told that as they had been unable to attack the *Tirpitz*, this operation would not count towards their tour. This was despite having been fired on at the Russo-Finnish border en route! The bomb aimer, Jimmy Parsons, would however receive some consolation when he was commissioned on 29 September. Like the rest of the surviving aircrew members, he would also receive a Russian decoration, although this had to wait until 1994, after the collapse of the Soviet regime.

Even now Fate had another sour trick to play. Flg-Off Levy of 617, in PB416 'V', who was also carrying two of Wyness' crew, wandered off track and hit high ground near Nesbyen in Norway, killing everyone on board. When the last Lancaster returned each one had covered a total of 4,905 miles from the beginning to the end of the operation.

The sense of frustration may have been mollified by the award of three DFCs – two to the PRU crew for carrying out eight sorties in quick succession and one to Flt Lt Melrose of 9 Sqdn, despite his crew claiming only a near miss at the time. Squadron rivalry inevitably played its part in this – although this operation had shown that they could fully support each other when necessary – and someone had decided that Melrose's crew had been responsible for the damage inflicted on the *Tirpitz*. It was the start of a controversy which has never been satisfactorily resolved.

It was also time for one of 617's long-standing characters to bow out. After twenty operations with 619 Sqdn and thirty with 617, Nicky Knilans was told he had operational fatigue and was grounded. The tree branch that had shot into his cockpit became an Officer's Mess trophy, with the caption 'Believe It Or Not.'

The JW mine had failed to inflict any damage at all, which was hardly surprising as protruberances on the mine's casing affected the airflow over it, making it very difficult to drop with any accuracy. Some twenty mines had been seen to hit the water and the rest were thought to have gone wide. Most either self-destructed or sank without trace, and this weapon was not used again. Not all had fallen into the fjord, for one was found on a slope above it in 1987.

The PRU coverage showed that a Tallboy had hit the battleship's bows, blowing an enormous hole in the starboard side. This covered much of the fo'c's'le and was 30ft deep by 50ft long, letting in a thousand tons of water. Damage had also been inflicted on the deck, on the fire-control instruments and the main engines.

By October it became known, from a former member of the ship's crew who was by then a prisoner, that a near miss from a second Tallboy close to the side of the fo'c's'le had pushed it in. The water level inside had risen to the ship's torpedo bulkhead and Torstein Raaby, a Norwegian agent who had kept a close eye on the anchorage, reported that the hole in the bows was big enough to accommodate a large motor boat. As two Tallboys had been involved, it seemed likely that both Tait and Melrose had been responsible for the situation.

Damage on this scale was crippling and *Tirpitz*'s captain proposed to Dönitz that she be taken out of service. However, Dönitz believed she still had a part to play as a floating gun battery, not in the north, but at the port of Tromsø, which was two hundred miles to the south. His decision was to seal the fate of not only the ship, but many of her crew, and he may have been influenced by Hitler's continuing belief, despite the Allied invasion of northern Europe, that the British would attempt a Norwegian landing. There was also the threat of the advancing Red Army in the Petsamo area of northern Norway. At a *Kriegsmarine* conference five days after the attack it was decided that the *Tirpitz* could not be made ready for sea again. She would be used to reinforce the Polar defences instead.

Despite the German admission of this damage, Dönitz maintained a defiant note: 'After successfully defending herself against many heavy air attacks, Battleship *Tirpitz* has now sustained bomb hits, but by holding out, her presence confounds the enemy's intelligence.'

This served only to confirm what Bomber Command's Intelligence already knew. Dönitz was not about to give in, but neither was Harris.

On 15 October, after her bows had been patched up, the *Tirpitz* moved south at a stately seven knots, escorted by every available German warship, reaching Haakøy island, just under four miles from Tromsø, the following day. This would be her new berth, and it would turn out to be her final one. Here the water was deemed to be so shallow that even if she sank, her guns would still be able to fire. Where she went, the torpedo nets and smoke canisters would follow. A further line of defence would now also be made available. Two *Staffeln* of JG 5, a fighter unit, moved their FW 190s to a nearby airfield at Bardufoss.

The battleship's arrival was reported by another Norwegian agent, Egil Lindberg, who operated from, of all places, an attic above the town's mortuary. This was quickly confirmed by another of 540 Sqdn's Mosquitoes on 18 October. This caused some relief at High Wycombe, for her new berth now put her within range of Lossiemouth. The good news was that there would be no further need to use Russian facilities, except for emergency purposes. The bad news was that the extra fuel tanks would still be necessary and with their reduced defensive armament the Lancasters would be vulnerable to fighter attack.

An Ultra intercept showed that the *Tirpitz* was no longer operational, but as far as High Wycombe was concerned that was of no importance. The Admiralty would be made to learn, once and for all, not only that battleships were outdated, but that Bomber Command could destroy this one when nobody else was able to. Since success was needed to make up for past failures, the raids would continue until she had gone down.

9

Dams and Dykes

Benign Reader, here is offered onto thy courteous acceptance, marking of sundry sorts, and to content divers humours. Who finds any fault in the composition, with courtesy let the same be concealed, or in friendly sort point out the errors, which shall be corrected in a future impression.

William Byrd, Lincoln, 1611

With the *Tirpitz* out of the running for the time being other matters nearer home could now be attended to. By September the Germans had been cleared out of France and Belgium, but anyone who had felt that the rest of the European war would be a pushover was disillusioned by the outcome of the Battle of Arnhem. This had been the culmination of Operation *Market Garden*, whose intention had been to advance rapidly through Holland and secure a bridgehead across the Rhine, which was the only natural obstacle to an invasion of north-western Germany. However, after severe treatment at the hands of two SS armoured divisions the remnants of the British 1st Airborne Division were withdrawn from Holland to rest and refit.

As the front line crept nearer to their western border, so German resistance stubbornly increased. Fighting in Holland continued throughout the autumn; a fact brought home to the staff at Woodhall Spa when, with just five minutes' notice, Dakota transport aircraft were seen in the circuit carrying men from the Border Regiment, who had more than earned the tea, sandwiches and cigarettes that were hastily provided for them. In the nineteenth century a French Army marshal had once observed, 'The British infantry are the finest in the world. Fortunately there are not many of them.' There were even fewer now.

Once again the bombing of communications had become a priority. For 617 this meant a return to what had been the scene of their blackest night a year before – the Dortmund-Ems Canal.

Today, now that the car has become king, most people are apt to regard canals as pleasant waterways to cruise along on holiday, forgetting how important they once were as a means of moving goods. The Dortmund-Ems had long been recognised as a vital communications link, not only for the German forces that had encircled Arnhem, but also as the main means of transporting coal, steel and iron ore to the Ruhr. Destroy the canal banks and two aqueducts near Ladbergen, where the water was above the level of the surrounding countryside, and it would be out of action for months to come.

23-24 September 1944
Targets 1. The canal banks and aqueducts near Ladbergen, as the primary target.
           To be attacked by 9, 50, 97, 61, 106, 463, 467 and 617 Sqdns.
        2. The night fighter base at Handorf, near Münster, as the secondary target.
           To be attacked by 44, 49, 57, 83, 207, 619 and 630 Sqdns
        3. The town of Münster, as a last resort.
Weather Ten-tenths' cloud over the target, with a base at 8,000ft, but good visibility below it.

Force 12 Lancasters of 9 Sqdn:

W4964 'J' Flt Lt J. D. Melrose	LM713 'Z' Flg-Off W. G. Rees
LM715 'O' Flg-Off R. W. Ayrton	LL901 'V' Flg-Off C. B. Scott
LL914 'U' Flg-Off W. Begg	PD198 'W' Flg-Off J. E. Stowell
LM548 'C' Flg-Off J. W. Buckley	PD213 'F' Flg-Off B. Taylor
LM448 'T' Flg-Off C. Follett	LM220 'Y' Flg-Off W. D. Tweddle
LL845 'L' Flg-Off S. Laws	PB289 'B' Flg-Off A. F. Williams

11 Lancasters of 617 Sqdn:

LM405 'N' Wg Cdr J. B. Tait	LM482 'Q' Flt Lt J. L. Sayers
LM489 'A' Sqdn Ldr J. V. Cockshott	NF923 'M' Flt Lt G. E. Stout
DV402 'X' Sqdn Ldr D. R. C. Wyness	ME559 'Y' Flg-Off J. Castagnola
ME555 'C' Flt Lt M. Hamilton	DV380 'P' Flg-Off P. M. Martin
ME554 'F' Flt Lt T. T. Iveson	ME562 'K' Flg-Off J. A. Sandars
DV393 'T' Flt Lt D. J. Oram	

Escort None.

Bomb Loads 9 Sqdn – six aircraft each carried one Tallboy with a No.47 pistol, giving a half-hour delay. These included Begg and Scott, although the identities of the other four Tallboy crews are not known. The other six carried twelve or fourteen 1,000lb MC bombs each, with the same fuse setting.

617 Sqdn – each aircraft carried one Tallboy, with the same delay as 9 Sqdn.

An additional 549 aircraft of 1, 3, 4 and 8 Groups would be bombing the town of Neuss, near Düsseldorf. 5 Group's strength was split between Ladbergen and Handorf. 9 Sqdn and 617 were part of a force of 113 Lancasters and eight Mosquitoes of 5 Group, which were to bomb the primary canal target, while another 120 aircraft attacked Handorf. Included in these totals were 83 and 97 Sqdns, who were to attack in three waves with cluster flares and red or yellow TIs, although some of their aircraft carried 1,000-pounders as well.

All the Neuss and 5 Group aircraft were routed south-east over Colchester and over the Essex coast at Clacton, to cross into Belgium just south of Ostend and from there to a point south-west of Brussels. Here, in an attempt to split the German night fighter effort, they would turn east, 5 Group diverging to head north-east from the Neuss force as they did so. 5 Group would head round the north side of the Ruhr, then east to Munster. After the attack, they would exit in the direction of Utrecht, dog-leg around Rotterdam and cross the coast at Over Flakkee, north-east of the town of Westkappelle.

To allow for heavy wartime barge traffic and to provide some insurance against one of the banks being breached, the Dortmund-Ems split into two parallel branches at this point, the original narrow one and to the west of it a broader second canal, both of which crossed over the river Glane by means of a pair of short aqueducts. An island formed by the two canals was thought to have flak positions on it. Well aware of the significance of this target, the Germans had spread camouflage netting over the distinctive S shape of the river at this point.

The canals were to be marked using red TIs, the airfield by green TIs and the third target, the last resort of Münster, by yellow TIs. If the canals could not be bombed due to bad weather or some other cause, aircraft other than the Tallboy carriers were to attack Handorf. If Handorf was not marked they were to attack the yellow TIs, which meant that what had been intended as a precision raid would become a Main Force area attack. If the canal could not be marked or discerned, the Tallboy crews were to bring their loads back.

The flight to the target area was fairly uneventful, although an alarming number of Main Force crews used their navigation lights en route, despite the presence of some

The Dortmund-Ems Canal's Glane bypass, pictured before the attack on the night of 23/24 September 1944. The difference between the older canal below and the wider modern one above can clearly be seen. Towards the left of the picture, the white stripes indicate camouflage netting over the river Glane, which passed under both canals at this point. (NA)

night fighters – one of which, a Ju 88, forced one of 61 Sqdn's aircraft to take evasive action. Some crews did not douse their lights until nearly H-Hour. Ground defences in the target area proved slight, but heavy cloud came near to frustrating the object of the raid and made controlling difficult.

Eight of 627 Sqdn's Mosquitoes had been given the tasks of controlling and marking. Four were despatched to Ladbergen under Wg Cdr Woodroffe of 54 Base, the other four going to Handorf under Sqdn Ldr Owen. In addition, the details of seven winds were to be passed to the flare and marking force, although they received only three. Flt Lt D. H. Shorter of 97, flying as Link 1, with the task of averaging these out, was unable to do so, although he did receive a bombing wind.

The problems really began when the controllers tried to make sense of what they glimpsed through the cloud below. Wg Cdr Woodroffe arrived late due to navigational problems and so took no part in the operation. Wg Cdr G. W. Curry, flying as Marker 1, assessed the flares dropped by 97's first wave as being too far south of the target, so he ordered the second and third waves to drop theirs three miles to the north. However, flares still fell too far to the south, so Flt Lt R. Oakley, as Marker 3, asked for more flares to the north. These were still to the south, so Oakley dived in an attempt to identify the AP. On his second run he thought he had done so and dropped a red TI.

Curry claimed afterwards to have seen the river Ems, despite camouflage, from four hundred feet up, and assessed Oakley's TI as a hundred yards south-east of the MP. The other two Mosquitoes detailed for the canal for some reason did not back up Oakley's marking. Perhaps these crews had their doubts, and if so they were to prove justified, for Oakley had inadvertently marked another pair of aqueducts that were seven miles north of the target.

Crews were ordered to bomb Oakley's red TI, but attempts to exercise R/T control were frustrated by strong German interference, attributed to Freya radar, on both the VHF channels that were in use. Using W/T as a back-up proved slow. The TR1196 set was in use despite previous experience of interference on it, but the TR1143 was also affected. The issue was further complicated by the cloud base not being as high as expected and by some more lower cloud creeping across the target, resulting in orders being given to bomb the glow of the TIs. In this situation, it looked as if the last-resort target was indeed going to be needed, so that when some of 83's and 97's crews were reassigned to drop TIs and bombs on Münster, they did so.

83 Sqdn, given the task of marking Handorf airfield, had been incorrectly told that it was a rocket base! A number of those crews detailed to bomb Handorf duly attacked it, although flares and the green TIs were scattered. Some crews said that the one green TI they glimpsed went out almost as soon as it landed. One of 627's Mosquito crews had satisfactorily marked the airfield, but due to a faulty radio the crew had been unable to pass on that fact.

This left only the last-resort target, which one of 83 Sqdn's crews claimed to be the first to mark. Other aircraft orbited first and then, on the controller's W/T instructions, bombed the yellow TIs for lack of anything else being visible, although these indicators were few and far between.

The Tallboy force's instructions were to operate at a height band of 14,000-16,000ft. Half of the aircraft were to overshoot and half to undershoot, each by one hundred yards, by means of false height settings on their bombsights. However, all this confusion ruled out a Tallboy attack and the controller put out a recall to 617's aircraft. It would also have applied to 9 Sqdn's Tallboy carriers.

Several runs were made by these aircraft, but not all were able to bomb before the TI finally burned out. Of 617's crews, Iveson had been the first to arrive in the target area, at 2145, but did not bomb as the TI disappeared under the cloud fifteen seconds before he would have done so. Sandars, Stout and Wyness did not bomb for similar reasons. Neither did Sayers, who was also handicapped by an unserviceable compass. The other six did not receive the message and so went ahead, Oram being the last at 2216. This meant a close shave for Flg-Off D. W. Meredith's crew of 106 Sqdn, when a Tallboy narrowly missed their aircraft. They were on the last trip of their tour – which nearly ended too soon when they were damaged by a fighter as well, but nevertheless reached home safely.

It is not certain from 9 Sqdn's ORB whether any of their Tallboy carriers bombed, although a survey carried out after the war said only six Tallboys were dropped, which if correct would mean that only 617 did. Their experiences would have been as mixed as those of 617 and it is likely that none of them did so, especially as only three made runs over Ladbergen. All that can be said is that two attacked Münster with what would have been 1,000-pounders, five brought back their loads, whatever they were, and two of the Tallboy aircraft went missing.

Flg-Off Graham Rees and his crew, on their second operation with 9 Sqdn, had a particularly hairy time, being attacked on the way by a Ju 88 and then hit by flak in the target area, damaging their starboard outer engine. After feathering this propeller, they made another run on the remaining three engines, dropped their twelve 1,000-pounders and came home.

Just after 2200 a VHF message ordered all aircraft to return to their bases, but night fighters were present in some strength as the bomber stream returned over Holland. 9 Sqdn lost two aircraft – the crews of Flg-Off C. B. Scott and P/O W. Begg, both coming down near the towns of Deventer and Wierden. Only one man survived, to be taken prisoner. For the reasons given above, it is doubtful whether these two aircraft had released their Tallboys over the canal.

617's only loss was the crew of Flt Lt Geoff Stout, who were returning with their Tallboy when a night fighter attacked, hitting three engines and starting a fire in the bomb bay. Stout's corkscrew evasion maneouvre came too late and an attempt to jettison the Tallboy resulted only in a lever coming away in the bomb aimer's hand.

The Junkers Ju 88 was without doubt the most versatile aircraft in the Luftwaffe's armoury. This C-6 night fighter model carries Liechtenstein airborne radar and the Flensburg passive homing device, which picked up the signals from the Monica tail-warning radar carried by RAF bombers until 1944. (Imperial War Museum, neg. no. HK2864)

Now just the starboard outer engine was left running, meaning that power was only available for the mid-upper turret – not much defence against what was thought to be a Bf 110. Flg-Off C. E. M. Graham, the navigator, had been wounded, as had the mid-upper gunner, Flt Sgt Peter Whittaker, and the flight engineer, P/O Allan Benting.

There was nothing for it but to bail out. While Stout held the aircraft as steady as he could a parachute was clipped to Graham's harness and he was pushed out of the stricken Lancaster. The rest of the crew quickly followed, but despite his own elbow and head wounds Whittaker went forward to clip a chute to Stout's harness. Stout then ordered Whittaker to jump, indicating that he would follow. All this was to no avail – Stout, Benting and Graham did not survive. The aircraft crashed near Lochem, in Gelderland.

Whittaker landed without further injury and later met up at a Dutch farmhouse with the aircraft's bomb aimer, Flg-Off Bill Rupert, who had sustained two broken bones on landing, one in his right foot and the other in his right shoulder. Flg-Off Ronald Allen, the wireless-operator, was taken prisoner. What happened to Whittaker at this point is uncertain, although it seems likely that as Rupert avoided the Germans, he was able to do the same. Flg-Off Reg Petch, the rear gunner, also evaded capture. Bill Rupert delayed his return home until the following year, having used his time to assist the Dutch Resistance with sabotage work. Whittaker, who had nearly sacrificed his own chance of escape from the aircraft in a last attempt to help his skipper, was awarded a DFM in December 1945.

Reactions from the surviving crews at debriefing were mixed. A number of the Main Force crews had orbited for twenty minutes but had heard no orders due to the jamming. Some thought the controlling had been good in the circumstances, while others expressed their views in a more robust manner. One of 49 Sqdn's crews

The same stretch of both canals after the attack, showing scattered bombing by 5 Group. Most of the damage that mattered was inflicted by the two Tallboy hits at A and B. These drained both canals, leaving a barge stranded at C. D indicates other Tallboy near-misses. (NA)

was surprisingly matter-of-fact, describing it as 'An uneventful trip, and not very successful.' A 207 Sqdn crew said, 'No control whatsoever,' and another, referring to Handorf, was not wrong when they declared, 'Impression gained that only 20 per cent of the force bombed the correct aiming point.'

97 Sqdn, the displaced Pathfinders, commented, 'In no way could the raid be described as a success ... It is hoped, however, that some damage was done to the enemy.'

It came as a welcome surprise to see that it had. Eighty-two aircraft were assessed as having bombed on or around the canals, with another twelve attacking the airfield. Photographs showed clearly that the aqueducts had not been destroyed, although the barge sitting on top of one of them told its own story. Scattered bombing by 5 Group north of the aqueducts had cratered the embankments of the eastern narrower canal and inflicted some minor damage on the broader western one, but what mattered were the two Tallboy hits that had drained both canals at this point. Five barges were aground in this section and at the southern approach to the target another seventy-three were drawn up in a stationary line.

A further check showed that over six miles of the canals had either been drained or lowered to the point of being impassable, stranding 100 barges. Water had escaped across the nearby fields, scouring a wide channel before reaching the river Glane. By 23 September, eighteen miles of the canal had emptied, from the Ems aqueduct to the junction of the Dortmund-Ems and Mittelland Canals at the town of Bevergen. The damage inflicted was easier to repair than if the aqueducts had been brought down, but even so this result was far better than had been expected. Flt Lt Oakley received a DFC for his part in this attack, although the fact that he had marked the wrong part of the right canal was the source of some amusement.

It is unlikely that Sir Archibald Sinclair, the Secretary of State for Air, knew of this when he sent a congratulatory telegram: 'The War Cabinet have instructed me to convey to you and to all concerned their congratulations on the outstanding success achieved in the recent attack on the Dortmund-Ems Canal. Pressed home with great determination against strong opposition and in difficult weather it constituted yet another major blow against the German war economy.'

In the months to come German repair attempts were frustrated by two further 5 Group attacks in November and March, as well as by a raid on the Mittelland Canal on 1 January 1945. During November 1944 Speer reported to Hitler that this bombing had prevented smelting coke from the Ruhr mines from reaching three important steelworks near Brunswick and Osnabrück. After the war he said that these raids, with the attacks on the railway system, had produced more serious setbacks to the German war industry at this time than any other type of bombing.

The canal attacks put further pressure on the railways in north-western Germany, which would in turn lead to 9 and 617 attacking their viaducts by day during 1945. By 1956 the canal was again in operation, but its broad modern western section was never reopened.

One of 9 Sqdn's crews would never forget the consequences of the loss of Flg-Off C. B. Scott. Flt Sgt Jim Brookbank was this crew's bomb-aimer:

> The door burst open and our Nissen hut was invaded by SPs, who promptly began gathering up items of personal property. It was only by sheer luck and providence that some of the crew were in residence at the time and challenged their actions. The SPs announced that Scott's crew had 'failed to return' and were detailed to collect the kit. They then recited the names of the crew, including mine.
>
> We finally managed to persuade them that we were very much alive and that they would be well advised to direct their energies to ensuring that the telegrams destined to be sent to our next-of-kin were cancelled. It was a great relief to know that this was in fact dealt with as a matter of urgency.
>
> Some days after this incident I was accosted in Lincoln High Street by a bomb aimer from another squadron, whom I had trained with in Canada. He approached

uncertainly and with some incredulity stabbed a finger into my ribs and announced, 'You are dead.' The situation then became hilarious. I found myself denying it. Apparently no one had corrected the report of my death in the 5 Group news sheets which were now distributed to all squadrons within the group.

His crew, captained by Flg-Off W. Scott, had been mistaken for the other one, six members of whom were indeed no longer alive. Those lost included Flt Sgt L. A. Harding, whose son Mike would later become well known as a folk musician and entertainer. Mrs Harding had become a wife, mother and widow, all in the space of a year.

On 23 September, after an unpleasant Channel crossing, a party of officers, consisting of Wg Cdr G. H. Everitt of the RAF, an RNVR officer and two USAAF officers, began an inspection of those U-boat pens that had so far been liberated. Everitt noted the intention to double roof thicknesses and the use of air spaces, with *Fangrost* concrete members, as bomb-traps. 'Unless a bomb directly hits one of these concrete members I feel that its passage would only be slightly affected before it reached the original roof below.'

While at Brest they examined the roof and were duly impressed by the size of the bomb craters. They did not consider the displaced concrete to be of high quality, although the reinforcing was. Two bombs had made holes twenty feet in diameter through the roof and two others had made smaller holes right through. Hits by 500lb and 1,000lb bombs had had 'no visible effect whatever'.

It was clear that none of the Tallboys had gone off inside the pens. The holes had been caused by them exploding after they had penetrated the concrete, forcing large pieces of the ceiling down into the pens below. There was no evidence of any damage caused by these concrete falls, except to any objects lying immediately below them.

Everitt concluded, 'Mr Wallis was correct when he estimated that a Tallboy Medium bomb would penetrate into reinforced concrete to a depth of eight to ten feet. At Brest, some of the bombs penetrated a few feet further than that. However, although the results were impressive, I am of the opinion the Tallboy Medium is unsuitable for attacks on U-boat pens where the roofs are constructed of reinforced concrete more than 10ft thick.' He recommended that Tallboy Large – the projected ten-ton bomb – be developed for use against such targets, and that the Brest pens be used as a trials target.

The first of these recommendations would be carried out in due course. Bufton commented, 'Everitt's report is an interesting one. These bombs aren't designed to penetrate concrete. A rocket-accelerated weapon seems to be needed; the Tallboy Large, to get penetration, must be dropped from 40,000ft and the Lanc at present won't make half that height.'

So far, Tallboy had done well, but when pitted against layers of concrete, for which it had not been designed, its success had been limited. Would its bigger brother, when it arrived, be able to overcome such constructions by sheer force?

During October Tallboy production would gather apace, with seventy British bombs, sixty of them filled, plus a further 110 from the USA, all of which were ready for use. This would rise to 150 by the end of the year. The rough appearance of the American bombs made them readily distinguishable from their smooth-cased British counterparts, and problems would be encountered when trying to fit tails made by Vickers or Short Brothers to some of them. Nevertheless, without the contribution made by the American steel industry the achievements of the two Tallboy squadrons would have been far less. Their support was all the more commendable given the fact that there was no American aircraft capable of carrying these weapons into action.

On 27 September, thirteen 9 Sqdn Lancasters took part with 214 other aircraft of 1 and 5 Groups in an attack on the town of Kaiserslautern. Two Tallboys are said to have been dropped on this target, but a check of 9's ORB gives no details and does not confirm this. It seems likely that any 12,000lb bombs used on this night were of the HC variety.

The island of Walcheren, off the mouth of the river Scheldt, remained in German hands after the Allies took the port of Antwerp, whose use would greatly shorten the Allied supply line. Shaped like a saucer, Walcheren was protected by dykes made of unmortared blocks of basalt on enormous wooden piles. Sand dunes were piled on top of these to a height of over forty feet. The garrison consisted of some 10,000 troops of the German 70th Division, who were not considered to be of very high quality, plus a large number of other men driven back over the causeway linking Walcheren with South Beveland on the Dutch coast. Unlike the Channel ports, this formed an obstacle that could not be bypassed.

Lieutenant-General Guy Simmonds, commanding 2nd Canadian Corps, which formed part of the 1st Canadian Army, had foreseen that the Germans were likely to partially flood the island. This would leave them the use of the embanked roads and dunes above the water, so making the attackers' job more difficult. Simmonds successfully argued that a complete flood would deny the Germans the use of the roads but would not hamper the Allies since American-built tracked amphibious vehicles such as the Buffalo and Weasel were available.

A Main Force daylight attack was therefore ordered on the Westkapelle dyke on 3 October. In addition, eight Lancasters and two Mosquitoes of 617 were involved, their route out being over Aldeburgh in Suffolk and their H-Hour 1000. They were only to bomb if their designated APs could be identified. However, before the Tallboy crews could reach the target the Main Force succeeded in breaching it. Tait assessed the situation:

> Reached target at 1455. Bombing by the Main Force was still proceeding. The wall was already breached and water had flooded inland to a distance of about one mile and into streets of Westkapelle. After consultation with the Deputy Leader I decided that the job was done and ordered the force to return.

Further Main Force attacks resulted in two other breaches, which the Dutch civilian population accepted as a price worth paying to get the Germans out. The assault had to wait until 1 November before all the conditions for it were right. It was successful, but 1st Canadian Army lost 12,873 dead in the fighting that followed. These included American, British and Polish troops under their command. Antwerp and the Scheldt estuary could thus be opened up, although only after an extensive minesweeping operation had been carried out. Like Arnhem, this operation was an indication of just how hard the Germans would resist as the ground fighting reached their own borders.

617's next operation would have the object of letting water out, rather than in. The Kembs barrage, on the Rhine near the town of Basle, provided hydroelectric power. It was 570ft long and about 30ft wide at the top, with an estimated height of 20ft of water behind it. It had three sluice gates, the destruction of any one of which would release the water behind it.

The significance of this was that the US 7th Army, who now occupied most of the area to the west of it, believed the Germans would open the sluice gates if they did not. Although it would subside after several hours, the resulting tidal bore would affect the Rhine – and any Allied units trying to cross it – as far as Maxau, opposite Karlsruhe. If it was breached now the water would have subsided by the time the Allies wanted to cross, and it would also cut off German units retreating towards the west bank.

At this point the Rhine ran north-west, being split into two equal and roughly parallel sections. One of these two channels then split a second time, with the target located at the point where they became one again and this channel swung north-east to rejoin the other. For this reason there was a long narrow strip of land in the middle of the river.

The American assessment of the barrage's importance had been passed to Bomber Command on 28 September and a request by Harris for more information was met

The Kembs barrage, photographed at low level before the attack on 7 October 1944. This shot is indicative of the dangers faced by PRU pilots, and the quality of their work. (Imperial War Museum, neg. no. C4685)

by General Vandenberg of the US 9th Air Force. To fit the US 6th Army Group's plans and to obtain maximum effectiveness, it would have to be breached no later than 15 October. After a slight delay due to the Walcheren attack having priority, Harris stated this raid could now go ahead, subject to suitable weather.

An attack with Upkeep was out, for *Chastise* had shown that it would take too long to retrain the crews in the specialised technique required. Wallis was confident that one Tallboy between the sluice gates would destroy the river barrage. He favoured a high-level attack as the full tamping effect would be obtained as well as penetration. With regard to a low-level attack, he felt that there was a possibility of the bomb ricocheting, although that was unlikely if it was dropped from above 500ft. There was, he said, no danger of the bomb prematurely detonating on striking the barrage's concrete ramp. Certainly if it was dropped from high level there was no risk to aircrew safety. Finally, he was not certain what effect the water would have on the fuse, but, again, if dropped from high level the problem would not arise.

Despite these arguments, it was decided to split Tait's force. An accurate attack could only be made in daylight. The barrage and a power station on the run up to it were heavily defended, so in an attempt to achieve surprise and offer a dispersed target for the flak there would be a high force and a low one. The seven aircraft of the high one would attack first, flying in a gaggle at heights between 7,300ft and 8,500ft, while the six aircraft of the low one would live up to their name by coming in at 600ft, which made them vulnerable to the light flak while denying the crews any chance of baling out if hit. It was hoped that the three Mustang squadrons that were to escort them would prove adequate for flak suppression.

7 October 1944
Target The Kembs barrage, also referred to as a dam.
Weather Cloud at 3,000ft, but a clear patch over the target.

Force 13 Lancasters of 617 Sqdn:

EE146 'D' Wg Cdr J. B. Tait	?	Flg-Off J. Castagnola
LM492 'W' Sqdn Ldr J. V. Cockshott	LM489 'A'	Flg-Off J. Gingles
EE923 'M' Sqdn Ldr G. E. Fawke	DV393 'T'	Flg-Off A. W Joplin
PB415 'S' Sqdn Ldr D. R. Wyness	DV391 'O'	Flg-Off P. H. Martin
LM482 'Q' Flt Lt C. J. G. Howard	ME562 'K'	Flg-Off J. A. Sanders
ME554 'F' Flt Lt T. C. Iveson	LM485 'N'	Flg-Off F. H. A. Watts
DV402 'X' Flt Lt J. L. Sayers		

Tait, Cockshott, Howard, Martin, Sanders and Wyness all made up the low force.
The remainder would act as the high one.

One 627 Sqdn Mosquito as a camera aircraft:
    KB215 'H' Flt Lt Hanlon and Flt Lt K. G. Tice

Escort 34 Mustang IIIs of 2nd Tactical Air Force's 133 Wing:
    129 Sqdn RAF   306 Sqdn (Polish)   315 Sqdn (Polish)

Bomb Loads Each Lancaster carried one Tallboy, with a 25-second delay for the high
    level force, and a half-hour delay for the low-level one.

The attack was scheduled for late afternoon and the rendezvous with the escort was
to be over Dungeness. Tait ordered the squadron to 4,000ft and then called Wg Cdr
Jan Zumbach, the fighter leader. Within a few minutes the Mustangs lifted out of the
cloud to meet them and the formation headed out across the Channel. 129 Sqdn were
to cover the high force, 315 the low force and 306 would strafe the flak.

Never a man to order others to do something he would not do himself, Tait was
leading the low force, leaving Fawke in charge of the high one. Patches of cloud as
they approached the target indicated that the seven Lancasters above him would have
some cover, but there would be none for his group. Although his attack height would
not be as low as that for *Chastise*, if anyone was seriously hit their only hope of survival
would be a crash-landing. The Rhine, covered by enemy fire, would not be a soft place to
ditch into. Not far away was the Swiss frontier, but this was not too welcoming either, as
Watts discovered when he flew too close and 'neutral' flak hit his starboard outer engine.
He feathered it, swung further to the left and kept going.

Apart from this, the flight to the French town of Besançon went smoothly enough.
At this point the low force did an orbit and 129 Sqdn went on with Fawke's group,
meeting only a little flak. Basle slid by below on their right, their bomb doors opened
and from the target three miles ahead Tait could see heavy fire being directed at
Fawke's formation, followed by a series of splashes as their Tallboys struck the river.

So far, so good, but the defences were heavier than expected and their luck could
not hold indefinitely. At his call 306 Sqdn's Mustangs dived out of the sun. For a
moment Tait thought the flak had not seen him, but then white tracer came wobbling
up from the east bank of the river. He felt the aircraft jump as the bomb dropped
away, slammed the throttles forward and heard his rear gunner open fire as they
passed over the barrage.

Tait commented afterwards, 'Weather was touch and go near the target, but the
target itself was clear of cloud below bombing height and visibility was good. The
high force had bombed before I reached the target and all traces of the bursts had
disappeared, so that I could not assess the high bombing and there appeared to be no
damage to the target. All of the sluices were closed. Our bomb landed in the correct
position ten yards short of the target. It did not bounce.'

Bomb release trouble caused several overshoots from the high force, two of whose Tallboys fell as much as 600 yards west of the barrage. Two more from the low one fell forty to fifty yards away. Tait's bomb was seen to hit the left side of the barrage. Watts overshot by fifty yards, as did Martin, after making a second run. Sayers also made two runs, but as he opened his bomb doors on the second one an electrical fault caused the bomb to fall off prematurely through one of them, buckling it. Cockshott hit Tait's slipstream and so his Tallboy fell wide. Sanders overshot by fifty yards, his bomb falling into the river behind the target, as did that of Joplin. Due to a late and manual release, Gingles' bomb fell onto a railway line. Iveson's Tallboy struck the bank some four hundred yards from the barrage, while Castagnola's fell between the first and second piers. Fawke had his hang-up on two runs, releasing it manually on the third, but it still fell five seconds late, onto the west bank of the river.

Two aircraft were lost – both, almost inevitably, from the low force. Wyness was hit repeatedly but dropped his bomb before crashing into the Rhine near the Franco-German border town of Chalampe. A hung-up bomb made Howard elect to make another low-level run and light flak blew his port wing off. The Lancaster crashed at the village of Efringen-Kirchen, just inside Germany. There were no survivors from either crew. One of 306 Sqdn's Mustangs was hit, but its pilot carried on and returned with the others. Three Lancasters came home damaged, including Tait's, with a hit in its port wing-root and a tyre shot away.

No less hazardous was the task of the Mosquito crew from 627. Flight Lieutenants Hanlon and Tice made two runs over the target, at 1740 at 3,000ft, then at 6,000ft eleven minutes later. On their first one they saw one bomb burst some two hundred yards south of the west end of the barrage, soon followed by another burst 'which appeared to blow out westerly span. Water started to pour through gap and there were ripples extending 200-250 yards upstream.'

This operation never attained the fame of *Chastise*, but it was no less demanding for those who ran the gauntlet that afternoon. It quickly became clear that it had been completely successful. The Tallboys had destroyed the iron superstructure above the first and second pillars on the barrage's west side, causing the water upstream to fall dramatically.

The German press could say little, but the Swiss *National Zeitung* reported:

> The breaching of the Kembs Dam has lowered the water level in the Rhine basin at Basle, necessitating the transfer of boats from the first basin to the second. At 2100 hours the level of the Rhine fell by three to three and a half metres. Below Kembs the water released is estimated at millions of cubic metres and has apparently caused flooding everywhere, for the German authorities have given the water alarm. So far it is not known whether navigation on the Rhine will be completely suspended.

For now it would, as the affects of this raid included Switzerland, whose barges were also stranded on the mud.

DFCs came thick and fast for this one; to Flg-Off Martin, to P/O B. A. McKay, Watts' bomb aimer, to Flg-Off Daniel, Tait's bomb aimer, and to W/O H. D. Vaughen, his rear gunner. Flg-Off Sanders and Sqdn Ldr Cockshott both received Bars to theirs. They were all well earned.

As a result of the Ladbergen breach, rail communications between northern and central Germany and the Ruhr had now become even more important, not only for the supply of industrial materials but also to those armies facing the Allied forces in Holland. One of the three main lines serving the Ruhr from the east was the Neheim-Schwerte railway, which had been one of the communications targets considered at the time of *Chastise*. It could be put out of action by the destruction of the Sorpe dam, just a few miles away.

The next use of Tallboy would be due to the idea that Wallis had put forward the previous May regarding further attacks on the Sorpe. In a letter of 12 September

Wallis had said of earth dams: 'If the balance of forces can be upset by relieving pressure on the air side of the dam, excess of pressure on the water side will produce a crack in the relatively thin concrete bulkhead and through this crack a stream of water will pour which will have the effect of eroding the rubble on the air side, thus accentuating the out of balance forces.' He felt this process might go on for days and would lead to the complete destruction of the dam.

This had been hoped for after the Upkeep hits. It sounded plausible, but who was going to try it out? While 617 licked their wounds, this time the honours would go to 9 Sqdn.

15 October 1944
Target The Sorpe dam.
Weather Nine-tenths' cloud in the area, but clear over the target.

Force 18 Lancasters of 9 Sqdn:

LM715 'O' Wg Cdr J. M. Bazin	EE136 'R' Flg-Off A. L. Keeley
ME809 'X' Sqdn Ldr A. G. Wiliiams	LM220 'Y' Flg-Off R. C. Lake
LM754 Flt Lt G. C. Camsell	PB596 'H' Flg-Off S. Laws
LL845 'L' Flt Lt A. M. Morrison	LM548 'C' Flg-Off D. Macintosh
PD198 'W' Flg-Off R. E. Adams	LM736 Flg-Off D. E. Marsh
NF937 'E' Flg-Off K. S. Arndell	NN722 'Q' Flg-Off E. C. Redfern
PB146 'A' Flg-Off J. J. Dunne	PB289 'B' Flg-Off J. E. Stowell
NF929 'P' Flg-Off M. L. T Harper	PD213 'F' Flg-Off B. Taylor
LM448 'T' Flg-Off A. F. Jones	PB594 'D' Flg-Off A. F. Williams

One 627 Sqdn Mosquito as a camera aircraft:
    DZ414 'O' Flt Lt B. D. Hanafin and Flg-Off L. A. K. Howard

Escort 58 Mustang IIIs of 2nd TAF's 133 and 150 Wings:

19 Sqdn RAF	129 Sqdn RAF
65 Sqdn RAF	306 Sqdn (Polish)
122 Sqdn RAF	315 Sqdn (Polish)

Bomb Loads Each Lancaster carried one Tallboy. Twelve bombs should have carried an 11-second delay pistol, and the other six a 30-minute one. However, it later emerged that at least two bombs had been fitted with direct-impact pistols.

PRU coverage by 542 Sqdn on 28 September had shown that the damage and discolouration left from the *Chastise* attack had gone. In response to the demands for all the German dams to be defended, there were now several barrage balloons over the lake, at least two on the parapet, with others over the compensating basin and the sides of the valley by it. There were also at least twenty-two flak positions, some on the parapet and many around the dam or behind Langscheid village at the side of it.

Despite all this it turned out to be a routine ride as far as 133 Wing were concerned. 129 Sqdn's diarist, not being aware of the demands of Tallboy, described the Lancasters as attacking from a height due to the barrage balloons. The bombing was considered spectacular, if delayed. 'Even so, from 18,000ft they made three craters right on the dam. No fighters and very little flak was seen, and so the squadron returned safely. It was the first time we had operated with 150 Wing today and we agree the R/T 'natter' nothing short of bloody awful. However, they may improve.'

150 Wing had had a good deal to natter about. Its three squadrons had only just moved to Andrews Field, near Braintree in Essex, the previous day, from Matlask in the wilds of Norfolk. This early morning duty caught them completely on the hop, as 19 Sqdn's diarist noted, 'Shambles. An early show with no ground crew, serviceability doubtful, parachuteless wing commander. The Wing finally staggered into the air, 19

Sqdn led by Sqdn Ldr Wright at about 0750. But not for long as the CO's wheels would not come up. The squadron was taken over by Flg-Off Staples (DFM), who was not a little inconvenienced by having no course chart.'

The parachuteless wing commander was one Bill Loud, who must have lived up to his name that morning!

65 Sqdn were no better off. 'For a change this morning the erks were allowed to sleep while harassed pilots ran up their engines, which they had previously uncovered with their own fair hands, and in some cases attempted to taxi out without first removing the chocks.'

Despite all this, a rendezvous was achieved and the uneventful flight that followed would have come as a relief to all concerned.

Twenty miles from the target, one group of six aircraft split from the other twelve. These twelve, with the 11-second-fused bombs, were to go in first, followed by the other six, with the 30-minute ones, two minutes later. All were to aim at the shore of the compensating basin, below the dam face.

As 9 Sqdn were not experienced in formation bombing they were to attack in line astern, each aircraft to be a hundred feet below and two hundred yards astern of the one in front. Wg Cdr Bazin would bomb first, from 15,000ft. Providing all aircraft flew at 210mph, the total time between the leader's bomb being released and its explosion would be just over forty-one seconds, which would be ample time for those behind him to aim their bombs accurately.

There was to be a false height setting on the bombsight, so that the bombs would strike a point fifty yards short of the crest of the dam on the air side. It was hoped that some of the second wave's bombs would land in the craters made by the first, so achieving very deep penetration. Although the dam's water level was fifteen feet lower than at the time of *Chastise*, it was still thought that there was a good chance of destroying it.

Of 9 Sqdn's eighteen aircraft, only sixteen bombed, two being jostled over the target by the others. Wg Cdr Bazin's bomb burst on top of the dam wall, leaving a crater that was noted at the time. Flg-Off Redfern turned to starboard to avoid another Tallboy dropped from overhead, which narrowly missed his port wing. He then made a request for a second run, which was denied. Flg-Off Williams also did not bomb due to another aircraft overtaking him and driving him off course to starboard. He too requested a second run, but received the same answer, so these two brought their bombs back.

A slight vector error caused the MPI to be some two hundred yards from the AP and several bombs overshot the dam crest, to fall in the water. Some crews reported hits around the compensating basin or in the dam lake, then saw large amounts of water fly over the parapet, leading one over-enthusiastic rear gunner to wrongly claim a breach. Hits were seen on the earth face as well, but at least one bomb was reported to have not gone off.

The final damage was two hits on the crest, with another three on the air side. None of these led to a breach. The fact that the Germans had lowered the level of the Sorpesee to reduce the pressure on the water side led someone within 5 Group to ruefully comment, 'If the water had been a little higher, the dam would undoubtedly have gone.'

The local population thought so too, for after this attack the Sorpesee was lowered by a further seventeen feet, so that it was now thirty-two feet below what it had been at the time of *Chastise*. Still, whoever had written that would have changed his mind if he had ever walked along the crest of the dam and seen how massive it was. Using Tallboy on it proved as futile as flinging Upkeep at the crest fifteen months before. This dam was strong enough to resist anything Wallis could devise for it, and it stands to this day. Sqdn Ldr A. G. 'Bill' Williams later related an odd story connected with this raid:

When we returned to Bardney, Richard Dimbleby was there, to make a record of the op, to go on the air for the BBC in London. To this end, I had a Lancaster and crew standing by to fly the record to Northolt in time for the nine o'clock news. However, I did not hear another word about the operation, whether the bombs went off, what happened to the dam or any detail whatsoever. I had to cancel the aircraft which was standing by, so the record, if it was actually made, did not get broadcast.

Although the dam had been damaged, this raid was clearly not the success that *Chastise* had been and what the crews had to say might not have been what those above them wished to put out. It seems likely that someone – perhaps the noted commentator himself – called his superiors and was told not to take the matter any further. If any recording was made, it may survive in an archive.

There was an unexpected sequel to this raid in December 1958, when the Tallboy that had been reported as not going off was found in the water at the foot of the dam. In January 1959 it was rendered safe in a joint Anglo-German operation – Herr Walter Mitzke, a former Luftwaffe officer whose experience dated back to 1925, and Flt Lt J. M. Waters of the RAF's 6209 Bomb Disposal Flight both safely extracted its three Number 47 30-minute delay pistols.

Gordon Maguire, who was still serving in the RAF, had cause to remember this incident:

> Flt Lt Waters was my former flight sergeant, now commissioned. He rang me up, asking how many aircraft had been involved. I couldn't go out to Germany as I was in accident investigation at the time and in the middle of a Vulcan crash. So I advised him to take the base plates out, then deal with the exploder pockets. I said the pistols were well greased and should come out without any problems, which they did.

Two weeks later two more Tallboys, this time with Number 58 direct-impact pistols, turned up in the mud below the dam. These pistols were considered less dangerous and this time the German bomb disposal organisation dealt with them.

During the latter part of 1944 Tallboys were needed for everything, and it was time for another change of target. Once the fate of the *Tirpitz* had been finally settled, there would be one last try at the Urft dam, after which the idea of using Tallboy on this type of target would finally be abandoned.

Each target posed a different set of problems, but there was one that was common to all of them: the release delay, which persisted despite all attempts to cure it. After *Paravane* and again after the Kembs barrage attack, both squadrons had made representations to 5 Group.

Besides a natural urge to support his men, Cochrane was well aware that the support that had been given to him could disappear if they failed to deliver the goods, for whatever reason. 5 Group therefore passed on these complaints to Bomber Command, Boscombe Down, the Air Ministry and Vickers. Each instance of a late release, or none at all, was duly gone into, but there seemed no clear solution to the problem. Flg-Off Dunne's hang-up during *Paravane* was put down to the bomb slip and strop taking on a 'set' after the aircraft had been bombed-up for some time, thus locking the release jaws. Sayers' misfortune over the Kembs barrage, when his bomb fell off on opening the doors, was thought to have been an accidental release.

The crews were not particularly impressed by this line of argument. To them it looked as if the workmen were being blamed, rather than their tools. No one doubted the ability of Tallboy to get results, or that of their sights to aim it correctly, but what use was that when this maddening fault stopped the bomb from landing in the right place?

Wallis took a keen interest, especially when Cochrane took it up directly with him, and a number of small modifications were made, but the problem persisted. 617's protests after the Kembs operation brought the long-suffering Air Commodore Bilney to Woodhall Spa on 10 October, followed by Reg Firman of Vickers, who, it will be remembered, had taken part in the timing tests at Bardney just before *Paravane*.

On 16 October Wallis wrote to Cochrane that he had found one bomb slip returned from 617 to be waterlogged – the armature had become corroded solid to the duralumin of the slip, making release practically impossible. He could therefore only suggest that the crews be warned to keep them dry – like any piece of electro-mechanical apparatus, they were delicate. By way of a sweetener, Wallis added,'You certainly are doing some marvellous things with Tallboy, and I am filled with admiration for your magnificent work. Please be assured that we will do everything we can to cure the hold-up trouble.'

Cochrane passed this on to the squadrons, to be politely informed by Bardney that they were already doing this by storing the slips in a warm dry atmosphere. So far, the only effect of this had been to add fifteen minutes to the bombing-up of the aircraft.

It was possible that the damp conditions at Yagodnik had contributed to the failures experienced during *Paravane*, although an effort had been made to stop the release gear taking on a 'set' by resting the Tallboys on the ground whenever possible. This, however, did not account for the other problems experienced before and since that operation.

By now this was having a bad effect on the morale of 617's bomb aimers, who had trained to a high standard on the SABS Mark III, only to see their efforts wasted in several instances. During the autumn of 1944 consideration was given to redesigning the release system. Following Bilney's visit, 'Talking Bomb' Richardson, who considered the existing system too delicate, had submitted a rough design for a new type of release gear – a wire strop suspending the bomb with a couple of barrage balloon cable cutters to sever it.

All this led to yet more trials – this time with Lancaster PD198 of 9 Sqdn at Boscombe Down between 20-22 October. The aircraft was fitted with two micro-timing recorders, a Cambridge Chronograph and a high-speed camera. It was noted, with mixed feelings, that each time it was activated the release gear worked efficiently, with an average delay of 25.93 milliseconds. This was equivalent to an error of eight feet on the ground at an IAS of 200mph, although the aircraft's height was not mentioned.

The release problem would never be solved and this trial result raised more questions than it answered. What would happen when the ten-ton bomb finally came into service?

10

Obviate and *Catechism*

It is known that the *Tirpitz* suffered severe damage during the attacks by Lancasters of Number 5 Group on 15 September 1944. This damage is known to have rendered the battleship unfit for seagoing operations, and it appears likely that the Germans may attempt to get the battleship back to a base in Germany, where the necessary repairs and refit can be carried out. So long as the *Tirpitz* remains afloat it continues to be a threat to our sea communications with Russia. It has therefore been decided that a further attack shall be made against the ship.

5 Group Operation Order B432

As previously stated, the Germans had decided to move the *Tirpitz* south from Kaafjord, with a view to using her as a floating fortress in the defence of Norway. Her new anchorage would be off Haakøy island, 150 miles south of her previous one and four miles west of the town of Tromsø.

It was there that she was found on 18 October by the pilots of seven Firefly fighter-bombers of the Fleet Air Arm's 1771 Sqdn, sent off from the carrier HMS *Implacable* on a shipping reconnaissance. They reported she was there in company with a flak ship, three destroyers and a repair vessel. This sighting was confirmed when a PR Mosquito of 540 Sqdn, briefed to check this area for the *Tirpitz*, also found her there on the same day.

A return flight to Tromsø from Lossiemouth was 2,260 miles. Tait calculated that a return trip would be possible, this time avoiding the delights of Yagodnik, but with very little safety margin in case of adverse winds. The same tank modifications could be used as for *Paravane*, this time for all aircraft of both squadrons, but it would mean loading so much fuel that each Lancaster would be taking off at two tons over its maximum permissible weight. This could be accomplished by fitting Merlin 24 engines to the aircraft of both squadrons, so giving them additional boost on take-off, but the problem was that aircraft so fitted were scattered around 5 Group's Main Force squadrons. A simple exchange was not possible as only those of 9 and 617 had the 'blown' bomb bay doors fitted to carry Tallboy.

There was therefore no alternative but to change 120 engines – a task accomplished by the erks, working in shifts, over three days! The engines that had been removed from 9 and 617's Lancasters also had to be fitted to the Main Force aircraft, and there were other modifications to follow. At Waddington, Flt Lt Buckham's camera aircraft had to have two 400-gallon long-range tanks fitted into the bomb bay.

On dispersals around Lincolnshire rumours were rife and grumbles many, especially concerning the preferential treatment given to 9 and 617 where new kit was concerned. All this took place as well as, not instead of, the usual routine of repairs, maintenance and testing. Small wonder that the erks' unofficial motto was 'There's Always Bloody Something.'

At least the Main Force squadrons were spared the additional work at Bardney and Woodhall Spa. While the engine exchanges were being carried out at the front, the rear and mid-upper turrets had to be removed so that the Wellington and Mosquito tanks could be slid in. Since each Lancaster would have to carry 2,406 gallons, a good deal of other weight had to go. The pilot's armour was removed, along with the portable oxygen bottles, and twelve of those that the crew would normally use while at their stations in the aircraft.

Out too went the nitrogen bottles, then the flare chute, followed by the guns and ammunition from the front turret. This might have seemed a foolhardy step, but avoiding the weight of these items, and leaving the mid-upper gunner behind, was deemed acceptable when weighed against the risk of head-on attacks; if such an event did occur two 0.303s would be little defence by day against a fighter's cannon armament. Finally the rear turret went back on again, this time with its ammunition supply reduced from 10,000 to 7,000 rounds. This left each aircraft with an all-up weight of 68,200lb.

The erks deserved the highest praise for having done so much so quickly. If motor races were usually won in the pits, then it becomes clear from efforts of this kind that the outcome of a wartime bombing operation could be decided on the ground before it began.

As with *Paravane*, the attack would be from the landward side, to achieve surprise – or so it was hoped. The ship's defences were now assessed as sixteen heavy and sixteen light guns. There were also twelve heavy and twenty light weapons on a radius of six and a half miles from Tromsø. The ship's deck armour had been designed to give maximum protection from bombs or plunging fire. Its first layer was two inches thick, backed up twenty feet below this by a second, just over three inches in thickness. This lower layer was increased over the gun turrets and ammunition magazines.

On 22 October a request was made to Coastal Command's 18 Group to provide facilities in north-east Scotland. This was promptly agreed to, enabling Lossiemouth, Kinloss and Milltown to be used. Any pilots in doubt of reaching these three bases on their return could divert to Scatsta in the Shetlands.

Any aircraft which suffered engine problems or had less than 900 gallons of fuel left on leaving the target could divert to either Yagodnik or Vaenga, although this would be very much a last resort as Yagodnik was 680 miles from Tromsø. Two Royal Navy destroyers would be used for homing purposes by the navigators, while also providing rescue for any crews forced to ditch. A third would be on immediate notice at the Shetlands for ASR use if necessary.

The same level of security prevailed as for *Paravane*, this time apparently with no leaks. At both Bardney and Woodhall Spa's briefing rooms there were recent vertical photographs of the target, with an Admiralty chart of the area around it, accompanied by maps showing the radar, flak and fighter airfields. These were not to be removed from the rooms until after both squadrons had left for their advanced bases. In the meantime access to them was limited to the crews and a small planning staff. To avoid any leakage from Soviet sources, permission to use Yagodnik and Vaenga was not sought until 27 October. This was granted the following day.

Now it was up to the weather. At this time of year the prevailing westerly wind brought stratus cloud in from the sea over Tromsø, leaving no more than three days in each month when it blew from the east, leaving the sky over the town clear for a few hours. All that the two squadrons could do now was to fly up to Scotland, in the hope that this would occur while they were there and that it would not change again before they reached Tromsø. They could not remain in Scotland indefinitely, for other targets might come up nearer home.

As if all this was not enough, there was, as with *Chastise*, a date beyond which the attack would not be possible. After 26 November the sun would not rise above the horizon at Tromsø, although for a few days after that there would be enough twilight to bomb at midday. Then there would be no light until the following spring. Finally word came on 28 October and the two squadrons moved north, once again under the command of Gp Capt. C. C. McMullen. Accompanying them, once again, came Flt Lt Bruce Buckham and his crew to film the attack. They had been sent first to Bardney and then to Lossiemouth, for 'special photographic duties', although it did not take much intelligence to work out what the destination and target would be.

It is hard to know what the RAF would have done without the Mosquito. At midnight a weather reconnaissance variant of this versatile aircraft sent back the news that the wind was veering to the east. An hour later the heavily-laden Lancasters rose into the air and Operation *Obviate* was on.

29 October 1944
Target The battleship *Tirpitz*, at Haakøy island, near Tromsø.
Weather Good en route, but patchy cloud at 15,000ft and 8,000ft over the target.

Force Twenty Lancasters of 9 Sqdn:

PD377 'U' Wg Cdr J. M. Bazin	NN722 'Q' Flg-Off A. L. Keeley
PD368 'A' Sqdn Ldr A. G. Williams	PB696 'V' Flg-Off R. C. Lake
NF929 'P' Flt Lt G. C. Camsell	NG235 'H' Flg-Off S. Laws
NF937 'E' Flt Lt J. J. Dunne	NG242 'C' Flg-Off D. Macintosh
NG206 'J' Flt Lt J. D. Melrose	PA172 'G' Flg-Off L. E. Marsh
NG845 Flt Lt A. M. Morrison	NG249 'S' Flg-Off E. C. Redfern
ME809 'X' Flg-Off R. E. Adams	NG220 'B' Flg-Off J. E. Stowell
NG252 'R' Flg-Off K. S. Arndell	PD213 'F' Flg-Off B. Taylor
PD198 'W' Flg-Off R. J. Harris	LM220 'Y' Flg-Off W. D. Tweddle
LM448 'T' Flg-Off A. F. Jones	NG223 'D' Flg-Off A. F. Williams

Nineteen Lancasters of 617 Sqdn:

NG180 'S' Wg Cdr J. B. Tait	NF920 'E' Flg-Off D. W Carey
DV405 'J' Sqdn Ldr G. E. Fawke	DV385 'V' Flg-Off J. Castagnola
ME554 'F' Sqdn Ldr T. C. Iveson	LM489 'A' Flg-Off J. Gingles
EE131 'B' Flt Lt L. S. Goodman	ME561 'T' Flg-Off A. W. Joplin
DV380 'P' Flt Lt B. A. Gumbley	NG181 'M' Flg-Off A. E. Kell
PD233 'G' Flt Lt M. D. Hamilton	PD238 'H' Flg-Off P. H. Martin
PB415 'O' Flt Lt R. E. Knights	ED763 'Z' Flg-Off D. J. Oram
LM492 'W' Flt Lt H. J. Pryor	ME462 'K' Flg-Off J. A. Sanders
DV402 'X' Flt Lt J. L. Sayers	LM695 'N' Flg-Off F. H. A. Watts
DV391 'Y' Flt Lt I. M. Marshall	

Escort None.

Bomb Loads 9 and 617 Sqdns – each aircraft carried one Tallboy, with an 0.07-second delay.

One 463 Sqdn aircraft to carry an F24 camera:
PD329 'Y' Flt Lt B. A. Buckham
In addition to its normal seven-man crew, Buckham's aircraft also carried Flt Lt Loftus and Flt Sgt Buckland as film cameramen.

From their bases the aircraft took off at +18lb of boost as opposed to the normal 14lb. Despite a light wind, none had any trouble in so doing and they climbed away with plenty of runway to spare. They then formed up at 2,000ft in what was described as a night gaggle, using their navigation lights until they were fifty miles from the occupied territory.

Again using the gap in the German coastal radar chain, they would climb steadily to 7,000ft to cross the coast. This height would be maintained until they reached the rendezvous point, which was to be an easily recognisable lake, although just to be certain it was to be marked with smoke bombs. The force would then climb to their bombing heights of between 13,000ft and 16,000ft. If there was cloud between these heights, they were to fly lower, but not below 6,000ft.

Four aircraft of 9 Sqdn were to find the winds for the rest of their unit, which meant setting course from the rendezvous point with 617 to orbit any well-defined landmark.

They would then rejoin 9 Sqdn and at H-6 pass their findings by VHF to Bazin, who would then average these out, issuing a bombing wind by R/T and W/T.

The attack was to be visual. If cloud or a smokescreen interfered with the bombing runs, the bombs were to be brought back. However, if there were clearly identifiable features visible in the vicinity of the target, and if its exact position relative to those landmarks was known to the bomb aimers, then the attack could continue. A listening watch was to be kept on the W/T control frequency at fifteen minutes and forty-five minutes past the hour, becoming continuous at H-20. At H-10 all aircraft were to switch their VHF sets to the appropriate channels, two different ones being allocated for each squadron, but R/T silence was to be maintained until H-6.

617 were to attack first, from H-Hour to H + 1, with 9 Sqdn following from H +5 to H +6. After the attack, whatever its results, the W/T half-hourly listening watch would resume and the aircraft were to dive rapidly to 1,000ft at the coast on the way out, though they could later climb to 4,000ft once they were clear of enemy territory. Royal Navy destroyers were standing by off the coast to pick up any crew forced to ditch. Tait and Bazin were to transmit details to Lossiemouth by W/T, using the following codes:

HFC Target sunk
VLR Target hit by one Tallboy
BAM Target hit by several Tallboys
CMB Target obscured by cloud
BYG Target obscured by smoke
ZPR Results unobserved
DRQ No attack made
AYF Target not in position

The bombers' low altitude over the sea restricted the Gee coverage and astro-navigation was made difficult by a cloudy sky, so most of the route was navigated by dead reckoning, although loop bearings were also used. A change of wind brought a landfall fifteen miles south of their intended track, but moonlight made accurate pinpointing possible and there were no more navigation problems until the return journey.

It was a measure of the importance attached to this raid that Buckham's aircraft was to fly direct to RAF Northolt in west London afterwards. However, he came near to not making it at all.

> We observed one of the stand-by RN destroyers at 6430N 0530E and altered course for the planned coast-in point. About halfway across the North Sea we experienced a terrific jolt, and in the early morning light we could see that the starboard main undercarriage leg was hanging down, the engine nacelles were flapping in the breeze and that there was a gaping hole in the wing. Apparently a shell had passed through the undercarriage bay and between the Numbers 1 and 2 fuel tanks without exploding.

Despite this they pressed on and their navigation turned out to be good – on making landfall a pinpoint confirmed that they were just 400 yards to port of track. In this Buckham's crew performed better than Tait's force and they reached the rendezvous point early, on their own.

Buckham finally spotted Tait's force, saying afterwards that he was lucky to see the others as they to port of track by at least twenty miles. He then flew to intercept them at position E, which was the final turn-in point. Realising its error, the force dog-legged, formed up at the lake as briefed and then flew along the fjord. Haakøy island was visible from five miles away, as was the ship within her torpedo nets, and the attack began.

It did not go according to plan. The windfinders climbed in loose formation when ten miles from Tromsø, but one arrived late in their orbiting area and consequently could not find a wind to pass to Bazin before the allocated time. The wind then complicated matters by becoming westerly again, causing patches of cloud to drift across the fjord at 6,000ft as the bombers made their way along it.

Although it was not really his business, Buckham felt sufficiently concerned to send a course correction by VHF at 0830, but as Tait and Bazin had their hands full at this time it was hardly surprising that he did not receive an acknowledgement. Descending from 14,000ft to 6,000ft, the Film Unit Lancaster's cameras began to turn.

> We saw the first bombs burst approximately 100 yards from the ship, which made us suspect that the edge of the cloud had obscured the target and that the bomb aimers had been forced to estimate the aiming point at the last minute ... We circled the target area until 0908 hours, during which time more bombs were dropped, two of which were seen to strike the anti-torpedo nets surrounding the *Tirpitz*. One pilot made several runs from different directions, but did not bomb due to the deteriorating weather conditions.

The *Tirpitz* was quickly hidden, and those who bombed her did so by aiming at the glimpsed gun flashes. Tait ordered a rerun, but the weather continued to deteriorate and as they flew away it was apparent that the ship was still afloat.

It was perhaps because of this, or the damage that he had sustained earlier, that Buckham returned to his home base at Waddington, not Northolt as originally ordered, landing on one wheel with his crew at their crash positions. Due to the poor weather only 150ft of film had been shot.

A high-level reconnaissance shot of the *Tirpitz* inside her torpedo nets at Tromsø, indicating the kind of view the bomb aimers would have had. (Imperial War Museum, neg. no. C4773)

Six aircraft did not bomb, five of them due to cloud or smoke at the target, despite several runs. These were two from 9 Sqdn and three from 617. The sixth one was flown by Flg-Off A. F. Redfern of 9 Sqdn, who did not attack due to his port inner engine seizing up en route. Redfern limped home on the other three, being the first of his unit to land. It was a measure of the determination shown that one of 9 Sqdn's crews bombed from 15,200ft despite a lack of oxygen for everyone on board except the pilot.

Despite the protracted attack there were no fighters, but four aircraft were holed by flak. Of these, the worst hit was NF920 'E' flown by Flg-Off Bill Carey, which took a hit in the starboard outer. With fuel streaming from his wing, Carey dived to get away, but then encountered more gunfire over the fishing village of Andenes, which hit another fuel tank and stopped the port inner. Then the hydraulics failed, causing the wheels, flaps and bomb doors to fall down.

So far, they had been fortunate not to catch fire. Deciding the sea was too rough to ditch in – and with the wheels hanging down the aircraft might have flipped over on impact – Carey headed for Sweden, dumping loose and secret gear en route. On seeing a boggy field near the Lapland village of Porjus, Carey crash-landed the bomber after its wheels had been cranked back up by hand. The Lancaster stood on its nose, then fell back. The crew walked away without a scratch, except for Carey, who had dislocated his knee when it hit the compass.

Subsequently the crew set fire to the aircraft, but only the forward section was burned out and some useful parts, such as the engines and the undamaged fuel tanks, were later salvaged. Fuel from the aircraft was sold locally. Being of a high octane rating, it was much appreciated by those who used it! NF920's tail section remained in the bog until it was recovered for the Swedish Air Force Museum in 1985.

The crew were interned for a while and the expected interrogations were conducted, but they were well treated by the Swedes, to such an extent that this episode came to be known within 617 as 'Carey's Swedish Holiday.' The pilot's knee was expertly reset by a Swedish surgeon and the crew flew back home during November.

Flg-Off A. F. Jones of 9 Sqdn was wounded by flak that smashed the port side of his canopy. His bomb aimer flew the aircraft home, although Jones was able to land it. A Warwick of 281 Sqdn, up from Banff on an ASR sortie to cover a strike being made by Coastal Command's Dallachy Wing, received word of a ditched Lancaster, but this turned out to be a false alarm. Apart from Carey, all the crews would return.

For three and a half hours after leaving Norway, navigation was once more by dead reckoning until the bombers again came within Gee's range. Presumably the three-letter codes were used, but someone at Lossiemouth must have been impatient, for Sqdn Ldr Williams of 9 Sqdn was interrogated while returning and reported, 'Hit on bow followed by explosion and cloud of smoke.' This was followed up by 'Target hit by one Tallboy', which later turned out to be correct, though not in the manner previously described. Perhaps the impatience had come from the Air Ministry's Public Relations department, for a BBC newsreader announced at one o'clock that the *Tirpitz* had been hit by a 12,000lb bomb. This was three hours before any of the aircraft touched down.

The track miles flown would have been 2,250; it was estimated afterwards that due to the strong winds the actual mileage had been 2,400. The bombers landed singly, their return times being spread over two and a half hours, but most returned with a reasonable margin of fuel. Some had been grinding along for over thirteen hours.

Frustrated at not being able to bomb, Kell had hung around waiting for a gap in the cloud, but there was none to be seen and so he was the last to leave the target area. He suffered problems with his hydraulic system and despite orders from the staff at RAF Sumburgh he landed there with his bomb still on board. Watts also opted to land his flak-damaged Lancaster there, as did five aircraft of 9 Sqdn, two of which had also been hit, although none had suffered any casualties.

A PR sortie later that day by a 540 Sqdn Mosquito showed that the *Tirpitz* was indeed still afloat and on an even keel. There had been a near miss at her stern, claimed by five crews. This had caused some damage to her port prop shaft and let in 800 tons of water. The ship could no longer steam under her own power and on the recommendation of her skipper, Kapitan Wolf Junge, her complement was reduced by 400 men, most of them engine-room staff, as the engines were now required only for the generators and domestic services.

There was another potential problem. Tallboy craters showed clearly that the bed of the fjord was mud, not rock as had been thought. Junge had no doubt that his ship would be attacked again and to prevent her capsizing arrangements were made for dredgers to dump rubble under her keel. He was then recalled to Berlin, to be succeeded by the ship's former gunnery officer, Kapitan Robert Weber. Junge's request to remain for the sake of his crew was refused and he left on 4 November. Despite German propaganda her crew were aware of the grim situation their country faced. They also knew that the bombers were bound to return. *Tirpitz* would retain her 'hang-dog' look until her last moment came.

Obviate had not sunk the battleship, but it had come close. A report to the Chief of the Air Staff stated, 'It appears that had the attack taken place half an hour earlier conditions would have been perfect. An unsuspected front was apparently approaching the target when the force arrived, bringing with it two layers of cloud … The target could be clearly seen on approach but cloud interfered on the bombing run … The SASO 5 Group considers that the force would have obtained some six hits but for the cloud.'

Cochrane was quick to contact the two squadrons. 'Congratulations on your splendid flight and perseverance at the target. The luck will not always favour the *Tirpitz* and one day you will get her.' The next day he congratulated Tait again, this time on the award of a Bar to the latter's DFC, though Tait could have wished he had seen the end of this troublesome target first.

Tallboy production in Britain continued, but demand, even by just two squadrons, continued to outstrip supply. Sgt Harrison, the flight engineer in Flg-Off S. Laws' crew at Bardney later commented, 'The only reason that we did not drop more was the fact that we could not get more. They used to arrive by lorry, still warm from the factory.'

At times turnover was such that any bombs that were still warm would not have had much time to cool down. By the beginning of November, Tallboys of American manufacture were starting to reach both squadrons, but some proved to be unserviceable as they were unable to accept a standard detonator container. They were, however, locally repairable if modified containers were used. Consequently, by 15 November it had been decided that all future Tallboys were not to go direct to the squadrons, but were to be checked by 233 MU at Market Stainton, where a standard or modified container would be fitted as necessary while the bomb was still on its vehicle. This was to be done by an armourer sergeant and his assistant, under the supervision of an inspector from the Air Inspection Department.

Once the fitting of one or the other was shown to be possible the bomb was to be off-loaded and fitted with its appropriate container before going on to either Bardney or Woodhall Spa. Any bomb unable to accept either one was to be sent directly to the Royal Ordnance Factory at Risley for rectification. In this regard it was noted that a Mr Beacham, the Vickers representative at Woodhall Spa, had been very active and much appreciated.

While this procedure was being sorted out, the other big question remained. Would the bomb fall at the right time? This was next aired at a meeting of eleven people at Woodhall Spa on the afternoon of 6 November.

Wg Cdr 'Talking Bomb' Richardson, as 5 Group's Armament Officer, was in the chair. Also present among the other officers were Tait, Sqdn Ldr R. Evans of AAEE, Flt Lt Tolfrey, who was Woodhall Spa's Armament Officer, and Reg Firman as the Vickers representative. By now Firman must have been asking himself if this matter would ever be resolved, or whether the bombs would have to saturate a target on a 'brute force and ignorance' basis to achieve any results at all. He must also have wondered what had led him to go into the design of bomb-slips in the first place, quite apart from what Wallis would have to say to him if the problem continued.

It was stated that the slip was still experimental – that it had been maintained and modified by Vickers. By now some modifications had been made to eliminate hang-ups due to a slightly inaccurate positioning of the release slip, which in the original design would have caused binding and release failure. The corroded armature that Wallis had previously described to Cochrane was thought to be due to the presence of zinc in wartime cadmium plating, or moisture, which could have entered at the point where the electrical leads were brought through the slip's casing.

By now Woodhall Spa's armourers were using locally-made covers to protect the slips when they were not in use and it was decided that they should also make canvas covers to fit over the release slip while the Tallboy was suspended in the aircraft. This had been tried previously, but earlier types had not stood up to the force of the airflow and had not been introduced to the squadrons as this failure had been detected during the initial AAEE trials. The new covers could either be removed before take-off, or left in position.

As previously stated, the most recent trials, conducted during October, had shown that the ground error would be no more than a few feet. No defects had been reported during *Obviate*, but this was not conclusive as few of the bomb aimers had been able to see the results of their attacks. The defects were classed as either hang-ups and partial errors which in turn led to huge overshoot errors, or sluggish release action, causing small but persistent errors of up to thirty yards. The suggestion of cable cutters or explosive bolts that had been made to the Air Ministry by Harris in October had led to the Directorate of Air Armaments stating that past experience had shown these to be unreliable. A wire cable strop, which had also been suggested, was considered more likely to cause distortion.

Everyone agreed that the next step was to carry out further tests under operational conditions, with either a Cambridge Chronograph of the type that AAEE had used in the October trials, or timing apparatus that was now being designed by Vickers. As only four Chronographs were available it was suggested that two of these and two of the Vickers items be made available for fitting to 617's aircraft. Richardson said that there should be no delay in doing so, as the SABS Mark IIA provided suitable points for the connection of electromagnetic relays to start the timing apparatus prior to bomb release.

Tait explained that during a concentrated attack it was difficult for his crews to identify their own bombs, and that there was no concrete evidence apart from the information in the failure signals afterwards. The spotlight now turned on to Reg Firman, who was asked to summarise the action that Vickers had taken so far.

Firman said that the trouble had originally been thought to be misalignment of the release mechanism, so it had been modified to overcome this difficulty. The possibility of the release belt around the bomb binding, which might have distorted the slip and caused hang-ups, had apparently been got round by modifying the release slip lug. The description by Wallis of the waterlogged slip was seen as misleading – Firman had dismantled it at Woodhall Spa in the presence of Richardson and other senior officers.

Flt Lt Tolfrey, anxious to defend his own department, stated that when not in use the slips had been protected by canvas bags. Apart from condensation running down the sides of the bomb, he could not understand how any moisture could enter the slips, though the prompt action of Mr Beacham had done much to cure the trouble.

On the following day an order was issued to the effect that the slips were to be removed from the aircraft of both squadrons and stored in a warm dry building when not in use. To cut down time spent bombing-up the aircraft, the slips were to be refitted while Tallboys were being prepared in the bomb dump.

It now seemed as if the trouble had been cured. The proof of that would only come on the next operation. No one had any doubts as to what the target would be.

Once again 9 and 617 were detailed to attack the *Tirpitz*, and all that had changed was the operation code-name – this time it was *Catechism*. It began with a request to station a Mosquito at Vaenga for weather reconnaissance purposes. This was agreed to. Then two destroyers were detailed for ASR duties in the North Sea. On 4 November both squadrons flew to Scotland again, but the operation was postponed the next day due to bad weather. They returned home on 6 November, giving Tait time to take part in Richardson's meeting. Briefing took place again on 10 November, with a view to attacking two days later.

On 11 November Tait was playing football with his crews when he was suddenly summoned to meet Cochrane. This came so suddenly that he had no time to change and consequently appeared in sports gear before his AOC in Woodhall Spa's operations room. So attired, Tait received the order to attack the *Tirpitz* again. In a few hours both squadrons were once more on their way to Kinloss and Lossiemouth, accompanied as before by Flt Lt Buckham's Film Unit Lancaster.

The preliminary forecast was for convection cloud over the Norwegian coast, which would have meant a low freezing level and a high risk of the aircraft icing up. There was also the threat of stratocumulus cloud getting in the way. Shortly after midnight the weather Mosquito landed at Lossiemouth and reported cloud over the lower half of Norway, with fog in the fjords. There was no convection cloud, but there were patches of stratocumulus. It was thought that Tromsø would be clear by dawn, but there was the possibility of icing conditions. None of this was particularly encouraging, but after discussion with the meteorologists Tait decided to go.

12 November 1944
Target The battleship *Tirpitz*, at Haakøy island, near Tromsø.
Weather Clear, with excellent visibility.

Force 13 Lancasters of 9 Sqdn:

PB362	Sqdn Ldr A. G. Williams	NF939	Flg-Off A. E. Jeffs
NF929 'P'	Flt Lt G. C. Camsell	NG242 'C'	Flg-Off D. Macintosh
PA172 'G'	Flt Lt L. E. Marsh	NG252 'R'	Flg-Off C. Newton
PB696 'V'	Flt Lt R. C. Lake	NG249 'S'	Flg-Off C. E. Redfern
PD198 'W'	Flt Lt H. Watkins	NG220 'B'	Flg-Off J. E. Stowell
LM448 'T'	Flg-Off D. A. Coster	LM220 'Y'	Flg-Off W. D. Tweddle
NN722 'Q'	Flg-Off M. L. T. Harper		

18 Lancasters of 617 Sqdn:

EE146 'D'	Wg Cdr J. B. Tait	PD233 'G'	Flg-Off M. B. Flatman
ME554 'F'	Sqdn Ldr T. C. Iveson	LM489 'A'	Flg-Off J. Gingles
ED763 'Z'	Flt Lt S. A. Anning	ME561 'T'	Flg-Off A. W. Joplin
PD371 'S'	Flt Lt B. J. Dobson	NG181 'M'	Flg-Off A. E. Kell
DV405 'J'	Flt Lt B. A. Gumbley	DV393 'R'	Flg-Off J. H. Leavitt
PB415 'O'	Flt Lt R. E. Knights	DV380 'P'	Flg-Off W. R. Lee
DV391 'Y'	Flt Lt I. M. Marshall	ME555 'C'	Flg-Off I. S. Ross
LM492 'W'	Flt Lt J. L. Sayers	ME562 'K'	Flg-Off J. A. Sanders
DV385 'V'	Flg-Off J. Castagnola	LM485 'U'	Flg-Off F. H. A. Watts

Escort None

Bomb Loads 9 and 617 Sqdns – each aircraft carried one Tallboy, with an 0.07-second delay.

One 463 Sqdn Lancaster as a camera aircraft:
PD329 'Y' Flt Lt B. A. Buckham
This aircraft also carried Flt Lt Loftus and Flg-Off Rogers as cameramen.

At 0300 the first of the Lancasters lifted off from Lossiemouth. This time the weather was fine and clear on take-off, which seemed like a good omen, but the crews were in a determined rather than optimistic mood. Once his course had been set, Tait engaged the autopilot and tried to catch up on some much-needed sleep while over the sea. This time his aircraft was the one he had flown on the Kembs dam raid, which he saw as lucky. Certainly he was more fortunate than 9 Sqdn's CO, Wg Cdr Jim Bazin, who due to icing problems was unable to leave the ground. Flg-Off Roy Harvey, the navigator in Sqdn Ldr A. G. 'Bill' Williams' crew, recounted what happened:

> Wing Commander Bazin's aircraft could not be made ready in time. The weather was atrocious and the ground crews had the task of cleaning the frost off the wings on a bitterly cold night. As the aircraft was so overweight with additional fuel and the Tallboy it would have been suicidal to have attempted to do so [without cleaning the wing surfaces first]. As it was , I seem to recall having to call out the airspeed well above the normal for take off before Bill finally managed to break the ground friction by 'bouncing' the aircraft off. I suppose it was suicidal any way, for to get the overall weight down the aircraft were stripped of all 'unnecessary' weight including the mid-upper turret and most of the ammunition for the rear turret. We had been informed at briefing that fighters had been sent to a nearby airfield to protect the *Tirpitz*!

This crew's problems were just beginning. Bill Williams was Bazin's deputy, so, with Gp Capt. McMullen's permission, Bazin broke radio silence to inform him that he was now in command of a depleted force; no less than seven of 9 Sqdn's aircraft had been affected by the weather and were unable to take part. In his curtained 'office' behind the pilot, Roy Harvey bent to his task: 'After take-off I found my Gee set was u/s, so had to navigate by drifts supplied by bomb aimer and rear gunner.'

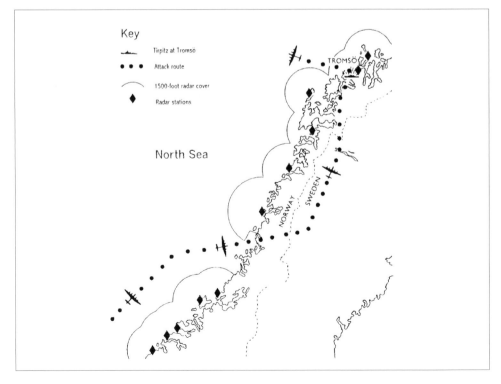

The attack route flown by 9 and 617 Squadrons during Operation *Catechism*. (Julie Anne Hudson)

An economical cruising speed resulted in a consumption of almost exactly one mile per gallon. Again the aircraft used their navigation lights for most of the way to keep station on each other, diligently dropping flame floats to check their drift. Once again they took advantage of the same radar gap in the district of Hortafjorden – it was surprising that the Germans had done nothing to fill it by now. They then flew on into Sweden, keeping the mountains between themselves and the local radar stations. The fighters that they had been warned of were FW 190s of JG5, who had moved into Bardufoss airfield, just thirty miles from Tromsø. No one wanted to meet them unless it was unavoidable. Twice now they had been lucky where fighters were concerned but – this time?

It was daylight now, with the sun streaming down onto a vast panorama of angular, dark-sided and snow-capped mountains. For the crews the sight would have been beautiful if their business had not been so grim.

Their rendezvous point was over the distinctive narrow Akka Lake, which was seen with a cloud the same shape over it. The cloud, like the lake, was just about the only one in the area. This time there was a clear sky over the *Tirpitz* and, blessed relief, no smokescreen. The pots were there, having just been brought down from Kaafjord, but the Germans had not yet had time to prime them. Construction of flak emplacements on the nearby hills had also been started, but these were not yet ready for use either.

Buckham later reported, 'There in front of us we could see Tromsø island, which appeared as a large snow-covered mound in the middle of the fjord. Some fifteen miles off, the massive outline of *Tirpitz*, anchored off Haakøy island, was clearly visible. Almost immediately, vast explosions appeared in and around the loose gaggle of bombers; *Tirpitz* was engaging us with her main armament, using short-delay fuses. As we got closer, we experienced sporadic flak from guns lining the fjord, which was soon supplemented by fire from two flak ships which were anchored in the fjord.'

At 0730 Kapitan Weber, aboard the *Tirpitz*, had received the first reports of Lancasters heading into Sweden, and alerted his anti-aircraft officer. At 0815 there was a further report of three Lancasters over Mosjoen, still a long way off, but heading towards the ship.

The water was as smooth as glass, there was not a breath of wind and unlike Kaafjord there were no high hills to screen the ship. Conditions were ideal for an air attack. Knowing that the FW 190s could be overhead in ten minutes, Weber ordered his signals officer to contact Major Heinz Ehrler, JG5's Gruppekommandeur at Bardufoss. This unit, known as the *Eismeer* (Frozen Sea) *Geschwader*, having spent much of the war in Finland, was used to operating in these inhospitable northern latitudes. The FW 190 had proved a tough proposition for even the RAF's Spitfires; the Lancasters, especially with their depleted armament, would be easy meat.

Next Weber ordered his crew to action stations, followed by the hoisting of a blue and yellow aircraft alarm flag, which was the signal for the flak batteries on Haakøy and around Tromsø to come to readiness. Perhaps this was it, but the *Tirpitz* was his ship and she would go down fighting.

Finally, at 0938, with the Lancasters visible as black dots in the south-eastern sky, Weber ordered his gun crews to open fire. As flak began to stain the sky around the anchorage, he enquired after the fighters and was told they had taken off.

Indeed they had. Eighteen FW 190s had been scrambled – only to head in the wrong direction. No one had told them that the *Tirpitz* had moved from her old anchorage. Apart from two flak ships, the Haakøy batteries and some fire from two other vessels, the ship was on her own now.

This time Buckham's crew would not be content just to film:

We went in at 6,800 feet as 'Willie' Tait and the others set up their bombing runs. We found this height too unhealthy, so I decided to descend to 2,000 feet, which secured us from the fire of the shore-based batteries. However, one of the flak ships was a real nuisance, so we shot her up from all three turrets, whereupon she upped anchor and moved to the other end of the fjord.

Flg-Off Terry Playford was the navigator of Knights' crew:

> I should think we could see the *Tirpitz* from about thirty miles out. Gin-clear sky
> and we could see the ship sitting there naked and we knew we were going to get her.
> As we neared the target, everyone was opening their bomb doors and the gaggle was
> still complete – we'd forgotten all about the fighters they warned us about. Over the
> target we could see the bombs of the other aircraft going down – you can't really see
> your own bomb going down, only the other ones. They were mighty close – and the
> splashes were tremendous – even at 15,000 feet they seemed to be coming right up
> at us. Then our bomb aimer shouted, 'We've hit her', and I was so pleased, and we
> went into orbit to try and see what damage had been done. And then to our delight
> we saw her gradually going over – though her guns were still firing, which impressed
> us very much. We knew we'd got her then. It made our day.'

Buckham vividly described what happened.

> By this time, the bombers were high above us and in the middle of a steady bomb
> run; the Tallboys clearly visible suspended under their bomb bays. The sight of these
> massive bombs as they fell away was quite remarkable. They appeared to travel in a
> graceful curve, remaining visible virtually to the point of impact. The first two Tallboys
> were observed as near misses, followed by a direct hit, which in turn was followed
> by two more direct hits only seconds later. Almost immediately, there was a massive
> explosion on board the warship, which appeared to heave itself out of the water. It
> was obvious, even from our height, that the *Tirpitz* was being badly damaged.
>
> At this point, throwing caution to the winds, we descended to 200 feet and with
> all cameras in action we flew round the unfortunate ship as more Tallboys rained
> down. Once it became apparent that all bombs had been dropped, we proceeded to
> fly over the *Tirpitz*, which was covered by a huge pall of smoke, reaching high into
> the clear sky. As we watched, we could see fires and more explosions on board and
> could clearly see a huge hole that had been blown out of the port side of the hull.

The attack was over in three minutes. One bomb hit abreast of the ship's B turret,
another penetrated amidships before exploding, then two others ripped the hole that
Buckham's crew saw, letting in thousands of tons of water. One of her officers was
Oberleutnant Bernard Schmitz:

> While I was eating in the mess, the sirens went, warning us of a coming air attack.
> I went to the bridge and was told that a large bomber squadron had been sighted.
> At about 8.30 I could see the planes, twenty-eight or thirty Lancasters, through the
> bridge telescope. Soon after, our 15-inch guns opened fire. We went into the armoured
> tower. Then the bombs began to drop. One hit the ship forward and another near the
> funnel. I stood on the starboard side and tried to balance myself by holding on to the
> gas-mask rack. But the ship shook so violently with the explosions that I suddenly
> found the rack in my hand. The brackets had torn loose with the armour plating.
>
> The ship was already listing to port. The signals officer ordered me to open one of
> the armoured doors, but it had got jammed, it was impossible. I tried the other side
> but that door was jammed too. I was given permission to go down to the chartroom,
> which was my proper action station. The captain and the other officers decided to
> stay in the tower as long as the guns were firing. On my way down the men asked
> me if there was any chance of the ship turning over. I told them it was impossible,
> we did not have enough water under the bottom. I must have been the last person
> to see the captain alive.

The noise abated as the Lancasters droned on. In the strange quiet that followed the
Tirpitz, like some great mortally wounded animal, turned over to port and Weber

ordered his men to jump. Abruptly her after 15-inch magazine blew up, hurling the massive 1,000-ton C turret into the air. For a moment the ship continued her slow roll until she lay on her side. Then, as more water flooded in, she rolled again until her upperworks touched the bottom. All that could be seen was her upturned and shiny keel, like an enormous red whale caught in a large pool of burning oil. The life of the *Kriegsmarine*'s biggest battleship had finally ended, but Bernhard Schmitz would not be trapped inside her:

> When I reached the deck, I saw the masts and main turret coming towards me. I didn't want to get buried under all the debris so I jumped into the water and swam away as fast as I could. I was still wearing my seaboots and full kit. Around me were a lot of men with their arms held high, and I saw them sink in front of my eyes, which was a terrible sight. I swam about 150 metres to the anti-torpedo nets and reached a buoy. Turning round, I saw the ship had listed over even further, to about 130 degrees. The torpedo tubes were level with the water. I don't know how long I stayed there, but it must have been one and half to two hours. My watch and my cufflinks were the only things I saved.

Tait, Castagnola and Gingles had been the first to bomb. Gingles scored a near miss, while there were indications that Tait and Castagnola's bombs both hit – the latter being a direct hit on the superstructure. Ross and Sayers claimed hits on the bows, while Flatman reported a direct hit amidships and Knights saw his explode just off the port quarter. Later, Lee was credited with a hit near the ship's catapult, Anning near the funnel and Kell at the bows. The time of their attack was recorded as 0842-0843.

Knights' crew later said that the first four bombs fell on or near the starboard quarter, the starboard bow, the port bow and near the funnel. Assessing their squadron's contribution as concentrated and accurate, they added that four bombs from 9 fell 200 yards, 500 yards, three-quarters of a mile and one mile off target, but added that after all 9 were using the Mark XIV sight(!).

Someone who appears to have had a better view, and perhaps a more objective one, was Sqdn Ldr Williams, leading 9 in behind 617. He said the first Tallboy fell slightly short, the second was a very near miss, the third hit the island to the left of the ship and the fourth hit directly amidships. Of his own unit, Tweddle and Newton both claimed near misses at 0845. Only eleven of 9 Sqdn's aircraft bombed; Camsell and Redfern did not attack as they were both late at the rendezvous point.

One of 9's aircraft, LM448 'T' flown by Flg-Off D. A. Coster, took a flak hit on the run-up, setting its starboard outer engine on fire. This was quickly put out and the bomb was dropped, but it was apparent that they were not going to get home and Coster headed for Sweden. They eventually reached the village of Vännäsberget, circled it, then crash-landed on a smooth river promontory. The muddy ground cushioned the impact and all six men scrambled clear with no injuries. Like Carey's crew, they were interned for a month or so before repatriation. Flg-Off Stowell came home with a flak-damaged port tailplane.

There were many near misses, which, like the Tallboys dropped on land, were probably as lethal as the direct hits. The final one of these put a sixty-foot-long dent, five feet deep, into the hull. It was generally agreed that the fourth Tallboy to fall hit the ship, knocking out her fire-control position, which was why gunfire from her became spasmodic just before she turned over. Even after this a flak unit on Haakøy continued to fire, but was silenced when a Tallboy fell on or near it (this raid's bomb plot and the probable sequence of events are described in Appendix 2).

Some spectacular footage was obtained by Buckham's camera aircraft. His film, held today by the Imperial War Museum, shows the *Tirpitz* under attack, with gun flashes. Then a Tallboy lands on shore with a big explosion, followed by what appear to be several hits, whose smoke smothers the flashes. The smoke hangs in the air in colossal pillars, but shock waves from those bombs that come down on land are momentarily visible as expanding white rings.

After the attack Buckham had turned away after having seen the battleship heel over towards the island, thinking that even after all this she would never sink. At this point his rear gunner, Flt Lt Eric Giersch, called out that he thought she was going to turn over.

> I immediately turned to port to see for myself and saw that she was indeed rolling over. Turning back, we went in again, flying at little more than fifty feet as we watched the last of Germany's battleships heel over to port and slowly settle upside down. The last pictures the camera crew took were of seamen standing on the upturned hull, while others were either jumping off the hull or already swimming in the icy waters of the fjord.

Buckham's crew returned to Waddington after being in the air for fourteen hours, to be met and questioned by Cochrane. For this he would receive a DSO to add to the DFC he already possessed and all his crew would be awarded DFCs as well.

The ship had grounded fore and aft after capsizing, but she had sunk amidships into a hollow, which carried away her port bilge keel. This was the area that had been filled by the dredger, but insufficiently, as it turned out.

Wg Cdr Richardson concluded afterwards that since 617 had attacked first, 9's bombing was bound to be hampered by the smoke from the explosions. Certainly 617's bombing was very concentrated, but the last few from 9 fell well away from the target. As the two squadrons again met over the lake Tait fired a Very light to signal the others to form a gaggle behind him.

Now to get home. Roy Harvey's navigational troubles were not yet over: 'On the return journey we received a radio message to say that ten-tenths' cloud had built up over the Shetlands (our first landfall) and our bases in north Scotland, so you can imagine my relief when I asked Bill to descend under the cloud, to see the tip of North Unst just ahead!'

At Bardney what was described as a tremendous party was laid on for 9 Sqdn. 617 touched down at Woodhall Spa to salutations from their erks and music from the Border Regiment's band.

At 1150 a 540 Sqdn Mosquito photographed the target area from 17,000 feet. On their return to RAF Dyce late in the afternoon the PRU crew reported the ship on its side within its nets, accompanied by a large streak of oil on the water and other ships standing round. The latest Ultra decrypt read, '*Tirpitz* blown and capsized'. Further confirmation, as if it was needed, was supplied by the Norwegian agent Egil Lindberg, who sent back a radio report from his attic above the mortuary where the Germans were beginning to lay out their dead.

For those able to quickly recover from the shock, it was time to ask what had happened to the promised fighter cover. Having been sent to the wrong anchorage, Major Ehrler's FW 190s had then lacked enough fuel to fly to the right one. The losses caused by this breakdown in communication meant that a scapegoat had to be found, so Ehrler's head went on the block. Following a court of enquiry, he was held responsible for the ship's loss and sentenced to three years' hard labour. Ater four weeks, due no doubt to the Luftwaffe's need for fighter pilots in the final weeks of the war, this sentence was waived and Ehrler went back into the air again, only to meet his death in an Me 262 jet fighter over Berlin in April 1945 at the hands of an American P-51 Mustang.

For the Norwegians it was a happy day, not least because there was no longer any danger of the RAF returning to this remote area. Parts of a Tallboy's casing were found on a beach afterwards and any bomb splinters quickly became prized souvenirs. At least one Tallboy fractured on impact, failed to go off and was dealt with by a German Bomb Disposal officer.

The capsized hulk of the *Tirpitz* at Tromsø in May 1945. Sections of armour plate and at least two of the three propellers have been cut away by the salvage gangs.

The *Tirpitz*'s upturned bow, a hundred feet of which was shattered by a Tallboy hit on 15 September 1944. (NA)

A German sailor on one of the salvage vessels gives scale to the huge hull, whose remaining armour plate shows a dent from a Tallboy near-miss. (NA)

The first rescue boats had arrived at the ship an hour after the bombing, finding hundreds of men, some of them wounded, swimming in the icy and oily water around the wreck. Still wearing his cap, Bernard Schmitz was hauled out. He had avoided death this time, but not those feelings that only survivors know:

> I lay in hospital for a few days after that, and was overcome for the first time with a deep depression. The ship had been our home. I had felt secure on board her, and I would have liked to have stayed with her. Now we had lost our home, and for the first time it became clear to me that this dreadful war, which I had hoped would have a satisfactory ending, was for us finally lost too.

600 men were pulled from the water, but the rescuers' primary concern was for those trapped inside the battleship, in a dark upside-down nightmare world whose only exit would be through its double bottom. Some were lucky; their hammering was answered by footsteps on the hull above them, the hiss of cutting gear and then the beautiful blue sky above their heads as they were hauled up. Eighty-seven men were saved in this manner and contact was made with another three, but special equipment would have been needed to reach them. As it was not available, they did not survive.

900 men died by one means or another. It is said that one trapped group sang *Deutschland über Alles* before succumbing either to the cold or the rising water. Gradually the hammering within the hull changed to a faint tapping. Then it ceased altogether.

Telegrams and decorations came thick and fast. Among them were plaudits from Churchill, the War Cabinet, the Chief of the Air Staff, Harris, the Admiralty, MRAF Lord Trenchard, Crown Prince Olav of Norway and one from Buckingham Palace:

Wing Commander 'Willie' Tait. After *Catechism*, he had something to smile about. (IWM, neg. no. CH14119)

'Please convey my hearty congratulations to all those who took part in the daring and successful attack on the *Tirpitz*.' There was one from the British Mission in Moscow, which said, 'Our warmest congratulations on sinking *Tirpitz*. Please pass to 5 Group and squadrons concerned, whose skill and tenacity have been fully rewarded. Russians most impressed and grateful that this menace to the convoy route has been disposed of.'

Stalin certainly was impressed. 'The news that British aeroplanes have sunk the *Tirpitz* has greatly delighted us. British airmen may legitimately pride themselves on this deed.'

They did. Tait was recommended for the VC, but instead he received a third Bar to his DSO – an unusual though not unique award. Someone coined the nickname '*Tirpitz*' Tait but, perhaps fortunately, this did not catch on. He was promptly summoned to the BBC to make a radio broadcast on the attack. Knights received the DSO and a DFC went to P/O Evans, Castagnola's bomb aimer. For all aircrew there was also a forty-eight-hour leave pass, which after their recent intense efforts would have been appreciated as much as any decoration.

There was another message, this time from Wallis to Cochrane, 'Very hearty congratulations to you and all officers and crews of 617 Sqdn on the magnificent success achieved yesterday. The tremendous courage and skill displayed has resulted in a major victory for Bomber Command.' Harris, no less, replied, 'Many thanks for your message. On the contrary, success due entirely to your perseverance with your bomb.'

It was later said that some high and mighty individual in the Admiralty had claimed that the *Tirpitz* was not really sunk because she had not disappeared completely beneath the water. If so, it was an opinion not likely to be entertained at High Wycombe.

Now, as far as the two squadrons were concerned, there was just one more score to settle. Just who had destroyed the *Tirpitz*? That controversy, which had begun after the single Tallboy hit during *Paravane*, would rumble on for years to come. Indeed, it has not been settled yet – but more of that later.

11

Pens, Shipping and Viaducts

The introduction of this large egg has been most successful but has entailed a lot of hard work and hard thinking by armament personnel.

V Group News, referring to Tallboy

By the beginning of December production of the said egg had improved, eighty-eight now being held by Bomber Command and a further thirty-two due within the next two weeks.

None of the targets that the two squadrons would attack over the next four months would be remembered in quite the same way as the *Tirpitz*, but nevertheless their destruction would be as important to the German war effort. As far as the crews were concerned the carrying out of these attacks would be no less demanding.

On the night of 26 November 9 were part of a 5 Group raid on the city of Munich, but on this occasion they carried 12,000lb HC bombs instead of Tallboys. Five of their aircraft carried out a similar attack on Heilbronn on 4 December, four of these carrying a 12,000lb bomb and the fifth a mixed load, with nothing bigger than a 4,000-pounder. These attacks have been mentioned as they occur in a file, now held by the National Archives, on the use of Tallboys by the two squadrons. Despite an admonition not to include raids in which 12,000lb HC bombs were used, it seems that some slipped through the net. 9 Sqdn's ORB is not specific on this, but correspondence with members of three crews shows clearly that they carried HC bombs on the Munich raid.

Of his two photos, the flight engineer commented in his letter to me:

I'm sorry I can't remember the names of the ground lads, but I can remember an incident that forever strengthened my faith in those boys. On an operation to Munich on 27 November 1944, carrying a 12,000lb 'cookie', we were struck by lightning over the Channel. It was preceded by a fantastic show of static, ending with a blinding flash, split-second silence, a slightly longer blackness, even the time for a thought of being blown to little pieces. The armourers had done their job, the sound of the 'horses' returned, the dash panel twinkled again and the voice of Newcastle exclaimed, 'The radio has gone for a ...'

(The Geordie WOp.)

It was not long before another target came along that was all too similar to the Kembs dam, and one to be attacked for the same reason. The dam in question was at the head of a valley in which ran the river Roer. By now American troops were just three miles away and preparing to cross it. As at Kembs, this one's teeth would have to be drawn before the Germans could use them.

8 December 1944
Target 1. The Urft dam, also referred to as the Heimbach dam.
   2. The Schwammenauel dam was an alternative target.
Weather Nine to ten-tenths cloud over the target.

The crew of Flying Officer Harry Anderson of 9 Squadron. From left to right, back row: armourer, Flight Sergeant Ashworth (mid-upper gunner), Flying Officer Anderson (pilot), three armourers. Front row: Flight Sergeant Loakes (flight engineer), Sumner (bomb aimer), Vivian (navigator), Cornfoot (wireless-operator), and Harrison (rear gunner). (W. D. Loakes)

Off duty. The NCOs of Flying Officer Anderson's crew 'outside the Bardney residence'. Pipers seem to have been de rigueur for 9 Squadron at this time! (W. D. Loakes)

Force 5 Lancasters of 9 Sqdn:

PD368 'A' Flt Lt L. H. Watkins	PB213 'F' Flg-Off B. Taylor
NN722 'Q' Flg-Off A. F. Jones	LM220 'Y' Flg-Off W. D. Tweddle
NG242 'C' Flg-Off D. Macintosh	

19 Lancasters of 617 Sqdn:

EE146 'D' Wg Cdr J. B. Tait	DV391 'Y' Flt Lt I. M. Marshall
DV385 'V' Sqdn Ldr J. F. Brookes	ED763 'Z' Flt Lt D. J. Oram
NG181 'M' Sqdn Ldr C. C. Calder	LM485 'U' Flt Lt H. J. Pryor
PD238 'H' Sqdn Ldr J. V. Cockshott	DV402 'X' Flt Lt J. L. Sayers
DV380 'P' Sqdn Ldr C. W. C. Hamilton	ME555 'C' Flg-Off M. B. Flatman
ME554 'F' Sqdn Ldr T. E. Iveson	ME561 'T' Flg-Off A. W. Joplin
PD371 'S' Flt Lt B. J. Dobson	LM695 'N' Flg-Off J. H. Leavitt
LM489 'A' Flt Lt H. V. Gavin	DV393 'R' Flg-Off P. H. Martin
NF992 'B' Flt Lt M. S. Goodman	PB415 'O' Flg-Off J. A. Sanders
DV405 'J' Flt Lt B. A. Gumbley	

Escort 39 Mustang IIIs and 50 Spitfire IXs of 11 Group:

1 Sqdn RAF	306 Sqdn (Polish)
19 Sqdn RAF	316 Sqdn (Polish)
65 Sqdn RAF	340 Sqdn (Free French)
165 Sqdn RAF	441 Sqdn (Belgian)

Bomb Loads 9 and 617 Sqdns – one Tallboy per aircraft, with an 11-second delay.

The intention was to breach the spillway alongside the dam. The two squadrons would attack after the Main Force, who would be using 1,000-pounders set for 0.025-second delay. These units were to attack first, in pairs, each pair to pass over the target in a three-minute period, with five minutes between each pair. Their approach was to be at right-angles to the overflow, with 9 Sqdn's five aircraft acting as windfinders. The importance accorded to this target can be judged by the fact that no less than 206 Lancasters from 5 Group had been assigned to it – and on a daylight raid, which was another indication of the Luftwaffe's decline.

The Germans, however, had another ally – the fickle northern European weather, especially at this time of year. It turned out to be clear over Belgium en route, but not where it mattered, and it was probably this which led to 5 Group's only loss on this date – a 630 Sqdn Lancaster in a collision over the target area with another aircraft which presumably survived.

Tait's report summed up the situation:

Ten-tenths stratocumulus cloud obscured the target and there was no chance of a break. The force orbited for some time, making runs in various directions, but it was impossible to bomb although the target could be glimpsed occasionally, and was definitely identified. Water was flowing down the spillway. There was no flak in the target area, but a solitary gun was firing somewhat north of the target. I therefore recalled the force at 1140.

By now 128 aircraft had bombed out of the 206 sent.

Three of 617's Lancasters sustained flak damage. Brookes, not realising Dunkirk had been by-passed and was still held by the Germans, flew over the port at 300ft on his return and was fortunate in that some of the flak thrown up at him bounced off the Tallboy beneath the aircraft. Hamilton and Joplin were also hit, the latter over the target, but both came back. Goodman tried homing to the target on Gee, making six runs, but was unsuccessful. Oram's crew was apparently the only 617 one to bomb at all, although his bomb overshot.

9 Sqdn fared slightly better, with three of their crews bombing. Watkins was unable to attack despite orbiting the target for thirty-six minutes, and Jones did not either – permission to bomb on his fourth run was refused by Tait at 1140, as he ordered everyone home. Taylor and Tweddle both bombed, the latter seeing black smoke from some of 5 Group's bombs in the dam's estimated overflow area. Due to the cloud he estimated the AP by the smoke and a jutting piece of land. Macintosh described the rest of 5 Group's bombing as wild, but even so he claimed to have seen two of their bombs hit the AP. He came home fuming with frustration when his Tallboy hung up on his first run and then failed to explode when it finally dropped away on his seventh.

Just to add to the day's difficulties, there was thick fog waiting for them on the other side of the Channel, forcing 9 to divert to RAF Odiham in southern England and 617, less Brookes, to make a dramatic but safe landing at Manston with the aid of FIDO. Brookes landed at a USAAF base at Sudbury, whose commander, staggered at the size of the Tallboy, refused his crew permission to lower it onto the grass, thereby easing the weight on the aircraft!

Whatever damage Tait had seen, it had not been enough to cause a breach. A PR Mosquito crew assessed it all as: 'Bombing seemed good and fairly accurate. One direct hit on 'apron', and one in water just above, and one at base of apron.' There had, it seemed, been one hit on the roadway at each side of the spillway, letting water out through both. Still, it had not been enough for a breach. For the next two days the weather was too bad to permit a return.

11 December 1944
Target The Urft dam.
Weather Five to nine-tenths stratocumulus cloud, with tops at 6,000-8,000ft, drifting across the target.

Force 20 Lancasters of 9 Sqdn:

PD377	'U'	Wg Cdr J. M. Bazin		
NF929	'P'	Flt Lt G. C. Camsell		
PA172	'G'	Flt Lt J. J. Dunne		
PB696	'V'	Flt Lt M. L. T. Harper		
PD198	'W'	Flt Lt R. J. Harris		
NN722	'Q'	Flt Lt A. E. Jones		
LL845	'L'	Flt Lt A. M. Morrison		
PD368	'A'	Flt Lt H. Watkins		
NG249	'S'	Flg-Off R. E. Adams		
NG206	'J'	Flg-Off K. S. Arndell		

ME809	'X'	Flg-Off R. W. Ayrton
NG223	'D'	Flg-Off J. W. Buckley
NF937	'E'	Flg-Off C. Follett
NG252	'B'	Flg-Off A. L. Keeley
NG235	'H'	Flg-Off S. Laws
NG242	'C'	Flg-Off D. Macintosh
NG257	'L'	Flg-Off P. W. Reaks
NG220	'B'	Flg-Off J. E. Stowell
PD213	'F'	Flg-Off B. Taylor
LM217	'O'	Flg-Off J. C. Wiley

17 Lancasters of 617 Sqdn:

EE146	'D'	Wg Cdr J. B. Tait
ME555	'C'	Sqdn Ldr J. F. Brookes
NG181	'M'	Sqdn Ldr C. C. Calder
PD238	'H'	Sqdn Ldr J. V. Cockshott
ME554	'F'	Sqdn Ldr T. C. Iveson
PD371	'S'	Flt Lt B. J. Dobson
LM489	'A'	Flt Lt H. V. Gavin
NF992	'B'	Flt Lt H. S. Goodman
DV405	'J'	Flt Lt B. A. Gumbley

DV391	'X'	Flt Lt I. M. Marshall
ED763	'Z'	Flt Lt D. J Oram
LM483	'U'	Flt Lt H. J Pryor
PD233	'G'	Flg-Off M. B. Flatman
DV402	'X'	Flg-Off A. W. Joplin
LM695	'N'	Flg-Off J. H. Leavitt
DV393	'R'	Flg-Off P. H. Martin
PB415	'O'	Flg-Off J. A. Sanders

Escort A total of 188 fighters from RAF Fighter Command, who covered two other Main Force attacks on the Osterfeld marshalling yards near Essen and two benzol plants at Duisburg, as well as this one. No other details are available.

Bomb Loads As per previous attack on 8 December.

One 627 Sqdn Mosquito as a PR aircraft:
KB362 'K' W/O R. W. Player and P/O C. B. Heath

Also included in this attack were 233 Lancasters of 5 Group and 5 Mosquitoes of 8 Group.

The plan was the same as on 8 December. Once again, the cloud caused problems, several runs having to be made while the crews bombed through gaps in it. 9 and 617 were to attack after the Main Force, smoke from whose bombs obscured the AP.

There was no fighter opposition, although some flak came up from the target area and to the north of it. One 57 Sqdn Lancaster was lost. Tait claimed his bomb hit dead centre on the dam's apron and saw another, probably that of Brookes, overshoot to the right. Iveson confirmed that the first Tallboy to fall, which was possibly Oram's, hit the dam about a quarter of the way down it. His own bomb fell in the water and did not explode, though another that followed it did. Gavin's bomb overshot due to a partial hang-up, solved by a manual release.

Of 617's crews, Cockshott and Sanders were the only ones not to bomb. Cockshott made five runs, then due to an unserviceable bombsight gave up and came home with his Tallboy still on board. Sanders made six, but claimed smoke from the Main Force bombing, then cloud later on, prevented him from releasing his Tallboy. He was finally ordered home by Tait.

All of 9 Sqdn's crews attacked. Buckley said he saw four Tallboy direct hits on the spillway and water coming over it in two places. 5 Group's bombing was scattered, with much of it to the west of the AP, although the Tallboy bombing appeared concentrated. Watkins summed things up fairly well when he said that the bombing was well concentrated, but apparently without making much impression and that 'Indications were that the water was not at such a high level as the previous attack.' Indeed, for the Germans had lowered it and the hoped-for eruption did not take place. This was despite thirty-five Tallboys being aimed at it.

Several Main Force sticks had straddled the dam and some direct hits were claimed, but there was no evidence of serious damage. There had, it seemed, been one hit on the roadway at each side of the spillway, removing thirteen feet of concrete from along the top of the dam, although this had not been enough for a breach.

Harris later commented, 'Many direct hits were in fact scored. This was not sufficient, although photographs showed that the top of the Urft dam was deeply chipped at three points. In one case the chip extended almost down to the water level, which at the time of reconnaissance was thirteen feet from the top. The enemy evidently manipulated the water-level so as to avoid erosion of the dam and spillway.'

Further attacks planned for 13 and 14 December were scrubbed due to fog at the RAF bases. Not surprisingly, it was then decided that this dam, like the Sorpe, was too strong to be destroyed by Tallboys.

15 December 1944
Target The Ijmuiden E-boat pens.
Weather Ten-tenths cloud over the target.

Force 17 Lancasters of 617 Sqdn:

EE146 'D' Wg Cdr J. B. Tait	LM483 'U' Flg-Off H. J. Pryor
DV391 'X' Sqdn Ldr J. F. Brookes	PD371 'S' Flg-Off J. Castagnola
PB415 'O' Sqdn Ldr C. C. Calder	PD233 'G' Flg-Off M. B. Flatman
PD328 'H' Sqdn Ldr J. V. Cockshott	LM489 'A' Flg-Off A. W. Joplin
ME554 'F' Sqdn Ldr T. C. Iveson	NG181 'M' Flg-Off A. E. Kell
NF992 'B' Flt Lt L. S. Goodman	DV393 'R' Flg-Off P. H. Martin
DV380 'P' Flt Lt B. A. Gumbley	ME555 'C' Flg-Off I. S. Ross
DV402 'X' Flt Lt I. M. Marshall	LM695 'N' Flg-Off F. H. A. Watts
ED763 'Z' Flt Lt D. J. Oram	

The E/R-boat pens at Ijmuiden after the Tallboy attacks of 24 August and 15 December 1944. One hit just west of centre and damage to the rear caused by the August raid is clearly visible, as is further damage to the side facing the harbour from the second attack. Another smaller hole in the south-western area was also inflicted during the second attack. A third hole near this one was possibly due to a rocket-propelled Disney bomb dropped by the US 8th Air Force. The large Tallboy craters at the rear of the pens were clearly not quite close enough to undermine them. Note the contrast between these and the size of the roof holes, indicating the strength of the building. (IWM, neg. no. C4885)

Escort 36 Spitfire IXs of 11 Group:
  312 Sqdn (Czech)   441 Sqdn (Belgian)

Bomb Loads Each aircraft carried one Tallboy, with an 11-second delay.

This daytime attack was preceded by three weather reconnaissances, each flown by a pair of Spitfires, from 229, 453 and 602 Sqdns. In each case the report was poor, with thick haze from halfway across the North Sea to Holland, reducing visibility to one mile. Nevertheless, 617 took off shortly after 1300 and arrived over the port two hours later.

A smokescreen hindered accurate bombing and this time the flak was much heavier than during the previous August attack. Pryor and Marshall were both hit, as was Calder, who took some light flak through his starboard main spar, although fortunately for him it held together. Watts ducked as flak struck the port side of his windscreen. It hit his front turret too, which meant a narrow escape for its occupant, Flg-Off Jewell, when part of a shell missed him. Hydraulic fluid dripping down from the turret's power lines did not help the bomb aimer's vision either, so that meant a return without bombing.

Tait saw his bomb fall near the centre of the southern pens. Brookes said, 'We had a hang-up over the target. The gyro toppled and we were under the impression the bomb had gone. We then circled south-west of the target for fifteen minutes waiting for the gyro to settle, but without effect. We were eventually instructed to return to base. We endeavoured to recock the bomb but it slipped and the bomb fell off in the sea about three to five miles west of the target.' Flatman suffered a hang-up during two runs and tried to jettison at the end of the second one. Then, as he opened the doors for a third attempt, his bomb also fell out, some two miles from the target.

Marshall came back with his bomb still on board. One of his starboard engines had caught fire, but by diving and using the extinguisher, he had put it out. On landing, his Tallboy, which had failed to release despite three runs, then fell out. It did not explode, but that did not prevent the crew from very quickly vacating the Lancaster!

Despite all this, the thirteen Tallboys that had been dropped had achieved a good deal. A hole fifteen feet across had been knocked through one roof. Part of it, 140ft by 33ft, over four pen entrances, had collapsed, due to one or two hits.

On 17 December, 9 were part of another 5 Group night attack on Munich. Of the twenty-three crews that they put up, eighteen carried a 12,000lb bomb and five a 4,000-pounder with clusters of incendiaries. As the 12,000-pounders were fused to detonate instantaneously, these are likely to have been HCs, not Tallboys.

Although he was unable to remember the date, it was probably during this last winter of the war that P/O Gordon Maguire had an unexpected demand made on his department:

One night Sqdn Leader Robinson, the Armament Officer at Waddington, rang me to say, 'We've got one of your birds here!' We both knew what that would mean – bombing it up with a Tallboy away from home, but there was very little we could say over an open line. Anyway, we arranged that he would provide some lighting and I organised a small convoy, with myself on a motorbike in front. The bomb on its trolley followed behind.

On the way we stopped at a pub at the village of Potter Hangworth, leaving the Tallboy outside. Then there was a complaint from a civilian that someone had left a 'bloody great rocket' outside!

Waddington was a large base with more than one squadron on it,* none of whom had seen a Tallboy before, so quite a crowd had gathered to watch the operation. We went into the bomb dump to fuse it. As arranged, there were lights to illuminate the Lancaster's bomb bay. I told my NCO, Corporal Spencer, that he had an audience. He, being something of an actor, twirled his moustache and said, 'Great!' It was all done in twenty minutes and there were cheers. Spencer bowed and the Armament Officer came across with a cap full of money! [*463 and 467 Sqdns, RAAF]

The Australians were suitably impressed. Their contribution was probably spent in the same pub on the way home.

The next Tallboy target would be a very different one. Under some pressure from the Ministry of Economic Warfare, Harris had in the past reluctantly mounted raids on targets whose destruction, he had been assured, would have 'vital consequences' for the German war effort. Among these had been the ballbearing plants in the Schweinfurt area, a Mosquito raid on the molybdenum mine at Knaben and of course *Chastise*. Despite what the civil servants had said, in each case a rapid German collapse had not followed and his comments concerning panacea targets had, he felt, been justified. It was therefore not surprising that he had reacted to demands for attacks on oil plants in the same way.

As Wallis had observed, Hitler's war machine was dependent on oil. Since Romania had now joined the Allied side the supply from Ploesti was denied to the Germans, making their home output of synthetic products more important than ever. The reputation of German chemists was second to none, and this type of oil was being produced by two different methods.

One was the Fischer-Tropsch process, in which molecules of hydrogen and carbon monoxide, obtained by breaking up coal with steam, were used to form oil molecules. However, there had been no expansion in the Fischer-Tropsch facilities since 1940;

their plants, being in the Ruhr, had been subjected to heavy bombing during area attacks.

A more important alternative was a process known as Bergius hydrogeneration, which involved the splitting of coal molecules, then forcing hydrogen into them at high pressure to produce liquid oil molecules. The Bergius plants were meeting almost the whole of the Luftwaffe's needs, for since 1940 they had more than doubled in production, turning out no less than 3.8 million tons of synthetic aviation spirit in the first quarter of 1944.

Two plants which between them produced over a third of the total Bergius output were those at Leuna, ninety miles south-west of Berlin, and at Pölitz, near Stettin. They had therefore been bombed by the US Eighth Air Force in May 1944, resulting in production at Pölitz being held up for two months. Repairs had been swiftly carried out and this plant was now in full swing again. Despite his misgivings, Harris had agreed to put them out of action once more.

21 December 1944
Target The Pölitz hydrogeneration plant.
Weather Good over target, despite some haze.

Force 16 Lancasters of 617 Sqdn:

LM489	'A'	Sqdn Ldr J. F. Brookes	DV380 'P' Flt Lt H. J. Pryor
EE146	'D'	Sqdn Ldr C. C. Calder	LM492 'W' Flg-Off J. Castagnola
PD238	'H'	Sqdn Ldr J. V. Cockshott	PD233 'G' Flg-Off M. B. Flatman
ME554	'F'	Sqdn Ldr T. C. Iveson	ME561 'T' Flg-Off A. W. Joplin
NF992	'B'	Flt Lt L. S. Goodman	NG181 'M' Flg-Off A. E. Kell
DV405	'J'	Flt Lt B. A. Gumbley	DV393 'E' Flg-Off P. H. Martin
PD371	'S'	Flt Lt I. M. Marshall	ME555 'C' Flg-Off I. S. Ross
ED763	'Z'	Flt Lt D. J. Oram	LM695 'N' Flg-Off F. H. A. Watts

This was part of an all 5 Group force of 207 Lancasters and one Mosquito. On this occasion 9 Sqdn carried conventional bomb loads.

Escort None.

Bomb Loads Each 617 Sqdn Lancaster carried one Tallboy, with an 11-second delay.

This was to be a night raid, and one that would be complicated by foggy weather at home. In anticipation of this, airfields in the Moray Firth area of Scotland had been allocated for diversionary purposes. Reflecting on their past Main Force experiences, 617 were not happy about the choice of target – or that it was at maximum range – but resolved to do what they could. Over at Coningsby the fog was so bad that 83 Sqdn could not even be seen taking off. At Bardney one of 9 Sqdn's aircraft would crash on its return, and several diversions would be necessary.

The plan, worked out by 5 Group's 54 Base, was that at eleven minutes to H-Hour the Primary Blind Markers were to drop two of a new form of white TI, which would flash V in Morse on the AP. This was intended to combat any enemy attempt at spoof marking. The plant was then to be marked with flares until four minutes to H-Hour. As soon as possible the visual marking aircraft were to drop a stick of five markers – three reds and two greens – across the AP. The Master Bomber, Wg Cdr Woodroffe, would then select the most accurate TI and order the Main Force to aim at this, using a false wind vector.

617's role was to fly with 9, 463 and 467 Sqdns in support, but at a lower height than these other units. They were to attack by the light of the flares between nine and four minutes to H-Hour, while flying on the same track as the flare force. After marking the supporting run, they were to orbit to port and then go in on the Main Force's heading. Elements of the Main Force would make a spoof attack on another target five minutes before the real one. A forest – the Politzer Stadtwald – to the south and the river Oder to the east were both conspicuous landmarks. If it was adequately marked, the plant, being a mile across, could hardly be missed. However, the crews had been warned of the proximity of a POW camp, making indiscrimate bombing out of the question.

The flight to Pölitz was for most crews without incident and the weather in the target area was reasonably good. The target was well lit by flares, but the red and yellow TIs were scattered, so some of the bombing was as well. A concentration of the force proved poor due to a wind change at a time when Loran fixes were unobtainable. Few crews saw the white Morse flashing markers. Some industrial haze and a smokescreen put up by the defenders did not help, although a decoy fire was quickly seen through, as it was started far too early.

It was considered afterwards that the Master Bomber had assessed the markers as being closer to the target than they were, so leading much of the attack astray. Gumbley summed it up well when he said afterwards, 'We could not see our bomb burst. The target area was very smoky. Impossible to assess bombing. The flares gave good illumination, but not over the AP.'

Watts did not bomb as his sight became useless ten minutes from the target, and neither did Marshall. Cockshott did four runs, finally bombing at 2210 despite a toppled gyro. Iveson had the same problem on his first run and brought his Tallboy back after further attempts. Brookes was hit by heavy flak, which prevented him from opening his bomb doors. Calder never reached the target at all, being forced to divert to Milltown after his port inner engine developed a fault.

Flg-Off Arthur Joplin had a very experienced stand-in bomb aimer, Flg-Off Arthur Walker, on what would be the latter's forty-fifth and final operation of two continuous tours of duty. Taking due heed of the Master Bomber's instructions, Walker aimed his Tallboy at the recommended red TI, without any visible result. Once the aiming-point photograph had been taken, Joplin's crew set course for the Moray Firth.

Once they had sorted themselves out after diversions to Scotland or just up the road to Metheringham, 617's crews later commented that although flares had illuminated the target, its construction was such as to deny the SABS the distinct aiming point that it needed. Of the eleven Tallboys dropped, it was thought that at least three had fallen in the target area, probably to the north of the plant.

Disgruntled though they may have been, at least these crews were still alive to talk about it. One Main Force Lancaster disappeared without trace and eight others were lost in crash landings, largely due to the fog that blanketed Lincolnshire. At the midnight meteorological conference, with the bombers not expected back for another hour, it had become clear that only two airfields would be safe for landing, so five others equipped with FIDO had been ordered to stand by.

One of the victims was Joplin and his crew. While returning, a message had been received from 54 Base ordering all aircraft to make for their respective bases. Diversions were inconvenient; they resulted in bombers scattered all over the country, making them unavailable for operations the next day or night. Clearly, someone on the ground had decided that to bring them home was worth the increased risk.

On the approach to Coningsby, which had been one of the two airfields still judged usable without FIDO, it became clear that fog would make a landing there difficult if not impossible, but Joplin's fuel situation now ruled out diverting to Scotland. Then the powers-that-be had another change of mind and put out a W/T message that 'Aircraft should now land at the first available airfield.' By now it was 0230 and the order to light FIDO was given. However, with visibility down to 400 yards, the best that could be done at RAF Ludford Magna, also in Lincolnshire, was to indicate the runway's position.

Joplin saw the red glow of the FIDO installation at Ludford Magna, ensured his aircraft was above the safety level of this airfield and called for permission to land. Not surprisingly, a lot of other 5 Group crews had had the same idea and this part of the night sky was now full of Lancasters.

While circling, Joplin's port wing struck something. He called for full power on all four engines, but felt it ebbing away. At the last moment they put out a distress call. Then they struck the ground with such violence that the rear turret was torn off. Five crew members were injured and the other two killed. One of them was the bomb aimer, Arthur Walker, who had insisted on doing this final operation of his tour.

Joplin survived with multiple fractures to both legs after being dragged out by his navigator, Flt Sgt Basil Fish. Having accounted for the rest of the crew, Fish tried to get the other two out, but was driven back by flames and exploding ammunition.

They had crashed at Tealby, three miles north-east of Market Rasen, in a particularly remote part of Lincolnshire, at 0245. Despite a head wound, Fish went off to seek help at a farmhouse, some three miles away. With the farmer's assistance he found a callbox and rang Ludford Magna, although only after a sharp exchange with an operator who wanted him to put twopence in the coinbox first! The injured men were treated in the RAF hospital at Rauceby.

The enquiry that followed was unjustly critical of both Arthur Joplin and Basil Fish, whom it found guilty of not following the proper Gee homing procedure. Both men received red endorsements in their logbooks. This censure went ahead despite the other surviving members of the crew being adamant that the Lancaster had collided with another unseen one, instead of hitting the ground. (A full account of this operation and its aftermath can be found in the book 617 Sqdn: The Dambusters at War by Tom Bennett.)

There was a feeling in the squadron that justice had not been done, especially when a plotting exercise conducted by them afterwards showed that if Joplin's Lancaster had followed Gee from the Lincolnshire coast it would not have had enough fuel to reach Woodhall Spa. It was some compensation for Fish that despite the black mark he had been given he received a commission the following year.

However, the findings of the court of enquiry stood. Those above 617 did not want to know. It was appalling treatment that added to Joplin's physical pain and mental anguish, especially when he learned that two of his friends had died. He was eventually cleared to fly again, but spent the final months of the war convalescing before being repatriated to New Zealand. His leg injuries would affect him for the rest of his life.

Had it been worth it? A PR sortie by 542 Sqdn indicated that the high level of activity shown a few hours before the raid had now dwindled to almost nothing. Dense black smoke covered the plant, but this could be discounted as it was issuing from what appeared to be oil fires at the southern end of the works; a ruse, as it was known that there were no oil tanks there.

Nevertheless, there were numerous hits within the plant area, one of which had felled a 320-foot power station chimney. A number of connecting pipelines had been destroyed, but the most important damage was to the power station. This would probably necessitate a shutdown for a fortnight, followed by production at about half-capacity. Further coverage the following month showed the plant to be working at about 50 to 75 per cent capacity again.

To use Tallboy on such an operation had clearly been a wrong decision; the 12,000lb HC bomb would have been of far more use against the piping, most of which was on or above the surface. It may also be asked why it had been considered necessary to mount this raid on such a vile night, particularly as the weather had already led to a postponement earlier in the day. Fortunately FIDO had been available to save many aircrew lives in what was turning out to be the worst winter of the war, but bad luck had robbed Joplin's crew of a safe touchdown.

At this point Tait was retired from command of 617. Like Cheshire, it was considered that he had done enough with them, and he was posted to 100 Group's headquarters. His four DSOs and two DFCs were indeed a record. Cochrane did not want to see him dead before victory was achieved.

His successor was Gp Capt. Johnny Fauquier, a French-Canadian former airline pilot in his thirties, who had stepped down from the prized rank of Air Commodore in order to command 617. Fauquier had previously served under Bennett and had made a name for himself as a tough individual of few words; his curt manner meant that he did not have to say a great deal. Although an able airman with the presence of a leader, he would not prove to be a popular one.

29 December 1944
Target The E-boat pens at Waalhaven, near Rotterdam.
Weather Clear.

Force 16 Lancasters of 617 Sqdn:

NG118 'V' Sqdn Ldr J. F. Brookes	ED763 'E' Flt Lt D. J. Oram
ME554 'F' Sqdn Ldr C. C. Calder	LM485 'U' Flt Lt H. J. Pryor
PD238 'H' Sqdn Ldr J. V. Cockshott	LM492 'W' Flg-Off J. Castagnola
DV380 'P' Sqdn Ldr C. W. C. Hamilton	PD233 'G' Flg-Off M. B. Flatman
PD371 'S' Flt Lt B. J. Dobson	NG181 'M' Flg-Off A. E. Kell
LM489 'A' Flt Lt H. V. Gavin	DV393 'R' Flg-Off J. H. Leavitt
NF992 'B' Flt Lt L. S. Goodman	ME555 'C' Flg-Off I. S. Ross
DV405 'J' Flt Lt B. A. Gumbley	LM695 'N' Flg-Off F. H. A. Watts

Escort None.

Bomb Loads Each Lancaster carried one Tallboy, with an 11-second delay.

As it would take a few days for Fauquier to settle in – especially after a farewell party in the Officer's Mess the previous night not only for Tait but also the outgoing Station CO, Gp Capt. 'Monty' Philpott – for the moment Sqdn Ldr 'Jock' Calder led 617 on this raid.

The pens were at the east side of Waalhaven, consisting of three sections with a total of sixteen pens each. Each pen presented a target 150ft long by 25ft wide. The roof, just over eight feet thick, was camouflaged to look like a green hill, though with some gun positions. The pens included the usual torpedo-loading facilities, stores, workshops and general servicing facilities. During this month ten E-boats were housed there.

The clear winter's afternoon made marking unnecessary. From bombing heights of between 16,000ft and 18,000ft, 617 could afford to ignore any light flak and there were no fighters to worry about. Although some aircraft found two runs necessary, there were several direct hits. Pryor said, 'One bomb undershot by two hundred yards and one was to the west. The rest hit the target.'

There were three direct hits on the southern portion of the pens, with a crater 25ft in diameter on the entrance to the southern shelter's roof. An enormous length of roof – 158ft by 20ft – was smashed over the entrance of the west side of the southern section.

Two out of the three sections had been damaged as the centre one took a direct hit on the roof, destroying two buildings over the shelter entrance. A large section of the roof over the entrance on the west side had collapsed. Other Tallboy craters to the east, north-east and north-west of the pens had destroyed several buildings along with a quayside, as well as cutting a railway track in several places.

There must have been relief that, after the sense of being misemployed at Pölitz, the squadron was now back to doing what it did best – pinpoint attacks on small but important targets by day.

The next day 617 paid another visit to the Ijmuiden pens, but ten-tenths cloud over the target meant that Calder ordered the force to return without bombing.

31 December 1944
Target The cruisers *Emden* and *Köln*, at Hortenfjord in Norway.
Weather Bright moonlight.

Force 12 Lancasters of 617 Sqdn:

EE146 'D' Gp Capt J. E. Fauquier	ED763 'E' Flt Lt D. J. Oram
NG118 'V' Sqdn Ldr J. F. Brookes	DV391 'X' Flt Lt H. J. Pryor
ME554 'F' Sqdn Ldr C. C. Calder	PD233 'G' Flg-Off M. B. Flatman
PD238 'H' Sqdn Ldr J. V. Cockshott	LM695 'N' Flg-Off A. E. Kell

The cruiser *Köln*, photographed pre-war, which was one of the targets at Oslo. (IWM, neg. no. HU1048)

NF992 'B' Flt Lt L. S. Goodman	DV393 'R' Flg-Off J. H. Leavitt
DV405 'J' Flt Lt B. A. Gumbley	ME555 'C' Flg-Off I. S. Ross

Escort None.

Bomb Loads Each Lancaster carried one Tallboy, with a 0.5-second delay, so that they would explode 100 feet under water.

Sixteen crews, eight from each of 83 and 97 Sqdns, would provide an illuminating force, carrying flares and four 1,000lb MC bombs each. TIs could not be used as they would not burn on the water.

The success of the Allied ground forces in north-west Europe during the last six months had not been achieved without a high cost, especially in infantry. Although what was left of the *Kriegsmarine*'s surface fleet did not present too much of a threat at this time, it could still be used to ferry troops home, away from the advancing Russians in northern Norway, to bolster up the German home defences. Deny them the necessary sea transport, and the Norwegian garrison would either have to sit impotently on one side, to be mopped up after Germany had surrendered, or fall into the Red Army's hands.

A small 5 Group force had previously attacked these two ships at Oslofjord on 13-14 December, but without result. It was known which islands in Oslofjord the cruisers used as anchorages, but both ships were active and constantly changed their berths.

The plan was to split the attacking force into two – Red Force to the north of the islands and Yellow Force to the south of them, to bomb by the illumination provided by the flare-droppers.

However, 617 had no experience of attacking moving targets at night. Flg-Off Brown of 83 identified the *Köln* in excellent visibility, dropping a red and green Wanganui flare over her. At this point she was steaming south on the east side of Basto island. On being informed, Fauqier said he would come and prove the ship's identity, but took his time doing so, so that at 0015 Brown called in the rest of the force on his own while dropping more flares. Fifteen minutes later Brown's flares were dying out, so after asking Fauquier's permission to fire Verys, he did that, firing six cartridges in two runs. The fact that Brown had to resort to this showed just how disorganised things had become.

Flt Lt A. P. Weber of 83 saw what he thought was the *Emden*, firing flak from amidships, bow and stern. He dropped a marker on it and then called Fauquier, who again was a long time in coming. Fauquier then ordered illumination, in answer to which Weber and one other 83 Sqdn crew dropped two sticks of flares. This ship was now going due north and Fauquier ordered a switch to the *Köln*, which was passing Mamo island. A Wanganui flare and a few 1,000-pounders fell from one of 83's aircraft, then a Tallboy passed them to starboard. Faced with this, the cruiser took evasive action and none of the bombs hit.

Several of 83's and 97's crews told similar tales of attempts to identify vessels, illuminate them, pass on details, and finally to sink them. One pilot described the whole action as confusing, which it certainly was. It might even have been amusing if one of 83's crews had not been lost in Oslofjord. The first flares had fallen north of Rano island and attempts by Fauquier to redirect them to the south resulted in an overcorrection, so in the end 617 were reduced to bombing by moonlight. He dropped his own Tallboy from 8,000 feet. It burst a hundred yards from the port side of the *Köln*, which promptly made off at high speed in a northerly direction.

As the last of the flares burned out, so crews ran in, using the ships' flak as a guide. Pryor made six runs but could not see the targets and did not bomb. Neither did Flatman, who described the weather as too murky. Both cruisers took evasive action at speeds of up to thirty knots – which was fast for their size – while firing back with everything available, and survived several near misses. Goodman tried to bomb what he thought was the *Emden*, missed it but then realised he had attacked the wrong one. Gumbley was probably the closest of anyone, as his bomb was a near miss on the port side of one vessel, which then swung to starboard and stopped abruptly.

All this took half an hour and it was as well that there was no fighter reaction. The three squadrons headed for home as the New Year began, each probably feeling like blaming the others, but really it was the sheer elusiveness of their targets that had caused a feeling of frustration. They were not to know that the *Köln* had in fact been hit off Horten and that the damage she had sustained would lead to her being dry-docked at the German port of Wilhelmshaven. She would be destroyed there by the 8th Air Force's bombs three months later.

This operation was not an auspicious debut for 617's new CO and just to add to all the uncertainty there were other changes pending further up the ladder. Cochrane, with two of his fellow Group commanders, would be moving on next February. Looking back over the last six months, it seemed a very long time since the successful bombing of the Saumur tunnel. Tallboy had brought all manner of previously unimaginable results, but it had not forced the enemy into surrender. The war could not last much longer now, but lives were still going to be lost before that happened. What was the New Year going to bring?

Over at 233 MU the answer had been coming from Uncle Sam – more Tallboys. However, these proved a mixed blessing for, as noted earlier, a number proved to be oversize and would not fit the British-made tail units intended for them. Following a visit from the RAF's Inspector of Explosives, who found some sixty Tallboys to be over gauge, the MU's CO was instructed not to issue the oversize bombs until tails could be specially made for them. To be fair, during December one of 617's British-made bombs had turned out to have the same fault after some fifty different tail units had been tried on it! To sort out the sheep from the goats, serviceable US-built Tailboys would now carry a white arrow on their noses. It was just one of those things that the armourers would have to find a way round.

As noted earlier, some Tallboys did not go through the MU at all, but were sent direct from the ROF to the airfields. P/O Gordon Maguire at Bardney recalled one snowy day when a load arrived that did not seem right:

The bombs were brought in in twos on a civilian ten-ton lorry. I saw one come in that had snow on the vehicle, but there was none on the tarpaulin covering the bombs. This was because they were still hot from filling, as I checked by putting a thermometer into the exploder pockets. The British-made bombs were fine-turned, but the American ones had a finish that had been ground. They came over empty and had to be filled here. Also, they had American screw threads, which caused problems. I went to modify some with a knife – when I whipped it out of my flying boot the Italian POWs who were dealing with them scattered in all directions, convinced a maniac was on the loose! I can't remember where that was – either Market Rasen or Norton Disney.

Norton Disney was actually Number 3 RAF Forward Filling Depot in Lincolnshire although, just to be awkward, it was not near the village of that name but close to the bomber base at RAF Swinderby. The filling in question referred to mustard gas bombs, although HE ones were also stored there.

Flt Sgt Jim Brookbank, the bomb aimer in Flg-Off W. Scott's crew, later summed up his squadron's position at this time:

> During 1945 and the concluding months of hostilities the squadron flew more and more daylight raids against the enemy, as opposed to night raids. These were always referred to as 'daylights' and our lives, in some respects, assumed a more normal pattern. We were now 'working' during the day, as it were, and sleeping at night, which was a refreshing change to the 'night shift' we had grown accustomed to and the inevitable disturbances experienced whilst trying to sleep during the hours of daylight.
>
> Also, from a bomb aimer's viewpoint, I always felt that a more accurate attack could be made in natural light, affording as it did a clearer, more distinct view of the aiming point of the target. All operations carrying the Barnes Wallis Tallboy bomb were carried out in daylight, our instructions being that if the aiming point was not identified we were to bring the bomb back.
>
> In those days we lived from one daylight raid to the next. It could be said that we were 'living daylights', which is what, on occasion, I could quite happily have 'knocked out' of the 'penguins' who persisted in doing their duties 'by the book'.

12 January 1945
Target The Laksevaag U-boat pens and shipping at Bergen, in Norway.
Weather Clear, with slight haze.

Force 17 Lancasters of 9 Sqdn:

?		Sqdn Ldr J. D. Melrose	?		Flg-Off R. W. Cook
NG206	'J'	Sqdn Ldr A. G. Williams	NG249	'S'	Flg-Off M. L. T. Harper
NG220	'B'	Flt Lt J. J. Dunne	NG242	'C'	Flg-Off A. E. Jeffs
PD198	'W'	Flt Lt R. J. Harris	NG384	'T'	Flg-Off A. F. Jones
PB696	'V'	Flt Lt R. C. Lake	LM220	'Y'	Flg-Off A. L. Keeley
PA172	'G'	Flt Lt L. E. Marsh	NF292		Flg-Off S. Laws
LL845	'L'	Flt Lt A. M. Morrison	NG257	'N'	Flg-Off E. C. Redfern
NG235	'H'	Flt Lt L. H. Watkins	LM217	'O'	Flg-Off J. C. Wiley
ME809	'X'	Flg-Off J. W. Buckley			

9 Sqdn's ORB incorrectly states that NN722 'Q' was flown by both Melrose and Cook on this date.

16 Lancasters of 617 Sqdn:

NG228	'V'	Sqdn Ldr J. F. Brookes	PD238	'H'	Flt Lt G. R. Price
EE146	'D'	Sqdn Ldr C. W. C. Hamilton	PD233	'G'	Flt Lt H. J. Pryor
NG181	'M'	Sqdn Ldr T. C. Iveson	LM492	'W'	Flg-Off J. Castagnola
LM695	'N'	Sqdn Ldr J. L. Powell	DV380	'P'	Flg-Off J. H. Leavitt
LM485	'U'	Flt Lt B. J. Dobson	DV393	'R'	Flg-Off P. H. Martin
ME562	'K'	Flt Lt H. V. Gavin	NF992	'B'	Flg-Off I. S. Ross
DV402	'X'	Flt Lt L. S. Goodman	LM489	'A'	Flg-Off J. A. Sanders
DV391	'Y'	Flt Lt I. M. Marshall	DV405	'J'	Flg-Off F. H. A. Watts

One 617 Sqdn Mosquito FBVI as the Master Bomber's aircraft:
NT205 'L' Gp Capt. J. E. Fauquier and Sqdn Ldr G. B. Ellwood.

Escort 13 Mustang IIIs of 13 Group:
315 Sqdn (Polish)

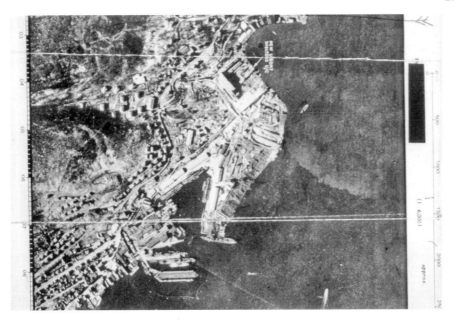

An overhead shot of the pens, with part of Bergen harbour to the south-east of them. (H. F. C. Parsons)

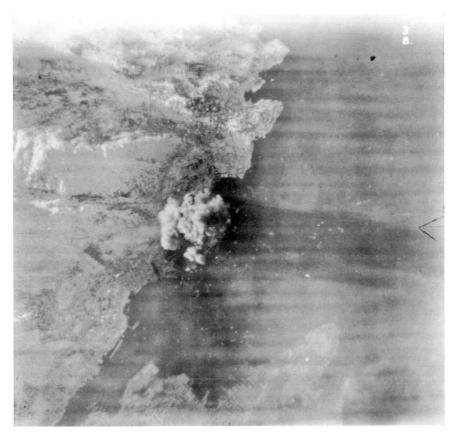

The strike photograph taken by Flight Lieutenant Ray Harris of 9 Squadron over Bergen harbour. By now the pens were completely covered in smoke. (H. F. C. Parsons)

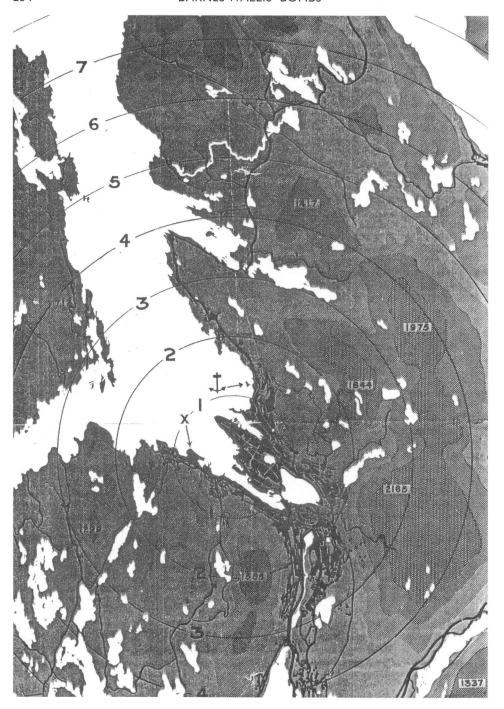

An RAF target map of the area around Bergen Harbour, with north at the top of the diagram. X indicates the position of the U-boat pens. The other numbers are spot heights, calculated in feet. (H. F. C. Parsons)

Two Mosquito FBVIs of 100 Group's 169 Sqdn RAF.
  These two aircraft, whose usual role was to support Main Force crews by night, were also to provide ASR assistance if needed.

Bomb Loads 9 Sqdn – each Lancaster carried one Tallboy, with an 11-second delay.
  617 Sqdn – each Lancaster carried one Tallboy, six of them with a 0.5-second delay, the remainder for 11 seconds.

The *Organization Todt* had determined the basic pen design, including the roof thickness. Construction had been by German sub-contractors, for whom the OT provided and housed the workforce. This was made up of either forced labourers from Occupied Europe, POWs or DPs from the east. In general Germans occupied the key artisan positions. On being interrogated after the war, the engineers said they did not know the size of bomb against which the original roof thickness was designed – this had been determined in Berlin. The use of increasingly heavy bombs had come as an unpleasant surprise, so the roof of the Bergen pens, constructed for the 11th U-boat Flotilla, had subsequently been modified.

  Measuring 435ft by 480ft, the pens had been constructed on igneous rock in a small bay on the south-west side of Bergen harbour. There were six pens, the first three of which were dry and the rest wet docks. Next to pen 6 was a dry bay, for oil storage and housing an emergency power plant. It was also to be a workshop, to supplement the three-floor one at the rear. Their external and division walls had been founded direct upon the rock, then built before the concrete floor had been poured.

  The original specification had called for the walls to be just under 10ft thick and the roof to give a total cover of 13ft of reinforced concrete. After Tallboy's arrival this had been changed to just over 16ft on the walls and 19½ft on the roof, to be finished by the summer of 1945. Perhaps the engineer in charge realised the idea behind the earthquake bomb; by the time of this attack the walls had been reinforced to nineteen and a half feet, while the roof was thirteen feet thick. The 6½ft-thick internal dividing walls were spanned by precast concrete reinforced girders, almost 5ft deep and curved on their outer surfaces. Although still incomplete, the structure had not surprisingly been deemed sufficient to resist bombing.

  These dimensions had been the original standard for all such constructions. Over pens 3 to 6, this had then been increased to thirteen feet of solid concrete. The workshop area and the remaining three pens had an air gap of just over eleven feet over them with an additional 4½ft-thick ceiling above them.

  The air space had come about as the result of an order from Berlin to provide accommodation for U-boat crews and essential stores, but clearly it was similar to the *Fangrost* system that had been used on the Biscay pens and would serve to check any damage inflicted from overhead during a raid. This requirement had been dropped when Tallboy came along, the resting U-boat crews then being quartered outside Bergen. Another order, in the light of increased Allied bombing, was to thicken the roof over the workshop area. This had not been fully carried out when supplies of cement ceased in April 1944, so that the full thickness of nineteen-and-a-half feet had only been achieved over the building's north-west corner. Additional shortages of concrete and steel had led to the substitution of large three-foot-square blocks of roughly dressed granite, hewn from a local quarry, being bedded in sand on the roof. As with the French pens, this extra thickness was never completed and at the war's end the roof would be left at varying heights.

  The building had other defences apart from these. Three quadruple 20mm flak guns had been mounted on the north-west side of the roof and over its southern corner a heavy steel cupola supported on a reinforced concrete structure was being erected as a defensive position to house mortars, with an all-round field of fire. Perhaps someone had considered a Commando attack a possibility. Just behind each pen's portal, suspended from roof rails, was a one-and-a-half-inch-thick steel plate door, although this was intended to enforce the blackout rather than give blast protection.

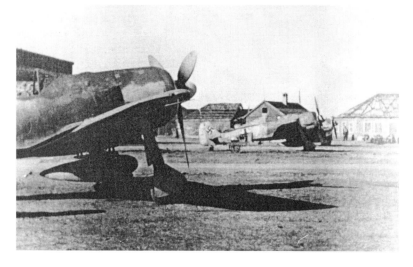

The FW 190s of 9/JG 5 in Norway, probably at Herdla airfield near Bergen. (H. Orlowski via R. Harris)

A close-up of an FW 190's nose, just showing the Geschwader's 'Eismeer' badge. The spiral spinner motif was a popular decoration. (H. Orlowski via R. Harris)

The pilots of 9/JG 5, complete with mascot, await their next scramble. (H. Orlowski via R. Harris)

This formidable structure's importance had increased when U-boats had been withdrawn from France to Norway during the latter part of 1944. An attack on the pens by 6 and 8 Groups the previous October had resulted a large number of Norwegian civilian casualties, many of them children, in Bergen. Despite thirty 500lb and 1,000lb MC bombs being aimed at them, five of which hit, the pens had suffered only minor damage. These hits had all occurred before reinforced concrete had been poured over the precast girders, but they had not been serious, for it had been added later. This raid had achieved more in the harbour, where four U-boats and four other vessels had been either sunk or damaged beyond repair.

As there were several targets, two different fuse settings had been used by 617's crews. Brookes, Dobson, Gavin, Goodman, Hamilton, Iveson, Leavitt, Marshall, Powell and Price were to attack the pens. Martin, Pryor and Sanders were to attack a U-boat in a floating dock, while Castagnola, Ross and Watts would go for any shipping they could find.

H-Hour was to be 1300, with 617 attacking first, immediately followed by 9 Sqdn. Fauquier was to ensure the aircraft withdrew in a tight gaggle. They were to do a left-hand orbit after bombing and were not to withdraw until Fauquier ordered them to do so. Bombing heights would be between 15,000ft and 18,000ft.

With the danger to Norwegian civilians in mind, those three aircraft allocated to bomb shipping would each select a target and attack on such a heading that any overshooting Tallboys would fall either in water or on open land. Ships were not to be attacked if they were within 150 yards of the quays or any built-up area. These three aircraft were also to keep straight and level, in order to get the best photographic results – all aircraft had been fitted with vertical cameras for this attack.

The three that had been allocated the floating dock target were to do the same thing, for the same reasons. There was the possibility of a hospital ship, distinctively marked in white with red crosses, being in the area, and if so this was on no account to be attacked. Neither was shipping outside the port, with the New Year's Eve fiasco a recent memory.

The remainder of 617 and 9 Sqdns were to bomb the pens. 617 were to aim direct, while 9 were to select a suitable AP away from the pens and calculate a false wind vector to hit them from it. As usual 9's five windfinders were to find an accurate wind at the Norwegian coast, although they were to avoid arriving there more than five minutes before the rest of the force. They were to orbit for that time, find the wind, pass it on, then join the rest of 9 for the attack.

RAF Intelligence knew that German fighters were based at Herdla, an airfield just twenty miles away from Bergen. They were the FW 190-equipped 9/JG 5 and 12/JG 5 – old adversaries from Bardufoss, now moved to southern Norway. The slip-up that had enabled the two squadrons to escape their clutches during *Catechism* was not likely to occur a second time. However, the escorting Mustangs were a match for any German fighter and everyone knew the martial spirit of the Poles.

At this time of year anyone who ditched in the North Sea could measure their survival in minutes rather than hours, so two ASR Warwicks from 279 Sqdn at RAF Fraserburgh would also be available, one accompanying the force while the other remained on stand-by at Sumburgh. Each would carry a lifeboat and Lindholme dinghy packs to drop to ditched aircrew.

The fighters and bombers rendezvoused off Peterhead, as arranged, in weather that remained clear throughout the operation. Flying to Norway took three uneventful hours. There was some slight industrial haze over Bergen, although some crews afterwards reported a smokescreen had been started. Below them the alarm had sounded at 1252 and once again the Norwegians sought what shelter they could while an intense barrage of light flak came up to meet the attackers.

Flt Lt Ray Harris of 9, one of the windfinders, arrived at the target five minutes early, flying over it in a wide triangle while his navigator worked out the wind speed and direction for transmission to the rest of the force. By now some cloud was drifting over the pens, so he called Fauquier on VHF for permission to bomb, which was given.

Flg-Off Roy Harvey, Sqdn Ldr Williams' navigator, was on this raid, and explained why, due to the different types of bombsight used, it was necessary for 9 to follow rather than lead: 'With a standard Mark XIV bombsight it was possible to use an offset aiming point upwind and a 'false' wind to overcome the effects of the actual target being hidden by earlier bomb blasts. It was for this reason that 617 Sqdn, with their later type of bombsight, which required a clear view of the target, always bombed first.'

Castagnola, the lowest of 617's gaggle at 14,850ft, reported, 'Our bomb fell on the stern of a vessel, which started to sink immediately. Approximately three minutes later the boiler (or something) blew up. The ship rolled over onto its side and went down. The first bomb to fall on the sub pens was an overshoot.' He had hit the German Minesweeper M1, which sank in Eidsvag Bay, killing twenty of its crew and wounding fourteen.

Brookes, who was leading 617's pen force, claimed to have dropped his bomb on the southern corner of the pens. Castagnola's overshoot observation was confirmed by Marshall, whose own bomb fell into the smoke below and was lost to sight.

This smoke, whatever its cause, led several aircraft to make more than one run. Dobson, Gavin and Powell all returned with their bombs as they were unable to see the pens. Goodman had a clear sight of it on his first run but was hampered by an unserviceable bombsight. He then made at least three more runs, but by now the pens were totally obscured and he too returned without bombing. 9 Sqdn, flying at the same mixture of heights as 617, saw some hits but could only aim at the smoke over the pens. One of their pilots, Flt Lt A. M. Morrison, did not bomb for this reason.

Inevitably, the smoke drifted out over the harbour, affecting the other two groups of three aircraft from 617. Sanders, despite five runs, was unable to identify the floating dock, so, in obedience to Fauquier's instructions, he attacked a ship instead. Watts damaged a German tramp steamer, the *Olga Sierus*, with a near miss. It had to be run aground at Sandvikena Bay to avoid sinking.

This delay in bombing would lead to death or imprisonment for members of four crews, as Roy Harvey recalled:

> After the first few 617 Squadron aircraft had bombed, the target was obscured, so the remainder of that squadron were unable to attack. By the time we had bombed it was even worse, but to allow the remainder of 617 Squadron to bomb we continued to circle over the target, waiting for the aiming point to clear. As this was likely to take some time, it was decided that those aircraft that had bombed should leave the target area and make for home. The Polish fighter pilots were chattering away in their own language and were thoroughly enjoying the grandstand view. When we left the fighter escort remained over the target. What we didn't know was that German fighters were waiting for us off the Norwegian coast.

They would not get away with it this time. Since the force had split up instead of remaining together, the returning Lancasters were especially vulnerable now. As these aircraft headed out over the coast, suddenly their rear gunners saw small black specks which at first they took to be the escorting Mustangs. No, these had angular wings, but they were too blunt-nosed. JG 5's FW 190s had been scrambled from Herdla. By day their four 20mm cannon would easily outrange the 0.303s that the Lancasters carried.

A prime target was Sqdn Ldr Tony Iveson's aircraft, which had already been damaged by flak over the harbour and forced to jettison its bomb over an uninhabited area. A fighter attack set Iveson's port inner engine on fire, riddled his port tailplane and rudder, then put the rear turret out of action, with its guns jammed. With no elevator or rudder trim either, Iveson called, 'Prepare to abandon aircraft!' Due to a misunderstanding both his gunners and the wireless operator bailed out over Norway, to be taken prisoner. His rear gunner, P/O Ted Wass, left via the crew entry door, but, unlike Tony Burcher during *Chastise*, escaped injury. By rights none of those who remained aboard this aircraft should have survived, but fate plays strange tricks and they would all do so.

Someone who would not be coming back was Flt Lt John Pryor. After six abortive runs over the target, he was told to do one more by Fauquier. As he swung the Lancaster round again he was attacked by an FW 190 and put the bomber into a diving turn to starboard. His port outer engine was then hit by a second fighter, which he had not seen. His flight engineer added to this by inadvertently feathering the starboard outer. Then, in trying to correct this error, he held the starter button in for too long, causing the engine to overspeed and costing them the power they needed at the critical moment.

The loss of the port outer had also deprived the rear gunner of the power supply to his turret, obliging him to use a crank handle instead. The second attack had left them with damage to the fuselage as well; a neat line of holes ran along along it just above the navigator's head. Now on two engines, only one of which was fully functioning, and with no gunnery defence left to speak of, there was only one way to go – down towards the fjord below. All this and they still had six tons of bomb on board.

Pryor stood the Lancaster on its port wing tip, causing the two FW 190s to overshoot, then opened the bomb doors, jettisoning the Tallboy to explode on an uninhabited hillside six miles from Bergen. Relieved of the weight, they climbed away round the mountains, still trying to avoid the persistent fighter pilots.

On being informed by the flight engineer that due to fuel loss they might make Scotland, but certainly not Woodhall Spa, Pryor decided on a crashlanding, then looked at the snow-capped mountains below and changed his mind. All that mattered now was to gain as much height as possible, then bail out. Perhaps one of the Luftwaffe pilots realised this, for he flew alongside them, apparently making signs that they should jump. Just in case he decided to attack again two red Very flares were fired, indicating an aircraft in distress.

They headed inland. At 1,500ft the nose hatch was opened and seven bodies went tumbling out through it. The last was Pryor, after turning the bomber out to sea again. He was all too close to the minimum safety height, but fortunately landed in a large snowdrift.

After flying over Litlelindas, to the north-west of Bergen, Pryor's Lancaster came down in an area of the sea known to the Norwegians as Fedjefjorden, between the islands of Austrheim and Fedje. According to a Norwegian eye-witness, the two fighter pilots did not survive, for there was an explosion which involved the Lancaster and one of the FW 190s, causing both aircraft to spin into the sea five miles from the coast. Possibly the fighter had flown too close to the crewless bomber, only to collide with it. The other pilot circled and must have called the German ASR services, but he stayed too long, ran out of fuel, then crashed into a fjord while returning to Herdla and died of exposure.

Four hundred miles of rugged country between Pryor's crew and the Swedish frontier precluded evasion. Rather than be hidden by the local people, against whom German reprisals could have been taken, six of the men surrendered, feeling that the war would be over soon. Someone who would not see the end of it was Flt Lt George Kendrick, the bomb aimer, who had apparently struck his chin on the hatch while going out. Unconscious, he had fallen to his death.

9 Sqdn also had their work cut out getting away from JG 5. The aircraft flown by Flg-Off Ray Harris would now owe its survival in part to 9's Gunnery Leader, Flt Lt Bill Gabriel, in the rear turret, and his deputy in the mid-upper, Flg-Off A. J. 'Mac' Williams. Bill Gabriel recalled what happened next in a letter to his former skipper in 1971:

When we first sighted the FW190s they were at such a distance I thought at first they were the Mustangs. It was not until they were getting near to fighting range that Mac and I positively identified them as 190s.

In the first attack, cannon shells ripped through the Lancaster. One narrowly missed the bomb aimer as it passed through the nose from left to right, severing a hydraulic pipe and sending the oily contents everywhere. This put the turrets out of action.

After the action started, I well remember the difficulty I had in bringing the guns to bear because you were throwing the kite around in your best 5 Group corkscrew manner. When my turret was hit, my oxygen pipe was severed and things went pearly-grey for a bit.

The seldom-used front turret seemed likely to be needed now. P/O H. F. C. 'Jimmy' Parsons, the bomb aimer, had disconnected his intercom to move forward into it, and as the bomber dived he thought a crash was imminent, so he reached for the nose hatch. In response to his pilot's frantic waving, he plugged in again.

Don't leave us, yet, Jimmy. Hold tight.

The Lancaster performed its second corkscrew before the front turret could be manned. In response to Bill Gabriel's directions the Lancaster was flung to port or starboard – any direction to get away from the fighters as they struck again and again. Just to add to the sense of impending doom, one FW 190 flew off their port wingtip, and Ray Harris saw its pilot grin at him!

Just when it seemed this fight could have only one end, a steep dive towards the sea led the four FW 190s to each fire a final burst and then turn for home, being by now at the limit of their fuel.

There had been fifteen attacks in all, but Bill Gabriel had continued to give directions despite sustaining leg and eye wounds. His defence and that of 'Mac' Williams, who had been hit in the legs, had prevented the Germans from pressing home their attacks. However, their problems were not yet over, for it needed the combined strength of the pilot and his flight engineer to pull out at 1,000ft, having lost 11,000ft since the attacks had started.

An intercom check led to a weak answer from Bill Gabriel, who was given first aid on the rest bed by Jimmy Parsons, assisted by the mid-upper gunner, despite his own injuries. There was just one other wound – the wireless-operator, Flg-Off W. E. Brownlie, had been nicked in the backside.

This would have been funny in other circumstances, but no one felt like laughing as Ray Harris and his flight engineer, Sgt Maurice Mellors, nursed the bomber home with three engines on full power, for the starboard outer was delivering only half its normal output. No further height could be gained and if their speed dropped below 160mph ditching would be inevitable, with little chance of survival.

The loss of the hydraulics would mean a reliance on the back-up CO_2 system. Trying the flaps produced no result, so their landing speed would be higher as well. The wheels might go down, or they might not, they might not stay locked down when the aircraft's weight settled on them, and the tyres might have been punctured.

Such a landing needed a wide and long runway. The emergency airfield at RAF Carnaby, near Bridlington on the Yorkshire coast, was the best option. Ray Harris used his VHF transmitter again.

Hello Carnaby, this is Rosen William. Am coming in to land. Wounded on board. Stall under 160mph. May not be able to use undercarriage.

As they lined up with the runway, fire engines and an ambulance could be seen making for the point where they should touch down. Much to everyone's relief the undercarriage had locked down and the landing was unexpectedly smooth. Bill Gabriel would receive help from an unexpected source:

I remember quite well coming in to land at Carnaby when Mac and I and some of the others got down on the floor of the aircraft in the recommended safety positions, leaving you up front to land the blessed thing. I also remember seeing you and the rest of the crew around my bed in Driffield hospital where I was taken direct from Carnaby. Incidentally, whilst there, I had a bit of an operation for the removal of shrapnel from my leg and the operation was performed, I understand, by a German POW doctor – rather ironic!

In March Bill Gabriel received a well-deserved DFC. While his operation was in progress the rest of the crew went to a pub in the nearby village of Lissett and consumed a large amount of beer. How strange it must have seemed to be fighting for their lives one minute, then in the next sipping the local brew in a rural hostelry. When Flg-Off Don Macintosh flew in from Bardney to bring them home, he looked at the state of their Lancaster and silently shook the hand of its pilot. PD198 'W' survived until 1947, but would see no further action.

Jimmy Parsons and Ray Harris were both on their second tour with 9. The bomb aimer had been recommended for a non-immediate DFC the previous November and would receive it in February. His skipper had been awarded the DFC a short time before and was now recommended for the DSO as well, but nothing came of this. Getting home after such an ordeal was enough.

Someone else lucky to return was Flt Lt L. E. Marsh of 9. His crew endured nearly twenty minutes of combat, beginning at the coast when no less than five FW 190s peeled off to attack. One hit his starboard outer engine, which began smoking, but Marsh had sufficient presence of mind not to feather it for now, so maintaining the power supply to his mid-upper turret. His feelings emerged in his report afterwards:

> We ended up at 900 feet and 360 on the clock after corkscrewing continuously. One FW 190 followed us finally at a safe distance, but gave up as we were flying into the sun. After seeing the fighter escort at the concentration we never saw them again, except for one which stood off and watched us near the end of the attacks. One Lanc seen shot down on fire and go straight into the sea from 16,000 feet.

The Lancaster Marsh's crew saw was probably that flown by Flg-Off E. C. Redfern, who was lost with his crew when they were brought down over the target area. Marsh's rear gunner, Flt Sgt P. R. Riches, returned the enemy's fire and gave a good commentary to his pilot as he did so. The eventual loss of the mid-upper turret's power supply put further pressure on Riches, but they came home and he received a DFM, with a DFC for Marsh, two months later.

Sqdn Ldr Williams had just one FW 190 to contend with, but that was enough. Roy Harvey again:

> We were lucky – a fighter did come in to attack and Bill put the nose down in a steep dive. I watched the needle of the ASI starting to go round the dial for a second time. He pulled out at sea level, when the tension disappeared as a 'wee voice' came over the intercom complaining he nearly got 'his feet wet' – it was our Scottish rear gunner! The fighter did not attack, so I can only assume that when he tried he was out of ammunition.

Some crews tried to attract the escort's attention with red Very flares. Although his crew did not take part in this raid, Jim Brookbank later described a curious incident during the air battle:

> The Very pistol was permanently positioned angled through the top of the fuselage near the wireless-operator's position. The trajectory of one such Very light 'arc-ed' back into the radial engine of an attacking FW 190, which quickly broke off the engagement and was last seen billowing black smoke and diving away rapidly.

Of the thirteen Polish Mustangs that had set off, two had returned early with mechanical trouble. Their Operations Record Book simply says, 'Operation went according to plan. Uneventful.'

It had certainly not been for everyone else. Afterwards, the German fighter pilots said they had never seen any Mustangs and were surprised to hear that they had been there. Complaints made by the surviving bomber crews were understandably bitter. It was their opinion that the Poles had forgotten their orders and had carried out ground strafing instead of remaining where they should have been – above their charges. However, it becomes apparent from what Roy Harvey witnessed that 315 Sqdn remained with those bombers that were circling over the harbour, apparently oblivious to the carnage being inflicted over the sea. If any calls for help went out, they may have been lost in the Poles' chatter over Bergen. Had they intervened most of the bomber losses might have been avoided. It was also said that Fauquier, flying an armed Mosquito, could have made an effort to defend the bombers, although to be fair to him it should be pointed out that he had not had a fighter pilot's training.

So much for the Mustangs. What had happened to the two Mosquitoes of 169 Sqdn, up from RAF Great Massingham in Norfolk to Peterhead, and no doubt feeling a little strange to be flying by day, instead of their customary nocturnal activities? Both these crews saw what was happening, but had problems of their own. Sqdn Ldr J. A. Wright and his observer Flt Lt H. B. Vine intervened in the fight and for their pains were chased by five FW 190s, relief for them only coming when the fighters broke off to attack a Lancaster – probably Marsh's aircraft.

The second Mosquito was flown by Flg-Off George Hart and Flt Sgt Scott. Like the Mustangs, they had taken off from Peterhead at 1155 and met their charges as arranged. Hart's combat report form is quoted here, its breathless style vividly illustrating the high speed and uncertainty of fighter combat:

We flew with the bombers to the target and at 1305 hours crossed out [over] the Norwegian coast at 15,000 feet. Just as we crossed five FW 190s went past me, below and crossing. They had not apparently seen me as I was in the sun. They did however see Sqdn Ldr Wright who was in the accompanying Mosquito and who was unfortunately about three thousand feet below me and about two miles ahead. They went into line abreast and started to chase him.

I yelled to Sqdn Ldr Wright to look out behind and gave chase to the FW 190s. All seven of us streamed off downhill, like dingbats. After about three minutes the enemy decided to leave Sqdn Ldr Wright alone and go after a Lancaster which was by itself, five or six miles to starboard. They went into line astern and I followed suit. They got to the Lancaster about half a minute before me and attacked it, breaking their attack, looping and diving down to attack again. I arrived on the scene ... and attacked one FW 190 as it came out of a dive, giving it a burst of about three to four seconds. I fired at range of 500 yards, down to about 250 yards, and saw no result. I broke away from this and jettisoned my drop tanks, and then attacked another FW 190. He went into a steep turn and I held him, firing all the time. I saw strikes just behind his engine, around his gills. I fired at him until he peeled off to port and passed beneath me. I fired at this aircraft for six seconds.

By now it was not only Wright and Marsh who were under attack.

I did not wait to see what had happened to him because meanwhile Flt Sgt 'Rubberneck' Scott had been telling me, in no uncertain terms, that a third FW 190 had looped around behind us and was uncomfortably close. All this took place between 9 and 10,000 feet. I opened the taps and went downhill extremely fast. We left him behind us after two minutes and after another minute or so we took stock, and having jettisoned 160 gallons of petrol, and not being able to receive on VHF, we decided to go home. This we did and landed at Peterhead at 1420 hours.

At 1400 a preparatory scramble warning was received at Sumburgh. There had been a report of a ditched Lancaster, which was now being circled by two others. Having obtained all the available information, the Warwick crew, skippered by Flg-Off David Duthie, became airborne at 1443. For some reason this message did not reach the Warwick accompanying the force, whose crew had seen Lancasters returning at intervals – indicative of the combat that had taken place. Just four minutes after the Sumburgh aircraft took off, this one began returning to Fraserburgh.

It was 1600 before Duthie reached the by now almost submerged Lancaster. Flown by Flg-Off Ian Ross, it had been the last of 617's crews to face fighter attack on this day. The crew were standing on top of it. The lifeboat was dropped, landing 200 yards upwind of the crew, one of whom swam to it. Duthie then decided to drop a Lindholme dinghy across their path, but to his horror it failed to deploy properly and sank. He then tried a second one, but the same thing happened. By now an FW 190 was nosing around, so Duthie made off at low level, but not before his crew had had the bitter experience of watching a Ju 88 strafe the lifeboat. There was no point in remaining; his crew had done all they could. Only the day before 279 had lost a Warwick to a Bf 109 off the Norwegian coast.

A winter's night comes early in these northern latitudes. Another of 279's Warwicks, flown by W/O Williamson, dropped a second lifeboat at 1725 in an area where red flares had been seen. More flares were then dropped, showing the lifeboat with a dinghy nearby, but contact was lost and not regained, despite Williamson's crew continuing the search until a shortage of fuel forced them to return.

279 had other commitments, including searching for a dinghy reported after a strike by the Dallachy Wing's Beaufighters. Two Coastal Command aircraft, one fitted with a powerful Leigh Light, searched during the night but failed to locate the lifeboat. Another search the next day also proved fruitless. Two months later the body of the wireless-operator was found by a Norwegian fisherman off the small island of Slyngen, having drifted towards the Arctic Circle, but no trace of Ross and the rest of his crew was ever found.

Meanwhile, Sqdn Ldr Tony Iveson and the remainder of his crew were struggling to get home. An FW 190 flew alongside them after three crew members had jumped and its pilot mockingly gave them the thumbs-down sign, then accelerated away, presumably thinking that the rest of the crew would also be bailing out. If not, then the North Sea would claim them as well. Damage to the Lancaster's port side made it difficult to fly straight and level, until the bomb aimer ran a rope from the port rudder control to the camera-housing in the nose and knotted it securely, allowing a grateful Iveson to relax his left leg a little.

With this problem mitigated, it was time for the remaining crew members to take stock. They had no rudder control and were flying on three engines. Large holes were torn in the port rudder, fin and tailplane. Vibration was severe, especially at the rear of the aircraft, which might well break up and sink quickly if they had to ditch. There was also no guarantee that the dinghy would still be usable.

Their VHF radio had been smashed, so they could inform no one else of the situation they were in, except by W /T. Although they lacked a wireless-operator, each crew member had some knowledge of Morse and would be able to send rudimentary messages. However, Iveson vetoed that on the grounds that the enemy would be listening and might send a fighter out to finish them off.

Sumburgh was less than ideal, being a small airfield whose local weather conditions were such that a landing often had to be made crosswind on the one runway. Any attempt to go round again meant a steep turn to avoid a hill near the town. Still, given their present fuel state, they could go no further. As Iveson's crew arrived, they fired off several Very cartridges in a variety of colours to indicate their distress. They then lowered the undercarriage, but with no green lights showing on the instrument panel there was doubt as to whether it had locked down. There was considerable relief when the wheels held as they touched down and Iveson landed with great skill, winning himself a DFC. It turned out to be his last operation with 617, as he was posted to a Lancaster Finishing School the following month.

After all that, had it been worth it? Back at Bergen, three Tallboy hits on the pen roof had caused severe damage to the workshops, stores and offices. However, in contrast to the four boats lost the previous October, this time there had been only slight damage to two: U-775 and U-864. Adequate shelter had meant that, apart from the minesweeper's crew, German casualties had been surprisingly light, twelve *Organization Todt* members being killed in addition to the two fighter pilots from 9/JG 5.

Both bomber squadrons had paid dearly for a raid that had not been particularly successful, although that was no fault of theirs. In contrast to the previous one, this time there had been no civilian deaths or damage.

Unlike the Biscay pens, there would be no retreat this time. The Bergen pens would continue in use until the war's end and the two damaged U-boats would return to service. U-775 was surrendered to the Royal Navy the following May and sunk by gunfire in December 1945 as part of Operation *Deadlight* – the disposal of the remaining U-boats. U-864 was torpedoed and sunk by the British submarine HMS *Venturer* a month after the Bergen raid.

An opportunity to inspect the damage came after German forces in Norway surrendered four months later. On 23 May a visit to the pens was made by a party of RAF officers under Air Commodore C. N. H. Bilney, including Sqdn Ldr Whitehead, who had witnessed the Tallboy trials just over a year before. They inspected the damage and interviewed Baurade Kumuli, who had been the *Organization Todt*'s Chief Engineer there.

There had been two Tallboy direct hits and two near misses. The first bomb to hit had landed between pens 2 and 3, leaving heavy spalling over a radius of 25ft. Below this, the internal dividing wall had been pushed nine inches out of the vertical. The archways in this wall were subsequently filled in. The roof over the crater was then brought up to the stipulated 19.5ft height by adding a block of reinforced concrete over the hole. From fragment strikes on vertical surfaces in the vicinity, it was clear that this Tallboy, which had had an 11-second delay, had exploded before its full length had become embedded in the roof, meaning that the pistols had either self-initiated or that the bomb had not fully penetrated before detonation.

The second had hit over the stores area near the north-east corner of the building, making a funnel-shaped crater 26ft across and over 16ft wide at its bottom. To reinforce this weak spot, a wall had been built under the crater afterwards, four heavy I-section girders being laid over the top to support the vertical reinforcement that was built into the crater before it was filled with concrete. Again, nearby strikes showed that this bomb had also gone off before fully penetrating.

One near miss was in a cutting forty yards away from the pens, on the approach road that ran up to their north-east corner. This had completely destroyed the roadway,

An oblique shot of the Bergen pens and the harbour behind them, in May 1945. Note the two half-sunken ships and the lines of surrendered U-boats in the harbour. (NA)

The pens viewed from their north-west side, with Bergen harbour in the background. Although in shadow, their entrances can just be made out, behind the remains of the anti-torpedo boom. (NA)

The Tallboy hole between pens 2 and 3, after repair. The wall on the left had been pushed nine inches out of the vertical, but it had not collapsed. (NA)

with some superficial damage to the outer pen walls. The other had demolished half a workshop bordering the south-west corner, burning out the remainder of it. As a result of this and his investigation of the wreck of the *Tirpitz*, Air Commodore Bilney was to recommend that future earthquake bomb bodies be forged, in order to penetrate without breaking up, and that any alternative to the sensitive Torpex was to be considered.

For Ray Harris of 9 Sqdn there was to be an unexpected follow-up to this raid, when he was able to correspond with one of his former attackers in 1998. Heinz Orlowski commented, 'Looking at your pictures, I can well imagine how good a pilot you were when we met near Bergen in 1945. Since this was my first and last meeting with a Lancaster bomber, I have never forgotten it.'

Neither would anyone else who survived that day. However, total war left little time for grief or recriminations; there was still a job to do. On 16 January, 9 took part in a raid on the synthetic oil plant at Brüx in western Czechoslovakia, but this time their ORB showed that conventional loads of MC and GP bombs were carried, the largest being of the 4,000lb type. Although the question has been raised of this being a Tallboy raid, during my research no evidence came to light in support of it. After Pölitz it may have been realised that HC bombs, whatever their size, were more effective than Tallboy against the piping of such a target.

3 February 1945
Target The E-boat pens at Ijmuiden (9) and the midget submarine wharf at Pootershaven (617).
Weather Good visibility at both targets.

Force 18 Lancasters of 9 Sqdn:

NF937	'E'	Wg Cdr J. M. Bazin	
NG486	'A'	Sqdn Ldr A. G. Williams	
NG278	'N'	Flt Lt R. E. Adams	
NF929	'P	Flt Lt G. C. Camsell	
ME809	'X'	Flt Lt R. J. Harris	
PB696	'V'	Flt Lt R. C. Lake	

NG206	'J'	Flg-Off C. M. T. Follett
NG419	'U'	Flg-Off M. L. T. Harper
NG384	'T'	Flg-Off A. F. Jones
NG495	'R'	Flg-Off A. L. Keeley
NG235	'H'	Flg-Off S. Laws
NG242	'C'	Flg-Off D. Macintosh

Unteroffizier Heinz Orlowski of 9/JG 5, one of the pilots involved in the air battle off the Norwegian coast. (H. Orlowski via R. Harris)

LL845 'L' Flt Lt A. M. Morrison	NG220 'B' Flg-Off J. E. Stowell
NG440 Flt Lt B. Taylor	LM217 'O' Flg-Off W. G. Rees
LM220 'F' Flt Lt W. D. Tweddle	NG487 'D' Flg-Off A. F. Williams

18 Lancasters of 617 Sqdn:

NG445 'E' Gp Capt. J. E. Fauquier	ME554 'F' Flt Lt R. M. Horsley
NG228 'V' Sqdn Ldr J. F. Brookes	DV391 'Y' Flt Lt L. M. Marshall
NG489 'M' Sqdn Ldr C. C. Calder	ED763 'Z' Flt Lt D. J. Oram
PD238 'H' Sqdn Ldr J. V. Cockshott	DV385 'T' Flg-Off J. Castagnola
PD371 'S' Sqdn Ldr J. L. Powell	EE146 'D' Flg-Off M. B. Flatman
LM485 'U' Flt Lt G. W. Bailey	DV393 'R' Flg-Off P. H. Martin
LM489 'A' Flt Lt H. V. Gavin	DV380 'P' Flg-Off G. R. Price
PB415 'O' Flt Lt L. S. Goodman	ME562 'K' Flg-Off J. A. Sanders
DV405 'J' Flt Lt B. A. Gumbley	LM695 'N' Flg-Off F. H. A. Watts

Escort 36 Spitfire IXs of 11 Group:
310 Sqdn (Czech)   312 Sqdn (Czech)   313 Sqdn (Czech)

Bomb Loads Each Lancaster of both squadrons carried one Tallboy, with a half-hour delay.

One 627 Sqdn Mosquito to film the Pootershaven attack:
KB362 'K' W/O R. W. Player and P/O C. B. Heath.

Although originally intended for E and R-boats, the Ijmuiden pens and what had been a private wharf at Pootershaven were now playing host to a new weapon – German midget submarines, one of which, known as the *Biber* (Beaver) can be seen in the Imperial War Museum today. These one-man craft would turn out to be as suicidal as their Japanese counterparts in the Pacific, but they constituted a threat to Allied shipping that could not be ignored.

At Ijmuiden 9 Sqdn's target was the new set of pens that had been meant for E-boats, at the north-western end of the Herring Harbour. Of a more elaborate construction than the old E/R-boat ones nearby, these were now to be attacked for the first time. The roof was 710ft by 315ft. It had been planned to fit a double one with an air space some 12ft high in between, but once again this was only partly completed. The upper roof varied from 10-12ft in thickness, while the lower one was from 2-4ft. This housed eighteen pens, each 240ft long, with workshops at the rear.

The squadron bombed in the late afternoon between 14,000ft and 17,000ft. The usual wind-finding procedure took place, but, due to the height at which it was dropped, a smoke float was seen as useless and details were only passed on after the bombers had orbitted twice over the port. The wind led to a slight overshoot, but as delay fuses were used some results were not seen at the time.

Bazin, handicapped by an unserviceable bombsight, was the only one not to attack. Williams had to feather his port outer engine after a flak hit, while Follett suffered some slight damage to his starboard wing tip and port inner engine nacelle. More serious were the experiences of Jones, who had to swing violently to port to avoid a Tallboy dropped from above, and Macintosh, who on the way home saw five bombs, including a 4,000-pounder, dumped by a Main Force Lancaster on his port quarter. PRU cover later showed no damage to the pens, although several bombs fell very close, and a Bombing Survey report compiled after the area had been liberated confirmed that there had been no hits.

The target at Pootershaven had originally been used by its Dutch owner, after whom it was named, for the transport of bulbs and other produce. Taken over by the *Kriegsmarine*, it consisted of a wharf, with some bunkers nearby that had been built to store torpedo warheads and mines. These were nowhere near as strong as the E and

U-boat pens; they have been described as no better than concrete Nissen huts. 617 met moderate heavy flak at the target before dropping all their bombs on the first run, from 12,000ft to 14,000ft. Three bombs fell close to the wharf, at least three more near the entrance to it and one, possibly Gavin's, overshot into a field.

Castagnola's Tallboy also overshot, but in so doing cut a railway line which ran along the shoreline to the north of the wharf. The rest of the bombing was very concentrated and smoke quickly covered the wharf, making observation difficult, but the crews claimed up to four direct hits.

Subsequent PRU coverage showed that this time they had been too modest; there had been at least twice that number, with several near misses. It would not be necessary to visit this target again. Surprisingly, one of the bunkers survived and has since been used as a cold store. There is also a preserved Tallboy crater in the vicinity.

There were some satisfied grins, and indeed smirks, from High Wycombe to the highest in the land. Photographs of this attack were shown by the Vice-Chief of the Air Staff to the War Cabinet. Air Commodore Bufton considered it magnificent and commented in a letter, 'I understand that Howard-Wilkins has given it the priority it deserves at 8th Air Force headquarters.'

The RAF liaison officer concerned had done his own career no harm by tactfully rubbing the Americans' noses in it, especially as the rocket-propelled Disney bomb, which they had tried from 8th Air Force B-17s, turned out to have little effect on these structures.

Precision bombing. The German midget submarine wharf at Pootershaven on 3 February 1945, as seen from the bomb bay camera of Flying Officer F. H. A. Watts' Lancaster. (NA)

During February SHAEF decided to renew an offensive to separate the Ruhr from the remainder of Germany. This resulted in the Ruhr Plan, which among other things listed eighteen weak links in the transport system, most of which were bridges and viaducts. Consequently, although this plan was not adopted until 10 February, 9 and 617 made the first of several excursions to two targets on 6 February with which they would become very familiar in the next month – the railway viaducts at Altenbeken and Bielefeld in north-west Germany. With the draining of the Dortmund-Ems Canal these had become even more important as a means of transport. Use Tallboys to destroy them and even the resilient Germans would be hard put to restore communications before Allied ground forces moved into the area.

The snag was the rarity of clear skies at this time of the year. On 6 February neither squadron would achieve its objective. 9 Sqdn found ten-tenths' cloud over their target area and all eighteen of their aircraft were diverted to the emergency airfield at RAF Woodbridge in Suffolk.

This ought to have been routine, but it meant another cross-country journey for Gordon Maguire and his merry men, as Sqdn Ldr A. G. 'Bill' Williams later recalled:

On landing, one of our aircraft picked up a large piece of metal in one of its wheels. It was considered that it would not be safe for the aircraft to move, so the armament team from Bardney was sent for to lower the bomb, so that the wheel could be changed. The aircraft was standing on grass and the armourers started lowering the bomb. A lot of interest was created among the Woodbridge airmen and Waafs, and a large crowd had gathered round the aircraft to have a look at this famous bomb.

Now, the bomb was being lowered when the Bardney armourers decided on a little fun. So they suddenly let the bomb go, with a thump on the grass. This horrified the onlookers and there was great consternation among them. They thought the bomb would go off and take them with it. Actually, the Tallboy was completely safe, their fears were groundless and we all had a good laugh. A good joke, we thought.

Many times we had to land with the monster on board, but this never troubled the Lanc, as it was a truly remarkable aeroplane.

It is not known whether Cpl Spencer, the moustachioed armourer of Waddington fame, was present on this occasion, but it certainly seems to fit his style.

617, after having four Lancasters suffer flak damage over the front line, were also recalled due to bad weather.

8 February 1945
Target The Ijmuiden E-boat pens.
Weather Good, with only small amounts of cloud at 2,000ft to 3,000ft in the target area.

Force 15 Lancasters of 617 Sqdn:

NG445 'E'	Gp Capt. J. E. Fauquier	LM432	Flt Lt D. J. Oram
NG228 'V'	Sqdn Ldr J. F. Brookes	DV380 'P'	Flt Lt G. R. Price
NG489 'M'	Sqdn Ldr C. C. Calder	DV385 'T'	Flg-Off J. Castagnola
PD238 'H'	Sqdn Ldr J. V. Cockshott	PD233 'G'	Flg-Off M. B. Flatman
ED763 'Z'	Flt Lt B. J. Dobson	PB415 'O'	Flg-Off P. H. Martin
NG340	Flt Lt L. S. Goodman	ME562 'K'	Flg-Off J. A. Sanders
DV405 'J'	Flt Lt B. A. Gumbley	LM695 'N'	Flg-Off F. H. A. Watts
LM485 'U'	Flt Lt G. W. Lancey		

Escort 33 Spitfire IXs of 11 Group:
310 Sqdn (Czech)   312 Sqdn (Czech)   313 Sqdn (Czech)

Bomb Loads Each Lancaster carried one Tallboy, with a half-hour delay.

This raid targetted the new pens, which 9 Sqdn had failed to hit on 3 February. 617 rendezvoused with the Czech Wing over the North Sea, the latter having taken off from a Continental base after escorting a Main Force raid the previous day.

The bombing took place in just four minutes, between 0932 and 0936. Despite the half-hour delays, at least three bombs exploded on impact. Fauquier claimed he saw two direct hits, which were confirmed by PRU coverage.

A survey after liberation showed that there had been two direct hits and two near misses. One Tallboy hit at the north corner of the pens had caused a major collapse of the neighbouring structure, destroying the thin roof and pen walls in that area. It had also damaged the harbour wall.

Another had penetrated the roof's southern edge and came to rest between the double outside walls – a feature which, like the burster slabs at Siracourt, indicated that someone had thought of near-misses at the time of construction. This Tallboy broke two-thirds of the way from the front. The empty front portion, showing little damage, was found lying on the ground, unexploded. The filling had either been shaken out or removed by a German Bomb Disposal team, although the bomb's tail was described as having blown some concrete from the roof's edge when it went off. Other instances of bombs breaking up in a similar manner would occur when the Arnsberg railway viaduct was bombed in the coming months.

On 12 February a signal was passed by Air Vice-Marshal Saundby to 5 Group, listing the following special targets for attacks 'as opportunity offers':

GH501 Bielefeld viaduct	GH504 Arnsberg viaduct
GH502 Neunbeken viaduct	GR3597 Hamburg/Finkenwerder shelter
GH503 Altenbeken viaduct	SN102 Bergen pens

Saundby stated that 'these targets are to be attacked in daylight with fighter escort, or, if opportunity and tactical considerations permit, in moonlight'.

This was to set the pattern of operations for both squadrons during the final two months of the European war. Apart from the weather, one possible handicap was the available fighter range, especially Hamburg, which was considered a borderline case by 11 Group, depending on routes and the use of advanced bases in north-west Europe. As noted earlier with the Czech Wing, these airfields had given the Spitfire squadrons a longer reach, but as most had only recently been shot-up by the Allies, then booby-trapped and abandoned by the Luftwaffe, their facilities left a lot to be desired.

On 14 February 9 and 617 again set off for the two viaducts at Altenbeken and Bielefeld, but were beaten by the weather for a second time. Flt Lt J. J. Dunne's crew of 9 Sqdn, in NF937 'E', did not return. Presumed lost to flak, their aircraft crashed at Sasserath, south-east of the spa town of Bad Münstereifel. There were no survivors. Flg-Off Graham Rees also returned with slight flak damage.

A further pointer to the future came from Air Commodore H. V. Satterly of 5 Group's 54 Base, who suggested on 17 February that attacks should be made on the remaining German naval units, which were now being pushed westwards by the Russians, on the grounds that these would be useful experience for Bomber Command in the Pacific war.

By now the two squadrons were committed to Altenbeken and Bielefeld as priority targets, necessitating a good deal of hanging around while waiting for the weather to clear. This led Satterly to become concerned at a deterioration in their morale. In due course his advice would be heeded, but there were other matters to attend to first.

22 February 1945
Targets The railway viaducts at Altenbeken (9) and Bielefeld (617), in north-west Germany.
Weather Slight haze but no cloud over Altenbeken, much haze at Bielefeld.

Force 16 Lancasters of 9 Sqdn:

NG459 Wg Cdr J. M. Bazin	NF929 'P' Flg-Off R. W. Ayrton
NG278 'N' Sqdn Ldr J. D. Melrose	NG384 'T' Flg-Off J. W. Buckley
NG486 'A' Sqdn Ldr A. G. Williams	NG206 'J' Flg-Off M. L. T. Harper
PB696 'V' Flt Lt R. C. Lake	NG242 'C' Flg-Off A. E. Jeffs
PA172 'G' Flt Lt L. E. Marsh	NG220 'B' Flg-Off D. Macintosh
NG442 'F' Flt Lt B. Taylor	NG249 'S' Flg-Off W. G. Rees
LM220 'Y' Flt Lt W. D. Tweddle	LM217 'O' Flg-Off J. C. Wiley
ME809 'X' Flg-Off H. Anderson	NG487 'D' Flg-Off A. F. Williams

18 Lancasters of 617 Sqdn:

NG445 'E' Gp Capt. J. E. Fauquier	DV391 'Y' Flt Lt I. M. Marshall
NG489 'M' Sqdn Ldr C. C. Calder	PD238 'H' Flt Lt G. R. Price
NG228 'V' Sqdn Ldr J. L. Powell	DV402 'X' Flt Lt J. L. Sayers
LM492 Flt Lt S. A. Anning	NG494 Flg-Off D. W. Carey
PB371 Flt Lt B. J. Dobson	DV385 'T' Flg-Off J. Castagnola
LM489 'A' Flt Lt H. V. Gavin	PB415 'O' Flg-Off J. H. Leavitt
ME554 'F' Flt Lt L. S. Goodman	NG340 Flg-Off P. H. Martin
DV405 'J' Flt Lt B. A. Gumbley	ME562 'K' Flg-Off J. A. Sanders
NG539 Flt Lt C. W. Hill	LM695 'N' Flg-Off F. H. A. Watts

Escort 115 Mustang IIIs of 11 Group:

64 Sqdn RAF	129 Sqdn RAF	306 Sqdn (Polish)	16 Sqdn (Polish)
118 Sqdn RAF	165 Sqdn RAF	309 Sqdn (Polish)	
122 Sqdn RAF	234 Sqdn RAF	315 Sqdn (Polish)	

Bomb Loads

9 Sqdn – each aircraft carried one Tallboy, with either a 0.25 or 11-second delay.

617 Sqdn – each aircraft carried one Tallboy, with an 11-second delay.

Surprisingly, in view of past events, it was not deemed necessary to bring one of 627 Sqdn's crews along to film this attack.

The twin-track viaduct at Altenbeken ran just west of the village from which it took its name, eight miles north-east of the town of Paderborn. Built of brick and sandstone, it was on the main line running west from Berlin and was assessed as the second most important German railway viaduct; the first, of course, was the Bielefeld one. The vital nature of the target was underlined by the fact that railway traffic from

A North American Mustang III of 306 (Polish) Squadron, and typical of those fighters which escorted 9 and 617 into Germany by day in the last months of the European war. A similar aircraft was used by Cheshire and Tait for low-level target marking. (IWM neg. no. HU4063)

three different directions all converged at this point. In normal times it was second in importance only to the Berlin-Hanover-Ruhr line.

Built in 1851 to bridge a valley with a small stream, the twenty-four-arch viaduct was 450m long and 33m high at its centre. At both ends the track curved through hills, then after running along embankments it curved again as it crossed the valley.

Beginning on 26 November 1944, the US 8th Air Force had attacked the viaduct three times, each time through cloud and from a higher altitude than 9 Sqdn were now going to do. The first of these attacks had destroyed four piers and five spans in the viaduct's centre. Repairs had begun the next day, indicating the value the Germans put on it. Three days later a second raid had resulted in two more damaged piers and cut track. A third on 9 February had not been effective.

All this had meant that no traffic had been able to cross for two and a half months. In an attempt to avoid losing it altogether if the viaduct was brought down, the Germans had started a single-track line to bypass the viaduct, but it would never be completed. Repairs had been delayed by cold weather, frustrated by red tape, then disrupted by numerous daylight strafing attacks and air-raid alarms at night. However, progress had finally been made with the installation of two steel piers to support a 35m steel bridge that now filled the gap. The viaduct had been back in action since 10 February.

After encountering heavy but inaccurate flak between the Rhineland cities of Bonn and Koblenz, 9 Sqdn's bombing at Altenbeken was generally concentrated along the eastern side of the viaduct, if tending to overshoot. Buckley claimed to have seen one Tallboy hit it, but afterwards there was much smoke. Jeffs, the last to bomb at 1603, was caught in another aircraft's slipstream and bombed the railway instead.

Wg Cdr J. A. Plagis, one of the escort wing leaders, dived down to take a look and thought the viaduct had been hit at one end, but was not certain. He was correct, for the span leaving the eastern abutment had been destroyed. The northern abutment had also been affected, the span supported by it had been cracked and part of the pier destroyed. There had been some Tallboy misses within thirty metres of the viaduct, but in this case only the hits mattered, which once again showed how critical a near miss could be. It was also interesting to note that it had been the old masonry at the ends of the viaduct that had fallen. Although some Tallboys had landed close to the new steel latticework, their explosions had had little effect on it.

It was probably on this occasion that Gordon Maguire, over at Bardney, had the chance to impress a visiting USAAF brigadier-general:

> He arrived in a Liberator and I took him to our headquarters. When he saw a Tallboy he said, 'What the hell is that?!' Then when he saw a Lanc's bomb bay and was impressed by its size, he said, 'You could get two in there!' He watched the armourers bomb one up in twenty minutes and reckoned that was pretty slick.
>
> After he was told we had gone to bomb a viaduct, he asked how many aircraft. When he was told 'Fifteen to sixteen,' he at first thought that was the number of squadrons. When we told him that we meant aircraft, he was aghast at the thought of so small a force.

There was one final shock in store.

> He was still at ops when a flight sergeant came in with a dripping print of a Tallboy hitting the viaduct!

617's target, between the industrial towns of Bielefeld and Herford, was more difficult to destroy as it consisted of two parallel twin-track viaducts. The first had been completed in 1847 and the second, in response to increased traffic, had been added by 1917, some of it having been constructed by POWs. By 1939 three hundred trains were crossing them every day, leading to no less than fifty-four raids on this area between 1940 and 1945.

After D-Day there had been several attacks on Bielefeld by B-24 Liberators of the US 8th Air Force's 2nd Bomb Division. During November 1944, 2,151 high explosive bombs and 33,000 incendiaries had been dropped, although to use incendiaries against stonework was ludicrous. It was hardly surprising that all that had been achieved was to damage two spans and one pier, or that the Germans had got round this by relaying track over girders that they had placed across the damaged sections. The 2nd Division's efforts had served only to heavily crater the ground around the viaduct, creating a muddy moonscape reminiscent of a First World War battlefield. Anticipating further raids, in the following month the Germans had begun to build a temporary loop line to bypass the viaduct altogether.

The problem was that viaducts were long, narrow targets. Whether the attack was by level or dive-bombing, they were difficult to hit even in good weather – Paul Brickhill later aptly described it as like trying to stick a dart in a line. Even if a stick of bombs landed close by, the multiple arches provided a means by which blast could pass through without doing any more than chip the masonry. Except during their first use at Altenbeken, the American 500lb and 1,000lb bombs had proved quite unsuited to this task. What was needed was something heavier, and although by now many Tallboys were of American manufacture, they could still only be dropped by the Lancaster.

The viaducts' defences consisted of a 20mm light flak battery on a nearby hill and smoke generators positioned two miles to the north-east. Perhaps these were responsible for some of the haze, which led to several aircraft bombing after two or three runs.

Fauquier's bomb, on his second run, overshot by fifty yards, at the northern end of the viaduct. One was believed to hit in that area, with at least three others coming down close to the centre of the west side. It was the combined shock wave from these that brought down three arches of the western most viaduct.

The track was cratered at the northern end, also causing damage to a road that passed under it at that point, but it had been the three near misses in the middle that mattered.

Despite the damage, the other viaduct still stood and the *Organization Todt*'s repair teams quickly succeeded in making good the damage to the track. It was going to need another attack – and an even bigger bomb, which by now was almost ready.

On 24 February a daylight raid was mounted against the same area of canal near Ladbergen that had been attacked the previous September, but once again unsuitable conditions forced a recall when the crews were just thirty miles away from it. The only

The double railway viaduct near Bielefeld after Tallboys had collapsed three spans on its western side. (IWM neg. no. C5085)

Tallboy to fall was one that was jettisoned by Flg-Off Wiley of 9 Sqdn, due to his need to feather a malfunctioning port engine. The weather now seemed determined to grant the Germans a series of last-minute reprieves, but this target, like the Bielefeld viaduct, was not going to be spared until it was so damaged as to be completely unusable before the area came under Allied occupation.

3-4 March 1945
Target The Ladbergen canal aqueduct, near Munster.
Weather Nine-tenths stratus cloud over the target at 4,000ft to 5,000ft.

Force 19 Lancasters of 9 Sqdn:

NF929	'P'	Flt Lt G. C. Camsell	NG202	Flg-Off M. L. T. Harper
LL845	'L'	Flt Lt A. M. Morrison	NG384 'T'	Flg-Off A. F. Jones
NG447		Flt Lt W. Oldacre	NG495 'R'	Flg-Off A. L. Keeley
NG442	'F'	Flt Lt B. Taylor	NG238	Flg-Off S. Laws
NG499	'W'	Flg-Off H. Anderson	PB696 'V'	Flg-Off D. Macdonald
NG206	'J'	Flg-Off K. C. Arndell	ME791	Flg-Off E. G. R. Morgan
LM220	'F'	Flg-Off R. W. Ayrton	NG220 'B'	Flg-Off J. E. Stowell
NG488	'A'	Flg-Off J. W. Buckley	LM217 'O'	Flg-Off E. I. Waters
NG249	'S'	Flg-Off D. A. Coster	ME809 'X'	Flg-Off R. B. Young
PA172	'G'	Flg-Off C. M. T. Follett		

Escort Support was provided by 11 Mosquitoes from the following units of 100 Group:
85 Sqdn RAF   141 Sqdn RAF   515 Sqdn RAF

Bomb Loads
9 Sqdn – each Lancaster carried one Tallboy, with a 0.5-second delay.

This was part of a 5 Group attack, totalling 212 Lancasters and ten Mosquitoes. There was also a raid on a synthetic oil refinery at Kamen by 4 and 8 Groups, as well as a feint attack against the coastal town of Emden.

617 were sitting this one out, which they were probably glad to do after their previous experiences in this area. It had been planned as a daylight raid, but such was the weather that during the morning its take-off time had been postponed to 1700. By 1100 it had become a night one, with H-Hour at 2200.

It was known that a smokescreen was now in place, and in the event of the primary MP being covered by it a second one had been allocated two and half miles away. 83 and 97 Sqdns were to act as the illuminators, locating the target by H2S and dropping green TIs as Primary Blind Markers, these in turn being backed up by three Mosquitoes of 515 Sqdn on target marking patrols. The two APs, to the north and south, were to be marked by nine of 627 Sqdn's Mosquitoes, using 1,000lb red TIs. Any inaccurate marking was to be 'scrubbed' by the use of yellow TIs.

The winds turned out to be northerly and stronger than forecast. Although the flares and the PBM green TIs were dropped a minute or so early, they were accurate. The smokescreen was deployed, but 627's Flt Lt J. E. Whitehead, as Marker 3, was able to pick out the primary MP through it and dropped one red TI. Flg-Off E. A. Saunders, as Marker 4, assessed this as accurate, so backing-up by the rest of 627's force was now ordered and quickly completed.

A few clusters of flares were dropped some distance from the canal, but they were considered to be spoofs. Other enemy counter-measures were dummy red TIs to the south-west, south-east and east of the canal, at least half a mile from it. All of these were recognized and ignored. The secondary MP was not affected by the smokescreen, but it was not considered necessary to mark it.

By now two groups of reds could be seen by the Lancaster crews. The issue was settled by the Master Bomber, who instructed them to attack the largest red glow seen through cloud to the north-west of the target area, and overshoot it by three seconds, which they did. As far as 9 Sqdn were concerned, everyone bombed except Coster and Keeley, both of whom felt that accuracy was not possible due to the cloud.

9 Sqdn were safely back by 0041 and in this they were fortunate, for although 5 Group lost seven Lancasters over the Continent, on their return the others would find that there was no security at home either. The 100 Group night fighters had had no contacts while over Germany and on their return they realised why. Their prey was elsewhere, for the Luftwaffe had mounted what was really the last fling of their night fighter force – *Unternehmen Gisela*, which was a long-range intruder operation over Britain's east coast, reaching up as far as Yorkshire.

This defiant gesture had been anticipated and on hearing the codeword 'scram' the crews headed for airfields outside the danger area. Even so, twenty bombers were shot down over their home territory, two of them being 5 Group Lancasters.

The canal was breached in two places, so that when photographed there was no water left in it. It had been put completely out of action and Bomber Command did not need to attack it again before the European war ended. As another raid had had the same effect on the Mittelland Canal, this deprived the Germans of one-third of their coal supply.

6-7 March 1945
Target The German naval port of Sassnitz, on Rugen island in the Baltic, north of Stettin Bay.
Weather Seven-tenths' thin cloud over target at 6,000ft.

Force 20 Lancasters of 9 Sqdn:

PB696	'V'	Flt Lt R. F. Adams	NG419	'U'	Flg-Off M. L. T. Harper
NF929	'P'	Flt Lt G. C. Campbell	NG495	'R'	Flg-Off A. L. Keeley
NG499	'W'	Flt Lt R. J. Harris	NG235	'H'	Flg-Off S. Laws
LL845	'L'	Flt Lt A. M. Morrison	ME809	'X'	Flg-Off R. C. Macdonald
PA172	'G'	Flt Lt W. Oldacre	LM217	'O'	Flg-Off D. McIntosh
NG384	'T'	Flg-Off H. Anderson	HK791	'M'	Flg-Off E. G. R. Morgan
NG206	'J'	Flg-Off K. C. Arndell	NG220	'B'	Flg-Off J. E. Stowell
NG486	'A'	Flg-Off J. W. Buckley	NG276		Flg-Off E. I. Waters
NG249	'S'	Flg-Off D. A. Coster	NG487	'D'	Flg-Off A. F. Williams
NG442	'F'	Flg-Off C. M. T. Follett	LM220	'Y'	Flg-Off R. B. Young

Escort None.

Bomb Loads
9 Sqdn – each Lancaster carried one Tallboy. Those carried by Flt Lt Harris and one other crew had a half-hour delay, the remainder having a 0.7-second delay fuse.

Aircraft of 3 and 8 Groups were also attacking the town of Wesel in preparation for the crossing of the Rhine.

The plan was similar to that used at Ladbergen, with flares and green TIs to be used for Primary Blind Marking by 83 and 97 Sqdns. They were to illuminate the town at first, so the dock area could be marked by 627 and bombed by the Main Force. Again, red TIs were to be used for marking and yellow ones to scrub them if necessary. There were three ships as targets. If the MPs could not be identified, the centre of the three targets was to be attacked. Failing this, the most accurate of the green TIs was to be bombed. H-Hour was to be 2300.

The raid started well, the flares and green TIs being both on time and accurate. 627's Marker 3, Flg-Off P. A. Saunders, identified the AP first and his TI fell 100yds east of it. It was then backed up by two other 627 Sqdn crews. The Marker Leader,

Flt Lt W. W. Topper, considering this sufficient, called off his other Mosquito crews, climbed to 8,000ft and estimated that cloud would pass over the target in two minutes. He then passed this to the Master Bomber, who told the Main Force to orbit for three minutes. A red TI two miles to the north-east was seen as a decoy and ignored. The target became clear again just before H-Hour, when the Main Force was called in.

Some seventeen ships were counted outside the harbour, but those within it merged with the coastline and could not be picked out. The Master Bomber ordered, 'Bomb as planned ... Attack on three large ships outside harbour.'

From 9 Sqdn's point of view, the markers were well concentrated, but cloud conditions had meant that no flame floats were seen, so no guaranteed wind could be found. Several small vessels were attacked and one large one that was thought by Buckley's crew to be a twin-funnelled liner, about 1,000yds off shore. Laws attacked a destroyer – evidently successfully as it was seen to have a 70-degree list afterwards.

At least three ships were seen making for the open sea – not surprisingly as the flares were visible from the Swedish coast and those on board felt very naked. Williams thought he hit a flak ship, although this too might have been the destroyer. Some of 97's crews saw a small vessel sunk by what they thought was a 1,000-pounder and a larger one near-missed by a Tallboy. Morrison's crew made two runs in twelve minutes over the shipping, but the large merchant vessel that was their target was obscured by cloud each time, so they headed for home without bombing. Coster was similarly handicapped, and after two runs over three small ships he bombed the dock area with the Main Force – this was probably the large explosion seen in the docks at 2327 by Anderson's crew.

Considerable damage was caused to the northern part of the town and three ships were sunk in the harbour, which indicated that if they had been hit while at sea, then someone had tried to beach them first. Two Main Force Lancasters were lost, one over the Baltic and the second in a crash at its base afterwards.

Meanwhile, 617 had been on standby to attack the Bielefeld viaduct again, as soon as the weather cleared. They would shortly have another weapon with which to do so, for on 5 March Fauquier had been trying out a new Lancaster, known as a BI Special.

The old hands would now be reminded of *Chastise*, for this aircraft had no bomb doors and no mid-upper turret. There the similarity ended, for there were a whole host of other modifications, from the obvious to the obscure. The reason for this was that the final Wallis earthquake bomb design had at last come to fruition. On 9 March another raid on the viaducts was scrubbed because of the weather, but this would be the last all-Tallboy raid to the Bielefeld area. Once again the weather had granted a reprieve, but it would only be for a few more days.

This did not mean that 9 would be idle, nor did their use of Tallboy exempt them from taking part in Main Force raids, as the three city attacks that followed during March would show. These were to Essen on 11 March, Dortmund on the 12th and Würzburg on the 16th. However, although the loads for these are described as '12,000lb MC' in 9's ORB, Bardney's and the Air Ministry War Reports for these three dates all say that the bombs used were 12,000lb HCs. This was confirmed by the log of Flg-Off Dennis Nolan, Flg-Off Buckley's bomb aimer, who flew on all three operations.

Meanwhile, a new and even bigger bomb had been arriving at Woodhall Spa.

12

Grand Slam at Last

The destruction of towns and cities behind the battlefront will have a direct effect upon the results of the land battles which the ground forces will have to undertake soon. The enemy will be denied the use of his most essential means of transport, shelter for his reserves and what remains of his armament production in the previously attacked areas. To achieve this, all Air Bombers must make sure that their bombs hit the areas they are intended for, and that means constant practice, a thorough knowledge of all equipment, and the ability to conform strictly to the plan of attack.

V Group News, September 1944

This still held true six months later. Although foreign troops were now on their soil and defeat was staring them in the face, the Germans, armed by Speer and terrified by Himmler, were resisting as fiercely as ever on the ground. Although seen less in public now that the outside world was closing in on him, Hitler had declared in a radio broadcast in January, 'The world must understand that this state will never surrender. The Third Reich may suffer setbacks, but never will it surrender in the face of hardship.' Casualties on both sides were not light and Bomber Command's firepower would have to be constantly used until the end.

It was now that the ten-ton Grand Slam bomb finally arrived on the scene. This title dated from 22 November; it had originally been known as Tallboy Large until the six-tonner's code-name had been compromised by appearing in the press. The biggest non-nuclear air-dropped weapon of the war and therefore, until Hiroshima, the most powerful, it represented the culmination of everything Wallis had worked for in bomb design over the last five years.

On 18 July 1943, in the wake of *Chastise*, the Controller of Research and Development at MAP had been given a requirement for twelve 4,000lb Tallboy Smalls and cases for sixty Tallboy Mediums. For some unknown reason MAP had placed an order for one hundred ten-tonners as well, but due to lack of production capacity the Chief of the Air Staff, with Churchill's approval, had ordered MAP to stop work on the ten-tonner on 30 September.

It was revived when the use of Tallboy during the summer of 1944 had highlighted that bomb's strengths and weaknesses. Inspection of various concrete structures had shown that this weapon was not sufficiently powerful enough to destroy them, except by undermining. Clearly the ten-tonner would have to be brought back into the picture, and so production of it had been resumed that July.

Despite this, Grand Slam had come close to not going into action at all because, as with Highball, questions had been raised as to what it was to be used against. In September 1944, just as Britain's defenders had got the measure of the V-1 flying bomb, a series of explosions began in the London area and elsewhere, followed by a strange noise in the sky. The V-2 rockets had now started to arrive. Travelling at 3,600mph through the stratosphere, they could be neither seen nor heard and could only be combated by bombing their mobile launching sites in Holland.

This attack had been expected ever since the RAF's bombing of a German research site at Peenemünde in the Baltic, and these elusive targets, code-named Big Ben sites, had been suggested as a possible use for Grand Slam before the first V-2 landed. With hindsight, it is probably as well that Grand Slam was not yet ready; to have used this massive weapon on so small a target would have been overkill and might have led to unnecessary Dutch civilian casualties.

It was at this time that a group captain in the Air Ministry's planning department had pointed out that by the time Grand Slam was ready there might not be any targets suitable for it. Aircraft modified for it would be unable to carry anything else, which inevitably meant fewer Main Force ones. Air Commodore Bilney replied and it says something for him that, despite the headaches Tallboy's problems had caused, he defended its bigger brother: 'I appreciate the introduction of Tallboy Large means locking up special aircraft capable of carrying only this or Tallboy Medium. The precedent for such action lies in the aircraft modified to carry Upkeep – a less versatile weapon than the Tallboy Large is likely to prove.'

The group captain stated – with some accuracy, as it turned out – that Tallboy Large was not likely to be available until November, and not in any numbers until the following February or March, but, remembering the euphoria after Tallboy's first use at Saumur, Bilney stuck to his guns:

> I am convinced that Tallboy Large will prove an excellent weapon, and one for which many targets will eventually be found. There is almost invariably a smokescreen put up against the introduction of a new weapon, but once it has completed a successful operation, there is an immediate clamour for its use against a multitudinous list of targets … I strongly recommend the use of Tallboy Large in spite of the lock-up of aircraft.

Wallis, who knew all about bureaucratic smokescreens, would have been proud of him.

At High Wycombe opinions regarding the new bomb were mixed. During September a production run of twenty-five bombs a month was proposed – not enough for Saundby, who wanted at least fifty and preferably seventy-five.

On being approached by Wallis over the ten-tonner, Harris, recalling his 'pink elephant' comment when the dams had been breached, had given a cautious approval. He was still not as enthusiastic as his deputy, considering these bombs suitable only for U-boat pens and 'large Crossbow sites' – which again meant the V-weapons. It was his view that production figures ought to be decided by the Air Ministry. An instruction to proceed with the cases was given towards the end of the month and, by October, 600 were on order – 200 in Britain and twice that number in America.

However, any jubilation was quickly stilled when British production was cancelled on 4 October. American production was maintained only after a protest by the RAF Mission in Washington, which had used its influence to get the Americans to produce the weapon and objected to a cancellation of the order. They suggested fifty cases, to which the Air Ministry, perhaps with reluctance, agreed. Four Lancasters were to be modified for them. The American cases, which had been ordered in September, were expected to be ready by the end of the year, and were to be filled in Britain. Then someone had another change of heart and the order for the four modified bombers was cut to one, for trials use.

If it is possible to imagine a ten-ton bomb hanging by a thread, then that was what was happening at this time. However, during December the Battle of the Bulge started and it became clear that Nazi Germany was not finished yet. There would be a need for the new bomb after all and Grand Slam was finally reinstated, albeit with an order much reduced from the previous September. There would now be 200 from America and twenty-five at home.

Changes were also afoot at Woodhall Spa. Gp Capt. H. S. A. Walmsley, 5 Group's SASO, suggested that the remaining ten Upkeep aircraft be sent to storage with 41 Group and that 617's establishment be increased to three flights. This was recommended by Cochrane and away went the last remnants of *Chastise* in the final week of 1944. The erks, who had come to look on them as no better than white elephants, were unlikely to have waved any fond farewells. The remaining Upkeeps went too, but still had to be available at one week's notice.

Saundby followed this up by putting forward the case for increasing 617 from its present two flights to three at the expense of one of 4 Group's Halifax squadrons, on the grounds that it could then achieve more than the Halifax flight could. The new establishment would then consist of two flights of Grand Slam aircraft and one of standard ones with blown bomb doors, making thirty Lancasters in all.

This was cleared with 4 Group's AOC, so that in February 51 Sqdn had to reduce itself to two flights and pass on the surplus manpower to 5 Group. If the uprooted erks' grumbled on their way down to Lincolnshire, they would have taken care not to do so too loudly, for 21st Army Group's infantry shortage at this time was such that some airmen had already gone to the depleted battalions; a move that was seen as no better than a death sentence.

So, the bombs would be along soon, but would the Lancaster be able to accept them? The first person to be persuaded was Roy Chadwick, and Eric Allwright was present at a meeting between him and Wallis.

> You'll find this reported as a Dutch auction, but I was there and it was very interesting. Wallis wanted a 22,000lb bomb – Chadwick said it wasn't on. Wallis was very persuasive – very clever on these things – and he gradually worked Chadwick up to 22,000lb ... Of course the Lancaster had to be strengthened.

It certainly did. This bomber's adaptability has already been mentioned when discussing the Tallboy modifications in Chapter 5, but it was necessary to go much further this time. A lot of kit would have to go, and Cochrane stressed the need to be ruthless in discarding it.

First the aircraft themselves had to be provided at a time when Avros were facing increased demand due to the conversion of some Main Force squadrons from Halifaxes to Lancasters. Because of the load that they would have to carry, there could be no question of adapting well-used Main Force aircraft; it would be necessary to start with new airframes. So an order for thirty-two BI Specials was placed with the Avro factory at Manchester, but even so things did not happen immediately. Quite apart from the problems the modifications posed, there were other forces at work.

Cochrane, who had kept a close eye on the situation, told Saundby that he had unofficially heard that the delivery dates for the Grand Slam aircraft had slipped due to an attempt by Avros to get their new design, the Lincoln, back to its production dates. He noted that it would be a pity if they missed the opportunity to attack more distant targets, such as the Rothensee Ship Lift, during the longer hours of winter darkness. His arguments echoed those of Bilney:

> As with the original Tallboy, I imagine that we shall have to drop a few before anyone will believe that they will go off and do damage, and then there will be a hectic rush to try and get them produced in numbers. That is why I suggest that we should urge on production of, at any rate, a few of the modified aircraft and of the bombs in order to get some dropped as quickly as possible.

Wallis went to Coningsby for a meeting during February 1945, clearly in connection with this activity, although it was also necessary to discuss the type of fuses to be used with Air Commodore Sam Elworthy of 5 Group. Just in case anyone still had any doubts after Tallboy's success, Wallis pointed out that one Tallboy crater took longer to fill than twelve 1,000lb ones. Grand Slam would therefore be ideal for attacking railway choke points and similar targets. Repairs would also be hampered by the limited number of men and machines that could work around the perimeter of the crater. Yes, the latest bomb had not yet been dropped, but trials were going ahead at Boscombe Down and there was every reason to believe that the first one would be successful.

The BI Specials began to be built on the Manchester line towards the end of January. By 13 February the first two were awaiting flight clearance, with twelve more likely to be available within the next ten days, increasing to twenty-four by the end of the month. Deliveries would continue into March, by which time the full thirty-two would have been supplied. The first one of this batch, PB995, went to AAEE for testing, in company with PB592/G, a BI from a batch that had been built the previous year at Manchester, and which would be modified to the BI Special standard.

Since these aircraft were received in 'ex-works' condition it meant that certain extra items did not need to be fitted in the first place. On the other hand, others had to be removed, leading to a bewildering number of rip-outs and reinstatements, with each item being weighed. A conference on 25 February was called to sort out the matter.

To fit or not to fit? Out went the front turret, to be replaced by a special fairing. Next, the mid-upper one, its fairing and the H2S radar. These removals might have been expected, but hard on their heels came the TR1196 R/T set, electric lighting, flare chutes, flame dampers, some fuel tanks, the rear gunner's armour plate, three of the bomber's fire axes, a tool kit and even the crew ladder! IFF? Get rid of it, Cochrane said. Aircraft could use a device called the VHF Bomber Fixer if in distress, and for identification when returning.

For operational reasons, some electrical items could not be avoided, adding to the load; this was a few years before transistors were invented and valves meant bulk as well as weight. Although it was likely that most if not all Grand Slam attacks would be by day, the northern European weather was nobody's friend and navigational aids would still be necessary. So it was decreed that Gee would go aboard, along with Loran, an aid similar to it but operating on a much lower frequency. The equipment fitted to the bomber would pick up synchronised pulse signals from master and slave ground stations, the aircraft's position being established by measuring the time difference in the signals received from each one. Loran gave wider coverage than Gee but proved easier for the Germans to jam – which they had begun to do by February.

A high-level radio altimeter and a low-level one would have to be fitted to each aircraft. Also deemed indispensable were recognition lights, some VHF signals equipment, instruments, essential modifications to the airframe, the rear guns and 6,000 rounds of ammunition for them, making 1,210lb in all. The bomb doors had been removed, but not just to save weight; the new weapon's girth was such that not even the blown variety could have closed around it. 1,000lbs of weight had been allowed for what was now a five-man crew; the mid-upper gunner and wireless-operator normally carried in each aircraft would not be needed.

Then there was the question of defence. Evasive action with such a load was out of the question. Fishpond tail-warning radar was ruled out, but, possibly because Me 262 jet fighters were now beginning to appear in some numbers over north-west Germany, AGLT, code-named Village Inn or the Z Equipment, was requested.

The Automatic Gun-Laying Turret, which consisted of a radar-directed FN121 four-gun rear turret, fitted with a gyro Mark II gunsight, had been under trial by the Bomber Development Unit since April 1944 and had been tried operationally by two Main Force squadrons. The idea was that it would automatically sight and fire at an unseen approaching night fighter. Desirable though this seemed, its inability to tell friend from foe and the fact that its installation restricted the gunner's view from the turret made it something of a two-edged sword. Priority for its fitting had originally been given to 1 Group, on condition that they used it only when allocated a target of their own, without other Allied aircraft being present.

A new form of IFF was therefore necessary, so as a result of a crash programme aircraft of 1, 5 and 8 Groups had all been fitted with Z Equipment transmitters by

August 1944. AGLT functioned best, not as a blind-firing device, but as an early warning one, with some accounts of night fighters being damaged and driven off by it. However, a move to equip all of 5 Group with it was stymied when it was decided that it would not be a requirement for use in the Far East to which, it was anticipated, some of 5 Group's squadrons would be going once the Germans had surrendered. The idea was therefore dropped, although 617's BI Specials were fitted with Z Equipment in the nose. Hopefully, none of them would accidentally be shot down should they find themselves behind an AGLT-equipped Lancaster.

After all this, with 5,120lb of fuel on board, each BI Special weighed 39,765lb. By 25 February the first of them had arrived at Woodhall Spa, but arguments continued over what equipment to put in them. Gee should have been added at the factory, but Avros had slipped up and it was definitely needed. Fauquier felt that Loran was not, but the bracket and wiring for it could be fitted, to allow for quick installation if necessary. Omission of the front turret was approved, along with the hydraulics for it. Heaters were needed for the rear guns. The SABS had normal Tallboy release gear but lacked the facility to drop small practice bombs – this would have to be incorporated. Out would go the TR1154 W/T transmitter and receiver, to be replaced by VHF R/T. The final result would be an aircraft that, on operations, would only be able to carry the two earthquake bombs.

There were more changes on the ground too. In recognition of Grand Slam's importance, Woodhall Spa's bomb dump, which until now had only been allowed a maximum of forty earthquake bombs, had this figure increased by another ten, the space for them being provided by removing surplus stocks of other weapons.

How would the new monster be brought to the aircraft, and what problems would there be in fitting it inside? This had been determined during February 1945 by AAEE trials on Lancaster BI PB592/G, as well as on the Type H bomb trolley, which had been specially designed to move both Tallboy and Grand Slam.

This aircraft's bomb bay walls had been faired with quickly removable panels running from the door hinges to floor level, to protect hydraulic pipes and other equipment from the slipstream. Metal plates formed a flat roof to the bay, whose front wall was provided with a fairing to provide a contour for reception of the bomb. The rear wall was also faired in to provide a clean airflow out of the bay.

The standard bomb switches were replaced by one master switch and a release button. For emergency use, a mechanical release cable and toggle were fitted to the port side of the cockpit. The bomb was located in the bay by a large spring-loaded dowel that protruded from the floor above. It was then held in place by two steel suspension links that hung from the floor to fit underneath it. These were coupled together midway by a special Vickers release unit, which could be operated either electrically or manually. These links could be adjusted from inside the aircraft. Fusing units in the bay roof incorporated all the necessary positions for either Tallboy or Grand Slam.

Both weapons were then tried. Tallboy fitted satisfactorily, but Grand Slam's design featured a metal skirt, made in two halves, which fitted between the body and its tail unit. The skirt's leading edge stood proud of the body surface, and the slipstream over it while falling could tear the halves off, with serious effects on the bomb's stability. The AAEE therefore recommended a redesign of this item.

A ten-ton Ransome Rapier crane performed satisfactorily when hoisting Grand Slam on concrete. The Type H trolley proved acceptable for Service use, provided that when loaded it was towed at no more than 10mph and its tyres were inflated to 80lbs PSI. It was necessary to modify the trolley by raising the front cradle, to prevent the bomb's fins from fouling the bomb bay roof on arrival beneath the Lancaster.

Six men would be needed to winch either type of bomb up into the aircraft – a process that would take thirty-five minutes from its arrival on the dispersal. Templates were provided to align the bomb on the fore-and-aft axis of the aircraft. The front one proved unnecessary, but the rear one was used, being hung from an anchorage point in the bomb bay roof. Another question was the possible problem of ice accretion on the bomb's nose in flight – something that might also affect its stability during descent.

So far, so good, but how would the BI Special handle in the air, and how long could it sit on the ground with ten tons of bomb slung underneath it? Part of the answer lay in the Lincoln – a larger and heavier offshoot of the Lancaster, which had first flown in June 1944 with a view to Far East service. At the beginning of March Lincoln wheels and tyres began to be fitted to the BI Special. The aircraft's maximum permissible all-up weight was to be no more than 72,000lb and except in an emergency its landing weight was not to exceed 60,000lb. Merlin 24s were to be fitted, with paddle-blade propellers, and take-offs were to be from smooth runways only, by pilots experienced on the type. Orders issued to those who would fly it contained a mixture of the obvious and the somewhat alarming:

> When the store is carried the aircraft is to be very carefully handled and is restricted to gentle maneouvres only. At weights in excess of 67,000lb there is a tendency for the aircraft to wallow, but use of the controls may aggravate this, and no move should be made to correct it.

There is, nevertheless, a story that a certain pilot barrel-rolled his BI Special – minus its load – around an American B-17!

The bomber's structure was to be carefully checked, especially the wing skin and the rear fuselage. Its centre of gravity was within limits when carrying either Grand Slam or Tallboy, provided only the rear turret was fitted. To keep the best relieving loads on the wings, the fuel was to be kept as far outboard as possible. The need for this would become apparent once it took to the air fully loaded.

To render the BI Special a little less conspicuous, 5 Group requested a day camouflage scheme, which was applied to the later aircraft. This meant replacing the Night undersurfaces with a very pale green tone known as Sky, while retaining the standard upper finish of Dark Green and Dark Earth. However, someone slipped up, so PB995, the AAEE trials aircraft, and the first few BI Specials issued to 617 arrived wearing their customary black coats. To differentiate them from the Tallboy aircraft, they were all allocated the code letters YZ; KC continued to be carried by the squadron's Tallboy carriers.

In the midst of all this, Cochrane finally bowed out as 5 Group's AOC, moving on to Transport Command. Such a posting did not imply criticism; it had been decided to give other officers of Air rank the experience of exercising command at Group level before the European war ended. His replacement was Air Vice-Marshal Hugh Constantine, a fit and hearty rugby-playing type, who was still in his thirties. A big man who had first made a name for himself by sorting out civilian contractors during his previous service with 1 Group, Constantine was the kind of man who led from the front, did not distance himself from those below him and refused to take no for an answer. He would prove a worthy successor to Cochrane.

Before all this could take place it had been necessary to go back to the weapon that Wallis had first envisaged. The need for Grand Slam had meant more squash court drawing work for Vickers section leader Eric Allwright and his team, which included Spud Boorer and Ernie Marshall.

> It was on a Sunday afternoon that Boorer and Marshall and I, and another chap, I think – Len Christmas – we actually drew the first ten-ton bomb full-size. Obviously someone had to decide how thick this thing was, and we were given a weight of the bomb, which we had to meet in the structure, so you could get the required amount of explosive in. I think they allowed something like 800lb for the tail – made out of aluminium alloy, you see.

Jack Froude, who appeared earlier in the Upkeep part of this story, was also involved.

As originally conceived it was 37 feet 6 inches long from nose to fins and 4 feet 6 inches in diameter. The reason I remember the dimensions in the old Imperial scales was that Wallis wanted to see a drawing of the bomb full-scale. Another draughtsman – a Mr Burke – and I repaired to the spectator balcony of the far squash court to make the drawing. We had a long drawing board, the width of the squash court, but of course drawing paper and boards were only 30 inches (2 feet 6 inches wide). We overcame this problem by joining two lengths of 30-inch paper edge to edge, giving us a roll of paper 60 inches wide, the join forming the centreline of the bomb. I remember the roll being very tricky to manipulate, especially as we could only get to it from one side, the other side being the vault of the squash court!

When finished the drawing was hung nose down for Wallis to survey in the badminton court, which was the only place with the necessary headroom. It was then taken away. As far as I know, no more detail design was done at Burhill. Presumably it went somewhere to an organisation that designed bomb casings.

Designing it was something completely new for Eric Allwright.

So we had to get a structure whose casing – and what did any of us know about bomb design? No one had done a thing like this before. So we worked on this on a Sunday – in the war you worked any hours at all – and we produced this from this thickness on the front, tapered down as much as we thought was sensible, and then it had to be thick enough at the back, with bosses, to take this huge end-plate, which was about two inches of solid steel. So we did all that, and we started off by a thickness at the front of fifteen inches, which was arbitrary if you like. That external shape was established, so we had to fair this in, which we did. It looked all right, and that's how they were made. The weight was right.

After the war, the Ministry of Aviation, or whatever, said they wanted these bombs productionizing, because they had aircraft-type drawings, for which I was responsible. So Farnborough wanted these things fully productionized, and in fact I had to take on the job if getting every part of these bombs drawn to the Farnborough design – a waste of time entirely … But the other thing which was done post-war was this. It was decreed that in view of the way we'd designed this bomb it could do with a check for the strengths of it. So – on the point of view of the bomb dropping vertically – we had to make sure it wouldn't crumple under the weight of the bomb behind. So I had the job of stressing it all the way through, with Boorer or Marshall – one of the two. You could hardly see the difference in what we had drawn and what we found out – it was amazing!

Our methods were right. What was nice was that we believed we'd made a contribution, whereas a lot of the Drawing Office was very busy all the war with chaps working very hard, but nothing they did ever came to fruition, because the shops were full of Wellingtons and Warwicks. There was no need for another one. It was only the Production Drawing Office that was producing things, in the way of mods. Those working for Basil Stephenson – we really produced something.

Although Tallboy's trials and use in action had established the soundness of the earthquake bombs' design, it was not simply a matter of taking a six-tonner and scaling it up. During 1944 Sheffield's English Steel Corporation had been working on this strange new project. It had been given the cover name of a boiler, but no one was fooled by that. Inevitably, the foundrymen had their suspicions, but memories of two heavy raids on Sheffield during 1940 provided enough incentive for them to keep their mouths shut.

Apart from the bomb's size, there was the question of what type of steel to make it from. This question was solved only after trying several different types until they found one that would stand up to the shock of impact. There were just two British firms capable of manufacturing it, which involved a painstaking process. An individual concrete core had to be made, to a ten-thousandth of an inch, then a sand-covered outer mould, into which the molten metal had to be poured. It was then necessary to wait for it to cool before the core could be chipped away.

- Working to copies of the drawings that the Vickers squash court team had produced, the Americans constructed these bombs by electric welding. Seeing the two bombs that are now part of the Broooklands Museum collection led Eric Allwright to contrast the two methods:

> This big plate went on the back and we had studs in here. Then we had these fuses – three of those. That was all cast in Britain – more than Sheffield, in the end. But there weren't too many factories that could cast that kind of thing. Rough machined on the outside, and the inside was left bare-fettled. [The Americans cast] about three pieces. These were all electrically welded, with welding five inches thick – I well remember the dimensions. Mind you, that's a far quicker method than casting this huge thing. When you cast ten tons of stuff, you had to wait a week while it cooled down! I've been in foundries, so I know.

Another drawback of casting was that hot spots on the casing could turn into weaknesses, leading to the bomb breaking up on impact, with perhaps partial detonation or none at all. American methods might be superior, but even so not all their bombs would be acceptable.

> I had to approve them or scrap them, in the usual Stress Office manner, if the defects were too significant. I acted as the designer, for strength as well as the drawings, for which my experience suited me. It's interesting, starting out to build as a constructional engineer – a builder, a civil engineer – then working on aeroplanes and ending up with big bombs.

Once it was ready, the British-built Grand Slam casing then had to be transported a hundred miles for machining. Although each bomb could be carried in two parts – the explosive-carrying nose section and the tail – special trailers still had to be provided as the railways lacked the facilities to handle them. Since there had been two fatal accidents with wagon loads of explosives in 1944 – at Soham, near Ely, and at Catterick station in Yorkshire's North Riding – the London & North Eastern Railway, who served Lincolnshire, were probably quite happy not to be involved. When filling the bomb, which began around the beginning of 1945, it was deemed necessary to stand the body, which was 12ft 1in long, on its nose and pour in Torpex explosive by the bucketful – all 9,200lb of it.

When assembled Grand Slam had an overall length of 25ft 5ins long, a maximum diameter of 3ft 10ins and a total weight of 22,400lb – like Tallboy, its official weight differed from this, describing it as a 22,000-pounder. Two other things it had in common with its smaller brother were its chrome-molybedenum steel casing and three different types of pistol to provide a range of delays. These would be as follows:

No.37 6-144 hours   No.53 30 minutes   No.53A 1 hour

An 11-second delay would also be made available in time for the first operational use of this weapon.

The first one reached Woodhall Spa on 20 January and it was expected that fifteen would be ready by the end of the following month. There could be no question of immediately rushing into action with this new weapon, for the aircraft modified to carry it were not yet available, nor had it been test-dropped by AAEE. Anyway, heavy snowfalls were hampering operations at this time, so the crews spent far more time using shovels on the runways than flying from them.

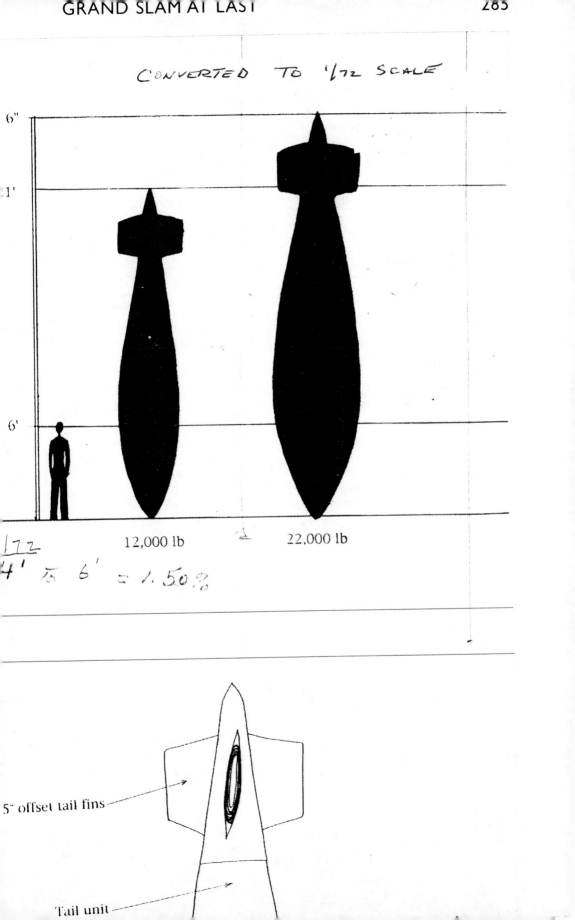

CONVERTED TO ¹/72 SCALE

6"

1'

6'

1/72
4' 5 6' = 1.50 %

12,000 lb   22,000 lb

5° offset tail fins

Tail unit

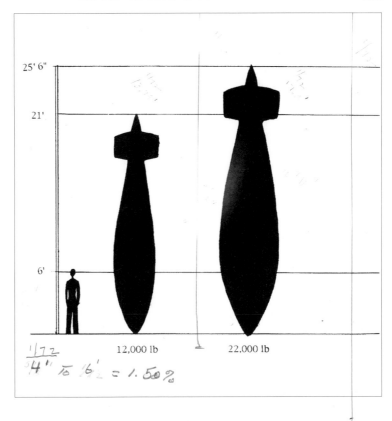

Scale drawing showing the sizes of Tallboy and Grand Slam, compared with a six-foot-tall airman. (Julie Anne Hudson)

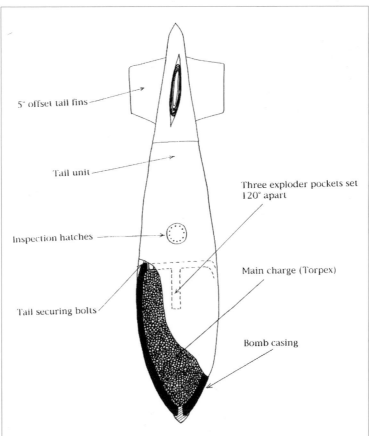

A cutaway drawing of Grand Slam (Julie Anne Hudson)

Even though Grand Slam had reached Woodhall Spa's bomb dump without incident, the problems it caused were not over. An Allen crane there proved dangerous, for its front wheels rose off the ground while lifting the bomb. There was no safety device to hold the weapon up and the brake was unable to control its downward descent onto the bomb trolley except by suddenly locking. This meant a snatching movement, causing the bomb to drop two feet at a time. The armourers had dealt with all shapes and sizes of bomb in their time, but their reactions to this one can well be imagined. Although AAEE's use of the Ransome Rapier crane had been noted, an American-designed type known as the Bay City was used by 617's armourers, proving satisfactory once a power-lowering device had been fitted in the late spring of 1945.

Like its predecessor, the only way to prove Grand Slam's effectiveness was to drop a prototype on the concrete target at Ashley Walk range, if possible from the ideal height, which had been calculated as 22,000ft. This time there would only be one; quite apart from the cost, the others were up in Lincolnshire with 617, who were standing by to hear the result, as they had not yet been cleared to use Grand Slam operationally.

What was described as the final trial installation of the ten-tonner aboard the other AAEE BI Special, PB995, now took place at Boscombe Down. Its pilot was the very experienced Gp Capt. H. A. 'Bruin' Purvis DFC AFC. For Purvis, carrying an unusual load designed at Weybridge was nothing new; during the so-called 'Phoney War' he had been the test pilot for the first of the minesweeping Wellingtons, which had flown with a large metal electric ring attached to them.

However, it was not PB995 which dropped the first Grand Slam but its sister, PB592/G. Bad weather meant that it was the beginning of March before the trial could at last take place, within 18,000 feet of the village of Godshill on the edge of the Ashley Walk range. The locals, in ignorance of the monster overhead, would soon receive an unforgettable wake-up call. Not yet, however. Reg Firman was present, to witness more delays.

> They had a big square block of concrete and they didn't think they were ever going to move it. So the man who was going to fly this colossal bomb – he thought he'd have a go. He flew over and we all went round to see what would happen. The machine came flying over, went round and round. Presently he said, 'This is no use. I cannot do anything in this!' The machine went back to Boscombe Down. It had been there a fortnight, in all weathers.
>
>   They said to me, 'What can we do? Have we got to take the bomb off and examine it, or put a new slip on?' I said, 'No, I think we'll be all right.' On the next fine day they went down again and the same thing happened again. In the spring there was misty weather and they couldn't see the bombing target for half a minute together. They gave it up at the second time. We'd been out there three weeks on the exposed ground of Boscombe Down.

Although his companions showed concern over wear and tear on the slip in use and asked whether they should change it on the next fine day, Firman decided they could continue to use the same one. Then they tried again on 13 March.

> It came flying over at the correct altitude, and he said, 'Shall I let it go?' I said, 'Let it go.' They did. It didn't land directly in line with this block – it was out of line to right or left, so that it left the block standing. But as far as the alignment and distance went it was correct.

The pilot may have been either Gp Capt. Purvis or Sqdn Ldr Hedley 'Hazel' Hazelden, who had been on trials work of this kind since the previous November. Having taken the bomb up before but been unable to drop it, Hazelden had become the first man to land a Lancaster with a ten-tonner on board.

The crater made at Ashley Walk bombing range by a Grand Slam in March 1945, just before this weapon's first operational use at Bielefeld. (Imperial War Museum, neg. no. E(MOS)1384)

On this occasion Eric Allwright was there as well, after witnessing a previous flight:

> So the poor old Lanc took off and ground away trying to reach some height ... There was a big target – a big hut of concrete, probably twenty feet square – and it landed within a hundred feet of it! Not bad, because bombs are different from what they are today.
>
> We had a job to see it when it came down. It was all marked in black and white, so you could see it rotating. Then there was this almighty explosion when it went into the ground. After that had settled a bit we all motored round to stand on the edge of this crater – it must have been 120 feet in diameter; and the same depth. Soil and stuff, and there were minor explosions, like a volcano going off, from the gases still coming up. So that proved the ten-ton bomb to be able to be dropped from a Lancaster, and to work.

His estimate of the crater's diameter was close to the mark – it was 124ft in diameter and 34ft deep. It was time for a celebration, so all concerned trooped off to the nearest pub, found a phone and rang Woodhall Spa, saying – according to Firman – 'Yes, we've passed the bomb. It works perfectly.' Official clearance would not come through until 22 March, but 617 would go into action with it on this day.

The Final Raids

13 March 1945
Target The railway viaducts at Arnsberg (9) and Bielefeld (617).
Weather Smoke and haze over Arnsberg, ten-tenths cloud over Bielefeld.

Force 18 Lancasters of 9 Sqdn:

NG485		Wg Cdr J. M. Bazin	?	'M'	Flt Lt L. H. Watkins
NG278	'N'	Sqdn Ldr J. D. Melrose	NG206	'J'	Flg-Off K. C. Arndell
NG486	'A'	Sqdn Ldr A. G. Williams	NG419	'U'	Flg-Off M. L. T. Harper
ME809	'X'	Flt Lt R. F. Adams	PA172	'G'	Flg-Off A. E. Jeffs
NF929	'P'	Flt Lt G. C. Camsell	NG299		Flg-Off A. F. Jones
NG499	'W'	Flt Lt R. J. Harris	?		Flg-Off A. L. Keeley
?	'O'	Flt Lt A. M. Morrison	NG235	'H'	Flg-Off S. Laws
LM217	'O'	Flt Lt B. Taylor	NG242	'C'	Flg-Off D. Macintosh
LM220	'Y'	Flt Lt W. D. Tweddle	NG220	'B'	Flg-Off J. E. Stowell

9 Sqdn's ORB incorrectly states that HK791 'M' was flown by both Watkins and Keeley on this raid. Morrison's crew are mentioned in the Bardney ORB but not the squadron one, showing that there was more than one 'O' on the squadron's strength at this time.

19 aircraft of 617 also took part, but are not listed as they did not bomb. They included two BI Specials – PD119 'J', flown by Gp Capt. J. E. Fauquier, and PD112 'S', flown by Sqdn Ldr C. C. Calder.

Escort 75 Mustang IIIs of 11 Group:

122 Sqdn RAF	118 Sqdn RAF	315 Sqdn (Polish)
129 Sqdn RAF	165 Sqdn RAF	316 Sqdn (Polish)
234 Sqdn RAF	309 Sqdn (Polish)	

Some Spitfire squadrons were also engaged on a sweep of the Osnabruck area, possibly as a cover for this raid.

Bomb Loads 9 Sqdn – each Lancaster carried one Tallboy, with an 11-second delay.
617 Sqdn – two Grand Slams were carried by Fauquier and Calder, with Tallboys for the rest. All the bombs had an 11-second delay.

It was necessary for Fauquier and Calder to use the whole of Woodhall Spa's runway to get airborne. By now 617 knew every inch of the country around Bielefeld, but 9 Sqdn still needed to exercise care, for at Arnsberg, twelve miles south of the town of Soest, there was a large Red Cross camp immediately south of the viaduct, which spanned the river Ruhr on the western outskirts of the town.

This was a fairly short viaduct, a twin-track seven-arch curving structure that was built of concrete, brick and sandstone. On the line from Kassel to the Ruhr, the viaduct crossed

Bombing up a Lancaster BI Special of 617 Squadron with Grand Slam, whose size is shown by the armourers riding on the trolley. (IWM neg. no. CH15371)

A Lancaster BI Special runs up its engines at dispersal. Two of the aircraft's three gun turrets have been removed and a sling holds the bomb in position in the doorless bomb bay. (IWM neg. no. MH4263)

a steep-sided valley, its western end terminating in an embankment. At its eastern side the line ran into a tunnel. Like Altenbeken and Bielefeld, it had previously been attacked three times by the US 8th Air Force, using 1,000lb and 500lb bombs. These had cut some track and fractured one pier's base but had still left the viaduct standing.

Flt Sgt Ken Rogers was flying in the CO's aircraft as a W/T controller. Always having an interest in radio, his expertise included knowledge of Morse code, the aircraft's Aldis lamp, the stars and the Lancaster's electrical system. He owed this position to his performance during an air exercise: 'The reason I was selected to be a W/T controller was that they sent one aircraft to lead and two followed. I had to send messages to them, which was really a mock raid. This lasted about two hours.'

Group Signals had been listening in. He was instructed to carry on: 'That's when I flew with Wg Cdr Bazin on the raid to Arnsberg. We left Bardney, I pulled the Very pistol, let off the colour of the day and the rest of the aircraft followed. When we got to the target Wg Cdr Bazin informed me to pass a message as to what height to bomb and all the other things during the raid on the viaduct.'

The only defences were some meagre inaccurate flak south-west of Arnsberg. Flt Lt R. E. Adams had trouble with his port outer engine constant speed unit, obliging him to feather it, jettison his Tallboy and return early. Bazin tried three runs, but poor visibility meant that only two crews bombed, neither doing any damage. Camsell bombed a bridge south-east of the target, claiming a hit, while the Tallboy dropped by Watkins overshot the viaduct to port.

Their return was not without incident. Morrison's crew had to jettison their Tallboy when smoke and fumes began to issue from the navigator's compartment, just behind the cockpit. Tweddle was diverted to the emergency airfield at Carnaby with his port outer engine on fire, landing safely with his Tallboy still aboard.

He was joined there by 617, including Fauqier and Calder, who also touched down safely on the single wide runway. With the exception of one clear patch over the Zuider Zee, they had met solid cloud all the way. The raid had been abandoned after 129 Sqdn had investigated the cloud over the target, the only excitement coming when one of 234 Sqdn's sections had chased an unidentified twin-engined aircraft away.

Anyone travelling on the Scarborough-Hull railway line past Carnaby that evening might well have wondered why these two apparently deformed Lancasters were parked among the other bombers in the airfield's dispersal loop, or what the dark-coloured shiny-tailed objects were beneath them. They would not remain there for long, as the Bielefeld viaduct's time had almost run out.

14 March 1945
Target The railway viaducts at Arnsberg (9) and Bielefeld (617).
Weather No cloud en route, but some on the north approach to Bielefeld, with much haze over both targets.

Force 15 Lancasters of 9 Sqdn:

NG278 'N' Sqdn Ldr J. D. Melrose	NG495 'R' Flg-Off A. L. Keeley
NF929 'P' Flt Lt G. C. Camsell	NG235 'H' Flg-Off S. Laws
LL845 'L' Flt Lt A. M. Morrison	NG490 Flg-Off R. C. Macdonald
HK791 'M' Flt Lt L. H. Watkins	NG242 'C' Flg-Off D. Macintosh
PA172 'G' Flg-Off R. W. Ayrton	NG206 'J' Flg-Off W. Scott
NG488 'A' Flg-Off J. W. Buckley	NG220 'B' Flg-Off J. E. Stowell
NG442 'F' Flg-Off C. M. T. Follett	NG419 'U' Flg-Off J. C. Wiley
NG384 'T' Flg-Off A. F. Jones	

Flg-Off W. G. Rees in PB696 'V' was unable to take off due to a punctured radiator.

15 Lancasters of 617 Sqdn:

NG228 'V' Sqdn Ldr J. F. Brookes	DV391 'Y' Flt Lt D. A. Rawes
PD112 'S' Sqdn Ldr C. C. Calder	DV402 'X' Flt Lt J. A. Sayers

PD371	Sqdn Ldr J. L. Powell	DV380 'P'	Flt Lt J. C. Warburton
LM492	Flt Lt S. A. Anning	NG489 'M'	Flg-Off D. W. Carey
NG494 'B'	Flt Lt L. S. Goodman	NG339 'G'	Flg-Off M. B. Flatman
DV405 'J'	Flt Lt B. A. Gumbley	PB415 'O'	Flg-Off P. H. Martin
LM489 'A'	Flt Lt C. N. Hill	LM695 'N'	Flg-Off J. W. Speirs
LM485 'U'	Flt Lt G. W. Lancey		

Escort 74 Mustang IIIs of 11 Group:

64 Sqdn RAF	126 Sqdn RAF	234 Sqdn RAF	315 Sqdn (Polish)
122 Sqdn RAF	165 Sqdn RAF	309 Sqdn (Polish)	316 Sqdn (Polish)

Bomb Loads With the exception of Calder's Grand Slam, all Lancasters of both squadrons carried Tallboys. All the bombs had an 11-second delay.

Eight of 8 Group's Oboe Mosquitoes had also been brought in for marking purposes, four each from the following units:

105 Sqdn RAF   109 Sqdn RAF

One 627 Sqdn Mosquito as a camera aircraft:

KB433 'Z' W/O H. W. Player and P/O C. B. Heath

When this operation began the two BI Specials flown by Fauquier and Calder were still at Carnaby. As they started up at 1415 Fauquier's aircraft became unserviceable, due to the SABS leaking oil and the starboard inner engine seizing up.

Fauquier leapt from his own aircraft and sprinted towards the other one. 'Jock' Calder realised what had happened. Not about to miss the big occasion or be displaced as his crew's skipper, he ignored the waving figure, pushed his throttles forward and took off, leaving Fauquier fuming on the tarmac behind him.

Carnaby's diarist commented, 'As his aircraft was carrying one of the new ten-ton bombs, Germany had short weight on this delivery. An opportunity of remedying this deficiency, however, will no doubt be presented in the very near future.'

As Calder met up with the rest of the squadron and settled down for the flight to north-west Germany the full impact of what he had done hit him. He would have to destroy the viaduct now – and even that might not save him from Fauquier's wrath on his return.

Calder's apprehension was nothing compared to that shown in the Tallboy aircraft around him. On the ground a Lancaster has no perceptible dihedral, but the ten-ton weight beneath his wings had caused them to lift in an arc. He could fly no faster than 210mph, for above this speed vibration became pronounced, due, it was thought, to the baffle plate fitted to the rear of the open bomb bay. Clearly visible beneath the bomber was the great dark green and silver missile, like some parasitic fish. Was the aircraft's main spar going to hold out until they reached Bielefeld? What about the engines overheating?

9 Sqdn's attack on Arnsberg resulted in a good concentration of Tallboys. Camsell thought the first overshot slightly and the fourth appeared to hit. Macintosh was almost the last to attack, but by now the viaduct was covered in smoke, so he bombed a secondary target, a bridge east of a tunnel, undershooting by some forty yards and to one side. Buckley, the last to attack, did not bomb as he could not make out the viaduct through the smoke. The secondary target was also out of the question, as the necessary run could not be made in time.

Perhaps Macintosh had done better than he knew, for according to the US Strategic Bombing Survey Report afterwards only one bomb did any worthwhile damage, by exploding in the centre of the track between the tunnel portal and the viaduct's eastern abutment, destroying thirty metres of track as well as part of the portal's face and the tunnel's lining.

The PFF Mosquitoes should have dropped yellow TI markers at Arnsberg, but none were seen. Two from each squadron had been allocated to each of the two targets, but three of 109 Sqdn's aircraft had developed technical trouble. Their fourth, a reserve, was not called in and the two 105 Sqdn Mosquitoes allocated to this target did not attack for some unstated reason. 109 Sqdn's diarist was apologetic: 'It was unfortunate that all our aircraft had technical failures, but as the targets were clear of cloud the heavies had good visuals and did a very good job.'

Not good enough, for despite all this the Arnsberg viaduct still stood. Perhaps the PFF contribution would have made a difference if it had gone ahead as planned.

Nor were the clouds entirely absent. After 617's gaggle had skirted Bremen and neared the lunar landscape at Bielefeld it was noted that Sod's Law had intervened and there was cloud on the north side. Calder therefore went round and approached from the south while Flt Lt John Benison, his navigator, gave the bomb aimer, Flt Lt Clifford Crafer, amended SABS settings in very quick time.

Behind and below them was the 627 Sqdn Mosquito, with its film crew. Crafer switched on the sight, then gave Calder a couple of minor corrections as they approached the viaduct. One of the two 105 Sqdn Mosquitoes had dropped four 250lb TIs, which gleamed yellow some 300yds south-south-west of the target.

Finally, at 1628 and from a height of 11,965 feet, Crafer pressed the release, allowing ten tons of alloy and Torpex to plummet earthwards. Like some monstrous black salmon, the Lancaster then leapt 500 feet, causing Crafer to bang his head on the top of the bomb-aimer's compartment. For thirty-five seconds the bomb fell, spinning as it went, and there was a brief spurt of mud as it speared into the battered marshy ground.

And the earth moved! The Bielefeld viaduct's remains after Squadron Leader Calder's Grand Slam near-miss on 14 March 1945. (IWM neg. no. C5086)

An undershoot, perhaps by no more than thirty yards. Was that enough of a near miss? Calder was past it now and turning. Another eleven seconds. Fame or a court-martial?

Abruptly a vast cloud of mud and smoke spewed skywards, quickly swallowed up by more eruptions as the Tallboys fell around the viaduct. Calder did not see the Grand Slam go up, but someone who did was W/O Player, the pilot of the film Mosquito. With a yell of 'You've done it!' in his ears, Calder peeled off from the gaggle to see what had happened.

Now the smoke wafted away and below him was something that looked like an ancient ruin. A total of 460 feet of masonry had collapsed from both the north and south viaducts, taking seven spans down into the mud below. Calder could see no debris between the piers. Had this bomb pulverised the stone? It hardly seemed possible.

Compared with that even the Tallboys seemed puny, although as they fell at around the same time they too may well have contributed to the collapse. Several crews claimed direct hits or near misses, while a hit by one on the south-western approaches blocked all the lines as well.

However, not all went smoothly. Carey's aircraft had to return without bombing when his sight became unserviceable just before his crew began their bomb run. Sayers began to open his bomb doors at 1612, only to have his Tallboy fall through and damage them. Rawes, unable to see the target, did a second run from Bielefeld, but followed a road to the south of it and dropped his bomb on an autobahn bridge, not realising what he had done until it was too late.

Coming along behind all of them to photograph the results was Flg-Off Fray of 542 Sqdn. His deep blue unarmed Spitfire was attacked three times by a pair of FW 190s, but he escaped them by dodging into cirrus cloud. A 540 Sqdn Mosquito's coverage also confirmed what had occurred.

It was later estimated that 20,000 tons of masonry had fallen, undermined by the Grand Slam and two of the Tallboys. In Calder's Lancaster the relief was considerable, but the real celebrations would have to wait until they reached home. The Grand Slam aircraft still had to be flown, and handled carefully. It would not do to have another accident now, especially not with Fauquier waiting to grill them at the other end.

Fauquier did indeed have a certain amount to say, but although he never quite forgave Jock Calder or his crew for stealing his thunder he was big enough to put his own feelings to one side and recommend Calder for a Bar to his DSO. There was surprise and relief all round. Constantine added to the celebratory atmosphere: 'You certainly made a proper mess of it this time and incidentally added another page to your history by being the first squadron to drop the biggest bomb on Germany. Good work. Keep up the training. We can't afford to put them in the wrong place.'

Following this raid the BI Specials were dubbed 'clapper aircraft', for, as the squadron put it, after you had dropped the Grand Slam the Lancaster went like the clappers!

After all his hard work, Reg Firman received a pleasant surprise when 617 passed Calder's bomb-slip on to him as a souvenir: 'It was a good way of thanking me. So we all had a drink.'

Others who had cause to breathe again were the inhabitants of the villages of Brake and Schildesche, near the viaduct. Now that it was in ruins there was no longer any danger of them being bombed. Perhaps they would see this war out after all.

15 March 1945
Target Arnsberg railway viaduct.
Weather Hazy conditions, with some thin cloud over the target.

Force 14 Lancasters of 9 Sqdn:

NF929 'P' Flt Lt G. C. Camsell		NG419 'U' Flg-Off M. L. T. Harper
NG384 'T' Flt Lt A. F. Jones		PA172 'G' Flg-Off A. E. Jeffs

The scene at Woodhall Spa's bomb dump as another Grand Slam is prepared for the attack on the Arnsberg viaduct on 15 March 1945. (IWM neg. no. CH15368)

NG486 'A' Flt Lt D. Macintosh	NG495 'R' Flg-Off A. L. Keeley
NG442 'F' Flt Lt B. Taylor	NG235 'H' Flg-Off S. Laws
LM220 'Y' Flt Lt W. D. Tweddle	HK791 'M' Flg-Off W. Scott
NG206 'J' Flg-Off K. C. Arndell	NG487 'D' Flg-Off J. E. Stowell
NG249 'S' Flg-Off R. W. Ayrton	PB696 'V' Flg-Off J. C. Wiley

Two Lancasters of 617 Sqdn:
PB996 'C' Sqdn Ldr C. C. Calder   PD114 'B' Sqdn Ldr J. V. Cockshott

Escort 34 Mustang IIIs of 11 Group:
234 Sqdn RAF   309 Sqdn (Polish)
306 Sqdn (Polish)   315 Sqdn (Polish)

Bomb Loads
9 Sqdn – all aircraft carried Tallboys, with an 11-second delay.
617 Sqdn – both aircraft carried Grand Slams, also with an 11-second delay.

One 627 Sqdn Mosquito as a camera aircraft:
KB433 'Z' W/O H. W. Player and P/O C. B. Heath

The Vlotho bridge, as seen from
Flying Officer A. L. Keeley's
Lancaster.

Although only four squadrons were employed as close escort, there was a total of 175
fighters in overall support, also covering a raid by 4, 6 and 8 Groups on the oil plants
at Bottrop and Castrop-Rauxel.

9 Sqdn were off at 1300, and met no opposition, but by the time they arrived over
Arnsberg visibility was poor. The 627 Sqdn Mosquito crew had the best overall view
of the attack. Player and Heath reported that the 'whole force made one run into sun
and one bomb seen to drop.'

This was probably Cockshott's Grand Slam, dropped from 13,600 feet at 1658.
It was followed one minute later by Stowell's Tallboy. Calder did not bomb due to
his Grand Slam being 'not required.' Player and Heath continued their observation:
'Second run into sun and one or two bombs fell. Individual runs then made. No direct
hits seen. Majority of bombs fell to the east.'

The first two Tallboys, the second of which was dropped by Macintosh, fell close to
the viaduct, leading him to claim that it had collapsed. However, it had not, and their
effect was to cover it with smoke, preventing any detailed observation. Macintosh
noted that the mouth of the nearby tunnel had been cratered, but this had been
inflicted by him the day before. The haze led Harper, Jones and Laws to all attack a
bridge at the eastern end of that tunnel.

Taylor failed to see the viaduct at first, then found it covered with smoke during
the reciprocal run, and so did not bomb. Neither did Scott or Wiley, for the same
reason. Jeffs did, and so did Ayrton, but he was the last to attack, his Tallboy falling
into the smoke. Arndell suffered his Tallboy dropping through the doors en route, but
nevertheless kept his place in the gaggle.

On his return Jones' port inner engine overspeeded and could not be feathered. He
ordered his crew to don their parachutes, and then, when oil flowing out from behind
the propeller caught fire, they were told to bail out fifteen miles south of Arnsberg.
Four did so, but after this the fire died out and Jones nursed the Lancaster down to a
safe forced landing at Gosselies airfield near Brussels, with assistance from Tweddle's
crew, who had obtained permission to stay with him and had then checked the
airfield's suitability by landing there first.

It seems likely that Calder had not attacked on the first run due to the haze, and
was doubtful of getting his Grand Slam close to the viaduct on subsequent runs, so he
flew back to Manston with it still on board. He had been fortunate at Bielefeld, but
was not about to push his luck a second time. The Arnsberg viaduct still stood, but
once again the reprieve would be a short one.

19 March 1945
Target Vlotho railway bridge (9) and Arnsberg railway viaduct (617)
Weather Up to four-tenths high cloud, with patches of thin cloud below.

Force 18 Lancasters of 9 Sqdn:

NG278 'N' Sqdn Ldr J. D. Melrose	PA172 'G' Flg-Off C. M. T. Follett
NF929 'P' Flt Lt R. E. Adams	NG419 'U' Flg-Off M. L. T. Harper
NG499 'W' Flt Lt R. J. Harris	NG486 'A' Flg-Off A. E. Jeffs
NG242 'C' Flt Lt D. Macintosh	NG495 'R' Flg-Off A. L. Keeley
LL845 'L' Flt Lt A. M. Morrison	NG235 'H' Flg-Off S. Laws
NG442 'F' Flt Lt B. Taylor	NG249 'S' Flg-Off R. C. Macdonald
LM220 'Y' Flt Lt W. D. Tweddle	PB696 'V' Flg-Off W. G. Rees
NG206 'J' Flg-Off K. C. Arndell	HK791 'M' Flg-Off W. Scott
NG220 'B' Flg-Off R. W. Ayrton	LM217 'O' Flg-Off J. C. Wiley

19 Lancasters of 617 Sqdn:

PD119 'J' Gp Capt. J. E. Fauquier	NC113 Flt Lt D. A. Rawes
NG445 'E' Sqdn Ldr C. C. Calder	PB997 'E' Flt Lt J. L. Sayers
PD238 'H' Sqdn Ldr J. Y. Cockshott	LM485 'U' Flt Lt K. L. Trent
PD121 'S' Sqdn Ldr J. L. Powell	LM489 'A' Flt Lt J. C. Warburton
PB998 'D' Flt Lt S. A. Anning	ME562 'K' Lt W. Adams USAAF
PD116 'A' Flt Lt J. B. Dobson	PD132 'X' Flg-Off D. W. Carey
PD131 'V' Flt Lt H. Y. Gavin	PD129 'O' Flg-Off M. B. Flatman
PD130 'U' Flt Lt S. Goodman	PB996 'C' Flg-Off P. H. Martin
PD126 Flt Lt B. A. Gumbley	PD415 'O' Flg-Off J. W. Speirs
PD118 'M' Flt Lt C. N. Hill	

From now on, due to the YZ codes used by the BI Specials, there would be some duplication of individual aircraft letters within 617 Sqdn.

Escort 88 Mustang IIIs of 11 Group:

118 Sqdn RAF	165 Sqdn RAF	306 Sqdn (Polish)
122 Sqdn RAF	234 Sqdn RAF	309 Sqdn (Polish)
129 Sqdn RAF		316 Sqdn (Polish)

Bomb Loads
9 Sqdn – all aircraft carried one Tallboy each, with an 11-second delay.
617 Sqdn – Fauquier, Gavin, Goodman, Gumbley, Flatman and Martin all carried Grand Slams. The remainder carried Tallboys. All bombs had an 11-second delay.

One Lancaster of 463 Sqdn RAAF as a camera aircraft:
PD329 'Y' Flt Lt T. A. Berry
In addition to its seven-man crew this aircraft carried two RAF Film Unit photographers, P/O Buckland and Sgt Peace.

Flg-Off Phil Martin, an RAAF pilot who had won the DFC and Bar during his two tours with 61 and 617, later vividly described his memorable introduction to Grand Slam:

'Remember', said the Groupie [Fauquier], 'if you have to bring the bomb back you can't drop the aircraft more than six inches on to the runway. If you do, the tyres will burst.' If anyone among us sitting in that Nissen hut had had a pin and dropped it, it would have sounded like an unexploded Tallboy hitting a steel floor.

Fauquier went on with his briefing. His previous comment was just one in a string of pearls of wisdom we mentally fingered as we came out of the briefing room, knowing we were to fly the op to obliterate the Arnsberg viaduct with one of the biggest bombs ever made – the awesome Grand Slam.

The first doubts had tip-toed into our minds when we saw the mother and father of all trucks wheel onto the airfield at Woodhall Spa, all big wheels and thick tyres. This was the beginning of our brief encounter with Barnes Wallis' ten-ton brainchild. On that truck was the business section of a monstrous bomb. Another truck followed, loaded with the Grand Slam's tail section. All this lethal ironmongery was eventually to be bolted together and hung under one Lancaster. Ours.

'No worries', said Chiefy, watching our faces as that incredible cavalcade inched past. 'We've fitted stronger tyres on the Lanc.' 'Fine', said the aircrew, 'but we've only got two wheels.' 'Well, don't corner too fast on the perimeter track', replied the flight sergeant.

We could think of no suitable retort but knew no normal aircraft could ever get off the deck with that weight hanging under it. The only kite that could even make a brave stab at the job, pregnant with this enormous bombload, had to be the Lancaster. And the Lancaster I was to fly was no ordinary Lanc. It didn't even look like a complete aircraft.

Probably because it was only the second of its type, the armament on PB996 was arranged differently from that on subsequent BI Specials.

Flown in from some other establishment, this machine had an orphan, unfinished look about it, as though it had been pushed out of the nest before it had properly hatched. The mid-upper turret was gone and the hole faired over. The front turret was minus one gun, the rear turret minus a brace of the comforting Browning foursome. There was ammunition for a two-second burst per gun. After that it was a case of disassemble the Brownings and hurl them at the enemy in an airman-like manner, no doubt.

We would carry no wireless-operator or W/T sets this trip. The navigator had been deseated from his normal alloy and leather throne, and was to ensconse himself in a cane chair as part of the fight against a ten-ton weight penalty. The pilot – me – was to feel rather exposed about his derriere with the armour plate taken out from under the driver's seat. I cannot recall if we were deprived of the Elsan's weight.

It might have led to unfortunate consequences if they had. 'Ordinary' trips were hairy enough, but this was something else.

The Lancaster's fuselage had been scooped out along the under belly from about the pilot's position, thirty-three feet rearwards to make a great gouge into which to fit the Grand Slam. Fuelling was a case of metering enough fuel for the flight out and back with no frills. Not even an extra one hundred gallons for the gremlins. When the bomb was hoisted into position and clutched in a pair of crane-grab arms secured with an electro-mechanical release unit, it looked lonely, almost appealing in its solitude, but also unbelievably lethal.

I looked at the loaded Lanc. All I could think of was, 'It looks as though we're carting a Spitfire fuselage. But it's probably the best armour plating we've ever had – no flak from below would ever get through to the cockpit.'

The day was fine as we started engines and began leaving dispersal. As we tried to move, we forgot the weather and wondered how much power we would have to apply to overcome the inertia and reach a satisfactory break-out force merely to move this massive load of nuts, bolts and high explosive.

We got underway – a loose term for a slow waddle; oleos bottoming at the slightest hint of surface undulation; flatfooted; incredibly lifeless and spongy. I knew – we all knew – that take-off would be a time of trying to coax a hopelessly overloaded aircraft off the runway in the face of logical impossibility.

It was. Full bore on the brakes after we had lined up. Release the binders, and begin lumbering forward like a tired carthorse pulling a loaded coal cart. Those four Rolls-Royce Merlins were building up to their superb crackling best as the throttle levers went forward like life members of the 'Throttle-Benders' Club.

Speed. More speed. And it came so slowly. The temptation to shove those throttle levers through the gate into emergency boost, but knowing we still had a long journey ahead of us. The runway's end at Woodhall Spa getting closer, literally looming ahead like the end of the world, and still no lightening feeling of wings taking over from the battering wheels.

This can't be flying. 'Wheels up!' as we trundled alarmingly slowly over the bitumen's end. We staggered. We wallowed. But the Lancaster was airborne, somehow and against all the rules of aerodynamics. Then came that sinking feeling as the wheels began retracting and wings were asked to promote an airflow which would somehow get this thing flying.

Wonder of wonders, it flew; if staggering though the English air in this fashion could even loosely be called flying. Then came the battle to actually gain a few feet of altitude. It was a fine day – most of us remember that. But we don't recall how many buildings, chimney pots, hayricks and what-have-you we flew round on that crazy departure from Woodhall Spa, en route to the coast.

We were proceeding at less than a hundred feet. In retrospect, I feel our climb pattern must have looked rather like the trace of a mad temperature chart graph, of a patient in extremis from triple influenza. Gain a few precious feet and try to stop counting grass blades. Milk up a few degrees of flap and loose that height again. Fly round a church, a building, Merlins howling, knowing full well that if we met a bus in the road we'd have to fly through the damned thing. This went on, sweat oozing into my battledress, until we had retracted flap and fed more fuel to the engines, thus lightening the load by a scant few pounds.

The Lancaster crossed the British coast at about 1,000 feet, the Tallboy Lancasters in our force beginning to form up loosely astern. Anyone looking down from above would have been justified in thinking this force was composed of mother taking the chicks for a flight. From memory, we crossed the enemy coast at about 6,000 feet, thanks to constant fuel consumption and precious little else apart from sheer hand-flying, feeling for each foot of height. But it still felt low enough to be clobbered by a rock thrown up by some stray German soldier or flak gunner.

H-Hour had been set at 1100 for both targets, and for most of the force the flight out would have been uneventful if it had not been for the loss of Flt Lt S. Sawicki, a Mustang pilot of 309 Sqdn, who due to engine trouble force-landed, while still carrying his drop tanks, in a ploughed field next to Essex City Hospital. The fighter caught fire and Sawicki died from burns despite being pulled clear by some of the hospital's patients.

129 Sqdn assessed the bomber formation as very compact, but noted that they flew in cloud at 14,000ft, which did not make the task of escort an easy one. There was some heavy flak in the Bonn area and from Alkmaar on the Dutch coast as the formation returned.

By now some SABS sights had come into use with 9 Sqdn, whose target spanned the river Weser, north-east of the town of Herford and near Minden. Ray Harris was late at a rendezvous point and was ordered to return to base. Morrison turned back when his starboard inner engine became unserviceable and Adams, being caught in someone else's slipstream, was unable to contact his leader until after the bombing was completed. Of the fifteen who did attack, Macintosh later said that the first Tallboy overshot by 300 yards, and according to Graham Rees it sank a barge. The next two were fifty-yard overshoots. Several then fell together, creating a concentration, but it was not close enough and the bridge was left standing, although one span had been blown out of alignment by a near miss which had exploded sixty feet away.

617 approached their target over what for them was historic territory. There was the Möhne dam below, with up to eight balloons around it and a smokescreen in use. Flg-Off Len Sumpter had recently returned to 617 after a spell on instructing at 85

OTU, and it would have been highly appropriate for him to take part in this raid. However, he would not be going back into action just yet.

Chastise seemed a lifetime ago. Events had moved on, and the target that now mattered had no defences apart from some flak, probably also from the hills around the dam, that now stained the sky ahead.

Flt Lt Berry's camera crew had been given the task of filming the attack made by Phil Martin's BI Special, and as he neared the target they were flying to starboard of him. Berry's Lancaster carried no bombs at all, so his bomb aimer, if he was still carrying one, may have felt redundant and perhaps envious of the awesome weapon about to be used in front of him.

One cameraman had been installed in Berry's front turret and the other in a position to film underneath his bomber. By this means it was hoped to film the ten-tonner as it fell away, followed by an accurate impact below. As they neared the target Berry fell back behind Martin, below his port quarter. Martin reflected on the advice given him by 617's Bombing Leader, who was accompanying his crew on this operation.

All through, I remembered the Bombing Leader's warning. 'Don't drop under 14,000 feet or you'll get the benefit of shock waves.' This was perhaps the funniest part of the whole operation. He might just as well have told us not to drop this bomb until we reached the black side of the moon.

We managed to coax this flying bomb up to about 12,700 feet. And there she stayed, governed by the law of gravity and that dam' great bomb hanging under there like an overgrown pilot fish under a whale's belly. We began attracting predictor-guided flak as the viaduct neared, and the bomb aimer set up his SABS sight. This was where the fun really began.

We were committed to a five-minute straight and level bombing run after the sight had been set up, win, lose or draw. I concentrated on flying the Lancaster to the tolerances demanded by the SABS sight – within half a mile an hour of airspeed, and plus or minus ten feet of height – during those five minutes. Everything had to be forgotten if the bomb was to go down on target. Everything but flying.

Behind him, in Berry's Lancaster the front turret camera started running. Martin braced himself for what was to come.

I had dropped Tallboys and knew what the upward spring was on release. But this Grand Slam was a beauty. I heard the release unit 'fire' with its usual sharp retort, and the slam of those great arms hitting the fuselage as they came free. That Grand Slam, spinning impeccably, went down. And we went UP. Lord, how we ascended. Most of us made it six hundred feet upwards, the Lancaster's wings flexing and reflexing like an overstrung bow – and we were the human arrow.

The Grand Slam release sequence that Berry's crew filmed has since become well known. The giant bomb fell away, starting to spin as it did so, the Lancaster leapt upwards out of the shot and the results were all that anyone could have wished for. Afterwards Berry reported that he 'saw Tallboy Large hit western span, and the whole span disintegrated, and roofs and houses disappeared, and on our second run round just a crater was left.' He also mentioned feeling a slight vibration at 13,000 ft, although he did not say whether this was due to the bomb! Back in the aircraft it had just left, Martin had something else to contend with.

Strange noises emanated from the bomb aimer's compartment down in the nose, as my bomb aimer, Don Day, and the man crouching by his shoulder-Bombing Leader Sqdn Leader Jim Moody – became entangled like a pair of Saturday night stadium all-in wrestlers. I couldn't see our Grand Slam descending. Regulations demanded that I fly the Lancaster straight and level until the bomb hit. As it struck the viaduct, I banked to

Bomb gone! One of the cameramen in Flight Lieutenant TA Berry's 463 Squadron Lancaster films a Grand Slam as it falls away from Flying Officer P. H. Martin's BI Special on 19 March 1945. This was one of six Grand Slams aimed at the Arnsberg railway viaduct. (IWM neg. no. CH15374)

port to see for myself what I had unleashed. In actual fact, no human thumb pushed the button – it had all been done by clockwork after the SABS sight was set on the target.

Down below, a magnificent pattern of concentric shockwave circles was shuddering out, the apex being where the viaduct had once arched. Tallboys were already slamming into the circles, creating cross-circle patterns. All the other bombs were released, in the air and curling wonderfully downward when the Grand Slam struck. An immense feeling of lightness and power flowed through the stick as the Lancaster drew breath, delivered of its mammoth babe. The aircraft felt light, responsive, full of bellowing power – in fact, like a Lancaster again.

Everyone bombed except Sayers, whose Tallboy had fallen out on 14 March. Now its successor could not be got rid of! Fauquier noted that the 'bombing had a tendency to overshoot, but about a third of the viaduct appeared to be down. There were two hits on the embankment to the north of the bridge.'

Two runs were considered necessary and there was a general opinion that the first four bombs overshot, but that the rest were well concentrated. Trent reckoned that part of the viaduct had definitely come down after the first run, while Goodman said that 'five bombs exploded together and were all around AP. About quarter of viaduct broken down. One wide bomb quarter mile south of target on 2nd run.' This was Gumbley's Grand Slam, which actually fell fifty yards to one side due to an SABS fault.

Arnsberg viaduct could finally be crossed off the list, as two arches and one pier in the middle had been destroyed. This time there was no crater in the centre, but a large cone of debris was left in the river. The track on the west bank had also been cut by a crater, part of an embankment had been shifted out of alignment and a tunnel entrance on the east bank had been blocked. Again, the nearby Red Cross camp was not touched. Phil Martin's crew turned for home along with the others.

Losing height on the way back, we broke out the Thermos. We had had no time or inclination to do so on the outward flight. And all the time, that Lanc was feeling more and more like a Spitfire on a fighter affiliation exercise – no weight, all urge and a dream to handle.

And so we came home, back to Woodhall Spa. A time of calling, 'funnel', remembering the other five aircraft in the circuit as we touched, feather-light, on the bitumen with no need to recall the group captain's doleful warning about not dropping more than six inches to the deck. It was one of the lightest landings I ever made. It felt rather as one does after having carried a heavy load – as if one was some inches off the ground, all hollow and indescribably airy.

We were back in time for tea. And I never flew that particular Lancaster again. Ours was a brief encounter, and I think she forgave us for the bawdy, curious looks we shot her when we saw her standing there, incomplete as if put together by someone who didn't care.

This time the intact noses of two earthquake bombs, one of each type, did not fully function and they came to light at the war's end. The Grand Slam still had some of its explosive filling in it. It was thought to have become unstable and landed on a road, causing part of the explosive to go off but leaving the rest in the nose intact. The Tallboy struck a masonry wall, whose structure caused it to break up and bury itself in the ground nearby without exploding.

Despite the increasing use of Grand Slam, there was evidently another Tallboy shortage at this time. On 20 March, 9 Sqdn, escorted by forty-nine 8th Air Force P-51s, attacked a railway bridge at Nienberg with 68 tons of 1,000lb MC bombs. Some sticks straddled and probably damaged it, but it was still standing afterwards. There was a sense of unfinished business here, as at Vlotho, but it would have to wait for now.

21 March 1945
Target The Arbergen railway bridge.
Weather Good visibility with little cloud.

Force 20 Lancasters of 617 Sqdn:

PD119	'J'	Gp Capt. J. E. Fauquier	NG494	'B'	Flt Lt C. N. Hill
PB996	'C'	Sqdn Ldr C. C. Calder	NG489	'M'	Flt Lt G. W. Lancey
PD114	'B'	Sqdn Ldr J. V. Cockshott	PD118	'M'	Flt Lt G. R. Price
PD115	'K'	Sqdn Ldr W. H. Gordon	PD113	'T'	Flt Lt D. A. Rawes
PD133	'P'	Sqdn Ldr J. L. Powell	NG445	'E'	Flt Lt J. L. Sayers
LM695	'N'	Flt Lt S. A. Anning	PD238	'H'	Flt Lt K. L. Trent
PD130	'W'	Flt Lt B. J. Dobson	PD128	'N'	Flt Lt J. C. Warburton
PD116	'A'	Flt Lt H. V. Gavin	PB997	'E'	Flg-Off D. W. Carey
PB998	'D'	Flt Lt L. S. Goodman	NG339	'G'	Flg-Off M. B. Flatman
PD117	'L'	Flt Lt B. A. Gumbley	PD129	'O'	Flg-Off J. W. Speirs

Escort 20 Mustang IIIs of 11 Group:
306 Sqdn (Polish)   309 Sqdn (Polish)
Five other 11 Group squadrons acted as escort to the Main Force raid on Bremen detailed below.

Bomb Loads Except for Fauquier and Calder, with Grand Slams, all aircraft carried one Tallboy each. All bombs had an 11-second delay.

133 Lancasters and 6 Mosquitoes of 1 and 8 Groups attacked the Deutsche Vacuum oil refinery at Bremen. Other Main Force squadrons raided the towns of Münster and Rheine.

The Arbergen railway bridge was a 200-yard-long double-track one, consisting of three spans of steel girders, which crossed the Weser near the town of Nienburg, south-east of Bremen. The line approached it from the south-west by an embankment until it was 460 yards from the river, when it crossed a flood meadow by a long low steel viaduct raised on piers.

Probably alerted by the Main Force attack, this time the defences were stronger and Fauquier's Lancaster was hit no fewer than six times by flak. Due to the same sighting fault that had affected Gumbley at Arnsberg two days before, his Grand Slam fell 200yds north of the bridge, although Carey put it and Calder's much closer. Gordon saw some Tallboys fall on the south end of the target, with three in the river close to the bridge.

Gavin had little luck – his SABS went unserviceable just after the bomb run started, so he followed the rest of the gaggle in and released manually. His port outer engine then caught fire, and as he turned away from the target he was shot at by a German jet fighter, but he put the fire out and returned.

Gumbley was hit by heavy flak in the target area and his crew dived earthwards in flames. Evidently their Tallboy was still on board, for the resulting explosion blasted a crater ten metres deep at Okel, near the town of Syke, some twelve miles south of Bremen. There had been no time for anyone to bail out. Price's crew had to swing to avoid the burning Lancaster as it fell ahead of them, but he quickly resumed his heading and carried on.

Flak hit four other aircraft. Sayers was unlucky yet again, being affected by someone's slipstream, so he aimed his Tallboy at a railway junction to the north of the bridge.

Timing had been tight and all the bombs that were dropped fell within one minute. Two spans of the viaduct on the south-western approach to the bridge were brought down by two Tallboy hits which caused their piers to collapse. The two bombs went

The destruction of the Arbergen railway bridge by Grand Slams and Tallboys on 21 March 1945, as Squadron Leader Cockshott's crew fly overhead. (IWM neg. no. C5102)

into the earth under these piers, causing them to collapse into the resulting craters. The shock of another Tallboy's near miss threw an adjoining viaduct span off its other pier. At the north-eastern end of this breach another adjoining span was thrown fifteen feet out of alignment. Other craters cut the river bank, causing flooding.

Although the bridge itself had not been brought down, the cutting of the viaducts at each side of it meant that it was now of no use to the Germans. It was later demolished in an attempt to make the Allies' passage across the Weser more difficult, although this did not hold them up for very long. It was, thankfully, one target to which 617 would not have to return.

22 March 1945
Target Bremen railway bridge (9) and Nienburg railway bridge (617).
Weather Clear, with good visibility.

Force 17 Lancasters of 9 Sqdn:

HK803 'Q' Flt Lt R. F. Adams	NG495 'R' Flg-Off A. L. Keeley
NF929 'P' Flt Lt G. C. Camsell	NG206 'J' Flg-Off P. C. Langdon
PA172 'G' Flt Lt L. E. Marsh	NG235 'H' Flg-Off S. Laws
HK791 'M' Flt Lt E. G. R. Morgan	NG242 'C' Flg-Off W. Scott
LL845 'L' Flt Lt A. M. Morrison	NG486 'A' Flg-Off J. E. Stowell
LM220 'Y' Flt Lt W. D. Tweddle	LM278 Flg-Off E. I. Waters
NG249 'S' Flg-Off H. Anderson	NG487 'D' Flg-Off A. F. Williams
LM217 'O' Flg-Off R. W. Ayrton	NG499 'W' P/O J. C. Graves
NG442 'F' Flg-Off J. R. Macdonnell	

Eighteen aircraft had been detailed, but Flg-Off Rees and his crew were unable to take part due to a burnt-out starter motor. 9 Sqdn's ORB states that LM220 'Y' was flown on this date by both Camsell and Tweddle, but this was corrected by the Bardney ORB.

20 Lancasters of 617 Sqdn:

NG445 'E' Gp Capt. J. E. Fauquier	PD238 'H' Flt Lt R. M. Horsley
NG225 'V' Sqdn Ldr J. F. Brookes	NG489 'M' Flt Lt G. W Lancey
PD115 'K' Sqdn Ldr C. C. Calder	PD135 'W' Flt Lt D. R. Price
PD114 'B' Sqdn Ldr J. V. Cockshott	PD997 'E' Flt Lt D. A. Rawes
PB996 'C' Sqdn Ldr W. H. Gordon	PD132 'X' Flt Lt J. A. Sayers
PD112 'Z' Sqdn Ldr J. L. Powell	LM485 'U' Flt Lt K. L. Trent
PD639 'P' Flt Lt S. A. Anning	PD138 'N' Flt Lt J. C. Warburton
PD134 'Y' Flt Lt H. V. Gavin	PD131 'V' Flg-Off D. W. Carey
PB415 'O' Flt Lt L. S. Goodman	LM695 'N' Flg-Off M. B. Flatman
NG494 'B' Flt Lt C. N. Hill	PD121 'S' Flg-Off J. W. Speirs

Escort Reputedly 114 Mustang IIIs and 69 Spitfire IXs of 11 Group, covering this as well as the four Main Force attacks, but no further details are available.

Bomb Loads
9 Sqdn – all aircraft carried one Tallboy each. Half of these had a delay of one hour, and the rest for 25-35 minutes.
617 Sqdn – six Grand Slams, with delays of 25-30 seconds, were carried by Cockshott, Gordon, Powell, Gavin, Rawes and Anning. The rest carried one Tallboy each, with a delay of either 25-35 seconds or one hour.

Including 9 Sqdn, eighty-two Lancasters attacked the Bremen bridge, the remainder being from 5 Group's 53 Base. On this day there were four other major Bomber Command attacks against the towns of Hildesheim, Dülmen, Dorsten and Bocholt.

The fact that all these targets could be attacked in daylight with the loss of just four Lancasters indicates how weak the Luftwaffe had now become.

The Bremen railway bridge, which crossed the Weser, was double-track, 720ft long and consisted of five spans of steel bowstring girders. 9 Sqdn's Tallboys fell amid the sticks of conventional bombs dropped by the rest of 5 Group, whose targets included a nearby road bridge and marshalling yards.

Tweddle did not attack as his port inner engine failed after take-off, necessitating a return to Bardney. On his run in Camsell was hit by heavy flak in his bomb doors, wings and fuselage as well as both his starboard engines, forcing him to jettison his Tallboy and limp back to RAF Ludham in Norfolk. Smoke was visible for up to ninety-five miles on their return, but as far as the railway bridge was concerned, neither the Tallboys nor the conventional loads did any useful damage and it remained standing.

617's bombing at Nienburg was tight, with most bombs falling within a minute. It had been arranged that the fourth and eighth rows of their gaggle would not bomb on the first or second runs. This meant that Brookes, Powell and Speirs did not bomb, but the five Grand Slams and twelve Tallboys that fell scored several direct hits, wrecking it from end to end. Flatman said, 'The first large bomb hit the bridge on the AP, and blew the bridge up. It collapsed into the water at the eastern end. There was a further direct hit in the centre.' Goodman commented that on their second run the whole bridge was seen to be submerged. All the spans had been either broken or torn off their piers.

Authority finally caught up with Grand Slam on this date, belatedly clearing the bomb for service, subject to the aircraft modifications and handling restrictions mentioned earlier.

23 March 1945
Target The railway bridges at Bad Oeynhausen (9) and Bremen (617).
Weather Clear – assessed as ideal for precision bombing.

Force 11 Lancasters of 9 Sqdn:

NG486 'A' Flt Lt E. G. R. Morgan	NG235 'H' Flg-Off J. R. Macdonnell
NG206 'J' Flt Lt B. Taylor	NG499 'W' Flg-Off W. G. Rees
LM220 'F' Flt Lt W. D. Tweddle	NG220 'B' Flg-Off J. E. Stowell
NG249 'S' Flg-Off H. Anderson	NG278 'N' Flg-Off E. I. Waters
PA172 'G' Flg-Off C. M. T. Follett	NG487 'D' Flg-Off A. F. Williams
NG495 'R' Flg-Off M. J. Irwin	

20 Lancasters of 617 Sqdn:

PD119 'J' Gp Capt. J. E. Fauqier	PD238 'H' Flt Lt R. M. Horsley
PD133 'P' Sqdn Ldr J. F. Brookes	NG489 'M' Flt Lt G. W. Lancey
PD112 'S' Sqdn Ldr C. C. Calder	PD113 'T' Flt Lt G. R. Price
PD114 'B' Sqdn Ldr J. V. Cockshott	PD132 'X' Flt Lt J. L. Sayers
PB998 'D' Sqdn Ldr W. H. Gordon	PD145 'K' Flt Lt K. L. Trent
PB996 'C' Sqdn Ldr J. L. Powell	LM695 'N' Flt Lt J. C. Warburton
PD118 'M' Flt Lt S. A. Anning	PD131 'V' Flg-Off D. W. Carey
PD134 'Y' Flt Lt H. V. Gavin	PB997 'E' Flg-Off M. B. Flatman
PB415 'O' Flt Lt L. S. Goodman	LM492 'W' Flg-Off J. H. Leavitt
NG494 'B' Flt Lt C. N. Hill	PD130 'U' Flg-Off J. W. Speirs

Escort 41 Mustang IIIs of 11 Group:
  122 Sqdn RAF   309 Sqdn (Polish)
  306 Sqdn (Polish)   316 Sqdn (Polish)
Seven other RAF Mustang squadrons gave overall cover to the Bremen force.

The Bad Oeynhausen bridge under attack, as seen from the 8-inch camera of Flying Officer J. E. Stowell's Lancaster.

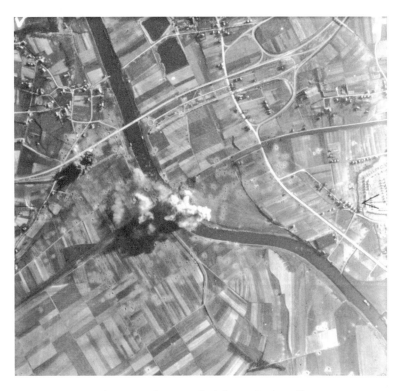

The same target, this time photographed from Flying Officer M. Anderson's Lancaster as the attack develops.

The last shot, taken by the 20-inch camera of Flying Officer Graham Rees, just after avoiding the Me 262.

Bomb Loads

   9 Sqdn – all aircraft carried one Tallboy each, with either an 11 or 25-second delay. 617 Sqdn – Fauquier, Calder, Cockshott, Powell, Gavin and Flatman all carried Grand Slams. The rest carried one Tallboy each. Half the Tallboys had a delay of 25-35 seconds and the rest for one hour. No details of Grand Slam fusing are available, but these were probably the same as for the previous raid.

9 and 617 were part of a force of 128 Lancasters of 1 and 5 Groups, most of which attacked the bridge at Bremen. Two Lancasters were lost from this raid. There was also an attack by 80 Lancasters of 3 Group on the town of Wesel, in preparation for the amphibious crossing of the Rhine that would shortly follow.

   The target at Bad Oeynhausen consisted of two bridges side by side. Like Vlotho, it was near the town of Minden in north-west Germany. (In their book *The Bomber Command War Diaries* Martin Middlebrook and Chris Everitt speculated that as both the Bad Oeynhausen and Vlotho bridges were near Minden, they might have been one and the same target. However, aiming point photographs taken by 9 Sqdn on 19 and 23 March show that this was not so.)

   The escort's rendezvous with the bombers went according to plan and twenty miles west of Bad Oeynhausen the bombers split into two formations, one flying to starboard while the other turned to port through 360 degrees. As the two formations regained their original course, seven Me 262s dived out of the sun and attacked 309 Sqdn, who lost no aircraft but claimed to have damaged one of the jets. This attack and the escort's response set the pattern for what was to follow.

Flg-Off Graham Rees described 9's version of the gaggle and what happened on the run up to the target, 'Four of our aircraft were fitted with windfinding equipment – 'O', 'S', 'W' and my own, 'V'.'

Looking at the eleven Lancasters 9 fielded on this occasion, it seems that only two of the above four were used, the other being flown by Flg-Off Anderson. However, according to 9's ORB Flg-Off Follett in PA172 'G' was also given the same task.

Two lines of aircraft would fly parallel in line astern, almost nose to tail, with no more than fifty feet difference in height between them. They would be stepped down, providing mutual firepower and in particular protecting the blind spot below the preceding aircraft. The first to bomb would be the highest, in the lead. The windfinders were always in the right-hand line, at the rear, and broke away. We rejoined the gaggle for the bomb run. This time I was to be at the back, half a minute behind the others, as I had a 20-inch wide lens camera fitted, to film the bomb bursts.

Before this the windfinding sequence had to be carried out:

You broke away from the gaggle, chose an easily distinguishable aiming point and ran up to it as for bombing. When the AP was in the bomb release position the bomb aimer would say, 'On', the navigator would switch on the machine and the pilot would fly on instruments, as accurately as possible, a Rate 1 turn, maintaining perfect height and speed, with neither sideslip nor skid, returning to the same AP in approximately three minutes, when, on the command of the bomb aimer the machine was switched to 'off'. It could be either way – I always turned to port.

The resultant windspeed and direction were then classified on a scale of one to four, depending on our estimate of the accuracy of the maneouvre. The results were sent to HQ by W/T, correlated there and the final figures transmitted to squadron, Group or Command, as the case may have been. The setting of a correct windspeed and direction as near as possible to the target was vital as the aircraft and the bomb travelled through air, which was always on the move.

Concentrating on instruments meant it was not possible for him to look out of the cockpit until the turn was completed. This time there was an unpleasant surprise.

Imagine my shock when looking out to port and seeing a silver Me 262 flying on my beam. I can only assume that he must have been puzzled by my strange behaviour in breaking away from the safety of my formation in a cloudless sky with perfect visibility and then performing this gentle turning circle. My gunners drew my attention to a US Mustang seen clearly on my starboard side, to whom I immediately gave a hand signal and received a 'thumbs up' in reply.

The escort were on a different radio wavelength, so I told the wireless-operator to put a red into the Very pistol. Then I took evasive action, diving under the Mustang and getting back into the formation, rolling the whole way – not corkscrewing as we couldn't see where the 262 was. It startled him when we fired the red flare.

I made my way rapidly to rejoin my squadron, now in bombing formation, and aimed for my allotted tail-end position, rolling all the while to search our underneath blindspot area. On joining the gaggle the Me 262 came up vertically from beneath, opened fire and hit the aircraft of Flying Officer Follett, who was directly in front of me. The Me rolled into a dive and was pounced upon by a line of Mustangs who came down at very high speed and disposed of him. A couple of days later I read an Intelligence Report of aerial combats for 23rd March 1945, which showed one Me 262 destroyed – credited on share to several USAAF officers.

Follett had just completed his windfinding and returned to the gaggle when the Me 262 attacked him. The impact of four 30mm cannon burst the Lancaster's tailwheel, hit its starboard elevator and trim tab, then ripped a hole some six feet square in his starboard wing. Through all this the four Merlins kept going, but his return flight to Bardney was only accomplished after the stick had been roped back and the Tallboy jettisoned.

Five other Me 262s orbited the target area but made no further attacks, probably due to the flak. These aircraft would have been from JG 7, the only Me 262 fighter unit available at this time. The identity of the Americans is not known. Some RAF escort pilots fired at other Me 262s, but only one kill claim was made.

Waters was hit by heavy flak on his bomb run, but pressed on despite his bomb aimer's sight of the bridge being hampered by a splintered clear vision panel. Hit twice again after bombing, he limped back to RAF Seething in Norfolk with two holed fuel tanks, both turrets and his port inner engine out of action.

Two other Lancasters were also hit, but despite all this 9 Sqdn's bombing was very concentrated. Irwin attempted a separate camera run but turned away without getting any shots as the heavy flak was becoming uncomfortably accurate. Graham Rees reported four Tallboys apparently on or close to the bridge, while Stowell described the results as three Tallboys overshooting, two very near misses and one possible hit. It was later seen that both parallel halves of this bridge had collapsed due to a near miss some sixty feet away. The squadron's accuracy was commended.

Now it was 617's turn to have their loads mixed in with the sticks dropped by 1 and 5 Groups. A smokescreen had been started, but it was just too late to prevent concentrated bombing. Fauquier saw two direct hits on the bridge, but smoke and debris quickly covered it. A problem with the constant speed unit on Powell's outer starboard engine had precluded him flying at the gaggle's speed, which meant an early return after he had reluctantly released his Grand Slam over a recognised jettison area. Calder bombed despite having his bomb aimer's clear vision panel also shattered by flak. Brookes, Gordon, Gavin and Horsley all reported at least three direct hits. Goodman's Tallboy overshot after hanging up for fifteen seconds after the cockpit's red light went out.

The Messerschmitt Me 262 jet fighter – an advanced design that made its delayed appearance in the daylight battles over Germany in 1945. It is indicative of the crumbling state of German morale in the final weeks of the war that this example was surrendered intact by a defecting Luftwaffe test pilot. (IWM neg. no. HU2744)

Three Tallboys were unused. Hill did not bomb as the bridge was obscured on his run-up and he was unsure of its exact location. Neither did Trent, who had experienced a complete oxygen failure and had been told by Fauquier to turn back. Sayers was unlucky again, also returning early with a failed starboard outer engine.

Anning and Warburton both claimed direct hits. Lancey's aircraft was hit ten seconds before bomb release, cutting the air pressure to the sight, but they released as soon as they had got back onto their run. No one on board was injured.

Despite the crews' claims it was found afterwards that just one bomb, probably a Tallboy, had hit the bank at the southern end of the bridge, about a hundred feet from the abutment. The earth shock from this had been enough to displace the abutment, causing its span to fall into the Weser. Another Tallboy hit the line north of the bridge and a third 250 yards to the south of it, but this was quickly repaired and track relaid over it. Finally the Germans demolished the remainder in a futile attempt to stop the Allies from crossing the river.

It was also on this date that three of the remaining *Chastise* Lancasters were brought back to life, not for another raid, but to dump the remaining live Upkeeps, minus their fuses, in the Atlantic. There was no longer any need to keep this weapon or its aircraft in reserve, for the dams that had been attacked in 1943 were going to be in the British Zone of north-western Germany once the war had ended. Further destruction of this sort would be pointless; there would be enough problems without the need to repair them a second time. It was a final acknowledgement by officialdom that *Chastise* had been a one-off.

As a result of this, no live Upkeeps are known to have survived. Those that are displayed in museums today are all concrete-filled practice ones that were salvaged from Reculver some thirty or more years after the war ended.

27 March 1945
Target An oil storage depot (9) and a U-boat shelter, (617) both at Farge.
Weather Clear visibility.

Force 15 Lancasters of 9 Sqdn:

HK803	'Q'	Flt Lt R. F. Adams	NG486	'A'	Flg-Off P. G. Langdon
NG499	'W'	Flt Lt R. J. Harris	NG235	'H'	Flg-Off J. R. Macdonnell
HK791	'M'	Flt Lt L. E. Marsh	PB696	'V'	Flg-Off W. G. Rees
LL845	'L'	Flt Lt E. G. R. Morgan	NG206	'J'	Flg-Off W. Scott
NG249	'S'	Flg-Off R. W. Ayrton	NG220	'B'	Flg-Off J. E. Stowell
NG487	'D'	Flg-Off M. H. Caven	NG419	'U'	Flg-Off E. I. Waters
NG442	'F'	Flg-Off C. M. T. Follett	LM217	'O'	Flg-Off J. C. Wiley
NG495	'R'	Flg-Off A. L. Keeley			

20 Lancasters of 617 Sqdn:

PD119	'J'	Gp Capt. J. E. Fauquier	PD129	'O'	Flt Lt J. H. Leavitt
PD131	'V'	Sqdn Ldr J. F. Brookes	PD115	'K'	Flt Lt I. M. Marshall
PD118	'M'	Sqdn Ldr C. C. Calder	?	'W'	Flt Lt J. C. McLaughlin
PD114	'B'	Sqdn Ldr J. V. Cockshott	PD128	'N'	Flt Lt G. R. Price
PD112	'Z'	Sqdn Ldr L. Powell	PD113	'Y'	Flt Lt. J. L. Sayers
PD139	'W'	Flt Lt S. A. Anning	PD116	'A'	Flt Lt K. L. Trent
PD238	'H'	Flt Lt G. L. Beaumont	LM695	'N'	Flt Lt J. C. Warburton
NG228	'V'	Flt Lt L. S. Goodman	PB997	'E'	Flg-Off D. W. Carey
LM485	'U'	Flt Lt C. N. Hill	PB996	'C'	Flg-Off M. B. Flatman
PD130	'U'	Flt Lt G. W. Lancey	NG539	'G'	Flg-Off J. W. Speirs

Escort 90 Mustang IIIs of 11 Group:

64 Sqdn RAF	126 Sqdn RAF	234 Sqdn RAF
118 Sqdn RAF	129 Sqdn RAF	316 Sqdn (Polish)
122 Sqdn RAF	165 Sqdn RAF	

Bomb Loads

9 Sqdn – all aircraft carried one Tallboy each, all with a half-hour delay, in order that smoke clouds would not obscure the target.

617 Sqdn – Beaumont, Goodman, Hill, Leavitt, McLaughlin, Warburton and Speirs carried Tallboys. The remaining thirteen aircraft carried Grand Slams. All these bombs had a delay of one hour.

9 Sqdn were part of 115 Lancasters of 5 Group, who attacked the oil storage depot. Other daylight raids were also made on the towns of Paderborn and Hamm.

Since the previous October construction work had been noted near the village of Farge, on the Weser five miles north of Vegesack and ten miles north-west of Bremen. Indeed, the building in question could hardly have been missed as it was a massive shelter, 1,375ft long by 315ft wide, built for the assembly of prefabricated Type XXI U-boat components. All this gave 1,400,000 cubic yards of space inside. Its walls and roof were almost 15ft thick, with a reinforced concrete roof. This, once again, was in the process of being increased to 23ft at the time of this raid. Two-thirds of it had already been carried out, and construction was continuing on the remainder.

During 1941, RAF attacks on the shipyards had led to the possibility of U-boat construction in bombproof shelters being looked at, and by November 1942 Hitler was demanding that they were to be built without delay. There had been two important yards in the Bremen area – Deutsche Schiff und Maschinenbau AG (Deschimag) at Bremen, and Bremer Schiff und Maschinenfabrik (Bremer Vulkan) at Vegesack. These were to be code-named *Hornisse* and *Valentin*.

The ground on which the Valentin shelter was to be built also came under Bremer Vulkan, although it was some distance from the Vegesack yard. Construction had started early in 1943, but just after this had begun a decision was made by the *Hauptausschuss Schiffbau* (Main Committee for Shipbuilding) in Speer's ministry for it to be converted to an assembly centre for the new Type XXI U-boat.

The shelter was sited close to the convex shore of a bend in the Weser, to minimise silting. Excavation and dredging had been carried out to a depth of 23ft, in order to get barged sections in and completed U-boats out. The eight sections of each U-boat of this type were to be fitted out at Hornisse and Wespe – the Blohm und Voss yards at Hamburg – with work being split between them. These parts would then go to Valentin for final assembly. There would therefore be no need for open slipways, which were vulnerable to Allied air attacks.

Sections would be brought to Valentin by barge and moved inside it by a 200-ton overhead crane. After twelve different assembly stages, a closing of gates would allow the dock the completed U-boat was now in to fill with water. It would then be floated to the thirteenth stage of final checking, and so out to the river.

The whole process was another version of the *Verbunkerung* technique. Component production was dispersed and U-boat sections were small targets whose final assembly would only take place under cover. Once again there would be little for the Allies to bomb.

The plan had been for U-boat production to begin in March 1945, with full capacity being attained by August. This would then have allowed the elimination of the Wespe and Hornisse yards. As things had turned out, production at Farge had not yet begun, but it was within two months of doing so and some machine tools had already been installed. Ninety per cent of the shelter had been completed.

The Type XXI U-boat turned out to be another might-have-been, but had it gone into action sooner it would have been a serious threat to Allied shipping. A very clean, modern design, it had been designed from the beginning for high submerged speed, attacking by sonar and hydrophone, without using its periscope. Due to its light, high-capacity batteries, it could remain underwater for up to three days without the need to surface. It was as well for the Allies that the deployment of these boats had been delayed by the need for lengthy crew training first. Only one patrol by a Type XXI, U-2511, would be made – from Bergen – before Germany surrendered.

Just how important *Valentin* could have been to the war at sea is indicated by the efforts made at the nearby Vegesack yard. This was the fifth most important shipbuilding plant in Germany, with seventy-eight Type VIIB and VIIC U-boats to its name. Several RAF raids had had little effect and a USAAF one in March 1943 had only stopped production for six weeks. Some U-boats had been hit but none had been lost and all had been delivered after repairs. After November 1943 this yard had concentrated entirely on production of three of the Type XXI's sections. The machine shops in particular were modern and well equipped, leading a US Strategic Bombing Survey team to comment that greater use could have been made of the yard's facilities. All this had been achieved despite the fact that this yard never received the protection that the assembly shelter did.

The oil storage depot was equally important, although not so well protected. Situated thirteen miles north-west of Bremen and two miles from the Weser it consisted of vertical and horizontal storage tanks with an estimated total capcity of 800,000 tons. All this was buried beneath a fir plantation and it was considered to be one of the best laid-out of Germany's oil storage centres.

9 Sqdn were off at 1037 and bombed the depot from between 16,000ft and 17,000ft. All attacked despite heavy flak, although Langdon had decided to bring his bomb back due to an unserviceable sight. Bombs falling from aircraft above led him to jettison it in order to get away quickly. Macdonnell was caught in someone else's slipstream, but bombed anyway. All fifteen bombs were dropped and the target was said to have been 'well covered', but three Tallboys apparently overshot by half a mile and exploded in a wood north of 9's AP, starting a fire. 617 went into the attack minus Goodman, who had had to turn back just after take-off, and Lancey, whose port inner engine had failed. Unable to keep up, he had been ordered to jettison his Grand Slam into the North Sea. They met moderate heavy flak, which hit Trent's aircraft eight times, wounding his navigator, but he bombed nevertheless. The gaggle was well dispersed, being spread over some 5,000ft of sky. Warburton was apparently the first

The U-boat shelter at Farge, near Hamburg, after the raid of 27 March 1945. This shows one of the two Grand Slam hits, which penetrated fourteen feet of concrete. The resulting fall of debris rendered the shelter unusable. (IWM neg. no. CL2607)

to bomb, quickly followed by Fauquier and Flatman. The rest of the bombs fell within a minute. Despite the delay fuses, three were seen to explode on impact. Two appear to have been Grand Slams dropped by Brookes and Powell, while the third may have been Speirs' Tallboy. One or two bombs fell in the water at the front of the shelter, but the rest were either on target or very close.

One of the bomb aimers was Len Sumpter, flying in Flt Lt Marshall's crew, and by now on his fiftieth operation. Like the others, he had to put up with a bang on the back of his head when the Grand Slam fell away and his Lancaster leapt upwards. Also with Marshall was Flg-Off Dougie Webb, another of 617's 'originals', who had been front gunner to Townsend's crew during *Chastise*. This crew claimed to have seen three direct hits – possibly those that prematurely exploded – and reckoned their own bomb fell on the south side of the shelter's roof.

Like Ijmuiden, this shelter's roof had been built using circular prefabricated concrete pilings. At the time of the attack it was almost 15ft thick at its west side, and had been increased to 23ft at the east side. As luck would have it, two Grand Slams struck the thinner west side portion. Both penetrated for just 8ft, but the force of their explosions was sufficient to bring down over 1,000 tons of concrete into the building, collapsing two travelling cranes inside. In spite of this, the blast from them did not penetrate the interior, which meant that an adjacent crane operator escaped injury.

These two bombs also caused considerable damage to the thicker part of the roof and to a reinforced concrete periscope testing tower. The US Strategic Bombing Survey report later commented, 'In all probability a twenty-three foot roof would withstand the 22,000lb bomb, but whether it is entirely proof against repeated hits by such bombs can only be determined by experiments.' Indeed, and just to make certain there had been a plan to increase it to 32ft! These comments were later acted on, for after the war Farge would be subjected to such experiments, using American and British weapons.

Another bomb caused damage to more lightly constructed electricity generating stations, concrete mixing plants and workshops on the shelter's north side. Twelve mis-aimed Main Force 1,000-pounders also fell on or near the shelter, but had little effect.

Although there was no evidence inside the shelter of damage by fragments, blast or earth shock, German marines who had been inside at the time later referred to the tremendous concussion of the explosions, saying that the subsequent morale effect was very great.

On 30 March, the US 8th Air Force followed this up by attacking the Farge shelter with the rocket-assisted 4,500lb Disney bomb. Over sixty were dropped, but only one hit the roof, leaving a small crater.

Astonishingly, attempts were made at this late stage to repair the damage, with I-section girders being put across one of the Grand Slam roof holes. The shelter would never be used, for 21st Army Group's 30th Corps would occupy Bremen after a five-day battle at the end of April.

After this, the next target seemed small indeed, but it was still important. A *Sperrbrecher* had reached the isolated German garrison at Ijmuiden, and SHAEF requested an attack on the grounds that it was intended as a blockship in the outer harbour, so denying the Allies entry to the port. Should it be so used, it was estimated that clearing it would take up to ten days.

The original Bomber Command plan was to use two squadrons, the first to be of up to ten aircraft with Tallboys and the second with 1,000-pounders. However, Harris was of the opinion that the use of stick bombing might cause unnecessary Dutch casualties, so he decided that the best way was to make a precision attack with one Tallboy squadron. To ensure success he stepped up the force from ten to fifteen aircraft.

On 6 April fifteen of 617's aircraft were detailed to sink the Ijmuiden *Sperrbrecher*, but bad weather over the port caused this raid to be postponed and the squadron returned without bombing. This would turn out to be another brief reprieve.

7 April 1945
Target The *Sperrbrecher* at Ijmuiden.
Weather No cloud, but a slight ground haze.

Force 15 Lancasters of 617 Sqdn:

PD132 'X' Sqdn Ldr C. C. Calder	PD130 'U' Flt Lt Lancey
PD114 'B' Sqdn Ldr J. V. Cockshott	PD129 'O' Flt Lt Leavitt
LM485 'U' Sqdn Ldr W. H. Gordon	PD134 'Y' Flt Lt I. M. Marshall
PD131 'V' Sqdn Ldr J. L. Powell	PB996 'C' Flt Lt J. C. McLaughlin
PD135 'W' Flt Lt S. A. Anning	PD135 'W' Flt Lt G. R. Price
PD238 'H' Flt Lt G. L. Beaumont	PD128 'N' Lt W. Adams USAAF
PB998 'D' Flt Lt L. S. Goodman	PD115 'C' Flg-Off J. Castagnola
PB997 'E' Flt Lt R. M. Horsley	

Escort 12 Spitfire IXs of 11 Group's 441 Sqdn RCAF.

Bomb Loads All aircraft carried one Tallboy each. No fusing details are available.

Two 5 Group Mosquitoes were also involved, one for weather reconnaissance and the other as a camera aircraft. 627 Sqdn did not take part in this operation.

This early evening attack was delivered from 13,200ft to 14,500ft in the face of meagre heavy flak, two runs being made. The first four Tallboys overshot, although of the first twelve none were more than fifty yards from the target. Three burst on a jetty to the south. Gordon and Beaumont both claimed direct hits, the latter on the ship's stern. Len Sumpter, again in Marshall's crew, believed his bomb was a near miss.

Leavitt was the last to bomb and also claimed a direct hit, which was confirmed by Cockshott and Anning as being on the bows. Those of Powell, Adams and Goodman fell between the ship and the harbour wall. When the smoke cleared the ship appeared to be still afloat, but later, as Beaumont had thought, it was seen to be well down by the stern and listing to starboard, with its after well deck awash.

Up to now Tallboy and Grand Slam had been officially referred to as DP (Deep Penetration) bombs, until someone in authority realised this description could be mistaken for Drill Pattern – meaning an inert weapon used for training – so they became MC bombs instead.

Their next objectives would consist of another naval one and a related target, but this time in response to a much more serious threat. On the night of 8-9 March 4, 6 and 8 Groups had attacked the Hamburg shipyards, the object being to disrupt production of the new Type XXI U-boat, whose parts had been prefabricated in dispersed inland factories. Due to the *Schnorchel* breathing tube and a new type of battery-driven electric engine, the Type XXI would be capable of remaining under water for long periods, with bursts of high speed when necessary. Its threat to Allied convoys was clear enough and, as Harris had once argued, it would be better to destroy such boats in the yards than for Coastal Command to hunt them at sea.

Due to cloud cover this raid had not been especially successful. Another on 31 March had achieved better results, resulting in considerable damage to houses and factories, but this was still not enough and a further daylight attack by the US 8th Air Force was ordered. This was to be immediately followed by another night one, then a daylight one on the U-boat pens. In addition, as part of the bombing offensive against German sources of synthetic oil, the plant at Lützkendorf was to be attacked as well. A maximum effort indeed, which was indicative of just how relentless the Allied bomber offensive became during the final months of the European war.

8-9 April 1945
Target The Wintershall synthetic oil plant at the town of Lützkendorf, near the city of Leipzig.
Weather Clear.

Force 18 Lancasters of 9 Sqdn:

NG442	'F'	Flt Lt P. G. Langdon		NG495	'R'	Flg-Off B. J. C. Graves
HK791	'M'	Flt Lt E. G. R. Morgan		NG419	'U'	Flg-Off H. L. T. Harper
LL845	'L'	Flt Lt M. Morrison		NG499	'W'	Flg-Off M. J. Irwin
HK803	'Q'	Flg-Off H. Anderson		DV393		Flg-Off J. R. Macdonnell
NG206	'J'	Flg-Off K. C. Arndell		PB696	'V'	Flg-Off W. G. Rees
ME555		Flg-Off R. F. Ayrton		LM217	'O'	Flg-Off J. C. Wiley
NG220	'B'	Flg-Off H. D. Barrowman		NG486	'A'	Flg-Off A. F. Williams
NG488	'A'	Flg-Off J. W. Buckley		NG235	'H'	Flg-Off R. S. Woolstencroft
NG249	'S'	Flg-Off D. A. Coster		NG384	'T'	Flg-Off R. B. Young

Escort None

Bomb Loads All 9 Sqdn aircraft carried one Tallboy each, with half-hour or, in the case of Graves and Young, one-hour delays.

At least one 9 Sqdn aircraft, flown by Flg-Off Rees, was briefed to windfind for 5 Group and also to mark the target with a yellow TI. As his three fellow windfinders, Flg-Offs Coster, Irwin and Wiley, were also present, it is likely that they too were similarly tasked.

Wallis had not been the only one to mark out oil as a source of power, and therefore a vital target. As far back as 1941 Lützkendorf had been listed by Bomber Command as one of seventeen vital German oil plants. 5 Group had raided this plant on 14-15 March 1945, but only moderate damage had been inflicted. On 7-8 April a benzol plant at Molbis, also near Leipzig, had been put out of action, but once again Lützkendorf had escaped serious damage.

9 Sqdn were part of a 5 Group force of 231 Lancasters and at least ten Mosquitoes. The plan was for four of 627 Sqdn's Mosquitoes to act as windfinders, dropping yellow TIs. Once this had been accomplished, fourteen Lancasters of 83 Sqdn and fifteen from 97 Sqdn were to act as Primary Blind Markers, dropping green TIs.

A further six of 627's Mosquitoes would then act as marker aircraft, dropping nine red and a few yellow TIs on the MP. For 5 Group's 'old lags' there were shades of Ladbergen and Pölitz, but this time 617 would not be taking part. They would be on the daylight raid the following afternoon.

It is not known why it was considered necessary to allocate the same task to two different squadrons, unless one was intended as a back-up for the other. In a letter to me in 1999 Graham Rees said that he had no knowledge of any activity by 627 Sqdn on this night. Possibly their use in the windfinding role was experimental.

H-Hour was 2245 and only moderate heavy flak was met in the target area. The Primary Blind Markers were assessed by 627 as accurate, if a minute early. Gp Capt. P. W. Johnson, flying with 97 Sqdn, identified the plant on H2S, dropping a green TI a hundred yards east of the MP. A quarter of a minute later a second green TI fell 200yds south of this one.

The Master Bomber's call for yellows was answered by the Marker Leader, Flt Lt W. H. Yeadell, who dropped a red and a yellow together on the MP. The remaining five Mosquitoes then backed this up and, with one exception, they achieved a concentration of red and yellow TIs 150 yards east of the MP.

During the Main Force's run-up the Master Bomber ordered flares to be dropped east of the greens. Although Wanganui sky markers were available as conditions were clear it was decided not to use them. Just to make things more interesting for those on the ground, 83 Sqdn added their loads of 1,000lb MC bombs, fitted with five-and-a-half-hour delay fuses. The target could be identified visually and by nearby quarries.

Morgan's crew bombed the MPI of red TIs on the north-eastern corner of the target area, as directed by the Master Bomber, using the vector wind. Other crews from 9 said afterwards that they were ordered to bomb red, or red and yellow TIs with eleven seconds' overshoot. Barrowman did not attack as his crew suffered a port inner engine failure ninety minutes before H-Hour. Despite pressing on he did not reach the target until it was too late to bomb, so he brought his Tallboy back. Macdonnell saw the yellow TIs that the windfinders had dropped, but as the wind turned out to be stronger than forecast he obeyed an 11-second overshoot that the Master Bomber had ordered. 627's concentration of TIs was also seen by a number of 9's crews before bombing, but as their windfinders had to cut into the bomber stream before the attack, Morrison was 'badly caught' in their slipstream.

Woolstencroft was brought down in the Berlin area, the only survivor being the rear gunner, who became a POW. As this crew made no signals it was not established whether they had bombed or not. Five other 5 Group Lancasters were also lost.

The consequence of all this was that several large explosions were seen in the target area at around 2254. Some concentrated bombing had rendered the plant 'inactive', which was not surprising, since a PRU sortie afterwards showed extensive damage to the compressor house, as well as to two buildings in the catalyst plant and one contact oven house. A bomb had damaged the gas purification plant, while fires burned from tanks in the hydro-generation plant. Several smaller buildings had been destroyed or damaged. This meant another source of oil disrupted at a time when the Germans most needed it, especially as March had seen the last stocks of fuel being issued to the fighter formations. Luftwaffe piston-engined aircraft were being grounded now and only the jets would continue for a little longer.

9 April 1945
Target The U-boat pens in the Finkenwerder district of Hamburg.
Weather Clear. Some haze, but excellent visibility, with a thin high layer of cirrus cloud over the city.

Force 17 Lancasters of 617 Sqdn:

PD119 'J' Gp Capt. J. E. Fauquier	LM695 'N' Flt Lt J. H. Leavitt
PD112 'S' Sqdn Ldr C. C. Calder	PD134 'Y' Flt Lt I. M. Marshall
PD115 'K' Sqdn Ldr W. H. Gordon	PD133 'P' Flt Lt G. R. Price
PD131 'V' Sqdn Ldr J. I. Powell	PD130 'U' Flt Lt J. L. Sayers
PD135 'W' Flt Lt S. A. Anning	? 'F' Flt Lt J. C. Warburton
NG339 'G' Flt Lt G. L. Beaumont	PD139 'L' Lt W. Adams USAAF
PB998 'D' Flt Lt I. S. Goodman	PD113 'T' Flg-Off J. Castagnola
PB997 'E' Flt Lt R. M. Horsley	PD118 'M' Flg-Off J. W. Speirs
PB996 'C' Flt Lt J. C. McLaughlin	

Escort 233 fighters, consisting of 120 Mustang IIIs, 30 Mustang IVs, 59 Spitfire IXs and 24 Spitfire XVIs, all of 11 Group.

64 Sqdn RAF	306 Sqdn (Polish)	441 Sqdn RCAF
118 Sqdn RAF	309 Sqdn (Polish)	442 Sqdn RCAF
122 Sqdn RAF	310 Sqdn (Czech)	602 Sqdn RAux AF
124 Sqdn RAF	312 Sqdn (Czech)	603 Sqdn RAux AF
129 Sqdn RAF	313 Sqdn (Czech)	611 Sqdn RAux AF
165 Sqdn RAF	315 Sqdn (Polish)	
234 Sqdn RAF	316 Sqdn (Polish)	

One of 602 Sqdn's Spitfire XVI pilots was twenty-three-year-old Flg-Off Raymond Baxter, later to become better known as a racing commentator and presenter of the BBC programme *Tomorrow's World*.

Bomb Loads Of 617 Sqdn, Fauquier and Calder each carried a Grand Slam. The rest carried one Tallboy each. No fusing details are available.

A raid by the US 8th Air Force at the end of March had already sunk five U-boats at Finkenwerder. The previous night's attack by 440 aircraft had also been intended for the shipyards, but some cloud had caused it to become dispersed. Nevertheless, a further five U-boats had been lost and two damaged during it. Those who crawled out of the rubble the next morning did not yet know that this had been the last major night raid by Bomber Command on their city. However, it was not quite all over yet, for a further two-pronged attack was to be made now. In addition to 617's shelter attack, forty Lancasters of 5 Group's 53 Base were to bomb oil storage tanks with 1,000-pounders.

The fighter escort seemed massive for such a small bomber force, but recent daylight attacks by the Me 262s had shown that they were not to be ignored. As yet the only Allied equivalent was the Gloster Meteor, but this was an inferior design, available to only a single squadron. For now, the fastest piston-engined fighters would have to do. Their pilots had strict orders not to engage in strafing, despite the number of targets parked on airfields below. The first jet-versus-jet battles would not take place until the Korean War, five years later.

Both the attacks were concentrated, meeting a good deal of heavy flak, which damaged six of 617's aircraft, although they all bombed and survived. Fauquier said his Grand Slam hit at the north-eastern corner and confirmed three other hits in the centre of the shelters. Calder's Grand Slam apparently hit on the west side. Before smoke covered them, direct hits were claimed by Anning, Beaumont, Castagnola, Goodman, Horsley, Leavitt, McLaughlin and Price.

Most of the buildings north and west of the U-boat shelters were destroyed or damaged. A plot photograph later indicated seven direct hits, four of which had penetrated the roof. Once again Len Sumpter was flying with Flt Lt Marshall's crew, who saw four hits, but did not claim any as their own.

The five Finkenwerder pens were in a building 500ft square, with a roof up to 11.5ft thick, this being reinforced with steel beams and trusses. A report compiled after the surrender showed that there had been six direct hits by Tallboys on the pens. The rest, including the two Grand Slams, were thought to have landed in the water. All six bombs had penetrated part of the way into the roof, struck a heavy steel girder, then blown holes through the ceiling, causing hundreds of tons of concrete to fall into the pens.

Their Commandant later said that six Type VIIC U-boats had all sustained damage, while a further two were put out of action by the destruction of a dry dock. Further research has indicated that only two U-boats, U-906 and U-1192, were damaged on this date, which if so meant that the others had become casualties the night before. At the time of the attack there had been 3,000 people in the pens – less than usual because it took place on a day when most only worked until 1600.

The interrogators must have found this hard to believe. Nazi Germany was within a month of collapse and yet 'Poet's Day' still applied. By contrast, twelve-hour shifts had been the norm in Britain since 1939! Germany's manpower problems were also illustrated by the fact that most of those in the pens had been foriegn workers, only one in ten being German. The attack, which took place at about 1700, killed twenty-seven people and seriously injured up to sixty others, causing panic. There was also considerable secondary damage in the vicinity – a pier, railway trucks, stores sheds, barracks and workshops had been wiped out.

The crews did not know this at the time and even if they had there were more immediate matters to be dealt with. Their heavy escort proved justified, for now some thirty Me 262s were seen. 467 Sqdn RAAF, flying on the oil tank raid, were already in a tight gaggle with a high risk of collision. Their leaders speeded up and turned away before their photographic runs were completed, so as a result 467 found themselves behind 617 on the way out. It had not been part of their flight plan to be there, and a bumpy ride through 617's slipstream did not help matters.

The Mustangs jettisoned their drop tanks. They were going to have to mix it this time, for 122 Sqdn had seen the Me 262s, circling like black sharks in the clear sky. After leaving the target area a number of 262s attacked the bombers, coming in from astern and below. The squadron bounced these, but the superior speed of the 262s enabled them to evade without much difficulty. No further attacks were made.

306, 309 and 315 Sqdns, after noting dust over the Hamburg targets and two columns of smoke, also did their best to intercept the Me 262s. Two Lancasters went down, one of which was seen to blow up in mid-air. In a fifteen-minute engagement the Poles claimed three Me 262s shot down and three more damaged.

One minute after an R/T warning Sqdn Ldr J. Zulikowski, 306's CO, saw an Me 262 some 3,000ft below, among the bombers. He dived towards this one which overtook the bomber formation, then turned for a head-on attack. Zulikowski fired from 200yds, causing the jet to break away. As he turned back he saw three more attacking, and two Lancasters on fire. These three turned to port and dived, whereupon Zulikowski fired at the nearest one, this time from 800yds, claiming to have shot it down. 309 Sqdn claimed three destroyed and some other units also tried their luck, such that there was a danger of the escorts colliding with each other! Four of the damaged U-boats were extracted from the pens and made seaworthy again, but they were not back in action before the war ended. The other two were still in there, one on its side and the other under water, when the Allies marched in. The destroyed workshops had contained components and large rear assemblies for three other U-boats.

Since heavy minelaying by Bomber Command in the Baltic had severely restricted the use of German and other shipping for some months, it may be asked why it was still thought necessary to attack the U-boat shelters at a time when the war was nearly over. However, as far as the Chiefs of Staff were concerned the surviving U-boats, and any facilities that continued to operate in support of them, would still be considered a threat until Germany was fully occupied.

There was another danger that they did not yet know of. During January 1945 U-234, a Type XB minelaying submarine and the largest of the *Kriegsmarine*'s U-boats, had begun to take on board an exotic cargo at Kiel. Apart from some senior German and Japanese officers as passengers, into the boat's mineshafts went a quantity of the latest German anti-tank weapons, a set of Me 262 parts and, intriguingly, ten cases of uranium oxide ore, which had been extracted from mines in Czechoslovakia. Well aware of the possibilities of atomic power, the Japanese had been working on a uranium bomb since 1941 and had requested these materials for their research.

This boat sailed to Christiansand in Norway and left there on 14 April for Tokyo. Fortunately for the Allies, it was captured by the Americans. On 24 July, just after the Americans had exploded their first atomic bomb in the New Mexico desert, the material was removed from the U-boat and sent immediately to a manufacturing plant at Oak Ridge in Tennessee. The uranium did indeed reach Japan in the end – it was in the bomb *Little Boy* when it exploded over Hiroshima. The possibility of the Germans or Japanese using atomic weapons first had been an Allied nightmare for the last two years.

It can therefore be seen that, one way or another, the U-boats remained a menace and that attacks on them were justified right up until the surrender. Even after this had occurred it was noted by the Royal Navy that their crews, many of them hard-faced Hitler Youth products, were surly in their manner and did not behave as if they had lost.

U-234 had already begun her ill-fated voyage as the Lancasters made their way home on the evening of 9 April. No nation, even one now governed by the iron hand of the SS, could hold out for much longer. One more month and it would all be over. U-boats were not the only naval targets that still needed attending to. A Main Force raid on Kiel on 9-10 April resulted in the capsizing of the pocket battleship *Admiral Scheer*, as well as damage to the cruisers *Admiral Hipper* and *Köln*. Three days later the first of three daylight attacks was staged against some more remnants of the *Kriegsmarine* – specifically, the heavy cruiser *Prinz Eugen* and the pocket battleship *Lützow* – at the Baltic port of Swinemünde.

The *Prinz Eugen* had become well known early in the war as an escort, first to the battleship *Bismarck* and then when she accompanied the battlecruisers *Scharnhorst* and *Gneisenau* in the 'Channel Dash' from Brest to Kiel in February 1942. Her luck had changed shortly after this when her stern had been heavily damaged by a torpedo from the British submarine HMS *Trident*. RAF bombing had kept her out of action for the better part of a year, but recently she had been involved in German evacuation operations in the Baltic.

The pocket battleship *Lützow*, originally known as the *Deutschland*, had last been in action when she had unsuccessfully attempted to intercept a Russian convoy in the Battle of the Barents Sea at the end of 1942. When Hitler had heard that his heavy cruisers had been driven off by British light cruisers and destroyers, he had flown into a rage, and, as seen in those chapters referring to the *Tirpitz*, he had ordered them to be paid off.

Consequently the remainder of Hitler's surface fleet had seen little action since, but they posed a threat other than the obvious one. The battlecruiser *Gneisenau*, which had survived the 'Channel Dash' only to be bombed by the RAF after she had limped into Kiel with mine damage, had had her armament removed to bolster the Atlantic Wall defences in Norway. Recently, on 27 March, the resulting hulk had been used as a blockship at the Polish port of Gdynia before the advancing Red Army occupied it. There was still the possibility that, as with the *Gueydon* at Brest and the *Sperrbrecher* at Ijmuiden, the Germans would try the same thing elsewhere.

On Friday 13 April – perhaps an ominous date – 9 and 617 Sqdns therefore set course for Swinemünde, but, despite the presence of four weather reconnaissance Mosquitoes, they were unable to find a way round the ten-tenths cloud that stretched all the way from the Elbe to the target. The raid was postponed again on the 15th, for the same reason.

16 April 1945
Target The pocket battleship *Lützow* and the heavy cruiser *Prinz Eugen*, at Swinemünde.
Weather Clear, with good visibility.

Force 18 Lancasters of 617 Sqdn:

PD119	'J' Gp Capt. J. E. Fauquier	PD133	'P' Flt Lt G. R. Price
PD130	'U' Sqdn Ldr J. F. Brookes	NG494	'B' Flt Lt E. Quinton
PD115	'K' Sqdn Ldr W. H. Gordon	PD371	'W' Flt Lt D. A. Rawes
NG228	'V' Sqdn Ldr J. L. Powell	NG340	'U' Flt Lt K. L. Trent
PD132	'X' Flt Lt S. A. Anning	PD128	'N' Flt Lt J. C. Warburton
PD116	'A' Flt Lt H. V. Gavin	PD139	'L' Lt W. Adams USAAF
PB997	'E' Flt Lt C. N. Hill	PD113	'T' Flg-Off J. Castagnola
PB998	'D' Flt Lt R. M. Horsley	PB996	'C' Flg-Off M. B. Flatman
PD114	'B' Flt Lt J. H. Leavitt	PD118	'M' Flg-Off J. W. Speirs

Escort 127 fighters, consisting of 90 Mustang IIIs and 37 Mustang IVs, all of 11 Group:

64 Sqdn RAF	234 Sqdn RAF	316 Sqdn (Polish)
118 Sqdn RAF	306 Sqdn (Polish)	442 Sqdn RCAF
122 Sqdn RAF	309 Sqdn (Polish)	611 Sqdn R Aux AF
126 Sqdn RAF	315 Sqdn (Polish)	

A pre-war photograph of the pocket battleship *Deutschland*, which, as the *Lützow*, would be sunk by a Tallboy near-miss at Swinemünde. (IWM neg. no. HU1033)

The heavy cruiser *Prinz Eugen*, the other target at Swinemünde (IWM neg. no. HU1016)

These aircraft would operate at the limit of their endurance, each spending over five hours in the air.

Bomb Loads Powell, Quinton, Rawes and Trent each carried twelve 1,000lb bombs. The remainder carried one Tallboy each. No fusing details are available.

The raid was accompanied by an RAF Film Unit Mosquito.

On the way the crews noted a great deal of German shipping in Lübeck Bay, Pomeranian Bay and off the estuary of the Elbe. Those who had seen action on Germany's Eastern Front, and many who had not, had no desire to fall into the hands of the Red Army. If escape to Sweden was not possible and the only alternative was to head westwards across the Baltic, running the gauntlet of RAF attacks en route, to throw themselves on the mercy of the Allies, then so be it.

There were, therefore, no lack of targets at Swinemünde, most of them being the thirty to forty ships lying offshore. However, the two that mattered were identified in the harbour itself, the *Lützow* lying along the west side of the Kaiser Canal at its northern end.

The escorting Mustang pilots hungrily eyed the many German aircraft on the airfields en route, but the no-strafing order still applied and everyone kept to their stations. The fact that most of the Luftwaffe was by now on the ground and not in the air showed how successful the attacks on the oil plants and the transportation system had been.

During the twenty minutes it took to run up to the port, 617 were assailed by moderate but extremely accurate heavy flak, so much so that Fauquier decided they would all run in at the same time, instead of in sections. Nevertheless, he deemed two runs necessary. Then he misidentified the target and bombed another vessel out of at least seven in the canal near Swinemünde. His bomb undershot by just ten yards.

Gordon said, 'We were hit by flak on run in, which severed throttle controls, causing carburettor butterfly valve to close and losing power on port outer. This threw our bombing run off and when we started a second bombing run it was not accurate enough so we scrubbed it. We found the engine was u/s and were unable to keep up with the gaggle. When the latter made their second run we were nearly ten miles behind and unable to catch up. We tried to make a run of our own but the target was obscured by smoke. We abandoned the run and rejoined the gaggle and were ordered to bomb any built-up area en route.' Their new target was a village fifteen miles west of the town of Prenziau.

They fared better than Powell, whose Lancaster shed its port wing after a direct hit and went spinning down in flames into a wood. One man jumped but his parachute apparently did not fully deploy and there were no survivors. Gavin was also hit and jettisoned his Tallboy in the target area, which it undershot by 450 yards.

Brookes said his bomb overshot, landing twenty-five yards off the *Lützow*'s bows. His crew claimed to have seen four other near misses. One Tallboy, which turned out to be the one that mattered, went off between the ship and the side of the canal. Anning, Castagnola and Warburton all reckoned that the ship's stern had been hit. Some crews thought the bombing was scattered and as usual smoke obscured the results. However, Speirs commented, 'Our bomb went into smoke and was followed by huge explosion and flying debris.'

Hungry for some final kills before it was all over, six Poles of 316 Sqdn chased a Me 410 after seeing it take off from Parchim airfield, but lost it at sea level. One FW 190 was destroyed by two Canadians from 442 Sqdn, while 611 Sqdn dived on some FW 190s, shooting down at least three. Two other fighters were seen in the target area, but these were Russian Yaks – a reminder that the Red Army was by now only a few miles away.

The *Lützow* did go down, although she took two days to do so. The near miss alongside had smashed in her armour plating below the waterline, and she settled by

The 9 Squadron memorial. (J. S. E. Brookbank)

the stern. As she had gone down in shallow water, her superstructure remained above it and some of her guns continued in action until the Russians occupied the port, whereupon she was blown up.

The *Prinz Eugen* survived this raid and was surrendered to the Allies at Copenhagen on 9 May. She was subsequently sailed to Bikini Atoll in the South Pacific and used as a target ship, along with several surplus American and captured Japanese vessels, in a 1946 atomic bomb test. As a result, she turned over completely off Kwajalein Atoll, lying upside-down for many years with only part of her keel and propellers showing. Once it was decided that the radiation count had dropped to a low enough level, one of those propellers was cut off in 1978 and taken back to Kiel as a memorial.

Most of 617's aircraft had suffered flak damage during this attack, so not surprisingly the squadron was stood down for three days to give time for repairs to take place.

19 April 1945
Target The coastal gun batteries on the island of Heligoland.
Weather Thin patchy four-tenths stratocumulus at 3,000-4,000ft.

Force 16 Lancasters of 9 Sqdn:

HK803 'Q' Sqdn Ldr J. D. Melrose	NG487 'D' Flg-Off J. W. Buckley
NG206 'J' Flt Lt C. M. T. Follett	NG249 'S' Flg-Off D. A. Coster
NG499 'W' Flt Lt R. J. Harris	NG220 'B' Flg-Off S. Laws
NG384 'T' Flt Lt D. Macintosh	NG419 'U' Flg-Off R. C. Macdonald
NG442 'F' Flt Lt L. E. Marsh	PB696 'V' Flg-Off W. G. Rees
LL845 'L' Flt Lt A. M. Morrison	DV393 Flg-Off W. Scott
NG481 Flt Lt Watkins	ME555 Flg-Off E. I. Waters
NG495 'R' Flg-Off H. Anderson	LM217 'O' Flg-Off J. C. Wiley

20 Lancasters of 617 Sqdn:

NG445 'E' Gp Capt. J. E. Fauquier	PB415 'O' Flt Lt J. H. Leavitt

PD118 'M' Wg Cdr C. C. Calder
PD121 'S' Sqdn Ldr J. B. Brookes
PD115 'K' Sqdn Ldr W. H. Gordon
PD135 'W' Flt Lt S. A. Anning
NG339 'G' Flt Lt G. L. Beaumont
PD116 'A' Flt Lt H. V. Gavin
NG494 'B' Flt Lt C. N. Hill
PB998 'D' Flt Lt R. M. Horsley
? Flt Lt G. W. Lancey

PD133 'P' Flt Lt I. M. Marshall
PD238 'H' Flt Lt A. E. Quinton
? Flt Lt D. A. Rawes
PD132 'X' Flt Lt K. L. Trent
PD128 'N' Flt Lt J. C. Warburton
PD139 'L' Lt W. Adams USAAF
PD134 'Y' Flg-Off J. Castagnola
PD114 'B' Flg-Off M. B. Flatman
LM695 'N' Flg-Off J. W. Speirs

617's ORB incorrectly states that NG340 was flown by both Lancey and Rawes on this date.

Escort 79 fighters, consisting of 11 Mustang IIIs, 42 Spitfire IXs and 26 Spitfire XVIs, from 11 and 12 Groups:

1 Sqdn RAF   310 Sqdn (Czech)   602 Sqdn RAuxAF
309 Sqdn (Polish)   312 Sqdn (Czech)   603 Sqdn RAuxAF
313 Sqdn (Czech)

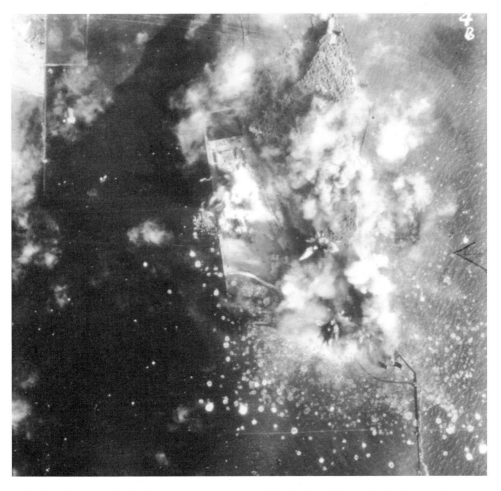

Heligoland, as seen by Flight Lieutenant L. E. Marsh of 9 Squadron early in the attack. Craters from the previous day's raid are visible at the top of the picture.

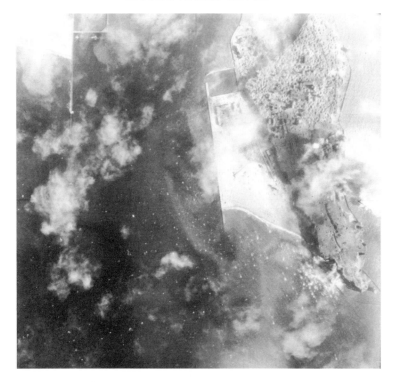

The view shot by Flying Officer Graham Rees as the attack develops. Cloud is now drifting in from the bottom of the picture, obscuring the APs.

The cloud continues to move across the island as Flying Officer R. C. Macdonald takes his shot. The Lancaster crew turning to starboard were fortunate not to have been hit from above.

Bomb Loads 9 Sqdn – all aircraft carried one Tallboy each, with a 25-second delay.
617 Sqdn – Calder, Brookes, Gordon, Anning, Castagnola and Flatman all carried Grand Slams. The rest carried one Tallboy each. No fusing details are available, but these were probably as for 9 Sqdn.

The raid was accompanied by a Film Unit Mosquito.

Heligoland had a curious history, having once been a British possession before being exchanged for Zanzibar in 1890. Just over two square miles in size, the island's highest ground consisted of red limestone cliffs, with a pronounced step between them and a lower area on which most of its buildings stood. Its civilian population had been evacuated earlier in the war.

Like Walcheren the previous September, the island's two 6-inch and 12-inch coastal gun batteries, with their associated radar stations, commanded the approach to river estuaries – in this case the Elbe and Weser on the north-western coast of Germany. On 18 April, in response to a request from SHAEF, 969 Main Force aircraft had devastated the naval base, town and airfield on this and a neighbouring island. Even so, neither the forty heavy anti-aircraft guns nor the coastal batteries on the island had been completely destroyed. It was therefore necessary for 9 and 617 to finish the job.

The gun emplacements were on the north and south of the island, which meant three APs. Two of these, labelled G and K, were to be bombed by 9 Sqdn; the other, H, was reserved for 617. Prior to the attack, six of 9 Sqdn's crews were to act as windfinders. This was a task they accomplished with practised ease, the windfinding leader broadcasting their findings to the rest of the squadron at H-5.

As they neared the island, the crews saw that the centre was still burning from the previous day's attack. After the pounding they had taken, it was not surprising that the defences were meagre – there were just four shots from one heavy flak gun – but nevertheless disaster nearly struck. On their run-in 9 Sqdn were forced to climb 1,000 feet when they discovered 617 were coming in at the same time! 9 then decided to delay attacking their target and orbit, partly due to the non-appearance of their fighter escort and to information from 617 that cloud was obscuring the target.

Eventually 9 did attack, but two of their crews brought their Tallboys back. Cloud cover prevented Morrison from failing to see the AP until it was too late, while Ray Harris was caught in someone else's slipstream.

617 did two runs and all aircraft bombed except Rawes, who was unable to get onto the correct heading in time. Fauquier's Tallboy exploded twenty yards east of the battery area, while the bombs dropped by Beaumont, Brookes, Horsley and Quinton all undershot. Adams claimed a direct hit on 617's AP, as did Warburton, who said he had seen four other bombs fall on it. Speirs considered the bombing had been poor due to the weather conditions.

Photo interpretation afterwards showed that only two direct hits had been scored on the gun positions. The near misses had caused further damage, but the job was still not considered complete, as a further Main Force attack was planned during the first week in May. It was not carried out due to Allied acceptance of the unconditional surrender at Luneburg Heath of all enemy forces in north-western Germany and Denmark. However, Heligoland had not seen the last of the RAF; the island would be used as a bombing range until the 1950s.

The next day both squadrons heard that PRU coverage had revealed that the *Lützow* had finally sunk. Unlike the *Tirpitz*, the pocket battleship had apparently gone down on an even keel. As it had been covered only from above, this had not been obvious to the interpreters until they had carefully compared photographs taken before and after the raid of 16 April. There must have been clearly audible sighs of relief at Bardney and Woodhall Spa. No more long hauls to Swinemünde for them! The loss of Powell's crew at this late stage had led to a good deal of bitter comment among 617's crews, especially as they were so near to the finish now. Even so, for them there would be one more raid before that day dawned.

25 April 1945
Target Hitler's country home above the town of Berchtesgaden in the Bavarian Alps, and other buildings nearby, including the SS barracks.
Weather Excellent visibility, except for mist in the valleys.

Force 17 Lancasters of 9 Sqdn;

NG495 'R' Sqdn Ldr J. D. Melrose	NG220 'B' Flg-Off S. Laws
LL845 'L' Flt Lt D. Macintosh	NG442 'F' Flg-Off C. M. T. Follett
PA172 'G' Flt Lt L. E. Marsh	ME809 'X' Flg-Off R. C. Macdonald
ME555 Flt Lt E. G. R. Morgan	DV393 Flg-Off W. Scott
NG499 'W' Flt Lt H. Watkins	NG419 'U' Flg-Off E. I. Waters
NG384 'T' Flg-Off H. Anderson	LM217 'O' Flg-Off J. C. Wiley
NG205 'J' Flg-Off K. C. Arndell	NG487 'D' Flg-Off A. F. Williams
NG486 'A' Flg-Off J. W. Buckley	PB696 'V' Flg-Off R. B. Young
NG249 'S' Flg-Off D. A. Coster	

16 Lancasters of 617 Sqdn:

PD131 'V' Sqdn Ldr J. B. Brookes	PB415 'O' Flt Lt J. H. Leavitt
PD121 'S' Sqdn Ldr E. G. Ward	PD134 'Y' Flt Lt I. M. Marshall
NG339 'G' Flt Lt G. L. Beaumont	NG494 'B' Flt Lt A. E. Quinton
PD116 'A' Flt Lt H. V. Gavin	PD135 'W' Flt Lt K. L. Trent
PB998 'D' Flt Lt L. S. Goodman	PD139 'L' Lt W. Adams USAAF
PB997 'E' Flt Lt C. N. Hill	PD114 'B' Flg-Off M. B. Flatman
PD127 Flt Lt R. M. Horsley	NG340 Flg-Off N. H. Frost
PD130 'U' Flt Lt G. W. Lancey	PD132 'X' Flg-Off J. W. Speirs

Escort At least 126 fighters, consisting of 82 Mustang IIIs and 44 Mustang IVs, all from 11 Group:

64 Sqdn RAF	165 Sqdn RAF	315 Sqdn (Polish)
118 Sqdn RAF	234 Sqdn RAF	316 Sqdn (Polish)
122 Sqdn RAF	303 Sqdn (Polish)	442 Sqdn RCAF
126 Sqdn RAF	306 Sqdn (Polish)	611 Sqdn R Aux AF
129 Sqdn RAF	309 Sqdn (Polish)	

Two US 8th Air Force Fighter Groups also took part, contributing a further 98 P-51Ds.

Bomb Loads
9 Sqdn – all aircraft carried one Tallboy each, with a 30-second delay. 617 Sqdn – all aircraft carried one Tallboy each. No fusing details are available, but these were probably as for 9 Sqdn.

Including these two squadrons, the total force would consist of 359 Lancasters and 14 Mosquitoes of 1, 5 and 8 Groups. Oboe and marking support would be given by 14 Mosquitoes and 24 Lancasters of the following 8 Group units:

105 Sqdn	109 Sqdn	405 Sqdn RCAF	635 Sqdn

The Main Force would attack on the instructions of the Master Bomber. Wg Cdr J. W. Fordham, or his Deputy, Sqdn Ldr G. C. Hitchcock, both of 635 Sqdn. These two would carry six 1,000lb red TIs between them, while their supporting crews would carry yellow ones.

This raid would be accompanied by a Film Unit Mosquito.

The Obersalzberg, a beautiful mountainous region tucked away in the south-east corner of Germany, close to the Austrian border, was one that had long appealed to

Hitler. His home, referred to on this raid by the RAF as the Chalet, was the only one he had ever owned. Following the Munich Putsch and his imprisonment, Hitler had stayed in the Obersalzberg, writing part of *Mein Kampf* there.

Royalties from the book's sale had enabled him to buy a house, called the 'Berghof', meaning 'a neat farm building with the characteristics of a mountain house.' It had suited Hitler to retain an apparent man-of-the-people image when he became Chancellor, but the building had been rebuilt on a lavish scale. Alterations to it had continued even during the latter part of the war, when building materials had been in short supply.

Other buildings in the area were the Platterhof Pension, rebuilt in 1938 as a hotel for those on pilgrimages to see their beloved *Führer*, plus houses for Martin Bormann and Hermann Göring. The best-known addition was the dramatically named 'Eagle's Nest', a tea-house that had been built by Bormann on Kehlstein mountain, apparently as an isolated conference building.

During the summer of 1939 Hitler had been at the Berghof, taking part in a series of increasingly tense meetings. On the evening of 23 August, just as a pact was being signed in Moscow to pave the way for the invasion of Poland, there had been a strange sight in the sky. The heavens had turned into an astonishing range of colours; from vivid greens, reds and yellows to a dull grey lead. As they had watched this spectacle a Hungarian woman whose apprehension of what was to come overruled her fear of speaking out said to him, 'My *Führer*, this augers no good. It means destruction, blood and more blood.' Shocked by the sight above him, but by now committed to his chosen course of action, Hitler had declared, 'If it has to be, then let it be now.' Now it would, in what until recently had been a peaceful corner of Bavaria.

In response to the increasing severity of Allied bombing, plans had been drawn up for an elaborate tunnel shelter complex. Göring, with an eye to his own generously proportioned skin, had started a shelter for himself as early as 1941. The complex had eventually consisted of over two miles of tunnels, equipped with, among other things, air conditioning and a private bathroom for Hitler's mistress, Eva Braun.

By 1945 what had originally been a retreat for Hitler had become a symbol: part of the National Redoubt that the Nazis would be expected to defend to the last man. However, unknown to the Allies as yet, Hitler was in the remains of his Chancellery in Berlin, ordering armies that no longer existed to stand and die. Whatever the outcome, he had decided to remain there. His state of mind had been indicated by his declaration that, 'We shall win because we must win! If we did not, world history would have lost its meaning.'

One man who now knew he would not see that victory was Hermann Göring. As someone who had fallen out of favour a long time ago, he should have known better than to send a telegram to Hitler stating that as Berlin was now surrounded he, Göring, should be given Hitler's powers to carry on as Germany's new leader. An accusation of treachery had been the answer, leading Bormann to order Göring to be placed under arrest at his Obersalzberg home. Nemesis would come soon – but not from his SS guards.

The British Special Operations Executive, acting on information from a POW who had been one of Hitler's staff, had put together a file on the layout of Hitler's home and the surrounding area with a view to assassinating him. This plan had been turned down, apparently on the grounds that had it been successful it would have turned Hitler into a martyr, but stories of the National Redoubt had probably led the War Cabinet into now deciding that bombing was an acceptable alternative. The operation had originally been planned for 21 April, but bad weather had put it off for four days.

For many of Bomber Command's squadrons, this operation would be their last and a fitting climax to a long, hard campaign. Tired as they were, everyone wanted to be on this one. It would mean a round trip of 1,400 miles, but the chance of killing Hitler was too good to miss.

Someone who had no choice but to stay behind was 617's CO. As usual Fauquier carried out the briefing, but for him it meant going through the motions; like Gibson, Cheshire and Tait before him, he was being forcibly retired from operations. 617 would be led by Sqdn Ldr Brookes.

The plan was for all the aircraft concerned to rendezvous over Paris, then fly to southern Germany, approaching Berchtesgaden at 0945 from the south-west by flying along the line of the Alps. The Oboe Mosquitoes were to drop red TIs on the SS barracks at H-4, 3, 2 and 1. Using these as a guide, the Master Bomber and his Deputy would then drop their own reds, backed up by the yellows carried by the rest of the two 8 Group squadrons. However, these were to serve as guides only; the targets were to be visually identified.

617 were to lead the Main Force, followed by 9 Sqdn, then everyone else. As before, the escort were forbidden to attack ground targets. Whatever remained of the Luftwaffe just might decide to make a last stand.

Set against a clear blue sky, the snow-capped Bavarian mountains made an unforgettable sight. As far as the 8 Group crews were concerned, all seemed well on the approach to the target, for the nearby lake and town of Berchtesgaden assisted in its identification.

Then the atmosphere changed to concern and anger as things began to go wrong. Despite flying at 39,000ft the 8 Group Mosquitoes could not receive any Oboe signals, due to the mountains intervening between them and a mobile ground station. They decided to drop their TIs anyway, but ground mist would mean that few if any of the Main Force crews would see them.

This was bad enough, but just to make the Master Bomber's task more interesting, communications between him and the Main Force were hampered by the 8th Air

Approaching the target. The Lancaster ahead and to the right already has its bomb doors open. (IWM neg. no. C5244)

Force's escort fighters using the same VHF frequency – a fact reported by crews afterwards, some saying they heard him clearly and others, including a few of the PFF ones, not at all.

Lacking the clear assistance of the Oboe Mosquitoes, it was now up to the red TIs carried by Wg Cdr Fordham and Sqdn Ldr Hitchcock to provide the primary target marking. As if to prove that troubles never come singly, some of the more eager Main Force crews chose to attack ahead of the PFF, while others were slightly late, overshooting their briefed turning point.

Ordering the rest of the PFF and the Main Force to orbit, Fordham approached and dropped his reds at 0946. These slightly overshot the AP, falling one hundred yards to the north-west of it, but the bombs he released with them were seen to burst on buildings on the AP's northern edge. Hitchcock was ordered in, to find himself handicapped by an unserviceable bombsight, but may have tried to mark anyway, for some other reds were seen to cascade onto the target a minute later. These were quickly followed by yellows and the attack began. The uncertainty caused one of 405's crews to hang onto their TIs and select bombs only. If there was an enquiry afterwards, nobody was going to blame them.

Fordham at first ordered everyone to bomb the centre of the smoke, but when an overshoot became apparent he corrected this, saying, 'Bomb upwind edge of the smoke.' One of 405's crews later reported that, 'Raid generally appeared successful, but not as good as it could have been. Master and Deputy were slow in identifying and crews report hearing, 'Bomb visually'.'

This confusion had led to two runs, the first at 0858-0910 and the second at 0945-1000. During the first, possibly due to the lack of marking, bombing tended to overshoot, although some Main Force sticks were seen to fall across the SS barracks – accounting for the fresh craters seen on the snow by some of 405's crews. Nine Tallboys were aimed at the Berghof and a further three at the Eagle's Nest, but smoke prevented the results from being assessed. Another three of 617's aircraft that should have attacked the Eagle's Nest were unable to pick it out.

As photographs later showed, those who had bombed during the first run had done better than they knew. Although most of the bombs aimed at it missed, the Berghof sustained much blast damage. At the SS barracks, one building was demolished and several others damaged.

These crews who went in on the second run had little difficulty in identifying the target and before smoke covered the AP a good concentration of bombs – at least four Tallboys as well as Main Force 1,000-pounders – had fallen across the barracks. There was no fighter opposition, but some predicted heavy and light flak, from hillside positions as well as the barracks, was accurate, bringing down two Main Force Lancasters.

As for the two Tallboy squadrons, 617 had come through some heavy flak, but despite that everyone seemed to want to bomb first! Brookes failed to identify his target in time. Neither could Ward or Gavin, and none of these three bombed at all. Goodman was hit by flak, but dropped his bomb anyway. Lancey cursed his luck when his bomb hung-up, then fell away to hit a mountainside. Hill attacked a last-resort target, identified by him as either the edge of a village or Army huts! After two runs Marshall still could not find the primary target, so he bombed a railway and road junction. His bomb aimer was Flt Lt Len Sumpter – probably the only 617 'original' to take part in that squadron's final wartime raid.

He was not the last to leave the target area, though. Leavitt had done one run and, not being satisfied, asked for permission to do another, but was unable to get through as by now Fordham had switched to another frequency. Being alone over Berchtesgaden as the rest of the gaggle had departed, he set course for home, dropping his Tallboy on a viaduct over a road en route in order to catch up with everybody else.

The last Tallboy target – Obersalzberg, above Berchtesgaden in the mountains of southern Germany. Taken after the attack, this shot shows the Berghof, Hitler's L-shaped house, at the bottom centre of the picture. The square-shaped house of his Deputy Führer, Martin Bormann, is well to its left. In the centre, in the form of a hollow square and partly obscured by cloud, is the SS barracks, which was 8 Group's aiming point. The large T-shaped building is the Platterhof Pension. On the day of the attack, a covering of snow and mist inhibited accurate bombing, except in the centre of the target area. (IWM neg. no. C5242)

A close-up of the Berghof and the nearby Gasthof Zum Turken, which had been a Gestapo headquarters, showing Tallboy and Main Force bomb damage. (IWM neg. no. C5253)

9 Sqdn's fortunes were similarly mixed. Ten of their crews bombed as intended, but Watkins commented, 'Raid marred by higher squadrons crowding above first and lowest squadrons, thus spoiling the bombing runs.'

There could have been few more chilling sights than seeing a Lancaster's enormous bomb bay open directly above you – and why get killed by your own side when it was nearly over? Faced with a bomb hurtling down from above, Melrose overshot and did not bomb at all. Neither did Macdonald at first, due to haze on the run up. The target cleared too late for him to correct his heading, so he aimed his Tallboy at a railway bridge instead.

Possibly due to an electrical failure, Williams' bomb had fallen through the doors as soon as it was selected and fused, exploding in a wood by the Rhine. Marsh did not bomb due to his sight becoming unserviceable. Neither did Wiley, being unable to identify his target through what he described as a thin cloud layer at 1,000ft. Arndell, who had difficulty identifying the direction he was supposed to take and also had his run interfered with by other aircraft, did not bomb and was told not to make a second run. Anderson claimed he was unable to identify the primary target early enough, so he bombed an alternative.

As some consolation for all this, Young claimed a hit on the northern corner of a house – possibly the Berghof, though he did not say so. V Group News later commented, 'Although it is believed that Hitler has since died elsewhere, it is to be hoped that some of his minions were present at Berchtesgaden to reap suitable benefit from this attack.'

From the German point of view, the attack had been heavy but the loss of life slight; just six people killed out of the 3,500 who had sheltered in the air-raid tunnels. The first 1,000lb bombs had fallen on the nearby housing estates of Buchenhohe and Klaushohe. It had been a further half-hour before Tallboys had begun to fall in the Berghof area. One side of the Berghof had been hit and there was damage to the homes of both Göring and Bormann, as well as a workers' camp.

At the SS barracks, the north-eastern building had been demolished, while the north-western and south-western ones were severely damaged. The headquarters building was on fire and the SS administrative head's residence had also been damaged.

Down in his shelter with his family and their captors, Göring survived the bombing, being taken to Austria by the SS. It was only a temporary reprieve; he would later surrender to the Americans and stand trial for war crimes at Nuremberg, but commit suicide by poison shortly before he was due to face the hangman. In Berlin, Hitler would soon die in his bunker, after saying that if the German people lost this war they would have proved unworthy of him.

Berchtesgaden was soon occupied by the US 3rd Infantry Division, despite the attempts of other American and French units to get there first. They found that the damaged Berghof had been set on fire by the SS, but this did not stop them from indulging in a souvenir hunt! Göring's train and his art collection were 'liberated' by the US 101st Airborne Division, who also went off with Hitler's Mercedes-Benz touring car. Those of more modest means and ambitions who 'acquired' pistols did a roaring trade.

This raid turned out to be the last one to use any of the Wallis bombs. On 8 May Victory in Europe Day was declared and at Woodhall Spa everyone paraded in a hangar at 1415 where a radio had been installed, to hear Churchill declare, 'We may allow ourselves a brief moment of rejoicing.' Afterwards, the Station Commander reminded them of future commitments with regard to Japan. In the evening there was an all-ranks party in the Sgts' Mess, with a pause for the King's speech at 2100. In an era of rationing the buffet was unforgettable, including iced Victory cakes, the biggest of which was resplendent in white and gold, weighing in at 200lb!

Someone who was not dancing round Piccadilly that day was a white-haired man bent over a drawing board at Burhill. For the moment Barnes Wallis was still there, although not long after the war ended he would move back to Brooklands, this time to the old race track clubhouse, which would not be needed again for its former purpose.

For him this was a normal working day. Compressibility and transonic flight were problems to others, but new opportunities for him. For those in the Services that rejoicing was indeed brief; there was still one more enemy to deal with. Tiger Force, a mixture of Lancasters and Lincolns, would be Bomber Command's contribution to the bombing of Japan. With the exception of those men deemed ineligible for Far East service, 617 would soon be on their way, and four other squadrons could expect to convert to Tallboy use shortly. Among the aircraft earmarked for this new role was PA474, a then-new Lancaster BI, which at the time of writing still flies as the centrepiece of the RAF's Battle of Britain Memorial Flight.

It was not to be. The following August two bombs deadlier than anything Wallis could have devised fell on the cities of Hiroshima and Nagasaki. Surrender followed on 15 August.

The war was over, and those who had lived for six years under a death sentence slowly came to terms with the fact that they were going to live. The airmen and women would receive their civilian suits, queue up for their rail warrants and depart for home, if home still existed. The aircraft would go to the scrap heap, while most of their bases would revert to the farmland they had been before 1939. And the bombs – what of those?

14

Aftermath

What a glorious thing must be a victory, sir.
The greatest tragedy in the world, madam, except a defeat.

The Duke of Wellington, 1835

To the US 79th Division, who took it in 1945, the Möhne dam was just another in a string of objectives. With its wartime repair still visible, the valley below it strewn with debris and guarded by a formidable array of defences, most of which had seen little or no use, it presented a forlorn picture. The towers had been cut down almost to the level of the parapet and with them had gone the two rooftop gun positions that had done their best to defend the dam on that fateful night nearly two years before.

To Wallis, allowed into Germany to see the damage his bombs had done, this was an important stop. At last he had the opportunity to check on the ground the target that had become almost an obsession over the two years up to May 1943. The snag was that the locals, some sullen, some resentful and some still fearing what might happen to them, hardly knew how to address the designer of a weapon that had caused a major disaster.

The best information Wallis could get out of anyone was that obtained from the proprietor of the Seehof Hotel, which was on the shore of the Möhnesee. Communication was difficult, for his German was not good and the man was only prepared to talk to him through the barred front door. However, Wallis did gather that only two Upkeeps had struck the dam, which confirmed what Maltby had observed at the time and what had been said in the reports afterwards. This meant that Young had breached it and that Maltby had widened the gap.

Bielefeld viaduct had been overrun by the US 5th Armored division on 2 April. On 22 May Wallis visited the ruins that Calder's Grand Slam and the Tallboys had created. Despite the bitter winds and icy rain, he described the bombing as 'marvellous'. It had taken six long years, but everything he had worked towards since 1939 had come about in the end.

A joint Anglo-American report on the pens and shelters hit by both types of earthquake bomb in Holland and north-western Germany showed that against such massive structures even Grand Slam had its limitations:

> The most that can be achieved is temporary and repairable damage, plus a large morale factor which cannot be assessed. The contents of the heaviest concrete structures may be severely damaged by the fall of concrete resulting from hits with six and ten-ton bombs. There is no evidence that fragmentation plays an important part in this role.

At the Ijmuiden pens, the lightest of these structures, the interior walls had only been pitted by falling fragments, while at others, such as the Farge shelter and the Finkenwerder pens, that had not occurred. Ijmuiden also provided evidence that Tallboy, and by implication Grand Slam, were liable to fracture some two-thirds of the way back from the nose after impact on such a hard target.

The Bielefeld viaduct from ground level, photographed just after the war's end. This was the sight that greeted Wallis when he came to look it over. (IWM neg. no. BU12138)

The vital necessity for extremely accurate bombing is apparent in all cases. Only direct hits or 'near' misses are effective and the targets are relatively small. The bombing at Hamburg is outstanding in this respect.

Someone who would have agreed with the comments on the weakness of the Tallboy's casing *was* the German Bomb Disposal officer who had dealt with one in Norway. The *Tirpitz*, still on her side at Tromsø, was checked over by six RAF officers, led by Air Commodore Bilney. From the air ten Tallboy craters were clearly visible and one broken bomb was found on the muddy shore.

This bomb was scoured on its nose and the body was slightly flattened, the fracture having occurred a few inches behind the spigot hole in the body. The German Bomb Disposal officer was interviewed and he expressed the opinion that this bomb had hit the ship and ricocheted approximately two hundred yards to its present position on the mud, which is where he found it, and attempted to burn out the main filling. This seems to be a highly probable explanation, as it is most likely that the bomb would have detonated in close proximity to the ship with 0.07 seconds' delay fusing – this would account for the third apparent hit shown on the strike photographs.

Bilney's party also interviewed two senior *Kriegsmarine* officers and Tromsø dockyard's Chief Engineer, as the surviving members of the *Tirpitz*'s crew were no longer in the area. They were told that after the Altenfjord Tallboy attack in September the Germans had given up all hope of repairing the battleship and had brought her south to be moored at the spot at which she now lay for use as a floating fortress. 'The informants expressed the opinion that the ship would not have capsized had not an internal explosion occurred, caused by a fire started from the second bomb hit.'

They went on to recommend that 'immediate steps should be taken to produce a forged steel design of the 12,000lb and 22,000lb MC bombs, to overcome failures due to the fracture of the case when subjected to side blows on passing through a labyrinthine target.'

The interviewees all agreed that when the *Catechism* attack started the first bomb to hit the *Tirpitz* struck her almost amidships, being quickly followed by a second direct hit abaft and to port of C turret, starting a fire. The ship had previously had a slight list to starboard, but immediately after this hit it took on one to port.

Due to the shock and speed of events, plus the fact that of 1,900 crew on board at the time over half became casualties, it was not possible from then on to give a clear-cut picture of the sequence of events, or of the damage sustained. The Tallboy hits had pushed the armoured deck downwards, opening up a gap between it and the side of the ship.

Twenty minutes after the first hit an explosion occurred and the cumulative damage tore a hole 120 feet long on the port side from deck to keel. Very shortly after this the ship had rolled over to port through 140 degrees, embedding the superstructure in the bottom of the fjord. It was said that the main armament had been in action, but that things had happened too quickly for anyone to be able to open the turret doors.

At the time of its examination the hull's starboard bilge keel was nearly vertical. Most of the armour had been removed from the starboard side and returned to Germany. One hundred feet of the bows had been destroyed and the hull plating had been pushed in for a further fifty feet aft of this, all of which had been inflicted during *Paravane*. Amidships, a near miss had severely dished in the outer bottom over a length of approximately fifty feet, just above the bilge keel. The mainframes were badly sprung inwards and serious damage would have occurred if the vessel had not been of welded construction.

The RAF officers had some interesting observations to make concerning the *Tirpitz*'s structure. 'In this ship the plates are butt-welded together, and they are also welded to the stringers, thus making a homogeneous but flexible structure. In spite of the fact that the outer bottom has been driven in to a maximum depth of approximately four feet, leakage was negligible, and in no case have the plates been torn apart. From the contour of this dishing, it is estimated that the 12,000lb bomb burst some sixty feet from the ship's bottom, and it is of interest to note that in spite of this near detonation of 5,200lb of Torpex, the ship's structure has stood up remarkably well.' This could have occurred during either *Obviate* or *Catechism*.

Reading between the lines in this report, it seems that Bilney's officers found it hard to believe that this supposedly unsinkable ship could have succumbed to just two bomb hits. It may also be asked why there were neither Royal Navy officers nor British ship designers in the party. Considering the fates of some British capital ships earlier in the war, they might have learned something. Did the Air Ministry still harbour critics of Wallis, who were reluctant to be proved wrong, and were their Lordships sulking because it was Bomber Command that had finished her off?

There were two other questions, which this report did not answer. Who had crippled the *Tirpitz* at Altenfjord and who had dealt the final blow at Tromsø? Neither 9 nor 617 were prepared to give ground on this issue, which was aggravated when a piece of armour plate was presented to them after the ship had been scrapped.

In 1999, a former 9 Sqdn bomb-aimer told me how this came about. On return to civilian life one of his aircrew colleagues had lived in the Grimsby area, making his living in the fishing industry. Being on one occasion obliged to put into Tromsø, he was made particularly welcome by the Norwegians when they realised he had been with one of the units that had capsized the ship. He asked for a souvenir and the grateful local population, unaware of squadron rivalries, passed the armour plate to the RAF as a gesture of thanks. Inevitably, both squadrons continued to claim the credit.

The presentation of two pieces might have avoided what followed, although undoubtedly some die-hards would not have been content with one. At first, joint ownership was not a problem, since both squadrons were stationed at RAF Binbrook with Lincolns. However, the time came for a parting of the ways when 617 disbanded for a while. Whoever held this trophy would be deemed to have sunk the ship, so it therefore became acceptable for each squadron to steal it from the other, using everything from guile to brute force. A Vulcan's bomb bay is said to have come in handy for illicitly shipping it from one base to another and 9's veterans have told the story of one 617 pilot who put his career on the line by using it for this purpose. This ceased once the Panavia Tornado came on the scene.

When the plate went to the RAF Museum that might have been thought the end of the matter. It was not, for an RAF wing commander and former latter-day 9 Sqdn CO told me that his unit had succeeded in charming the museum into parting with it. When he relinquished command it had been firmly cemented into the guardroom wall at RAF Laarbruch in Germany.

However, 617 somehow removed the armour plate from there and carted it off in triumph to their base at RAF Marham in Norfolk. In 1994 they took on a maritime role and moved to Lossiemouth, taking the plate with them to a new and very appropriate location. According to Rob Owen, the 617 Sqdn Association's official historian, it is now protected by several elaborate warning devices, including seismographs – better than the Crown Jewels, in his opinion, and just as valuable to whoever holds it.

Something less contentious was one of the ship's anchor chain links, which in 1992 was presented to the RAF Museum, forming part of a display on the *Tirpitz* in the Bomber Command Hall.

However, these are not the only pieces of the ship to have survived. 617 Sqdn historian Jim Shortland was to have a hand in the preservation of other items. In 1994 he had met a Norwegian, Knut Tessem, at Tromsø. Subsequently, while driving round Haakøy island, Mr Tessem came across a farmer who was replacing some fencing posts in a field. He noticed that the Malay teak wood that had been used had been taken from the *Tirpitz*'s deck. The farmer's late father had used any wood available after the war, as materials were in short supply. Mr Tessem rescued the wood from being burnt and arranged for the Scandinavian Airlines System airline to ship the pieces to Britain, which they did free of charge. They were subsequently passed to Jim Shortland. My thanks to Ken Rogers, formerly of 9 Sqdn, who kindly loaned one to me and passed on this story.

My research has led me to certain conclusions as to who got the *Tirpitz*. However, this is one block I am not prepared to stick my head on. The saga of the armour plate, like Agatha Christie's *Mousetrap*, looks set to run indefinitely.

Wallis had not been the only one to visit Bielefeld, for, as mentioned earlier, a five-man team from the US Strategic Bombing Survey would also pick over the remains of the bridge and viaduct targets. As the biggest bomb the US 8th Air Force had used on them had been the 1,000lb GP type, the Tallboy and Grand Slam craters greatly impressed them, as did the economy of force used by the RAF in delivering these weapons. Also apparent was the great effort made by the Germans to clear up and rebuild, even after the earthquake bomb attacks. Their country, gripped by fear after the failed attempt on Hitler's life, had resisted almost to the end.

It will have become apparent that neither Upkeep, Tallboy nor Grand Slam were all-conquering wonder weapons, capable of winning the European war on their own. When pitted against hard targets the two earthquake bombs showed a tendency to either prematurely detonate or break up – but it should be remembered that they had been designed with earth in mind, not concrete. Given the data Wallis had on German concrete constructions, and his deduction that the U-boat pens would use roof bomb-traps, it is surprising that he did not allow for this in their design.

Despite this, it is clear that they achieved what other Allied bombs, even in large numbers, could not. Although they could not break the German will to resist, they could seriously disrupt the means to do so. In the last year of the war Tallboy and Grand Slam assisted greatly in defeating a resilient and ruthless enemy, frustrating any attempts on his part to prolong resistance by the introduction of new technology. Apart from the first atomic weapons, the earthquake bombs were the most effective air-dropped weapons used during the Second World War. Furthermore, with some exceptions, this was accomplished without high civilian casualties.

However, what really mattered was not the suitability of the Lancaster, the size, shape and speed of the bombs, the hardness of the targets or any other statistics. It was the skill of those who produced the bombs, those who serviced them on the ground and the courage of the crews who went into action with them. Although 9 and 617 were posted to the Far East as part of Tiger Force, the end of the war did not mean the end of the earthquake bomb trials. Those men of 617 who were deemed ineligible for overseas service were posted to C Flight of 15 Sqdn, taking their BI Specials with them. PD137, one aircraft that had not seen action, was allocated to the Bomb Ballistics Unit at Woodbridge in December 1945, later going to the RAE.

It fell to 15 Sqdn to take over 617's mantle, as they now had the only bomber crews in the UK who were experienced in the use of both the earthquake bombs and the SABS sight. Watten, previously used for Disney bomb practice, was apparently now used for Grand Slams as well. In May 1946 15 Sqdn took part with a USAAF B-29 Superfortress unit in Operation *Front Line* (known to the Americans as *Ruby*), during which a number of Tallboys and Grand Slams were once again dropped against Farge and an unspecified target on Heligoland – probably whatever remained of the coastal gun batteries.

Both USAAF and RAF reports after the 1946 trials stated that none of the bombs dropped had turned out to be suitable against heavily reinforced concrete targets, and recommended further bomb tests against them. Of the thirteen bombs dropped, only two had hit. It was considered that there was a pressing need to resume trials in 1947, with Farge once again as the target. This would take place after 15 Sqdn had dropped fifteen bombs in a battleship trial with the Royal Navy – it is not known against which ships or what type of bombs were used.

By now the squadron had only six Lancasters, four of which were BI Specials and not suitable for the 1,650lb model bomb which was to be tested. Two other Tallboy aircraft would have been, but the unit was about to re-equip with Lincolns. There was a requirement for six of these new aircraft, modified at Scampton and RAF Mildenhall, to be fitted with SABS and radar altimeters.

However, not all of the British bombs would be dropped by them, nor would they be the first in the queue. Once again three of the US Strategic Air Command's B-29s would be involved, as it had been deemed necessary to drop a 1,650lb model bomb from 30,000ft, which the SABS was unable to do. Also due to be test-dropped by the B-29s were two new US 25,000lb bombs, known as Amazon II and Samson. Although initially referred to by the Americans as Ruby II, these trials later became known as the *Harker Project*.

Using PRU coverage obtained by 542 Sqdn in February 1945, just before the Grand Slam attack, the parameters for the trials were laid down. Red flags would indicate the danger area, which included part of the nearby river, and cameras would follow each bomb's progress. Even though the bombs were inert, jettisoning in the target area could be carried out only in cases of emergency. Attacks from the north and east sides were forbidden because of the danger to nearby housing – which must have led to a few wry smiles among the veterans who manned these aircraft! The war had been over for just two years, but the official attitude towards German civilians had changed.

The trials began on 4 August, with the B-29 crews obtaining six hits from 30,000-35,000ft with the RAF 1,650-pounders. There were also five hits out of fifteen Amazon IIs dropped from 17,000ft. Six Samson bombs were apparently also due to be tested, but no further details of these are available.

From 20 September 15 Sqdn's Lincolns also tested the 1,650lb model, obtaining seven hits, although some broke up on impact with the 4 1/2-metre-thick roof. There were also further trials with an unspecified type of 1,000lb bomb, obtaining three hits out of seven. The RAE rated all this as beneficial and satisfactory.

As the world took stock after the war and changed, so Bomber Command found itself having to change with it. The Lancaster was relegated to maritime reconnaissance and lifeboat dropping with Coastal Command until it finally bowed out of RAF service in 1956. Its successor, the Lincoln, although it soldiered on through the anti-terrorist wars in Malaya and Kenya, was outdated as soon as jet fighters came on the scene.

With the arrival of atomic weapons and the West now seeing the Soviet Union as a threat, Bomber Command had to alter its thinking. After witnessing the second atomic raid on Nagasaki, Leonard Cheshire had summed up the feelings of many people by saying, 'We've got to have the biggest and the best bombs. That's the first principle of survival.' For a country which had nearly lost the Second World War due to its neglected defences, but which had ultimately triumphed against a ruthless enemy, there was no question of accepting the idea that only the Americans should have atomic energy. Also, there was as yet no campaign for nuclear disarmament.

In 1947 work began on an atomic device called Hurricane, which was successfully exploded in 1952. This in turn led to Blue Danube, a British nuclear bomb whose smooth aerodynamic shape clearly owed much to the lessons learned by Wallis and his team. This weapon finally showed that the day of the thousand-bomber raid was over. Provided they got through, one aircraft and one bomb could cause far more damage. That applied to the Russians as well. The prospect of a nuclear war was a chilling one, but it was doubtful whether Britain could rely on the USA to protect her against any future Soviet aggression, especially if there was the threat of atomic weapons being used. Whatever might be said in public, there was still the feeling that the Americans might not take part in any future European war. After all, they had taken their time coming into the last two.

These doubts were underlined by the Suez crisis in 1956, which led to the unprecedented spectacle of both the American and Soviet United Nations delegates condemning the actions taken by Britain and France. Should the button be pushed, there would be no time for Churchillian appeals to the New World to come forth to the assistance of the old. For the time being there was a large American presence in Europe, but isolationism was still a recent memory and the possibility of some future White House administration withdrawing their forces into 'Fortress America' was not one that could be ignored. A nuclear war would not drag on for six years; if it began it would be fought by whoever happened to be on duty at the time, using whatever was available.

Bomber Command therefore needed not only these new weapons, but also a new generation of bombers to carry them. The arrival of the first jet fighters had shown the way forward and when the three V-bombers – the Vickers Valiant, the Avro Vulcan and the Handley Page Victor – had come into service, the RAF once again had aircraft that were comparable to any in the world.

The new situation also meant that the Command had to rethink its methods as well. Once the Soviet Union had exploded its first bomb, putting Britain onto four minutes' notice of Armageddon, it was pointless having a bomber force that would be incinerated before it could get off the ground. A fast response would be necessary, which meant that aircraft would have to be kept at readiness, to be dispersed to distant airfields in times of crisis. Bomber crews would have to get used to scrambles. This was all reminiscent of the Battle of Britain and it needed some high-ranking Fighter Command officers, moved into bomber circles, to make it happen.

Although the V-bombers were designed primarily for nuclear weapons, there was still provision for conventional bombs to be carried. Indeed, these were used on the first and only time the Valiant went into action, at Suez. However, neither the Valiant nor the Vulcan could carry either of the earthquake bombs. The Victor's cavernous bomb bay could, as an alternative to the bulky Blue Danube, accommodate either one Grand Slam or two Tallboys! It is not known whether it was ever tested with either of these loads; it would have been an impressive sight to see.

In this new nuclear world there was little place for either Tallboy or Grand Slam. Large air-dropped weapons finally went out of favour when Blue Danube was replaced by the Blue Steel stand-off nuclear missile in 1963. Jack Froude, who, it will be remembered, had helped to draw them at Burhill, witnessed Grand Slam's final demise:

Many years later, while working for Faireys after the war, I had occasion to visit Westcott aerodrome to supervise the static firing of some test rockets. A lady manager showed me the route to the test site, and over to one side there were the unused ten-tonners being 'steamed out.'

When the V-Force bowed out in favour of the Polaris missile-carrying submarines in 1969 there was no longer a need for these weapons either. At almost the end of its career the Vulcan finally went into action in the Falklands in 1982, but each aircraft dropped twenty-one 1,000lb retarded bombs; a far cry from the Wallis designs of nearly forty years before.

Several references have already been made in the text to the manner in which *Chastise* was depicted in the film *The Dam Busters*. Directed by Michael Anderson and made by the Associated British Picture Corporation in the early 1950s, it was based on Paul Brickhill's best-selling book, the screenplay bemg provided by R. C. Sheriff.

Guy Gibson was played by Richard Todd – a part he probably enjoyed more than any other – and which, as he delved deeper into the character, he felt privileged to do. Michael Redgrave played BarnesWallis. Other parts were played by the Australian actor Bill Kerr as Mick Martin, Derek Farr as Gp Capt. Whitworth and Basil Sydney in a suitably domineering mood as Harris. Robert Shaw, who would go on to become an actor and playwright of some note, played the part of Sgt John Pulford, Gibson's flight engineer. The real Gp Capt. Whitworth acted as the film's technical advisor.

A considerable research effort was made before and during filming. Copies of the script were sent for approval to some of 617's surviving wartime members, while Richard Todd visited Gibson's home and watched film of him, noting his personal characteristics. There was some hilarity when Wallis and Michael Redgrave first met, as Redgrave did not really resemble him! However, make-up can achieve all sorts of wonders and a fair likeness resulted. Redgrave said to Wallis, 'I'm not going to imitate you, you know,' to which Wallis replied, 'No, you must not do that, you will have to create me.'

Attention to detail was evident throughout the film, which begins with Redgrave shooting marbles across a tin bath, using the original catapult, which is now on display in the RAF Museum at Hendon. It then goes on to illustrate some of the wrangles that Wallis had with various officials in the early days. When he was asked whether this part had not been overdone, Wallis replied, 'The half has not been told.'

Many of the original locations were made available for the film. These included the No.2 ship tank at the National Physical Laboratory at Teddington, complete with the original 1942 catapult made by Wallis and his team for shooting the model Upkeeps along the surface. A beach at Skegness doubled for that at Reculver, although, as the film was being shot in black-and white, the original test films could be used. The scene where Richard Todd, as Gibson, watches a Mosquito drop an early Highball is real, the only difference being that the aircraft he 'sees' through his binoculars had completed its flight eleven years before!

The lack of suitable aircraft meant that the same thing had to be done with regard to the early Wellington drops at Chesil Beach. By 1954, when the film was being shot, the Wellington was on the point of going out of RAF service. The best the film makers could do was to provide one shot of a Wellington TX, MF628, flying down the runway towards the camera. However, this shot was spoilt by the fact that this aircraft still wore its post-war Training Command colours, being resplendent in bright silver dope with yellow bands! Richard Todd is then shown the original 1942 film, featuring the camouflaged Wellington BIII that was used at the time.

Three weeks of filming were carried out at Scampton in May 1954. Most of those taking part had worn other uniforms at one time or other – Richard Todd had seen action in Normandy as a Parachute Regiment officer – and had no trouble in recreating the atmosphere of a wartime bomber station. Actors playing officers were constantly saluted by real RAF other ranks, so they decided to respond in kind rather than take time explaining!

The Lancaster had not yet departed from the RAF's inventory, so four BVIIs – NX673, NX679, NX782 and RT686 – were collected from a Maintenance Unit at Aston Down, then flown to RAF Hemswell and made ready. These had all been built by Austin Motors late in the war and had seen no action. It appears that Boscombe Down's photographic Lancaster, NX739, also took part, as Richard Todd remembered five aircraft flying over Scampton in perfect vic formation.

The arrival of the Lancasters set the tone for what was to come, as they then proceeded to beat up the airfield, to the approval of the watching cast. This unexpected display was brought to a breathtaking finish by a formation landing on the grass alongside the runway.

Most of these aircraft would retain their serial numbers during filming, though NX679 masqueraded as ED932 for a re-enactment of the famous shot of Gibson's crew by its entry door. Three of them were converted to resemble the *Chastise* aircraft, while NX782 remained standard, being marked up as the 106 Sqdn aircraft that appeared in Richard Todd's debut scene. RAF Lincolns, although bigger than the Lancaster, had a similar silhouette and were parked in the background to give the effect of a full squadron.

There was a problem over the shape and size of the bomb. Upkeep was still on the Secret List at the time and as film of the early test drops had shown its original spherical shape, this was the version mocked-up to go into the Lancasters' bomb bays. It resembled a giant cheese, larger than the real thing and hanging down further below the aircraft.

So began the legend that the bomb that was dropped on the dams was completely round. Over the years since then I have heard countless people say, when confronted by the real thing:'But I saw the film, and it looked nothing like this!' Indeed, and deliberately so. There is a story that certain gentlemen from some secret government department visited Scampton during the filming, inspected the mocked-up bombs and departed, satisfied with them! None of the Wallis bombs came off the Secret List until 1962.

The film's star was allowed to start a Lancaster and taxi it, although he later admitted that he did have an RAF instructor crouched down beside him. Indeed, Richard Todd was so thoroughly coached in all aspects of heavy bomber flying that he felt he could have coped with a real emergency.

Air-to-air scenes were shot from a modified Vickers Varsity trainer, the Lancasters being flown by Lincoln crews from Hemswell. Flying in formation with each other, and also with regard to the camera aircraft, had its hairy moments, but all concerned were determined to get it right. The Derwent reservoir near Sheffield doubled for the dams and the Morse for the soundtrack was supplied by none other than Wg Cdr W. Dunn, who had received it at Grantham on the night of the raid.

Interior scenes were shot in a mocked-up cockpit at the studios at Elstree, which meant that those who were playing pilots or flight engineers had to sweat it out under arc lights for up to four hours at a time. Included were models of the Möhne and the Eder, made with the same attention to detail as the originals. Erected on one of the huge sound stages, these were sealed off from any outside noise by locked steel doors.

The water the model dams held back had been treated with washing powder to encourage it to foam when a charge went off. Alongside each model was a two-foot track with a trolley on which a camera had been mounted. On command, the camera would race down the track, giving a wide view of the approach to the dam. As it came level with it a high column of water would rise into the air. The camera would continue to move, filming water spilling over the top of the wall until the trolley reached the end of its run.

The film received its UK premiere on 16 May 1955 – the twelfth anniversary of the attack. It was an immediate and lasting success. One reviewer commented, 'There has never been a film like this, or quite as good.' Although events were telescoped – the unsuccessful attack on the Sorpe is only briefly referred to – and the special effects would hardly stand comparison with today's computer-generated marvels, it has a sense of atmosphere and period that other more modern war films lack.

The Dambusters March, specially written by Eric Coates, was successful in its own right and is frequently heard on the concert platform today, but music is kept to the minimum during the attack sequences; the crews' terse comments, backed by the drone and sudden bellow of the Merlins, supply enough tension in themselves.

For me the most memorable scenes come towards the end, with a series of shots shown for the most part in almost complete silence, letting the story speak for itself without music or commentary. Martin's Lancaster taxies in apparently intact, but at the last moment severe flak damage to his starboard wing becomes apparent, leading you to wonder how he flew it home in that state. A letter left behind by an airman who will not return sits on his dressing table, waiting for someone to collect it. Australian actor Bill Kerr, as Martin, and one of his crew members return to their room, to stretch out fully clothed on their beds with understated but clear signs of fatigue.

Perhaps the most poignant scene of all is the final one, where Michael Redgrave asks Gibson if it was all worth it, to receive an encouraging reply. Richard Todd then announces that he has some letters to write – and indeed he has, all fifty-six of them – and strides off, a single figure, into the distance. The loneliness of command is well illustrated.

In the early 1990s Richard Todd commented, 'The film stands up well to the passage of time, nearly forty years, and I think this is largely due to the fact that we had jolly good story, firmly based on the facts and told in a believable way.'

Although he became friendly with Michael Redgrave, Wallis was not entirely happy with the way he had appeared in the film, feeling that Redgrave had played him as a rather mild-mannered but determined old buffer. Someone who passed that opinion on to me was John Bridger, who as a sixteen-year-old draughtsman met Wallis on three occasions at Brooklands while delivering drawings from a City firm, Brewer & Son, for his post-war projects. John was told this conversation and formed the impression that Wallis had been a good deal more forceful than the film had made him out to be. To judge from the comments made in their interviews, it was a description that Reg Firman and Sir George Edwards would have agreed with, although both had always respected him.

Some two years after their filming parts had been completed the Lancasters went for scrap. No one thought of preserving them, though luckily someone had the wit to hang onto the Wellington, which can be seen today in the RAF Museum's Bomber Command Hall, restored to its original 1944 camouflage finish. Nearby is a display on the Dambusters, featuring test items used by Wallis and a film consisting of still shots, narrated by – who else? – Richard Todd.

A story of this kind would be incomplete without a mention of what happened to the main characters later on. Vickers made Barnes Wallis Chief of Aeronautical Research and Development of their Aviation Section. After the war his department moved from Burhill into the Brooklands race track clubhouse which due to the closure of the track, was no longer needed for its original purpose. Wallis took over the office that until 1939 had been used by Percy Bradley, the last Clerk of the Course.

While Rex Pierson and George Edwards in the nearby factory took up the challenge of designing the Valiant and the Viscount airliner, Wallis continued to work on a variety of exotic projects. These included a flight model of the ill-fated Miles M52 transonic aircraft, a flying model named *Wild Goose*, which pioneered the use of variable-geometry, the *Green Lizard* guided missile and the *Heyday* rocket-powered torpedo, whose body had been designed to reduce drag. His last project was a Mach

Sir Barnes Wallis, photographed post-war in his study at the Brooklands Clubhouse. The airship painting, bomb and aircraft models around him bear witness to his varied contributions to British aviation. (Author's collection)

The Brooklands Museum Clubhouse, photographed during the 1980s, shortly after the Museum Trust had taken possession. Displayed against the wall are the two earthquake bombs. Also visible is the Fiat Panda that inadvertently came into contact with the smaller one. The post-war office used by Wallis was on the first floor, at the left of the building. (S. Flower)

5 airliner, which could have flown from London to Australia in three hours. None of these ever came to fruition, despite the fact that Wallis was often proved right and indeed to be ahead of his time, which did not always endear him to some of the lesser mortals around him. His swing-wing work, despite initial government disinterest, led to the General Dynamics F-111 and the Panavia Tornado. This aircraft was to serve the RAF well in the Gulf War of 1991 and over Kosovo eight years later.

Although Wallis had received a CBE as a result of *Chastise*, it may be asked why there were no further rewards after the war for his bomb designs. Harris recommended a knighthood for him, but it has been said that this was blocked by certain jealous individuals within Vickers. Nor were his enemies confined to his own company. The post-war Labour government contained at least one member – Sir Stafford Cripps – who did not like him, and some of Whitehall's warriors could not get over the fact that he had shown them how wrong their bombing theories were. A cash award did come his way, but, mindful of the sacrifices that others had made when taking his bombs into action, he promptly put it all into a fund at his old school, Christ's Hospital in Sussex, to help educate the sons of men who had died serving in the RAF.

There was also that revulsion from all things military which was the inevitable aftermath of six years of total war. Future British governments would not care to be reminded of the fact that they had had to take the war to Germany in order to win it, and the deaths of German civilians by British bombs was something to be pushed into the past, along with those who had made it possible. It was for that reason that, unlike those Fighter Command aircrew who had taken part in the Battle of Britain, the men of Bomber Command never received the campaign award that they deserved. The RAF's sole airworthy Lancaster flies today under the banner of the Battle of Britain Memorial Flight, not that of Bomber Command.

In 1968 the contribution that Wallis had made to aviation in general was belatedly recognised and he received a knighthood; an honour he courteously accepted. He was not about to let his new title go to his head; when asked at the start of a 1973 television documentary what he would like to be remembered as, he immediately replied, 'As the grandfather of twenty grandchildren.'

Wallis finally retired at the age of eighty-four, but continued to work from home. This was hardly surprising as when Richard Todd had asked him whether he would retire, he had replied, 'No. I still have nine years' work on my drawing board.'

Although increasingly frail in appearance, his mind remained as active as ever, continuing to veer in new and unexpected directions. This extract from what was probably the last filmed interview of him is indicative of that. Wallis was working on his drawing board at home and the young lady who interviewed him was off camera.

> *Interviewer* 'What are you working on at the moment, Sir Barnes?'
> *Wallis* 'I'm working out the age at which I will die.'
> *Interviewer* (unsure whether to take him seriously) 'And what age will that be?'
> *Wallis* 'Ninety-three.'

Sir Barnes Wallis went into hospital for a rest in October 1979 and died peacefully in his sleep on 30 October at the age of ninety-two. As usual, his calculations had been close to the mark, if not actually on it.

Norman 'Spud' Boorer retired as Chief Executive in 1981, having worked at Brooklands for Vickers, the British Aircraft Corporation and British Aerospace for fifty years. This included post-war work in the Clubhouse with 'Wally' – he must have been one of very few people to use that nickname. One of his many memories was of being at dinner in Norfolk after the war and finding the German lady sitting next to him had been on the receiving end of the floods caused by *Chastise*! After retirement he became an active supporter of the Brooklands Museum and was one of the team involved in the salvage of a Wellington bomber from Loch Ness in September 1985.

Joseph 'Mutt' Summers, Vickers' Chief Test Pilot, retired in 1951, his final task being the first flight of the Valiant. He subsequently went into hospital for what should have been a routine operation, but did not survive it. It was a sad end for someone who had followed a dangerous occupation for over twenty years.

George Edwards, the Experimental Department Manager, had nursed a ambition to run the Vickers factory at Weybridge ever since his arrival there in 1935. Eventually he was to achieve that and more , retiring at the end of 1975 as the Chairman of the British Aircraft Corporation. In 1956 he too was knighted for his services to aviation, especially for the highly successful Viscount airliner.

Sqdn Ldr Maurice 'Shorty' Longbottom, the cottage-demolishing Highball pilot referred to in Chapter 4, continued to fly with Vickers and was killed on 6 January 1945 while testing a Vickers Warwick. On the approach to land at Brooklands the aircraft's rudder overbalanced and it descended in a flat spin into a nearby railway cutting.

Roy Chadwick, without whose Lancaster none of this would have been possible, continued as Avro's Chief Designer. He was killed on 23 August 1947 when taking part in the flight test of an Tudor airliner prototype whose aileron controls had been fitted the wrong way round. His boss, Roy Dobson, was knighted in 1945. A fierce defender of his company's interests, but who nevertheless found time for active involvement with several others, Dobson died in 1968.

Air Chief Marshal Sir Arthur Harris was promoted to Marshal of the RAF and was made a baronet – a small reward, some thought, for Bomber Command's achievements under his leadership. He left the RAF to become a businessman in Rhodesia and died in retirement at Goring-on-Thames in 1984 at the age of ninety-two. He remains a controversial figure and when a statue of him was unveiled outside the RAF church at St Clement Danes in London's Strand, there were those who protested, Among those who witnessed this incident was David Shannon, who said of them, 'With people like that about I sometimes wonder if we weren't all wasting our time.'

Air Vice-Marshal the Honourable Sir Ralph Cochrane rose to Air Chief Marshal and was twice knighted again after the war. He died in December 1977 at the age of eighty-two.

Wg Cdr Jim Bazin relinquished command of 9 Sqdn in May 1945, shortly after VE Day. The following September his leadership was recognised by the award of a DSO. After the war he returned to his old unit, 607 Sqdn, commanding it until 1951. He later lived at St George's Hill, close to Brooklands, and died in 1985. P2617, a Hurricane flown by him during September 1940, is preserved in the Battle of Britain Museum at Hendon.

Wg Cdr Guy Gibson took up a staff job at the Air Ministry, which largely consisted of writing his classic book *Enemy Coast Ahead*, whose style indicates his aggressive character. Duty done, he then became 54 Base operations officer and badgered his superiors for more action. They reluctantly allowed him one more operation – as Master Bomber to a raid on Mönchengladbach on the night of 19-20 September 1944, for which he borrowed one of 627 Sqdn's Mosquitoes from Woodhall Spa. Gibson and his observer, Sqdn Ldr J. B. Warwick, were both killed in a crash on the way home.

What happened that night can never be fully known. Gibson's unpopularity with 627 has already been mentioned, leading one writer to suggest that some disgruntled ground crew member had deliberately sabotaged his aircraft. There is no reason to believe that such an event occurred, but several indications that it did not.

Firstly, Warwick was by all accounts a popular officer and there was no reason why anyone at Woodhall Spa should have wanted to kill him. Secondly, Gibson did not take KB213, the aircraft intended for him, nor did he take the spare aircraft as he did not consider it up to scratch. He and Sqdn Ldr Peter Mallinder of 627 then exchanged aircraft, which meant that Gibson would now fly KB267. Gibson's responsibility had been to cover the red target area with three TIs of that colour, which KB213 had carried. However, KB267 carried three greens, which he could not drop, so these were quickly removed from the bomb bay. All this extra activity, carried out at very short notice, would have ruled out any possibility of sabotage.

Gibson had not acted as a Master Bomber since *Chastise*, over a year before. Since then he had not been in action – officially – and he had just over eleven hours on the Mosquito, having flown it for the first time on 31 August. Warwick, though an experienced officer with a DFC, had been screened from operations and so had no experience at all of this type of aircraft. The two men had little if any experience of working as a team.

627's Chief Technical Officer was W/O Alan Webb, whom I met twice in the course of researching this book. He had been giving Warwick a last-minute briefing on the Mosquito from inside its cockpit when Gibson had arrived and curtly ordered him out of there. Alan Webb was the last man on the airfield to see either of them before the crash, as it was he who closed the hatch on them before take-off.

This was asking for disaster. It added up to a hastily-planned operation by an out-of-practice scratch crew while flying an aircraft that neither was fully familiar with, one of them an out-of-practice Master Bomber who no longer had any means of indicating the target. Gibson's most recent experience of 'twins' had been in part on the Lockheed P-38 Lightning, when 5 Group had tried one as an experiment. However, the Lightning was in some respects easier to fly than the Mosquito; an aircraft which did not forgive mistakes and which had to be flown the whole time. He would have to do that while also trying to direct 237 bombers over the target.

Over Mönchengladbach a 97 Sqdn bomb aimer saw two marker Mosquitoes. Gibson could see the AP but was of course unable to mark it, while the other crew could mark it but not see it. Gibson told them to follow him, saying he would flash his navigation lights when over it. This he did and was later heard to congratulate everyone, then order them home.

The crew of a 61 Sqdn Lancaster subsequently heard Gibson say that he had lost an engine, but that he would try to make home. A story that Gibson had not dropped his own TIs due to a hang-up could not have been true, for, as seen above, he was no longer carrying any. On the return his aircraft crashed at the van der Rhiet farm near Steenbergen-en-Kruisland in Holland. A witness reported that the Mosquito was seen to dive into the ground, that both engines had stopped and that the crew were silhouetted by a light in the cockpit.

German night fighters made no claims for this aircraft. Perhaps there had been a hit by light flak as they returned at low level. Alan Webb's opinion was that the aircraft's fuel supply had been mismanaged, especially as the area where it crashed was where he calculated the tanks would have to have been changed over. Also, a fire after landing indicated that there had still been fuel on board. The fuel cocks were behind Gibson's seat and accessible only to Warwick, whose lack of Mosquito experience has already been noted. The cockpit light that was seen may have been a torch switched on in an attempt to remedy this situation.

At first it was thought that only one man had been in the aircraft. Then Heer van der Rhiet found Gibson's wallet, which he should not have been carrying in action, and took it from the crash site before the Germans cordoned it off. Gibson s rank and decorations were not known to the Dutch at the time and it was not until after the war that the story, or most of it, could be pieced together.

In 1985 plans were unveiled for a new industrial site at Steenbergen. Due to the posssible presence of explosives at the crash site, the Recovery Unit of the Royal Netherlands Air Force checked the area, finding only some instruments and part of the Mosquito's tail.

A factory has since been built on this ground but there is a small memorial, placed nearby by Holt's Battlefield Tours in 1992. As Gibson had been a Scout this ceremony was attended by a Dutch troop – the Gibson Patrol – in pale blue uniforms. In addition three street names – 'Gibsonstraat','Warwickstraat' and 'Mosquitostraat' – remain to

Flight
Lieutenant
Len Sumpter
taking part in
a wreath-laying
ceremony at
the graves of
Gibson and
Warwick
in 1989.
(S. Flower)

The graves of
Gibson and
Warwick.
(S. Flower)

commemorate what happened. The Dutch are a peaceful race, but the effort made on their behalf by the Allies during the war years has never been forgotten.

It was not surprising that Alan Webb strongly objected to the sabotage theory, regarding it as offensive not only to himself, but to the men he worked with. Only hearsay supports it, and it can be treated with the contempt that it deserves.

Sqdn Ldr Harold Martin rose to become Air Marshal Sir Harold Martin KCB CB DSO and Bar DFC and two Bars AFC. In 1970 he became Commander-in-Chief RAF Germany, which meant that among the targets he had to defend were the Ruhr dams! He retired from the RAF in 1974 and died in November 1988.

Wg Cdr Leonard Cheshire regained his former rank of group captain and, as noted above, was present as an RAF observer at the second atomic bomb strike on Nagasaki. He left the RAFVR after the war and had some difficulty in settling down until he began the now famous Cheshire Homes, catering for the terminally ill. Although one of these was sited at Nagasaki, taking in survivors suffering from radiation sickness, he always insisted that this was not an act of reparation. Cheshire received a warm welcome from the inmates when he visited them, though the post-war Japanese government frowned on his visit. He would have been first to admit he would have achieved little without the support of his second wife, Sue Ryder.

Cheshire's health had been affected after the war by tuberculosis which, despite a 'rest cure' in the clear air of the Canadian Rockies, had left him with a gaunt appearance. Towards the end of his life he also contracted motor neurone disease. It was typical of him that he almost seemed to welcome it, saying that instead of speaking of 'The disabled', he could now say 'We, the disabled.'

Leonard Cheshire died on 31 July 1992 at the age of seventy-four. A remarkably courageous man.

Wg Cdr James 'Willie' Tait rose to group captain and was an ADC to the Queen after the war. He retired from the RAF on his fiftieth birthday in 1966, opting for the quiet life in South Wales.

Gp Capt. John Fauquier regained his old rank of air commodore before retiring from the RCAF to become a businessman in Toronto. His business, strangely enough, was building concrete structures – perhaps his experience of knocking them down came in handy. He died in 1981.

Flt Lt David Shannon, Len Sumpter's baby-faced pilot on both Lancasters and Mosquitoes, rose to Sqdn Ldr and later became a London businessman. He was proud of his RAAF service, especially when his portrait was hung in the Australian War Memorial in Canberra. Plagued by ill health in his later years, he died in April 1993, just before the fiftieth anniversary of *Chastise*.

Someone also not well enough to make that date was Flt Lt Len Sumpter, who had left the RAF in 1946, only to rejoin for four years as a physical training instructor with the rank of warrant officer. He too died in 1993. His one-time adversary, Karl Schutte, and Dougie Webb, the other 617 'original' who saw action again in 1945, lived on for another four years.

The three men who had survived being shot down on that unforgettable night over the dams are no longer alive. Hopgood's rear gunner, P/O Tony Burcher, once he had recovered from his spinal injury and been given new porcelain teeth to replace the ones he had lost during interrogation, was sent to *Stalag Luft III* POW camp. After surviving a gruelling forced march in the war's final days, he was repatriated in May 1945. Typically, he decided not to wait for transport home but made his own way to the Hook of Holland and boarded a ship for Harwich. On the way home he imbibed freely and his false teeth went over the side!

Burcher recommended Hopgood for a VC, but this was turned down as a second witness was necessary and he could not provide one. He returned to Australia the following year and subsequently transferred to the RAF. Later he lived with his wife, a former WAAF, in Cambridge before moving to Tasmania. He died in August 1995.

A story, possibly apocryphal but worth repeating, says that Tony Burcher returned to the Möhne in the 1950s. He found that the powerhouse immediately below the dam had not been rebuilt but, noting another at the side of the compensating basin, he somehow obtained access and talked to the staff without saying who he was. One of them said, 'Yes, we remember the raid very well. Some fool blew up the powerhouse and it caused us problems for years afterwards!' He did not have the heart to tell them that it was his own crew that had done it.

The bomb aimer responsible for that, P/O J. W. Fraser, also went to Stalag Luft III. After the war he became a forest ranger, dying in a road accident in the 1960s.

Sgt Freddie Tees, the rear gunner in Ottley's reserve wave aircraft, and the only crew member to live when it was shot down near Hamm, was treated in hospital for severe burns. He eventually went to a POW camp at Heydekrug on the Baltic coast. It is clear that he felt that sense of guilt that only the sole survivor can know, and two years behind barbed wire, on top of the pain he had suffered, could not have helped. He returned in 1945, only to learn that his mother had been killed by a crashing Stirling hitting the laundrette in which she worked.

The consequences of tragedy pursue some people to the grave. Freddie Tees handed in his uniform, got his ticket, became a hairdresser and, like everyone else in the post-war world, did what he could to move on. However, as books on *Chastise* were published and the film became popular, he began to receive enquiries about his part in the raid. His escape from Ottley's aircraft had been miraculous, but had he been saved just for this? It became clear to him that the past could not be left behind, for the letters, arriving at the rate of two or three a week, were causing him to constantly relive it. The pressure caused by them only ended with his death in 1982. He was, perhaps, the last victim of Operation *Chastise*.

My first visit to the Möhne and Eder dams had been in the summer of 1977 while working in West Germany. I had been staying at the town of Werl and one of the first things I had learned when I arrived was that the Möhnesee was just over the next ridge. So, that evening my driver and I took the road over that hill and as we drove along towards the village of Günne I saw the Möhne for the first time.

It was a dramatic glimpse through the trees of the air side of it, facing directly towards me, with the towers clearly visible. When we reached the restaurant at the side I realised just how massive it was. It hardly seemed possible that after reading about it so many years before, I was now actually there. My driver was Scottish and had seen several dams in his home country, but even he was impressed by this one. I looked for evidence of where it had been repaired, but the wartime scar had blended in with the original masonry to give a uniformly dark appearance, with moss growing on the air side.

There was no memorial on the dam to what had happened. The only signs of it were some postcards in the shop at the north side. I later learned that in the powerhouse that had been built at the side of the compensating basin in 1953, there were blinds that could be lowered, with drawings showing the attack. Subsequently we spotted the Eder on a map and spent a good part of one Sunday driving round trying to find it. This time the semi-circular repair that had been made was more obvious, due to two missing drainage slots.

When my father heard of this, he commented, 'I wouldn't have liked to have been British and lived round here after the war.' Perhaps it had been an uncomfortable time. However, I had the chance to see local civilians and BAOR personnel mix freely during a Saturday evening Tramps' Ball at a nearby Army camp. Whatever happened in the past has been forgiven if not forgotten.

In 1989 Capt. Paul Snook of Holt's Battlefield Tours organised a trip to the Ruhr dams, with a very special guest – none other than Len Sumpter, who would be returning to the area for the first time since the 1950s. He turned out to be a very down-to-earth character with a delightful sense of humour.

The Möhne dam in 1989. (S. Flower)

The scene as Len Sumpter, facing the camera, meets Karl Schutte for the first time since 1943. (S. Flower)

There were two coaches and only one special guest. Fortunately for me Len was on mine for most of the time, although this did mean some repetition of anecdotes later on, which he carried out with good humour. The long drive to Bochum was something of an endurance test, but our minds were taken off it by a showing of *The Dam Busters*. It was strange to be near to Len while he watched the actor playing him reacting as the film Lancaster rose up out of what was meant to be the steep-sided Eder valley. After all these years, a slight shake of his head showed that he still could not believe he had survived that.

Consequently, when we drove to the Möhne on Sunday 21 May there was a strong feeling of excitement. Juggling a tape-recorder and camera on the dam wall was not easy, particularly when several other enthusiasts were bent on doing the same thing. Thankfully I was able to record a good deal of what Len had to say, not only while we were on the dams, but also in transit between them.

The weather was beautiful and it was an unforgettable day, the climax of which undoubtedly came on the Möhne wall between the two towers, where Len proceeded to entertain us with the story of his improvised bombsight, amid a good deal of audience laughter. What he had to say has already been quoted in Chapter 3.

It was at this point that he was introduced to Karl Schutte, who since the war had lived nearby. The German television company WDR were also there to record the scene as they met for the first time since May 1943.

The two men made a strange contrast. Len, as befitted an ex-Grenadier Guardsman, was over six feet tall, with a considerable physical presence. Karl, on the other hand, was a foot shorter and looked as he would be incapable of hurting anyone, let alone bring down a Lancaster. However, the Iron Cross he had brought along, and had been persuaded to wear, spoke for itself. Several members of the audience, myself included, now had the job of trying to photograph this meeting and trying to record it at the same time, while trying to avoiding being trodden on by two coach-loads of applauding people on the wall.

Neither man spoke the other's language, which meant that a female relative of Karl's had to interpret, but that clear and unspoken bond between them was immediately apparent. I had heard of this happening elsewhere, but had not seen it until now.

It became impossible to do any further taping or filming on the dam; each man had no end of questions to ask the other, and we made our way back to the coaches behind

Together on the dam wall for the photographers. (S. Flower)

them, through the north tower, where Karl's gun had been mounted. While back on board I watched the two men talking nearby, then suddenly embrace; a spontaneous act of affection for which no words were necessary. Very few people saw that happen and for me it summed up the whole trip.

It was not over yet, for we still had the Eder to cover and Len had not been back there since the night he had attacked it. On the way he talked amusingly about the night he and Dave Shannon marked Munich in a Mosquito, then followed this by describing his experiences while attacking the Eder. On the dam he signed a photograph I had of the dam's final breach. That evening he also signed a painting of Gibson's Lancaster that I had nursed halfway across Europe. We toasted Bomber Command and Len managed to control his voice long enough to reply, 'On behalf of absent friends, thank you.'

On the way home we called at the Reichswald Commonwealth War Graves Cemetery, near Kleve in north-west Germany; the final resting place of 3,971 RAF and Commonwealth airmen. A minute's silence was observed, the Last Post being sounded by author Alan Cooper, a former Brigade of Guards musician. As Paul Snook climbed back aboard our coach he commented, 'It's strange, but every time I come I get the feeling they know we're here.'

During the early 1990s wartime fiftieth anniversaries came thick and fast. VE Day, remembered early in May 1995, was not something most Germans would have cared to celebrate, but amid the commemorations there was some humour.

A story told on BBC Radio Two's *Jazz Score* programme by the musician Roy Williams illustrated this. At around this time he had been playing at the Möhne, when a German in the audience asked him if he knew *The White Cliffs Of Dover*. He said yes, and would sing it. The German said, 'No, I'll do the vocals,' which led his accompanist to play with a sense of foreboding.

It was justified, for the song now went as follows:

There'll be Heinkels over
The white cliffs of Dover.
Tomorrow
Just you wait and see!

The Eder dam in 1989,
showing the missing
drainage slots. (S. Flower)

The Reichswald cemetery provides a sombre reminder of the bomber offensive's human cost. In the left foreground of this shot is the grave of Flight Lieutenant Bill Astell, lost during Operation *Chastise*. To his left is that of his flight engineer, Sergeant John Kinnear. (S. Flower)

The audience fell about laughing. Who said the Germans have no sense of humour? Dame Vera Lynn's rendition of it will never seem the same again.

The 1989 tour was a hard one to follow, but the fiftieth anniversary one in 1993 came close to it. I already knew from Paul Snook that Len's health precluded his being with us this time. On Monday 17 May the weather was good and there was some hilarity when during Paul's speech at the Möhne, a Tornado (of 617?) flew across the lake behind him. 'That was clever, Paul. How'd you manage that?' said I, amid laughter.

Although everyone has an enjoyable time, these tours always have an element of the pilgrimage and a serious mood is never far away. This time Karl Schutte met the sister and niece of Flt Lt John Hopgood. Everyone was aware of how awkward this meeting could have been, but it went off well. In a simple but memorable ceremony two wreaths, made by disabled former Servicemen and women at the British Legion's poppy factory at Richmond in Surrey, were cast down the side of the dam, towards two circular concrete markers in the basin below, where the old powerhouse had been.

The first wreath, from Holt's Tours, landed the right way up. The second, from the Royal Air Force Association's City of Derby branch, struck the side, turned over and hit the water upside-down. Three poppies separated from it and floated away, red against the shimmering blue water. Not for the first time I thought how appropriate the poppy was as a symbol of remembrance.

A drive up to the edge of a field near Ostonnen followed; the field over which Hopgood's Lancaster had exploded. Nearby stood a modern windmill, its streamlined appearance and three whirling blades to me a reminder of a Merlin in action. There was a simple cross here too, where a minute's silence was duly observed. What went through the minds of Hopgood's relations I can never know, but I would like to think that the presence of all these spectators, most of them not even alive in 1943, had some sort of comforting effect.

We also paused at the remains of the village of Himmelpforten – the first one to be swept away by the water. Father Berkenkopf's action in ringing his church bell had meant that there had been just seven fatalities, including himself. The rest of the villagers had had enough time to escape to high ground.

With the exception of one small but incomplete building, which had apparently survived because it was protected by rising ground between it and the dam, the village had been wiped off the map. The church, which had been consecrated by the Pope in 1249 and so was almost 700 years old when it was destroyed, had been reconstructed in outline, with a large cross as a memorial. Although it was much smaller, several people remarked on how much it reminded them of Coventry Cathedral.

For me there was also a reminder of the French village of Oradour-sur-Glane, deserted since the SS had massacred most of its population in the summer of 1944. Now nobody lived at Himmelpforten and the area where the village houses used to be had become a children's playground. It had been pleasantly landscaped and grass had grown over the scars, but the sense of sadness lingered on.

This trip included the Sorpe, which showed no signs of the Upkeep and Tallboy attacks. Indeed, with its rock-strewn straight edge and lack of towers, the Sorpe did not look like a dam at all. It was only the presence of the compensating basin, a long way down the scrub-covered hill on our left as we walked along it, which served to indicate its purpose.

On Tuesday 18 May we visited the Boselagerschen Wald, near Hamm, and walked to the spot on its northern edge where P/O Warner Ottley's Lancaster had crashed. The crash site had been found by a Hamm police officer in response to an enquiry from the Dambusters Research Association. Some 20mm ammunition had been found in the wreckage – evidence of the Lancaster's crash onto the ammunition dump as no striker marks were found on it. Local scouts had cleared the area and built a memorial cross in 1981.

Among those who had attended the memorial ceremony in 1982 was Freddie Tees, invited by the local Burgomaster. He had had mixed feelings about going and had expected to have to lay a few ghosts, but said afterwards that it had all been tastefully done. The memorial bears a simple inscription:

Bewahret Den Frieden. Krieg Ist Grausam.
(Take Care Of Peace. War Is Terrible.)

The drive along the winding lakeside to the Eder was different this time because the lake had dropped a considerable distance, exposing some islands that had probably not been seen for the last fifty years. Again thanks to Paul I knew what was coming, but even so it was a sight not to be forgotten.

This dam was being reinforced. In 1991 it had been found to have moved forward by up to 10cm. With over 200 million tons of water behind it, this had caused a great deal of concern.

Building work on the parapet made crossing it impossible this time, but we drove round to the far side, in the process going through the valley that the water had followed in 1943. At the dam we were fortunate enough to speak to the young chief engineer. Tall, sun-tanned and fair-haired, he spoke good English and performed well for the camcorders – obviously not for the first time.

One thousand people had built the Eder, starting in 1912 and taking two years. Good stone had been used throughout and set in concrete, with 200 people employed just to wash the stone before use. There had been no question of a dressed outer surface which was rubbish inside – this had been good material all the way through. The quality of the wartime repair had been as good as the original.

Around 1961-1962 a lot of water a seemed to be getting through the dam, so holes had been drilled in it and it had been regrouted with cement. This had worked well enough, but recently more measurements had been taken. When the Eder had first been built, the likely high-water mark over a hundred years had been taken into account. Now, the mark over a thousand years was what counted, hence the need to reinforce the dam.

This was being accomplished by drilling down through it to the rock below. Anchors, 80m in length and weighing 150 tonnes, each big enough to hold a weight of 4,500kg, would then be put through. They were the biggest of their type in Europe. It had been done elsewhere in the world and so was not a unique idea, but the Eder anchors were longer than any others.

The engineer lived at the site during the week, going home to Aachen at the weekends. He said there was pressure on them because of the need for both water and tourism. This had led to a system of twelve-hour shifts day and night, but only during the week. They had been given two years to carry out a job that should have taken twice as long. We could only hope that it was carried out correctly, but the deadline seemed not to bother him and he apparently bore his responsibilities lightly. Even so, he was clearly a professional.

This conversation had come about as the result of noting that a large amount of old concrete was coming out of the dam in small pieces. As these would make unusual souvenirs, researcher Jim Shortland had scrounged a wheelbarrow full of them for us by the simple method of going to the engineer and asking for it. His attitude was, 'If you don't ask, you don't get'. To his amusement, this promptly earned him the nickname of 'Jim'll fix it. ' So I now have my own piece of the Eder's history; a lump of concrete and masonry, semi-circular in section, a blend of the original and the wartime repair, some five inches long, picked up fifty years and one day after the breaching of it.

We drove on to Affolden, one of the villages that had been in the path of the Eder's water, where ten civilians and one soldier had died. At once it became clear that the 'Wasser-Katastrophe' was still a recent memory, and for some people a raw one. At the local cemetery there were two wreaths, one of oak leaves from the German War Graves commission and the other from the Mothers of Britain, to which we added our own spray. It was there that we met Heinz Baumann, whose experiences are detailed in Chapter 3. He had seen our coaches, came across and spoke to one of our guides, Linda Storrie, and myself in the churchyard. My German is basic, but it comes back surprisingly quickly when you need it.

It was time to board the coaches and go home. There was a reflective silence as we did so. As Paul Snook said afterwards, the whole tour had been something of a pilgrimage.

What remains today in Lincolnshire? Bardney was used for a short while by the Army after 9 Sqdn moved to Waddington in the summer of 1945, but reverted to farmland after the war. All that is left now is 9's memorial, consisting of a black spinner and three-bladed propeller.

Of the three airfields associated with 617 Sqdn, Scampton was in use by the RAF, including 617's Vulcans, up until the early 1990s, with a small wartime museum and the grave of Gibson's dog, Nigger. At the time of writing Scampton has gone onto 'care and maintenance' and its future remains uncertain, although it is to be hoped that his historic site does not become another business park or gravel pit, as has been the fate of so many other famous airfields in the past. There is a Heritage Centre in the village, opened in the mid-1990s and run by the local post office.

Coningsby is still an active RAF base, and at the time of our visit was being used as an Operational Conversion unit by Tornado crews, although it maintains its wartime connections by acting as the home of the Battle of Britain Memorial Flight. One hangar houses several different marks of Spitfire, a Hurricane Mark IIC and PA474, the Flight's Lancaster. Until the 1990s a Shackleton had been used to give post-war RAF aircrew the appropriate four-engined piston experience, but when 'the Grey Lady' finally went into retirement, she was replaced by a Dakota that also acted as a support aircraft for the BBMF.

When I visited in 1997 the Lancaster was wearing the colours of 9 Sqdn's W4964 WS-J, the original of which, as noted earlier, had taken part in Operation *Paravane*

Above and below: Photos of a recovered Upkeep and Tallboy nose. The Upkeep is a practice one, recovered from Reculver. The Grand Slam nose came from the attack on the Valentin U-boat assembly plant at Farge on 27 March 1945. (Will Stewart)

A preserved
Tallboy
at RAF
Coningsby in
October 1997.
(S. Flower)

A Grand Slam
at Coningsby,
its size
indicated by
the visitors
next to it.
(S. Flower)

and a good deal else. Its black sides gleamed with a glossy polyurethane-based paint, which, although not strictly authentic, was used to preserve the aircraft. The BBMF hangar is open to the public at certain times, but only for tours conducted by some very knowledgeable guides. Part of the centre fuselage of the real W4964, which had been used as a garden shed, was later recovered and has been on show at the Newark Air Museum since 1974.

Woodhall Spa closed for flying in December 1945 and was used for bomb storage. In the late 1950s it was partly reactivated for Bloodhound missile use and continued in this role until 1965. The rest was sold for agricultural use or gravel extraction. A visit in October 1997 – yet another of Paul Snook's tours – led us to the last wartime relic on the airfield, which was a piece of sliding door runner left in the ground where 617's hangar had stood. This was on the point of being gobbled up by the gravel company.

The former missile site is currently used by a detachment from Coningsby to service Tornado engines. The BBMF's spares are held there as well, so in one sense the Lancaster is still around. It also boasts a nine-hole golf course, which is open to civilians.

Away from the airfield, No.1 Communal Site's brick huts, used to house 617's NCOs and 627 Sqdn, still survive, some of them now being part of Thorpe Camp Visitor Centre – another small but interesting museum, run by volunteers and well

The 617 Squadron Memorial at Woodhall Spa village in October 1997. (S. Flower)

worth seeing when it is open during May to September on Sunday afternoons. Today, Lincolnshire takes pride in its aviation heritage.

In the village of Woodhall Spa the Petwood Hotel still thrives. Built among pine and deciduous trees in mock Tudor style during the Edwardian era, it has a bar specially devoted to 617 Sqdn. This hotel has plenty of atmosphere and in my opinion deserves better than the three stars the AA gave it. No wonder 627 Sqdn were envious!

Stories of ghosts are still told and on the late afternoon of my arrival in 1997 I was startled to look out of a first-floor window to see a grey-haired wing commander in service dress, complete with ceremonial sword! Several other young officers could be seen and I was amused when I heard that there had been a wedding at Coningsby that afternoon. The bride and groom were spending their wedding night at the hotel. Was there a better place to start a new life together? I silently wished them good luck.

Nearby, on the site of the Royal Hotel, which was destroyed by Luftwaffe bombing in August 1943, stands an unusual and unmistakeable memorial, in the shape of a breached dam. The names of squadron personnel who were lost are listed on it in alphabetical order, without ranks or titles. Gibson's name is included, although he was no longer serving with 617 when he was killed.

Another relic worth visiting is a delightful very early picture house called the Kinema, nicknamed 'Flicks In The Sticks' by its wartime patrons. This boasts a display of 1940s film star photographs, as well as an organ that rises out of the floor, to be played by its young manager. It has now gone 'Multiplex', with a second cinema at one side, but again the sense of the past is still strong. There were also two pianos, on one of which one of my tour companions could not resist playing 'Thanks For The Memory'. How appropriate.

The fate of the live Upkeeps and Highballs has already been mentioned. Only a few casing fragments of the bombs dropped during *Chastise* have come to light since 1943. One of these was found twenty miles downstream from the Möhne in the summer of 1970. However, in 1973 an article in *After The Battle* magazine mentioned that fifteen of the original concrete-filled practice Upkeeps could be seen either on the beach at Reculver, or were under the sea nearby. Two years later the Rayleigh branch of the British Sub Aqua Club decided to salvage some of them. Although a raft was tried, using oil drums and scaffolding, this was unsuccessful and when contacted the RAF said it was too heavy for them to lift. The US Air Force's 67th Sqdn at RAF Woodbridge in Suffolk was contacted and they provided a Sikorsky HH53 'Jolly Green Giant' helicopter. After two attempts four bombs were removed.

In October 1977 three more were recovered, one being used as a fund-raising venture in Blackpool for the Cheshire Homes before being flown to Amsterdam for permanent exhibition. A second one went to the RAF Museum, which already had one from the 1975 operation, and the third went to the Imperial War Museum's airfield at Duxford in Cambridgeshire. The following year German author and film-maker Helmuth Euler, who had carried out intensive research into *Chastise*, was given another casing fragment by an old school teacher. It had been given to him by a German soldier who had found it near the Möhne. There is also a fragment on display outside the Petwood Hotel, although a Tallboy would have been more appropriate.

Another chapter was added to this saga in June 1997, when four more bombs were recovered with the assistance of three squadrons of 101 Engineer Regiment, a TA unit which today carries out bomb disposal. These proved particularly interesting as they consisted of a full-size Upkeep, two scaled-down versions of it and a Highball. On the scene was Barnes Wallis Junior, who showed a marked resemblance to his father, both in appearance and in temperament, when asked some particularly inane questions by the media.

The Highball was earmarked for the Mosquito Museum at Salisbury Hall, near London Colney in Hertfordshire, while the Upkeep was claimed by Barnes Wallis Junior for a display commemorating his father's work at the Yorkshire Air Museum, at the former bomber base at Elvington, near York. One of the two scaled-down Upkeeps was to be displayed in the Reculver area and the other was to go to Scampton.

Today, several Upkeeps can be seen. One of the two passed to the RAF Museum now forms part of a display that also shows the contents of Wallis' post-war Clubhouse office. Brooklands Museum has the other, on loan from Hendon. East Fortune airfield in Scotland has one and there is another at the Lincolnshire Aviation Heritage Centre at East Kirkby airfield. This small but interesting museum, run entirely by voluntary labour, also has NX611, a fine example of a Canadian-built Lancaster BX, whose engines can be run. Yet another Upkeep can be seen at the Imperial War Museum's out-station at Duxford airfield in Cambridgeshire, in company with Lancaster BX KB889 and Mosquito B35 TA719.

Exactly how many Tallboys and Grand Slams remained to be disposed of is not known, but some escaped this process and also found their way into various museums. Examples of both bombs can be seen in the Bomber Command Hall at the RAF Museum, displayed alongside other weapons near to R5868, a veteran PFF and Main Force Lancaster BI with at least 135 operations to her credit. Proudly and defiantly displayed on her side is Hermann Göring's boast, 'No enemy plane will fly over the Reich territory.'

Also held in store by the RAF Museum is an example of the original type of Tallboy tail cone, which lacks the offset fins fitted to the later ones. They also hold the complete suspension linkage and one of the aircraft anchor points for it. A small museum next to the Battle of Britain Memorial Flight's hangar at Coningsby also has examples of Tallboy and Grand Slam displayed outside.

One museum where many visitors will be surprised to see examples of such weapons is that at what remains of the famous Brooklands race track, between Weybridge and Byfleet in Surrey. For many years after the war, two of the earthquake bombs were displayed on their noses outside the Brooklands Clubhouse, close to the pre-war Clerk of the Course's office window. As previously stated, the first floor office was later used by Wallis, the room below it becoming a store for a number of his papers and films, although unfortunately much damage was done to these by a flood in 1968. The museum's photographic archive includes a hilarious shot of Wallis rowing across the old Paddock area, near the Clubhouse's front door, in a small boat, while water laps just below the lower office window. He still had work to do and something as minor as a flood was not going to stop him from getting there. Amy Gentry would have been proud!

These two bombs consisted of one of the twelve 4,000lb Tallboy Smalls that had been made for the initial AAEE trials work, and a Grand Slam. Both were empty and their noses rested on circular plinths on the ground, their tails being secured by brackets to the brickwork. For a time after Wallis had retired this building was used by British Aerospace's Photographic Department and then it passed to Brooklands Museum when this was set up in 1985.

In 1989 two incidents occurred which led to the removal of the bombs. The first was due to an accident that, looking back, was hilarious, but it could all too easily have been fatal.

Outwardly, the clubhouse at Brooklands still looks very much as it did in the 1930s and is frequently used as a backdrop for photographic shoots of cars past and present. On this occasion the Paddock area in front of it was required for just such a shoot; one in which the now late Denis Jenkinson was involved. 'Jenks', as he became known to everyone, had been a pre-war Brooklands motor mechanic, was well known as Stirling Moss' co-driver in the 1955 Mille Miglia and had become one of motor racing's characters.

There was a problem. Parked just to the left of the front door, in front of the 4,000-pounder, was a white Fiat Panda car owned by the Museum's Director. Jenks duly went in and asked her if she would mind moving it. She handed him the keys, he moved it and replaced it in the same spot once the shoot was over. However, by now

The 4,000-pound Tallboy Small and Grand Slam at Brooklands Museum in 1997 (G. Lewis)

the Panda was facing away from the building and, inexplicably for someone who had been around cars all his life, Jenks had left it in reverse gear.

That evening, the Director came out of the Clubhouse, got into her car, neglected to check that the gear lever was in neutral and turned the key. The Panda leapt backwards and struck the 4,000-pounder, knocking its nose off the plinth and towards the wall. Fortunately for her the tail bracket held, otherwise it would have toppled onto the car with gruesome results. It was also just as well that she had rammed the smaller bomb. The Panda was repaired, although the insurance claim form must have made interesting reading!

The bomb, with some damage that was later made good, was removed, leaving the Grand Slam in solitary splendour. It remained in this position until the following October, when the filming of a 'Hercule Poirot' film for ITV led to it being removed as well.

For this the clubhouse was meant to look as it had done in 1934 and the film company spared no effort to make it so. Using a crane and a set of airliner steps to gain access, the tail was taken off and the bomb removed. A check behind one of the circular bomb pistol access plates revealed a starling's nest, but luckily it was not in use at the time.

As a result of all this the two bombs went to a wartime-built hangar on the race track's Finishing Straight, where they may still be seen today, together with the loaned Upkeep already mentioned. The 4,000-pounder, now probably the only survivor of its kind, has been repainted in the black-and-white quartered scheme it would have worn for photographic purposes during the trials at Orford Ness in 1944. The Grand Slam sits on a trolley, its body resplendent in dark green finish, with the tail in natural metal. Sleek, deadly and purposeful, they illustrate the contribution that Wallis made to the air war in a manner that that no other artefact can.

Be careful not to get too close to these weapons. You might end up writing a book about them.

APPENDIX 1

The Avro Lancaster

The Lancaster was developed from the unsuccessful Manchester, a twin-engined design whose Rolls-Royce Vulture engines had proved unreliable. The Chief Designer, Roy Chadwick, 'acquired' four tried and trusted Rolls-Royce Merlin engines for the 'Manchester III', which, renamed the Lancaster BI, first flew on 9 January 1941. Lancasters began to reach the squadrons of 5 Group at the end of that year, first seeing action with 44 Sqdn the following March.

BIs and BIIIs were used by 9 and 617 Sqdns, the latter mark differing only in their use of Merlins built under licence by the American Packard company.

Technical details (BIII)
Span	102ft
Length	68ft 11in
Height	19ft 6in

Power Plants Four Packard-built Rolls-Royce Merlin 28 or 38 twelve-cylinder vee liquid-cooled engines, whose additional functions were as follows:

Port outer – drove a hydraulic pump for the rear turret, with a generator for Gee and Monica tail-warning radar when fitted. The propeller could be windmilled if the engine was put out of action. This gave some turret power but would give drag as well.

Port inner – drove a compressor that powered the autopilot and a hydraulic pump for the ventral turret when fitted.

Starboard inner – drove a hydraulic pump for the front turret, radiator shutters, super-charger rams and also the air compressor for the brakes. It became usual to start this engine first, in order to have brake pressure from then on.

Starboard outer – drove a hydraulic pump for the mid-upper turret, plus the electrical generator for the H2S blind-bombing and Fishpond tail-warning radars when these were fitted. It could also power Monica if needed.

The inner engines both drove a vacuum pump from which the blind flying instruments and the Mark XIV bombsight worked. A similar arrangement, possibly using more powerful compressors, is believed to have applied to the SABS sight as well. They also powered several other functions, including the bomb doors, flaps, fuel jettisoning, propeller feathering mechanisms, undercarriage and generators to charge the W/T set. The dinghy, which was inflated by them, was carried in the starboard wing, although this could also be activated by an immersion switch in the aircraft's nose. Individual dinghy packs could also be carried by crew members.

Armament Eight 0.303-in Browning machine-guns, as follows:

Two guns in the front turret, with 1,000 rounds per gun.

Two guns in the mid-upper turret, with 1,000 rounds per gun.

Four guns in the rear turret, with 2,500 rounds per gun.

A ventral turret was fitted to some Main Force aircraft, but there are no reports of such fittings being used by 9 or 617 Sqdns.

Bomb Load Normally 14,000lbs. When modified for the earthquake bombs, up to 22,000lbs.

Weights When normally loaded, 53,000lbs. Maximum overload 65,000lbs.

Performance At normal weight, the maximum speed was 270mph at 19,000ft. The cruising speed was 210mph with a ceiling of 21,500ft.

Camouflage and markings Standard Bomber Command camouflage of the period consisted of Dark Green and Dark Earth over the upper surfaces, with Night (matt black) on lower fuselage sides and underneath. This was replaced on most of the BIs modified for Grand Slam, by an unusual daylight scheme of Sky (a very pale green).

Code letters and serial numbers were in Dull Red, although by 1945 several 5 Group squadrons, including 9 and 617, had embellished theirs by outlining them in yellow. At the time of *Paravane*, at least, 9 also displayed their code letters on the upper surfaces of their aircraft tailplanes, to be read from behind. Some of their flight leaders also indicated their status by painting the outer surfaces of their fins white. 9 Sqdn carried the letters WS for most of the war, while 617 began with AJ. These letters were apparently only carried by aircraft modified for *Chastise*, as by 1944 they had changed to KC. YZ was carried by the Grand Slam BIs.

The Mosquitoes used by 617 would have been camouflaged in Medium Sea Grey overall, with irregular Dark Green stripes over their upper surfaces. Other aircraft, such as the BIVs borrowed from other units in mid-1944, would have continued to carry their normal owners' code letters, with Dark Green and Ocean Grey over their upper surfaces, being either Sky or Black underneath. The above would have applied to 618, except when their aircraft went to Australia; these apparently were in natural metal finish overall with black code letters and the two-tone blue roundels peculiar to the RAF's South-East Asia Command.

Of the two Mustangs issued to 617, both are believed to have been finished in the then standard RAF day fighter colours of Dark Green, Ocean Grey and Medium Sea Grey. One is known to have carried the full 'invasion' black and white stripes in the summer of 1944, as well as a Malcolm hood – a British modification which greatly improved visibility from the cockpit. At that time this aircraft did not carry any squadron codes. The other was probably similarly adorned, although the code letter N is believed to have been carried by one of them when Cheshire flew it.

Many aircraft carried bomb tallies – in some instances up to 100 – and other personal embellishments on the nose.

APPENDIX 2

Operation *Catechism*
12 November 1944
Tirpitz Bomb Plot

Apart from the ship's own armament the defences consisted of flak from four other vessels as well as from the batteries on Haakøy island. As plotted by the RAF photo interpreters, the sequence of falling Tallboys was as follows:

No. 1   A direct hit on the ship, near the port end of the athwart ships catapult.

No. 2   Landed in the water just outside the southern end of the boom.

No. 3   Landed one second later on the southern tip of Haakøy island.

No. 4   Another hit, one-eighth of a second later on the port side, probably in the region of the ship's after rangefinder. This caused a brilliant flash, then an explosion. Flak that had been coming up from amidships now became spasmodic and ceased during the final stages of the attack.

No. 5   Landed in the water off the ship's port beam at the same time as No.4.

No. 6   Landed two seconds later between the boom and the shore.

No. 7   Landed inside the boom, close to the starboard side of the ship.

No. 8   Landed between No.6 and the shore.

No. 9   Was a very near miss off the port quarter, close to Y turret (D turret to the Germans). This quickly produced a column of black smoke – a reaction produced by no other bomb in the water. One and a half seconds later there was a bright flash seen amidships. This was possibly exploding ammunition as it was not preceded by a bomb burst. Also, a thin concentrated jet of steam was now seen rising amidships. It was thought to have been from a burst boiler, or from the inrush of water into a boiler room.

No. 10   Fell close inshore, causing a great disturbance to the water between the ship and the shore.

Nos 11-13 Landed in the water at least 1000ft east of the ship. The attack was now in its later stages.

No. 14   Fell close behind the ship's stern.

No. 15   Landed on the east side of Haakøy Island.

No. 16   Landed in the water, slightly south of No.12.

By now the ship was hardly visible, being covered by smoke from her own funnel and guns as well as by bomb explosions. Consequently, the remainder of the twenty-nine bombs that fell around her could not be plotted, and some of these may have inflicted further damage. The last pictures taken by the 463 Sqdn Lancaster showed the ship capsized, as by now much of the smoke had blown away.

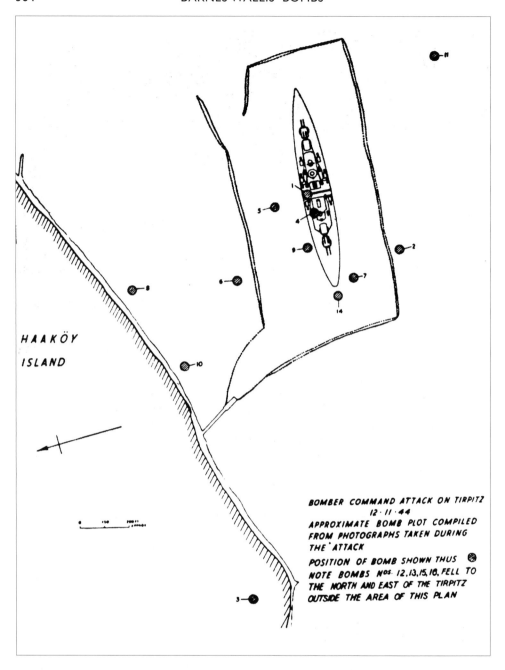

HAAKÖY
ISLAND

BOMBER COMMAND ATTACK ON TIRPITZ
12·11·44
APPROXIMATE BOMB PLOT COMPILED
FROM PHOTOGRAPHS TAKEN DURING
THE ATTACK

POSITION OF BOMB SHOWN THUS
NOTE BOMBS Nos. 12,13,15,16, FELL TO
THE NORTH AND EAST OF THE TIRPITZ
OUTSIDE THE AREA OF THIS PLAN

APPENDIX 3

Number of Tallboys Dropped on Active Service by 9 and 617 Sqdns 1944-1945

The categories are as follows:

A Bombs aimed at the target, including those that wholly or partly failed to explode.

B Bombs dropped accidentally en route to, near or on returning from the target.

C Bombs deliberately jettisoned or abandoned due to aircraft crash-landing (as in Operation *Paravane*).

D Bombs carried in aircraft that were shot down without dropping them, as far as is known.

Date		Target	Cat A	Cat B	Cat C	Cat D
8-9	June 1944	Saumur tunnel and bridge	19	-	-	-
14	June 1944	Le Havre E-boat pens	22	-	-	-
15	June 1944	Boulogne E-boat pens	11	1	-	-
19	June 1944	Watten V-2 liquid oxygen plant	17	1	-	-
24	June 1944	Wizernes V-2 launching bunker	16	-	-	-
25	June 1944	Siracourt V-1 launching bunker	16	-	1	-
4	July 1944	St Leu d'Esserent V-1 storage dump	8	-	-	-
6	July 1944	Marquise/Mimoyecques V-3 long-range gun site	13	-	1	-
17	July 1944	Wizernes V-2 launching bunker	16	-	-	-
25	July 1944	Watten V-2 liquid oxygen plant	15	-	1	-
31	July 1944	Rilly-la-Montagne V-1 store	12	-	-	-
5	Aug 1944	Brest U-boat pens	14	-	-	-
6	Aug 1944	Lorient U-boat pens	11	-	1	-
9	Aug 1944	La Pallice U-boat pens	12	-	-	-
12	Aug 1944	Brest U-boat pens	8	-	-	-
13	Aug 1944	Brest U-boat pens	5	-	-	-
18	Aug 1944	La Pallice U-boat pens	6	-	-	-
24	Aug 1944	Ijmuiden E/R-boat pens	8	-	-	-

At this point 9 Sqdn also became a Tallboy unit, so from now on the totals for the two squadrons are combined.

Date		Target	Cat A	Cat B	Cat C	Cat D
15	Sept 1944	*Tirpitz (Paravane)**	15	2	14	-
23-24	Sept 1944	Ladbergen canal banks and aqueducts	6	-	-	3
7	Oct 1944	Kembs barrage	12	-	-	1
15	Oct 1944	Sorpe dam	16	-	-	-
28-29	Oct 1944	*Tirpitz (Obviate)*	33	-	-	-
12	Nov 1944	*Tirpitz (Catechism)*	29	-	-	-
8	Dec 1944	Urft dam	3	1	-	-
11	Dec 1944	Urft dam	35	-	-	-
15	Dec 1944	Ijmuiden E-boat pens	13	-	3	-
21	Dec 1944	Pölitz hydrogeneration plant	11	-	-	-

Date	Target	Cat A	Cat B	Cat C	Cat D
29 Dec 1944	Waalhaven E-boat pens	16	-	-	-
31 Dec 1944	Cruisers *Emden* and *Köln* near Oslo	10	-	-	-
12 Jan 1945	Bergen U-boat pens and shipping	26	-	2	-
3 Feb 1945	Ijmuiden E-boat pens	17	-	-	-
3 Feb 1945	Pootershaven E-boat pens	18	-	-	-
8 Feb 1945	Ijmuiden E-boat pens	15	-	-	-
14 Feb 1945	Altenbeken viaduct (aborted)	-	-	-	1
22 Feb 1945	Altenbeken viaduct	16	-	-	-
22 Feb 1945	Bielefeld viaduct	18	-	-	-
24 Feb 1945	Ladbergen aqueduct (aborted)	-	-	-	-
3-4 March 1945	Ladbergen aqueduct	17	-	-	-
6-7 March 1945	Sassnitz port area and shipping	19	-	-	-
13 March 1945	Arnsberg viaduct	2	-	1	-
14 March 1945	Arnsberg viaduct	14	-	-	-
14 March 1945	Bielefeld viaduct	12	1	-	-
15 March 1945	Arnsberg viaduct	10	1	-	-
19 March 1945	Vlotho bridge	15	-	-	-
19 March 1945	Arnsberg viaduct	12	-	-	-
21 March 1945	Arbergen bridge	17	-	-	1
22 March 1945	Bremen bridge	15	-	1	-
22 March 1945	Nienburg bridge	12	-	-	-
23 March 1945	Bad Oeynhausen bridge	10	-	1	-
23 March 1945	Bremen bridge	11	-	-	-
27 March 1945	Farge oil storage depot	14	-	1	-
27 March 1945	Farge U-boat shelter	6	-	-	-
7 April 1945	*Sperrbrecher* at Ijmuiden	15	-	-	-
8-9 April 1945	Lüzkendorf/Wintershall synthetic oil plant	16	-	-	-
9 April 1945	Hamburg/Finkenwerder U-boat shelters	15	-	-	-
16 April 1945	*Lützow* and *Prinz Eugen* at Swinemünde	13	-	1	-
19 April 1945	Heligoland coastal gun batteries	27	-	-	-
25 April 1945	The Berghof, Eagle's Nest and SS barracks at Berchtesgaden	25	1	-	-
Totals		835	8	29	7
Total number of Tallboys expended on active service		879			

*This Category C total includes the five Tallboys abandoned at Yagodnik after the raid.

This does not include those Tallboys used in trials prior to this weapon's first operational use in June 1944.

APPENDIX 4

Number of Grand Slams Dropped on Active Service by 617 Sqdn in 1945

Date	Target	Bombs aimed at target	Bombs deliberately jettisoned
14 March	Bielefeld viaduct	1	-
15 March	Arnsberg viaduct	1	-
19 March	Arnsberg viaduct	6	-
21 March	Arbergen bridge	2	-
22 March	Nienburg bridge	5	-
23 March	Bremen bridge	5	1
27 March	Farge U-boat shelter	12	1
9 April	Finkenwerder U-boat shelters at Hamburg	2	-
19 April	Heligoland coastal gun batteries	6	-
Totals		40	2

Total number of Grand Slams expended on active service   42

As was seen in Chapter 12, one Grand Slam was dropped at Ashley Walk before the Bielefeld attack and an unknown number of others were expended in post-war trials.

The Witnesses

The titles are those in use at the time. Some of the witnesses quoted here have previously been interviewed by other authors.

Eric Allwright, section leader, Vickers-Armstrongs, Burhill, Surrey.
Heinz Baumann, schoolboy, Affolden village, near the Edersee, north-west Germany.
Flg-Off Tom Bennett, navigator, 617 Sqdn, RAF Woodhall Spa, Lincolnshire.
Norman 'Spud' Boorer, draughtsman, Vickers-Armstrong, Burhill, Surrey.
Flt Sgt Jim Brookbank, bomb aimer, 9 Sqdn, RAF Bardney, Lincolnshire.
Flt Lt Bruce Buckham, pilot, 463 Sqdn, RAF Waddington, Lincolnshire.
George Edwards, Experimental Department manager, Vicker Armstrongs, Foxwarren, Surrey (later knighted).
Reg Firman, draughtsman, Vickers-Armstrongs, Burhill, Surrey.
Jack Froude, draughtsman, Vickers-Armstrongs, Burhill, Surrey.
Sgt Guy Hammond, navigator, 9 Sqdn, RAF Bardney, Lincolnshire.
Flg-Off Ray Harris, pilot, 9 Sqdn, RAF Bardney, Lincolnshire.
Flt Sgt, later Flg-Off Ted Harrison, flight engineer, 9 Sqdn, RAF Bardney, Lincolnshire.
Flg-Off Roy Harvey, navigator, 9 Sqdn, RAF Bardney, Lincolnshire.
Cpl Frank Hawkins, armourer, 9 Sqdn, RAF Bardney, Lincolnshire.
Sandy Jack, Chief Inspector of the Lancaster Group, AV Roe and Company Limited, Lancashire and Boscombe Down, Wiltshire.
Flt Sgt W. D. Loakes, flight engineer, 9 Sqdn, RAF Bardney, Lincolnshire.
P/O Gordon Maguire, armament officer, 9 Sqdn, RAF Bardney, Lincolnshire (later Sqdn Ldr).
Clive Marler, factory worker, Royal Ordnance Factory Swynnerton, Staffordshire.
Flg-Off Phil Martin, pilot, 617 Sqdn, RAF Woodhall Spa, Lincolnshire.
Flg-Off Dennis Nolan, bomb aimer, 9 Sqdn, RAF Bardney, Lincolnshire.
Unteroffizier Heinz Orlowski, fighter pilot, 9/JG 5 *Eismeer*, Herdla, Norway.
Flt Sgt, then P/O H. F. C. 'Jimmy' Parsons, bomb aimer, 9 Sqdn, RAF Bardney, Lincolnshire (later Flt Lt).
Flg-Off Terry Playford, navigator, 617 Sqdn, RAF Woodhall Spa, Lincolnshire.
Flg-Off Graham Rees, pilot, 9 Sqdn, RAF Bardney, Lincolnshire.
Flt Sgt Ken Rogers, wireless-operator, 9 Sqdn, RAF Bardney, Lincolnshire.
Oberleutnant zur See Bernard Schmitz, officer, battleship *Tirpitz*, Tromsø, Norway.
Gefreiter Karl Schutte, anti-aircraft gunner, Luftwaffe, Möhne dam, north-west Germany.
Flt Sgt, later Flt Lt Len Sumpter, bomb aimer, 617 Sqdn, RAF Scampton and RAF Woodhall Spa, Lincolnshire.
W/O Alan Webb, chief technical officer, 627 Sqdn, RAF Woodhall Spa, Lincolnshire.

Glossary

AAEE	Aeroplane and Armament Experimental Establishment, at Boscombe Down in Wiltshire.
Airborne Cigar	Code-name for the disruption of German night fighter communications by jamming their radio frequencies.
AOC	Air Officer Commanding – which usually referred to a Group commander.
AP	Aiming Point, or Armour Piercing (bombs).
API	Air Position Indicator – a device, new in 1944, into which was fed airspeed, elapsed time and direction from an aircraft compass, to keep track of the aircraft's 'air position' – the position that it would have been in if there had been no wind.
ASR	Air/Sea Rescue.
ASV	Air to Surface Vessel radar.
BAOR	British Army Of the Rhine.
Category E	Aircraft written off, or struck off charge as being beyond repair.
Cookie	Nickname for thin-cased 4,000lb High Capacity bomb, also available in 8,000lb and 12,000lb sizes. Also referred to as a 'blockbuster'.
DFC	Distinguished Flying Cross.
DFM	Distinguished Flying Medal.
DPs	Displaced Persons – refugees.
DSO	Distinguished Service Order.
ECM	Electronic Counter-Measures.
Elint	Electronic intelligence – listening in to enemy radar and radio wavelengths.
Erks	RAF ground crew members.
FIDO	Fog Investigation and Dispersal Operation – the use of burning petrol at the side of a runway to burn off fog when aircraft were taking off or landing.
Flg-Off	Flying Officer.
Flt Lt	Flight Lieutenant.
Flt Sgt	Flight Sergeant.
Gardening	Code for a minelaying raid.
Gate	Slang for the wire fitted to an aircraft's throttle, to prevent too high a speed, with consequent engine damage. Breaking the wire, known as 'going through the gate', was used only in emergencies, and then for no more than a few minutes.
Geschwader	A Luftwaffe Group, made up of three or more Gruppen. There was no RAF equivalent.
Gp Capt.	Group Captain.
GP	General Purpose.
Gruppe	A Luftwaffe formation, consisting of three Staffeln (squadrons) equivalent to an RAF Wing.
HC	High Capacity – see Cookie.
H-Hour	Time on target

IFF	Identification Friend or Foe – a radio device which altered the shape of an aircraft's 'blip' on radar screen, indicating its nationality.
JG	Jagdgeschwader – a Luftwaffe Fighter Group.
Loran	Long Range Navigation – a radar-based aid, used from October 1944 by Bomber Command.
Mae West	RAF slang for lifejacket, derived from the pneumatic figure of a certain American lady film star.
Mag drop	Erks' slang, indicating a magneto problem.
Mandrel	Jammer to disrupt German early warning radar.
MC	Medium Capacity
MGB	Motor Gunboat.
MP	Marking Point.
MPI	Mean Point of Impact.
MRAF	Marshal of the Royal Air Force.
MTB	Motor Torpedo Boat.
MTU	Mosquito Training Unit.
MU	Maintenance Unit.
NAAFI	Navy, Army and Air Force Institute – the Forces' caterers.
Oboe	Blind-bombing system used by some PFF Mosquitoes.
OKW	Oberkommando der Wehrmacht – the Headquarters of the German Armed Forces.
ORB	Operational Record Book – an RAF unit's war diary.
ORS	Operational Research Survey.
PBM	Primary Blind Marker – PFF aircraft which dropped TIs before the start of a Main Force attack.
Penguin	Non-flying RAF officer.
PFF	Pathfinder Force (8 Group).
P/O	Pilot Officer.
POW	Prisoner of War.
PR(U)	Photographic Reconnaissance (Unit).
QDM	A request for navigational assistance, in which an aircraft's wireless-operator sent out a contiuous note, on which receiving stations could take bearings and then transmit the aircraft's exact position to it.
R Aux AF	Royal Auxiliary Air Force. Although its squadrons retained their county titles of the time, they were absorbed into the RAF's order of battle on the outbreak of war.
R/T	Radio-Telegraphy (voice radio).
RAAF	Royal Australian Air Force.
R-boat	Raumboot – a type of German minesweeper.
RDX	Research Department Explosive.
ROF	Royal Ordnance Factory
SASO	Senior Air Staff Officer.
See	German word for lake.
Serrate	System fitted to 100 Group's night fighters, to home onto emissions of German night fighter radars.
SHAEF	Supreme Headquarters Allied Expeditionary Force.
Sperrbrecher	German merchant vessel adapted as a flak ship.
SP	Service Policeman.
Sqdn Ldr	Squadron Leader.
TI	Target Indicator – a coloured marker flare.
TNT	Trinitrotoluene – a type of explosive.
Ultra	Allied code-name for information obtained by breaking the German Enigma code.
VC	Victoria Cross.

VHF	Very High Frequency.
VR	Volunteer Reserve.
W/T	Wireless-Telegraphy (Morse).
Wg Cdr	Wing Commander.
Window	Code-name for tin foil dropped from aircraft to 'blind' German radar by producing multiple echoes on the operator's screen.
W/O	Warrant Officer.
WOp/AG	Wireless-Operator/Air Gunner.

Chronology

October 1937	The Air Staff first consider the Ruhr dams as future targets.
October 1940	A series of model dams tests begins at the Road Research Laboratory in Harmondsworth.
March 1941	Wallis writes *A Note on a Method of Attacking the Axis Powers*, pointing out the dependence of German industry on coal oil and water.
April 1942	Wallis begins experiments on a bouncing weapon, at first with marbles and a tin bath. His experiences lead him to write *Spherical Bomb – Surface Torpedo*, enabling permission to be given to use the William Froude Laboratory at Teddington.
June 1942	Bouncing experiments in tank at Teddington begin, continuing until September.
24 July 1942	Nant-y-Gro dam in Wales successfully breached by a contact charge.
2 December 1942	Four experimental bombs are spun in a modified Wellington.
4 December 1942	The Wellington drops two bouncing bombs at Chesil Beach.
January 1943	Wallis writes *Air Attack on Dams*.
15 February 1943	An Air Ministry meeting gives permission for one Lancaster to be modified for the Upkeep bomb.
22 February 1943	MAP approves two Mosquitoes to be modified for Highball bomb use.
26 February 1943	Wallis is told at a MAP conference that work is to go ahead as a priority. An order is placed for three trials Lancasters, followed by twenty-seven operational ones, to be delivered by 1 May.
27 February 1943	Work begins on the first full-size Upkeep drawings at Burhill.
March 1943	The first three inert Upkeeps are delivered to Brooklands. By now sixty inert and sixty live Upkeeps are on order.
15 March 1943	Cochrane is ordered by Harris to form X Squadron at Scampton.
26 March 1943	X Squadron is renumbered as 617.
1 April 1943	618 Squadron forms at Skitten to use Highball.
8 April 1943	The first trials Lancaster arrives at Farnborough, and the first modified operational one at Scampton.
13 April 1943	First Wellington and Lancaster Upkeep trials at Reculver. Two modified Mosquitoes also drop Highballs. During this month, Highballs are also tried against land targets on the Ashley Walk bombing range.
18 April 1943	Second Lancaster Upkeep trial at Reculver. Wooden casing removed and Upkeep becomes cylindrical.

29 April 1943	Further satisfactory Upkeep trial at Reculver.
May 1943	Screens erected on shore at Reculver to simulate dam towers.
	Satisfactory 'attacks' made towards shore with inert Upkeeps. Highball trials begin against target ship *L'Amiral Courbet* at Loch Striven.
13 May 1943	First live Upkeep satisfactorily dropped off Broadstairs. A progress meeting on Highball and Upkeep shows that the former is not yet working satisfactorily. Doubt as to whether Operation *Chastise* – the dams raid – should go ahead.
14 May 1943	The Chiefs of Staff give permission for Upkeep to be used immediately without waiting for Highball. Operation *Servant* – the use of Highball against the *Tirpitz* – is postponed.
16/17 May 1943	Operation *Chastise* – 617 Squadron attacks the Ruhr dams. Two dams are breached and eight aircraft lost.
11 July 1943	At a MAP conference Wallis is given the go-ahead for the Tallboy bomb.
18 July 1943	MAP's Controller of Research and Development receives a requirement for twelve Tallboy Smalls and cases for sixty Tallboy Mediums. An order for 100 ten-ton bombs is also placed.
30 September 1943	The Chief of the Air Staff orders MAP to stop work on the ten-ton bomb.
6 October 1943	Highball is tried in South Wales tunnel bombing trials.
December 1943	The 4,000lb bomb, known as Tallboy Small, is first tried by AAEE at the Orford Ness range. Its fins are offset as a result of this and a tougher casing used.
12 February 1944	617 Squadron are ordered to pass one Lancaster to the AAEE at Boscombe Down for Tallboy modifications. By the end of this month twenty Lancasters had been modified.
18 April 1944	First live Tallboy trial at Ashley Walk range, in the New Forest.
24/25 April 1944	Six live Tallboys dropped at Ashley Walk.
11 May 1944	Two more live Tallboys are dropped.
15/17 May 1944	Further Highball trials, this time against the battleship HMS *Malaya*, with the first double releases on 17 May.
8/9 June 1944	First Tallboy raid – railway tunnel near Saumur in France.
14 June 1944	First daytime Tallboy raid – E-boat pens at Le Havre.
19 June 1944	First use of Tallboy against a V-weapons site – the liquid oxygen plant at Watten.
June 1944	The Chiefs of Staff redirect 618 to train for use in the Pacific.
July 1944	Production of the ten-ton bomb is resumed, in the light of experience with Tallboy.
5 August 1944	First use of Tallboy against U-boat pens – Brest.
29 August 1944	Order that the next twelve Tallboys to be filled were to be issued to 9 Squadron, who now become the second Tallboy unit.
11 September 1944	9 and 617 Squadrons fly to Yagodnik in northern Russia, to attack the battleship *Tirpitz* from there.
15 September 1944	Operation *Paravane* – the first Tallboy attack on the *Tirpitz* by 9 and 617 Squadrons. The ship is damaged beyond repair by one hit on the bows and a near miss.
23/24 September 1944	First use of Tallboy on a canal target – Ladbergen, by 9 and 617.

September 1944	US production of the ten-ton bomb, to be known as Tallboy Large, is arranged. By the end of this month 600 are on order – 200 in Britain and 400 in America.
4 October 1944	British production of the ten-ton bomb is stopped. US production is maintained but limited to fifty bomb casings.
7 October 1944	First Tallboy attack on a dam target – the Kembs barrage, by 617 Squadron.
29 October 1944	Operation *Obviate* – the second Tallboy attack on the *Tirpitz* by 9 and 617 Squadrons. Further damage is sustained, but the ship is not sunk.
October 1944	618 Squadron are shipped to Australia with the intention of using Highballs against Japanese naval targets.
12 November 1944	Operation *Catechism* – the third Tallboy attack on the *Tirpitz* with the 9 and 617 Squadrons. The ship capsizes after several hits and near-misses.
22 November 1944	The ten-ton bomb, previously known as Tallboy Large, is renamed as Grand Slam.
December 1944	Due to continuing German resistance, production of Grand Slam is increased, with 200 from America and twenty-five from home production. One Douglas A-26 Invader is shipped to Britain for Highball modifications.
20 January 1945	The first Grand Slam bomb is issued to 617 Squadron at Woodhall Spa.
January 1945	Towards the end of this month the first of thirty-two BI Special Lancasters, to drop Grand Slam, begin to be manufactured.
22 February 1945	First Tallboy attacks against German railway viaducts 9 Squadron attacks Altenbeken, destroying masonry at each end of it. 617 Squadron attacks Bielefeld, destroying one of two parallel twin-track viaducts.
February 1945	AAEE trials begin on the first BI Special Lancaster.
13 March 1945	The first Grand Slam bomb trials take place, successfully, at Ashley Walk range. This is immediately followed by this bomb's first operational use, by 617 Squadron, who destroy the remaining Bielefeld Viaduct with it.
22 March 1945	Grand Slam is now officially cleared for use.
16 April 1945	Tallboy attack on the port of Swinemünde by 617 Squadron. The pocket battleship *Lützow* is partly sunk by a Tallboy near-miss.
19 April 1945	Attack on coastal gun batteries on the island of Heligoland by 9 and 617 Squadrons. This is the last raid to use Grand Slams.
25 April 1945	Attack on Hitler's house at Berchtesgaden by 9 and 617 Squadrons. This is the last raid to use Tallboys.
July 1945	618 Squadron is disbanded, without seeing action.
16 May 1955	Premiere of *The Dam Busters* film.
1962	All four of the Wallis bombs are removed from the Secret List.
30 October 1979	Death of Sir Barnes Wallis.

Index

TARGETS

WEAPONS

The headings for each weapon are listed in chronological order: